JAMES V

Jamie Cameron (1962–1995)

The Stewart Dynasty in Scotland

JAMES V:
The Personal Rule 1528–1542

Jamie Cameron

edited by Norman Macdougall

This short run edition first published in 2011 by
John Donald, an imprint of Birlinn Ltd

West Newington House
10 Newington Road
Edinburgh
EH9 1QS

www.birlinn.co.uk

First published by Tuckwell Press in 1998

ISBN 978 1 904607 78 6

Typeset by HewerText Ltd, Edinburgh

Printed and bound in Great Britain by Bell & Bain, Glasgow

Contents

List of Illustrations

The title page illustration, a silver groat showing a profile of James V wearing an imperial crown, is reproduced by permission of the National Museums of Scotland

Foreword

Until comparatively recently, the character and policies of James V suffered from both scholarly and popular neglect. Little was written about the personal rule of this elusive Stewart monarch, perhaps because the careers of his more famous father James IV, and his internationally renowned daughter, Mary Queen of Scots, offered more immediately attractive themes for historians of the sixteenth century. Furthermore, the personal rule of James V stands alone, separated in time by fifteen years from the disaster of Flodden and the elimination of James IV with a large part of his nobility in 1513, and by close on nineteen years after James V's death in 1542 until the personal rule of his daughter Mary.

Fortunately a number of recent scholarly works have helped to shed light on some of the obscurity hitherto surrounding the reign. These include Carol Edington's masterly study of the period, *Court and Culture in Renaissance Scotland: Sir David Lindsay of the Mount* (1994); the wide-ranging volume of essays on Scottish literature, music, and heraldry contemporary with, and in some cases emanating from, James V's court, edited by Janet Hadley Williams under the title *Stewart Style 1513–42: Essays on the Court of James V* (1996); and Athol Murray's magisterial Edinburgh thesis (1961) on Exchequer and Crown Revenue (1437–1542), parts of which have been published over the years. Forthcoming is a major study of James V's court by Andrea Thomas.

All these works indicate an encouraging growth of interest in this hitherto neglected reign; but none of them is, or claims to be, a study of crown-magnate politics during the personal rule, an aspect of the reign which has long cried out for scholarly analysis. Instead of such analysis, we have Caroline Bingham's racy, readable, and inaccurate portrait of the king (*James V, King of Scots, 1513–1542* (London, 1971)), heavily dependent for its views on the post-Reformation chronicler Robert Lindsay of Pitscottie. More important is Gordon Donaldson's hugely influential chapter on King James's policies in *Scotland: James V – James VII* (The Edinburgh History of Scotland, volume Three: 1965); but its influence has hardly been beneficial, for other scholars have not really sought to challenge Donaldson's view that James V should be regarded with revulsion as a vindictive king who created a sense of insecurity amongst his subjects and who ultimately practised something of a reign of terror against his nobility. Far too much of this is surely the result of reading history backwards rather than forwards; James V, as the committed representative of the Auld Alliance and of Catholicism, has to be condemned in order to justify the Scottish Reformation and its political corollary, alliance with England. Thus the savaging of the king's reputation began early with the malicious outpourings of John Knox, and has been sustained, with few exceptions, down to the present day. All that has been salvaged is the image of James as a poor man's king, an elusive concept which might be applied to many Stewart kings, or at least to one view of themselves which they sought to publicise.

Dr. Cameron offers us a different portrait of James V, seeing him as a ruler whose policies bear a strong resemblance to those of his popular father. Thus both kings exploited the wealth of the Church in order to finance their wars; both relied heavily on the pursuit of feudal casualties in order to build up royal income; both indulged in legal sharp practice to extract money from their subjects; both ultimately adhered to the Franco-Scottish alliance because it proved financially lucrative to them; both mixed Arthurian myth and the reality of the Anglo-Scottish marriage of 1503 to remind Henry VIII of their closeness to the English throne; and both expended huge sums on the outward trappings of monarchy – on palaces, pageantry, even a royal navy.

These are striking similarities; however, there exists one major difference between father and son, namely the circumstances in which each came to power. James IV succeeded aged fifteen, and took over the reins of government, early in 1495, at the relatively advanced age of twenty-two, without conducting any purge of household or state officials. No such luxury was possible for James V. Succeeding as an infant of eighteen months, he had to endure close on fifteen years of fractious minority, in which – not for the first time – the king became a pawn in the struggles of the major political players – Albany, Arran, Angus, and the queen mother Margaret Tudor – and found himself effectively a prisoner of the Angus Douglases from 1526 to 1528. Dr. Ken Emond has argued that, given the divisions amongst the key political players in 1526, Archibald, sixth earl of Angus, probably felt that he had no option but to retain the person of the young king as a bulwark to the Douglases' continuing power; the alternative was to sacrifice political influence and risk being overwhelmed by rivals and enemies. Hence Angus's *coup d'état* of 1526, and his subsequent lavish distribution of offices in household and state to his family, including the Chancellorship for himself.

Thus the young James V, on taking control of government in the summer of 1528, had no option but to do so by staging a further *coup d'état* with the objective of removing Chancellor Angus and his entire family. This was a messy and only partially successful operation, involving an abortive royal siege of Angus's castle of Tantallon in 1528, protracted military and diplomatic efforts to drive the earl out of southern Scotland, and, once Angus had taken refuge in England, to prevent his return. This lack of a clean break in 1528 certainly coloured James V's relations with his magnates and with the English for much of the personal rule; but as Dr. Cameron shows, the Scottish king did not act in an irrational or vindictive way towards the Second Estate. It is true that he warded most of the principal Border lords in 1530; but this was an essential process given that the threat from Angus remained very real and that the king had to begin by securing a clear acknowledgement of his authority in the south. Significantly Robert, fifth Lord Maxwell, one of the most prominent of the borderers, remained loyal in spite of being warded; indeed, he was subsequently granted control of Liddesdale, made Admiral of Scotland, and as the king's trusted counsellor escorted Mary of Guise to Scotland in 1538.

The classic exception to this general rule of a loyal nobility during the personal rule is the young and foolish Patrick Hepburn, third earl of Bothwell, who in December 1531 offered to assist Henry VIII in an invasion of Scotland. Given his blatant treason, Bothwell's punishment – warding followed by exile – was light, and hardly serves as a demonstration of the king's supposed vindictiveness. And Bothwell's treasons stand out sharply from the norm, which was of a Second Estate supportive of James V from beginning to end of the personal rule, so much so that the king could confidently appoint four of them to govern the country during his absence in France for close on nine months in 1536–7.

It would seem, therefore, that, as Dr. Cameron argues, the extent of crown-magnate tensions during the personal rule has been grossly exaggerated. Certainly there were instances of Stewart sharp practice directed against weak targets amongst the nobility – the earls of Crawford and Morton are cases in point – but royal threats of disinheritance were not carried into effect, and James V seems simply to have been extending his popular father's forceful use of the device of recognition – that is, to make money, not to strip his subjects of their inheritances. Unlike James IV, however, James V was hardly generous in his distribution of royal patronage.

The modern perception of James as a grasping and vindictive king is based, as Dr. Cameron shows, on rather selective use of contemporary evidence. That great mine of information about the court, the Treasurer's Accounts, becomes much less effusive in this reign than in the previous one, with the result that one tends to turn for evidence to the 'bible' of the period, the published letters and papers, foreign and domestic, of Henry VIII, with their wealth of Scottish material. Uncritical reliance on this source, however, carries its dangers, due to an understandable English bias in the reporting of Scottish events. James V was, after all, a king who made two French marriages, flouted his English uncle's wishes, and resolutely opposed any return to Scotland of the English-backed Archibald, earl of Angus. Thus English comments on James V's policies and character are frequently severely critical of the king. For example, Thomas Magnus's 1529 warning to King James about the dangers of using 'yong Consaill', citing the fate of the Scottish king's grandfather as a result, is not only threatening in its language but also quite inaccurate in content; while the Duke of Norfolk's notorious remark of 1537, much quoted out of context, that 'so sore a dread king, and so ill-beloved of his subjects, was never in that land', is to some extent English wishful thinking and needs to be taken with a very large pinch of salt.

However, the English were not alone in seeking to condemn James V for his supposed cruelty. The Scottish border ballad of the reiver Johnie Armstrong – updated in recent times by John Arden's play 'Armstrong's Last Goodnight' – presents us with the 'graceless face' before which Armstrong pleaded in vain for mercy; but this was surely also the face of a resolute Stewart monarch perform-ing one of his primary duties as king, that of punishing thieves and reivers. James V's ruthlessness in performing this task again recalls his father's driving of the justice ayres; and generations of writers on kingship, from Bower to Boece, would certainly have approved. Nor, as Dr. Cameron also shows, is there any need to explain the executions of the Master of Forbes and Lady Glamis as evidence of a streak of sadistic cruelty in the king's nature. An alternative approach, followed here, is to assess the reasons for their indictment, and to consider the question of their guilt or innocence.

There are problems, too, in accepting the post-Reformation view that James V was a 'priestis king', in the pocket of the First Estate and swimming stubbornly against the inexorable tide of religious change. It is true that scholarly opinion is likely to remain divided over the extent and importance within Scotland of laymen with reforming opinions; but Dr. Cameron is surely right to be deeply sceptical of the existence of the king's 'black list' of heretics – 360 of them, with the earl of Arran at the head of the list and including most of the major Scottish magnates. Significantly, this list was first mentioned in March 1543, after James's death, by Sir Ralph Sadler, the English ambassador in Scotland, and Sadler's information may be no more than a gross inflation of earlier English reports that there had been disputes in the Scottish king's council in 1542.

However, such tensions as there were did not deprive James V of very wide support from the First and Second Estates in the autumn war of 1542. In the course of this, the Earl of Huntly won a battle at Hadden Rig, the Duke of Norfolk abandoned invasion plans and went home in October, and in a side-show on the Solway in November, Lord Maxwell was defeated and captured by Sir Thomas Wharton. Early in December, King James made plans to renew the conflict. It was his death at Falkland on the 14th of that month, more likely from cholera or dysentery rather than excessive nervous or mental stress brought on by the news of Solway Moss, which created an immediate crisis at court and made possible early assaults on his reputation.

Yet, as Dr. Cameron shows, acting as an advocate in James V's defence can easily be overdone. Wide magnate support for his policies does not in itself make him a popular king; indeed, there is virtually no trace of enthusiastic endorse-ment of James V in the few surviving contemporary Scottish sources. Even the praise of Sir David Lindsay, employed by the king throughout the personal rule and eventually promoted to Lyon Herald, is rather muted. In 'The Complaynt', Lindsay, it is true, makes approving noises about James's enforcement of law and order in the Highlands and on the borders; but in the 'Testament of the Papyngo', Lindsay's lavish praise of James IV – as 'the glore of princelie governyng', as the king who 'daunted' the 'Savage Iles', Eskdale, Ewesdale, Liddesdale and Annandale, and as the prince whose tournaments attracted contestants from all over northern Europe – leaves us in no doubt as to the identity of the poet's Renaissance paragon. And it may be no accident that while Lindsay credits James IV with organising famous jousts (one of which, at Holyrood in 1508, the poet may have witnessed), the best he can manage for James V is a contest between two Household servants, James Watson and John Barbour.

This rather homely image may simply suggest that, in the early years of the personal rule, James V did not fire Lindsay's imagination to the same extent as the king's father. Yet even as early as 1530, Lindsay reflects on the Arthurian imagery of the 'tabyll rounde' at Stirling, and offers conventional advice to the king on the guidance of his 'Seait Imperiall'. Both these themes would be developed by James V in the latter stages of his reign, and there can be little doubt that the French visit and marriage of 1536–7 marks the watershed of the personal rule. Before 1536 James had been preoccupied with domestic issues, with the continuing problem of the Earl of Angus, and with the spectacular opportunities afforded to him by the playing off of a heretic England against a Catholic Europe. On his return from France in May 1537, he had resolved these issues, had indeed acquired a more prestigious French marriage than had seemed possible even a few years before. Even Madeleine's speedy death did not impair the Franco-Scottish alliance, and James V was soon in receipt of another enormous dowry for his second wife, Mary of Guise-Lorraine.

Thus in what proved to be the last years of the reign, King James displayed an aggressive confidence which was reflected in his renewal and extension of 'imperial' themes whose origins, as Roger Mason has shown, can be traced back to James III in 1469. These themes centre round representations of the closed imperial crown, depicted, for example, on the contemporary portrait of James V and Mary of Guise, and on the superb gold 'bonnet piece' of 1539; while early in 1540 the Scottish imperial crown was itself remodelled and enriched for James V's use at the coronation of his queen at Holyrood in February 1540. These very tangible examples of the Bartolist concept that the king is emperor within his own realm were complemented by the astonishing royal building programmes at Falkland and Stirling, essentially the creation, at enormous cost, of French Renaissance palaces within the short time frame of 1537–1542. And King James's circumnavigation of his realm in the summer of 1540 may in part reflect his 'imperial' view of his kingship; this was a voyage made to emphasise the prestige of a prince in control even of the remotest areas of his kingdom.

In the last analysis, our view of the character and policies of James V is probably formed by our response to the simple fact of his very early and unexpected death. Had he lived, a clearer and probably more complimentary verdict would have been delivered on the personal rule; for the 1540s would then have developed with a young, powerful, and solvent Scottish king in full command of his realm, facing an ageing and ailing English ruler whose legacy was a disputed succession, deep religious divisions, a hostile Europe, and an empty treasury. In the fullness of time, Mary of Guise would have added to her tally of royal Stewart children, securing a smooth adult succession; and the close alliance with France would have led to the earlier enjoyment by the Scots of those huge financial outlays which the French deployed in Scotland in the late 1540s and 1550s, and which Marcus Merriman has so graphically described.

It was not to be. All Stewart kings took some unfinished business with them to their graves; but perhaps James V took more than most.

Norman Macdougall
Series Editor

EDITOR'S NOTE

The tragic death of Jamie Cameron in April 1995 not only deprived us of an able and thoughtful historian whose skills were still developing, but also created the immediate problem of deciding what to do with his work on James V; for Jamie had barely started on the lengthy process of converting his successful Ph.D. thesis into a book. However the importance of the subject, the author's original and challenging views, especially on crown-magnate relations and Anglo-Scottish diplomacy, and the encouragement of friends and colleagues, soon convinced me that Jamie's work ought to be edited and published as quickly as possible. If this is not the finished book which Jamie Cameron himself would have produced – he would, for example, have developed important themes such as the relationship between church and crown and the king's policy towards Ireland – it is nevertheless an important and in many ways radical review of royal policy in a reign which until recently was neglected by scholars and which is still widely misunderstood.

As editor I have tried throughout to avoid being too interventionist, largely leaving the author's work to speak for itself, which for the most part it does extremely eloquently. Here and there I have altered passages for the sake of clarity; I have removed some of the scholarly scaffolding necessary to sustain a thesis, but perhaps less welcome in a book; and I have added an index.

I should like to record my thanks to Aileen Cameron, the inspiration for this publication of *James V* from the very beginning; to John and Val Tuckwell, that ideal publishing duo for harassed writers; and to Margaret Richards, who having undertaken the complex and often problematical task of word-processing the thesis, found herself reliving the whole experience for the book, and did so with unfailing patience, skill, and good humour.

Norman Macdougall
Editor

DEDICATION AND ACKNOWLEDGEMENTS

This book is dedicated to my father-in-law Joseph G.S. Cameron, W.S., who as Jamie said 'would have liked to have done this sort of thing'. This is the dedication on Jamie's doctoral thesis.

Like his father Jamie had a good academic brain. He graduated from St. Andrews University with M.A. Honours in History, then from Edinburgh University with LL.B. with distinction. He was a qualified solicitor at the time of his death. He completed his doctorate at St. Andrews University under the supervision of Dr. Norman Macdougall. Jamie had a great love of Scottish History and believed strongly in its importance.

I am grateful for the opportunity to record my thanks to Norman Macdougall, without whose patience, understanding, guidance and tolerance this book, and in fact its source (the Ph.D.), would not have been completed. Jamie had great respect and affection for Norman and was grateful to him for all his efforts and indeed inspiration. Thanks must also go to Simone Macdougall (and Bonnie) for her friendship throughout the years.

Jamie was lucky to have excellent flatmates, and I would like to thank Dr. Bruce F. Gordon and Dr. Andrew Colin on Jamie's behalf for the good times they had together.

Finally Jamie would also have liked to have thanked his long time friends Andrew Gardner and Dr. Andrew Petersen for the many long and detailed academic discussions they had, whether it was in the hills he loved, our home in Edinburgh, or at Balgonie with Celia, Jamie's mother.

In recognition of Jamie's concern for Scotland, the Scottish people and Scottish History, its study and research, a settlement on Trust was made after Jamie's death. The Trust is called the Dr. Jamie Stuart Cameron Trust, and it was set up to assist postgraduate students of Scottish Mediaeval History. The net proceeds of the sale of this book will benefit the Trust Fund, which is administered by Anderson Strathern, W.S., Edinburgh.

Aileen A. Cameron
Edinburgh, 6 February 1998

CONVENTIONS

Dates are given according to the modern calendar with the New Year beginning on 1 January.

Wherever possible the contractions used in the text to describe printed works are drawn from: *List of Abbreviated Titles of the Printed Sources of Scottish History to 1560* (*SHR*, Supplement, October, 1963). Otherwise, abbreviations are as cited in text and bibliography.

CHAPTER ONE

'Ill Beloved'? James V and the Historians

The received view of James V is of a king who was very successful at making money: this was commented upon by Lesley and Buchanan, writing in the latter part of the 16th century, and again by Donaldson and Mitchison four hundred years later. Indeed these latter two historians have considered the pursuit of wealth to be the prime driving force behind all of James' policies.[1] A quick look at the account books for the reign confirms this impression. Total revenue in 1530–31 was under £24,000 Scots. In 1539–40 it was over £50,000 Scots, almost four times as much as it had been in 1525–26.

Casualty income doubled between 1530 and 1542, while Household costs and other expenditure rose to keep pace with this income.[2] Other sources of revenue were available to the king in the form of taxation (of the Church, burghs and laity); two vast marriage dowries (together worth almost £170,000 Scots); and the appointment of his illegitimate sons to vacant benefices (perhaps yielding £10,000 Scots each year).[3] James' expenditure on royal palaces was partially financed from casualties, but largely through taxation of the Church.[4] A great proportion of this income did not even pass through the account books. When the king died in 1542, he left £26,000 in his treasure chest at Edinburgh castle, which sum was quickly dispersed in his daughter's minority. Knox narrated how in his last few weeks James made an inventory of all his wealth.[5]

In the context of crown-magnate relations this pursuit is said to have made him extremely unpopular. Through blending financial extortion with unpredictable strikes against some magnates James managed to alienate the bulk of his nobility. By taking the counsel of members of the royal Household (and its sub-department the Scottish church[6]) he denied the 'natural' advisers of the monarchy – the Second Estate – the opportunity of remedying the situation. The personal rule ended in humiliation at Lauder in the course of the last week of October 1542. There the decision was taken to disband the Scots host, despite the recent presence on Scottish soil of the 'auld enemy', engaged in burning Kelso abbey and the neighbourhood some twenty-five miles to the south east. The inference taken from this episode is that the lords of Scotland had been driven into refusing to acknowledge that most fundamental feudal concept – to support the king in war. Less than a month later, the fiasco of Solway Moss provided enough good copy for later historians to complete their demolition of James V's political career; at Solway Moss, a Scots army was supposedly thrown into confusion by the efforts of a member of the royal household – Oliver Sinclair – to get himself appointed as its captain. The man supposedly in command – Lord Maxwell – was captured by the English together with two earls and four other lords. Later it was revealed that Maxwell allowed himself to be taken and in fact held Lutheran views. He and his magnate colleagues had taken advantage of the confusion to defect to the 'auld enemy'. In Scotland James V's chief regret was that Sinclair was also captured. James died of nervous exhaustion – or perhaps of a broken heart? Few regretted the passing of this 'terrifying' and 'vindictive' Stewart king.[7]

The verdict is that the king could not establish a working relationship with his magnates, hence their lack of support for him at the end of the reign. James V is seen as an example of complete failure.[8] John Knox simply stated that some called him a murderer of the nobility.[9] James' approach to crown-magnate relations was epitomised in dramatic form in 1537 with the executions of the Master of Forbes and Lady Glamis, and emphasised in 1540 by the execution of James Hamilton of Finnart – all three found guilty of treasonably plotting regicide. The burning of Lady Glamis on the castle hill at Edinburgh has particularly excited the pens of some historians (though the contemporary chronicler Adam Abell was content merely to note the bald facts[10]). Their judgements have ranged from 'an accident' through to 'almost unprecedented vindictiveness'.[11] Whether or not she was guilty (even if only on the balance of probabilities) is almost an afterthought. However, it was in the context of the events immediately following her death that James was dubbed 'ill-beloved' by the Duke of Norfolk.[12]

Other examples of James' approach to politics include his exiling of the third earl of Bothwell and annexation of his lands; and his imprisonment of the fourth earl of Argyll in 1531, of the archbishop of St. Andrews, James Beaton, in 1533, and of the third earl of Atholl in 1534. This last earl, according to Pitscottie and Bingham, had in 1530 entertained the king in a palace especially built for the royal visit. There the king, together with his mother, Margaret Tudor, and the papal ambassador, were wined and dined (with gingerbread, claret and swans on the menu) at Atholl's expense – which amounted to £3000 Scots in total.[13] Additionally, James hounded the eighth earl of Crawford for nonentries – reducing him, in Michael Lynch's words, 'to a near cipher of the court'.[14] In 1541 James attempted to relieve the disabled third earl of Morton of his earldom. Further down the social scale, in the early summer of 1530 the king warded several of the Border lords and lairds – including all three wardens of the Marches – and hanged the notorious Johnnie Armstrong of Gilknockie. The ballad recording this event inspired one historian to thunder that James had the attitude of a schoolboy. Possibly less well known is that in July of the same year, Lord Maxwell, newly out of ward, presented James with a fresh sturgeon, perhaps by way of a thank you for the gift of the escheat of the late John Armstrong.[15]

The Armstrong episode also reflects the image of James V as 'the poor man's king' (first noted by Knox and Chalmers). Bishop Lesley and Buchanan credited James with ease of access to the poor and a sense of justice that drove him to act against their oppressors. This is partially borne out by several civil cases brought before the newly created court of session by 'puir tenants'. James also revived the idea of legal aid, by appointing an 'advocate of the poor'.[16] Records show that the king visited the Borders in almost every year of the reign, and that justice ayres were frequent and lucrative. The wardens were urged to apprehend thieves, but it was Johnston of that Ilk – a trouble maker under Angus – whom the author of the *Diurnal of Occurrents* credits with the capture of George Scott of the Bog. Donaldson has used Scott's execution by burning at the stake to illustrate graphically James' cruelty rather than his sense of justice.[17]

The touchstone to crown-magnate relations throughout the entire personal reign of James V is considered by some historians to be the tension between the king and the Douglases. This theme is sustained throughout – from the sixteenth century author of the *Diurnal*, commenting that the king had a 'great suspicion' of where his temporal lords' sympathies lay, to Dr. Wormald, who comments on the king's 'hounding' of those bearing the surname Douglas.[18] (It is perhaps worth noting here that in 1540 Patrick Hepburn, bishop of Moray, remarked on how James appeared to penalise those of the surname Hepburn[19]). Dr. Kelley considers that James' malice in the last few years of the reign reached 'illogical and alarming proportions', shown by his gullible reactions on hearing rumours of Douglas-inspired treason.[20] Certainly the adult rule of James V caused a hiatus in the Scottish career of the sixth earl of Angus, and possibly it is the obviousness of this fourteen year gap which creates the touchstone. Magnate domination was totally incompatible with adult Stewart monarchy, as the Boyds had discovered in the reign of James III.[21] Purging those families which held power in the minority was nothing new in James V's reign. However, Dr. Emond has argued that the memory of earlier minorities was not a major influence on the consciousness of either the Douglases or the king.[22]

The majority rule of James V can be measured against the reigns of his forebears. The trend set by Wormald and followed by Lynch has been to compare and contrast the individual careers of the first five Jameses against the background of 'a growing corporate image of the Stewart dynasty'. Each individual king simply refined and extended the methods employed by his predecessors to make money. Each moved towards a position of autocracy. Each died before achieving this position, and the subsequent minority restored the balance in Crown-magnate relations.[23]

The greed of the royal Stewarts was first encountered in James I's reign. The act of revocation, which enabled the Crown to re-acquire land granted out in a royal minority and regrant the same (at a price), was first passed by James II. He also saw that ready cash could be made from feu farming. Apprising – the forced sale of land for debt – first occurred in James III's reign. He also experimented with recognition – the repossession of a fief by the superior for illegal alienation by the vassal of the greater part. In James IV's reign 119 instances of apprising and 149 instances of recognitions are recorded in the great seal register. Apprisings were not necessarily for debts owed to the Crown; but exacting payment to avoid recognition was a great money spinner for the Crown as well as being extremely unpopular.[24] So it is perhaps surprising that James V did not use this method of financial extortion, although he was well aware of the legal theory.

The vast majority of the two thousand-odd great seal charters issued in the reign relate to confirmation by the Crown of sales and grants made by third parties. However there are recorded numerous grants, confirmations of grants, and grants in feu farm. Of the one hundred-odd grants of apprised lands only a handful represent debts due to the Crown – almost invariably for nonentries. Nonentry payments affected, amongst others, the earls of Lennox and Crawford, dating from the death of their forebears at Flodden. One extreme example was the attempt to recover one hundred and fifty years' worth of nonentries for the lands of Kincraig in Fife from Walter Lundy of that Ilk, which was reduced by the Lords of Council and Session to fifty-two years.[25] The Crown raised numerous summons of error, not all of which were successfully pursued. Compositions for ward, relief, marriage and nonentry made up a significant portion of the Crown's casual revenue – some £2500 out of £13,000 in 1530, and £6000 out of £25,700 in 1542. Other compositions for charters were of much less significance, save for exceptional ones such as the £1333 paid by the fourth earl of Huntly for the feu of Braemar, Strathdee and Cromar in 1530. The proceeds from justice ayres and remissions were of greater importance.[26] Taxation supplemented these feudal methods, as it had for James IV.

James V followed the example of his ancestors in making money out of his revocation. He also used forfeiture – most notably of the Douglases – to obtain land. Kelley has pointed out that with the sole exception of the Regality of Abernethy – granted to the earls of Argyll – all of the forfeited Angus lands were either in the direct or indirect control of the king long before their formal annexation to the Crown in 1540.[27] This points up the other factor at issue in the manipulation of magnates' resources by any Stewart king – their redistribution in the form of patronage to win support. This was something that James III was bad at and James IV good. The received opinion of James V is that he 'did not love the nobility', and in this respect was akin to his maternal grandfather.[28]

Patronage reflected the individual style of each Stewart king. If the methods employed by James V to make money can be said broadly to have followed along the same lines as those of his predecessors, then it was rather the style of politics practised by him that earned him his reputation amongst his contemporaries and produces the verdict of later historians. There was of course the question of circumstances. In James V's case the coinciding of his adult rule with the growth of the European Reformation has provided various verdicts on the reign[29]. The growing influence of the Lutheran doctrine prompted the Church to begin examinations of heretics, and these on occasion directly involved the king. Abell

[4]

recorded the presence of James V at the trials of Mr. Norman Gourlay and David Stratoun in Holyrood Abbey in 1534. Both men were subsequently burned. Such repression incited the fury of John Knox, who described James as an 'indurate tyrant'.[30]

Others have criticised the king for his religious policy. Bingham considered that James's early death saved him from increasing unpopularity through its pursual.[31] That religious issues played an important part in Scottish diplomacy is certain; negotiations between James and his uncle, Henry VIII, involved debates over doctrine and the advantages or disadvantages which would result from dismantling the monasteries. James also wrote reassuring letters to the Papacy and received the approval of Charles V. The effect on Crown-magnate relations of Lutheranism is more difficult to gauge. It was a useful political ploy for James to threaten his over-taxed clergy with the fate of their English colleagues under Henry VIII if they did not toe the line. Possibly the supposed existence of a 'blacklist' of heretical laymen (headed by the name of the man who first advised Sir Ralph Sadler of its existence, namely the second earl of Arran, governor of Scotland in 1543) made an impression. Perhaps Lord Maxwell used the ploy of coming out as a Lutheran to impress his English captors in 1542. In any event, it is claimed that the most damaging aspect of religion on James' politics was that he was seen to be closeted in the counsel of the First Estate to the exclusion of the Second. Pitscottie's version of the failure of 1542 has the nobility saying of the king that 'he was ane better preistis king nor he was thairis.'[32] Hence the verdict on James' career is that he had the makings of a financial tycoon but as managing director was not popular with the rest of the board.

There are problems with this verdict. It is not necessarily inaccurate. The temptation is to leap to the defence of the Stewart likened to a Tudor.[33] Contemporary English reports dissuade one from so doing. There are virtually no traces of approval – though there are also virtually no contemporary Scottish opinions. Exceptions include Sir David Lindsay, whose works were written in the knowledge that his annual salary of £40 as herald was paid from the Household.[34] In the 'Complaynt' he praises the king for the law and order brought to the Borders and Highlands. The performance of the Epiphany 'Interlude' at Linlithgow in 1540 emphasises the need for the clergy to toe the line. The anonymous 'Strena' praises James unreservedly, but dates from 1528.[35] Adam Abell appears to be strictly factual, in that his account is substantiated by other records. He devotes the greater part of his work to damning Henry VIII; but he also narrates James' use of disguise in his visit to the duke of Vêndome's court in 1536. (The theme of disguise was taken to extreme lengths by Scott with his tales of 'the guidman of Ballengeich').[36] The events of the reign are well recorded in primary sources (though the principal unpublished sources – the *Acta Dominorum Concilii* and *Acta Dominorum Concilii et Sessionis* – are not user-friendly); and it must be admitted that the events upon which the hostile verdict of James V is based did, by and large, occur.

The first problem is that the verdict rests upon too few premises. Instances of oppression, extortion and execution are used rather in the manner of stepping stones to arrive at the verdict. This ignores other events of the reign. The second problem is that these stepping stones themselves may not be as wholly secure as they appear. For example the downfall of Sir James Hamilton of Finnart – seen as the last straw in political relations by some historians – was considered by Buchanan to be no great loss and Knox passed no judgement.[37] The third problem is one of contradictions, best illustrated in the careers of individual magnates. The 'Lutheran' Maxwell was one of James' staunchest supporters, acting as vice-regent in 1536–37. The exiled Bothwell was responsible in part for the expulsion of Angus in 1528–29. The imprisoned Argyll and disaffected Moray of 1531 were reliable warlords on the Borders in later years. The fourth problem is that other events of the reign suggest stable relations and co-operation between the king and his nobility. James spent nine months in France in 1536–37 without worrying about sedition back home, and in 1540 attempted the daunting of the Isles with magnate support. The fifth problem is in the interpretation of 1542. Lynch has suggested that the nobility refused to fight in defence of the realm; others have considered that the Scots army was refusing to go on the offensive; contemporary reports suggested a dire shortage of supplies for English and Scots armies alike.[38]

The final problem is that the verdict of failure in Crown-magnate relations relies more on description than on explanation. Such explanation as there is is general – whether due to religious policy, the culmination of the sharp practice of Stewart monarchy over the previous four reigns of adult kings, or simple greed. There has to be more to the rule of James V than this.

NOTES

1. J. Lesley, *The History of Scotland from the Death of King James I in the Year* 1436 to the Year 1561 [Lesley, *History*], (Bannatyne Club 1830), 167; G. Buchanan, *The History of Scotland* [Buchanan, *History*], translated J. Aikman (Glasgow and Edinburgh, 1827–1829), 2 vols., ii, 265; Rosalind Mitchison, *A History of Scotland* (2nd edn. 1982), 93; Gordon Donaldson, *Scotland: James V - James VII* (Edinburgh History of Scotland, vol. 3, 1965), 44.
2. *Accounts of the Lord High Treasurer of Scotland* [*TA*], vols. v-viii (1515–1546) ed. J.B. Paul (Edinburgh, 1903–1908), v, 407, 462; vii, 250, 361; viii, 10, 117; *The Exchequer Rolls of Scotland* [*ER*], vols. xv-xviii (1523–1542), ed. J.P. McNeill (Edinburgh, 1895–1897), xvi, 127–45; xvii, 269–97; Atholl Murray, 'Exchequer and Crown Revenue of Scotland, 1437–1542' [Murray, *Revenues*] (Ph.D., Edinburgh University, 1961), 120.
3. Murray, *Revenues*, 322, 340–1; Donaldson, op.cit., 46; cf. Michael Lynch, Scotland: A New History (London, 1992), 164, estimates over £40,000 Scots from benefices *per annum*.
4. *TA*, v, 389, 433; vi, 33–4, 151, 232, 363; vii, 231, 502; *Accounts of the Masters of Works* [*MW*], vol. i (1529–1615), ed. H.M. Paton (Edinburgh, 1957), 114, 195, 234, 263, 292.
5. *Registrum Secreti Sigilli Regum Scotorum* [*RSS*], vols. i-ii (1488–1542), edd. M. Livingstone and J.B. Paul (Edinburgh, 1908–1921), ii, no. 383; Murray, *op.cit.*, 346; John Knox, *The*

History of the Reformation in Scotland [Knox, *History*], ed. W.C. Dickinson (Edinburgh 1949), 2 vols., i, 33.

6. Lynch, *op.cit.*, 155.
7. Donaldson, *op.cit.*, 52 (vindictive); Jenny Wormald, *Mary Queen of Scots: a Study in Failure* (London, 1988), 32 (terrifying).
8. Lynch, *op.cit.*, 165; Wormald, *Court, Kirk and Community: Scotland 1470–1625* [Wormald, *Court*], (New History of Scotland vol. iv, London, 1981), 12; Donaldson, *op.cit.*, 60; Mitchison, *op.cit.*, 89; Caroline Bingham, *James V: King of Scots*, 1512–1542 (London, 1971), 184, 188, 191; also comments on James V in Henderson, *The Royal Stewarts* (London, 1914); S. Cowan, *Royal House of Stuart* (1908); P.F. Tytler, *The History of Scotland from the Accession of Alexander III to the Union* (Edinburgh, 1868), v, 299; P. Hume Brown, *History of Scotland to the Present Time* (Cambridge, 1911), i, 314–6; J.D. Mackie, *A History of Scotland* (Penguin, 1969), 140; less damning are Andrew Lang, *A History of Scotland from the Roman Occupation* (Edinburgh and London, 1900), i, 453; and Eric Linklater, *The Royal House of Scotland* (1970), chapter 4.
9. Knox, *History*, i, 35.
10. National Library of Scotland, [NLS] MS 1746 (Adam Abell, 'The Roit and Quheill of Tyme'), f. 126v. The portion of Abell's work which relates to the reign of James V has been translated and assessed by Alasdair M. Stewart, 'The Final Folios of Adam Abell's 'The Roit or Quheill of Tyme' in Janet Hadley Williams (ed.), *Stewart Style*, 1513–42: Essays on the Court of James V (East Linton, 1996), 227–253.
11. Sir Walter Scott, *Miscellaneous Works of*, vol. xxiii, *Tales of a Grandfather*, (II *History of Scotland*, Edinburgh, 1870), 45; Lynch, *op.cit.*, 164.
12. *Letters and Papers, Foreign and Domestic, of the Reign of Henry VIII* [*LP Henry VIII*], 21 vols. (1509–1547), edd. Brewer *et al* (1862–1932), xii pt. ii, no. 696.
13. R. Lindesay of Pitscottie, *The Historie and Cronicles of Scotland* [Pitscottie, *Historie*], (STS, 1899–1901), 3 vols., i, 335–8; Bingham, *op.cit.*, 89–90.
14. Lynch, *op.cit.*, 153.
15. Cowan, *op.cit.*; *TA*, v, 380; *RSS*, ii, no. 702.
16. Knox, *History*, i, 35; *Chronicles of the Kings of Scotland* (Maitland series, 1830), 86; Lesley, *History*, 167; Buchanan, *History*, ii, 264. Instances of poor tenants being represented at Court can be found in Scottish Record Office [SRO], CS6 ('Acts of the Lords of Council and Session') [ADCS], xi, f. 133 ('poor tenants of Nisbet'); xii, f. 139 ('poor tenants of Bothwell'). The idea of legal representation for the poor dates from a 1424 statute; cf. *Introduction to Scottish Legal History* (Stair Society, xx), 417. The appointment of an '*advocat vocatus pauperum*' took this one stage further: SRO, *ADCS*, vi, f. 62; cf. *RSS*, ii, no. 3261.
17. *A Diurnal of Remarkable Occurrents that have passed within the country of Scotland since the death of King James the Fourth till the year 1575* [*Diurnal of Occurrents*], 15; Donaldson, *op.cit.*, 62.
18. *Diurnal of Occurrents*, 12; Wormald, *Court*, 12.
19. Fraser, *Grant*, iii, no. 91.
20. Michael Kelley, 'The Douglas Earls of Angus: A Study in the Social and Political Bases of Power of a Scottish Family from 1389 until 1557' [Kelley, *Angus*] (Ph.D., Edinburgh University, 1973), 748.
21. Norman Macdougall, *James III: A Political Study* (Edinburgh, 1982), 85.
22. William K. Emond, 'The Minority of King James V, 1513–1528' (Ph.D., St. Andrews University, 1988), ii, 360.
23. Wormald, *Court*, 9–13; Lynch, *op.cit.*, 152–5.
24. Macdougall, *James IV* (Edinburgh, 1989), 160–3; Nicholson, R., 'Feudal Developments in Late Medieval Scotland', *JR*, 1973 (1), 13, 17.
25. SRO, *ADCS*, xv, f. 96v.
26. *TA*, v, 338, 344–9, 356; viii, 6, 12.

27. Kelley, *Angus*, 494–5.
28. Donaldson, *op.cit.*, 55, 62.
29. Lynch, *op.cit.*, 162, subtitles his chapter 'James V: new problems, old solutions?'
30. Knox, *History*, i, 22.
31. Bingham, *op.cit.*, 194–6.
32. Pitscottie, *Historie*, i, 402.
33. J.H. Burton, *The History of Scotland* (2nd ed., Edinburgh, 1873), iii, 186; Donaldson, *op.cit.*, 62.
34. *ER*, xvi, Pref. xlv-li, 12, 464.
35. *LP Henry VIII*, xv, no. 114; *The Works of Sir David Lindsay of the Mount*, 1490–1555 (ed. D. Hamer, S.T.S., 1930–36),[Lindsay, *Works*], i, 50; 'Strena Ad James V', in *Bannatyne Miscellany*, iii (Bannatyne Club, 1827–55).
36. Abell, *op.cit.*, f.125v; *LP Henry VIII*, xi, no. 631; Scott, *op.cit.*, 21–5.
37. Buchanan, *op.cit.*, ii, 261; Knox, *op.cit.*, i, 22; cf. Donaldson, *op.cit.*, 58; Wormald, *Court*, 12.
38. Lynch, *op.cit.*, 165; cf. Lang, *op.cit.*, i, 453; Bingham, *op.cit.*, 183; Donaldson, *op.cit.*, 59; *LP Henry VIII*, xvii, nos. 996, 1025.

CHAPTER TWO

The Assumption of Royal Authority

In June 1528, James V was sixteen years old and Scottish affairs were directed by his thirty-eight year old Chancellor, Archibald Douglas, sixth earl of Angus.[1]

Angus had been the dominant figure in Scottish government since at least July 1525. The scheme then devised by the lords in parliament was for the physical custody of the royal person to be rotated amongst his subjects. The safekeeping of the young king was entrusted to one group of leading politicians for a three-month period only, at the end of which a second group would take over for the following quarter succeeded in turn by a third and fourth group. Angus, his kinsman James Douglas, third earl of Morton, and Gavin Dunbar, archbishop of Glasgow, were principal amongst the first group whilst James Hamilton, first earl of Arran and Hugh Montgomery, first earl of Eglinton, headed up the second. James Beaton, archbishop of St. Andrews, and Colin Campbell, third earl of Argyll were in the third group; and John Stewart, third earl of Lennox, William Graham, second earl of Montrose, Cuthbert Cunningham, third earl of Glencairn, and Robert, fifth lord Maxwell, led the fourth.[2]

The scheme fell apart as Angus simply failed to hand over the young king to Arran at the end of the first quarter, in effect executing a simple 'coup d'état'.[3] In June 1526 Angus moved to legitimise his position. It was declared in parliament that James was now fourteen years old and hence of an age to exercise his royal authority personally. Accordingly all prior delegations of such authority were annulled.[4] The king had thus reached his 'majority' – technically responsible from there on for his own decisions, but actually controlled by Angus and a royal Household that shortly was to provide positions for Angus' relatives. Angus' brother, George Douglas of Pittendreich (Elgin) was appointed as carver to the king; their brother-in-law, James Douglas of Drumlanrig (Dumfries), became master of the wine cellar, and their kinsman, James Douglas of Parkhead (Lanark) was made master of the larder.[5] These titles were largely meaningless; the significant point was that the king was under physical supervision of Angus' own supporters.

Angus also secured the offices of state, taking the vacant Chancellorship for himself in 1527 (James Beaton having the previous year resigned office in outrage at Angus' sabotage of his campaign to be promoted as Cardinal) and appointing his uncle, Archibald Douglas of Kilspindie (Perth) first as Treasurer and then also as keeper of the privy seal.[6]

Emond has argued that Angus' coup d'état was not staged primarily as a bid for sole power at a time when the country lacked an adult king, but rather in an effort to preserve his own position as one of the lords of Scotland.[7] Faction fighting was perhaps the principal feature of the minority of James V. Royal authority was intermittently exercised in the form of the governor, John, duke of Albany (first cousin once removed of the king). Albany's third and final tour of duty in Scotland ended in May 1524. Control of government was then exercised by Margaret Tudor with the support of Arran. This was contested by Angus, supported by Lennox. The rotation scheme drawn up in parliament in 1525 reflected current divisions amongst the leading magnates. By holding on to the king's person, Angus obtained not only legitimacy – the declaration of the king's 'majority' in 1526 was a tactic which had been used in 1524 by Margaret's supporters – but also protection. An attack on Angus could be interpreted as an attack on the king.[8]

The first challenge to Angus had come in January 1526 when there was a confrontation between Angus' and Arran's supporters near Linlithgow. Arran backed down. Later in the same year he lent his support to Angus.[9] On 21 June 1526 a secret council was appointed in parliament to advise the king. Its members included Angus, Argyll, Lennox, Morton, Glencairn, Lord Maxwell and Gavin Dunbar, archbishop of Glasgow. Five days later James V obliged himself to Lennox to take the earl's advice on all important occasions 'fyrst and befor ony man'.[10] The second challenge to Angus came in July 1526 with an attempt by Sir Walter Scott of Buccleuch to abduct the king. The skirmish at Darnick, near Melrose, between the Scotts on the one hand and the Humes and Kerrs in Angus' company on the other, resulted in the death of Andrew Kerr of Cessford.[11] It is not clear whether or not Buccleuch at this point was acting in league with Lennox, but later in the same year he joined that earl in a fresh attempt to abduct the king. However, by this time not only had Lennox changed sides but so also had Arran. In September 1526 Lennox's attack on the forces about the king at Linlithgow was beaten off and Lennox himself was killed. The official criminal record stated that the attack was made upon the earl of Arran's supporters. Sir James Hamilton of Finnart was suspected of being Lennox's killer. The contemporary chronicler, Adam Abell, interpreted the clash as being between Lennox and Angus. In the parliament of September 1528, a charge of treason was laid against Angus and his supporters for '. . . exponying of our soverane lord to battell he being of tendir age . . .' on the fields of both Melrose and Linlithgow.[12]

For Emond the agreement reached between Lennox and James V on 26 June 1526 was the first unmistakable sign of the king showing an independence of action, not in accord with his custodians.[13] Certainly, the intention in parliament was to have Angus, not Lennox, appointed as the chief counsellor of the king.

The bond with Lennox was therefore made without Angus' knowledge, and Emond has observed that it is significant as being the only bond made between James and an individual magnate, possibly indicative of his desperation to be free of the Douglases.[14] However, it is equally possible that the initiative lay with Lennox, who had perhaps pretensions of staging his own coup d'état and thus aligning the royal cause with his own. The Lennox Stewarts were next in line to the throne after the Arran Hamiltons, and thus outranked the Angus Douglases. At Linlithgow, Arran and his 'part-takers, there assembled for the preservation and defence of the king's person',[15] might well have welcomed an opportunity to repulse Lennox and his supporters. The ward of the Lennox earldom was initially distributed equally between Angus and Arran.[16]

The failure of the Lennox abduction in September 1526 prompted Angus to strengthen his control of both Household and government. This in effect meant a narrower concentration of power, with Angus both unwilling either to trust or appeal to Lennox supporters and unable to maintain solidarity with Arran, who attended the sessions of the Lords of Council at Edinburgh on just two occasions after Linlithgow.[17] Emond has argued that from that point onwards the failure of the Angus Douglas régime was inevitable, with the king only waiting for an opportunity to escape.[18] In his interpretation the 'failed policies' of the Angus government rendered it 'dispensable' once the king and Angus were no longer 'compatible'.[19] This suggests that the king's desire to escape from his Chancellor and his dissatisfaction with his Chancellor's policies were not necessarily correlated. In fact, the opportunity to escape and the motive which lay behind it both originated in 1528; the rationale, that the king had been held against his will by the Douglases since Linlithgow, was not the central issue at stake.

One of the substantive charges brought against Angus, which his lawyer and Secretary, John Bellenden, had to answer in the first parliament held under the personal rule (September 1528), concerned an incident in the Borders. The charge was of:

> . . . treasonable art and part of assistance and maintenance given to John Johnston of that ilk bound in service to Angus to harry and burn with company of thieves and evil doers diverse times by day and night in the month of June bipast corns, lands and lordships and houses in sheriffdoms of Annandale and Niddesdale, pertain to James in property and other diverse buildings lands and houses within said sheriffdoms. . . .[20]

The particular concern was with an attack made by Johnston on the royal lands of Duncow in Nithsdale. The underlying issue was that Angus was failing to give good government in the Borders.

Angus was warden of the East and Middle Marches from 15 March 1526 until July 1528.[21] In the East March he succeeded Lennox who had been appointed in September 1524. The traditional wardens were the lords Hume; however the third lord had been executed for treason in 1516 and George, fourth lord Hume, at best acted as deputy-warden. In the Middle March Angus succeeded Andrew Kerr of Cessford, who acted as deputy until his death at Darnick. On the West March Lord Maxwell had acted as warden since 1515, and his suitability for this task – being the chief man of the area – was never seriously questioned by those in power, whether or not they were in agreement over other issues.

The Angus earldom embraced various border territories. In the east, in Berwickshire, Angus held the regality of Bunkle and Preston and the lands of Dye forest. In East Lothian was the lordship of Tantallon. Further south lay the barony of Selkirk and regality of Jedburgh-forest.[22] To the south-west of these areas was Liddesdale. Formerly a possession of the earls of Angus, in the reign of James IV the lordship had been exchanged for the lordship of Kilmarnock, then a possession of the Hepburn earls of Bothwell.[23] Patrick Hepburn, third earl of Bothwell, was of an age with James V and he was tutored by his great uncle, Patrick Hepburn, prior of St. Andrews, whilst his affairs were managed by his uncle, the Master of Hailes.[24] Hailes was thus charged with giving good order for Liddesdale in 1518, and again in September 1527.[25] However Angus took it upon himself to intervene in the pursuit of good government. In February 1526 he assumed responsibility for the area; in April and then again in June he led punitive expeditions against thieves.[26]

A punitive raid had also been directed against Hailes' own house of Bolton in East Lothian in 1524, in the course of which the house was destroyed by fire. The raid was conducted by Angus, Lennox, Maxwell, Malcolm, third lord Fleming, and the Master of Glencairn or Kilmaurs. It was declared by act of parliament in June 1526 that this had been authorised by the king for the purpose of detaining rebels in Hailes' company. Hailes was aggrieved; and in January 1529 he petitioned the Lords of Council that the terms of the declaration might be reduced in acknowledgement of the service that the Hepburns could offer the new administration. The lords agreed to look into the matter, but nothing further happened during James V's reign; not until fourteen years later, in 1543, when Hailes made supplication to parliament that the 1526 ruling be revoked. If this were done then Hailes could pursue Angus through the civil courts for compensation for the destruction of Bolton. Hailes claimed that the late king had intended to revoke the act in his majority but was unable to do so because of the influence of enemies of the Hepburns.[27] Interference in their border territory and burning their castle hardly endeared the earl of Angus to the Hepburns, and a further insult was the appointment in June 1526 of Comptroller Thomas Erskine of Haltoun as king's Secretary in place of Patrick Hepburn, prior of St. Andrews.[28]

In the period of his domination of Scottish government, Angus assumed a large measure of responsibility for the keeping of good order in the Borders. As well as raids on Liddesdale and other Hepburn territory, in July 1526 he took the king with him to Peebles and Jedburgh, in order to hold justice ayres. The intention was apparently to proceed to Whithorn, but the itinerary was disrupted by Buccleuch's attack.[29] Angus had at least the co-operation of his deputies. Lord Hume, Andrew Kerr of Fernieherst, Mark Kerr of Littledean and Andrew Kerr in Littledean were all in November 1526 given thanks in parliament for their support of the king – and Angus – in resisting the attacks by first Buccleuch and then Lennox. In the same year they gave redress for their respective Marches, the Kerrs carrying out the duties on behalf of the young Walter Kerr of Cessford.[30] Cessford himself was appointed as chief cupbearer in the Household in succession to the discredited Buccleuch.[31] However this co-operation did not stretch far enough for Angus to maintain credibility as an effective controller of the Borders.

In the summer of 1527 the English rebel, Sir William Lisle, broke free from gaol at Newcastle and headed for refuge into Scotland accompanied by an assortment of Border thieves, both English and Scots. Lisle then proceeded to conduct raids into England (he had originally been apprehended for sedition and inciting anti-government riots in Northumberland), using the debatable lands of Canonbie (Dumfriesshire) as a base. The Council of the North suspected that he was being aided and abetted by the Armstrong family, whose heartland was in Liddesdale. The Scottish government accordingly began to be bombarded with requests for its co-operation in detaining Lisle and suppressing the copy-cat disturbances created by his activity. These letters were initially addressed to Angus, who in August 1527 replied that both he and his fellow warden, Maxwell, had been ordered by their king to detain Lisle. He suggested, however, that as Lisle appeared to be operating from the debatable lands, the problem could not be pinned solely on Scotland.[32] This did not impress the English wardens, who then demanded redress for crimes committed by the Armstrongs, claiming that they were offering shelter to Lisle and his followers in Ewesdale.[33]

Maxwell staged a warden court in September with the English deputy, Sir Thomas Clifford, and further meetings were planned to address issues arising from disturbances in Tynedale and Redesdale.[34] However Lisle remained at large. In November and again in December Angus sent letters apologising for the failure of his colleagues and offering to meet his counterpart, the earl of Northumberland, in person to resolve outstanding difficulties.[35] Both sides then entered into discussions as to a suitable meeting place. In the course of this dialogue, in January 1528, Lisle and several Scotsmen, including various Armstrongs, voluntarily surrendered themselves to Northumberland's forces. Under interrogation, Lisle's kinsman, Nicholas Lisle, alleged that no steps had been taken at all by either Angus or his colleagues, Maxwell and Bothwell, to pursue Lisle and detain him. This was perhaps little more than idle boasting, but it prompted a reproving note from the English government addressed to both Angus and James V, urging them to be more diligent in the detention of rebels in the future.[36] To underline the point Lord Dacre, the English warden in the West March, conducted a raid into the debatable lands with the intention of flushing out more of Lisle's supporters. Lord Maxwell retaliated by raiding into Cumberland and burning Netherby. In March 1528 both wardens met to give redress for these incidents, but Dacre was not satisfied with Maxwell's attitude at the day of truce and subsequently wrote a letter of complaint to Angus, expressing his surprise that Angus had not seen fit to order Maxwell to give satisfactory redress. Angus' response was to attempt to gather a force together to lead a punitive expedition against Liddesdale, but he had to retire to Edinburgh for lack of support.[37]

The Lisle episode served to discredit Angus. The three year truce between England and Scotland concluded in January 1526 had entered into its final year and the parties had to have mutual confidence in their abilities to liaise over cross-border disturbances. The English questioned Angus' grasp of the situation; he appeared unable to communicate effectively with Maxwell, made excuses for not acting decisively to detain Lisle, and would not commit himself to a definite meeting with Northumberland. More importantly, the episode served to prompt James V into signs of independent thought. He, as well as his Chancellor, received the letters of complaint and sent back suitable apologies. Probably his own letters were vetted before they went out – possibly they were even dictated for him – but he could be in no doubt that the Scots government was not presenting a very smart public image. Sixteen years old on 10 April 1528 – older than his father had been at the beginning of his reign – James' memories of earlier chaotic government during his minority were presumably overlaid by current issues.

On 16 April 1528 a session of the Lords of Council met at Edinburgh, presided over by the Chancellor. Also in attendance were George Leslie, fourth earl of Rothes, and Lords Forbes and Somerville; the Treasurer, Douglas of Kilspindie; the king's advocate, Adam Otterburn of Auldhame; the Comptroller, Sir James Colville of Ochiltree, and the Secretary, Thomas Erskine. The recorded business of the session was purely judicial in nature.[38] However further business was dealt with off the record at around this time. Writing some nine months later, James described how he had confronted his Chancellor at Easter time before members of his Council and called him to task for his '. . . abusing of our auctorite . . .'.[39] The outcome was the proposal that the king in person should lead an expedition against Liddesdale. This was scheduled to take place in June.[40] The impression being given was of a king now willing to participate actively in governing his country and prepared publicly to upbraid his Chancellor. Of course there was probably an element of exaggeration in James' own account of the Easter showdown, and if this did indeed occur in the course of the April session, the presence of one earl, two lords and a handful of officers of state did not create a full public occasion. However by the end of May, the Lords of Council had made full arrangements for a royal expedition. Proclamation was made for the lieges to convene on 20 June to pass with the king against thieves and traitors in the south,. The session opened on 18 May with Angus, Montrose, David Lindsay, eighth earl of Crawford, and lords Fleming, Erskine and Somerville in attendance. James himself sat on the afternoon of 20 May, though this was simply to hear pledges for good behaviour being lodged on behalf of one Walter Stewart of Balquhidder. Business arising out of arrangements for the forth-coming raid took place in his absence. By the close of the session, on 28 May, the earl of Rothes and lords Cathcart, Lindsay and Hume had put in appearances, with Bothwell requesting absolution from all responsibility for Liddesdale whilst the raid was in progress.[41]

Whilst the Lords of Council were deliberating in Edinburgh, further tit-for-tat raids were taking place on the West March. After the Armstrongs and Irvines burnt Artureth in Cumberland, Lord Maxwell was reported by Lady Dacre to be in such trouble with his king that he dared not appear in Edinburgh and was sending his wife instead.[42] Then, in early June, John Johnston of that Ilk attacked the royal lands of Duncow. These lands were looked after by Maxwell, who acted as steward for Duncow as well as for Kirkcudbright, and also as captain of Threave and Lochmaben castles.[43] Again it appeared as if Maxwell was failing in his duties. In fact Angus took the blame. Defending him in parliament in September 1528 Bellenden argued that Johnston's crime had arisen out of a private feud with Maxwell, and quite reasonably pointed out that if there had been treason committed then surely the principal parties involved should also be charged.[44]

The tie-ups amongst the various Border families proved to be too intricate for Angus simply to expect his instructions for law and order to be obeyed. Maxwell had enlisted the support of the Armstrongs in his feud with the Johnstons. The Armstrongs themselves had their own grievances against the Johnstons, one John Johnston in 1527 failing to answer a summons for the murder of one Simon Armstrong.[45] In 1525 Maxwell had received from one John Armstrong and his heirs, kin, friends and servants, a bond of manrent given in exchange for Maxwell's grant of the non-entry of lands in Eskdale. It was of little concern to Maxwell were his supporters to engage in cross-border raids, whatever the concerns of central governments. This laissez-faire attitude was shown clearly in repeated English complaints. Maxwell simply ignored Angus' instructions to proclaim the Armstrongs as rebels.[46] In fact the Johnston raid on Duncow was in retaliation for an earlier attack on them by the Armstrongs, in which three Johnstons died. Maxwell was reputed to be lying in wait to assassinate Johnston of that Ilk should an opportunity arise out of the skirmish.[47]

The Armstrongs also had links with the Kerr family, who were responsible for the Middle Marches. Angus' failure to launch a raid on Liddesdale in March 1528 was attributed to the Kerrs' refusal to support him because '. . . thaye were under bonnde of assuraunce with the said Armistrounges . . .'.[48] Nor could Angus place much confidence in his deputies on the East March, the Hume family. George, fourth lord Hume, whose main lands lay in the south-east, was also the superior of the lordship of Ewesdale in the south-west. There, Maxwell held land of Hume, together with the patronage of the kirk of Ewes.[49] The Armstrongs were also tenants of Hume; on 10 June 1528 he granted forty pounds worth of land in feu farm to David and Ninian Armstrong, receiving their bond of manrent the following month. Both former tenants promised that they and their heirs, kin and dependants, would take Lord Hume's part against all others excepting only the king and Lord Maxwell. The bond was perhaps given to guarantee their future good behaviour as holders of the land, but the grant of the lands themselves was made before the breach between Angus and the king became public knowledge.[50] The Hepburns, for their part, were not only disaffected from Angus, but anxious to dissociate themselves from any liability for Liddesdale whenever punitive expeditions were proposed by the royal government.

Hence, for all Angus' efforts to deal with the problem of Liddesdale and the Armstrongs, his reward was to be condemned for his association with the criminal activity of their enemies, the Johnstons. Bellenden's point was perfectly valid – neither Johnston of that Ilk nor the Armstrongs' ally, Lord Maxwell, had been summoned as the principal parties involved in the burning of Duncow. Furthermore, there was no evidence suggesting either a connection between Johnston and Angus or any involvement by Angus in the incident. Nevertheless, the whole issue of border control provided the king with a plausible motive for dissociating himself with his Chancellor's policies. On 23 June 1528, shortly after the breach, James wrote to Henry VIII:

> Derrest uncle, Ze sall understand ye Estatis of oure Realme and Consaile ar in ane parte disconentit of ye ordoure of justice ministrat in tyme bypast be ye Erle of Angus aure Chancellaire. . . .

He then went on to lay the blame for recent disturbances on Angus.[51]

Lack of good government provided both the stimulation and an excuse for the king to begin to act independently of his Chancellor. The rationale for the change in circumstances was given in a further treason charge against Angus examined in the September parliament:

> . . . the tressonable art and part of the holding of our soverane lordis person aganst his will continualie be the space of twa yers last bipast and aganst the decreit of the lordis of his parliament quhor it was ordanit that our soverane lordis persaine suld have in keping be for devidit Parts in the yeir in the hands of certane lords as thair course come unto the month of June last bipast in to the which month our soverane lord putt himself to liberty. . . .[52]

This referred back to the scheme of rotation devised in the July 1525 parliament. The implication being made in the charge was that this scheme was acceptable; in July 1525 the king was thirteen years old and the parliamentary arrangements made for his custody for one full year until he reached the age of fourteen were not being challenged. However the continuation of his custody for a further two-year period constituted treason. After all, in the parliament of

June 1526 James had been declared as reaching his majority aged fourteen – this being determined by Angus. Clearly then the king had been illegally held captive by Angus for the first two years of that majority.

The wording of the charge thus neatly hoisted Angus with his own petard – he had declared the king to be of age in order to legitimise his own position in 1526; now after two years he was legitimately accused of treasonably contravening that declaration. By focusing only upon the previous two years, a veil was also drawn over earlier events of the minority; James' sole concern was with the treasons committed by the immediately preceding régime. Arran and others who had collaborated with the Douglases were also presumably relieved that it was only Angus and his immediate supporters who were the subjects under focus in the September parliament. At the same time the charge at once validated the 'rescue' attempts made in 1526 by Buccleuch and Lennox. The choice of words used also indicates that the treason lay not only in holding the king against his will, but also against the terms of the 1525 act of parliament, that is, before the majority of the king (at fourteen years) had been declared.

Bellenden's answer to the charge of holding the king against his will was one of robust denial. He argued that the Douglases had done no such thing; for the past three years (not just two), James had been free to ride where he pleased with as many or as few retainers as he wished, and often with never a Douglas in his company, '. . . as is well kent . . .'. In any case the Douglases held a remission granted in 1520 for all crimes before that date, and no treasons had been committed after it.[53] The verdict of the chroniclers, on the whole, did not support this contention. Abell twice spoke of the king 'expelling' Angus from him; the *Diurnal* cautiously described the 1526 'rescues' as being made because the king was '. . . held aganis his will, as said is . . .'. James then '. . . by flicht wan away fra the Douglassis . . .'. Lesley described the king as '. . . nocht willinge to remane langer under the tutell and governement of the erle of Angus and his cumpanye . . .'. Pitscottie provided a dramatic tale of an escape by James made in darkness from the palace of Falkland from under the nose of James Douglas of Parkhead. Buchanan described how the Douglases felt quite secure both in the king's affections as they allowed him to indulge in allurements and improper pleasures (which accounted for his ruined character in later years) and in government, as there was no faction to oppose them nor any fortified place for any opposition to use.[54]

The charge that James had been held against his will suggests a king meekly waiting for two years for an opportunity to escape. However it was not until 1528 that the first clear signs of royal initiative appeared. It is tenable that, since the Lennox attempt of 1526, the king had been denied such an opportunity, but the circumstances of 1528 – the king reaching the age of sixteen with his Chancellor unable to control the border situation against the background of the expiring truce with England – present a more credible argument for this being the year of James' realisation that he should now assume power. There can only be speculation on the outcome had Lennox succeeded in 1526 – whether he would have replaced the Angus régime with members of his own faction or whether, in Emond's words, the king would have established a 'broad based' personal rule.[55] Possibly the Hamiltons might not have resisted Lennox at Linlithgow had they anticipated the latter outcome. This would surely have resulted in treason charges brought against them. The charge in the September 1528 parliament that James had been 'exposed at tender age' to the battle of Linlithgow avoided the suggestion that the Hamilons as well as the Douglases were thereby treasonably implicated. This gives the distinct impression that the 'rescues' of 1526 had more to do with a struggle for supremacy amongst magnates rather than a royal attempt to assume power.

The motive and rationale for the royal assumption of power were both present by June 1528. James also required an opportunity. This was provided for him by his mother, Margaret Tudor. For some years Margaret had been seeking divorce from Angus, and by December 1527 she no longer regarded herself as being married to him. A copy of the decree in her favour reached Scotland early in April 1528, the petition for divorce having been heard over a year earlier in Rome. By April Margaret was already married for the third time, to Henry Stewart, brother of Lord Avandale. This marriage was not seen as politic in so far as it impinged on Anglo-Scottish relations. Cardinal Wolsey strongly urged his master's sister to stay with Angus. Angus himself took steps to prevent the two from physically meeting. John, fifth lord Erskine, sheriff of Stirling and keeper of its castle, was instructed to blockade the stronghold to prevent Henry Stewart from entering. Stewart was apparently detained, and by May the queen was to be found in Edinburgh and the Chancellor issuing charters in Stirling.[56] In Abell's words:

> . . . when he [the king] grew to man's age first he was apparently moved against Harry Stewart that married his mother after divorce between the foresaid earl [Angus] and her. . . .[57]

This related to the position in April and early May, with the king achieving the age of sixteen and Erskine patrolling Stirling castle. However on 17 July Margaret and Stewart were granted the free barony of the lands of Methven in recognition of their marriage and in reward for services both past and future. Both Stirling castle and the lands of Methven were part of Margaret's estates granted in liferent at the time of her first marriage. Stewart was created Lord Methven.[58]

Details of James V's movements in the summer of 1528 are not comprehensive, largely due to the absence of the Treasurer's accounts for the years 1527 to 1529. In the place of an authentic, verifiable record there has arisen Pitscottie's story of an escape from Falkland palace which cannot be substantiated by the official records – although it has been accepted by some historians in recent years. Lang first put forward a more tenable account of the escape from the Douglases, using the dating of the great seal as an indication of the timing of events.[59]

During the May 1528 session of the Lords of Council, eight charters were issued under the great seal. Only one entry in the register – on 20 May – cited a witness list, the rest simply noting the witnesses being as for other charters. The witnesses were Angus, as Chancellor; James Beaton, archbishop of St. Andrews; George Crichton, bishop of Dunkeld; Gavin Dunbar, bishop of Aberdeen and clerk register; Patrick Hepburn, prior of St. Andrews; William Douglas, abbot of Holyrood and brother of Angus; Archibald Douglas of Kilspindie, Treasurer and keeper of the privy seal; James Colville of Ochiltree, the Comptroller; Thomas Erskine of Haltoun, the Secretary; and the earls of Arran and Rothes. The charter was issued from Edinburgh, as indeed were all the great seal charters for the duration of the session, the last charter being dated 25 May.[60] On 27 May Angus wrote from Edinburgh to Lord Dacre informing him that the royal expedition against Liddesdale would take place on 22 June. Angus then closed the session on 28 May with Rothes, Kilspindie and Bishop Crichton also sitting.[61] The king's presence in Edinburgh was recorded on 20 May. He next appeared in the records on 19 June, writing from Stirling to advise that the expedition was to be postponed owing to disturbances '. . . in the inland of our realm . . .'.[62] Four days later, again writing from Stirling, James pointed the finger at his Chancellor as being to blame.

The breach was now public. The place of issue of royal charters also switched from Edinburgh (25 May) to Stirling (from 30 May to 26 June).[63] The clerks in the chancery office, however, did not take cognizance of any change in circumstances until 26 June, when new names appeared as testifiers. The witnesses cited for the charter issued at Stirling on that date were Gavin Dunbar, archbishop of Glasgow, as Chancellor; Malcolm, third lord Fleming as Chamberlain; the Comptroller, Secretary and Clerk Register all as before; the prior of St. Andrews and bishop Crichton as before; with the latter now acting keeper of the privy seal; the abbot of Dryburgh; and the earls of Arran (again as before), Argyll and Eglinton.[64] Beaton, Angus, Rothes, Kilspindie and the abbot of Holyrood had come off the register. James was describing Angus as his Chancellor as late as 23 June, and the decision to replace him presumably was made between 23 and 26 June. The author of the *Diurnal* recorded that Kilspindie lost the office of keeper of the privy seal as late as 2 July. Crichton, the new privy seal, in fact only moved to Stirling after 20 June, as after the session closed on 28 May he presided over two daily meetings in Edinburgh attended only by lawyers.[65] His appointment was made probably at the same time as Archbishop Dunbar became Chancellor. Letters under the privy seal were issued from Stirling on 28 May and from Edinburgh on 31 May.[66] The great seal was moved from Edinburgh to Stirling between these two dates, and it is tempting to suggest that in making the requisite entries in the privy seal register the clerk mistakenly entered the placenames round the wrong way, as otherwise the privy seal appears to have been travelling in the opposite direction from its big brother. This illustrates that the movements of king, court and government did not always coincide. However, in noting that the great seal charters registered as being issued from Stirling on 31 May and 3 and 23 June were testified 'ut in aliis cartis', the chancery clerks were surely referring to the list of 26 June and not to the list of 25 May, as otherwise the implication would be that Angus and his supporters simply moved with the king from Edinburgh to Stirling and were dismissed from Stirling. For the charter issued at Stirling on 1 June the clerk entered in the testification clause 'ut in cartis precedentibus', suggesting that this did happen. However this was a conventional phrase, used as an alternative to 'ut in aliis cartis'. If the register was being written up with reference to the witnessed charter of 26 June, then it may have slipped in by error.

Contemporary report indicated a royal escape between 25 May and 19 June:

> . . . the kinge of Scotts rode en secret and guyett maner frame Edynburgh to Stirling with the nomber of V or VI horses. . . .[67]

This report of an escape by her son from her ex-husband originated with Margaret Tudor, who sent a despatch from Stirling to the earl of Northumberland. This was undated, but the context set the events described as occurring at this time and indicates that it was written in June:

> . . . Furst that the kynge of Scotts haith takyn the towne of Sterlyng frome the quene by the partyall Counsaill whiche was bequested her in the testament of the late kynge of Scotts her husband. . . .[68]

Abell continued his account with the information that Margaret voluntarily surrendered Stirling castle to her son: '. . . And by his mother's request after he [Henry Stewart] was forgiven and she deliverand the castle . . .'.[69]

In July 1528 the session met at Stirling and '. . . the lordis consalis the kingis grace to mak his principale residence in this toune . . .'. Reference was made in the Comptroller's account the following year to the transfer of maintenance expenses for the castle and gardens from the queen's household to the king's household.[70] Lang, working on the assumption that where the great seal went the king was also to be found, suggested that the surrender was prearranged between mother and son at Stirling in early May, where charters were issued between the 9 and 12 of the month. This seems unlikely given that Angus, as Chancellor, also accompanied the great seal; besides, Margaret was in Edinburgh on 11 May.[71] Using the same assumption Lang then placed the king's secret ride to Stirling between 28 May (at the close of the Edinburgh session) and 30 May (charter issued Stirling).[72] This is plausible. Angus was in Edinburgh on 30 May, writing to Lord Forbes on the subject of the wardship of the earldom of Huntly;[73] the great seal charter registered as being issued from Stirling on that date almost certainly was testified by the new group of witnesses. Hence, unless Angus rode to Stirling on 30 May, the great seal had travelled there without him, taken by James.

Whether or not the king was expected by his mother to turn up secretly in

Stirling, she had reason to welcome him, estranged as she was from Angus and anxious to secure recognition of her third marriage. Whilst the narrative clause of the charter registered on 3 June is conventional in style, the idea that the subject matter – a grant in feu farm of lands in Stirlingshire in favour of the Comptroller – was being made with the consent of the king's mother could perhaps be taken literally on this occasion.[74] The reception at Stirling gave the king his opportunity to establish an independent power base from which to begin his personal rule. Buchanan's account of the escape echoes Abell; all that James had lacked until this point was a fortified place from which to challenge the Douglases, and this was provided him by his mother as part of a private bargain. On 18 July the Lords of Council indeed advised the king to make Stirling his headquarters until parliament opened in September.[75] Clearly the creation of the Methven lordship in July was a reward for this service.

If Lang's argument is accepted, then the king was in Stirling on 30 May, now physically free from his Chancellor, who remained in Edinburgh. However there followed a period of nearly three weeks, until 19 June, before James made his next move – to postpone the royal Borders expedition scheduled for 22 June. In the absence of any record of events occurring during that period, it can be conjectured that there was no official pronouncement of the breach between king and Chancellor. Proclamation had already been made for the lieges to convene to pass with the king on the Borders expedition; it can be hazarded that at some point before 19 June, Stirling was stipulated as the place of convention. James' letter of postponement prompted Northumberland to send a spy into Scotland to find out what was going on. The spy reported that James was in Stirling acting on the advice of Margaret Tudor, Archbishop Beaton, the earls of Arran, Argyll, Moray and Eglinton and other unspecified persons.[76] This list almost coincided with Margaret's own report on the king's advisers in Stirling; she listed Arran, Argyll, Eglinton, Moray, Lords Avandale, Sinclair and Maxwell, and Sir Hugh Campbell of Loudoun, sheriff of Ayr, '. . . and other dyverse lordes that used not ye courte sith the tyme that the Erle of Lymoges [Lennox] was slayne . . .'.[77] Arran, Argyll and Eglinton were witnesses to the great seal charter issued on 26 June, and in all likelihood of the four earlier charters issued from Stirling. It is tempting to speculate that these four earlier charters may have been drawn up and entered on the register prior to their being issued; the charter of 3 June has noted in the margin the phrase 'nondum levatur' (not yet raised). If that were the case, then the testing clause was added as the various testifiers arrived at Stirling.

It is also possible that the English spy may have confused his archbishops, as it was Dunbar, as Chancellor, rather than Beaton, who testified on 26 June. Argyll's presence at Stirling was recorded on 18 June.[78] Maxwell's appearance, fresh from his activities in the West March, suggests a confidence belying Lady Dacre's report on 2 June that he had sent his wife to court (presumably at Edinburgh) to face the king's wrath in his stead. Possibly Lady Maxwell returned home with the news that Angus and James were no longer acting with one accord. Margaret's reference to persons arriving at Stirling who had boycotted the court since 1526 certainly suggests that news of the estrangement between king and Chancellor had filtered through the country by 19 June. Though she was no doubt using the term 'court' loosely, her despatch also served as a reminder of the distinction between court and government; Moray and Arran had both been lords of the articles in the parliament of November 1526, whilst they had both acted as witnesses to great seal charters since then, as had Argyll, Eglinton and Maxwell – all testifying after Angus. Arran, of course, had acted as witness in Edinburgh on 20 May 1528.[79]

Margaret's report from Stirling continued '. . . by this forsaid apperance in the countrey it is supposed that ther wol be a chaunge in the Courte of Scotlande . . .'. This was verified by Northumberland's spy who stated that James was to hold a meeting with his lords on 29 June at Stirling, and from there proceed to Edinburgh. James himself, on 23 June, writing to his uncle from Stirling, confirmed that a convention would be held to examine his Chancellor's maladministration. However this would take place on 10 July with Edinburgh as the venue.[80] Northumberland's spy also added that on 29 June, proclamation was made at Stirling by the king that Angus should not come within seven miles of him because of his failure to keep justice and his misrule. This proclamation was also noted by both Buchanan and the author of the *Diurnal*.[81] In the parliament of September 1528, John Bellenden attempted to answer the charge levied against Angus of:

> . . . the treasonable art and part of the convocatione of our soverane lords legis within his burgh of Edinburgh viii dais continualie befor the first day Julie. . . .

The charge was amplified in the trial of Angus' supporter, Alexander Drummond of Carnock (Stirling), who was accused of:

> . . . art and part of the giving of counsale favour and assistence to Archibald Erle of Angus and George Douglas his brother, to invaid oure soverane lands persone and the baronis that ware with him for his defence in the burgh of Stirling in the monthe of Junie last bipast. . . .

In December 1528, a similar summons was raised against Janet Douglas, Lady Glamis, John Hume of Blackadder (Berwick), Hugh Kennedy of Girvanmains (Ayr), and Patrick Charteris of Cuthilgurdy (Perth) for their

> . . . arte et parte consilii assistencie auxilii et favoris prestit et exhibit archibaldo olim comiti Angusie ad convocando legios regios et barones apud burgo de Edinburgh acto diebus continuis precedens primum diem mensis Junii [sic]. . . .[82]

The clear inference was that Angus breached the terms of the proclamation. Buchanan and Pitscottie both state that Angus attempted to pursue James V (from Falkland) to Stirling before retiring to Linlithgow, and thence to Edinburgh.[83] In fact Angus' movements between 30 May, when he was at Edinburgh, and 18 July when he was at Dalkeith, are unrecorded. It is possible that he had left Edinburgh by 27 June. On this date a further charter under the great seal was granted at Edinburgh in favour of the Master of Glencairn, Angus' cousin. This concerned the apprising and assignation to the Master of forty shillings' worth of land formerly held by the earl of Eglinton in lieu of non payment. On 28 May the Lords of Council had fined Eglinton the sum of £1,000 for breach of a decreet arbitral declared in 1524 between the Montgomeries and the Cunninghams. The issue of the charter provided a link in continuity between the ruling made under the old régime and the first actions of the new one, despite the change in the political climate. (This continuity in business is also suggested by the judicial meetings of the session at Edinburgh on 15 and 20 June). Eglinton himself witnessed the charter as did Arran, Argyll, Lord Fleming, the prior of St. Andrews, Alexander Myln, abbot of Cambuskenneth, the Secretary and the Comptroller.[84] By this date Angus was no longer Chancellor, and proclamation had been issued against him. It seems remarkable that he should be in a position to convene the lieges at Edinburgh against the king between 23 June and 1 July, given that the machinery of government evidently had shifted back there from Stirling on 27 June. Bellenden's answer to this charge of treason was again a simple denial, to which was added the assertion that Angus and his supporters had departed from Edinburgh at the king's will.[85]

The English warden, Lord Dacre, sent a servant to Edinburgh to follow up on the report received by Northumberland. Dacre's spy reported that the Scots king and his supporters first made their entry into Edinburgh on 6 July, giving the impression that throughout June the headquarters were at Stirling. This impression was shared by later chroniclers; both the *Diurnal* and Lesley gave 2 July as being the date of entry, Lesley adding that Angus remained in Edinburgh throughout June. (Curiously, the parliamentary record left the date of entry blank).[86] If Edinburgh did remain in Douglas hands, then it appears remarkable that the great seal should have been returned there on 27 June. Further charters were issued at Edinburgh on 3, 4 and 5 July, and on 4 July Arran was to be found there receiving a bond of maintenance from Scott of Buccleuch. On the same day Maxwell was appointed as chief carver to the king in the royal household, replacing Sir George Douglas of Pittendreich.[87] The clear indication is that James' supporters were in residence in Edinburgh before 6 July, indeed as early as 27 June. The alternative interpretation for the use of the great seal at Edinburgh on 27 June is that the changeover in government did not provoke as much confrontation between supporters of the ex-Chancellor and those about the king as the charges of treason suggested. The fact that George Crichton, bishop of Dunkeld, had been able to come and go freely between Edinburgh and Stirling in June, as also that the charter issued on 27 June took up business left off on 28 May, indicates that the administration did not grind to a halt simply because the king and Chancellor had parted company. It is feasible that Angus simply remained in Edinburgh throughout June, wondering what was going to happen next, but with little belligerent thought. Pitscottie's account, although misleading on locations, indicated a man completely caught off balance by events: '. . . the king was nocht thair . . . [they returned to headquarters and] tuik consulltatioun quhat was best to be done. . . .'[88]

Nonetheless, the report by Lord Dacre's spy showed that the king was anticipating some aggression from Angus. He reported that:

> . . . all the tyme the King was in Edinburghe he was nightlie watched with sundrye lordes in their moste defensible arraye; and one night the King watched hym selfe in like arraye, for fere of the Erle of Angwys and his partie. . . .[89]

The group described as entering Edinburgh had at its service three hundred spearmen, evidently not considered a force sufficient to challenge Angus' 'partie' physically. Dacre's spy went on to describe how the king spent his first days in the capital, closely guarded in the house of the archbishop of St. Andrews. If Angus was no longer in Edinburgh by July, he was evidently close by. For the charge of treasonable convocation to have any substance, both parties would have to be in the same area. Abell spoke of the king 'expelling' Angus, but perhaps this was a metaphorical rather than a physical expulsion; the *Diurnal* narrated that the Douglases withdrew from the capital – which was more in accordance with Bellenden's answer to the charge of treasonable convocation of the lieges.[90] Dacre's spy made no reference to any signs of such convocation, let alone of actual confrontation. It is not evident how much support Angus might have been able to command. After his forfeiture in September, English reports suggested that he could at best command two hundred men in contrast to the king's five hundred[91], but in late June and early July the figure may well have been higher, hence the security precautions taken for the royal person. In fact Angus may well have been on the defensive. In the September parliament Bellenden was required to defend the charge of:

> . . . treasonable art and part of the munitions of the castle of Tantallon and of the king's fortress of Newark with men, artillery and victuals against the king's authority. . . .

Bellenden again denied the charge and argued that any man who possessed a house had a right to fortify it in case of threat from his enemies. Furthermore, saving the right of inspection by the king's officers in instances of suspected reset, there was no law requiring an individual to surrender up his house.[92] Given the proximity of Tantallon, Angus may well have retreated there in late June or early July.

James had informed his uncle that he would be convening his lords in Edinburgh on 10 July. In fact the session of the Lords of Council opened on 6 July. The king presided in person. Those present were his new Chancellor,

Archbishop Dunbar; his new keeper of the privy seal, Bishop Crichton; Gavin Dunbar, bishop of Aberdeen and Clerk Register; the abbots of Cambuskenneth and Scone; the earls of Arran, Argyll and Eglinton and the lords Maxwell and Erskine. For the afternoon session these were joined by the earl of Rothes and lords Glamis, Gray, Hume and Seton as well as Hume's brother, the abbot of Jedburgh. Several of these men had attended the May session; Rothes had sat almost every day alongside the former Chancellor. Lord Dacre's servant, erroneously describing this day as being the date of the king's arrival in Edinburgh rather than the opening of the session, nevertheless produced a comparable list. Those said to have accompanied the king from Stirling were his new Chancellor; Bishop Crichton; John Hepburn, bishop of Brechin; Henry Wemyss, bishop of Galloway; the earls of Arran, Argyll, Eglinton, Rothes and Bothwell, and the lords Maxwell, Avandale, Seton, Forbes, Hume and Hay of Yester.[93] James might not yet feel secure in Edinburgh, but the numbers of magnates about him appeared to be growing.

The business of the session was substantial. Lord Maxwell was confirmed in his post as warden of the West March. Lord Hume was appointed warden in the east, in place of Angus. Buccleuch was exonerated for his stance at Darnick back in 1526. The decision was taken to draw up communications for Henry VIII and the earl of Northumberland. Angus' brother, the abbot of Holyrood, was ordered to desist from building a fortified residence on the Borders near Coldingham. This activity was construed as being potentially threatening to the '. . . commoune weale of [the] realme. . . .'

Finally, a new king's 'consale' was appointed with a remit for:

> . . . thre or foure of thir to remane evir with the kingis grace with his officiaris for the direction of all materis that sall happin to occur concernyng his grace realme and liegis and utheris ways. . . .[94]

The councillors were the Chancellor, the bishop of Aberdeen, Arran, Argyll, Eglinton, Moray, Rothes, Alexander Stewart, abbot of Scone, Alexander Myln, abbot of Cambuskenneth, and Lord Erskine, as well as the keeper of the privy seal and the Secretary. The witnesses to the two great seal charters issued the following day were drawn from this group with the addition of the prior of St. Andrews, the Comptroller and, strangely on one charter, the abbot of Holyrood. Given that William Douglas had on the previous day been given a formal warning by the council and proceedings were about to continue against his brothers, his appearance as a witness on 7 July is remarkable, demonstrating either that the political situation in Edinburgh was not as dramatically defined as other pronouncements by the new government suggested or, alternatively, that the entry in the great seal register was misplaced and should be of an earlier date.[95]

On 7 July the session sat again, with the king on this day remaining at Archbishop Beaton's house. Those present were all members of the newly appointed council, namely the Chancellor, the keeper of the privy seal, the bishop of Aberdeen, the abbot of Scone, and the earls of Arran, Argyll and Eglinton. Angus was ordered to place himself in ward:

> . . . for the sure keping of our soverane lordis maist noble persoune. . . in the ferr partis of his realme in sic placis as it sall pleis his grace and ay and quhill he be fred be his hienes. . . .[96]

Letters were ordered, charging him to place himself north of the river Spey within six days of their receipt. The council also ordered that either his uncle, Kilspindie, or brother, Sir George Douglas, should enter himself in ward at Edinburgh castle, the other to keep at all times a distance of twelve miles from the king. In the September parliament, in explanation for the failure of the Douglases to carry out the council's orders, Bellenden argued that James had been advised '. . . be counsale of our unfrenndis . . .', and that the Douglases would have been risking their lives to have obeyed such orders. It could not therefore be treasonable to have disobeyed.[97] Possibly Angus was intended to have warded himself in his brother's house in Morayshire, or in the royal castle of Darnaway, held by Moray. The intention was to dislocate him from the estates of his earldom and thus from the areas from which much of his support was derived, which would certainly prove dangerous for him. It was curious, perhaps, that the king had not presided over the business of the session on the day that the order to ward was made; this laid him open to Bellenden's argument on behalf of the Douglases.

On 8 July the same group of councillors met again at the Tolbooth, on this occasion discussing matters arising from the management of the Lennox ward. On 9 July they were joined by Montrose and lords Maxwell, Erskine, Seton, Hume, Glamis and Lindsay. Order was made that, owing to the fact that Angus was currently able to obtain '. . . knawlege of the secretis of the court . . .', in future no person was to communicate with the earl without royal licence under penalty of death. All retainers of the earl were to leave the city within six hours under the same penalty.[98]

On 11 July the king once again attended the session. A parliament was called for 2 September for '. . . ordaining all materis concernyng the weile of oure said soverane lord his realme and liegis . . .'. The question of English diplomatic relations was again raised. This resulted in a formal letter of state being forwarded to Henry VIII on 13 July. In it James stated that Angus had achieved power in Scotland with English support. He had subsequently abused his offices of Chancellor and warden of the Marches and his position generally:

> . . . aganis our Baronis and uyer our liegis yat wald nocht entir in bond of manrent to him . . . applyand all commoditeis and accidentis of our Realme to his singulair proffit . . . sa stark of power yat We suld nacht be habil to regne as his Prince. . . .[99]

There followed the explanation that Angus had refused to enter into ward and was at present fortifying his strongholds. If he sought aid from England, James requested that this be refused. Six days had elapsed since the order to ward had been made. The implication was that the order had been served on Angus on the same day that it had been made – 7 July – which in turn meant that he was within a day's ride of Edinburgh and that his whereabouts were known.

13 July was a bad day for the Douglas cause. The new régime had shown its full hand to Henry VIII and attempted to discredit the former Chancellor fully in the English king's eyes. On the same day the session again sat. The king presided. In attendance were his Chancellor, keeper of the privy seal and clerk register; the abbots of Cambuskenneth, Scone and Coupar Angus; and the earls of Arran, Argyll, Eglinton and Rothes – all, save Coupar Angus, members of his new council. Donald Campbell, abbot of Coupar Angus and kinsman of Argyll, was perhaps there to assist the lawyers present – Sir William Scott of Balwearie, John Campbell of Lundy, and Adam Otterburn of Auldhame, king's advocate. Otterburn was instructed to draft a full summons against Angus. The indictment included all six major propositions of art and part treason: – exposing the king to battle during his minority; keeping him against his will; assisting the Johnstons; convening the lieges at Edinburgh; fortifying his strongholds; and failing to enter ward. Kilspindie, Sir George Douglas and Drummond of Carnock were also accused. The hearing was appointed for 4 September in parliament. The summons was drafted, sealed with the great seal, and announced in Edinburgh, all on 13 July. Lyon King of Arms served the summons in person on Angus at Dalkeith on 18 July.[100]

Early in 1529, James V gave his own version of the events of the preceding summer to Dr. Thomas Magnus, English ambassador to Scotland. He claimed that at Easter 1528, in the presence of members of the council, he had attempted to take Angus to task for his abuse of authority and failure to execute justice. Angus' reaction had been to propose a royal expedition to the Borders in June. According to James, this proposal had been a sham and merely a cover for Angus to root out and eliminate those who were suspected of putting the king up to challenge his Chancellor. Therefore James had removed himself to Stirling, so that he would:

> . . . incurrit nacht mair subjectioun unto ye tyme We send for our wyse
> Lordes and Barones of all estatis, and be yer advise substantiuslie or
> ordourlie devisit ane conventioun to be in Edinburgh. . . .[101]

Presumably what was meant was that whilst the king was away in Liddesdale, Angus or his supporters would arrange for a purge of the royal Household. This was perhaps feasible; throughout the minority positions in the Household were filled by supporters of the régime in power, and early on in his personal rule James carried out his own purge. In the absence of the *Treasurer's Accounts*, the identity of the five or six persons who first accompanied the king on his ride to Stirling can only be guessed. The allegation of a sham does, however, credit Angus and his supporters with a Machiavellian cunning that was not demonstrable at any other time in 1528, and, of course, it was an allegation made for effect and with the benefit of hindsight. The effort that Angus had put in earlier

[27]

in 1528 to maintain credibility with the English as an effective Borders manager, and the preparation put in hand for the royal expedition in June 1528, amounted to it being more than a sham. Interestingly enough, however, there was no sign of James' own involvement in this preparation; his one appearance at the session council in May was in connection with a separate matter.

The initiative in 1528 appears to have been with the king at all times. By removing himself to Stirling at the end of May, when proclamation had been made throughout central Scotland[102] for the lieges to convene for a royal raid on the Borders, James caught Angus completely off guard. In the three-week period between the end of May and the announcement that the raid was being postponed, it might be imagined that those magnates ready to lead their contingents to Edinburgh decided to head for Stirling instead to find out what was happening. Arran, for one, had in May requested leave from the expedition to deal with his own local difficulties in the west.[103] (Brodick castle had been burnt down). Maxwell, engaged in his own private feuds on the West March, headed north notwithstanding that he was extremely unpopular with Angus' government. The ease with which James attracted magnate support in the course of the month of June showed great certainty on their part that the circumstances were changing. This was an entirely different phenomenon from the Lennox rising of 1526. Then, there had been a challenge by one party against those about the king. Visibly in 1528 the challenge was being made by the king himself. Discounting the burning of Duncow, there was no violence committed from the time of James' escape until the issue of the summons of treason, an indication that the faction fighting of the minority was generally recognised to be at an end. The summer of 1528 was the period in which James began his personal rule. With the delivery of the double whammy against Angus on 13 July, the royal assumption of power was complete.

NOTES

1. Dunbar, *Scot. Kings*, 224, n.3; *Handbook of British Chronology*, [*HBC*], edd. F.M. Powicke and E.B. Fryde (2nd ed., London 1961), 467. (Angus was born circa 1490).
2. *APS*, ii, 294.
3. Emond, *op.cit.*, 487.
4. *APS*, ii, 301.
5. *ER*, xv, 272, 381.
6. *TA*, v, 281; *RMS*, iii, no. 358; *APS*, ii, 354; *Diurnal of Occurrents*, 11.
7. Emond, *op.cit.*, 629–30.
8. *Ibid.*, 493.
9. *Ibid.*, 493, 506.
10. *APS*, ii, 304; Fraser, *Lennox*, ii, no. 138.
11. *APS*, ii, 312, 330; Wormald, *Bonds*, App. B, no. 34; *LP Henry VIII*, iv, pt. i, no. 2335; Fraser, *Buccleuch*, ii, no. 136; *Diurnal of Occurrents*, 10.
12. *Ibid.*, ii, 325; Abell, *op.cit.*, f. 117; Pitcairn, *Trials*, i, pt. i, 134; Fraser, *Lennox*, ii, no. 146; *Diurnal of Occurrents*, 12.
13. Emond, *op.cit.*, 630.

14. *Ibid.*, 528.
15. Pitcairn, *Trials*, i, pt. i, 134.
16. *RSS*, i, no. 3500.
17. Emond, *op.cit.*, 550.
18. *Ibid.*, 626, 630.
19. *Ibid.*, 528–9.
20. *APS*, ii, 325.
21. Thomas I. Rae, *The Administration of the Scottish Frontier*, 1513–1603 (Edinburgh, 1966), App. 2.
22. *RMS*, iii, nos. 635–675 *passim*, no. 2233; Kelley, *Angus*, examines in detail the various Angus landholdings.
23. *RMS*, ii, nos. 2072–4.
24. *Scots Peerage*, ii, 159.
25. *ADCP*, 122, 124; *LP Henry VIII*, iv, pt. ii, no. 3404.
26. *ADCP*, 257, 259; Rae, *op.cit.*, App. 6.
27. *ADCP*, 302; *APS*, ii, 307, 432.
28. *RMS*, iii, nos. 351, 358.
29. *ADCP*, 244; *RSS*, i, nos. 3449–51; *TA*, v, 277–8.
30. *APS*, ii, 312; *LP Henry VIII*, iv, pt. ii, no. 2449.
31. *ER*, xv, 203, 289, 380.
32. *LP Henry VIII*, iv, pt. ii, nos. 3338, 3344, 3358, 3370, 3383, 3404; cf. also R.G. Eaves, *Henry VIII and James V's Regency* 1524–1528: A Study in Anglo-Scottish Diplomacy (University Press of America, 1987), which also relies heavily on English correspondence as source material.
33. *LP Henry VIII*, iv, pt. ii, nos. 3404, 3407, 3545.
34. *Ibid.*, iv, pt. ii, no. 3477.
35. *Ibid.*, iv, pt. ii, nos. 3545, 3704–6, 3762, 3777, 3795–7.
36. *Ibid.*, iv, pt. ii, nos. 3849–50, 3914, 3924.
37. *Ibid.*, iv, pt. ii, nos. 3972, 4014, 4020, 4134.
38. SRO, *ADC*, vol. 38, ff. 94–5.
39. *SP Henry VIII*, iv, pt. iv, 548.
40. *LP Henry VIII*, iv, pt. ii, no. 4298.
41. *ADCP*, 275–6; SRO, *ADC*, 38, ff. 100–117; RH 2.1.9, *passim*.
42. *LP Henry VIII*, iv, pt. ii, no. 4323.
43. *RSS*, i, nos. 2697, 2821, 3277; Fraser, *Carlaverock*, ii, 445, no. 6, 459, no. 7.
44. *APS*, ii, 325–6.
45. Pitcairn, *Trials*, i, pt. i, 137.
46. *LP Henry VIII*, iv, pt. ii, no. 4134; Wormald, *Bonds*, 335. App. A, no. 16.
47. *SP Henry VIII*, iv, pt. iv, 492.
48. *Ibid.*, iv, pt. iv, 492.
49. *RMS*, iii, nos. 100, 1484; *RSS*, ii, no. 1696.
50. *HMC*, xii, App. viii, 143, no. 154; Fraser, *Buccleuch*, ii, no. 143.
51. *SP Henry VIII*, iv, pt. iv, no. clxxxiii.
52. *APS*, ii, 325.
53. *Ibid.*, ii, 323.
54. Abell, *op.cit.*, f. 117; *Diurnal of Occurrents*, 10; Lesley, *History*, 140; Pitscottie, *Historie*, i, 323–6; Buchanan, *History*, ii, 238, 265.
55. Emond, *op.cit.*, 528.
56. *James V Letters*, 136, n. 142; *LP Henry VIII*, iv, pt. ii, nos. 4130, 4134; *SP Henry VIII*, iv, pt. iv, 4901; *HMC, Mar 38*.
57. Abell, *op.cit.*, f. 117.
58. *RMS*, iii, no. 614.
59. Pitscottie, *Historie*, i, 323–6; Lang, *op.cit.*, i, pp. xiii-xvi; Falkland is given as the place of escape by Eaves: *op.cit.*, 152; cf. Bingham, *op.cit.*, 73–4, where the choice is left to the reader.

60. *RMS*, iii, nos. 589–596.
61. *LP Henry VIII*, iv, pt. ii, no. 4298; SRO, *ADC*, vol. 38, f. 117.
62. *LP Henry VIII*, iv, pt. ii, no. 4298; SRO,RH 2.1.9; *ADC*, vol. 38, f. 102.
63. *RMS*, iii, nos. 596–601.
64. *Ibid.*, iii, no. 601.
65. *Diurnal of Occurrents*, 11 (Crichton had been keeper in earlier years prior to Kilspindie's taking office, *RMS*, iii, *passim*); SRO, *ADC*, vol. 38, ff. 117, 120, 121; RH 2.1.9.
66. *RSS*, i, nos. 3967–8.
67. *LP Henry VIII*, iv, pt. ii, no. 4532; the full text is given in Lang, *op.cit.*, i, pp. xv–xvi.
68. *Ibid.*
69. Abell, *op.cit.*, f. 117.
70. *ADCP*, 280; *ER*, xv, pp. lv, 550.
71. Lang, *op.cit.*, i, p. xvi; *LP Henry VIII*, iv, pt. ii, no. 4253.
72. *Ibid.*
73. *Illustrations of the Topography and Antiquities of the Shires of Aberdeen and Banff* (edd. Spalding Club 1847–69, 5 vols.) [*A.B. Ill*], iv, 415.
74. *RMS*, iii, no. 599.
75. Buchanan, *History*, ii, 238; *ADCP*, 280.
76. *LP Henry VIII*, iv. pt. ii, no. 4457.
77. *Ibid.*, no. 4532; Lang, *op.cit.*, i, pp. xv–xvi.
78. Glasgow University, Argyll Transcripts, III, 217.
79. *APS*, ii, 308; cited as witnesses in *RMS*, iii, e.g. nos. 412, 486, 489, 507, 589.
80. *LP Henry VIII*, iv, pt. ii, nos. 4397, 4411–2, 4457.
81. *Ibid.*, iv, pt. ii, no. 4457; Buchanan *History*, ii, 239; *Diurnal of Occurrents*, 10–11.
82. *APS*, ii, 325, 327, 331; in the charge against Janet Douglas and others the month is meant to be July. (June and July are frequently confused in the parliamentary record; cf. e.g. *ibid.*, 325, where "June" is scored out and replaced by "July" in the dating of summons against Angus - in 1543 this mistake was ingeniously exploited by the Douglases as part of their legal argument for their restoration: *ibid.*, 416–7).
83. Buchanan, *History*, ii, 239; Pitscottie, *Historie*, i, 323–6.
84. SRO, Glencairn muniments (GD 39) no. 42; *RMS*, iii, no. 602; *ADCP*, 276.
85. *APS*, ii, 323.
86. *LP Henry VIII*, iv, pt. ii, no. 4531; Abell, *op.cit.*, f. 117; *Diurnal of Occurrents*, 10–11; Lesley, *History*, 39; *APS*, ii, 323.
87. *RMS*, iii, nos. 603–5; Wormald, *Bonds*, 307, App. A, no. 7; Fraser, *Carlaverock*, iv, 518, no. 82.
88. Pitscottie, *Historie*, i, 326.
89. *SP Henry VIII*, iv, pt. iv, 501–2; also *LP Henry VIII*, iv, pt. ii, no. 4531.
90. Abell, *op.cit.*, f. 117; *Diurnal of Occurrents*, 11.
91. *LP Henry VIII*, iv, pt. ii, no. 4830; *SP Henry VIII*, iv, pt. iv, 517.
92. *APS*, ii, 322, 325 (quotation is anglicised here).
93. SRO, *ADC*, vol. 38 f. 122v; RH 2.1.9., *passim*; *LP Henry VIII*, iv, pt. ii, no. 4531.
94. *ADCP*, 276–7.
95. *Ibid.*; *RMS*, iii, nos. 606–7.
96. *ADCP*, 277–8; SRO, *ADC*, vol. 38, f. 123v; RH 2.1.9., *passim*; *SP Henry VIII*, iv, pt. iv, no. clxxxv.
97. *APS*, ii, 323.
98. *Ibid.*, 278–9; SRO, RH 2.1.9., *passim*.
99. *APS*, 278; *SP Henry VIII*, iv, pt. iv, 499.
100. SRO, *ADC*, vol. 38, f. 131v; RH 2.1.9., *passim*; *ADCP*, 279; *APS*, ii, 325.
101. *SP Henry VIII*, iv, pt. iv, 548.
102. *ADCP*, 276 - lieges were required to attend from the west.
103. *Ibid.*; Pitcairn, *Trials*, i, pt. i, 139.

CHAPTER THREE

The Struggle for Power: July to November 1528

The summons against Angus drawn up on 13 July 1528 included the charge of treasonable fortification of Tantallon and Newark castles. On the same day the council ordered that these should be surrendered by their keepers within forty-eight hours, as should also the strongholds at Kilmarnock and Cockburnspath. Tantallon was part of the Angus Douglas earldom, but the other three castles were controlled by Angus by virtue of his marriage to Margaret Tudor. With its termination the strongholds now reverted to her. Angus' written reply reached the council four days later, and was to the effect that as no-one was now allowed to communicate with him without licence and he himself was prohibited from approaching the king, consequently he could not defend his rights to hold on to the fortresses. Accordingly he hoped he '. . . mycht optene the kingis favouris and comper and ansuer for him self . . .'.[1] The council's reply is not extant but as James never again set eyes on his former Chancellor after May 1528, clearly the request was denied. No answer may have been made at all, given that the summons was already on its way.

Angus needed to hold on to his strongholds. He had lost the control of the royal person that had for the last three years been his shield against challenges from his rival peers. He was then confronted with the spectacle of the king returning to Edinburgh in the company of sixteen magnates and prelates and with a bodyguard of three hundred spears, all for the purpose of holding a convention to examine his mismanagement of government. With his receipt of the summons there was little that Angus could do other than stay on the defensive until parliament met in September. Neither side was completely certain of its ground. The summons was served in person by Lyon King at Dalkeith. Angus' usual whereabouts were unknown but he was probably based at Tantallon. The complete absence of any armed confrontation in this period suggests that neither party was confident of its position. Angus could perhaps command more troops, but the king had succeeded in attracting magnate support. However, several of these men had previously been willing to cooperate with the Douglas régime. What was required was not an overnight coup d'état but one that was legitimised by the authority of parliament. To resort to violence at this stage might not only lead to trouble with the English but within the ranks of James' own supporters as well.

The fear of Douglas-inspired violence prompted the king's return from Edinburgh to Stirling on 14 July. Prior to his departure he presided over the session's appointment of the Kerrs and Scott of Buccleuch as wardens of the Middle March, and the reassignation to the Hepburn family of responsibility for Liddesdale.[2] Angus had now lost all his official positions. Lord Dacre's servant reported the breaking up of the convention on 14 July. James returned to Stirling accompanied by his mother and 'the lordes roade their owne countreys . . . in disorder . . .'. In fact the session continued until the following day with judicial business being presided over by Gavin Dunbar, bishop of Aberdeen and clerk register.[3] The anxiety felt for the king's own safety in Edinburgh did not extend to all the members of his newly appointed king's council. The session then reconvened in Stirling on 17 July and the next day advised:

> . . . the kingis grace to mak his principale residence in this toune of Striveling quhill the parliament swa that his grace pas na ferthir na he may return agane her within v or vi houris at the ferrest.

The lords also ordained that:

> . . . gif the erle of Angus and his frenndis will make any insurrectioune aganis our soverane lord or convocatioun againis him . . .

then Arran, Eglinton, Maxwell, Hume, the Kerrs, Buccleuch, Ninian Crichton of Bellibocht and Hugh Campbell of Loudoun should be alerted immediately. It was further declared in the king's name that anyone giving assistance to the earl would forfeit his life, lands and goods.[4]

The chief magnates in attendance on this occasion were Argyll, Eglinton, and Rothes. Arran, Maxwell, Buccleuch and the Kerrs had all attended the Edinburgh session on 14 July. Arran put in one further appearance on the session on 20 July before departing elsewhere. Eglinton also ceased to sit on the same day.[5] The provisions made by the Lords of Council on 18 July were to ensure the king's safety whilst his magnate supporters dealt with their own local disorders. For the earl of Arran this meant returning west to deal with an uprising on the isle of Arran which resulted in Brodick castle being burnt down; for Eglinton the problem was with the Cunningham family who had just burned down his family home.[6] The Kerrs and Scott of Buccleuch were detailed off by the council to clear Teviotdale of thieves encroaching from Liddesdale. Maxwell, for his part, was responsible for the West March, and on 10 August met the English deputy warden, Sir Christopher Dacre, at Lochmabenstone. Dacre demanded the return of an English outlaw detained by Maxwell. Maxwell refused. Dacre then wrote in complaint to James V and also demanded redress for Liddesdale and the return of one of his servants imprisoned in Hermitage castle. Bothwell was detailed to respond to this letter, and in effect admitted that he was totally unable to control Liddesdale. Maxwell in the meantime skipped a further truce day scheduled for 24 August and at his next meeting with Dacre, on 2 September, he refused to give redress for his brother, Edward. Ironically on the eve of the parliament that was to forfeit the Douglases on the charge of, *inter alia*, treasonably assisting Johnston of that Ilk, the English grievance was with a Scots raid led jointly by Edward Maxwell and Johnston. Lord Maxwell's attitude was to avoid any responsibility and refer all matters to a later date.[7] These were the disorders in the country which faced the lords riding out of Edinburgh on 14 July 1528.

For the most part the king himself remained in Stirling in July and August.[8] The session continued to meet regularly, with the earl of Argyll leaving on 20 July and the earl of Moray – also one of the newly appointed king's councillors – putting in his first appearance on 27 July. The stipulation made on 6 July, that the king should at all times be attended by three or four of his council, was acknowledged in as much as members of this body regularly appeared on the session. The king himself put in only one recorded appearance on the session at Stirling, on 10 August. He did not even sit on 18 July to acquiesce in the proposals made by the Lords of Council for his security. Rather, the concern of the session on 10 August was with royal finances.[9]

The first meeting of the auditors of the exchequer – a group headed by the new Chancellor – was at Edinburgh on 6 July. By that date the annual return from the Irvine bailies had been received and more accounts were coming in. The account for the Edinburgh customs was made up for the year to 13 July and was in the name of the city's provost and custumar, Archibald Douglas of Kilspindie. Ironically this was also the date of a royal summons being drawn up against him. The account was handed into the exchequer by a deputy accountant, whilst Lyon King, unable to find Kilspindie in person, proclaimed summons against him from Haddington market cross at 11 a.m. on 18 July.[10] The exchequer rolls were then transported to Stirling and auditing continued there. In all, twenty-seven burghs returned bailie accounts with fifteen of these also providing customs accounts, these figures being comparable with the previous year. By 1542 returns were being received from thirty-one burghs – the highest number in James's personal rule. Therefore the returns figures for 1528 were fairly respectable. In monetary terms the amount received from customs in 1528 was £2689 Scots, up over £100 from the previous year, whilst the bailie figure slipped slightly, from £188 to £145. In 1542 the amount recorded as received by the Comptroller from customs was £4763, with the bailie figure again under £200.[11]

There was a less smooth transition in the accounts received from Crown lands, though the picture here was partly distorted as some accounts were made up on a biennial basis. The king's Secretary, Thomas Erskine, for example, returned two years' accounts for Brechin and Navar in 1528. In the same year the earl of Argyll's accounts for Roseneath, Cowal and Kintyre covered the three year period from 1525. By comparison Andrew Murray of Blackbarony, bailie of Ballencrieff (East Lothian), submitted an account in 1532 covering the previous five year period. He had simply ceased accounting after 1527; almost certainly he was a Douglas sympathiser. In 1542 he was eventually required to purchase a remission for his earlier support of Douglas of Kilspindie. Overall the receipts from crown lands in 1528 amounted to over £5000 Scots, an increase of one thousand pounds on the previous year's total.[12]

Changes in the royal Household were reflected in the 1528 accounts. James Douglas of Parkhead, master of the larder, lost his job to David Wood in Crag (who later rose to become Comptroller). Sir John Stirling of Keir, who was to be found with the king at Stirling as early as 18 June, now became master of the wine cellar in place of James Douglas of Drumlanrig. One John Douglas continued as groom in the wine cellar, but the butcher, Robert Douglas, was replaced by Walter Stewart. The provost of Glasgow, Sir Robert Stewart of Minto, re-entered the Household as principal marshal after a two-year absence. In 1527 the earl of Arran had received from Stewart a bond of manrent to last for as long as Stewart remained provost, excepting only allegiance to the archbishop of Glasgow. Hence Stewart was part of the affinity of the king's supporters in 1528. His uncle, William, was later to serve as Treasurer. In the meantime the Treasurer appointed to replace Kilspindie on 19 July was Robert Cairncross, who was provost of the collegiate church of Corstorphine and before the end of the year was to become abbot of Holyrood.[13] One of his first tasks as Treasurer was to allocate £2000 Scots from casualty to enable Sir James Colville of Ochiltree to balance the exchequer accounts. This was the piece of council business that required the king's presence at the session on 10 August.[14]

All in all, the changes in the Household personnel in 1528 amounted to little more than a handful out of a body of over eighty persons, and most of those who lost their positions were Douglases. In 1527 there were six Douglases in the Household; in 1528 there remained two, John Douglas in the wine cellar and one Walter Douglas, cupbearer in the hall. This was not a full purge of the Household, but rather an attempt to weed out a few suspect individuals in response to the directive of 9 July from the Lords of Council to prevent 'knawledge of the secretis of the court' from leaking out. Almost certainly those Douglases who lost their jobs were no longer at Stirling, but had departed with Angus at the time of the July expulsion order. The tone for the revision made in the summer of 1528 was set on 8 July with the royal confirmation of the earl of Argyll as hereditary Master of the Household. At the same time he was confirmed as justiciar of Scotland.[15]

The great seal register suggests that the king found time to visit Glasgow in July 1528 – a place no more than five or six hours' journeying time from Stirling. A charter was issued there on 25 July. The witnesses were cited 'ut in aliis cartis'. The last witness list given in full was issued at Stirling on 20 July, when Arran, Eglinton, Argyll, Lord Fleming, the prior of St. Andrews, the abbot of Cambuskenneth, the Clerk Register, the Comptroller, and the royal Secretary added their names to that of the Chancellor. The Glasgow charter was presumably attested by some at least of that group. The purpose of the charter issued on 25 July was to confirm two charters held by William Carmichael of

Crookston (Renfrew). The first charter concerned a grant by the eighth earl of Crawford of half of the lands of Ethiebeaton in Monifieth in the regality of Kirriemuir (Forfar). Ethiebeaton was held by Crawford of the earl of Angus, and the lands were sold to Carmichael by him in 1525. The second charter concerned half of the lands of Carpen in Abernethy (Perth), granted by Angus himself to Carmichael, again in 1525. These grants were now confirmed at Glasgow with the additional clause that for his good service Carmichael was now allowed a quitclaim of the lands, which would henceforth be exempt from all process of forfeiture to follow. The same additional clause appears in a confirmation issued at Edinburgh on 11 July in respect of five charters held by Peter Carmichael of Dron (Perth) and spouse, again relating to lands held in Abernethy. The 'extraordinary generosity' by the king (the phrase used by Michael Kelley) was significant for two reasons. Firstly, the Edinburgh charter appeared before the summons against Angus was drawn up and issued. There was clearly an anticipation amongst the lawyers stipulating terms that the earl was to lose his lands. Secondly, the new régime was attempting to undermine support for Angus by ensuring that his tenants' land rights would be protected whatever happened to the earl himself. A similar clause appeared in a letter of confirmation under the privy seal issued on 12 July in favour of Alexander Livingston of Dunipace (Stirling), who held his lands of Alexander Drummond of Carnock.[16]

In August 1528 the king had occasion to visit Falkland and Perth, again both places within reach of Stirling.[17] The reason for the Falkland visit may simply have been recreational (the *Treasurer's Accounts* are not extant for this period). The trip to Perth was in connection with disturbances created by Patrick Charteris of Cuthilgurdy. The Charteris family had been preying on the city of Perth for several years; indeed, burgh accounts had not been returned since 1524 owing to their disruption. On 10 July, James V signed a writ for their expulsion from Perth, condemning the brothers as:

> misgydit personis and of evill mynd, haivand na rentis nor gude ways to sustene thame bot be refe and oppressioun maid be thame daylie upon our trew liges, merchandis and burgessis of our said burgh, and commoune gude tharof, usurpand the provestry. . . .

The writ ordered that the Master of Ruthven be appointed as provost to restore order. By September William, first lord Ruthven, was holding the office of provost and was appointed as constable and custumar. The exchequer received returns in 1529 for the five outstanding years. Evidently the royal visit in August 1528 had made an impact.[18] However the Charteris brothers remained at large.

Royal authority had thus been asserted in both Glasgow and in Perth in the summer of 1528, and the provosts of both cities were now associated with the new government. There remained the problem of controlling Edinburgh, perceived by the king's advisers as still being a place of danger for the king. Lord Maxwell had previously served as provost of Edinburgh in the minority, and now he was appointed to the position again, in place of Douglas of Kilspindie.[19] His manner of taking up his appointment was extraordinary, and colourfully described by Roger Lascelles, English captain of Norham castle, in despatches sent by the earl of Northumberland to Cardinal Wolsey. Taking time off from his responsibilities on the West March, Maxwell arrived in Edinburgh in late August. He immediately headed for the provost's house and surrounded it. Inside, his predecessor was in the middle of hosting a dinner party for his nephews George and William. The new provost '. . . with a small company of men, clapped about the hows . . .' and the Douglases instantly beat a hasty retreat, heading out of the city for Tantallon castle. Maxwell then returned to the Borders to meet his next appointment, on 2 September, with Sir Christopher Dacre.[20]

Buchanan and the author of the *Diurnal* both offer the same interpretation of this incident, namely that the Douglases sent out a force of some one hundred horsemen from Tantallon to Edinburgh on 26 August. Their remit was to prevent the king from entering the city and so sabotage the chances of any parliament being held. In the ensuing struggle with Maxwell's men the Douglases came off worse and 'heirat was mony hurt with hagbuttis'.[21] The inference was clear; the summons against Angus required him to appear personally in parliament to answer the charges of treason and he had no faith in its finding in his favour. This was already indicated by the confirmations made to his tenants and, as Lascelles reported:

> . . . they are comonyng who shall have the Erles landes. And so at thys Parliament he shal be attaynted, both bloode and landes. . . .[22]

Angus had already opened up a line of communication with the English. His version of the breach with James had reached Cardinal Wolsey on or before 11 July. The Cardinal had also received the letter of state dated 13 July, prepared by the Lords of Council at Edinburgh and sent down to London with Patrick Sinclair for presenting to the English government. The English government appears to have written back in August directly to Angus. The replies are not extant but were encouraging enough for Angus to write on 10 September to thank Henry VIII for his support, and to add that he would endeavour to send Henry's letter on to the Scots king.[23] After Maxwell's strike on Edinburgh, William Douglas was sent to Norham to request possible refuge of Lascelles should the outcome of the imminent parliament prove unfavourable. Clearly the Douglases were pessimistic as to this outcome. Lascelles, trying to imagine his superiors' reactions, was cautiously encouraging, and suggested that a room in the outer ward of the castle might be available on a temporary basis if required. Then, on the day of the pronouncement of the forfeiture, 5 September, William and Angus appeared together on the Scottish side of the river Tweed across from Norham castle and again hailed Lascelles. In the shouted exchange which followed it was agreed that accommodation could be made available for all three Douglas brothers; Kilspindie and his wife, Janet Hoppringle; Margaret,

Angus' daughter by the queen; and the young George Gordon, fourth earl of Huntly.[24]

This last character was about the same age as the king and, unlike him, had yet to escape from the guardianship imposed by the earl of Angus. On the death of the third earl of Huntly, in 1524, the ward of the estates of the earldom had passed to Margaret Tudor. On her estrangement from Angus, she had assigned the ward over to the earl of Moray. Moray's first request in the September 1528 parliament was that the forfeiture of Angus, as former husband of Margaret, should in no way jeopardise his, Moray's, supervision of the Huntly estates.[25] Angus' last letter before the breach with the king was written to Lord Forbes on 30 May 1528. In it he thanked Forbes for the payment of one hundred merks for the grant of part of the Huntly earldom to Forbes. Angus continued:

> and be this my writing quitclamis and dischargis yow of the said ward landis during the tyme of the ward and gifis yow my full power to intromett with the said ward landis to your use and profit.

Angus then went on to say that he had to have one of Forbes' hawks to kill the herons that were plaguing his lands at Douglas. He concluded:

> Beleif weile I sall do for your gud matir as I wald do for myn awin. . . .

It was clear from the cosy terms of this letter that Angus, rather than either Moray or the queen, was then in *de facto* charge of the Huntly earldom. Indeed, just over a year later an interlocutor was served on Lord Forbes, requiring him to produce any evidence he had of his rights in the wardship. Almost four years after that, in 1533, Huntly brought an action against Forbes for wrongful intromission with the profits of the earl's lands in the barony of Strathbogie. Forbes produced a 'writing' by the earl of Angus granting him the gift of ward – perhaps the letter written on 30 May 1528.[26] There had been a scheme afoot in 1524 for Moray to marry Angus' and Margaret Tudor's daughter, Margaret, which was scotched by her father[27]; by hoping somehow to spirit Huntly and Margaret away to Norham castle in 1528, perhaps Angus intended to make the fourth earl his son-in-law.

Angus wrote three further letters to the English in the week following his forfeiture. His first, written at Coldingham on 10 September, as well as thanking Henry VIII for his intervention on his behalf, advised that James V had taken his uncle's intervention badly, and consequently Henry's support and protection was needed more than ever before. To Wolsey, Angus explained that he was in this precarious situation because his enemies in Scotland did not believe that the English king would intervene on his behalf. He trusted that the English would give no credence to the propaganda being put out against him by his enemies. In his letter to Northumberland, delivered by Sir George Douglas, Angus requested that the English Borderers be allowed to come to his support. In all these communications emphasis was laid on the idea that it was Angus' enemies – 'evil disposit personis' – who were responsible for the changed circumstances, and not the king himself.[28] Perhaps Angus really believed this. Certainly he had to accept that he had lost control of the king's person, but his letters make it clear that, in his view, the king was now simply in the hands of a group opposed to him, rather than exerting royal authority.

This view was shared by the English. In July, in a letter to Cardinal Wolsey, Lord Dacre described James as being advised by 'Lord Maxwell, and the laird of Buccleugh, chief manteiners of all misgyded men on the Bordours of Scotlande . . .'. Wolsey then recommended that negotiations should begin for the renewal of the Anglo-Scots truce, this having first been proposed by Angus in early 1528. Thomas Magnus, archdeacon of the East Riding, was appointed as the English negotiator, with instructions to seek a reconciliation between the Scots king and his former Chancellor. Wolsey noted that James was not yet as mature as he could be. In August Wolsey wrote direct to James V. He chose to misconstrue the terms of the Scottish letter of state presented by Patrick Sinclair. He regretted that the breach between James and Angus had been instigated by men who were liable to damage the king's interests more than Angus ever would, and denied that any attempt had been made by Henry VIII to control his nephew through the earl, claiming rather that Angus had done much to promote good understanding between the two sovereigns. After the forfeiture Lascelles provided a report for Northumberland, naming those who had:

> sat and concludit uppon the Erle of Angus forfataur, Spirituall and Temporal . . . all thies . . . that was the Erle of Angusis great enemys, the lordes in Scotland. . . .

The list corresponded almost exactly to the persons appointed as lords of the articles in parliament.[29]

Neither Angus nor the English had grasped the central tenet in the treason charges, that the king had been held against his will until he had 'putt himself to liberty'.

James V entered Edinburgh on 29 August after spending the night at Linlithgow. The return was calculated as a show of solidarity for the king, and proclamation was made for the lieges to accompany him on his entry. A handful of lairds from Ayrshire and Renfrew promptly had their goods escheated for 'biding at hame fra our soverane lordis oist . . .'. The main beneficiary was Ninian, third lord Ross. A further proclamation at the Market Cross warned the lieges to wait in Edinburgh for further orders, under penalty of death.[30] Parliament was opened on 2 September. Business began the next day and the record provides a list of sederunts for that day.[31] In the First Estate was the Chancellor; eight of the nine bishops, the one absentee being the bishop of Orkney (the bishopric of Moray was vacant at this point); and twelve abbots and one prior (under half of the total number). This was a higher turnout than for any parliament held in the minority. There are also extant parliamentary sederunt lists for 1531, 1532, 1535 and 1540/1541, and the average attendance figure for the First Estate is roughly twenty.

There were nineteen lords of parliament in attendance in 1528. Again this exceeded the turnout for parliaments in the minority. During the personal rule there were thirty-two persons designed as 'lords' (including the Lord St. John, preceptor of Torphichen). James himself made only one creation, that of Lord Methven. The attendance figure dropped to thirteen in 1531, six in 1532 and seven in 1535. Nineteen lords attended the December 1540 parliament which was the forum for the king's confirmation of his Act of Revocation, made at Rouen on 3 April 1537, and also for the Act of Annexation, extending the crown's lands. This parliament also ratified the forfeitures of, amongst others, the Douglases. It was prorogued to 1541 when twenty-two lords attended. The percentage turnout for lords in 1528 and 1540 was almost 60%, comparing favourably with that for the general council held at Perth after Flodden, when thirteen lords or their heirs were present.[32]

There were twenty-one earldoms in Scotland in 1513, and no new creations were made in the entire reign of James V. Nine earls were listed as parliamentary sederunts in 1528. This was rather less than had been present in 1525, when plans for the king's keeping were set out. Twelve earls were not listed. Two of these, Sutherland and Caithness, had never attended parliament in the minority and were absent again in September 1528. Their preoccupations were entirely with local difficulties. The liferent of the earldom of Sutherland was held by the sister of the ninth earl, with the fee being held by her son, Adam Gordon and his spouse. The caput, Dunrobin castle, had been seized in 1516 by her half-brother, resulting in a family feud over its possession, in the course of which the countess enlisted the support of the Mackays of Strathnaver only to end up falling out with them. Adam died in possession of Dunrobin in 1530, leaving a five-year-old heir. Wardship passed to the earl of Huntly in 1536.[33] The Sinclair family had similar problems. John Sinclair, third earl of Caithness, was given appointment as justiciar and Chamberlain of Caithness in 1526. In conjunction with his kinsman, William, fourth Lord Sinclair, he appears to have sought to extend his commission into Orkney. This provoked a violent reaction by the Orcadian Sinclairs, and William Lord Sinclair was thrown out of Orkney in 1528. In May 1529 the earl and lord returned armed with royal letters commanding the rebels to surrender. They refused and in the ensuing battle at Summerdale the earl was killed. Ward of the earldom went to Alexander Stewart, abbot-commendator of Scone.[34]

The non-appearance by Angus and Huntly was self-evident. Also absent was Matthew Stewart, fourth earl of Lennox. He was aged around eleven in 1528, and wardship of the earldom had been divided between Angus and Arran after Lennox's father's death at Linlithgow in 1526. Lennox himself was in France for much of the personal rule.[35] Gilbert Kennedy, third earl of Cassillis, was slightly younger than Lennox. Ward of his estate had been gifted to Douglas of

Kilspindie in 1527. Cassillis was also overseas for part of the personal rule.[36] Of great pertinence in September 1528 was the perception that both Sir James Hamilton of Finnart and Sir Hugh Campbell of Loudoun – the suspected killers respectively of the third earl of Lennox and the second earl of Cassillis – were lending their support to the king. Even younger than these absentees was William Hay, sixth earl of Erroll, aged nine or ten, whose ward was assigned in 1529 by Elizabeth, countess of Huntly (widow of the third earl) to Alexander Lyon, cantor of Moray.[37]

The remaining absentees were adults. Cuthbert Cunningham, third earl of Glencairn, was aged around fifty. His absence was primarily due to the presence of his veteran adversary, the sixty-eight year old Eglinton. Glencairn was, moreover, married to Angus' aunt, Marion Douglas. In July 1528 the Master of Glencairn had been ordered to remove himself and his retinue from Edinburgh, no doubt for fear that he might support his first cousin. However his business matters were still being attended to in Edinburgh, for in September a request by him for exemption from a royal summons of error raised against the Loudoun estate in Ayrshire was lodged before the session.[38]

James Douglas, third earl of Morton, who was aged about forty-eight, was also suspect; the summons against Angus had been served at Dalkeith, the caput of the Morton earldom. Alexander Graham, second earl of Menteith, was perhaps over fifty years old and had attended just one parliament in the minority, as had David Lindsay, eighth earl of Crawford, who was perhaps of similar age. Crawford did however attend the session at Edinburgh held on the Monday immediately following the close of parliament, which suggests that he may well have attended parliament after the roll call had been taken. He was amongst those vassals of Angus who on 5 September sought exemption for their land-holdings from the forfeiture.

The final missing name in 1528 was that of William Graham, second earl of Montrose, then a man aged around thirty. His absence was rather more surprising as he had attended the session of the Lords of Council on three consecutive days in July at Edinburgh, and had indeed been present when the date for the parliament was announced, on 11 July. He had also attended further sessions at Stirling.[39] Again, he may have attended the parliament after the clerks had noted names.

Thus the attested turnout of nine earls at the parliament of 1528 was respectable. Five were members of the king's council, namely Arran, Argyll, Eglinton, Moray and Rothes. John Stewart, third earl of Buchan, aged thirty, had already received a royal confirmation of his entire lands, and for 'singular favour' the king had erected these as the free barony of Glenquithle (Banff). John Stewart, third earl of Atholl, aged around twenty-one, and William Keith, third Earl Marischal (eighteen years old), were both present on the session at Stirling in July. The young Bothwell had also attended the council.[40] Of the twelve who were not on the parliamentary roll, four could be classed as political lightweights

– that is, they never or rarely attended parliament – namely, Caithness, Sutherland, Menteith and Crawford. Three were under the age of sixteen, namely Lennox, Cassillis and Erroll. Angus was under sentence and Morton and Glencairn probably identified with him, whilst the under-age Huntly was still under his control. If there could be said to have been one desertion, then this was Montrose, a man of little discernible political bias. Eight earls attended parliament in 1531 and 1532, eleven in 1535 and ten in 1540–1541. Hence in 1528 magnate representation in parliament was almost as high as James V would ever achieve.

The parliament lasted just three days. On Thursday, 3 September, proclamation was made charging all lords, barons, freeholders and others in Lothian, Haddington, Teviotdale, Selkirk, and Tweeddale to prepare for fifteen days' war commencing on the following Monday. The muster-point was to be Haddington. The declared objective was the 'ordering of matters concernying the commonweel and pacifying of the country'. Declaration was made that Douglases should have safe passage to attend parliament on Friday and would not be charged of any crimes save those contained in the summons already served on them. This declaration could have provided little comfort for Angus, as clearly he was the target of the 'pacifying'. On Friday, Master John Bellenden put forward the defence case. The parliament was illegal as it was being held in a holiday period without royal dispensation. A trial could not be valid as no advocate had been appointed for the defence. Bellenden then rehearsed the answers given by the Douglases for each individual charge of treason.[41] These arguments were rejected, and the lords in parliament reiterated that the Douglases should appear in person. Bellenden then proposed that pledges for their safety should be made, with Lord Maxwell, the Master of Argyll and Sir James Hamilton of Finnart being held hostage by Angus' friends until the trial was over. This proposal was also rejected. On Saturday sentence of forfeiture of life, lands and goods was passed on the earl of Angus, Sir George Douglas of Pittendreich, Archibald Douglas of Kilspindie and Alexander Drummond of Carnock. (Carnock had been charged on all six points save for the alleged assistance given to Johnston of that Ilk and also on the further treason of acting as spy for the period in which the king was in Stirling). Parliament then turned its attention to the lengthy list of appeals for exemption from forfeiture lodged by Angus' vassals.[42]

The lords of articles elected by the three Estates to preside over proceedings were Arran, Argyll, Eglinton and Moray; Lord Maxwell; Gavin Dunbar, archbishop of Glasgow and Chancellor, Gavin Dunbar, bishop of Aberdeen and clerk register, George Crichton, bishop of Dunkeld and keeper of the privy seal, and James Hay, bishop of Ross; Patrick Hepburn, prior of St. Andrews; Master Thomas Erskine of Haltoun, royal Secretary; Master Adam Otterburn of Auldhame, king's advocate, and Nicholas Clark of Oxgangs, deputy advocate. Lascelles' list of the names of 'Angusis great enemys' almost coincided with this group, though he did not consider the lawyers worth mentioning and confused

[41]

one or two of the bishops. Angus considered that the 'evil disposit personis' who had forfeited him were Arran, Argyll, Maxwell, Sir James Hamilton of Finnart, Sir Hugh Campbell of Loudoun, Sir Walter Scott of Buccleuch and Sir John Stirling of Keir.[43]

Almost immediately after the close of parliament, a reward of one hundred marks worth of land was offered by the Lords of Council for the capture of Angus. George and Archibald Douglas were valued at forty marks' worth of land apiece, and Drummond had a price of £100 on his head. This decision was taken on 7 September, with Bothwell, Argyll, Eglinton, Atholl, Crawford and Rothes sitting, as well as six bishops, nine lords, two abbots and the prior of St. Andrews, all fresh from attending parliament. The Lords of Council then declared that the king, with 'certane barouns and lordis', would be passing towards 'the westland for certane materis concyrning the weile of his hienes and realme'. He would be away for four days and in his absence Maxwell was to be responsible for Edinburgh, Bothwell for Lothian, and Lord Hume for the Merse. Letters were directed to all the sheriffs in Scotland to charge the lieges to be ready in Edinbrugh on 20 October for a twenty day campaign against Tantallon.[44]

This was a change of plan. The intention up until the week before had been for a campaign against Tantallon commencing immediately upon the close of parliament.[45] Lascelles suggested that the change of plan was made at the instigation of the earl of Argyll and in fact was the cause of some disagreement between the king and his lords, although the official explanation given, again according to Lascelles, for not proceeding immediately against Tantallon was that '. . . they wold not destroy the carne . . .'.[46] It is also possible that at this stage the king neither had sufficient forces or firepower at his disposal to mount a siege against Tantallon castle, hence the direction to sheriffs throughout the country. Sir Alexander Jardine of Applegarth, master of the artillery, appeared before the Lords of Council on 7 September to emphasise the poor state of the royal armoury (which led to directions for its refurbishment, necessitating the procurement of a barrel of Orkney butter to grease the gun carriages).[47] Presumably this was only found out during the course of the September parliament. Nevertheless, however sensible the reasons, the change of plan at the last minute was indicative of how the king's hopes over-reached what was practicable; his expectations on entering Edinburgh in force at the end of August were to proceed almost at once against Angus in the east of the country, and to be told that this was not possible may well have caused disagreement. The fact that James did not attend the session on 7 September suggests that he was still preparing to set out for the royal muster at Haddington. Lascelles also reported that there was some delay in getting the new campaign off the ground; originally this was scheduled to commence on 10 September, but a fresh proclamation was then made at the Market Cross in Edinburgh for the army to reassemble the following day in order to set off on 12 September.[48] In fact the army was on the move by Friday, 11 September and that night James V was at Lanark.[49] After two false starts and possibly some disagreement the offensive against Angus was under way.

The objective was to capture Douglas Castle, caput of the lordship of Douglas in Lanarkshire (and the place where Angus had been plagued by herons). The summons of treason had in July made reference to fortification of the houses of Douglas, Newark, Cockburnspath and Tantallon. In the final verdict, reference to Douglas and Cockburnspath was dropped. A royal confirmation of a grant of land made by Angus in the lordship of Douglas was made on 29 August which, as with the grants of lands in the regality of Abernethy, contained a clause protecting the recipient from the subsequent forfeiture. Further grants were made immediately following the forfeiture,[50] but Lascelles reported that the castle remained in the hands of Douglas supporters. The outlook for the defenders was poor, as the inhabitants of the surrounding area were seemingly hostile towards the Earl of Angus; furthermore, the house had little defences, though Lascelles reported that Angus had determined that he would keep it unless James V brought in artillery.[51] Lascelles credited the earl of Argyll with the conduct of the siege. The king's Household remained at Lanark, just up the road, for at least three days.[52] Lascelles was writing before the outcome of the siege, and there exists little further information on Douglas castle until January 1530, when William Symington was confirmed as its keeper as well as bailie of the lordship. The royal confirmation was of an earlier charter made by Angus, which suggests that if the siege was unsuccessful then Symington afterwards capitulated on terms favourable to himself. The king was first recorded as visiting the castle in 1531, and the first returns of the Chamberlain were received by the exchequer a year later.[53]

The fate of Newark Castle, in Ettrick Forest, is also unclear. On 26 September, George Nisbet of Dalziell (Ayrshire), and George Crow of Reston, James Ramsay in Foulden and William Reidpath – all from Berwickshire – were fined for not appearing to answer the charge of:

> . . . riding with their friends, tenants, and servants, and fortifying and assisting Archibald, formerly earl of Angus and his accomplices, for raising the siege of the castle of Newark; and for art and part with him therein. . . .

Just as with Douglas castle, so also is there neither any indication as to the outcome of the siege of Newark, nor any further mention of the castle until 1530, when the earl of Moray offered to serve as royal lieutenant in the Borders on condition that:

> the kingis placis upoun the borders beand redy to me and the hous of New Werk to duell intill peace indurand betuix the twa realms. . . .

Presumably Moray was simply requesting the use of the queen's castle rather than proposing to capture it. Possibly Scott of Buccleuch conducted the siege in

1528. In April 1527 he had been in temporary possession of the castle, and was given charge of this section of the Middle March by the Lords of Council in July 1528.[54]

The Lords of Council had demanded that Kilmarnock castle be surrendered. This was also part of Margaret Tudor's conjunct-fee. In May 1529 she gave her bond of maintenance to Robert Boyd to maintain him in his peaceful possession of the land and lordship of Kilmarnock. She also allocated him a lump sum of five hundred marks and a further one hundred marks *per annum* to maintain the castle.[55] It was perhaps more than coincidence that this grant was made a week after her former husband left Scotland. There is no record of a siege of the castle, and it is possible that Boyd, like Symington, surrendered it in return for the bond guaranteeing his position as keeper. It is feasible that all three houses – Douglas, Newark and Kilmarnock – remained in the hands of Douglas supporters throughout 1528 and well into 1529.

The king had returned from Lanark to Edinburgh by 16 September. On that day he presided over the Lords of Council with Moray, Rothes, and Lords Maxwell and Methven in attendance. Order was made for the royal artillery to be overhauled. Perhaps at Douglas James had seen for himself that its use was required and had abandoned the siege entirely to Argyll. At any rate, he returned to Stirling on 18 September and spent the rest of the month there, making just one excursion to Falkland.[56] There is no record of him venturing towards Newark.

Nor is there any record of Angus being at Newark. After his forfeiture he took refuge at Coldingham Priory. The attention of the king and his Lords of Council had turned towards an offensive in the 'westland'. This gave Angus an opportunity to strike in the east. On 10 September, he despatched eighty horsemen in the direction of Edinburgh. Their targets were the villages of Cranston and Cousland, near Dalkeith. Lascelles reported that the purpose of the raid was to provide the king with '. . . light to see to risse with all upon Fryday in the mornyng ...' and the author of the *Diurnal* recorded that the raiders 'did great skaith to mony puir commonis'.[57] The intention may also have been to punish Sir James Crichton of Cranston-Riddell who, as captain of Edinburgh castle, was turning over the armoury to the king. The raid was conducted by the Charteris brothers, until recently the terrorisers of Perth. On 1 November 1528 a remission was granted to the Charteris brothers and their supporters for these crimes.[58] Clearly, therefore, the Douglas resistance attracted support from other insurgents.

Coldingham priory was under the control of William Douglas, who in July 1527 had obtained tenure by means of excambion with the previous incumbent, Adam Blackadder.[59] William had been ordered in July by the Lords of Council to pull down the fortification which he was building to the south of the priory. This erection, known as Cawmills (or Eddrington), lay two miles north of the border at Berwick-upon-Tweed. In 1533 it became a major point of contention during talks for renewal of the Anglo-Scottish truce. The English then paid Sir

George Douglas at least £2000 to repair and occupy the building.[60] In early October 1528 Cawmills may have provided a refuge for Angus when the first royal attack was launched against him.

At the end of September 1528 James V returned from Stirling to Edinburgh and on the following day moved to Haddington. On 2 October he was reported to be heading for Dunbar.[61] However on 3 October he attacked Coldingham priory with five hundred men supplied by George, fourth lord Hume. However, Angus managed to escape from the priory before the royal raiders struck. Lord Hume and his brother, John Hume, abbot of Jedburgh, took possession of the house, and James V turned north again towards Dunbar. Before the Humes could settle into the priory, Angus returned and drove them out before pursuing the king northwards. He then gleefully reported to the earl of Northumberland that:

> the Kyngis grace durst nocht remane half one houir, but ramussit bakworts be al his mane and deligens and was richt afferit and never lechtit of his hors oneto he came to Dunbar.

There was an element of exaggeration in this account, Angus claiming that he had repulsed a superior force with only two hundred men. Northumberland's own interpretation was that up to three hundred Scots and English Borderers had assisted the earl once night had fallen, and their identities could not be recognised by the forces of the king. The raid had failed, but it alarmed Angus enough to send his daughter to Norham castle for safety (without Huntly who appears to have been able to free himself by this time). Also, William Douglas was found lying dead at Coldingham priory.[62] The manner of his departure was not recorded, but as Angus passed no judgement and made no protest, it can only be concluded that William died immediately before the raid, of natural causes. His death left vacant the wealthy abbacy of Holyrood, which was filled by the new Treasurer, Robert Cairncross. Also vacant was the priory of Coldingham.

On 9 October the abbot of Jedburgh was sitting in Edinburgh as one of the Lords of Council. The session was presided over by the Chancellor, and the only magnates present were Rothes and Lord Erskine. The business of the day was to consider and approve the terms of a contract drawn up between the king and the Humes. By this, the Humes agreed to undertake the task of expelling the Earl of Angus and his supporters from Coldingham and Cockburnspath and to hold these places themselves. Angus was also to be expelled from the Merse and prevented from re-entering Scotland. In return the abbot of Jedburgh was to receive the priory of Coldingham – in agreement with its former possessor, Adam Blackadder – and a nineteen-year lease of the lands and fortress of Cockburnspath from the queen mother. Lord Hume himself was promised Angus' former baronies of Bunkle and Preston. The Humes were to have powers to grant remissions to supporters of Angus to attract their support; and the escheat of the goods of those who continued to support Angus. Sixty spears were offered by the king for the Humes' use, and twenty-four culverines with their equipment. Over four hundred men were to assist in the taking of Coldingham, and all subjects of the king in the area were commanded to support the Humes in their task. The act of Twizelhaugh was to be invoked to protect the heirs of those slain on campaign.[63]

The Lords of Council had already appointed Lord Hume as warden of the East March and charged him with the safekeeping of the Merse during the siege of Douglas castle. Each of these directives had been considered by a much larger group of sederunts. According to Lascelles, Hume had refused the latter charge on 7 September '. . . wherewith the Kyng hath takyn a highe dyspleasure'. His refusal was undoubtedly because he was excluded from the initial scheme for division of Bunkle and Preston. The Comptroller, Colville of Ochiltree, in fact already held a charter of entitlement to half of the lands of Preston and neighbouring Lintlaws. Mark Kerr of Littledean was promised the remainder of the lands of Preston, whilst the earl of Moray was promised the superiority of Bunkle.[64] Evidently Hume's support could only be won with the offer of an incentive, and, given the limited supply of lands available, a degree of double-banking was necessary, which had to be dealt with discreetly. Given the proximity of the Humes' lands to Angus' strongholds, it was appropriate to seek the support of the former in driving out the latter. The lieges could only be commanded in the field for a fixed period, and both the burning of Cranston and Cousland and the raid on Coldingham demonstrated that the campaign to get Angus out could not be achieved solely by the use of siege tactics. James' aim was to get rid of the threat posed by Angus on the Borders, and to do so he used what means he had at his disposal; if this included making promises to border magnates, he was prepared to do this, on paper. A further incentive for the Humes was provided by a string of respites and remissions for members of the family involved in the rebellion by David Hume of Wedderburn against the Duke of Albany in the minority. Pledges were also taken, and various Humes were temporarily held in Edinburgh castle.[65]

The death of William Douglas also provided an excellent opportunity to win the Humes to the king's cause. The Humes had coveted the priory of Colding-ham for generations. The abbot of Jedburgh's namesake and uncle had been in possession until 1505; his brother, David, was recommended for the position in 1514. In 1517 David was judged to be a traitor, and Robert Blackadder, parson of Glasgow, was empowered by the Duke of Albany to uplift the fruits of the benefice, until a lawful prior could be appointed. First Robert and then David were assassinated. Patrick Blackadder of Tulliallan (Perth) succeeded his kins-man as claimant to the benefice and fell into dispute with the Humes over entitlement to the fruits. In turn, Patrick was assassinated in 1525. The third Blackadder, Adam, was thus not unwilling to exchange the priory with William Douglas in return for the provostry of Methven (Perth) and the priory of St. Mary's Isle. This agreement fell on the first death. As part of their service contract with the king, the Humes insisted that the preliminary paperwork should be carried out for the making over of the benefice by Adam to them. Blackadder instead sought an exchange with the unscrupulous John Roule, prior of Pittenweem. Roule succeeded in swindling Blackadder out of the benefice, and thus Blackadder was forced to go to Rome to recover it. In 1531 the king wrote to the cardinal of Ravenna to express his hopes for success in this journey and recommended that John Hume, abbot of Jedburgh, should be the most suitable candidate if Blackadder was still desirous of an exchange. John Roule continued until 1537 to try to obtain Coldingham, and James again wrote to discourage this appointment, especially because of the strategic position of Coldingham in relation to the border. Eventually in 1541 James V offered the vacant abbey of Dundrennan to Blackadder, and recommended to Rome that his nine-year-old illegitimate son, John Stewart, be appointed as prior of Colding-ham. Accordingly, during the personal rule, the Humes never achieved their ambition.[66]

As James V turned at first for support from the Hume family in Berwickshire, so he also turned to the young earl of Bothwell, sheriff of Lothian and Haddington. He and his chief supporters in the area – George, lord Seton, Robert Lauder of Bass, and Gilbert Wauchope of Niddrie-Marshall amongst them – were charged by the Lords of Council on 10 October to keep Lothian free from Angus and his supporters, and to see that Tantallon castle was cut off from outside assistance until the siege began. Again, the session was chaired by the Chancellor, and Bothwell, himself, was the only magnate in attendance. He protested that he 'culd tak nane of thai twa materis upon hand, bot that he wald do his diligence to resist the saidis rebellis'.[67] The Hepburns were by now beginning to earn a reputation for evading responsibility in Lothian as well as in Liddesdale.

The king had returned from Dunbar to Edinburgh on 4 October, and remained there for the week in which Lord Hume and Bothwell were before the council. James spent the following week in Stirling and returned to Edin-burgh on 18 October in order to prepare for the Tantallon campaign.[68] The start of this campaign was delayed for a few days. It was scheduled for 20 October, but the final details were still being gone over by the Lords of Council two days later. The king was absent from this session, but the earls of Argyll, Arran, Moray, Eglinton, Rothes, Montrose and Buchan were in attendance together with Maxwell, Avandale, Methven and twelve other lords. This was the highest turn out by magnates at a meeting of the council since before James' escape from Angus. Clearly, the proclamation had proved successful. The strategy drawn up was twofold. The earl of Bothwell and Lord Hume (who was not present although his brother, the abbot, was) were to assemble their forces at Cock-burnspath on 26 October and move against Coldingham. Their contract of 9 October was noted in a minute added to the record of the session; this perhaps indicates that the terms were not examined in detail on the day. It was also apparent that their remit included the taking of Cockburnspath itself. The

Scottish host was to be used against Tantallon castle. The king was to raise his standard at North Berwick to the west; the earl of Arran was to station his forces at Tynninghame to the south, and the earls of Argyll and Moray were to position themselves at Dunbar. The object was to cut off the castle from Cockburnspath and Coldingham where Angus was based. The prelate counsellors were to remain at Edinburgh to raise supplies for the besieging army. Each night of the siege three hundred men were to be placed to guard the artillery, and others would watch any possible escape routes for the castle's defenders.[69]

The scale of the operation was greater than anything that James V had yet attempted. Lascelles had estimated the Scottish host as being eight thousand men strong when assembled on 7 September for the aborted campaign against Tantallon; there is no indication of the size of the army which went to Lanark – but that was an operation involving only the earl of Argyll. The raid on Coldingham priory involved hundreds rather than thousands of men. For this campaign, however, Northumberland reckoned that James was set upon taking the field with twelve thousand men. Northumberland's information was not first-hand, but nevertheless he received reports from Lascelles, captain of Norham, and was also in contact with Angus' brother, Sir George Douglas – as had been the case with the Coldingham raid, so again the Douglases were the principal source of information for this campaign against them. The Scottish government's activity was impressive enough for Cardinal Wolsey to order Northumberland to take defensive measures. Hume's progress towards Coldingham, supported by Bothwell, prompted Northumberland to suspect that possibly a hostile move against England was intended, and he ordered that all men in the country should be ready upon an hour's notice.[70]

The siege itself employed four cannons from Edinburgh castle and further artillery from the castle of Dunbar. Members of the French garrison there, left over from the days of Albany's campaigns in the minority, appear to have aided the operation. The siege was one of the few national events of the period to be recorded in the Perth Chronicle, but its fame either did not spread as far as Aberdeen, or was not considered newsworthy by the chronicler there; and Adam Abell does not mention it. According to the author of the *Diurnal*, it lasted for ten days, from 25 October to 5 November.

English dispatches reported that the castle remained untaken. After venturing out from North Berwick to inspect the progress of the siege, James V abandoned the scene on 4 November, ordering that the artillery should follow him back to Edinburgh. Angus, with one hundred and sixty horsemen, fell upon the men dismantling the guns. David Falconer, captain of the footguard, was killed; Robert Borthwick, acting master of the artillery, was captured with his guns, and the second captain of the footguard was also taken. Angus released both Borthwick and his charges after ensuring that all the guns were spiked.[71]

Following the failure of the siege, several remissions and respites were allowed for those who had failed to answer the summons.[72] The death of David Falconer was noted both in the *Diurnal* and in Lesley's *History*. Buchanan and Bingham both make the claim that his murder drove the king wild with fury against the Douglases. Certainly an inquest was carried out as late as 1532 to find the culprits, and remissions were being granted until 1537 'and hundis putting in umquhile David Falconer alanerie exceptit'. However, it was not unusual for the repercussions of a murder to endure for this length of time; the criminal records contain several such examples, not necessarily inspired by the Crown. What is more significant is that Falconer is one of only two recorded fatalities in the entire effort to defeat Angus, and his death was to give rise to English concerns that arrangements for renewing the truce might be delayed.[73]

The Lords of Council met again at Edinburgh on 6 November, with the Chancellor presiding. Arran, Argyll, Moray, Eglinton, Bothwell, and Rothes attended, as did Lords Maxwell, Fleming, Erskine, Somerville, Forbes and Ross. All of these men 'swor be thar gret aith the haly evangellis tuichit that thai suld nevir labour at the kingis handis nor solist for Archibald Douglas'. Furthermore, they should make no communication with the earl and would use their efforts 'without any dissimulatioune to the utir distruction of the said Archibald and his part takaris'. This oath was also taken by the Chancellor, the bishops of Dunkeld, Aberdeen, Orkney, and Argyll; the abbots of Coupar Angus, Dryburgh, Jedburgh and Holyrood; Sir Alexander Jardine of Applegarth; Sir James Hamilton of Finnart; Sir Hugh Campbell of Loudoun; Sir John Stirling of Keir, and Nicholas Crawford of Oxgangs. It was made before the king, who in turn swore that Angus should never be reinstated except on the advice of these lords.[74]

Following on as it did from the failure to take both Tantallon castle and Coldingham priory, this 'grete aith' smacked of desperation on the part of the new régime. Since the July session, the tenor of the decrees issued by the council had been anti-Douglas, from the first demand for his warding through to the instructions for ordering the Tantallon campaign. The new government had legitimised its position in parliament and the Douglases were already declared forfeit of life, lands and goods. To resort to drawing up this bond or promise, which carried no penalty for breach, should have been an unnecessary step and a waste of paper. However, the attempt to remove Angus by force had so far achieved nothing, and perhaps it was felt necessary by the king and his Lords of Council to set out their position as at 6 November. There was also the material fact that communications had already been made between the new régime and Angus, as an aside to the diplomatic activity which was taking place at this time.

NOTES

1. *ADCP*, 279–80.
2. *Ibid.*, 279.
3. *SP Henry VIII*, iv, pt. iv, 501–2; SRO, *ADC*, vol. 38, f. 132; cf. RH 2.1.9., *passim*.
4. *ADCP*, 280.

5. SRO, RH 2.1.9., *passim*.
6. *ADCP*, 276; Pitcairn, *Trials*, i, pt. i, 139; *RMS*, iii, no. 708.
7. *ADCP*, 279; *LP Henry VIII*, iv, pt. ii, no. 4727.
8. *RMS*, iii, *passim*; cf. *ADCP*, 281–2; (note *SP Henry VIII*, iv, pt. iv, no. clxxxvi- letter by James V from Jedburgh dated 23 July - is wrongly placed in 1528. The correct year is 1526: cf. *LP Henry VIII*, iv, pt. ii, no. 4551).
9. *ADCP*, 281–2; RH 2.1.9., *passim*.
10. *ER*, xv, Preface p. xlviii, 438; *APS*, ii, 325–6; SRO, RH 2.1.9. (*ADC*, vol. 38, f. 122).
11. *ER*, xv, 357–71, 374–5, 436–54, 465; xvii, 457–72.
12. *Ibid.*, xv, 344, 375, 430–1, 434, 454; xvi, 222; *RSS*, ii, no. 4591.
13. *ER*, xv, 289, 460–3; xvii, 269; Wormald, *Bonds*, 307, App. A, no. 5; *TA*, v, Preface, p. xvii; *ADCP*, 281; Glasgow University Argyll Transcripts, iii, 210.
14. *ADCP*, 281–2; an account of the difficulties faced by royal financial officers in balancing the books is given by Athol L. Murray, 'Financing the Royal Household: James V and his Comptrollers 1513–43' [Murray, *Household*] in *The Renaissance and Reformation in Scotland*, edd. Cowan and Shaw (Edinburgh, 1983).
15. *HMC, Fourth Report*, 484, no. 242; *ADCP*, 278.
16. *RMS*, iii, nos. 610, 615, 617; Kelley, *Angus*, 479; *RSS*, i, no. 3982.
17. *Excerpta e libris*, App., 13.
18. *ADCP*, 281, 291; *ER*, xv, 63, 524; *RMS*, iii, no. 683.
19. *RCRB*, ii, p. i; *Edin.Recs.*, iii, 289.
20. *SP Henry VIII*, iv, pt. iv, 509.
21. Buchanan, *History*, ii, 240; *Diurnal of Occurrents*, 11.
22. *SP Henry VIII*, iv, pt. iv, 509.
23. *Ibid.*, iv, pt.iv, 510; *LP Henry VIII*, iv, pt. ii, no. 4546.
24. *SP Henry VIII*, iv, pt. iv, 509–10. Janet was more usually known as Isobel Hoppingle.
25. *ADCP*, 219, 253; *RSS*, i, no. 2538; *APS*, ii, 328.
26. *A.B. Ill.*, iv, 415 (it is not entirely clear here whether Angus is talking about Forbes' business *matters* or his *mother* who, if still alive, must have been an octogenarian).
27. Discussed in Kelley, *Angus*, 396.
28. *SP Henry VIII*, iv, pt. iv, no. clxxxvii; *LP Henry VIII*, iv, pt. ii, nos. 4718–9.
29. *SP Henry VIII*, iv, pt. iv, nos. clxxxv, clxxxix; *LP Henry VIII*, iv, pt. ii, nos. 4541, 4622.
30. *Excerpta e libris*, App., 13; *RSS*, i, nos. 3984, 3986; *ADCP*, 283; Pitcairn, *Trials*, i pt. i, 138–9.
31. *APS*, ii, 321.
32. *APS*, ii, *passim*; information on the lay magnates of this period, and an indication as to their likely ages, can be found generally in both *Scots Peerage* and *HBC*. Information on the prelates is contained in *Fasti Ecclesiae Scoticanae Medii Aevi ad annum* 1638, ed. D.E.R. Watt (St. Andrews, 1969), [Watt, *Fasti*] The 1531 parliament dealt with diplomatic and commercial matters. Alexander Drummond of Carnock was restored in the 1532 parliament, which also instituted the College of Justice. In both the 1535 and 1540–41 parliaments there was an outpouring of legislation dealing *inter alia* with the administration of Crown lands, burgh matters, and proclamations against heresy. In between full sessions, parliamentary committees met on a regular basis, mainly to continue business arising from the previous session.
33. *RMS*, iii, nos. 520, 577; Wormald, *Bonds*, App. B, nos. 20–1; *RSS*, ii, 1976; Fraser, *Sutherland*, iii, no. 80.
34. *ER*, xv, 639; *RSS*, ii, nos. 156, 3151; Records of the Earldom of Orkney, 1299–1614, ed. J. Storer Clouston (*SHS*, 2nd series, no. 7, 1914), 57, no. xxv; Lesley, *History*, 141; cf. P.D. Anderson, *Robert Stewart, Earl of Orkney, Lord of Shetland: 1533–1593* [Anderson, *Orkney*] (Edinburgh, 1982), 22–23.
35. Fraser, *Lennox*, ii, no. 149; *RSS*, ii, no. 1309.
36. *RSS*, i, no. 3878; ii, no. 642.
37. *Ibid.*, i, no. 4029.

38. *ADCP*, 278; SRO, *ADC*, vol. 38 f. 162.
39. SRO, RH 2.1.9. (*ADC*, vol. 38, ff. 129–131v, 141v-144).
40. *Ibid.*, *passim*; *RMS*, iii, no. 625.
41. *APS*, ii, 321–2. Bellenden claimed that parliament was being held in 'feriat time', meaning that the courts were on vacation: cf. *ADCP*, 380, 'feriat tyme of harvist'. The parliamentary record describes Bellenden as acting as Angus' Secretary rather than as his advocate.
42. *Ibid.*, ii, 323–8.
43. *SP Henry VIII*, iv, pt. iv, 513; *LP Henry VIII*, iv, pt. ii, nos. 4718–9.
44. *ADCP*, 283–4; SRO, RH 2.1.9. (*ADC*, vol. 387, f. 162).
45. Pitcairn, *Trials*, i, pt. i, 138–9; *APS*, ii, 321.
46. *SP Henry VIII*, iv, pt. iv, 509–10.
47. *ADCP*, 284–5.
48. Pitcairn, *Trials*, i, pt. i, 138–9; *SP Henry VIII*, iv, pt. iv, 510.
49. *Excerpta e libris*, App., 13.
50. *RMS*, iii, nos. 629, 650; a detailed account of the distribution of the estates of the Angus earldom is given by Michael Kelley, in 'Land Tenure and Forfeiture: A Sixteenth Century Scottish Example', *Sixteenth Century Journal*, ix, pt. 3 (1978) [Kelley, *Tenure*].
51. *SP Henry VIII*, iv, pt. iv, 512.
52. *Excerpta e libris*, App., 13; *RMS*, iii, no. 684.
53. *ER*, xvi, 290; *RSS*, ii, no. 521; *TA*, v, 419, 436; *Ibid.*, v, Pref. lxiv, suggests that the castle was not captured.
54. Pitcairn, *Trials*, i, pt. i, 13; *ADCP*, 257, 323.
55. Wormald, *Bonds*, 360, App. A, no. 3; SRO, Boyd Papers (GD 8), no. 69.
56. *ADCP*, 284–5; *Excerpta e libris*, 121–2, App. 13–14.
57. *SP Henry VIII*, iv. pt. iv, 510; *Diurnal of Ocurrents*, 11.
58. *RSS*, i, no. 4005; Pitcairn, *Trials*, i, pt. i, 141.
59. *RSS*, i, no. 3839.
60. *LP Henry VIII*, vi, nos. 146, 744, 1162 and *passim*.
61. *Ibid.*, iv, pt. ii, no. 4819; *Excerpta e libris*, App., 14.
62. Fraser, *Douglas*, iv, 136, no. 120; *SP Henry VIII*, iv, pt. iv, no. cxciii.
63. *ADCP*, 286–8; SRO, RH 2.1.9. (*ADC*, vol. 38, f. 177).
64. *SP Henry VIII*, iv, pt. iv, 509, 513; *RMS*, iii, no. 673.
65. *ADCP*, 286, 293–4; *RSS*, i, nos. 4002, 4057, 4068–70; ii, nos. 19–27.
66. *James V Letters*, 13, 76–8, 188–8, 234–5, 426–8; *ADCP*, 61, 207, 210, 293; *HMC, Twelfth Report*, pt. VIII, 161, no. 255; *Scots Peerage*, iv, 450; cf. the Humes' attempts to win the priory in the reign of James III in N. Macdougall, 'Crown versus Nobility: the Struggle for the Priory of Coldingham, 1472–88' in K.J. Stringer (ed.), *Essays on the Nobility of Medieval Scotland* (Edinburgh, 1985) [Stringer, *Nobility*]. John Roule, prior of Pittenweem, was implicated in a separate murder charge in 1531: cf. Pitcairn, *Trials*, i, pt. i, 157.
67. *ADCP*, 288; SRO, RH 2.1.9. (*ADC, vol.* 38, f. 178).
68. *Excerpta e libris*, App. 14; *LP Henry VIII*, iv, pt. iv, nos. 4839, 4860.
69. *ADCP*, 289–90; SRO, RH 2.1.9. (*ADC, vol.* 38,f. 184).
70. *SP Henry VIII*, iv, pt. iv, nos. clxxxix, cxc, cxciv.
71. *Ibid.*, iv, pt. iv, no. cxcv; *ADCP*, 285, 289; *Chronicle of Perth* (Maitland, 1831); *Diurnal of Occurrents*, 12.
72. *RSS*, i, nos. 4009–10, 4063; ii, nos. 206, 444, 447, 461, 503, 513.
73. *Ibid.*, ii, nos. 985, 1396, 1893; *SP Henry VIII*, iv, pt. iv, no. cxcviii; *Diurnal of Occurrents*, 14; Lesley, *History*, 141; Buchanan, *History*, 242; Bingham, *op.cit.*, 80. The other man who died was also killed at Tantallon, but his death was overlooked by the chroniclers. The victim was Henry Borthwick, gunner. There are later references to his 'puir barnis' in the judicial record: cf. SRO, *ADCS*, i, f. 104; viii, f. 43v; *ADCP*, 404. He was related to Captain Robert Borthwick.
74. *ADCP*, 290.

CHAPTER FOUR

Royal Victory?

Two days after the swearing of the 'grete aith', the Lords of Council proposed that a new 'secret counsale' be appointed for 'the ordouring of sic materis as occurris concernying the weil of the kings grace, his realme and liegis'. The main change in personnel was that Rothes was dropped and Bothwell appointed. Rothes was present at this session and assented to his dismissal, the reason for which may have been his absence from the Tantallon siege. (He obtained a remission for this in 1536). As one of the signatories of the 'grete aith' he could however still be classed as a supporter of the king. The new list of counsellors was put before the king for his approval, and on 17 November he signed an ordinance giving the names of 'the lordis . . . ordanit to be apoune our secret consale' to advise on 'all and sindry gret materis'. The dismissal of Rothes was approved, but the appointment of Bothwell was rejected.

The new secret council was now headed by Arran, Argyll, Eglinton, Moray and Lord Erskine, who all simply continued as before. On the prelates' side, the archbishop of St. Andrews was named in the ordinance, joining the Chancellor and other bishops and abbots. No time limits were stipulated for the duration of this council. Its predecessor had lasted for just four months, but the composition of the second body was almost the same. It was not explicitly stated that three or four counsellors from this second council should 'remane evir with the kingis grace', as had been provided for in July, although this was perhaps simply taken for granted; rather the royal ordinance gave express directions that the named persons were to find a royal lieutenant. This ordinance did not imply that the first secret council was now dissolved, but it did indicate a more active role for the king in choosing his counsellors and making use of them. The main purpose in the revision appeared to be an attempt to have Bothwell appointed. This was not for his own sake – he was no older than the king and hardly in a position to give counsel – but rather because of the strategic importance of his lands in the campaign against Angus.[1]

The royal ordinance of 17 November ordered that the revised secret council was to prevail upon Bothwell to take office as lieutenant within the bounds of Lothian, the Merse and Teviotdale. Failing this they were to find 'uthir personis convenient' who would serve in this capacity.[2] The choice of 'uthir personis' was limited. Six earls took the oath to destroy Angus. Of these, Arran was perhaps one of the most obvious candidates for lieutenant, in that the Hamilton and Douglas families had had ample experience of fighting each other in the minority. Against this, at the age of fifty-three, Arran had only four months left to live, and illness may have ruled him out. After his attendance to approve the appointment of himself as councillor, Arran can only be found sitting on the session on a handful of occasions in the latter part of January. If he was not ill, then his enthusiasm for the new régime was waning.

Arran had his own difficulties elsewhere. Back in May 1528 Sir James Hamilton of Finnart had requested that his father be excused from the proposed royal expedition against Liddesdale. This was because 'divers hieland men of Bute, Arane, Ilis and uthiris partis' had attacked the earl's house at Glenkill, on the Isle of Arran. Twenty-five persons, including the keeper of Glenkill, George Tait, were killed. By September Fergus and Thomas Macdowall, both lairds in Wigtownshire, had been detained for their association with Robert and Archibald Stewart, two of the seven sons of Sir Ninian Stewart, sheriff of Bute. In 1528 they were both outlawed for the murder of George Tait and for the burning down of Brodick castle. Proceedings against the Macdowalls were sisted pending the Tantallon campaign, and they were ordered to appear before the justiciar at the next Wigtown justice ayre. In December 1528 over seventy lairds from Wigtown and Galloway were outlawed for failing to answer the royal proclamations for the sieges of Douglas and Tantallon. These included Andrew Agnew, the sheriff of Wigtown. In January 1529 various members of the Neilson family were outlawed for communicating with the king's rebels in Bute, Arran and Carrick. The fates of all these numerous Wigtownshire lairds is not extant; however it was perhaps somewhat over-ambitious of the new régime to expect a full response from such far-flung corners of Scotland, especially given that many were apparently actively siding with the Stewart brothers against Arran. This dispute was one of long standing, over actual possession of the Isle of Arran. As far back as 1505, an armed royal ship had been sent to Brodick bay in order to persuade one Walter Stewart to surrender possession of the castle. With the first earl's death the dispute abated, and in 1535 Sir Ninian Stewart and all seven of his sons gave their bond of manrent to the second earl. The dispute would flare up again in the reign of queen Mary.[3] In 1528 this local difficulty provided a distraction for the first earl from the problems facing the king in the east, as well as depriving the Scots host of the service of the Wigtownshire lieges.

Likewise, the elderly earl of Eglinton had his own local concerns. His castle had not long before been burnt down by the Master of Glencairn in retaliation for Eglinton's failure to pay the full £1000 Scots fine imposed upon the earl by the Lords of Council in May 1528. The Lords of Council set aside the first day of December to hear all actions by Eglinton against Glencairn.[4]

The king's half-brother, Moray, was also at feud, with the clan Chattan. The chief of the clan, Lauchlan Macintosh, was killed in 1525, leaving as heir the under-age William. Lauchlan's wife, and mother to William, was Jean Gordon, half-sister to Moray (though not related to the king!). Lauchlan's half-brother, Hector, had received letters of legitimisation from the Angus government in 1526, and the gift of ward of the Macintosh estates the following year. His intention was probably to replace his nephew, William, as chief of the clan. At any rate, he attempted to forge alliances through offering his bond of manrent to Argyll, Argyll's brother, John Campbell of Cawdor (who was married to the sheriff of Nairn's daughter), Hector Munro of Foulis, Hutcheon Rose of Kilravock, and also to MacDonald of Sleat and the chief of the clan Cameron. Moray accordingly placed William (who was his nephew too) under the protection of Alexander Ogilvie of Findlater, and arranged for Jean Gordon to marry Ogilvie's heir.[5] Lesley records that the clan Chattan then attacked Moray's castle of Darnaway and the neighbouring village of Dyke, as well as the Ogilvie strongholds of Petty and Hawhill. Several Ogilvies were killed. With a change of government, Moray was able to have his revenge. On 10 November 1528 James V issued under signet a 'fire and sword' letter to his half-brother. Moray was appointed lieutenant in the north with authority to raise the lieges against the clan Chattan. Lord Forbes, Lord Fraser of Lovat and the earls of Sutherland and Caithness were commanded to assist, as were the sheriffs and captains of the clans. Moray was entitled to 'mak utir exterminatioun and destructioun' of the Macintoshes, and also to:

> tak the wemen and barnis of the said clan to sum partis of the sey, nerrest land, quhair schippis salbe forsene on our expenssis, to saill with thame furth of our realme and land with them in Jesland, Zesland, or Norway; becaus it wer inhumanite to put handis in the blude of wemen and barnis.

This instruction was said to be determined on the advice of 'oure consale', which at this time included Moray. Carrying it out occupied him until at least April of the following year, when Hector Macintosh paid forty pounds for a remission for all crimes – specifically for treasonable art, part and assistance to Angus. His bond of manrent was received by Moray at Darnaway in November 1530.[6] The principal casualty of this devastation of the clan Chattan appears to have been Hector's brother, William. The letter of fire and sword was directed against William and associates rather than against Hector. William is said to have been hanged at Tordarroch (Banff), with eighteen other ringleaders of the clan.[7] However, there was no direct connection between the Macintoshes and the Douglases. The most that can be argued is that Angus' government may have promoted Hector at the expense of the rightful chief, his nephew William. The letter of fire and sword spoke generally of the Macintoshes daily committing arson, murder, and 'heirschippis', and wasting the country. The specific incident was an attack on lands pertaining to James Dunbar of East Tarbert in the Brae of Moray. Dunbar held these lands by great seal charter, and also feued East Tarbert (in Ross) from the Crown.[8] He was probably kinsman to the sheriff of Moray, James Dunbar of Cumnock. There was no obvious reason for his being targeted by the clan Chattan, nor any tie-up with the Douglases. However, through marriage, George Douglas of Pittendreich had come to hold extensive lands in Morayshire, which in September 1528 were granted to the earl of Moray. In the previous year the Angus government had had reason to order Moray to surrender Spynie castle, to which Douglas of Kilspindie then held title.[9] The antagonism between Moray and the Douglas family ran in parallel with the clan Chattan dispute, but the two were distinct matters. However, by diverting Moray's attention to local difficulties at a time of national strife, the Macintoshes could, perhaps, be justly accused of giving treasonable assistance to the Douglases.

One common feature between the 'fire and sword' letter and the 'grete aith' sworn four days earlier is the vehemence of the tone employed. Both the Macintoshes and the Douglases were to be reduced to their 'utir distructioun'. In neither situation was this violence of language on paper fully enacted out in practice. The letter was given under the signet. There were three signets in use: one by the justiciar on justice ayre; the second by the Lords of Council, and the last by the king. The letter is denoted as arising 'out of deliberation of the Lords of Council'. The 'grete aith' itself is not extant, but rather its terms appear as an entry in the books of the Acts of the Lords of Council.[10] It is a reasonable conjecture to suppose that both items were drawn up by the same author, but merely speculation that the words came unedited straight from the lips of a young king disappointed at the failure of a major campaign.

The other magnate signatories of the 'grete aith' included Rothes, Argyll and Bothwell. Rothes was not at the siege of Tantallon and was no longer one of the secret council. The choice was between Argyll and Bothwell. It was, of course, feasible to turn to one of the lords who had sworn the oath. Forbes was ruled out as he was charged to assist Moray. Maxwell had both Edinburgh and the West March to look after. John, fifth lord Erskine, and Malcolm, third lord Fleming and Great Chamberlain, were both ubiquitous characters in government administration throughout the personal rule, the former as auditor and judge (he was again selected as a session judge on 15 November 1528) and the latter in the chancery office (he had an almost perfect record as a charter witness).[11] These activities suggest the characters of civil servants rather than warriors. Besides, Fleming too had his own local difficulties in Peeblesshire, where the hereditary sheriff John, third lord Hay of Yester, was failing to keep satisfactory order. In November, the council instructed Fleming to 'pass hame in his cuntre and put ane gude ordour and reule in the samin'.[12]

Hugh, fourth lord Somerville, attended the session primarily in order to pursue his action against his kinsman, John Somerville of Cambusnethan. Cambusnethan had been forfeited in 1522 for his part in the 'Cleanse-the-Causeway' episode of 1520, and Lord Somerville had gained by this; the forfeiture had then been rescinded in 1525. Subsequently the lord claimed that his kinsman had appropriated forty pounds worth of land from him in the barony of Carnwath. On 7 November 1528 the Lords of Council made an interim ruling in favour of Cambusnethan, obliging Somerville to request Finnart to stand as surety for his compliance with the decree. However, the dispute between the two Somervilles continued into 1533.[13] Lord Somerville was one of the lords of parliament in September 1528, and was present on the session dealing with judicial business on the 26th of that month. His swearing of the 'grete aith' on the day after decree was made against him may have been in order to curry favour for his suit against his kinsman.[14]

Ninian, third lord Ross of Halkhead, also took the oath. His sole claim to fame in the personal rule was to add his name as one of the nine ratifiers of the Anglo-Scottish peace treaty at Holyrood on 30 June 1534.[15] In any case, the notion of employing a lord of parliament, rather than an earl, as the king's lieutenant would have been to ignore the accepted view of social rank amongst the Second Estate. There were other adult earls who might have been considered; the sources refer only to Arran, Argyll, Moray and Bothwell being involved in the Tantallon campaign, but Buchan and Montrose had been at the session of the Lords of Council on 22 October to help plan the strategy, and almost certainly took part in its execution. There was only a handful of remissions granted to absentees from 'our soverane lordis oist and army of Temptalloun'. With two exceptions, the purchasers were of lairdly status or less, and most came from Renfrew, Ayr and Wigtownshire; some, at least, of the seventy-odd lairds underlay the law at the 1529 Wigtown justice ayre. (The two exceptions were Rothes and Lady Sinclair, whose remissions were both obtained in 1536). Thus the feudal army would appear to have been drawn from at least these areas in the west of the country.

That other areas were fairly represented in the Scots host is indicated by the attendance of fifteen lords at the session of 22 October, giving a good geographical spread – from Lords Ogilvie, Forbes and Fraser of Lovat in the north to Lords Maxwell, Fleming and Hay of Yester in the Borders. Therefore, it can be supposed that Montrose and Buchan were each commanding contingents from the north during the Tantallon campaign. Whether or not they were of high calibre as military commanders can only be guessed at. Montrose, as well as Rothes and Atholl, served on the Borders in 1532 under the lieutenancy of Moray. Possibly Moray possessed greater skills as a military commander. Probably, as the king's half-brother, he outranked both Montrose and Buchan in status. However, Montrose was considered to have the requisite skills and status to serve as joint vice-regent in 1536–37.

The reasonable choice of a lieutenant to lead the campaign against Angus was from amongst those earls most closely associated with the new régime, either as one of the oath-takers or as a secret councillor, or both. The choice lay between Bothwell and Argyll. Argyll was shrewd enough to point out to the Lords of Council on 24 November that his ability to carry out the task was compromised by two factors: firstly that he 'had his bundis in fer partis', and secondly, as a consequence of this fact, he 'mycht nocht convene his servandis and frenndis towartis the bordouris bot be generale gaderingis quhen all the kingis liegis ar chargit'. Accordingly he could only be judged in this light.[16] This was eminently more reasoned than Bothwell's continual attempts to evade responsibility; and it was small wonder that he should be excluded from the secret council. The terms upon which Argyll would accept the commission were laid before the Lords of Council on 28 November. He was to have his expenses borne by both male and female landholders in Lothian and the Merse. These would amount to two hundred pounds for every twenty days which the earl was on campaign. He was to have pledges from those in this area who would serve. He would have power to execute justice and issue remissions to all, the Douglases 'alanerly exceptit'. The act of Twizelhaugh was to be applied. Any reward of lands to the persons who took or killed the Douglases had to be approved by him. He was to have 'four small falconis' on campaign when these were available, and 'gret artalzery' when it came to taking the enemy's strongholds. These terms were accepted on 29 November, and the arrangements for paying Argyll's expenses were put in hand on 15 December.[17]

Running in tandem with the appointment of a royal lieutenant for the East March was the Hume enterprise to take Coldingham. They had failed to do this on two occasions – with the king in early October and again during the Tantallon campaign. It was also by no means clear that Cockburnspath had been captured. Accordingly the Humes put forward to the Lords of Council on 16 November the latest draft of their proposals. The main revision was that they now requested that proclamations be made for the lieges of the Merse, Lauderdale, and Teviotdale to assist them. They also gave their assurance that they would cooperate with 'quhat lord that beis made lietenent'. However, their main concern was that Colville of Ochiltree and Kerr of Littledean should immediately give up their claims to the lands of Preston and Lintlaws. They also wanted arrangements for the transfer of Coldingham priory to be put in hand.

On this occasion the session was attended by Arran, Argyll, Moray, Eglinton and Bothwell. Tactfully the Humes did not also demand that Moray should give up any claim he had to Bunkle. Their offer of service was accepted and arrangements made to find the four or five hundred men they required.[18]

The Hume 'contract' was eventually honoured, but only in part, by the Scots government. In September 1529, Lord Hume received the escheat of all of the goods in the Merse formerly held by Angus and Sir George Douglas, and the profits from the baronies of Bunkle and Preston from the spring of that year up to September. His brother, the abbot of Jedburgh, had to wait until 1531 to receive a five-year tack of half of the lands of Preston and Lintlaws, at which point he was also granted the power to hold bailie courts in the barony. In September 1529 the lands of Cockburnspath were granted in feu farm to Margaret Tudor's third husband, Lord Methven.[19] Coupled with their failure to obtain the priory, this meant that the Humes were forced to compromise their original demands. Whether or not all of these demands came out into the open at the session on 16 November is a debatable point. First proposed before a session made up predominantly of prelates and royal officers on 9 October, they had been dealt with by minute thereafter. Given the Hume record in the minority – murdering Albany's lieutenant, De la Bastie, in 1517 – the group of magnates on the session on 16 November may not have relished conceding that the Humes' assistance was necessary. Added to this was the fact that the Humes had achieved probably nothing to date by way of securing Angus' 'utir distruction'. The length of time which it took the Lords of Council to commission Argyll suggests that the new régime was swithering over the best way forward in terms of advancing the military offensive, and persistent pressure by the Humes ensured their place in this on their own terms.

Before any further campaigning took place, a five-year truce was concluded with the English, at Berwick on 14 December.[20] Prior to his breach with the king, Angus had opened up the possibility of the truce being renewed. This desire was also expressed in the letter of state dated 13 July and placed before Henry VIII and Cardinal Wolsey by Patrick Sinclair. The letter of state also sought to explain why Angus had been removed, mentioning that the English king was partially responsible for his rise to power. Wolsey, whilst welcoming arrangements for the renewal, and appointing Dr. Thomas Magnus as English negotiator, sent back a letter deploring the removal of Angus. This required a tactful response from the new régime. James wrote to Wolsey in September, and was at some pains to dispel the unfavourable impression given by Sinclair. The new Chancellor, Gavin Dunbar, wrote directly to Henry VIII after the September parliament to state categorically that Angus had been found guilty of treason and had been forfeited by authority of the three estates.[21] At this time, Roger Lascelles, the Earl of Northumberland's man based at Norham, reported to his masters that the Scots feared that the English king would actively support the forfeited earl, and that were Henry VIII to pursue a subtle approach, then whole-hearted compensation could be obtained from the Scots in the matter of redress for the complaints being made by Sir Christopher Dacre and other English border officers. Lascelles stated confidently that the Scots would agree to anything to prevent Henry VIII from intervening on Angus' behalf and added that:

> . . . Scotland was never so eith to wyne as it is nowe, nor never so ferde; for they feyre the King will take part with th'erle of Angis. . . .[22]

This was in line with the placatory tones of James' letter to Wolsey, though not with the more assertive response received by Henry VIII himself from the archbishop of Glasgow.

Northumberland wrote on 17 September to both James V and his mother, Margaret Tudor, to agree that a commission should be set up to negotiate the terms of a renewal of the truce. The letter to Margaret perhaps went some way to calm the fears that she had expressed right at the outset of the change in circumstances, when she had written:

Item the quene makes instance and desire to my Lorde [Northumberland] that ther be noo cause shewed of the Inglisshe borders, to provok any waire against the Kynge of Scotts and her'.[23]

Northumberland also urged that there should be no delay in setting up the commission, as the Borderers were showing signs of unrest, not only because Angus was now based in the Merse but also because they regarded the last truce as now at an end, and hence were carrying out raids without fear of reparations having to be made. He mentioned the raid carried out on the motte of Liddale in Nichol forest (Cumberland) by Edward Maxwell, towards which Edward's brother, Lord Maxwell, had taken such a cavalier approach at the truce day on 2 September.

Before any arrangements could be made, James struck at Angus at the priory of Coldingham. Angus repeated his request for English intervention, but Northumberland refused to act until he had further instructions from Wolsey.[24] Northumberland then received Sir George Douglas, who had been sent into England by his brother armed with Angus' earlier requests for help. Sir George arrived in London in the middle of October, was there granted one hundred pounds by Wolsey, and was sent north again with instructions that the English Borderers should be allowed to ride with Angus should they so wish. Northumberland commented that it would be hard to stop them, as 'th'Erle is soo welbeloved in England'.[25] This had perhaps already been illustrated in Angus' successful recapture of Coldingham priory.

Despite James' letter to his uncle Henry VIII, assuring him that redress would be given and that his nephew already had in hand the case of the capture of an Englishman on pilgrimage en route to St. Ninians,[26] the English had little confidence in the new government. Northumberland had already concluded:

'I can not see that any redresse woll be maid uppon the Borders, except the Erle of Angois be put in auctorite agayne'.[27]

Magnus was given his instructions on 5 October. He was to make it clear to any Scottish representatives that Henry VIII was only agreeing to a commission as a royal favour to his nephew. Redress had to be given before a truce could be agreed. At the least, Lord Dacre's servant, Miles Halton, held in Hermitage castle, must be released. If Angus were not reinstated, a separate article was to be drawn up allowing for his withdrawal into Scotland.[28]

Magnus was also instructed to deny any rumour that Angus had ever intended kidnapping the Scottish king and delivering him into his uncle's hands. This last point had already been stressed by Wolsey in answer to the Scottish letter of state. The instructions given to Patrick Sinclair in fact made no reference to a kidnapping plot. Possibly in presenting the Scots case to the English government, Sinclair had allowed his imagination to run away with him. The idea is reminiscent of abortive schemes concocted in the 1490s to kidnap the king's father James IV. It is difficult to see any purpose in its being raised by either side, other than in an attempt to seize the moral high ground. Sinclair may have been expressing the sentiments of some of the more conservatively minded Lords of Council. The kidnapping rumour again circulated in later years when proposals were being put forward for a summit conference between Henry VIII and his nephew, at a venue to be mutually agreed. In 1541, the Scottish First Estate was reported in diplomatic correspondence to be completely against such proposals.[29]

James replied to Northumberland's letter of 17 September on 5 October. He proposed a commission meet at Berwick-upon-Tweed on 8 November, and named as the Scots representatives Thomas Kerr, abbot of Kelso, and Adam Otterburn, royal advocate. He trusted that details of this meeting should not be circulated too freely, for fear that this would give rise to trouble from Angus.[30] By this was meant that there should be no opportunity allowed for Angus to recover influence in Scotland by forcing his way to the negotiating table. This was how the English government chose to interpret the king's request. Further instructions were issued to Magnus; if James V was fearful of Angus' restoration, then the prospect of this was to be used as a lever to secure full redress. This line had already been suggested by Lascelles. If it were not possible for Angus to be restored, then a separate article could be drawn up later determining his fate, once Henry VIII had had an opportunity to consider the point. Magnus was also briefed on Scottish foreign policy. If the Scottish king were seeking overseas allies then Angus had to be reinstated. Angus could cause more harm acting as Henry's agent in Scotland than he could in England. Were the Scots to become an ally of the German emperor, the benefits which this might bring them would be more than matched by the damage which Angus could cause.[31]

The background to this last concern of the English was the continuing effort by the Scots to secure a bride for their king.[32] The Scottish government had first approached Francis I of France in 1516 and in the following year concluded the defensive treaty of Rouen, by which they were promised a royal French princess for their then four-year-old king.[33] This treaty had been secured by the Duke of Albany. Since then, Henry VIII had tried to woo the Scots away from the 'auld alliance' with the offer of his daughter, Mary Tudor. Anglo-French relations had fluctuated during James' minority, and in 1527 England and France had agreed to treaty.[34] Nevertheless this alliance was not so well founded for the English to be complacent at the thought that the treaty of Rouen might be fulfilled. The rumour in 1528 that Albany (who still styled himself 'governor of Scotland') might return to Scotland alarmed both English and Scots alike.[35] His pro-French line had not been acceptable to Angus, who in the spring of 1528 had sent William Hamilton of Sanquhar to the French court. Whilst he was in France, James V assumed power in Scotland. In September Francis I advised Hamilton that he would endeavour to prevent Albany's return. This was welcome news for the new Scots government; Albany would simply complicate an already tense situation in Scotland. Hamilton was also advised that France could not oblige on the treaty of Rouen, because of her treaty with England.[36] Accordingly he passed into Flanders to investigate the possibility of an imperial bride for his king. The target was either Dorothea or Christiana, the daughters of the deposed Danish king, Christian II, and nieces of Charles V. Albany, however, intervened to prevent this.[37] News of Hamilton's moves reached the English government through their French allies. Anglo-Imperial relations were strained, and Henry VIII did not want his nephew to marry an imperial bride.

Before the meeting of the commissioners at Berwick could take place, there occurred a meeting between Sir George Douglas and Archibald Douglas of Kilspindie on the one hand, and Sir James Hamilton of Finnart and Sir Hugh Campbell of Loudoun on the other. This took place at Cockburnspath, at the height of the Tantallon campaign. The queen's stronghold was not yet taken by the Humes. What was discussed at this meeting is not extant, but Angus told Magnus that he had made:

'. . . mooste humble and mooste lowly offers, as it apperteynneth to a subjecte to use hym to his Soveraine Lorde. . . .

James then wrote to Magnus, saying that under advice from his uncle and from his Lords of Council, and for other reasons,

'. . . we condiscendit to gif graice to ye saidis rebellis, conforme to ye said Archibaldis desyr onder his hand wryte and signet. . . .

This referred to the mediation carried out between the king and his former Chancellor by Andrew Cairns, minister provincial of the order of Friars Observantine. With preparations underway for the Tantallon campaign, Angus wrote to James from Coldingham priory, and his letter was presented to the king by Cairns. In this letter, Angus offered to surrender Tantallon castle and his other fortresses in return for his restoration to his full honour and heritage. The English dispatches attest that James accepted this offer. Angus wrote again to promise that he would fulfil his side of the bargain, but was unable to speak for his relatives. James answered that he would receive them also if they would surrender. Abell records that the earl 'has asked forgiveness at the king by other brothers but he has not obtained it yet'. Magnus then reported the Cockburn-spath meeting to Wolsey, stating that the Scots king was:

'. . . pleased to receive and accept into his gratious favour the saide Erle, his broder, and uncle, upon theire oune offers and submissions; copy whereof your grace sent unto me; and after the said Erle revoked the same. . . .

Wolsey had received copies of these submissions from Sir George Douglas at their meeting in the middle of October. Whilst Andrew Cairns was acting as mediator between Angus and James, George was making his way back from Northumberland into Scotland, carrying with him Wolsey's assurance that the

English were sympathetic towards their cause. It is not clear why Angus rejected the peace offer which he had instigated. Possibly he considered that he could achieve even better terms at the forthcoming truce talks, and perhaps be reinstated as Chancellor with English approval. The failure of the Tantallon campaign may have convinced him that the new régime had no hope at all of defeating him. However this failure hardened rather than softened James' attitude. He wrote to Magnus:

> '. . . yai refusit ye samyn [offer] and dyd us displeasour at our returnyng fra
> ye sege of Tamtalloun, in murdering apone ye nycht ane noble man. . . .

By this, the king meant the death of David Falconer. The author of the *Diurnal* comments that with Falconer's death at the failure of the siege, the king 'haid greit suspicioun of the temporall lordis becaus thai favourit sum pairt the Douglassis'.[38]

The immediate result of this 'suspicioun' was the swearing of the 'grete aith' by, amongst others, Finnart and Loudoun. It is clear from this extraordinary interlude in the middle of a full-scale campaign that the Scots government was trying to pursue war and peace simultaneously and was displaying 'dissim-ulatioune' to a high degree. It is likely that the king knew of the Cockburnspath meeting, less so that he had authorised it. The 'other reasons' referred to in his letter to Magnus were not stated, but the king may have been responding to a situation beyond his control. Amongst his supporters there were those who favoured peace talks with the Douglases, whilst others were responsible for drafting the 'bond' calling for their destruction. It would become more apparent in later years whether the king's own character was more accurately reflected in the correspondence exchanged with Magnus or in such items as the 'fire and sword' letter and 'grete aith'.

The commissioners met, as agreed, at Berwick on 8 November. The meeting was not a success. The Scots had come briefed only to treat for a renewal of the truce for three years until the king should be of an age to conclude a full peace. Magnus had a more complex remit. He began by asking for redress. The Scots replied that this was a reasonable request, but admitted that their king could hardly control Liddesdale. Magnus answered that in that case, Henry VIII should have powers to deal with Liddesdale apart from any truce arrangements. The Scots conceded the reasoning in this. The English then asked what James V proposed to do about Angus, given that Henry VIII was showing him favour. The Scots replied that this was not part of their brief, but they were surprised that the English king should favour a rebel. Magnus responded that if James V so 'rigorously in his youth shulde persecute his noble men and Peers of his Realme, for noone higher cause nor transgression thenne yet appereth', then how would be behave in later years? He suggested that the king's council at the time consisted of Finnart, murderer of Lennox; Loudoun, killer of Cassillis; Scott of Buccleuch, who despatched Andrew Kerr of Cessford; and Maxwell, the chief maintainer of offenders. Hence Henry VIII was rightly concerned for his nephew's well-being. The Scots stated that they had come to renew the truce and that if this could not be achieved then Henry VIII would not be acting honourably. A further meeting was scheduled for 9 December.[39]

Faced with this unyielding stance by the Scots, Magnus recommended to Wolsey that 'it were not good to refuse peax for th'Erle of Angus, conseidering the warre of Scottlande is never to the proufite of Einglande'. He considered each side to be equally to blame for matters requiring redress, and observed that few English Borderers were assisting Angus, though they were authorised so to do by their government, and few more would unless directly ordered. Magnus then met the Douglas brothers and their uncle at Berwick. He assured them of a refuge in England, but avoided putting this promise in writing for fear that this would open the floodgates for all Scottish outlaws. Angus promptly requested the use of two or three hundred Borderers to ride with him. Magnus refused, reminding him that his brother had already received £100 from the English government which was surely adequate to buy support, if Angus indeed had any in Scotland. Probably Magnus considered that Angus had already thrown away his best chance of making a Scottish comeback by backing out of the Observantine sponsored talks. Angus resolved to use their mediation again before the next commission meeting.[40]

Magnus also found time to give his version of the Berwick meeting, and give an update on the list of outstanding matters requiring redress, in letters sent to James, Margaret Tudor, and Gavin Dunbar. The response was encouraging; on 19 November the Lords of Council ordered Bothwell to release sixty English prisoners who had been taken by Liddesdale men, and reassurances were given that the date of the next meeting would be kept. George Crichton, bishop of Dunkeld, requested that Magnus should secure the release of one of his servants, captured by the Douglases and incarcerated in Norham castle, together with 'ane barne called John Murray, quhilk was ane chylde, passing to the scule with his maister, and innocent of all crymes'.[41]

Adam Otterburn and the abbot of Kelso returned to Edinburgh. As a member of the secret council, Otterburn was then designated the task of finding a royal lieutenant. The English view of who was counselling James V at this time was rather less than accurate, although three of the people mentioned by Magnus had joined in the 'grete aith'. Magnus also picked up a piece of perhaps spiteful gossip from his meeting with Angus, namely that upon the return of the Scots commissioners to report their failure to negotiate a renewal of the truce, James had burst into tears 'insomyche that the lordes of his counseill were gretely mooved'.[42] If this were true it would be consistent with the frustrations felt by the king in the middle of November 1528. The military campaign was achieving nothing; negotiations to reach a compromise with Angus had failed, and foreign policy was getting nowhere.

On 5 December the Lords of Council instructed Otterburn, Scott of Balwearie, and Andrew Kerr of Ferniehirst to return to Berwick with instructions, if necessary, to concede to a separate article providing for the Douglases to withdraw into England, on condition that they surrendered Tantallon and all other strongholds still in their hands. The instructions concluded with the dour warning that 'Ingland sall ansuer for all the evil that thai sall happin to do in Scotland fra the type thai be ressett in Ingland'.[43] After a week of negotiation, a five-year truce was concluded. A separate article allowed for the English to invade Liddesdale if the Scots could not give redress for the area. Despite a letter from Magnus to Otterburn on the subject, the Scots succeeded in excluding any reference to Angus in the truce, but agreed to arrangements for his reset by way of separate article. They also argued that William Hamilton of Sanquhar had visited Flanders purely in order to negotiate terms for the Scottish staple at Veere, and contended that any suggestion that he was in fact searching for an imperial bride for their king must have been at Angus' instigation; this last point had caused such concern in England that there had been consideration given to the possibility of again offering Mary Tudor as a royal bride for the Scots king. Finally arrangements were made for the holding of regular truce days by the wardens, beginning in January 1529.[44]

Magnus headed south after concluding the treaty, but on 27 December received instructions from his masters to go north to Edinburgh to make one last attempt to intercede on Angus' behalf. The Observantine friars had again been busy on the earl's behalf. Magnus was kept waiting at Edinburgh until James returned there on 17 January 1529, having spent Christmas at Stirling. On 22 January the sixty-five year-old diplomat had a private meeting with the king. James prevaricated over the question of Hamilton of Sanquhar's diplomatic activities. He listened politely to the homily given by Magnus on the subject of 'private light and yong Counsaill', which had been responsible for the fall of the king's grandfather, James III. Magnus then opened discussion on the subject of the Douglases. James replied that his former Chancellor had already turned down the offer of a rapprochement 'granting unto thayme thair lyves, landes and honoures', which offer the king had 'mooved in good and gentill maner'. He claimed that the earl had committed the further crime of plundering the wreckage of the Scots trader the *Litill Martyne*, wrecked in November off Innerwick, and already the subject of claims for recompense by those merchants having goods aboard her. James concluded that all that Angus had to do was comply with the terms of the separate article drawn up at Berwick. Magnus' last tactic was to offer a bribe to the king of £2000, 'as I was required and mooved frome the said Erle of Anguse . . . for reconsiliation'. This was neither 'regarded accepted nor taken'.[45]

Unable to achieve anything further, Magnus returned south in early February, noting on his way through East Lothian that fierce fighting was going on between Bothwell's followers and the Douglases. He took with him, to show to his master, James' version of the events that had led him to break with his former

Chancellor, narrating the confrontation in Easter 1528, followed by the king's withdrawal to Stirling for his own safety.[46]

The fighting which Magnus witnessed was conducted by Bothwell, now acting as lieutenant of the East March. Bothwell's terms of service were laid before the Lords of Council on 26 January and came under the scrutiny of Arran, Argyll and Eglinton. The deal was that he would take commission for one year in the first instance, with full powers to issue remissions to all supporters of the Douglases, and with all firearms (he was issued with twenty small hand-guns) supplied by the royal master of artillery, and all royal strongholds made available for his use. His task was to surround Tantallon and hold the country down around the castle until it surrendered, and thereafter to expel the Douglases 'furth of the boundis of Lothiane and hald thame furth of the samin'. By achieving this, the Hepburns would demonstrate to the king and the Lords of Council 'their trew service without dissimulation'.[47]

Argyll's campaign in December 1528 had been directed against Coldingham. Assisted by his brothers, Archibald Campbell of Skipness and Sir John Campbell of Cawdor, Argyll spent his own money in hauling the royal artillery down the east coast. The campaign appeared to be successful; this is implicit in Argyll's appearance at the session on 3 January when he handed in his expenses account and offered to continue the offensive against the houses of Blackadder, Billie and Hutton Hall, all held by Douglas supporters. Answer was made to Argyll that:

> the kingis grace and lordis declaris and grantis that it salbe na cryme nor accusation to the said erle nor hurt nor prejudice to his honour albeit he pass nocht forwart at this tyme to fulfill the premissis becaus he can nocht be furnist with munitionis and money. . . .[48]

This was a roundabout way of admitting that at the present time the new régime could not afford Argyll's services at £20 a day. The earl was requested to be ready to resume his duties once more weapons and money were found. The Lords of Council may also have decided at this time to concentrate their efforts against Tantallon. At this juncture, the five-year truce had been signed but not yet ratified, and the first truce days had yet to be held. Lord Hume was given his instructions on this subject on 22 January. As warden of the East March, his task was to apprehend thieves. It would not be appropriate at this stage for him to be seen engaged in assisting the royal lieutenant in military activities just across the border from Berwick. His opposite number, the earl of Northumberland, had panicked the last time that Hume had taken an army into the Merse. Furthermore, Magnus was in Edinburgh, waiting for a private interview with the king on the subject of the earl of Angus.

Argyll received his reward for good service in the form of a royal charter to Abernethy; his brother Sir John was appointed as sheriff of Nairn. Argyll's reward came on 6 December – that is, apparently before he took the field. This was also the case for Bothwell, appointed as lieutenant on the day of ratification of the truce.

Bothwell was gifted the lands of Tantallon in feu farm, with the feu duty set at the attractive price of one hundred marks per annum.[49] This was cheaper than paying Argyll's expenses, and had the effect of killing two birds with one stone; like the Humes, the Hepburns were to capture their reward. The securing of Bothwell's service at the end of January accomplished the direction given to the secret council in November. It appears that his commission was preferred to Argyll's in January 1529. By then the new régime had concerns beyond the expulsion of Angus, with the need to meet its commitments under the new treaty. On 21 January, Maxwell was charged to meet with Dacre in the West March, Hume to order the East, and Mark Kerr of Dolphinton to answer for East Teviotdale. On 4 February, Maxwell was directed to secure the cooperation of his rival, Johnston of that Ilk, in giving redress in the west.[50] Argyll, as justiciar general, had the responsibility of holding justice ayres. In November 1528, he had presided over ayres held at Edinburgh, Haddington and Linlithgow, and in March the Lords of Council decreed that further ayres should be held in May at Jedburgh, Selkirk and Peebles.[51] The giving of redress presented problems. In his letter of 3 February to his uncle, James commented that in the east the Borderers 'will rather procure inventiones and mater to movis the weir, thane paix'. Of Liddesdale, the king asked for patience, as there were difficulties in securing order because of Bothwell's youth; Bothwell was required to meet the English wardens at Kershopemouth (Roxburgh) on 24 February.[52] He was being expected to carry out two jobs at once, given that he was simultaneously acting as lieutenant in the east. This suggests that the task of expelling the Douglases was no longer the sole royal concern.

The campaign against the Douglases also lost momentum because there was already a solution agreed between the two governments for his departure. In military terms, stalemate had been reached. The remaining Douglas strongholds could not be taken by force, and Tantallon was still holding out against the king. Angus could no longer look to the English government to back him in his attempts to fend off attacks.

On 11 March Bothwell and Hume were again charged to expel the Douglases from the Merse without delay, and to take the houses of Blackadder, Billie and Hutton Hall. Bothwell's great-uncle, the prior of St. Andrews, protested that this task could not be achieved as quickly as the Lords of Council were seeking.[53] The way forward was to resume negotiations with Angus.

On 6 March, Robert Barton of Over-Barnton was appointed to the two chief financial positions in Scotland, replacing Colville of Ochiltree as Comptroller and the abbot of Holyrood as Treasurer. One of his first actions was to obtain a letter under the privy seal giving him sole authority to execute all royal grants of casualty or property. On 12 March, a further letter cancelled all gifts of escheat made:

> through wilfull errour or uthirwayis gevin be circumventioun and agains resoun, of certane personis of the quhilkis the crymes wes nocht convictit nor dilatit in the tyme of the saidis giftis. . . .[54]

This letter held out some hope for the earl of Angus of recovering his lands at some point in the future, should he ever receive a royal pardon. Armed with this authority, Barton made contact with Angus, and on 23 March a deal was struck. Angus would surrender Tantallon and all other houses held by him and withdraw into England, in accordance with the separate article agreed at Berwick. In return, the Crown would undertake to resume possession of his estates and any regrants should only be made to its servants or to members of the royal household. Angus thus had a promise that his earldom would not simply be broken up and gifted in perpetuity. In addition he was granted licence to take away with him into exile, all of his moveable goods.[55] This licence proved to be of little value, as Lord Hume was later granted all those goods which Angus left in Berwickshire.

By 1 March 1529, seals had been exchanged confirming the ratification of the truce by both governments. With both sides anxious to carry out redress, Angus' presence in the Merse was now an obstacle for the English as well as the Scots. Following on from Barton's offer, the Scots government gave Angus a month's grace in which to withdraw.[56] On 27 March the lands of Tollcross in Edinburgh were granted to John Murray and Walter Scott. These were part of the conjunct-fee of the wife of Archibald Douglas of Kilspindie, Isobel Hoppringle. The grant was made 'quhill the said Archibald be our soverane lordis fre liegeman and relaxit fra his horne'.[57] This conditional gift admitted the possibility of such an outcome for the uncle of the earl of Angus, illustrating that the new régime, on paper, was prepared to honour the deal struck by Barton.

On 2 April the king rode first to Haddington and then to North Berwick. On the following day he took possession of Tantallon castle. The occasion was marked by seven remissions granted for supporters of Angus. Drummond of Carnock had obtained his remission on 31 March.[58] Angus, however, continued to hold out in the Merse, and on 21 April the Lords of Council, at a session chaired by the Chancellor and attended by Bothwell, Rothes, Lord Erskine and also, as a comparatively recent newcomer, the earl of Huntly, ruled that proclamation be made to:

> persew and invaid the saidis personis [the three Douglases] for thar slauchtir and utir distruction sa that thai be nocht sufferit to cum nor hant within this realme.[59]

On the same day the decree was underlined by the execution of the first of the Douglas 'partakers', one David Hope, hanged for his part in keeping Tantallon castle against the king. Alongside him was hanged William Inglis, for treasonable assistance to the Douglases.[60] On 18 May, Angus wrote from Preston (Berwickshire) to Henry VIII. He offered his service to the English king, and lamented that 'sa scherply I am persewit, and the treux sa extremly takin in my contrar, that I ma nocht weill remane in this realme.'[61] By the end of the month he was in Berwick-upon-Tweed.[62]

It had taken the Scots king and his supporters a year to achieve the removal of their former Chancellor. The royal assumption of power marked the end of the faction fighting of the minority, but for the first year of his personal rule James V was faced with a new task, that of coordinating his magnates against one of their number. This had not been achieved; Angus had negotiated his way out of Scotland and the call for his 'utir distruction' became mere rhetoric. The future actions of the king would be largely determined by the events of the first year of his personal rule. The initiative had at all times been with the king and his supporters. The Douglases had been forfeited with the endorsement of parliament, and the confidence of the English had been won. However, the assumption of royal authority had not been endorsed by an unequivocal defeat of the former régime. The killer punch had not been delivered. This was hardly a promising start.

NOTES

1. *ADCP*, 290, 295; *RSS*, ii, no. 2002.
2. *Ibid.*, 295.
3. *Ibid.*, 276; Pitcairn, *Trials*, i, pt. i, 139; SRO, *ADC*, vol. 38, f. 174; Wormald, *Bonds*, 88–9, App. A, 308, no. 8; Macdougall, *James IV*, 234.
4. *Ibid.*, 276, 295; *RMS*, iii, no. 708 ('not long ago' being the phrase used in the charter – '*nuper combusta fuisse*').
5. *RSS*, i, nos. 1593, 2704, 2769, 3462, 3800; *RMS*, ii, no. 3145; iii, no. 163; Macfarlane, *Genealogical Coll.*, i, 214; 'Chronicle of Fortirgal', in *Taymouth Bk.*, 118; *Scots Peerage*, ii, 459; v, 103; Wormald, *Bonds*, App. A, 181, no. 17, 382, no. 33; *Family of Rose*, App. 200.
6. Lesley, *History*, 137–8; *Spalding Miscellany ii*, 83–4; Wormald, *Bonds*, App. A, 345, no. 3; *RSS*, ii, no. 13.
7. Macfarlane, Genealogical Coll., i, 212–4; A.M. Shaw, History of the Macintoshes and Clan Chattan (London, 1880), 189.
8. *RMS*, iii, nos. 248, 372.
9. *TA*, v, 173; *RMS*, iii, no. 665; *ADCP*, 271.
10. *RSS*, ii, 3444; cf. SRO, *ADC*, vol. 38, f. 187 for the 'grete aith'; the 'fire and sword' letter does not appear in this record.
11. Cf. *ER*, xv-xvii; *TA*, v-viii; *RMS*, iii; and SRO, RH 2.1.9, all in *passim*.
12. *RMS*, iii, nos. 671–2; *ER*, xv, 529; SRO, Hay of Yester Writs (GD 28), nos. 462–5; *ADCP*, 295, 302.
13. SRO, *ADC*, vol. 38, ff. 176, 187; vol. 39, ff. 36, 61v; *Acta Sessionis* (Stair), case 37; *APS*, ii, 298; Emond, *op.cit.*, 260–1, 301.
14. SRO, *ADC*, vol. 38, f. 172; *APS*, ii, 321.
15. *LP Henry VIII*, vii, no. 911.
16. *ADCP*, 296.
17. *Ibid.*, 296–8, 299; Glasgow University, Argyll Transcripts, III, p. 217. The 'Act of Twizelhaugh', whereby the heirs of those killed on royal campaigns would come into their inheritances free of feudal casualties (wardship, relief, or marriage) takes its name from the Northumberland campaign of 1513 by James IV, when the act was invoked in the royal army at Twizelhaugh, three miles from Norham.
18. *ADCP*, 292–4; SRO, RH 2.1.9; *ADC*, vol. 38, f. 199.
19. *RSS*, ii, no. 896; *RMS*, iii, no. 840; *HMC, Twelfth Report*, App. VIII, 179, no. 39.

20. *LP Henry VIII*, iv, pt. ii, nos. 5029–30, 5045.
21. *Ibid.*, iv, pt. ii, nos. 4715–6.
22. *SP Henry VIII*, iv, pt. iv, 511.
23. *LP Henry VIII*, iv, pt. ii, no. 4532 (text in full in Lang, *op.cit.*, i, Preface, xv–xvii).
24. *SP Henry VIII*, iv, pt. iv, nos. clxxxix, cxciii; *LP Henry VIII*, iv. pt. ii, no. 4812.
25. *LP Henry VIII*, iv, pt. iv, no. cxciv; *LP Henry VIII*, iv, pt. ii, no. 4859.
26. *LP Henry VIII*, iv, pt. ii, no. 4829.
27. *SP Henry VIII*, iv, pt. iv, no. cxc.
28. *Ibid.*, iv, pt. iv, no. cxcvii; *LP Henry VIII*, iv, pt. ii, no. 4892.
29. Cf. e.g. *LP Henry VIII*, xvii, no. 1183; xviii, no. 219.
30. *SP Henry VIII*, iv, pt. iv, no. cxci.
31. *LP Henry VIII*, iv, pt. ii,no. 4892.
32. A full account of the diplomatic efforts to find a bride for James V is given in E. Bapst, *Les Mariages de Jacques V* (Paris, 1889).
33. *James V Letters*, 51–2.
34. *LP Henry VIII*, iv, pt. ii, no. 3080.
35. *Ibid*, iv, pt. ii, nos. 3794, 3805, 3816, 3924, 4700; *James V Letters*, 143–4.
36. *James V Letters*, 148; *LP Henry VIII*, iv, pt. ii, nos. 3794, 4051, 5044.
37. *James V Letters*, 147–8; *SP Henry VIII*, iv, pt. iv, no. cxcix.
38. *SP Henry VIII*, iv, pt. iv, 536, 549; nos. cxcviii, cc; Abell, *op.cit.*, f. 117; *Diurnal of Occurrents*, 12.
39. *SP Henry VIII*, iv, pt. iv, nos. cxcvii, cxcviii, cc; *LP Henry VIII*, iv, pt. ii, no. 4541.
40. *Ibid.*, iv, pt. iv, nos. cxcvii-viii, cc.
41. *Ibid.*, iv, pt. iv, 536–7; *LP Henry VIII*, iv, pt. ii, nos. 4951, 4952, 4953, 4963, 4965, 4970–2, 4974.
42. *SP Henry VIII*, iv, pt. iv, no. cc.
43. *ADCP*, 299.
44. *Ibid.*, 300–1; *SP Henry VIII*, iv, pt. iv, 543–4, no. cxcviii; *LP Henry VIII*, iv, pt. ii, nos. 4995, 5030, 5044–5.
45. *SP Henry VIII*, iv, pt. iv, no. cciv; *ADCP*, 296, 299; *LP Henry VIII*, iv, pt. ii, nos. 5070, 5086.
46. *SP Henry VIII*, no. ccii, 547–9.
47. *ADCP*, 301–2, 304; *RSS*, i, no. 4072; SRO, RH 2.1.9. (*ADC*, vol. 39, f. 61).
48. *ADCP*, 300–1. In the latter months of 1528 Angus had written most of his letters from Coldingham priory; in 1529 he moved to Preston (Berwickshire).
49. *RMS*, iii, nos. 716, 723, 738; *LP Henry VIII*, iv, pt. iii, no. 5233.
50. *ADCP*, 300–1, 304.
51. *Ibid.*, 285, 306; the absence of the Treasurer's accounts for this period leaves some uncertainty as to whether or not all the ayres were held.
52. *Ibid.*, 301; *SP Henry VIII*, iv, pt. iv, no. ccii.
53. *ADCP*, 307.
54. *RSS*, i, nos. 4104, 4109, 4117.
55. *ADCP*, 524.
56. *Ibid.*, 308–9.
57. *RSS*, ii, no. 4.
58. *Ibid.*, ii, nos. 7, 8, 13, 30–4.
59. *Ibid.*, 308–9; SRO, RH 2.1.9.; *ADC*, vol. 40, f. 12.
60. Pitcairn, *Trials*, i, pt. i, 142.
61. *SP Henry VIII*, iv, pt. iv, no. ccv.
62. *Ibid.*, iv, pt. iv, no. ccix.

CHAPTER FIVE

The Assertion of Royal Authority in the Borders

I. AUTHORITY AND ACQUIESCENCE: 1528–30

The English did not really believe that James had been in control of events during the struggle for power in 1528–29. This view was expressed by Thomas Magnus in his meeting with the Scots king at Edinburgh in January 1529. Magnus explained:

> howe it was reapoorted and sayd in Einglande, that a private and yong Counsaill dooth moore rule aboute His Grace thenne do the auncient and honourable Lordes of his Counsaill. . . .

and then warned James about:

> the fall and distruccion of King James the 3de his graunte fader, in that tyme totally advised ruled and governed by a light and a yong Consaill.[1]

Some of the advisers whom Magnus may have had in mind had been mentioned by Lord Dacre's spy in Scotland as early as July 1528. James was said to be ruled and advised at Stirling by Margaret Tudor, her husband, Henry Stewart, Lord Maxwell, and Scott of Buccleuch, 'cheif manteiners of all misguyded men on the Bordours of Scotlaunde'; and Campbell of Loudoun, the killer of Cassillis.[2] After being forfeited in the September 1528 parliament, Angus named his enemies as being Argyll, Arran, Maxwell, Hamilton of Finnart, Campbell of Loudoun, Scott of Buccleuch, and Stirling of Keir.[3] In November 1528, meeting with the Scottish truce commissioners, Magnus had cited the king's counsellors as being Finnart, killer of Lennox; Loudoun, killer of Cassillis; Buccleuch, killer of Andrew Kerr of Cessford; Maxwell, 'cheiff maytaner of all offenders'; and Henry Stewart.[4]

Apart from the fact that most of these individuals were not particularly young, there was a grain of truth in the English perception of the struggle for power. On 1 July 1528 at Stirling, Campbell of Loudoun and his followers had been granted remission for their involvement in the Lennox revolt at Linlithgow in 1526 and for the death of the second earl of Cassillis.[5] Soon afterwards, Scott of Buccleuch gave his bond of manrent to Arran, and was exonerated for his part in the Melrose episode in 1526.[6] On 14 July 1528, James Stewart, brother of Henry Stewart, became captain of Doune castle, and three days later Henry was created Lord Methven.[7]

All these grants were confirmed in the September parliament.[8] The new government was buying the support of those discredited under the Angus régime.

However, the composition of the first 'kingis consale', appointed on 6 July with 'thre or foure of thir to remane evir with the kingis grace . . . for the direction of all materis', suggests a body of 'auncient and honourable Lordes'. The archbishop of Glasgow, the bishops of Aberdeen and Dunkeld, and the abbots of Scone and Cambuskenneth were joined by the royal officers and Arran, Argyll, the truly 'auncient' Eglinton, Rothes, Moray and Lord Erskine.[9] All these councillors were to serve consistently in the chancery office as royal charter witnesses. The second body, designated by royal ordinance of 17 November 1528 as a 'secret consale', showed minimal changes, the main ones being the addition of the archbishop of St. Andrews, and the dropping of Lord Rothes.[10] From this body were drawn the lords of articles who presided over the September parliament, together with Lord Maxwell and Patrick Hepburn, prior of St. Andrews.[11] Angus could justly identify some of these men as his enemies, but they hardly constituted a 'private and yong' council.

What is evident is that the earls of Arran and Argyll were the guiding influences in Scottish government in the first year of the personal rule. Arran signed the Treaty of Berwick;[12] Argyll was pre-eminent in the struggle to capture Angus' strongholds. It remains a matter for speculation as to who were the 'hawks' and the 'doves' on the council in the effort to remove Angus. When Arran died – before Angus' final withdrawal from Scotland – the English considered that he had advocated a policy of reconciliation. His son, Hamilton of Finnart, met the Douglases to negotiate peace terms during the Tantallon siege. After its unsuccessful outcome, both Arran and Finnart signed, in the king's presence, the 'grete aith' calling for the 'utir distruction' of Angus and his family.[13] This was one of the few occasions in 1528–29 on which the king sat with the Lords of Council; possibly he was sponsoring the 'grete aith'. For most of 1528–29, James can be found at Stirling, designated as a place of safety by the Lords of Council. In the summer of 1528, whilst Lord Maxwell was clearing the Douglases out of Edinburgh, the king was presiding over the exchequer at Stirling. At the siege of Tantallon, the king was based at North Berwick, though he did venture out to inspect its progress in person. Arran, Argyll and Moray were in charge, the whole stratagem having been drawn up by the Lords of Council in the king's absence. In contrast, the earlier raid on Coldingham priory appears to have been a royal initiative, with James being supported by the Humes, and little apparent preparation being made beforehand.

In the credence dated 13 July 1528, and sent to the English government with Patrick Sinclair, James narrated how his former Chancellor, as warden of the East and Middle Marches and as lieutenant, had:

procurit divers radis to be maid upoun ye brokin men of our Realm, [but] he usit our autorite nocht aganis yame, bot aganis our Baronis. . . .[14]

In a further justification to Henry VIII, entrusted to Magnus on his return to England in February 1529, the king wrote how he had called Angus to task in Easter 1528, to answer for his 'abusing of our auctorite'.[15] Angus had then returned from an abortive raid against Liddesdale; the Kerrs had refused to support him against the Armstrongs, and Lord Maxwell had failed to execute royal letters to proclaim them rebels.[16] A fresh expedition, which the king was to lead, had been proposed for June.[17] With the change of government, this had been postponed. James wrote from Stirling castle on 19 June 1528 to the earl of Northumberland, that the postponement was due to disturbances 'in the inland of our realm'.[18] In fact, in previous years, Angus had executed a number of successful Borders raids; in 1525 he had captured one Simon Armstrong *alias* 'Sym the Laird', and David Armstrong, *alias* 'Davy the Lady'.[19] In April 1527 he carried out a raid against Teviotdale, killing eighteen thieves and hanging a further fourteen from a convenient bridge.[20] The episode to which the credence appeared to refer was the clash between the Scotts and the Kerrs at Melrose in July 1526. Angus had been discredited by his failure to detain the English rebel, Sir William Lisle; but in the negotiations leading up to the treaty of Berwick, the English had their doubts as to whether he should be excluded from the treaty's terms, given the lack of a proven track record for the new Scots government in controlling the Borders.

The treaty's terms contained an option for the English wardens to invade Liddesdale should the Scots be unable to give redress.[21] Since the capture of Lisle by the English, Lord Dacre had been happily engaged in burning the debatable lands around Canonbie. The Armstrongs and Irvines retaliated by burning Netherby, with Lord Maxwell's connivance. Lord Dacre burnt down the Armstrong tower at Hallhouse (Hollows tower). The Armstrongs burnt down Gilsland Mill.[22] Andrew Armstrong and Richard Irvine were captured and held in Carlisle castle. In turn, two of Lord Dacre's servants, Miles Halton and Jeffrey Middleton, were captured and held at Hermitage castle.[23] In the late summer of 1528, John Johnstone of that Ilk and Edward, brother of Lord Maxwell, attacked Liddale motte. Sir Ralph Fenwick intercepted a raid launched from Liddesdale by the English outlaw, Edward Noble.[24] It was small wonder that Magnus should bring the issue of redress for Liddesdale to the negotiating table in November 1528.[25] Fenwick had captured one Quentin Armstrong. This prompted 'Sym the Laird', again at liberty, to request a meeting with the earl of Northumberland at Alnwick in December 1528. According to Northumberland, the Armstrongs held the new Scots government in contempt, and considered that they could lay waste the Scottish Borders and 'not a man in Scotland durst remedy the same'.[26] The results of Northumberland's interview with 'Sym the Laird' must have been communicated to Magnus. At his meeting with James and after his homily on light and young counsel, Magnus raised the Armstrong question. He reported:

I moved this to the said King of Scottes, shewing that withoute justice and due correccion to be had withynne His oune reaalme, He couth not contynue and reigne like a King, and therupon inferred, howe that the said Armstrongges avaunted thaym selves to be the destructioun of twoe and fifty parisshe churches in Scottlande, besides the unlawfull and un-gracious attemptates by thaym committed withynne Einglande. Wherfore the said King of Scottes stoode, and was bounden to make aunsuer.[27]

In July 1528, Maxwell undertook to give good rule as warden for the West March, Bothwell for Liddesdale, Kerr of Dolphinton, Kerr of Cessford, Kerr of Fernieherst and Scott of Buccleuch as wardens for the Middle March, and Lord Hume as warden for the East March. Scott and the Kerrs were charged with the task of expelling all Liddesdale men dwelling in Teviotdale.[28] In November 1528, the Humes, Kerrs, Scotts, and 'hedismen' of Lothian were required by the Lords of Council to enter pledges for their support in the 'expulsioune and persute' of the Douglases. The issue of good rule in the bounds of their wardenries was obviously considered secondary to the campaign against the Douglases. The earl of Argyll was appointed as lieutenant in Lothian, the Merse and Teviotdale.[29] Following on from the signing of the treaty of Berwick, in January 1529, the Kerrs were instructed to give redress for East Teviotdale with their opposite numbers in England. Lord Maxwell was to meet with Lord Dacre; Lord Hume was to meet with the English wardens of the East March; and Bothwell undertook to give redress for Liddesdale.[30]

This last responsibility was a problem. Bothwell's services were also required in the east in the campaign against the Douglases. On 3 February 1529, James wrote from Edinburgh to Henry VIII 'tuichand ye rewill of ye Bordouris'. According to James, the West and Middle Marches were in good order; the East March 'brocht to sum towardnes', though the loyalty of the lieges there was suspect; but James required his uncle's forbearance with regard to Liddesdale, until his nephew could make 'due reformation'.[31] This letter was taken away by Magnus, who had to thread his way carefully southwards to Berwick-upon-Tweed, avoiding confrontation between the supporters of Bothwell and Angus 'moore by grace and fortune, thenne otherwise'.[32]

On 6 March 1529, the Lords of Council announced that justice ayres would be held in Lauder, Jedburgh, Selkirk and Peebles, commencing on 24 May.[33] By this latter date Angus had at last left the country, and his great rival, Arran, was dead.[34] Possibly the elimination of both these magnates made James now feel more free than at any previous time in his reign. At any rate he made his first recorded appearance on the Borders in the personal rule, at Jedburgh and at Peebles, in June 1529.[35] He was accompanied by his Lords of Council, including the earls of Montrose and Rothes, and Lords Fleming, Erskine, Lindsay and Somerville.[36] This was hardly a light and young council. A string of remissions was granted at both ayres.[37] At Jedburgh, the Kerrs undertook to give good rule and assist each other in the Middle March. Scott of Buccleuch also gave his bond for good rule. On 25 June at Peebles, Bothwell gave his bond for good rule in Liddesdale. Pledges, or hostages, were taken and held at Edinburgh castle.[38] Back at Edinburgh on 23 and 24 July, Lord Maxwell undertook in the royal presence to give good rule for the West March and to deliver the two border thieves, George Scott of the Bog, and Hector Scott.[39] In August, Lord Hume was fined for failing to surrender John Hume of Blackadder and ninety-eight others for their part in a convocation between Gilbert Wauchope of Niddrie-Marshall and John Edmonstone of that Ilk, this failure constituting a breach of Lord Hume's bond to give good rule.[40]

In September 1529, James went hunting in the Meggetland in Ettrick forest.[41] In November, he was at Dumfries. A series of justice ayres was carried out in the southwest of the country towards the end of 1529. Again, a string of remissions was granted at Dumfries, Whithorn, Kirkcudbright, and Wigtown.[42] The returns from the ayre at Annandale or Dumfries were £932; the Kirkcudbright ayre yielded £480, and £468 was collected at Wigtown. Lords Maxwell and Erskine; William Scott of Balwearie, justice-clerk; Henry Wemyss, bishop of Galloway; James Colville of Ochiltree, Comptroller; and David Beaton, abbot of Arbroath and keeper of the privy seal, presided.[43] At Dumfries, on 5 November, James wrote to his uncle to accuse the English border officers of being dilatory in the giving of redress.[44] However, waiting for him upon his return to Edinburgh was a letter from the earl of Northumberland, informing him that on 19 November, the Liddesdale men had raided Birkshawes. Eighteen of the earl's servants had been captured and a further four slain. Northumberland demanded that James remedy the matter and warned that 'I must advertise the Kinges Highnes my Maister therof'.[45] James wrote to Henry VIII to assure him that redress 'is the thing We desire maist ardentlie'.[46] Possibly it was the awareness that the Birkshawes raid had been carried out whilst James was presiding over justice ayres further to the west, that provoked a royal ordinance, put before the Lords of Council on 9 January 1530. On the session were the king; the archbishops of Glasgow and St. Andrews; the bishops of Aberdeen, Ross, Caithness and Orkney; the prior of St. Andrews; the abbots of Holyrood and Dryburgh; Thomas Erskine of Haltoun, the royal Secretary; the earls of Bothwell and Rothes; Lords Erskine, Hay of Yester and Maxwell; and Hamilton of Finnart. The ordinance again called for the holding of days of truce by the border officers 'sa that the liegis of Ingland sall hae na caus of complant'.[47]

Shortly afterwards Johnston of that Ilk and Edward Maxwell received £50 for bringing the head of a thief to Edinburgh.[48] In February, Bothwell, Maxwell and Hume were again summoned to convene in Edinburgh.[49] On 20 March, before a session of the Lords of Council which included James, Bothwell, Rothes, and Lords Ross, Somerville and Oliphant, the earl of Moray offered to serve as lieutenant for all three Marches, to pursue thieves, give redress in terms of the Anglo-Scots truce, and 'keip the kingis trew liegis in pece and rest unhurt'. The offer was accepted, the Lords of Council agreeing in return to place Newark castle at Moray's disposal and to grant him heritable tenure to the Crown lands of Ardmannoch, which he then held in tack. For his part, Bothwell undertook to give good rule for Liddesdale.[50]

In fact, Moray never carried out this commission, and did not obtain a charter to Ardmannoch. In the latter part of 1530 he was engaged in military operations in Caithness and Sutherland, as lieutenant of the north. Moray, 'our derrest brother and counsalour', was authorised to lead the king's lieges, and borrowed a cannon from Edinburgh castle.[51] The disturbances there were probably connected with the death of the earl of Sutherland, in feud with the Mackays of Strathnaver. The earl of Caithness was also dead, and there may have been a power vacuum in the area. In September 1530 Thomas Stewart, Treasurer of Caithness, and Andrew Peter, vicar of Wick, were amongst a group of clergy all summoned to appear at the Inverness justice ayre for their slaughter of William Sutherland of Duffus. Moray was granted the ward of Sutherland's estates in Elgin, Forres and Nairn on 26 April 1530.[52]

On 16 May 1530, in the royal presence at Edinburgh, William Cockburn of Henderland was convicted on charges of theft and treasonable in-bringing of Englishmen into the realm. He was executed. Two days later, Adam Scott of Tushielaw, in ward at Edinburgh castle, was convicted on charges of black-mailing, amongst others, the poor tenants of Howpasley. This 'king of thieves' was also beheaded.[53] It is possible that these two border reivers had been apprehended by one or other of the Scottish wardens, but the fact that James had been hunting in Ettrick Forest in the previous autumn suggests that he may have been responsible for their detention. Cockburn of Henderland had been warded for eighteen months in 1518–19. Scott of Tushielaw had been charged to ride with Angus against Liddesdale in 1525.[54] On the day after Tushielaw's execution, the 'lordis of the secrete consale' met in session to 'sitt upoun grete materis as he [the king] has presentlie ado'. These lords were the two arch-bishops; the bishops of Orkney, Galloway, Ross and Dunkeld; the abbots of Cambuskenneth and Arbroath; William Stewart, provost of Lincluden; Robert Barton, Treasurer; Scott of Balwearie, justice-clerk; Adam Otterburn, king's advocate; Nicholas Crawford of Oxgangs, Master Francis Bothwell and Master James Lawson, these last three being regular legal advisers; the earls of Moray and Rothes; Lords Erskine, Fleming and Gray, and Hamilton of Finnart.[55] Again, this group of councillors amounted to something more than a 'light' and 'young' council.

The Lords of Council ordained that the king and his true barons and lieges should ride 'endlangis' his Borders to punish thieves, pacify the country, and execute justice. For this purpose the chief border magnates should remain in ward.[56] Arrangements were then made for the distribution of the warded individuals. Bothwell, Maxwell and Hume were to remain in Edinburgh castle. John Johnston of that Ilk and Robert Scott of Wamphray were to pass to Doune.

Scott of Buccleuch and John, eldest son of Andrew Kerr of Ferniehirst, were assigned to Falkland. Mark Kerr of Dolphinton, John Hume of Coldenknowes and Patrick Lumsden of Blanerne went to Blackness. Alexander Hume of Polwarth and David Renton of Billie passed to Dumbarton. James Douglas of Drumlanrig and Stirling of Keir were placed in Inchgarvie. One John Forester went to Alloway. Lord Hay held responsibility for the son of the executed Cockburn.[57]

In all sixteen individuals had been detained, just one more than the number reported to the Duke of Milan by the Venetian ambassador in England. The ambassador thought that their imprisonment and the two executions were a reaction either to a Douglas plot, or Douglas incitement of unrest on the Borders.[58] In fact the wardings and executions were only part of a more general process of establishing central authority over the Borders. At the same time as the council was sitting, a great number of lairds from Roxburgh, Berwick, Selkirk and Peeblesshire pledged to underlie the law for all crimes that might be imputed against them. These included Lord Hay, sheriff of Peebles; Walter Kerr of Cessford, joint-warden of the Middle March; James Douglas of Cavers, sheriff of Roxburgh; and Patrick Murray of Fallowhill, sheriff of Selkirk. It seems unlikely that all fifty named individuals appeared in person at Edinburgh on 18 and 19 May, when their pledges were given; probably their undertakings were made in writing or by representatives. The substance of the matter was a failure to do 'their utmost diligence to fulfil their bonds'.[59] The whole warding process of 1530 laid emphasis on the need for the Borderers to affirm the bonds given in 1529. No attempt appears to have been made to enforce the pledges made by the fifty lairds to underlie the law.

By the time of the meeting of the Lords of Council on 19 May, the chief Borderers were already in ward. However their internment had been very recent. Lord Hume had been on the council on 15 March, and Bothwell sat on 28 March.[60] The Kerrs and Scott had been summoned to appear before the king at Stirling on 22 April, probably in order to have a royal ratification of their recently concluded indenture of friendship.[61] Kerr of Dolphinton and Scott of Buccleuch served on an inquest on 16 May in Roxburghshire.[62] Between 12 and 25 May a messenger was paid for passing to collect a thief detained by Lord Maxwell, which suggests that he was still in the west in the middle of the month.[63]

The most coherent account of the wardings is given in the *Diurnal*. The lords met in Edinburgh in a 'greit conventione' on 16 May. On the same day the border magnates entered into ward at Edinburgh castle and Cockburn of Henderland was executed. On 18 May Scott of Tushielaw was executed and the border magnates were distributed amongst the various royal castles.[64] The author of the *Diurnal* thus has the council meeting, executions and wardings occurring almost simultaneously.

At this time, amongst other things, James appears to have been watching 'the

Egiptianis that dansit before the King in Halyrudhous'.[65] It is difficult to imagine that the mass warding was achieved by force. The earl of Moray was still in Edinburgh, but no arrangements had been made to convene the Scots host to assist him in carrying out his commission as lieutenant of the Borders. Possibly his appointment was resented by the border magnates; the wardens would see this as undermining their local authority. The alternative was perhaps more bearable, namely to afford the king the opportunity of carrying out a royal raid two years after this had been promised to him. The king could not remain in the Borders indefinitely; conceivably his half-brother could, under royal instruction and using Newark as a base. The council ordinance of 19 May was so phrased as to suggest that, metaphorically, the decks were being cleared in the Borders for the duration of the king's expedition. The expectation of the border magnates would be that once the royal raid was over, they would return to their homes. This expectation was realised. It is doubtful whether the government had the means to achieve a general warding by using military force. The third earl of Argyll, war commander in the struggle for power, was dead.[66] The fourth earl was preoccupied with achieving Campbell domination in the Isles at the expense of his rival, Alexander MacDonald of Islay.[67] It is conceivable that an effort could have been made to find another general, possibly the earl of Montrose, who featured in the council's visit to Jedburgh and Peebles in June 1529. However, the fact that Moray was appointed lieutenant and then went on to deal with disturbances in the far north, suggests that the government did not regard the 'daunting' of the border magnates as a military operation. If it had been so regarded, then it would have been of more immediate concern than whatever was happening in Sutherland and Caithness, and Moray's active service would have been required on the Borders.

The initiative for the royal expedition may well have come from James himself. His presence on the Borders would impress his personal royal authority both at home and in the eyes of the English government. If he had used his half-brother's services, James might well have reinforced the earlier English impression that the Scots king was not yet visibly ruling his realm in person. Throughout the minority, a succession of royal lieutenants had conducted expeditions to the Borders, sometimes taking the king with them. Latterly these expeditions had been led by Angus.[68] In 1528, James appears to have pressed Angus into allowing him to lead a further expedition, probably with a view to promoting his personal authority at Angus' expense. The 1530 warding, executions and subsequent royal raid were the culmination of the assumption of royal authority in 1528. The delay had not been of James' own making, with one year spent in struggling for power, and the second year in attempting to give redress and live up to English expectations in the ordering of the Borders. The groundwork had been done in 1529, with the obtaining of the bonds of good rule from the border magnates. In 1530 the exercise was to enforce these bonds. The seriousness of James' intent was underlined by the executions of Henderland and Tushielaw.

Thus far, the Scottish wardens held office largely by default, there being no realistic alternatives. They had everything to lose by resisting the Crown; as James grew older, presumably his personal authority would increase and for Lord Maxwell and his colleagues it was politic to demonstrate early loyalty and cooperation. The alternative might be royal revenge in later years, resulting in their dismissal from office and possibly worse measures. It is also unlikely that the border magnates could have displayed uniformity in resisting ward; their individual interests did not coincide. In the West March, Maxwell can only have been regarded as *primus inter pares*, his chief rivals being the Johnstons and the Armstrongs. In the Middle March, the Scotts and the Kerrs had only just reached an accord after their skirmish at Melrose in 1526. In the East March, Lord Hume's kinsman, John Hume of Blackadder, had in October 1529 offered to come to terms with the Scottish government.[69] For any one individual to resist could have resulted in the Crown using the others to coerce cooperation. This in turn could have led to the worst scenario being realised –civil war, the return of Angus, and the discrediting of royal authority, essentially the revival of the faction fighting of the minority. The border magnates had everything to gain by accepting a brief period of warding to allow the eighteen-year-old king his head. One other possibility is that the Borderers were arrested without warning, upon their arrival in Edinburgh. This seems unlikely; it would hardly be a politic course for James' government to take. The Borderers would then become disaffected and unlikely to prove responsive to royal authority in the future.

On 19 May the Lords of Council 'devisit' that as Henderland and Tushielaw were now 'put to deid' and the king was to pass in 'propir persone' throughout the Borders to 'put gude reule' and pursue thieves and traitors, an armed force should accompany him. All landed persons of the inland and Borders were required to bring their households into readiness for a forty day campaign. The areas from which the force was to be drawn ranged from Kincardine and Forfar in the north east, through the central belt to Berwick and Roxburgh in the south. The army was to meet at Edinburgh on 26 June and pass to the Borders on the following day. Lord Hay, sheriff of Peebles, was ordered to summon the men of Peebles, Selkirk and Ettrick Forest, and also to put the castles of Neidpath and Crammald in readiness. All men between the ages of sixteen and sixty in Dumfries, Kircudbright and Wigtown were to mobilise.[70] After the raid, a number of escheats were made of minor individuals. The Master of Crawford was gifted the escheat of the goods of one John Robertson, *alias* 'Barroun Reyd'. John Douglas, servant in the wine cellar, was another beneficiary, as were David Lindsay, Snowdon Herald and John Scrimegeour, macer. So too was James Douglas of Drumlanrig, one of the warded Borderers. These escheats suggest that the turn-out for the muster was as wide as required. The narratives also indicate that the muster took place when scheduled, and that the army passed to the Borders on 1 or 2 July.[71]

The king's own movements during the raid can be traced through the

Household Books. On 2 July he moved from Linlithgow to Peebles. On 3 July he was at the Douglas burn in Ettrick Forest.[72] The Lords of Council were then at Peebles, and proclaimed that the army was not to break ranks. All the leaders were to convene with their households at 2 p.m., 4 July, outside St. Bride's Church.[73] On 5 July James was at Carlinrigg. On 7 July he was at the Allan water.[74] On 8 July he and the Treasurer signed a letter of gift, under the privy seal, to Lord Maxwell – then in ward – of all goods and assets of:

> umquhile Johnne Armstrang, bruthir to Thomas Armstrang of Mayngertoun [Mangerton, Liddesdale], and now pertenyng to our soverane lord be resoun of escete throw justifying of the said umquhill Johnne to the deid for thift committit be him, etc.[75]

On 10 July James moved south through Ewesdale, arriving at Staplegordon, in Eskdale, on 12 July. He then appears to have made a much more rapid withdrawal north to Crammald castle, arriving there on 13 July. A further letter was issued under the privy seal at Peebles on 18 July, and on 20 July the king returned to Linlithgow.[76]

James' visit to Staplegordon suggests that the man executed on or before 8 July was one John Armstrong, who held £5 worth of land in Langholm of Lord Maxwell, 14 marks of the scheilds of Dawblane, 5 marks of Balgray, 10 marks of the lands of Staplegordon, and 20s. in Staplegordon burgh. All of these were in Eskdale, and, with other areas, were apprised on 15 April 1532 for forty-three years of non-entries, valued at 10,335 marks and sold to Lord Maxwell.[77] On 2 November 1525 this John Armstrong had given his bond of manrent, on behalf of himself and his heirs, to Lord Maxwell in return for the gift of the non-entries.[78] On 3 March 1528, Lord Dacre had met with Maxwell to give redress; Dacre held a bill of complaint against John Armstrong, George Scott, William and Peter Moffat, and Andrew Little, all accused of burning Netherby. Lord Maxwell held a bill of complaint given in by John Armstrong of 'Stabilgate', accusing Lord Dacre of burning Hollows Tower. Dacre responded to this by claiming that Hallhouse was not in Scotland proper, but lay in the debatable lands.[79] Although Maxwell and Dacre met on subsequent March days to give redress, this particular episode never appears to have been addressed. After all, Armstrong was Maxwell's man.

The incident prompted Angus' abortive raid against Liddesdale, which in turn led to James insisting on leading a further expedition. Liddesdale was a major sticking point in the negotiations leading to the conclusion of the 1528 treaty of Berwick. Shortly afterwards, in his capital city, James was advised by the Englishman, Dr. Magnus, that 'he couth not contynue and reign like a King' whilst the Armstrongs were busily engaged in destroying all the parish churches in the West March. James was then apparently tongue-tied, unable to think of an appropriate response. The death of Armstrong of Staplegordon in Teviotdale, two years after the assumption of the personal rule, was a delayed answer. This was an execution prompted by the desire of the king to assert his own authority. As such it is comparable with the May executions of Henderland and Tushielaw. Perhaps Armstrong's death was something more, containing an element of royal revenge; for he represented a family whose activities had delayed the conclusion of the Anglo-Scots treaty. The English had considered that the earl of Angus should be included in that treaty, as a man capable of controlling the Borders. The Scots had to concede a separate article allowing for Angus to be reset in England. Angus had then managed to hang on in Scotland until May 1529, and was eventually negotiated out of the country without being defeated in battle. Indirectly, the Armstrong activities had contributed towards the outcome of the struggle for power. Possibly one of the strengths of Stewart kingship lay in the ability to wait until the right political circumstances arose before making the desired move. James had waited two years for this expedition, but it achieved the result he wanted.

The manner of the death of Armstrong of Staplegordon latterly became something of a legend. The two chronicles closest in time to the event make no mention of it. Adam Abell refers to a 'chase of Yarrow' in 1534, during which the chieftains of the Borders were warded.[80] The author of the *Diurnal* narrates that on 26 July 1530 the king made a raid upon the thieves and took thirty-two of the greatest of them, including Armstrongs, Elliots, Littles and Irvines. [81]Lesley states that in June 1529 the king, with a great army, passed to the Borders and took forty-eight thieves, with their captain, John Armstrong, all of whom were hanged upon 'growand trees'. Armstrong's brother, George, was pardoned, turned king's evidence, and agreed to be a royal informant. Also:

> thair was ane notabill thiff brint, wha had brunt ane housa, with ane woman and mony her barnis being thairintill.[82]

Pitscottie has the king hunting in the Meggetland in June 1528:

> and I hard say he slew in the boundis 360 of hairttis. Efter this huntting he hangit Johnne Armestrang and his compleces to the number of 36 persouns of the quhilk thair was werie mony sorrowfull bath in Ingland and Scottland.[83]

In Buchanan's version, set in 1529, the king has an army of 8000 men. John Armstrong was chief of a band of freebooters. The English paid him tribute. Lord Maxwell dreaded his power and sought his destruction by any means. John and fifty unarmed attendants were enticed by the royal servants into meeting the king. John had neglected to procure a safe-conduct. He was hanged with the greater part of his attendants. The courtiers had advised the execution and spread the rumour that John had promised to tyrannise the local areas under English instruction. On the contrary, the English were delighted at his death. Six of his retinue were spared.[84]

In *The Ballad of Johnnie Armstrong*, Armstrong becomes 'laird o' Gilnockie', murdered at Carlinrigg after asking 'grace at a graceless face' of the king who had 'movit his bonnet tae him', and who 'ween'd he was a King as well as he'.[85]

The story then grew into a tale of royal deception, complete with men wearing or not wearing hats, and withered trees which never grew again.[86]

Possibly the most significant reference to the incident is made by Sir David Lindsay of the Mount in the Epiphany performance of the *Interlude* at Linlithgow in 1540. Lindsay has his Poor Man looking for the king of Scotland, and being able to identify him as the man who hanged John Armstrong with his fellows and later hanged Sym the Laird.[87] This piece of flattery, and the later reference to the rope that hanged Armstrong in the *'The Satyre of the Thrie Estaitis'*, presumably gave rise to the interpretation of the death given by John Arden in *'Armstrong's Last Goodnight: An Exercise in Diplomacy'*, in which Lindsay plays a key part.[88] However, the fact that Lindsay, as a royal courtier, should have thrown in the reference in the *Interlude* demonstrates the impact which the death made upon the Court's view of the king. It is highly unlikely that James saw the death as being the single most important act of his personal rule, but it may have been his greatest personal achievement since the ride from Edinburgh to Stirling in 1528. If so, his royal person would find the 1540 reminder highly amusing. Hanging a notorious local troublemaker like Armstrong of 'Gilknockie' probably enhanced the royal image as a 'puir man's king'.

As an exercise in pacifying the Borders to the standard required by the English government, the royal expedition was not in itself of significance. Such progresses became a secondary issue for James in 1531, but in the latter part of 1532 there were cross-border raids and demands for redress from both sides. It was only after James eventually imposed his half-brother, Moray, as lieutenant of the East and Middle Marches, complete with the Scots host, that order was restored in 1533, and a perpetual peace was finally concluded in May 1534. As an exercise in establishing James's authority within Scotland, the 1530 warding and royal raid were a useful learning ground. In 1531, James invited, and received offers of submission from, the chieftains of the Isles. He contemplated a royal expedition there, first removing the fourth earl of Argyll as chamberlain of Kintyre, and then turning down his offer to daunt the Isles. Argyll was then briefly warded.

The executions of Henderland, Tushielaw, and Armstrong were only the beginning of a sustained effort to daunt the Borders. In the royal raid of July 1530, there were taken prisoner Adam Nixon and Robert Elliot. Lord Hay was entrusted with their safekeeping. They escaped and Lord Hay lost his job as sheriff of Peebles.[89] Archibald Armstrong was also taken, by George Hoppringle of Torwoodlee, and held by Lord Erskine.[90] Possibly he was kinsman of Janet or Isobel Hoppringle, wife of Douglas of Kilspindie. Isobel received lenient treatment from the king considering that she was married to a man whom James had sworn to pursue to his 'utir distruction'. On 1 April 1531, another John Armstrong, *alias* 'Blak Jok', was hanged with his brother, Thomas. Both were convicted of theft and reset. Blak Jok had had his family's houses in Liddesdale burnt down by Sir Christopher Dacre in May 1528.[91] Possibly both Armstrongs had been taken during the royal raid. In October 1531, Scott of Buccleuch and Bothwell were both charged with either securing the release of an English prisoner, one David Shafton, from the Liddesdale men, or with securing the imprisonment of 'Sym the Laird' and Dick Henderson of Liddesdale and 'Dave the Lady' of Howpasley in Edinburgh castle. Both Buccleuch and Bothwell were to enter ward for their own default, on penalty of treason. Buccleuch failed so to do, indeed he appears to have been kidnapped himself by Sym the Laird, as well as being warded in Edinburgh castle for his failure to enter Dave the Lady. Sym the Laird received a remission for both kidnappings.[92] Buccleuch redeemed himself by entering John and Adam Turnbull into ward at Blackness in 1534. In the same year one John Turnbull, *alias* 'Blak Sow', was hanged for theft and reset.[93]

Sym the Laird appears to have been a survivor; on 30 October 1535 he and several other reivers were outlawed for failure to underlie the law for cattle thieving and also for breaking their bonds made to the king. The various others included Thomas Armstrong of Mannerton and his Caruther and Elliot servants, and also 'Lang Penman', servant to 'Dikkis Wille'.[94] Lang Penman had in fact been captured once already by Buccleuch prior to the royal raid of 1530.[95] Sym the Laird was eventually convicted and sentenced to be drawn to the gallows and hanged on 21 February 1536. *Inter alia* his crimes included cattle stealing whilst in the 'King's ward' in August 1535; an arson attack on Howpasley town and stealing cattle from Scott of Howpasley; stealing royal sheep from Ettrick Forest, and treasonable assistance afforded to Alexander Armstrong, *alias* 'Evill-willit Sandy', who was a 'sworn Englishman'. On 13 March 1536, a third John Armstrong, *alias* 'John in Gutterholis', was convicted of theft, reset, 'outputting and inputting' in England and Scotland, treasonably inbringing Englishmen, murder and arson. Not surprisingly, the sentence of drawing and hanging was passed on him and his accomplice, Christopher Henderson.[96] Lindsay of the Mount had plenty of material for his plays.

To misapply Donaldson's phrase, Pitcairn's *Criminal Trials* is (naturally) 'very largely a catalogue of convictions and punishments'.[97] However, the extracts from the *Books of Adjournal* omit the execution of one whom Donaldson has called 'a certain thief'. This was George Scott of the Bog, presumably one of the individuals who had assisted Armstrong of Staplegordon in the burning of Netherby, and also the man whom Maxwell had promised to arrest in 1529 for theft and murder.[98] The author of the *Diurnal* credits Johnston of that Ilk with Scott's capture. According to this chronicler, this 'greit theif' had done 'greit skaith to the commouns, byrnand thair houssis, wyfis and bairnes queik'.[99] This presumably was the same man to whom Lesley referred in his account of the royal raid. The *Diurnal* notes that Scott's own execution was a novelty in that he too was burnt to death. Donaldson's phrase correctly applies to the *Diurnal*, and his assessment of what is contained therein is a matter for personal evaluation. However it is curious that Donaldson should have found the manner of Scott's death so significant. It is cited by Donaldson as being one of James' 'instances of brutality towards lesser men'. In drawing his conclusions on the policy of James V, Donaldson has used the example of Scott to suggest that the king had 'a streak of sadistic cruelty in his nature'.[100] A more enlightened interpretation would be to cite Scott's execution as an instance of apposite royal justice.

2. MAGNATE RESPONSES TO THE WARDING OF 1530

Whilst in ward in 1530, Scott of Buccleuch was presented with two-and-a-half elns of silver cloth, worth £22.10s., in reward for the entry of 'Lang Penman'.[101] On 24 July, at Edinburgh, Buccleuch, Johnston of that Ilk, Lord Maxwell and others, signed a bond to keep good rule, the king having graciously granted remission for crimes.[102] Buccleuch then offered to give good rule in Teviotdale, and also in Eskdale, Ewesdale and Wauchopedale, 'geif my lord Maxwell will nocht tak the reule'. He offered to give redress in terms of his bond given at the 1529 Jedburgh justice ayre and to ride against Liddesdale with the earl of Bothwell 'or ony uthir as pleis the kingis command to put gud reule in that cuntre'. Buccleuch entered two of his kinsmen as pledges, and he and Robert Scott of Wamphray were released from ward.[103] Subsequently, Buccleuch was employed – unsuccessfully – to catch Armstrongs. In the cross-border raids of 1532–33, the earl of Northumberland burned down Buccleuch's principal house of Branxholm.[104] After the conclusion of the perpetual peace in May 1534, the English warden of the West March, Lord Dacre, was charged with committing treasons during the recent confrontation. One point was that he had arranged with Thomas Armstrong and William Elliot in Liddesdale to attack the English lands of his rival, William Musgrove. A second was that he had met Lord Maxwell in the debatable lands, and the two had made a pact of mutual non-aggression against each other's lands. A third claimed that he had come to a similar accord with Buccleuch in Liddesdale, preventing Musgrove from attacking Buccleuch's lands, and allowing Buccleuch to attack Northumberland's lands. After a period of imprisonment, Dacre paid 10,000 English marks for a pardon.[105]

There was a reciprocal charge brought against Buccleuch in the Jedburgh justice ayre of April 1535. He was accused of giving treasonable assistance to Lord Dacre in the burning of Cavers and Denholm in Roxburghshire during the 1532–33 hostilities. After the trial, Adam Otterburn, king's advocate, supplied the earl of Northumberland with a copy of Buccleuch's indictment.[106] Northumberland appears to have been the man at odds with Lord Dacre in England. It is not so clear who first made the accusations against Buccleuch. He was on bad terms with the Armstrongs, the Turnbulls, and even with his kinsmen, Scott of Allanhaugh and Scott of Howpasley. He had already been in and out of ward for failing to give good rule for Teviotdale. Now he was warded again, being released in May 1536.[107] After that date there is an ominous lack of reference to Buccleuch. He was not summoned to Edinburgh for the king's homecoming from France in March 1537. Probably he was back in ward. He was in Edinburgh castle in May 1540, and given licence to continue a lawsuit against Howpasley's widow, notwithstanding his own ward.[108] In August 1541 the king ordered him to go to Elgin, and he obeyed.[109] As he was away from home Buccleuch was unable to protect his family. In January 1541 he raised an action against Scott of Allanhaugh, who shortly before the previous Christmas had attacked Buccleuch's wife with a long Jedburgh staff. 'Had she not been ready, the butt end had slain her'. Allanhaugh then returned to Buccleuch's house on Boxing Day and drove away all of the cattle.[110]

Thus the king did not rate Buccleuch's service very highly in the personal rule, for all that the English had identified him as a royal supporter in 1528. Buccleuch had held the honorific Household position of royal cup-bearer in 1525 and 1526. After Andrew Kerr of Cessford was killed in the Melrose skirmish in 1526, when Buccleuch was allegedly attempting to liberate the king from the Douglases, Cessford's heir became the cup-bearer and held the position at least until 1536.[111] It is possible that the royal disregard for Buccleuch was based upon events in 1528. According to the captain of Norham, Lord Maxwell had cleared the Douglases out of Edinburgh in August 1528. Lascelles added that 'the Lord of Buclugh shuld have taken the towne with the Lorde Maxwell, ande he cam not to night'.[112] Buccleuch had let the king down. After James' death, Buccleuch took his compensation for being exiled to Elgin by rounding up the royal sheep flocks at Melrose abbey and driving them home, alleging that the king had earlier stolen his own sheep.[113]

During his ward in 1530, Lord Maxwell received the escheat of Armstrong of Staplegordon. Possibly by way of thanks, one of Maxwell's men brought James a gift of a fresh sturgeon.[114] Maxwell used his time in Edinburgh castle to arrange his son's marriage with Beatrice Douglas, daughter of the earl of Morton. James granted Morton a licence for the marriage at Falkland on 17 June 1530.[115] Maxwell's grant of lands to Beatrice on 25 July was deemed to be valid, notwithstanding that he had been in ward. At Edinburgh on 21 July, James consented to the betrothal, but added that 'we purpose to take him [the Master of Maxwell] fra his fadir and bring him up in our awne house'.[116] On 24 July, Maxwell signed the bond for good rule. On 5 August the Master of Maxwell, with consent of his curators, agreed 'of thair awne fre motive [and] will' to enter into ward until Maxwell found security for his bond. The Master was subsequently brought up in the royal Household.[117] The king then invited Lord Maxwell to submit his proposals for giving good rule. On 10 August, Maxwell offered to 'tak the gyding' of Ewesdale, Eskdale, Wauchopedale and Annandale and to make them as peaceable 'in tyme cuming as Lowtheane and as uthir partis of your gracis realme'. Douglas of Drumlanrig and Lord Somerville put up security of £6000, and Maxwell's offer was accepted. The Lords of Council decreed that the lieges of the West March be charged to ride with their warden 'as thai salbe requirit'.[118]

Thereafter, Maxwell's career in royal service thrived. He was vice-regent of the realm in 1536–37. In 1537 he intercepted Margaret Tudor on her flight towards England and returned her to Stirling. He sat as a juror on the three major treason trials of the personal rule. In 1538 he escorted Mary of Guise from France to Fife. In 1540 he was on the royal expedition to the Isles. The foundation of Maxwell's success in royal service lay in the fact that he had been loyal during the critical period of the struggle for power, had entered into ward, and had allowed James to kill Armstrong of Staplegordon.

John Johnston of that Ilk took the bond for good rule on 24 July 1530 with his hand at the pen.[119] In the minority, Johnston had killed 'Mikill Sym Armstrong', and in March 1528, Lord Maxwell had encouraged the Armstrongs in their feud against Johnston. Maxwell himself apparently tried to ambush Johnston.[120] This three-cornered feud was one of the elements contributing towards Angus' failure to carry out a successful raid against Liddesdale. Johnston had then attacked the royal lands of Duncow, and Angus was charged with treasonable art and part assistance in the attack. On 11 February 1529, at Lochmaben, Johnston settled his differences with Maxwell and gave the warden his bond of manrent.[121] In November 1529 he received a general remission for crimes committed in the minority.[122] Johnston's reconciliation with Maxwell, and subsequent pardon, were critical factors in the demise of Armstrong of Staplegordon. Johnston would wish to see Armstrong dead. Maxwell had come to terms with his chief rival and so abandoned his former retainer, probably tearing up Armstrong's bond of manrent.

At Peebles on 16 August, Johnston gave in to the Lords of Council his (subscribed) obligations for good rule in Moffat, Lochmaben and other areas under his influence.[123] Johnston then captured the notorious George Scott of the Bog and other thieves, in conformity with his bond.[124] However, he appears to have defaulted at times; in September 1536 he was again in ward in Dumbarton castle, although released in time to be summoned for the king's homecoming in March 1537.[125] At the Jedburgh justice ayre of May 1541, he found caution to re-enter ward in Dumbarton town, under penalty of 10,000 marks. Presumably he was again in breach of his bond. He appears to have obeyed the royal order, and the English reported his release on 7 December 1542.[126] Possibly he was so harassed by the king because of the greater influence of Maxwell, and because he had been busy attacking Duncow at a time when the king was assuming his personal rule.

The Kerrs were also released in August 1530, making similar pledges and finding Hamilton of Finnart as cautioner.[127] Mark Kerr of Dolphinton and Walter Kerr of Cessford were both in ward again in 1536, but released together with Scott of Buccleuch.[128] The three leading Kerr families acted on occasion as a triumvirate in office as wardens of the Middle March, but Andrew Kerr of Ferniehirst – who appears to have escaped ward in the personal rule – was the pre-eminent figure.[129] Lord Hume took slightly longer to find cautioners able to put up the sum of £10,000 but he too was out of ward by the end of 1530, and resumed office as warden of the East March.[130] Both Lord Hume and Lord Maxwell received their warden's fee of £100 each in 1530.[131]

The greatest casualty of the general warding was Patrick Hepburn, third earl of Bothwell, aged around eighteen in 1530.[132] The earl of Angus had on occasion taken control in Liddesdale in the minority, but on 27 May 1528 endorsed an undertaking by Bothwell to resume the keeping of good rule there. In July 1528, Bothwell was charged by the new government to continue answering for Liddesdale.[133] On 2 January 1529, he was ordered by the Lords of Council to meet the English wardens at Kershopefoot for the giving of redress, but four days later offered to take up the lieutenancy of Lothian and the Merse and expel Angus from Tantallon castle.[134] Accordingly he was granted the lordship of Tantallon in feu farm for an annual fee of 100 marks, but in July 1529 this was superseded by a charter to the royal Secretary, Thomas Erskine of Haltoun, who took up the feu for an annual fee of 200 marks.[135] Whilst Bothwell was engaged – unsuccessfully – in the Douglas campaign in the east, he was excused from responsibility in Liddesdale. In James' letter of February 1529 to Henry VIII, he requested his uncle to have patience over the issue of Liddesdale, as Bothwell was busy elsewhere and still in his 'youtheid'.[136]

In June 1529, Bothwell gave his bond for good rule at Peebles and promised to go to Liddesdale in person to give good rule.[137] At this stage his importance to the king was acknowledged by his being designated as one of the three earls who were to:

> sit apon our secret consell and assist till our chancelar continually in ordorying all sik thingis as concernys justice, our honour, the common weill of our realm and our proffitis.

The other two earls were the third earl of Argyll and Moray. However, provision was made that their places could be taken by legal deputies when duties called the magnates elsewhere.[138] The 'secret consell' was no longer a group of the greatest lords required to attend the king daily, as had been the case in July 1528. It appears on this occasion to have become a body charged with assisting the Chancellor in administration, rather than with giving advice to the king.

In March 1530, when Moray offered to serve as lieutenant of all three Marches, Bothwell again affirmed his obligations to answer for Liddesdale.[139] However, Bothwell was warded for the duration of the royal expedition, and at Peebles on 16 September 1530, he again undertook to give good rule, under penalty of £10,000 for default.[140] At Dundee on 8 October he requested a general remission for all of the inhabitants of Liddesdale, and this was granted, George Scott of the

Bog being specifically excepted. The Liddesdale subjects were also given free licence to 'do thare lefull erandis and besynes'.[141]

Bothwell then became a regular attender at sessions of the Lords of Council, sitting from October 1530 until November 1531.[142] In July 1531, Scott of Buccleuch made what he claimed was a retaliatory raid into Liddesdale, and brought an action against Bothwell as the man responsible for the area.[143] Both men were then charged with securing the release of David Shafton, or with the detention of 'Sym the Laird' and 'Dave the Lady'. Buccleuch was warded for his failure to capture the latter man, and again charged with the release of David Shafton. On 5 December 1531 the Lords of Council ruled that Bothwell was to ensure that the men of Liddesdale relieved Buccleuch for his expenses in the exercise.[144] The Shafton incident took place against the backdrop of a joint Anglo-Scots commission into the issue of giving redress for Canonbie and the debatable lands, which achieved little success in the winter of 1531–32.[145] As Sym the Laird subsequently received a remission for his involvement in the Shafton incident, it appears that he too was detained, though it is doubtful whether this was due to Bothwell.[146]

Bothwell was summoned to a convention which met at Edinburgh on 26 January 1532 to debate the issue of Canonbie. The Chancellor presided. Those present included Huntly, the fourth earl of Argyll, Lennox, Rothes, Eglinton, Montrose, Marischal; Lords Fleming, Hume, Gray, Hay, Somerville, Erskine, Ross, Saltoun, Lindsay, Lyle, Elphinstone, Livingston, Avandale, Methven, Herries, and Crichton and Hamilton of Finnart.[147] The Lords of Council unanimously declared that Canonbie was 'undowtit propir landis of Scotland'.[148] Three days later, another suitably august body of councillors, including Huntly, Moray, Argyll and Atholl, ruled that the archbishop of St. Andrews had 'committie falt' in correspondence with the English at this time, the two countries 'standand apoun the punct of weir'. As the archbishop had failed to advise the king of this correspondence, there was now 'ane suspitioun aganis him', and he was required to remain in Edinburgh pending further inquiry.[149] The archbishopric of St. Andrews had in 1531 made its contribution of £200 towards the king's expenses for his projected Isles expedition.[150] Throughout the personal rule James exploited the wealth of the Church on various pretexts, most notably to establish the College of Justice. Probably James Beaton was aggrieved that the Crown should find in the First Estate a reliable source of income; and this grievance formed the basis of a complete breakdown in relations between the king and his senior archbishop, leading to the latter's disappearance from the council and eventual warding in 1533.

Although Bothwell was summoned to the January 1532 convention, he did not appear. The likelihood is that the king required him to appear in order to place him in ward. The presence of so many lords in Edinburgh may have been in order to endorse this decision, as well as to give an opinion on Canonbie. For on 21 December 1531 at Dilston (Northumberland), Bothwell had moved far beyond

[87]

the normal give-and-take of Borders diplomacy; he met with the earl of Northumberland and signed a paper in which he offered to bring 6000 commoners and 1000 gentlemen to the service of Henry VIII, should that monarch wish to invade Scotland. The earl of Northumberland then passed this communication on to Henry VIII.[151] By June 1532 Bothwell was in ward in Edinburgh castle, and appears to have remained there until May 1535, when he was ordered to remove himself to Inverness. In 1539 he received a royal licence to travel from Aberdeen to the Continent. After April 1541 he was in Venice. In April 1542, after turning down an offer of service with Charles V and being turned down by Francis I, out of that monarch's regard for James V, Bothwell approached Henry VIII. After King James' death, in the 1543 parliament, the earl was accused of aiding the English.[152] The warding of Bothwell was based not upon 'ane suspitioun aganis him', but on the awareness that he had committed blatant treason.

The earl of Northumberland asked Bothwell in December 1531 why he was so aggrieved against his king. Bothwell listed various reasons. James had kept him in his 'nonage' (he was still under twenty-one in 1531), and paid little regard to the service of himself and his forbears; James had imprisoned him for the best part of six months for his rule of Liddesdale; part of his heritage had been given to the Kerrs; the king was likely to put him to death if he could.[153] It was true that Bothwell had had a dispute with the Kerrs over the profits of the lands of Fairnington and Ferniehope, and eventually lost his case after an interim decree in his favour.[154] Possibly he had not given a creditable performance with regard to the Shafton incident. For the rest, Bothwell appears to have been both a victim of circumstances, and a young man who misjudged the political situation in December 1531. He considered that James had erred in banishing Angus, and had compounded this error in seeking to disinherit the earl of Crawford and in imprisoning the earl of Argyll. Whilst the king's advocate in December 1531 was about to commence an action for non-entry against the Crawford earldom, and Argyll was experiencing obstacles in his campaign to daunt the Isles, in the event both magnates were to prove loyal to the Crown. Bothwell had completely miscalculated their reaction to royal provocation. Possibly this was due to his own inexperience in Scottish politics, leading him to assume that because he felt aggrieved and ready to rebel, so too would others. He was wrong.

The initial approach to Bothwell appears to have come from the earl of Northumberland, on the instructions of Henry VIII. Possibly the information on the state of Scottish politics in 1531 was derived from the communications of the archbishop of St. Andrews. Strategically, the earldom of Bothwell lay in the area which had been at the centre of the 1528-29 struggle for power. The Hepburn family had been induced to serve against Angus with the promise of the reward of Tantallon if successful. They were not successful and never set foot in Tantallon. For Henry VIII, advised by Angus, this may have been seen as a reason for Bothwell to resent the Crown. Added to this, the 1531-32 row over

Canonbie and the debatable lands turned on the question of controlling the Armstrongs of Liddesdale. Nominally, Bothwell was in charge, but his dispute with Buccleuch indicates that he could take little credit for controlling the activities of the numerous curiously named Armstrongs, George Scott of the Bog and others. That King James should have made a point of referring to Bothwell's youth in writing to Henry VIII in February 1529 suggests that the Scots king considered that a more experienced man was required in Liddesdale. In 1529, the circumstances were that Bothwell was required in two places at once, and in this sense became a victim, unable to make his own personal impression in Liddesdale. That he should appear as one of the 'secret consell' at the age of seventeen in 1529, reflected the political importance of the areas under his nominal authority rather than his own abilities. The leniency with which Bothwell was treated suggests that the king felt he was more a victim of circumstances who had been exploited by the earl of Northumberland than a willing and active rebel.

After Bothwell had committed treason, his uncle, the Master of Hailes, initially took control of Liddesdale for the Hepburn family. Bothwell protested that as he himself was in ward he could not give good rule there 'sa weile as and he war present', but would 'do his extreme power'.[155] However, in August 1532, Sir James Sandilands of Calder was appointed as captain of Hermitage castle, receiving the monthly fee of £80. Bothwell requested of the Lords of Council that Sandilandis' appointment should not affect his (Bothwell's) heritage.[156] Lord Maxwell took charge from November 1533 to July 1534, before relinquishing control to the Hepburn family, shortly after the conclusion of the perpetual peace.[157] Lord Maxwell was again in charge by August 1535, in conjunction with Lord Fleming, the latter man assuming sole responsibility during Maxwell's stint as vice-regent in 1536–37.[158] From 1537 onwards, Lord Maxwell administered law and order both internally and externally.[159] The lordship was formally annexed to the Crown in the December 1540 parliament. So too was the greater portion of the earldom of Angus.[160] The superiority of Liddesdale had passed from the earls of Angus to the earls of Bothwell in 1492. The grant by James IV to the first earl of Bothwell had been made at that earl's own initiative, and reduced the influence of the fifth earl of Angus on the Borders.[161] In annexing Liddesdale in 1540, James V was taking away what his father had bestowed, and probably the king considered that it was logical that the lordship should fall to the Crown, together with the Angus earldom.

With the head of the family in ward, the rest of the Hepburn family fared neither well nor badly during the personal rule. Margaret Hepburn, Lady Sinclair, remained as lessee of Orkney and Shetland until 1540. Sir Patrick Hepburn of Waughton was convicted in January 1536 for an attack on James, brother of William Sinclair of Roslin.[162] He paid £1000 for a remission and was restored to his lands in May 1536. The money went to Hamilton of Finnart for building works at Blackness castle.[163] Waughton and his retainers then received a further general remission for crimes committed in the minority.[164] His namesake,

Patrick Hepburn, prior of St. Andrews and great-uncle and former tutor of the earl, was a regular charter witness from June 1528 until November 1538.[165] In 1538 he became bishop of Moray and abbot-commendator of Scone.[166] The bishopric provided a less lucrative living than the priory, which was bestowed upon the king's illegitimate son, James *secundus*, then aged eight.[167] In the period prior to Hepburn's admission to his new posts, in 1537–38, the Crown was able to collect almost £3700 in revenues from the vacant bishopric.[168] In February 1540, the Comptroller, David Wood of Craig, approached the bishop at his Edinburgh house and insisted that Hepburn feu part of the bishopric's lands in Strathspey to John Grant of Ballindalloch and his brother. Hepburn wanted to feu these lands to James Grant of Freuchy, but his visitors insisted that the king wished otherwise. After the Comptroller had left his house, Hepburn had his notary public record the altercation and note that in his opinion the king was acting with great severity to all those of the surname Hepburn.[169] Possibly Hepburn had in mind the ward of his former pupil, and was aware that Liddesdale was shortly to be annexed to the Crown. Alternatively, he may simply have been making a silent protest against the Crown's attitude towards the revenues of the Church. King James and his financial staff had a somewhat cavalier attitude towards the bishopric of Moray.[170] In November 1541, the bishop had to protest to the Lords of Council to suspend royal letters obtained by the sheriff of Elgin for a weaponshowing within his regality.[171]

The earl of Bothwell remained as the titular sheriff of Haddington and Berwick, notwithstanding his ward. In April 1541 he was faced with a bill of around £670, representing uncollected castlewards, for the past twenty-eight years, for twenty-one castles. The individual sums were trivial, and Bothwell had the right of relief against the principal debtors – amongst them Angus' sister, Alison Douglas, who owed £7 for Wedderburn. Nevertheless he protested to the Lords of Council that he had been 'in continuale subjectioun' since Flodden.[172] There were precedents for this effort by James' financial staff to collect the Crown's feudal and proprietorial dues. Upon achieving his majority, the earl of Cassillis was also faced with the task of recovering uncollected castlewards. In August 1532, the Master of Hailes, as acting deputy-sheriff for Bothwell, was required to pay the sum of £19. 10s. 10d. to the Comptroller.[173] Donaldson has asked whether or not it was so reasonable for the Crown to seek payment in 1541. The question is largely irrelevant; legally the sums were due to the Crown, and it is apparent that Bothwell and his family had been neglecting their shrieval duties. That it had taken the Comptroller so long to come round to collecting the debt was unremarkable by sixteenth century standards. A comparison can be made with a dispute between the earl of Crawford and the bishop of Moray in 1553–54 over the collection of teinds in Perthshire for the twenty year period between 1514 and 1534.[174]

Also in 1541, Bothwell was attempting to recover a backlog of feudal casualties for the king, amounting in all to over £6300. Amongst others, the earl of Huntly owed the Crown £1900 for entry to his Berwickshire estates of Fogo, Gordon and Huntly, of which he had taken possession in 1537.[175] There is no indication that he ever paid Bothwell or his deputies any of this. Possibly, therefore, it was a relief for Bothwell to be granted licence to leave the country and leave the financial headaches to others. Notwithstanding the loss of part of his heritage, and the large amounts of money which he was expected to collect for the Crown, he had got off lightly considering his treasonable default in December 1531.

Liddesdale was as much a liability as an asset for the Crown. The Comptroller's rental assessment at Hermitage castle in May 1541 revealed an annual rental value of £132. Several lands were vacant, possibly due in part to the royal policy of thinning out the Armstrongs and other thieves over the years.[176] In the aftermath of the 1533 hostilities, the annual payment to the keepers of Liddesdale rose to £100. By 1539 it had dropped to 40 marks. In this latter year Maxwell was allowed £100 for repairs to Hermitage castle.[177] In 1542, with hostilities again imminent, gunners were sent to the castle.[178] Together with the debatable lands, Liddesdale caused problems for both the English and the Scots. In January 1536, Lord Maxwell invited the earl of Cumberland to accompany him in a joint expedition to drive out thieves. By 1538, both sides were able to report that some order had been restored. In 1541 the English border officers suggested that they might deal with Tynedale and Redesdale, whilst the Scots attended to Liddesdale.[179]

The king regularly returned to the Meggetland in the month of September to go hunting.[180] In August 1531 he went hunting there with Lord Hay, Elizabeth Hepburn, prioress of Haddington, and the men of Lothian and Menteith.[181] In May 1532 he was again in the area, and the English border officers reported that the 'common brute and voice was [that he] was to have made a roode upon the Debatable grounds and Liddisdale men'. They also reported that Margaret Tudor was in Ettrick Forest to hold a court of justice and was refused entrance to Newark castle by Scott of Buccleuch. The king ordered Buccleuch to surrender the keys to her.[182] Possibly it was on this occasion that Johnston of that Ilk caught Scott of the Bog. In June 1534, a further English report was that the king was to hunt in Eskdalemuir with Lord Maxwell. In December of the same year James wrote from Edinburgh to his uncle to say that he had punished his border thieves.[183] On 12 May 1535, the Danish Ambassador, Peter Suevenius, met the king after Mass at Melrose abbey, James still dressed in his hunting clothes.[184] This was shortly after the Jedburgh justice ayre at which Argyll presided as justiciar, and at which William, brother of Andrew Kerr of Ferniehirst, was granted remission for various thefts of sheep and cattle.[185] At the same ayre Buccleuch was charged with communicating with Lord Dacre. The king may have been at his trial.[186]

In November 1535, James was at Frendraught during the Dumfries ayre, where Argyll presided, assisted by the earl of Montrose. The ayre raised £814.[187] After this year there was a hiatus in the king's personal appearances on the Borders until November/December 1539, when he appears to have visited Kelso, Melrose, Peebles, and Lochmaben, presumably again in conjunction with the justice ayre circuit.[188] At Falkland on 19 December 1539, James reported to his uncle: 'We have in our proper persoun riddin alangis all our Marchis'.[189] In November 1540 the lairds of Lothian were charged to ride with the king to the Borders. This later gave rise to a rumour that the Scots king had attempted to flee into England. In pursuit of a falcon, James crossed the river Tweed and was spotted by the Berwick garrison. They invited him into the castle for a glass of wine, but the king declined.[190] At the end of 1541 the English again expected James to make an appearance on the Borders,[191] but his next expedition appears to have been to Peebles in July 1542.[192]

One of the hallmarks of successful Stewart monarchy was that the king should be seen to be active in person throughout the country in the giving of law and order and execution of justice. This was something upon which James III fell down, and at which his son displayed great skill and energy. In this respect, James V was more akin to his father than his grandfather, not only regularly visiting the Borders, but later paying visits to the more far-flung parts of his realm. The executions of at least four Armstrongs and Scott of the Bog can only have contributed to his later reputation as a 'puir man's king'.[193] Furthermore, the death of Armstrong of Staplegordon or Gilknockie was a visible example of the assertion of royal authority in person.

In terms of Crown-magnate relations, Armstrong's demise mattered little. The interesting feature is the general warding. In the later careers of those border magnates warded in 1530, there is a full spectrum, ranging from the loyalty of Lord Maxwell, through Lord Hume, the Kerrs, Johnston of that Ilk and Scott of Buccleuch, to the treason of the earl of Bothwell. It is doubtful whether Bothwell's ward made much of an impression on any other individual, saving perhaps his great-uncle. If anything he was treated leniently. James demonstrated a shrewd awareness of those whose services were valuable to him. Thus Maxwell, despite being implicated for similar offences as those for which Buccleuch was warded, remained as the most important magnate in the south-west, and as one upon whose service the king could rely. By contrast the physical presence on the Borders of the young and inexperienced Bothwell proved unnecessary. His command of Liddesdale was taken over by Maxwell, and his other offices exercised by his kinsmen. It was fitting that he should lose the office of great admiral to the king's 'traist cousing and counsalour', Lord Maxwell, who carried out the function literally in escorting Mary of Guise to Scotland.[194]

The general warding of 1530 is remarkable both for its extent and for the circumstances giving rise to it. It demonstrates a degree of trust and cooperation between Crown and magnates at an early stage in the personal rule, when the king had only recently emerged from the dominant influence of those who had assisted him in his struggle for power. Clearly Maxwell interpreted his own ward in this manner, whilst Bothwell did not. For James, it was a success not because he had forced his magnates into submission, but because he had secured an incontrovertible acknowledgement of his own authority.

NOTES

1. *SP Henry VIII*, iv, pt. iv, no. cciv.
2. *Ibid.*, iv, pt. iv, no. clxxxv.
3. *LP Henry VIII*, iv, pt. ii, nos. 4718–9.
4. *SP Henry VIII*, iv, pt. iv, no. cxcvii.
5. *RSS*, i, nos. 3969–79.
6. Wormald, *Bonds*, App. A, 307, no. 7 (4 July 1528); Fraser, *Buccleuch*, ii, no. 139; cf. *ADCP*, 276 (6 July 1528).
7. *RMS*, iii, nos. 612, 614.
8. *APS*, ii, 329–30.
9. *ADCP*, 277.
10. *Ibid.*, 294.
11. *APS*, ii, 321–2.
12. *LP Henry VIII*, iv, pt. ii, no. 5045.
13. *Ibid.*, iv, pt. iii, no. 6305 (wrongly placed in 1530); *SP Henry VIII*, iv, pt. iv, no. cxcviii; *ADCP*, 290.
14. SP Henry VIII, iv, pt. iv, no. clxxxiv.
15. Ibid., iv, pt. iv, 548.
16. *Ibid.*, iv, pt. iv, no. clxxix.
17. *LP Henry VIII*, iv, pt. ii, no. 4298; *ADCP*, 276.
18. *LP Henry VIII*, iv, pt. ii, no. 4397.
19. *SP Henry VIII*, iv, pt. iv, no. cxxx; cf. W.A. Armstrong, *The Armstrong Borderland* (Galashiels 1960), 62, where the designation 'of Whithaugh' is given for Simon Armstrong.
20. *LP Henry VIII*, iv, pt. ii, no. 4186 (wrongly placed in 1528); *ADCP*, 257–8, 492 (given as 1526); cf. also Rae, *op.cit.*, App. 6.
21. *LP Henry VIII*, iv, pt. ii, no. 5045.
22. *Ibid.*, iv, pt. ii, nos. 3972, 4014, 4020, 4420, 4323. The colourful details of these episodes can be found in Armstrong, *op.cit.*, 71–3 *et passim*, and in G.M. Fraser, *The Steel Bonnets* (Collins, 1971), Chap. xxvi.
23. *LP Henry VIII*, iv, pt. ii, nos. 4531, 4727.
24. *Ibid.*, iv, pt. ii, nos. 4727, 4747.
25. *Ibid.*, iv, pt. ii, nos. 4925, 4951.
26. *Ibid.*, iv, pt. ii, no. 5055.
27. *SP Henry VIII*, iv, pt. iv, no. cciv.
28. *ADCP*, 276, 279.
29. *Ibid.*, 291, 296.
30. *Ibid.*, 300–1.
31. *SP Henry VIII*, iv, pt. iv, no. ccii.
32. *Ibid.*, iv, pt. iv, no. cciv.
33. *ADCP*, 306.
34. *SP Henry VIII*, iv, pt. iv, no. ccv (Angus' last letter at Preston, Berwickshire, written on 4 May); *RSS*, ii, no. 6 (ward of the Arran earldom to Finnart, on 31 March 1529).
35. *SP Henry VIII*, iv, pt. iv, nos. ccvi, ccviii (Jedburgh, 22 June; Peebles, 29 June); *James V Letters*, 154–6 (Jedburgh, 1 and 20 June; Peebles, 28 June).
36. SRO, RH 2.1.9. (*ADC*, vol. 40, ff. 55, 56, 59); *ADCP*, 311.
37. *RSS*, ii, nos. 151–190 (Jedburgh, 9–23 June), 197–203 (Peebles, 28 June - 1 July).
38. *ADCP*, 311, 333.
39. *Ibid.*, 312; Pitcairn, *Trials*, i, pt. i, 142–3.
40. Pitcairn, *Trials*, i, pt. i, 143.

41. *TA*, v, 357, 363.
42. *RSS*, ii, nos. 387–434 (Dumfries, 26 October - 10 November), 435 (Whithorn, 12 November), 437–8 (Kirkcudbright, 13 and 20 November), 444–8 (Wigtown, 1 and 6 December).
43. *TA*, v, 354, 387.
44. *SP Henry VIII*, iv, pt. iv, no. ccxi.
45. *Ibid.*, iv, pt. iv, no. ccxii.
46. *Ibid.*, iv, pt. iv, no. ccxiii.
47. *ADCP*, 320; SRO, RH 2.1.9. (*ADC*, vol. 40, f. 153).
48. *TA*, v, 387.
49. *Ibid.*, v, 386.
50. *ADCP*, 323–5; SRO, RH 2.1.9. (*ADC*, vol. 41, f. 29); *RSS*, i, no. 3296 (tack of Ardmannoch to Moray, 1524).
51. *ADCP*, 330–1; *RSS*, ii, no. 776; *TA*, v, 450; *ER*, xvi, 114.
52. Pitcairn, *Trials*, i, pt. i, 149. The earl of Atholl acted as their cautioner; *RSS*, ii, no. 660 (gift of ward to Moray).
53. Pitcairn, *Trials*, i, pt. i, 145; the appellation given Scott by Lesley, *History*, 141.
54. *ADCP*, 148, 218.
55. *ADCP*, 327.
56. *Ibid.*, 327.
57. *Ibid.*, 327–8; Pitcairn, *Trials*, i, pt. i, 147. The unidentified laird of Keir probably hailed from Dumfriesshire, and was not Stirling of Keir.
58. *SP Venetian*, iv, no. 584.
59. Pitcairn, *Trials*, i, pt. i, 146–8; Rae, *op.cit.*, App. 1.
60. SRO, RH 2.1.9. (*ADC*, vol. 42, ff. 8, 40).
61. *TA*, v, 378; Wormald, *Bonds*, App. A, 382, no. 34, at Ancrum, 16 March 1530. This was to settle their differences arising out of Scott's killing of Andrew Kerr of Cessford at Melrose in 1526.
62. SRO, Lothian Writs, [GD 40/3], no. 494, serving James Crichton of Cranston-Riddale as heir to the lands of Nisbet, Roxburgh.
63. *TA*, v, 379.
64. *Diurnal of Occurrents*, 13–14.
65. *TA*, v, 379, paid 40 shillings on 25 May.
66. Before the end of 1529: cf. *RMS*, iii, nos. 861 (still alive 5 November 1529), 932 (fourth earl in possession by 15 January 1530.
67. *ADCP*, 326–7.
68. Cf. Rae, *op.cit.*, App. 4, 6.
69. *ADCP*, 318–9.
70. *Ibid.*, 328–9. Rae, *op.cit.*, App. 6, gives a useful indication of all areas from which military forces were raised for Border expeditions.
71. *RSS*, ii, nos. 704, 407, 714, 719, 721. Some of the place names are obscure:- John Wood of *Balbegrenoch* (?Barbegno, Kincardine) received the escheats of John Wischart in *Auchearny* (?Acharnie, Aberdeen) [not an area summoned for the muster], and David Strachan in Over *Craiginestoun*; Douglas of Drumlanrig (Dumfries) received the escheats of Alexander Gordon of the *Holme*, Thomas Grear in Bariarg (Barjarg, Dumfries), and Thomas Welsh in *Bracho*; the heralds received, *inter alia*, the escheats of David Blair in *Schangy* and William Moncur in *Nevay*. David Lindsay of the Mount was a herald in 1530 (*ER*, xvi, 12; *TA*, v, 432), and Edington, *op.cit.*, 47, identifies him as being Snowdon Herald.
72. *Excerpta e Libris*, App., 31.
73. *ADCP*, 331 A great seal charter was issued at Peebles on 4 July, indicating the presence of the Chancellor, and others in the chancery office: *RMS*, iii, no. 954 (test *ut in aliis cartis*).
74. *Excerpta e Libris*, App., 31.

75. *RSS*, ii, no. 702.
76. *Excerpta e Libris*, App., 31; *RSS*, ii, no. 705.
77. *RMS*, iii, no. 1199.
78. Wormald, *Bonds*, App. A, 336, no. 15; cf. also Fraser, *Carlaverock*, ii, no. 84, *et passim*.
79. *LP Henry VIII*, iv, pt. ii, no. 4014.
80. Abell, *op.cit.*, f. 121v.
81. *Diurnal of Occurrents*, 14.
82. Lesley, History, 143.
83. Pitscottie, Historie, i, 335. The editor, A.J.G. Mackay, comments that sixteen manuscripts were examined to produce the STS edition: *ibid.*, lix. A more flamboyant version of Pitscottie's description of Armstrong's death is cited in Pitcairn, Trials, i, pt. i, 153–4. This gives substantially the same story as the Border Ballad, complete with embellishments.
84. Buchanan, History, ii, 244.
85. Quoted in Bingham, *op.cit*, App. A.
86. Presumably due to Sir Walter Scott of Buccleuch, and the proliferation of Pitscottie manuscripts.
87. Quoted in Bingham, *op.cit.*, App. B; cf. also, Edington, *op.cit.*, 189.
88. Performed by the Royal Lyceum Theatre Company as part of the 1994 Edinburgh International Festival; first performed at the Glasgow Citizens Theatre in 1965.
89. SRO, Hay of Yester Writs [GD 28], nos. 462–465; Pitcairn, *Trials*, i, pt. i, 149.
90. *ADCP*, 343.
91. Pitcairn, *Trials*, i, pt. i, 154; *LP Henry VIII*, iv, pt. ii, no. 4323.
92. *ADCP*, 364, 367; Fraser, *Buccleuch*, ii, no. 152.
93. Fraser, *Buccleuch*, ii, no. 153 (placed in 1534 by Fraser); Pitcairn, *Trials*, i, pt. i, 169.
94. Pitcairn, *Trials*, i, pt. i, 171.
95. *TA*, v, 380.
96. Pitcairn, *Trials*, i, pt. i, 172–3.
97. Donaldson, *op.cit.*, 62.
98. Pitcairn, *Trials*, i, pt. i, 142–3.
99. *Diurnal of Occurrents*, 15, placed chronologically in 1532.
100. Donaldson, *op.cit.*, 62.
101. *TA*, v, 380.
102. *ADCP*, 332. The others were Jardine of Applegarth, Grierson of Lag, Charteris of Amisfield, and Crichton of Bellibocht.
103. *Ibid.*, 333, 336.
104. *LP Henry VIII*, vi, no. 125.
105. *Ibid.*, vii, nos. 674, 962, 1601.
106. *Ibid.*, ix, nos. 64, 88; *APS*, ii, 414, 433.
107. *SP Henry VIII*, v, pt. iv, no. ccxcvi.
108. *ADCP*, 519; Fraser, *Buccleuch*, ii, no. 157 (Fraser estimates the year to be 1540 in the undated document which he reproduces).
109. Fraser, *Buccleuch*, ii, no. 160.
110. SRO, *ADCS*, xiv, f. 86.
111. *ER*, xv, 203, 289, 389, 544; *ER*, xvi, 134, 480E. Fraser, *Buccleuch*, i, 83–4, suggests that an attempt was made by the king to have Buccleuch reappointed in 1527.
112. *SP Henry VIII*, iv, pt, iv, 509.
113. *HP*, i, no. 263.
114. *TA*, v, 380.
115. SRO, Morton Papers [GD 150], nos. 284–5; *Mort. Reg.*, i, no. i (no year given, but in accordance with the Morton Papers).
116. *RMS*, iii, no. 956; *Mort. Reg.*, i, no. ii (again no year given).
117. *ADCP*, 332, 337; *TA*, vi, 35, 91, 203 (liveries for the Master).
118. *ADCP*, 334, 337–8.

119. *Ibid.*, 332. Others who did so were Grierson and Jardine.
120. *SP Henry VIII*, iv, pt. iv, no. clxxix.
121. Wormald, *Bonds*, App. A, 336, no. 17.
122. Fraser, *Annandale*, i, no. 26, specifically for his absence from the army at Solway.
123. Pitcairn, *Trials*, i, pt. i, 148–9; *ADCP*, 341.
124. *Diurnal of Occurrents*, 15; *ADCP*, 413; *TA*, vi, 141, 220.
125. *TA*, vi, 307, 312.
126. Pitcairn, *Trials*, i, pt. i, 229–230; *HP*, i, no. 248. He first found caution in March 1541, and again in November and December. The English described him as 'the Lorde of Sanct Johnston'.
127. *ADCP*, 323–3, 336, 338–9.
128. *SP Henry VIII*, v, pt. iv, no. ccxcvi.
129. Rae, *op.cit.*, App. 2.2.
130. *ADCP*, 342, 345; Rae, *op.cit.*, App. 2.1, latterly acting through deputies, also Humes.
131. Rae, *op.cit.*, App. 3. Probably the Kerrs were paid as well, but no record survives of it.
132. *Scots Peerage*, ii, 157.
133. Rae, *op.cit.*, App. 2 (4); *ADCP*, 276, 279.
134. *ADCP*, 301–302, 306.
135. *RMS*, iii, nos. 738, 806
136. *ADCP*, 302; *SP Henry VIII*, iv, pt. iv, no. ccii.
137. *ADCP*, 311.
138. *Ibid.*, 315.
139. *Ibid.*, 323.
140. *Ibid.*, 340–1.
141. *Ibid.*, 341; *RSS*, ii, no. 745, 753.
142. SRO, RH 2.1.9. (*ADC*, vol. 41, ff. 115, 134, 160; vol. 42, ff. 19, 192; vol. 43, ff. 53, 92 *et passim*).
143. *ADCP*, 360; *ER*, xvi, 539.
144. *ADCP*, 364, 367.
145. *LP Henry VIII*, v, nos. 411, 463, 480, 513–7, 763, 854.
146. Fraser, *Buccleuch*, ii, no. 152. No year is given for the remission.
147. *TA*, vi, 56; *ADCP*, 370; SRO, RH 2.1.9 (*ADC*, vol. 43, f. 140).
148. *ADCP*, 370.
149. *Ibid.*, 370; SRO, RH 2.1.9. (*ADC*, vol. 43,f. 141).
150. *TA*, v, 450.
151. *LP Henry VIII*, v, nos. 595, 609.
152. *ADCP*, 379, 439, 445; *LP Henry VIII*, vi, no. 885; xiv, pt. ii, no. 131; xvi, no. 1182; xvii, no. 702; SRO, Morton (of Dalmahoy) Papers [GD 150], nos 1404–5; Fraser Papers [GD 86], i. no. 99; *RMS*, iii, nos. 1984, 1999, 2038, 2045.
153. *LP Henry VIII*, v, nos. 595, 609.
154. SRO, *ADC*, vol. 39, ff. 137v-8; *ADCP*, 309–11 (Decision 1529, in Bothwell's favour); *RMS*, iii, no. 1228 (grant in favour of Janet Rutherford, widow of Thomas Kerr of Mersington, after an apprisal on 28 August 1532).
155. *TA*, vi, 59; *ADCP*, 379.
156. *TA*, vi, 165–6, 314; *ADCP*, 381–3.
157. *TA*, vi, 217, 237; *ADCP*, 425–6; cf. *RMS*, iii, no. 1402 (charter preamble thanking Maxwell for his service).
158. *TA*, vi, 265; *ADCP*, 455.
159. *ER*, xvii, 749, 760; Rae, *op.cit.*, App. 2(4).
160. *APS*, ii, 404; *RMS*, iii, no. 2233.
161. Macdougall, *James IV*, 91.
162. *ER*, xvi, 602; Pitcairn, *Trials*, i, pt. i, 172; *APS*, ii, 352; cf. *ADCP*, 526.
163. *RSS*, ii, nos. 2019, 2027; *ADCP*, 452–3.
164. *RSS*, ii, no. 2033, specifically for support of David Hume of Wedderburn.

165. *Scots Peerage*, ii, 157ff; *ADCP*, 123; *RMS*, iii, nos. 601, 1862, *et passim*.
166. *James V Letters*, 342–3; *RSS*, ii, nos. 2493, 2772.
167. *James V Letters*, 343, 399; *RSS*, ii, nos. 3097, 3125 (in 1539). In 1533 the bishopric of Moray was required to pay £176 in tax for one term. The priory of St. Andrews paid £441 in the same period: *TA*, vi, 144, 146.
168. *TA*, vi, 378; vii, 85, 248–9, 386, inclusive of the temporalities from Scone and also the abbey of Inchaffray.
169. Fraser, *Grant*, i, 107–110; iii, no. 241.
170. Cf. Athol L. Murray, 'The Revenues of the Bishopric of Moray', in *Innes Review*, xix (1968).
171. *ADCP*, 510.
172. *Ibid.*, 502–3; SRO, *ADCS*, xv, f. 145.
173. *ADCP*, 381.
174. Donaldson, *op.cit.*, 53, poses the question of reasonableness presumably in an attempt to equate acceptable Stewart monarchy with the exercise of financial leniency. Cf. *ADCP*, 627, 633, for teind dispute.
175. SRO, *ADCS*, xv, f. 105v; *ER*, xvii, 735.
176. *ER*, xvii, 697–702.
177. *TA*, vi, 237 (to Maxwell in 1534); vii, 275, 289.
178. *Ibid.*, viii, 110–11.
179. *LP Henry VIII*, x, no. 160; xiii, nos. 547, 720; xvi, nos. 1212, 1326.
180. *TA*, v, 442 (1531); vi, 137 (1533), 215 (1534), 264 (1535); vii, 87 (1538). It is not always entirely clear whether this was to the Megget water south of Peebles, or to the Meggat water in Eskdalemuir.
181. *Ibid.*, v, 445–6; *RMS*, iii, nos. 1059 (Crammald, 18 August), 1060 (Peebles, 18 August).
182. *SP Henry VIII*, iv, pt. iv, no. ccxxvi.
183. *LP Henry VIII*, vii, nos. 829, 1585.
184. *Ibid.*, viii, no. 1178.
185. SRO, Lothian Writs [GD 40/13], nos. 2, 6.
186. Cf. *RMS*, iii, nos. 1468–9 (Kelso, 2 May), 1471–2 (Jedburgh, 6 and 7 May), indicating that the Chancery office was in the area shortly after the ayre.
187. *TA*, vi, 245, 265–7.
188. *Ibid.*, vii, 51, 259 (Kelso and Melrose); *RMS*, iii, no. 2041 (Peebles, 1 December); *RSS*, ii, nos. 3211 (Kelso, 17 November), 3212 (Peebles, 23 November), 3213 (Lochmaben, 25 November). Returns from ayres at Dumbarton and Dumfries only are noted in the *Treasurer's Accounts* in 1539–40: *TA*, vii, 250.
189. *SP Henry VIII*, v, pt. iv, no. ccclxi.
190. *TA*, vii, 406; *LP Henry VIII*, xvi, no. 483.
191. *HP*, i, nos. 106, 108.
192. *Ibid.*, i, no. 122; *TA*, viii, 92; *RMS*, iii, nos. 2726–7 (Peebles, 10 July); *RSS*, ii, nos. 4771–4 (Peebles, 9–12 July).
193. Cf. contrasting views expressed in Armstrong, *op.cit.*, 87–91, and Donaldson, *op.cit.*, 61–62, where attempts are made to equate these executions with the entirely unrelated executions of the Master of Forbes and Lady Glamis.
194. Fraser, *Eglinton*, i, no. 126 (Bothwell as great admiral in August 1533); *RSS*, ii, no. 2556 (Maxwell as great admiral in May 1538).

CHAPTER SIX

Poisoned Chalice? The Douglas Connection

T he repercussions of the struggle for power in 1528–29 and the expulsion of the Angus Douglases were still being felt as late as 1533, when Scotland and England nearly went to war. Angus retained some support in Scotland, and King James had to address the problem of how to dissolve his former Chancellor's continuing influence.

I. GENERAL REMISSIONS

Disorder was a major feature of the first year of James' personal rule. The campaign against the Douglases was the principal concern for the king, but there were distractions elsewhere for the magnates on his secret council, with the rebellion by the clan Chattan in the north-east, the Stewart attacks on the Isle of Arran, and the ongoing Glencairn-Eglinton feud. These local disturbances do not appear to have been directly connected with the Douglas cause, but probably came to a head as a result of their instigators seizing their opportunities at a time when the Crown's military offensive was directed primarily against the Douglases. With the achievement of the renewal of the Anglo-Scots truce in December 1528, the new régime's concern was to consolidate its position with minimal recriminations.

Only two people are known with any precision to have died as a result of the fighting in the Douglas campaign. These were David Falconer, captain of the footguard, and Henry Borthwick, gunner, both apparently killed by Douglas supporters after the failure of the Tantallon siege. The hangings of David Hope and William Inglis at Tantallon in April 1529 can be seen as a tit-for-tat reprisal. There are no other recorded deaths, save that of Angus' brother, William Douglas, found dead at Coldingham priory. The record of the privy seal register attests to a policy of leniency, with some forty letters of remission granted over the year from December 1528 to December 1529.[1] The recipients were almost without exception men of lairdly, or lesser, status and their servants. Of note was the remission given to the burgh of Dunbar generally on 7 April 1529,[2] suggesting less than wholehearted support for the Crown at the time of the Tantallon siege. The typical phraseology used in the wording of these remissions did not specify the exact nature of the support given by the grantee. Thus, one John Dunlop was granted respite in December 1528 for the crime of:

> tresonable art, parte and assistence gevin be him to Archibald sumtyme erle of Angus, his brother and eme [uncle], and thare complicis in thare tresonable dedis. . . .

Who John Dunlop was, or when his support to Angus was given, is not clear. Possibly he was John Dunlop of Hunthall in Cunningham, Ayrshire, but his connection with Angus, if any, is not apparent.[3] Arguably, his crime was to be involved in the disturbances in the west which served to preoccupy Arran in the summer of 1528. The king was unable to secure a full turnout from the lieges of Ayrshire prior to his entry into Edinburgh to hold parliament in September 1528. It has already been suggested that Hector Macintosh, chief of the clan Chattan, had no direct involvement in the campaign against the Douglases. The remission afforded to him and his servant, Alan Keir, on 4 April 1529, was again for treasonable art and part assistance of the Douglases.[4] Clearly the harm being addressed here was that the rising in the north-east had served to deprive the king of the service of his half-brother, Moray, potentially one of the most eligible candidates for the lieutenancy of the East March.

It is apparent that the crime of art and part assistance could be loosely applied towards malefactors in the first year of the personal rule. This was perhaps the case for William Barclay of Touch (Stirling) who was denounced rebel for his part in the murder of John Vallance of Pitreadie (Fife). Also accused were Robert Clarke in Dysart, Robert Melville, goldsmith, and John Melville. The date of Vallance's death is not recorded in Pitcairn's *Trials*, but the escheat of the goods of his suspected killers was made in May 1529. The following month Clarke and John Melville obtained a nineteen year respite for the 'crewell slauchter', whilst Barclay's respite was for 'tresonable intercommonying [with] and assisting' the Douglases as well as for all other actions.[5] It is possible that Vallance was another, otherwise unrecorded, fatality of the Douglas campaign, but the more likely sequence is that Barclay was outlawed for murder and subsequently became associated with the Douglases. Similarly, the Charteris brothers were engaged in unrelated crimes and were incriminated for being associated with the Douglases only after being driven out of Perth in August 1528.

The privy seal register also indicates that remissions were being granted to individuals from those areas where the estates of the Angus earldom were concentrated. In Berwickshire, John Hume of Blackadder, Alexander Hume of Polwarth, and James Cunningham in Coldingham were all granted remissions in 1529.[6] Power to grant remissions to Douglas supporters had been allowed to Argyll, Bothwell and Lord Hume in the course of their respective campaigns in the Merse and East Lothian. Prior to Angus' eventual departure from the Merse, in May 1529, the policy of remission granting served to undermine his position by removing his support. Hence Alexander Hume's remission, on 11 April 1529, embraced sixteen unnamed others, presumably his servants.

Those who received remissions can also be identified as former tenants of the earl of Angus. William Carmichael of that Ilk held lands in the lordship of Douglas. Upon the forfeiture of his superior in September, these were distributed to the Comptroller, James Colville of Ochiltree, and to Hugh Crawford. However, on 8 March 1529, Carmichael and three of his servants received remissions, again for art and part assistance. Carmichael was restored to his estates and, for his good service, these were erected into the free barony of Carmichael.[7] Thus the supporter of the discredited earl now became a tenant-in-chief of the Crown.

This was a quick transformation, but not otherwise unique. Alexander Hume of Polwarth's son and heir, Patrick, was granted, again for good service, half the lands of Kimmerghame (Berwick) in 1532. These had been held by his father and had fallen to the Crown on Angus' forfeiture.[8] Robert Lauder of the Bass (on 10 October 1528 ordered by the Lords of Council to assist Bothwell) was granted remission with eleven others on 7 April 1529. His estate of Omachie in the regality of Kirriemuir was granted to the king's secretary, Thomas Erskine of Haltoun, but in 1538 Lauder was able to buy the lands back from Erskine and receive confirmation of the transaction under the great seal. In the same year he also recovered the lands of Horschopcleuch in the Lammermuirs, which he had also lost on the forfeiture of Angus.[9] In studying the pattern of redistribution of the earldom of Angus following on from the earl's forfeiture, Kelley has shown that many of the vassals of tenants of the former earl were able to maintain possession of their lands.[10] This group included those who were suspected of supporting him in 1528 and 1529. It is not possible to gauge how active this support was; it may well have been the case that Angus' tenants feared that they would lose their lands entirely through the forfeiture of their superior and that this fear was removed by the generous treatment afforded to Carmichael. Again, remission was for the crime of art and past assistance, suggesting both that Angus' former tenants deemed it prudent to obtain such a letter, and that such letters were readily available, at a price. The *Treasurers Accounts* are not extant for the year 1528–9, but in the following year the record shows that the treasury received or was expecting to receive over £5000 Scots from the sale of remissions at the most recent (1529–30) circuit of justice ayres in Dumfries, Kirkcudbright, Wigtown, Ayr, Renfrew, Roxburgh, Selkirk and Peebles. Over £2000 of this was from the January 1530 ayre at Ayr; £400 was entered as arrears from the Berwick ayre as sums which were not ingathered in time to be entered in the previous year's accounts.[11]

The same factors which prompted Angus' former tenants to obtain remissions may also have moved the various members of the Douglas kindred who were also recipients, amongst them Hugh Douglas in Longniddry and his brother James; William Douglas of Whittinghame (East Lothian) and his servant James;

James Douglas in Hardrig (Douglas); and (in 1530) Thomas Douglas, former cook in the royal Household (removed in the summer of 1528).[12] Amongst Angus' servants, John Bellenden was one of those individuals whose assistance to Angus was blatant and recorded in the parliamentary record for September 1528. As Angus' secretary, he must have been relieved to receive his remission on 26 April 1529.[13]

Around forty letters of remission and respite were granted in the year from December 1528 to December 1529. Seventeen more appeared by 1535. A further three were issued after 1540. In all, one hundred and forty-six people were explicitly pardoned for their support of the Douglases.[14] Only one of these was of higher rank than laird. This was John Hay, third lord Hay of Yester. His remission was obtained on 8 April 1529 together with those of his kinsman, William Hay of Tallo (Berwick) and fourteen other persons. The specified crime was 'treasonable communication, reception, favour, counsel, and assistance given and shown to Angus, George Douglas, and Archibald Douglas and their accomplices in their treasonable actions'.[15] This apparently more heinous crime than mere art and part assistance was, in fact, simply a variation on the theme. Thus the burgh of Dunbar was granted remission on the same terms as were Lord Hay and his servants, whereas Hugh Kennedy of Girvanmains, John Hume of Blackadder and Alexander Drummond of Carnock, all of whom were summoned to answer for their crimes in parliament, were granted remission for art and part assistance. The charge for which Drummond was forfeited was 'art and part of the giving of consale favour and assistance'.[16]

2. THE CASE OF LORD HAY

Lord Hay could be condemned as a Douglas supporter because he had been married to one for at least twenty years. His wife was Elizabeth Douglas, sister of Angus and Sir George Douglas.[17] In fact, the probable cause of his problems lay with his own relatives rather than those of his wife. Lord Hay's career in the minority of James V had been undistinguished. In April 1522 he had served on the Borders under the duke of Albany's administration. His more familiar territory was the tolbooth at Edinburgh; he appeared on the sederunt list of the Lords of Council in every year from 1513 onwards, a record suggesting a complete lack of political bias.[18] His family were the hereditary sheriffs of Peeblesshire, and the third lord had held office since 1518, faithfully and regularly returning the annual accounts to the exchequer.[19]

Lord Hay appeared on the session partly to pursue his own suits. In April 1526 his grandmother, Elizabeth Cunningham, Lady Belton, appointed him as factor over her estates. Lady Belton possessed the lands and castle of Belton as her widow's terce, and held these lands of her grandson. In return for managing the lands and their profits, Lord Hay agreed to provide her basic maintenance and allow her to remain in possession of her house. The arrangement broke down, and in December 1527 Lady Belton obtained a decree from the Lords of Council ordering her grandson and his brother, John Hay, to deliver her estate to her new factor. This was her son, and Lord Hay's uncle, George Hay of Menzion (Peebles). This letter was produced before the session by Lord Hay on 24 July 1528; he asserted that the arrangement between his grandmother and himself had been freely entered into by both parties and that she was under no form of coercion from himself. He then proposed that his grandmother was in fact illegally occupying Belton castle. On 19 August an investigation into the matter was ordered by the Lords of Council.[20] This appeared to find in Lady Belton's favour, for on 10 October an offer was tendered to the Lords of Council on Lord Hay's behalf, whereby he would allow his grandmother to keep the castle in return for his continuing to factor the lands. He also offered her compensation.[21] This did not work, and in December 1528 Lord Hay protested to the Lords of Council that his grandmother continued to withhold the profits of the estate from himself. Hay of Menzion then lodged a counter-claim to the effect that Lord Hay had been in wrongful possession of the profits of the lands from 1527 onwards. The dispute over which branch of the family was entitled to the profits of Lady Belton's estate dragged on into 1531, by which time she was dead and Lord Hay was arguing that his uncle had taken forcible entry of Belton castle in 1527.[22] But Lord Hay had already lost the financial battle. In August 1529 an inquest found in favour of Hay of Menzion and ruled that £3,345 be paid to him by his nephew, being the new balance due after setting off the appropriations made by each on the other's lands. The profits from Lord Hay's own estates, as well as those from Belton, were assigned to his uncle to meet the debt, together with nearly five hundred sheep and cows valued at £200. In 1531 the lord was forced to sell land in order to meet the payment.[23]

Thus Lord Hay lost his suit against his uncle, with the judicial process going against him and putting him under some financial duress. However this was not a political matter, and in no sense was he being 'punished' for his Douglas connection. Elsewhere in the judicial records there can be found rulings being made without any reference to political circumstances, for example in the dispute between Lord Somerville and his kinsman, John Somerville of Cambusnethan; the former was a signatory of the 'grete aith' on 6 November 1528, whilst the latter had been forfeited in 1530 for art and part assistance of the earl of Angus.[24] Cambusnethan sought exemption from Somerville's barony court jurisdiction in Carnwath. The Lords of Council found in his favour in November 1528 and again in 1533.[25] This example of judicial impartiality towards a man with Douglas connections was not an isolated one. In his detailed examination of the fortunes of the Douglas kindred, Kelley has shown that several, including Isobel (also called Janet) Hoppringle, first wife and then widow of Archibald Douglas of Kilspindie, were able to pursue court cases successfully before the Lords of Council.[26] This is an indication that, lacking political direction, the lords dealt with business on a purely legal footing.

However, there were political considerations in another dispute in which Lord Hay became embroiled in the early years of the personal rule. This concerned his tenure as sheriff of Peebles. In November 1528 the king had ordered the Lords of Council to release Malcolm, third lord Fleming, from his attendance at the session in order that he might:

pas hame and put ordour in the cuntre . . . harmyt and distroyit be thevis and tratouris throw his absence. . . .

The lords complied with this order. Two months later Lord Hay protested that Fleming had procured a private commission of justice, and armed with this,

tharwith takis and justifiis in Bigar and uthir partis quhar he pleisis ony persouns within the . . . scherefdome that he lufis nocht. . . .

With Fleming's consent the commission was suspended, and the two lords were appointed joint deputy justiciars under the earl of Argyll.[27] Fleming's consent makes it clear that he was acting with royal approval; the royal order of November to the Lords of Council indicates that Fleming's commission was 'private' only in the sense that it had come direct from the king without consultation with the council; as the newly appointed lord chamberlain[28], Fleming was close to the centre of government.

Lord Fleming – who was married to the king's illegitimate sister, Janet Stewart – was at feud with the Tweedies of Drumelzier, who had killed his father in 1524 and who were linked by marriage to the Angus Douglases.[29] He had already succeeded in having them excluded from any remission which, in October 1528, Lord Hume was authorised to grant to Douglas supporters in the Merse and Teviotdale. He then obtained a decree ordering the Tweedies to desist from visiting slaughter and destruction upon his tenants.[30] On 7 April 1529, John Tweedie of Drumelzier and several members of his family undertook to appear at the next justice ayre in Peebles. Lord Hay undertook to act as guarantor for their appearance. Again Lord Fleming's consent was required for this step, as outlaws were not technically entitled to offer such guarantees. The differences between the Tweedies and Lord Fleming were eventually resolved by arbitration, with final agreement being reached in March 1531, to the effect that the Tweedies agreed to endow the appointment of a chaplain at Biggar to say prayers for the soul of the long-deceased second Lord Fleming, and also agreed for some of their kin to go into voluntary exile. Fleming agreed to appear arm-in-arm with John Tweedie and his son before the king and the session to demonstrate their new-found accord.[31]

Fleming was possibly embarrassed by this showy display of affection for his former enemies, but if so he found consolation in his appointment as sheriff of Peebles on 1 December 1530.[32] Lord Hay had already probably been less than diligent in his pursuit of the Tweedies – he had a tenuous family connection with them through the Stewarts of Traquair[33] – and in the summer of 1530 he again lapsed in his duties. In May of that year he was ordered to convene the landowners of Peeblesshire in readiness for the royal border expedition against thieves.[34] But in August he was in ward in Linlithgow palace, vicariously liable for his brother's negligence. John Hay had been entrusted by the king with the custody of two thieves, Adam Nixon and Robert Elliot, but had allowed them to escape. Lord Hay received a royal pardon the following month, but at the same time was relieved of his duties as sheriff.[35] If this judgement seems a little harsh, it was understandable in the context of the elaborate preparations being made in the summer of 1530 for the royal raid. Lord Hay thought it unjust, and lodged an appeal in 1531 against the decision. The suit continued until July 1534, when arbitrators were appointed from amongst the Lords of Council. Hay argued that he was not culpable for the incident leading to his dismissal, which in turn had led to his incarceration in Linlithgow:

> where I susteinit gret truble in my person and gat seikness and malady quhilk I will never recover.

Fleming argued that the dismissal had been carried out legally, and in any case would serve as an example for all negligent sheriffs.[36] No decision was taken. In March 1535 Hay again pleaded his cause, and this prompted a royal direction to the Lords of Council to make a decision. In 1536 a royal warrant was prepared, directing that Hay should be reappointed by letter under the privy seal, but there is no entry in the register confirming issue of such a letter. Rather, on 11 March, the king instructed his advocate, Adam Otterburn, to have proceedings suspended, in order that Otterburn might deal with diplomatic matters. The case was not taken up again. Fleming retained office and accompanied the king on his visit to France in September 1536. Lord Hay's hopes of regaining office were probably finally dashed by the anti-Douglas backlash after the king's return in 1537. On 21 February 1540 Fleming received a letter under the privy seal confirming his appointment. However this was to endure only for his life; the earlier appointment of 1 December 1530 was a hereditary one. Clearly, Hay's protests had made some impact. Early in 1543 the Lords of Council restored the office to Hay, ruling that he should not have been held responsible for the negligence of his brother thirteen years earlier.[37]

Finding a sheriff vicariously liable for the negligence and conduct of his deputies was a legal principle laid down by act of parliament in 1469.[38] In June 1529, John, fifth Lord Lindsay of Byres, had lost his position as sheriff of Fife to the fourth earl of Rothes, despite a provision by the Lords of Council that Lindsay and his brother should have an opportunity to reduce the ruling for misconduct made against them.[39] In 1538, James contemplated reappointing Lindsay, drawing up a letter of instruction for the chancery office to this effect. However James was a man who liked to hedge his bets. The letter came endorsed with a memorandum to his secretary:

Secretar – we charge you incontinent signet the letter maid on this signatour with the signet ye kep your self and kep this signatour that na persoun get knawlege tharof quhil we think tym it be diwlgat.

The letter was never divulged to the Chancery. Instead, in 1540 Rothes and his heirs were confirmed in the office by charter under the great seal.[40]

That the office of sheriff was not to be regarded purely as an inviolate hereditary privilege for the incumbent magnate was illustrated in a privy seal letter of 1 March 1536 to Patrick, third lord Gray and sheriff of Forfar. The Lords of Council had found Gray vicariously liable for the misconduct of his deputies in the office, and accordingly had ruled that he should be warded for this in accordance with the law. However, on this occasion the king declared himself to be 'perfitlie informit' that no misconduct had occurred and accordingly over-ruled the decree, restoring the lord 'to his honour, dignite and fame'.[41] Gray's position was no different from that of Lindsay and Hay. In Lindsay's case the Lords of Council were prepared to allow him to prove his innocence, but were pre-empted by Rothes' appointment. In Hay's case the law applied strictly and the king simply lost interest in Hay's supplications. By the time Gray's case came up, it appeared that the king was not willing to allow appeals against dismissal. Accordingly, the lords were caught wrong-footed by the royal reinstatement of Gray. Clearly, the choice of sheriff was a political matter, whatever the act said. Just to underline the principle that the office was his to bestow, when Gray died in 1541 James appointed John Stewart, fourth lord Innermeath, as sheriff of Forfar for a year or longer at the king's will. Innermeath's appointment did last only one year, and the office was granted in 1542, together with Lord Gray's estates, to Patrick Gray of Buttergask.[42]

Lord Hay stands out as being the only magnate to receive a remission for the crime of assisting the Douglases. His career during James V's majority was not successful; he lost out financially to his kinsman, Hay of Menzion, and was displaced as sheriff for the lifetime of Lord Fleming, a man closely identified with James' government. He suffered more from neglect than persecution, the king in 1536 losing interest in his suit to recover his office as sheriff. It is apparent that he was pardoned on 8 April 1529 principally for his perceived incompetence in this office; significantly his remission was granted the day after he acted as guarantor for the Tweedies. He was by no means a committed Angus supporter and indeed was identified by Lord Dacre's servant as being one of the lords who accompanied the king in the move from Stirling to Edinburgh in July 1528. His marriage to Angus' sister was not the factor hampering his career.

Hay continued to haunt the courts; in 1542 he was pursuing the second earl of Arran for the earl's destruction in June 1541 of eighty yards of a boundary dyke erected along the south side of the Calder water in Ayrshire. Its destruction had been accomplished by eighty of Arran's men armed with spades and axes 'under silence of night'. The case was continued.[43]

Appearances at court in the latter part of the reign were made by others with Douglas connections. In December 1542 decree was made in favour of William Douglas of Whittingham over a croft dispute on the west side of Haddington; his possession of the house and land was unsuccessfully challenged by the son of Patrick Hepburn of Bolton. In June 1541 Patrick Hume, son of the pardoned Alexander Hume of Polwarth, brought a case on his wife's behalf against the sheriff-depute of Berwickshire. Amongst those related by marriage to the Angus Douglases, Angus' aunt, Isobel Hoppringle, was pursuing with success a case over land ownership, in May 1542, against George Hume of Wedderburn.[44] Amongst the former Angus tenants, John Carmichael of that Ilk, heir to the deceased William, and his tutors were ordered in July 1540 to produce before the session their charter to their lands in the lordship of Douglas. These were reduced in court, as being granted during the king's léssage in 1529. However, the following month Carmichael was regranted these lands as a free barony.[45]

Amongst those others who received remissions were Angus' tenants, his servants, and those of the surname Douglas who were lairds in East Lothian, the battleground for much of the Douglas campaign. These men had little in the way of an identifiable affinity with magnates other than Angus.[46] The only man who appears to have given his bond of manrent to another lord was Hector Macintosh, to Argyll in 1527.[47] The clan Chattan revolt had little, if any, connection with the Douglas campaign; in any case Argyll was a leading magnate of the new régime.

3. THE CRAWFORD CASE

On 24 June 1529, David Lindsay of Edzell received a remission for his treasonable assistance to the Douglases at Edinburgh . Edzell received a further remission in 1543 for his absence from the king's host at Tantallon in October 1528.[48] Edzell held the lands and barony of Dalbog of David, eighth earl of Crawford, who had been served heir to the earldom in 1517, on the decease of his father, the seventh earl, Alexander.[49] Alexander in turn inherited from the sixth earl, John, who was killed at Flodden. The succession was unusual in that Alexander was the uncle of John, and the eighth earl was consequently first cousin to the sixth earl. John had no male heirs.[50] In 1528 the liferent of the earldom was held by David, with his son, Alexander, Master of Crawford, his designated heir from September 1527.[51]

Crawford does not appear to have had a close Douglas connection; indeed in 1526 he had been summoned for treason by the Angus government for his suspected involvement in the Lennox revolt.[52] The charge was abandoned, and no further steps were taken against Crawford, who was to be found at the session in the last days of the Angus government in May 1528. Under the new régime, he did not appear in the September parliament, but he was on the session immediately after its close.[53] Crawford held of Angus the lands of Ethiebeaton in the regality of Kirriemuir, and a request was made in the September parlia-

ment that his interest should be protected despite Angus' forfeiture. This plea
was ignored, and the lands were granted to Sir John Stirling of Keir on 5
September 1528.[54] Crawford had sold the west half of Ethiebeaton to William
Carmichael of Carpow in 1525, retaining his interest as mid-superior. This sale
was confirmed by the king under great seal charter on 25 July 1528 at Glasgow,
and again in April 1529 when Carmichael received a letter under the privy seal
confirming his entitlement and discharging the gift of the lands made to Stirling
of Keir. Possession of the lands by the Carmichaels was confirmed again in 1541.[55]
However, Keir still retained his interest as superior, which he resigned to the
king in 1532. The superiority of Ethiebeaton was then granted to the royal
secretary, Sir Thomas Erskine of Brechin.[56] The Crawford interest as superior
disappeared after 1532 with the resignation by Keir to the Crown. Technically,
Keir was holding Ethiebeaton from Crawford, and Crawford was the tenant-in-
chief. However all reference to Ethiebeaton as a possession of the earldom had
disappeared by 1541.[57]

The Master of Crawford has been dubbed 'the Wicked Master'.[58] He had
caused his father problems in 1526 and 1527, primarily through his sponsorship of
one David Douglas, who appears as a witness to the Master's charters in 1527 and
1530, as does one Patrick Campbell.[59] At the justiciary court of Dundee on 16
February, held by the depute justiciar, Sir John Campbell of Lundy, the Master,
David Douglas, Patrick Campbell and others were charged with convening the
king's lieges and oppressing the estates of the earldom of Crawford. In May 1533,
Crawford brought a successful action for damages against David Douglas. The
earl claimed that in July 1527 Douglas had attacked and burnt down the gates of
his castle of Dalbog, causing £100 worth of damage; furthermore he had
kidnapped the earl and held him against his will for twelve weeks in his own
castle of Finavon. Crawford also sought compensation of £150 for rents lost
through Douglas attacking the barony of Glenesk for three years in succession,
from 1528 to 1530. However there was no attempt made by the earl to sue his own
son.[60] David Douglas, who had earlier been warded in Dunbar castle, was
released in July 1531 on condition that he remained west of the river Tay and made
no attempt to communicate with either the earl of Crawford or the Master. The
editor of Stair has made the suggestion that Douglas was the son of Sir George
Douglas of Pittendreich, but there is no evidence to confirm this, nor as to the
outcome of Crawford's action against him.[61] The Master himself was initially
favoured in the personal reign. On 10 July 1530 he was given a gift of the entire
goods of one John Robertson, alias 'Baron Red', whose estate was escheated for
his failure to attend the Scots host during the royal Borders expedition of that
summer.[62] The degree of disharmony between the earl and the Master made it
possible for the Crown to put pressure on both.

On the day before the charge brought against the Master at Dundee, Crawford
himself was arraigned for a whole series of criminal incidents, commencing with
art and part rape and oppression of Margaret, dowager countess of Montrose and

widow of the fifth earl of Crawford, whilst the good lady was on her way home to her house in Dundee.[63] When these incidents were supposed to have occurred is not recorded, but the criminal process against the earl was simply a precursor to the civil action brought against him the following year. Robert Barton of Barnton had held his lands of the earls of Crawford since 1511, but had failed to enjoy undisputed possession, and hence to collect his rents. His action for payment against the eighth earl was first raised in 1527, and Barton obtained authority to collect his debt in December of that year, by which time the earldom was technically held in fee by the Master, with the liferent alone reserved to the earl.[64] Barton thus raised an action against the Master as well. In December 1528 he obtained decree from the Lords of Council allowing the apprisal of Crawford's lands, notwithstanding the 'pretended infeftment' made by the earl to the Master of the earldom on 2 September 1527. On 16 March 1529 Barton received a royal charter assigning to him the lands of Kirkbuddo in lieu of the sum of £646 deemed to be due to him by way of uncollected rents over the years.[65] By this time Barton had newly been appointed as both Comptroller and Treasurer, and it is possible that he instigated the investigation that followed into the earldom of Crawford, following on from what was disclosed by the valuation of the lands of Kirkbuddo.

An action was brought by the Crown on behalf of Janet Gordon, widow of the deceased John, sixth earl of Crawford. The Crown's interest apparently lay in its concern that its tenants were being oppressed by the eighth earl. The king was thus interfering as the feudal over-superior. In January 1531, the Lords of Council found that the profits from Janet's terce of the earldom of Crawford were owed to her by the earl and Master from the time of her husband's death.[66] This was followed in February by an action for payment brought against the eighth earl by John Lindsay, illegitimate son of the sixth earl. The Lords of Council found that the eighth earl had intromitted with the profits of the lands in the barony of Downie granted to John.[67] A case was then brought by William Bonar of Ross, requesting that the eighth earl release goods which he claimed were due to him through his holding of lands of the earldom in Perthshire.[68] Rather than making a decision on the merits of Bonar's case, the Lords of Council required the earl to enter into ward, and a decree arbitral was pronounced on 16 July 1531 interdicting the Master from alienating the lands of the earldom.[69] A full investigation then began into the manner of the eighth earl's possession of the earldom.

In December 1531 the earl of Northumberland wrote to Henry VIII that Crawford was reputedly being dispossessed by James V.[70] This turned out to be correct. In May 1532, armed with possession of the rental books of the earldom of Crawford,[71] the Crown brought its case against the eighth earl and the Master. The Lords of Council held that the entire earldom fell to the Crown by reason of nonentry since the decease of the sixth earl at Flodden. The seventh earl had not been correctly served as heir, and thus the eighth earl was not infeft.[72] The effect was that all profits from the lands of the earldom since 1513 – more than £15,000 Scots – were due to the Crown.[73] The lords also ruled that this burden should fall on the earl and the Master alone, ordaining that they should re-enter all tenants and vassals holding charters of lands in the earldom 'freely as they held of before with certification to them'.[74] This ruled out the possibility of a redistribution of the lands of the earldom; primarily the intention of the Crown was to extort money from the eighth earl, rather than to dispossess his tenants. However, £2700 was raised in 1532–33 by way of composition paid for the gift of non-entries by the Crown to former tenants of the earldom.[75] Patrick, third lord Gray, paid £274 for the lands and forest of Alicht; Lord Ogilvy of Airlie paid £133 for his lands in the barony of Alicht; David Lindsay of Edzell was required to find £400 of the non-entry of the lands of Edzell. These gifts were made 'ay and qhuill the lauchfull entre of the richtuis are'.[76]

Crawford managed to reach an agreement whereby the non-entry of the earldom would be purchased from the Crown, on payment of £1000. In 1533 he paid £867, and he succeeded in finding the remaining amount by February 1536, when he obtained a letter of non-entry to the estate.[77] However he also had to find the arrears of non-entries for the greater part of his tenants. Accordingly much of the estate was mortgaged; the barony of Downie was valued at over £3500 and assigned in 1533 to the king's secretary, Sir Thomas Erskine of Brechin.[78] Crawford's inability to obtain legal repossession possibly accounted for his attempt to sue David Douglas. This financial crisis for the earl was such that, at the height of the confrontation between England and Scotland in September 1532, Northumberland wrote to Henry VIII suggesting that Crawford was a suitable target for possible subversion.[79] The sheriff of Forfar – Lord Gray – was also put under financial pressure, being required in 1535 to enter in the charge column on his balance sheet the sum of £16,325, and managing to discharge just £800, carrying forward as arrears almost the entire amount. In comparison his counterpart in Kincardine (the Earl Marischal) had a total charge of just £141 in the same year.[80] It was unsurprising both that Lord Gray should come under censure from the Lords of Council for misconduct and be reprieved by the king in 1536.

Crawford had managed to retrieve the situation by 1536. The Master, however, was left out on a limb. Interdicted from alienating the estate, he could only stand on the sidelines whilst Crawford set about restoring the family's possessions. The Master's exact legal status was at first unclear. On 20 May 1532 he contracted with Lindsay of Edzell to renounce lands to Edzell in the event of his being 'restorit to ye said erledome and obteinit heritable infeftment thereon'.[81] This suggests that the non-entry had reduced his fee, and that his father was left with the duty of restoring it prior to their both carrying out the order of the Lords of Council to re-infeft their tenants and vassals. The interdict was thus a safeguard to prevent the Master from dissipating the estate beyond recovery. In December 1535 the Master appeared before the Lords of Council to request lifting of the interdict against him in respect of a payment of £80 owed to one Thomas Cullos, and this was allowed by the lords. The Master was in a position to fulfil his contract with Edzell by 26 May 1535, suggesting another lifting of the interdict.[82] In 1533 his accomplice, Patrick Campbell, was freed from ward at Dumbarton castle, on the condition that he would not join with the Master, and with security of 300 marks.[83] This suggests that the Master was at that point an outlaw, either for his criminal activities against his father or for protesting too strongly against the summons of error, or for both. He was rehabilitated by 1535, as shown by his charter to Edzell, and also by a letter to him from the king on the subject of rents held by the Friars Preachers of Montrose which began 'welbelovit friend, we greitt you weil . . .'.[84] There was perhaps a touch of irony in this greeting, for in March 1537 the Master was required to renounce all rights that he held to the earldom.[85] It is not clear why he was required to do this, but undoubtedly the renunciation was connected with the earlier interdict of 1531.

The beneficiary of this legal emasculation of the Crawford earldom was the Crown. The story picked up by the earl of Northumberland from Bothwell in December 1531 was that Crawford lost his lands to William Wood of Bonnington; his brother, David Wood of Craig; and Henry Kempt of Thomastown.[86] Bonnington held the position of gentleman of the inner chamber in the royal Household, whilst his brother was master of the larder, and later became Comptroller. Kempt was described as 'special familiar' of the chamber in 1529.[87] In fact, only the first named of these three men benefitted. The royal confirmation of the grant from the Master to Bonnington was followed in August 1531 by a further confirmation of a grant by the earl to lands in Finavon and by the royal gift of the barony of Kinblathmont, and then, on Christmas Eve 1532, Bonnington received confirmation of his purchase of lands in the barony of Fern.[88]

The other royal servant who gained was the royal secretary, Sir Thomas Erskine of Brechin. His acquisition of the Downie barony followed on from his purchase from Robert Barton of the lands of Kirkbuddo, valued at £662. Sir William Scott of Balwearie also picked up seven marks' worth of annual rents from the barony of Strathmiglo.[89] However, the report which Northumberland received in December 1531 reflected a trend occurring elsewhere in Forfar. Whilst Kempt had not gained from the discomfiture of Crawford, on the day of Angus' forfeiture he had received the lands of Torburnes and Glaswell in the regality of Kirriemuir. Also on 5 September 1528, William Wood of Bonnington had been granted the lands of Kingennie, Petmowe, Balnagarro, Chapelton and eight acres in Whitefield. David Wood received the remainder of Whitefield and a third brother, Andrew Wood of Largo, obtained the lands of Ballindarg and Drumshed. James Atkinhead, master of the aviary in 1529, received Balmuir.[90] On the following day Bonnington was gifted further lands in the regality and the royal secretary also became a landholder there. In this manner various tenants of Angus were dispossessed, amongst them Lord Forbes, who lost Whitefield, and

Robert Lauder of the Bass, who received remission as a Douglas supporter, and ten years later, bought back the lands of Omachie from Sir Thomas Erskine. Crawford lost Ethiebeaton. In the lordship of Abernethy, another element in the Angus earldom, John Tennant, who was later to become the keeper of the royal purse together with Henry Kempt, was granted the lands of Mylecroft on 15 April 1531.[91] Although Kelley has shown that of the thirty-four new tenants infeft by James V in the estates of the earldom of Angus, only eleven remained so infeft in 1542[92], it is clear that their introduction was intended to reinforce the Crown's presence in Forfar. This was achieved both directly, by the new appointments, and indirectly by confirming the existing tenancies, either immediately or by their reintroduction. These changes were already visible in Abernethy and in Kirriemuir by the time the earldom of Crawford fell into the Crown's possession through non-entry. The technique learned by the Crown in the disposal of the Angus Douglas estates was applied again with the Crawford estate.

The question is whether there was a Douglas connection at work in the treatment afforded to the earldom of Crawford. Of the one hundred and forty-six people granted remission for treasonable art and part assistance to the Douglases, only a handful were identified with areas outwith East Lothian and the Merse. Amongst this handful were the Gray brothers, receiving a remission for their support of the Charteris brothers in the September 1528 burning of Cranston and Cousland.[93] The Charteris brothers came to aid the Douglases after being driven out of Perth. George Wedderburn, brother of James Wedderburn *senior* of Dundee, also received a remission in 1528. The Wedderburn family held lands in the barony of Fern, but directly of the Crown rather than through the mid-superiority of the earls of Crawford. James Wedderburn *junior* received a further charter to lands in Dudhope in 1533, again held direct of the Crown.[94] Robert Lauder of the Bass was a tenant of Angus in Kirriemuir. The only other Forfar landholder was Lindsay of Edzell, holding of the earl of Crawford. Of the fifteen remissions granted for not attending the royal host at the siege of Tantallon, only one was obtained by a Forfar land-holder. This was William Graham of Fintry, who paid sixty-six pounds in January 1530 to be pardoned, and at the same time re-infeft in his lands in the regality of Kirriemuir.[95]

There were other Forfar landholders who held both of the regality of Kirriemuir and of the earldom of Crawford. Sir Henry Lovell of Ballumbie was confirmed in his holdings in the regality on 11 May 1529, and in July 1532 received the gift of the non-entries for his Perthshire lands in the earldom.[96] Both Robert Maule of Panmure and Thomas Fotheringham of Powrie had lost their regality holdings in 1528 to Sir Thomas Erskine and James Atkinhead respectively, which suggests that they were Douglas supporters. But both men had recovered their lands by the time they received gifts of the non-entries to their Crawford holdings.[97] Neither received remissions for either art and part assistance of the Douglases or for being absent from the siege at Tantallon.

Given the paucity of remissions, it is not possible to prove that any individual in either the Angus estate or the Crawford earldom actively supported the Douglases in the first year of the personal rule. However it is worth noting that in May 1529 Lord Gray, as sheriff of Forfar, was ordered to take measures to expel rebels in Forfar, and in October of the same year there were disturbances in Menteith.[98] This disorder paralleled the disruption in the Merse at the same time, and in the case of Forfar occurred in the month of Angus' final withdrawal into England. However, persecuting Douglas supporters was not the prime aim in Forfar. The policy was more subtle. By introducing new tenants and allowing the existing tenants to retain possession despite the difficulties of their superiors, the Crown was undermining the local affinity of these superiors generated by feudal ties. Effectively, the Crown stood in place of both Angus and Crawford in Forfar. The intention was to 'saturate' the county with landholders whose loyalties would be to the Crown rather than to either earl. Should Angus ever be restored to his estates in Forfar – a possibility envisaged in the deal struck between him and Robert Barton in March 1529 – his neighbours would be men whose tenure had come under threat by forfeiture or non-entry of their superior, but had been protected by the Crown.

The troubles faced by Crawford were initiated by the Crown. As early as 1515, the two sisters of the then infeft seventh earl had brought an action against their brother to investigate the findings of the inquest that had served him as heir to the sixth earl. Nothing further happened in this respect until 1532 when, after being summoned before the session, the members of this inquest were found to have erred in ignorance.[99] Thus seventeen years after the first attempt to investigate the service of the seventh earl, the matter was fully exploited by the Crown. James was capitalising on the internal problems of a family that was at feud with itself, both in the field and in the civil court. There is no contemporary suggestion that the dispute between the eighth earl and the Master was in any way connected with support or lack of it given to the Douglases.

What is almost certain is that at least one of them did not support the king at the siege of Tantallon. Their whereabouts in October and November 1528 cannot be traced from the records, but the fact that they were in dispute until 1530 suggests that both would not turn out for the Scottish host. Probably they both stayed away. Unsurprisingly neither man was mentioned as serving on the Borders during the Anglo-Scots war of 1532–33. Moray was then serving as lieutenant, and proclamation was made in January 1533 for the sheriffs of Perth (Lord Ruthven) and Forfar to summon the lieges to convene at Edinburgh. All barons of both counties were also charged to attend.[100] Crawford was in Edinburgh in attendance at the session in September and October 1532 to 'heir the propirtie of the haill erledome of Craufurde reasesit in the Kingis handis for the by-runin nonentres'.[101] English sources reported that, by February 1533, Moray had received reinforcements from Forfar, Perthshire, Strathearn and Fife, and was accompanied by several lairds from north of the Forth. The lords in his company at Teviotdale in February were named as being the earls of Montrose and Rothes; Lords Gray, Ogilvie of Airlie, Ruthven and Drummond. Also present were James Scrimegeour, constable of Dundee; Graham of Fintry; Melville of Raith and Wemyss of that Ilk.[102]Atholl was also summoned to serve in this quarter and had arrived by March. James Stewart, brother of Lord Methven, was already there.[103] Crawford was conspicuous by his absence.

It is possible that the legal attack made on the Crawford earldom was motivated by revenge on the king's part, because the earl had not been at Tantallon. However there was more to it than this; Rothes, another absentee, simply received a remission in 1536, without any such upheaval.[104] Crawford's circumstances were such that he was a 'soft' target; the earldom had been in financial straits since the latter part of James IV's reign, when the sixth earl had sold the sheriffship of Aberdeen to the earl of Erroll.[105] The king was exploiting this situation in 1532 in order to intrude into Forfarshire, to destabilise the earl of Angus' influence there.[106]

The lords on the session who found against Crawford on 7 May 1532 were almost entirely composed of clergy and lawyers. Gavin Dunbar, archbishop of Glasgow and Chancellor, presided. In attendance were Henry Wemyss, bishop of Whithorn; John Hepburn, bishop of Brechin; Patrick Hepburn, prior of St. Andrews; Alexander Milne, abbot of Cambuskenneth; Robert Reid, abbot of Kinloss; John, fourth lord Erskine; George Dundas, lord of St. John of Torphichen; William Stewart, bishop-elect of Aberdeen and Treasurer; James Colville of Ochiltree, Comptroller; James Foulis of Colinton, clerk register; Mr. Richard Bothwell, parson of Ashkirk; Henry White, rector of Finavon; Adam Otterburn of Auldhame, king's advocate; Nicholas Crawford of Oxgangs, justice-clerk; Thomas Scott of Pitgormo; Francis Bothwell, and James Lawson. Many of these men were to become the first senators of the College of Justice. The first appearance put in by any magnate, other than Erskine, was on 10 May when Argyll and Rothes both sat, by which time decree had been issued against their peer.[107] This does not suggest necessarily that the sederunt list on 7 May was 'fixed', but it is indicative of the growing specialisation in the council's functions. The legal expertise of these lesser men was being made full use of by the king. The summons of error had achieved the same result in the civil court as had the earlier forfeiture of the Douglases in parliament for treason.

4. SUMMONS FOR TREASON

There were five individuals summoned for treason in 1528 besides Angus, Sir George Douglas and Archibald Douglas of Kilspindie. Summons was served on Alexander Drummond of Carnock on 20 July 1528. The charges against him contained all the points of treason upon which the Douglases were convicted, save that of assistance to Johnston of that Ilk for the raid on Duncow. There was one further charge specific to him: this was art and part treasonable 'advertising and exponing' of information on James' strength and power at Stirling in June 1528, thus enabling the Douglases to 'decern when it were most gainful to fight with him or desist therefrom'. For these crimes he forfeited his life, lands and goods.[108]

The only connection which the Drummonds had with the Douglases was that Angus' maternal grandfather was John, first Lord Drummond. However, Alexander Drummond of Carnock was not a close relative of the lord. On 1 February 1516, Carnock had received the fee of £200 from the duke of Albany's government for the keeping of Stirling and Tantallon castles. Lord Drummond had been captain of the latter castle immediately prior to his being charged with treason by the Albany government in July 1515. The payment of this sum of £200 six months later to Carnock, suggests that he did not support the lord in opposition to the government of the day. Lord Drummond died in 1517.[109] There is no further trace of Carnock acting as keeper of either castle in later years, for example under the Angus government from 1526 to 1528. As a Stirlingshire landholder, he perhaps was in a position to supply the Douglases in Edinburgh with details of the king's activities in Stirling in the last week of June 1528, and if there was indeed a plot to 'invaid oure soverane lords persoune', then Carnock may have had some useful information on how to achieve this without pre-cipitating a siege of Stirling castle. He presumably had some expertise in supplying and fortifying strongholds, particularly Tantallon, and this was one of the general points of treason on which he and the Douglases were convicted.[110] However, it appears that most of the points in the summons against Carnock were simply copied over from the sheet drawn up for the Douglases. For example, it is unlikely that he played any significant role in holding the king for two years against his will.

The beneficiary of Carnock's forfeiture was Sir John Stirling of Keir, who on 13 December 1528 received a charter to the estates for his good service and in part compensation for his own earlier forfeiture. Keir had been forfeited in 1526 for his support of Lennox, and had already, on 5 September 1528, received grants from the forfeited estates of Angus and Sir George Douglas, with the explanation that these were to compensate him for his financial loss of £4,000 from his own downfall.[111] He had joined the king at Stirling at least as early as 18 June 1528, shortly afterwards replaced Sir James Douglas of Drumlanrig as master of the wine cellar, and was described by Angus as being one of the men responsible for his downfall.[112] In 1526 Sir George Douglas had benefitted from Keir's forfeiture, and thus the grants to Keir of the Douglas lands in September 1528 were in some part a genuine compensation.[113] In 1535 Keir and Carnock were in dispute before the session, with the latter claiming that he had letters of entitlement to the former's lands of Keir, but the Lords of Council ruled that these letters had no effect.[114] It is possible that Carnock's claim dated from 1526, and thus that Stirling of Keir's grant in December 1528 of Carnock's lands was compensation of similar kind to his Crown gift from the estates of Sir George Douglas. Hence Carnock's forfeiture may have been in large part due to antagonism with Stirling of Keir. He was granted a remission in April 1529 and formally restored to his estates in parliament in 1532.[115]

Hugh Kennedy of Girvanmains was summoned for treason in December 1528, and again in January 1529. The charge was of assisting the Douglases in Edinburgh for the last eight days of June 1528.[116] His being singled out in this way may have been due to the favour that Hugh Campbell of Loudoun, sheriff of Ayr, enjoyed under the new régime. Like Stirling of Keir, Campbell was identified by Angus as being one of those responsible for his downfall.[117] On 1 July 1528 Campbell and twenty-five others were granted remissions for the slaughter of Gilbert Kennedy, second earl of Cassillis, in 1527. Campbell's remission was ratified in the September parliament.[118] The Kennedies had retaliated against the assassination of their lord by murdering Robert Campbell in Lochfergus (Kirkcudbright), Alexander Kirkwood, and Patrick Wilson. On 28 July 1528, no fewer than seventy-five members of the Kennedy kindred were summoned to answer for this crime. Kennedy of Girvanmains was not specifically singled out in this summons, but in 1526 he had been granted a respite for his involvement in three other murders.[119] He was near neighbour to Campbell of Loudoun in the lordship of Galloway.[120]

The disturbances created by the Kennedies following Campbell's assassination of Cassillis may have intensified when Campbell was granted a remission; hence the poor turn-out of landholders from the west for the king's host at Stirling in late August 1528. Kennedy was granted a five-year respite in June 1529 for treasonable assistance of the Douglases, on condition that he passed into exile to France within two months after being warned so to do by the king.[121] In fact, this exile was delayed until Campbell received judgement in his favour from the Lords of Council for payment of 300 marks in compensation for damages caused to his lands in February 1528.[122] This judgement was given in March 1531. A licence and letter of safe-conduct had been granted in the previous year for the young third earl of Cassillis to pass overseas under the supervision of his tutor, the abbot of Crossraguel, and in the company of several of the Kennedy kindred, including Girvanmains.[123] The indication is that Girvanmains' real crime in 1528 was his involvement in the problems in the west of the country, rather than his Douglas connection, if any. On 16 December 1528 no fewer than seventy-one lairds from Galloway and Wigtownshire (including Andrew Agnew, sheriff of Wigtown) were declared rebels and outlawed for non-appearance at Stirling, Douglas and Tantallon.[124] Whilst Girvanmains had held the position of gentleman in the royal Household in September 1524,[125] prior to Angus taking power, he had become little more than a problem by 1528. The king was probably perfectly happy to export the troublesome Kennedy kindred in 1530; ward of the Cassillis earldom had passed back to the Crown on Kilspindie's forfeiture.[126]

Patrick Charteris of Cuthilgurdy was also summoned for assistance afforded to the Douglases in June 1528. His principal crime, after pillaging Perth, was to attack Cranston and Cousland in September 1528. Also he was associated with Janet Douglas, Lady Glamis, the fourth person summoned in December 1528.

The final individual to be summoned for treasonable art and part assistance given to the Douglases in June 1528 was John Hume of Blackadder.[127] He was brother of the deceased David Hume of Wedderburn, who had been married to Alison Douglas, sister of Angus. In 1517 Wedderburn had assassinated the duke of Albany's lieutenant, De La Bastie.[128] His kinsman, the fourth Lord Hume, had secured the contract to drive Angus from the Merse in the winter of 1528–29. Part of the deal was that Blackadder's brothers, Alexander, Patrick, Andrew and Bartholomew were obliged in October 1528 to enter into ward at Edinburgh castle, each finding security of £2500. In November this was modified to one of the four remaining in ward:

> apoune his heid that all his four [sic] brethir with their kin . . . Blackatir alanerlie except, that thai suld serve the Lord Hwme. . . .[129]

John Hume of Blackadder apparently remained at liberty, and in September 1529 Lord Hume undertook to expel his troublesome kinsman from the Merse within twenty days.[130] Blackadder's latest crime was art and part convocation of the lieges for an attack on Gilbert Wauchop of Niddrie-Marshall. Ninety-eight lieges assisted Blackadder. This was a local dispute – or 'deadly feud' – between Wauchop and John Edmonston of that Ilk. Wauchop, who had on 10 October 1528 been charged by the Lords of Council to assist Bothwell in the expulsion of Angus, was convicted for his attack on Edmonston. So too was Lord Hay's rival, George Hay of Menzion. This and other disturbances, such as the attack of James Guthrie, captain of Crichton castle, upon Lord Hay's sheep grazings in the same month,[131] led to Lord Hume being appointed as lieutenant of the Merse.[132] Blackadder retreated to Horncliff, in Northumberland. There he prepared a petition to the Lords of Council, offering to go into overseas exile 'endurand the kingis will' and under a penalty of £3,000 for default, in return for his being granted a remission. The petition was allowed, and in October 1529 a respite for nineteen years was granted to Blackadder and sixteen others, with the order that they should depart by Easter 1530. Lord Hume agreed to provide security.[133] However, Blackadder had returned to Scotland by 1532, and his brother Alexander, tutor of Wedderburn, was compelled, under penalty of 1000 marks, to secure his appearance before the king at Falkland palace on 3 December. The intention of the king was apparently to satisfy himself of Blackadder's innocence of the murder of David Falconer, for a remission was issued under the privy seal giving full remission to him and three others for all assistance to the Douglases, as well as for treasonable communication and assistance given to the English, 'our enemies'. This was made conditional upon Blackadder's appearance before James V to prove that he did not kill Falconer.[134] Blackadder passed the test, and in June 1533 was charged with his brother,

Alexander, to assist Lord Hume in his duties as warden of the East March, in keeping order there pending the renewal of the Anglo-Scots truce.[135] However, he was again in ward in 1542, probably because he was a security risk on the East March in times of hostility.

Blackadder's career is illustrative of the ambiguous position in which the Humes found themselves in 1528. Their service in the Douglas campaign was secured by a carrot-and-stick method; the promise of the prize of Coldingham priory for Lord Hume's branch of the family was combined with the coercion of the Wedderburn branch. Alexander Hume of Polwarth was also granted remission as a Douglas supporter in 1529, whilst the goods of one Paul Hume were escheated and granted to a Cuthbert Hume.[136] Both branches of the family had supported Angus in the minority in opposition to the government of the day. The third lord had been executed in 1516 for opposing the duke of Albany, and the fourth lord had given his bond of manrent to Angus in June 1526.[137] As part of his conditions of service Hume requested, in October 1528, a general remission for himself, 'his kyn, frendis and part takaris now dependand on him for all times bigane'. Remissions for supporters of himself and David Hume of Wedderburn in the minority were granted in April 1529[138], but there is no extant remission for the lord himself. His 'de facto' restoration in 1522 had been confirmed in parliament in 1526, but it was not until June 1535 that his legal entitlement was formally acknowledged by the king at 'his perfect age of twenty three', through the technical device of revoking all charters to lands granted out of the forfeited estate of the third lord and regranting these to the fourth lord, at a cost to the latter of £1000.[139] Until 1535 Hume was only 'de facto' forgiven for his activities in the minority.

5. A STATE AKIN TO WAR

Lord Hume's charter was granted a year after the Scots and English signed a peace agreement in London, on 11 May 1534, the Scottish representatives being William Stewart, bishop of Aberdeen, and Adam Otterburn. The peace was to endure for the joint lives of both sovereigns and for one year further.[140] This was as much a watershed for the Douglas cause as had been the earlier treaty of Berwick; for relations between England and Scotland had been beginning to deteriorate by the summer of 1532, partially at least due to Angus' encouragement of the English border officers. After withdrawing from the Merse, Angus took up residence at Newcastle, supported by a pension from the English government.[141] Despite the rejection by James of Magnus' overtures in January 1529, the English government had again attempted to plead Angus' cause. A further ambassadorial visit to Scotland was made by Sir Thomas Clifford in the autumn of 1529; but again the request for Angus' reinstatement was rejected, both James and the Chancellor, Gavin Dunbar, writing to this effect direct to Henry VIII.[142] Nevertheless, Angus' proximity to the Merse served to stimulate disruption there until November 1531, when he moved down to London.[143] Blackadder's brother, Alexander, tutor of Wedderburn, was induced to serve under Lord Hume's lieutenancy only under threat of a penalty of £2000 and ward in Edinburgh castle for non-compliance.[144] His sister-in-law – and Angus' sister – Alison Douglas, Lady Wedderburn, was ordered to leave the family home of Wedderburn in January 1531 and to remain in Edinburgh with her eldest son 'for divers causis of suspicioune'. In February 1532, she was granted licence to return home to attend to the needs of her younger 'barnis', under penalty of £1000 should she fail to return by 8 April.[145] Hume of Wedderburn was given charge of the family home during her ward.[146]

The lack of any clearly defined loyalties amongst the Merse landholders in the period after Angus' withdrawal from Scotland was demonstrated by others as well as the Humes of Wedderburn. David Renton of Billie was obliged in November 1529 to offer security for Blackadder's good faith; he himself had been warded a year earlier for failing to serve under Lord Hume against the Douglases, and he was warded again in 1530. Patrick Lumsden of Blanerne (in the Angus barony of Preston and Bunkle) also acted as security for Blackadder, and was also warded in Blackness castle in 1530.[147] Alexander Hume of Polwarth had been granted remission in April 1529 for art and part assistance but was also warded in 1530, together with John Hume of Coldenknowes. Polwarth was again required to enter into ward in January 1531, with George Hume of Ayton, Alexander Hume, tutor of Wedderburn, and Gilbert Wauchop of Niddrie-Marshall, all protesting in the king's presence that they should not be 'cautioun nor souritie for his remanying, but him self suld ansuer'.[148] George Nisbet of Dalzell (Lanark) had been fined on 26 September 1528 for failure to underlie the law for his part in attempting to relieve the siege of Newark castle. He was given a nineteen-year respite on 2 August 1529 for art and part assistance of the Douglases.[149] His kinsman, Adam Nisbet of that Ilk, was outlawed in April 1529 together with son, Philip, for art and part assistance. In November 1529, Philip acted as security for Blackadder.[150] One John Nisbet was with Blackadder at Horncliff in October 1529, as was William Reidpath, another man who had attempted to relieve Newark castle.[151] Further west, James Douglas of Drumlanrig – married to Angus' sister, Margaret – was warded in Edinburgh castle in July 1529, under penalty of £1000, and again at Inchgarvie (Fife) in May 1530. However, in August 1530 he received two gifts from the king by letters under the privy seal, one of the escheated goods of two outlaws in Craigdarroch and Castlefern (Dumfries) and the other of a ward in Kirkcudbright.[152] William Stewart of Traquair – who was married to Lord Hay's daughter and Angus' niece – had been granted a remission on 28 December 1528. Four years later his mother, Janet Rutherford, Lady Traquair, was denounced as a rebel for treasonable assistance to the Douglases and for:

> resetting, supplying, and Intercommuning with them, and daily conversing with them, within the kingdom of England, and secretly in Scotland.[153]

[118]

Whilst attempts were being made by James' government to secure the loyalty of the men (and latterly the women) of East Lothian and the Merse through a mixture of wardings, remissions, outlawings and pledges, the dialogue between Henry VIII and his nephew over the subject of Angus continued into 1531. Through his envoy, Thomas Scott of Pitgormo, James argued that Angus was the main cause of disturbances and that his removal was necessary, as:

> to have hym resident nere to the Borders . . . he myght more facilly make poursute to the said King of Scottes.[154]

Although Angus went to London in November 1531, he returned to join the earl of Northumberland at Wark in September 1532, having secured from Henry VIII the promise of an annual pension of £1000 (sterling) in return for his services against the Scots. He informed Northumberland that the Scots king was in fear of his own subjects and unable to raise a large army. Both Teviotdale and Liddesdale could be won over to support the English, and in addition the earls of Argyll, Bothwell and Crawford might be induced to do the same.[155] The reasons for these optimistic predictions were that Crawford was being hounded for non-entry, Bothwell had been warded in 1530, and Archibald Campbell, fourth earl of Argyll, had been forced to surrender his heritable office as chamberlain of Kintyre in 1531.[156] Angus' speculations were based on second-hand information. Writing in London at the same time, Chapuys, imperial ambassador to Henry VIII's court, had a different perspective, drawn from information received by papal envoys recently in Scotland. He predicted to Charles V that James would be able to put an army of twenty thousand men in the field, a force sufficient to divert England's attentions away from the Continent.[157]

The Douglas connection both entangled internal loyalties and threatened to ensnare Scotland and England in a war. In an attempt to cut the Gordian Knot, James appointed a new lieutenant for the East and Middle Marches. The first earl of Arran had died before 31 March 1529. The third earl of Argyll had died by the end of the same year.[158] Both had held this commission. The second earl of Arran was a minor; the fourth earl of Argyll was temporarily under a cloud through loss of office in Argyll.[159] The best available candidate was James' half-brother, James Stewart, earl of Moray. He had been appointed for this role in 1530,[160] and had experience of command as lieutenant in the north in campaigns against the clan Chattan and in Caithness.

Moray was appointed in September 1532, the same month in which Angus returned to the Borders.[161] Lord Hume and the Kerr family were appointed as his deputies in the East and Middle Marches respectively.[162] Letters were sent out by the Lords of Council charging the sheriffs of Linlithgow, Perth, Stirling, Kincardine, Edinburgh, Selkirk, Peebles and Lanark to be prepared to summon the lieges and hold weapon-showings. Already in September, the sheriffs of Fife and Forfar had been charged to meet the king at Haddington.[163] Northumberland reported that Moray had been promised three thousand troops, but that the king had been refused a tax to pay for them.[164] In fact the bulk of the army was raised by the traditional method. This was illustrated in two court cases raised in the summer of 1533. In the first, on 23 May 1533, Robert Logan of Restalrig pursued Elizabeth Wardlaw, lady of Riccarton and holder of one third of his grandfather's land by terce, for his expenses of four marks for thirty days' service by himself in the previous month in defence of the Borders against the English. In the a second case, a month later, Alexander Leslie sought payment from Margaret Fraser, again a terce holder, for three periods of thirty days' service, at Tantallon, in a raid on Caithness conducted by Moray in 1530, and on the Borders.[165] These two cases were raised on the strength of a decree by the Lords of Council on 5 May 1533 that landholders should have the right of relief from lands held by terce in their holdings.[166] The only extant tax levied for Moray's tour of duty was on the burghs, who together had to furnish three hundred footmen at ten shillings a day each, commencing on 5 January 1533.[167]

Moray did not move to the Borders until 1533. The latter part of 1532 was taken up by cross-border raids. In August, Northumberland gave details to Henry VIII of three Scots raids into English territory. The first was by sixty Armstrongs of Liddesdale. Two were captured and held in the hope that they could somehow be utilised in bringing Liddesdale to the English side. The second raid was by Andrew Kerr, son of the deputy-warden of the Middle March, Mark Kerr of Dolphinton, who led seven hundred men in an attack on Felkington. Three English were killed. The third raid was an attack on Tynedale by an assortment of Kerrs, Rutherfords and Davidsons. The English claimed one hundred and twenty Scottish casualties and twelve prisoners taken for hanging.[168] On 10 October, Lancelot Kerr raided into Northumberland and burned Alnham and Newstead, capturing two hundred cattle and twenty prisoners and killing two people.[169] In diplomatic exchanges, the Scots claimed for their part that Lord Dacre and Northumberland had attacked Scott of Buccleuch's house of Branxholm.[170] James complained that his uncle was deliberately allowing Angus to remain on the Borders as a source of antagonism. Henry replied that by the treaty of Berwick, Angus had been allowed reset in England until a reconciliation between him and James could be achieved. Henry would be more willing to remove Angus were James to show more signs of attempting to meet the truce conditions and give redress.[171] Accordingly James ordered the Kerr family, as deputy wardens of the Middle March, to detain their kinsman, Lancelot, and charged him with treasonably assisting the Douglases.[172] This bizarre accusation reflected how James wanted these disturbances to be interpreted; Scotland and England were not at war, rather the problems created by Scots raids could be traced to the Douglas connection. James also wrote to Henry to assure him that he was willing to give redress, and that indeed he had sent his Comptroller and Thomas Scott of Pitgormo to meet with the English border officers at Kelso in October for this purpose. However, the English had refused a meeting.[173]

The attempt to blame the Douglases for the raids was not convincing, for on 20 November 1532, Northumberland reported a further Scots raid at which the banners of all three Kerr deputy-wardens and Scott of Buccleuch were identified by his garrison. Northumberland informed Henry VIII that notice should be taken of this, for the Scots king had proclaimed the previous week that all offenders save the Douglases were pardoned.[174] However it was not until 16 December that James issued a full summons of the Scots host 'for resisting of our saidis auld enemyis'.[175] This was in direct response to the English raid of 11 December on East Lothian and the Merse, a raid conducted by Northumberland with the assistance of Sir George Douglas and Douglas of Kilspindie. Northumberland reported successful attacks on no less than fifteen settlements, from Oldhamstocks down the coast to Ayton. Two thousand cattle and four thousand sheep were taken, as well as many prisoners and 'all the insight, coyn, imployments of houshold, estemed to a great somme'.[176] This raid, employing at least eleven hundred Englishmen as well as the Douglas retinue, was greater in scale than the earlier Scots raids. It was followed by the capture by Northumberland of Cawmills, just before Christmas.[177]

William Douglas, abbot of Holyrood in 1528, had been ordered by the Lords of Council to cease from fortifying Cawmills (Edrington) castle. The place had then been placed under the charge of Robert Lauder of the Bass. In February 1532 Alexander Hume, tutor of Wedderburn, was ordered to hold the place.[178] Perhaps it was indicative of the inability of James to ensure full control of the Merse that these two dubious characters should have been entrusted with its safe-keeping, and that apparently no attempt was made to meet Wedderburn's request to the Lords of Council in October 1532 for extra support in its upkeep:

> for and it owthir left waist or tane be Englishmen, it may be verray prejudiciale to the realme and half the est part of the Mers waist.[179]

The English at first did not know whether to repair Cawmills or cast it down, but eventually turned it over to Sir George Douglas.[180] The Scots demanded its return in July 1533. In September 1533 Francis I wrote to Henry VIII urging him not to allow peace to be held up over the issue of its return, and by the terms of the perpetual peace of May 1534, it was returned.[181]

Moray arrived at Melrose abbey early in January 1533 with two thousand men and distributed his force amongst Melrose, Jedburgh, Kelso and Hume castles. Initially, according to English reports, he was accompanied by James Stewart, brother of Lord Methven, and Sir James Hamilton of Finnart.[182] By February he had been reinforced by the first quarter of the lieges, from Forfar, Fife, Strathearn and Perth, and the Scots army was reckoned at six thousand Borderers and between two and four thousand further from the 'inland'.[183] Again according to English reports, Atholl and Montrose were with Moray until March, when their places were taken by the next quarter, led by Huntly, Argyll and Marischal, commanding one thousand five hundred men from Inverness and the north-east, together with the Islesmen.[184] Moray received £300 each month in expenses, from January to April inclusive, to pay for a permanent footguard of two hundred men, commanded by James Stewart, and stationed at Kelso.[185] His arrival at Melrose was said by Chapuys to amount to a declaration of war.[186] The English border officials watching his manoeuvres were uncertain as to whether he intended to attack or defend.[187] He was rumoured to intend authorising raids, but in fact those that did occur were not credited to him.[188] His rôle was one of deterrence rather than of aggression. In March 1533 Henry VIII ordered his officers to suspend raids as his nephew was reported to be at Melrose abbey. English rumour had it that he was either waiting to hear from Francis I or was on the hunt for Mark Kerr of Dolphinton's concubines.[189]

Neither Henry VIII nor James V appears to have been whole-hearted about the prospect of engaging in conflict. From the English point of view there was the prospect of exploiting the alleged ill relations between the Scots king and his magnates. Northumberland informed Henry VIII that he had spoken to one Scottish informant, at Berwick, who had advised that the Scots king was as much loved in Scotland as any of his ancestors.[190] This cryptic remark from an anonymous source was taken by Northumberland to mean that the Douglas connection could be used to English advantage. However, the predictions of both Northumberland and Angus proved over-optimistic. The deployment by James of his half-brother presented the English with the possibility of war rather than the capitulation of the Scots king and Angus' reinstatement.

For James, the confrontation presented opportunities as well as the threat of a Douglas return. His warlike manoeuvres attracted interest from both the Empire and France. In April 1532 Charles V had invested the Scots king with the Order of the Golden Fleece,[191] and James was in the marriage market, with an Imperial bride being a distinct possibility. Also there remained outstanding the fulfilment of the 1517 Treaty of Rouen.[192] Henry VIII, however, had little wish to see James becoming allied with either France or the Empire.[193] He enjoyed good relations with France in 1532 and 1533. Chapuys, imperial ambassador to London, held lengthy discussions with Adam Otterburn in the course of the latter's visit to London in 1534 to conclude peace. The gist of these talks was that Scotland should abandon both France and England and join with the Empire instead.[194] As Henry had just divorced the emperor's aunt, Catherine of Aragon, the thought of an Imperial-Scottish axis was most unwelcome, and accordingly by 1534 he was prepared to countenance James marrying Madeleine of France, rather than an Imperial bride.[195] Neither did the French king relish an Imperial alliance with Scotland. In February 1532 Francis I had written to James V to lament this prospect;[196] and his envoy, Monsieur de Beauvais, was despatched, first to Henry VIII and then to James, with the brief to persuade them to reconcile their differences. His arrival at Edinburgh in May 1533 played a major part in persuading James to dispatch a peace commission to Newcastle in June.[197]

That James was not wholly on the defensive was illustrated by his movements in 1533. In February he joined his half-brother and his army at Lauder and accompanied them first to Melrose and then Peebles.[198] In March he again visited Moray at Melrose, on this occasion purportedly concerned as much with recreational pursuits as with war.[199] In April he met de Beauvais on the Borders and returned with him to Edinburgh. Moray then issued a proclamation that no further Scots raids should take place, and withdrew from Jedburgh in May.[200] With peace talks underway in Newcastle in June, James next passed to Glasgow, through Ayr and down to St. Ninians. There, he was reported as test-firing three pieces of artillery abandoned by the Duke of Albany in the minority; he was accompanied by lord Fleming, Lord Avandale, and William Stewart, bishop of Aberdeen, and Treasurer in 1533.

From Dumfries, James moved next to Lochmaben and then to Peebles.[201] His intention was to meet with the Welsh refugee, James Griffyd ap Powell, who claimed to be the son of Sir Rhys ap Thomas, until his death the most prominent leader in Wales. Thomas was succeeded by his grandson, Sir Rhys ap Griffyd, who in 1531 was executed by the English government for treason.[202] Powell claimed to be the uncle of ap Griffyd and was implicated in his revolt. After being imprisoned in the Tower of London, Powell was pardoned and granted leave to travel to Ireland to buy horses for Anne Boleyn. Instead of returning to England, as ordered, he arrived with his wife and children at Whithorn in July 1533. He intended to request James' aid for another Welsh revolt against Henry VIII.[203] However, whilst he gave shelter to Powell, James was reported to be more interested in his daughter than in his revolution, although the latter idea incited English rumours about the imminence of an Imperial-sponsored combined Welsh and Scottish invasion.[204] From Scotland Powell passed overseas to the Empire in May 1534, after extracting the sum of £160 from the Scots Treasury.[205] His timing was out; had he arrived in Scotland six months earlier he might well have become a *cause célèbre* of war in the manner of Perkin Warbeck in the reign of James' father.[206] As it was, the perpetual peace was concluded just after Powell left Scotland.

Thus, the tension between Scotland and England in 1532 and the first half of 1533 had, in part, been inspired by the Douglas connection, but James came out of it very well. He had renewed Imperial interest in having Charles V as a potential ally; he had demonstrated to France that he did not regard himself as slavishly tied to her interests under the Treaty of Rouen, and he had won full peace with England. His magnates had not failed him in the crisis, and the Douglas cause was no further forward; indeed the lack of any sign of instability in Scotland in 1533 might well have discredited the Douglases in the eyes of Henry VIII. Therefore it was in a confident frame of mind that James V received Douglas of Kilspindie in Scotland in August 1534.[207] Chapuys wrote that Kilspindie sought to obtain a pardon from James V without the knowledge of Henry VIII.[208] Possibly he hoped to take advantage of the peace treaty made between England and Scotland to seek clemency. James evaded this attempt at reconciliation – if indeed that was Kilspndie's intention – by commanding that Kilspindie should be conveyed overseas by ship. The captain of any ship that was proposed to take him was fully assured that no recriminations should fall upon him for thus aiding a rebel, because Douglas of Kilspindie had '. . . optenit his hienes presens . . .'.[209]

There were repercussions for others. By 8 February 1533 Kilspindie's wife, Isobel Hoppringle, had been 'at the horne' for one year and a day for her assistance of the Douglases. Her lands of over-Menzion (Peebles) were gifted to Lord Fleming on that date. On 2 January 1536 she was regranted her conjunct-fee of the lands of Woodhall and Little Fordall in Ayrshire:

> havand consideratioun, conscience and piete of the grete truble and skaith sustenit be hir in hir said spous defalt, in recompensatioun of ane part tharof.[210]

Another who had gained part of her lands in April 1529 was Sir James Sandilands of Calder. In 1535 the former keeper of Hermitage castle found it needful to obtain a letter of protection on his departure overseas 'for doing of his pilgramage'. In March 1541 he obtained a remission for treasonable communication with the Douglases, and also for supplying Kilspindie with two horses.[211] In April 1542 Andrew Murray of Blackbarony (Peeblesshire) – the man so tardy in 1532 in entering his returns for Ballencrieff – received a remission for his assistance given to Douglas of Kilspindie and to his wife Isobel Hoppringle.[212] Finally, in February 1535, the earl of Cassillis was forced to go to court to obtain a ruling as to who had the right to the avail of his marriage, Sir John Campbell of Cawdor, or Kilspindie's illegitimate daughter, Janet Douglas, each of whom claimed to hold the ward of his marriage.[213]

In the early 1530s, then, the Douglas connection revealed itself in various permutations and affected Angus' tenants, family and neighbours. For some it proved an inconvenience, for others a poisoned chalice, while for James V himself it provided opportunities as well as problems. It can be seen to have influenced James' foreign policy and, internally, his handling of the earl of Crawford. What it had not done in the first half of the personal rule was permanently damage Crown-magnate relations.

NOTES

1. *RSS*, i-ii, *passim*; Emond, *op.cit.*, App. J.
2. *RSS*, ii, no. 33.
3. *Ibid.*, i, no. 4015; *RMS*, ii, no. 1530.
4. *Ibid.*, ii, no. 13.
5. *Ibid.*, ii, nos. 61, 71, 115, 155, 197.
6. *Ibid.*, ii, nos. 39, 209, 378.
7. *Ibid.*, i, no. 4111; *RMS*, iii, nos. 671, 672, 761.
8. *RMS*, iii, no. 1232.

9. *Ibid.*, iii, nos. 1824, 1868; *RSS*, ii, no. 31.
10. Kelley, *Angus* and *Tenure*, *passim*.
11. *TA*, v, 354–5; each individual remission in the Register of the Privy Seal indicates the sum levied for the actual grant of the letter itself (occasionally 'gratis') rather than the sum required for the compositon.
12. *RSS*, i, no. 4088; ii, nos. 30, 195, 593.
13. *Ibid.*, ii, no. 56; that Bellenden was employed over a period as secretary by Angus is suggested in *Boece*, edd. E.C. Batho 38; H.W. Husbands (*STS*, 3rd series, no. 15, 1541), App.
14. Excluding the citizens of Dunbar.
15. *RSS*, ii, nos. 34, 35 (original in Latin).,
16. *Ibid.*, ii, nos. 7, 154, 378; *APS*, iii, 327.
17. *RMS*, ii, no. 3378; *Scots Peerage*, i, 189.
18. *LP Henry VIII*, iii, pt. ii, no. 2186; Emond, *op.cit*, 301, App. F.
19. *ADCP*, 130; *ER*, xv, 84, 195, 283, 374, 452, 529.
20. SRO, Hay of Yester Writs (GD 28), nos. 427, 437, 439; *ADC*, vol. 38, f. 139.
21. Hay of Yester Writs, nos. 441, 442; *ADC*, vol. 38, f. 179.
22. Hay of Yester Writs, nos. 443, 447, 451, 470, 471; *ADC*, vol. 39, f. 149v; vol. 41, f. 89; vol. 42, f. 130.
23. Hay of Yester Writs, nos. 451, 453; *RMS*, iii, nos. 892, 1047.
24. *ADCP*, 290; *APS*, ii, 293; cf. Emond, *op.cit.*, 260–1.
25. *Acta Sessionis* (Stair), case 37; SRO, *ADC*, vol. 38, f. 187.
26. Kelley, *Angus*, 500–514.
27. *ADCP*, 294–5, 302–3.
28. *RMS*, iii, no. 601 (26 June 1528), is the first charter where he is so designed.
29. *LP Henry VIII*, iv, pt. i, no. 762; cf. Emond, *op.cit.*, 426–7. Fleming was married by 1524: *RMS*, iii, nos. 515, 1119.
30. *ADCP* 287; SRO, *ADC*, vol. 42/25.
31. Pitcairn, *Trials*, i, pt. i, 141; *ADCP*, 352.
32. *RSS*, ii, no. 768.
33. *Scots Peerage*, viii, 434–5.
34. *ADCP*, 328–9.
35. SRO, Hay of Yester Writs [GD 28], nos. 462, 465; Pitcairn, *Trials*, i, pt. i, 149.
36. Hay of Yester Writs, nos. 486, 492, 493, 503, 504, 507.
37. *Ibid.*, nos. 514, 516, 530; *ADCP*, 450–1, 525; *RSS*, ii, no. 3392.
38. *APS*, ii, 94.
39. SRO, *ADCS*, ii, f. 110; *ADCP*, 317, 321; *RMS*, iii, no. 798.
40. *RMS*, iii, no. 2227; *Spalding Miscellany*, ii, 189–90.
41. *RSS*, ii, no. 1957. The Lords of Council had ruled that Gray had been in default for three years: *ADCP*, 450 (February, 1536).
42. *RMS*, iii, nos. 2346, 2650.
43. SRO, *ADCS*, xvii, f. 137v; xviii, f. 86; xix, f. 9.
44. SRO, *ADCS*, xv, f. 148v; xix, f. 86; *AD*, i, f. 124v.
45. *Ibid.*, xiii, f. 174; *RMS*, iii, no. 2191.
46. The best exposition of magnatial affinities is given by C.A. Kelham, 'Bases of Magnatial Power in Later Fifteenth Century Scotland' (Ph.D., Edinburgh University, 1986).
47. Wormald, *Bonds*, App. A, 195, no. 78.
48. *RSS*, ii, no. 191; West Register House [WRH], Inventory of Scottish Muniments at Haigh, [NRA (S) 237], i, ff. 49, 51.
49. *Ibid.*, ii, no. 1460; WRH, Haigh Inventory, i, *passim*.
50. *Ibid.*, i, nos. 2866, 2908; *RMS*, iii, no. 1334; WRH, aigh Inventory, i, f. 57, *et passim*; *Scots Peerage*, iii, 23 ff.
51. *RMS*, iii, no. 494; WRH, Haigh Inventory, i, ff. 79–80.

52. *TA*, v, 264, 315–6; cf. Emond, *op.cit.*, 510.
53. SRO, RH 2.1.9. (*ADC*, vol. 38, ff. 105, 107, 162v).
54. *APS*, ii, 329; *RMS*, iii, no. 651.
55. *RMS*, iii, nos. 617, 2388; *RSS*, ii, no. 48.
56. *RMS*, iii, no. 1132.
57. Cf. *ibid.*, iii, no. 2484.
58. Cf. *Scots Peerage*, iii, 25–27; the designation was apparently given by a later family historian; cf. F.D. Bardgett, *Scotland Reformed: the Reformation in Angus and the Mearns* (Edinburgh, 1989), 11.
59. RMS, iii, nos. 543, 1057.
60. WRH, Haigh Inventory, i, f. 81; SRO, *ADCS*, ii, f. 175; *RMS*, iii, no. 1542.
61. *ADCP*, 358; cf. Acta Sessionis (Stair), Case 56 (the editors of the RMS do not make a connection between David and Sir George).
62. *RSS*, ii, no. 704.
63. WRH, Haigh Inventory, i, ff. 74–5; (the fifth earl was created Duke of Montrose by James III: cf. Macdougall, *James III*, 252–3).
64. *RMS*, ii, nos. 3647–8; cf. W. Stanford Reid, *Skipper from Leith* (OUP, 1962), 67, 1322–3, 221.
65. SRO, *ADC*, vol. 39, f. 21; *RMS*, iii, no. 765.
66. *ADC*, vol. 42, f. 13.
67. *Ibid.*, vol. 42, f. 43.
68. *Ibid.*, vol. 42, f. 192.
69. *Ibid.*, vol. 42, ff. 194v-196; *ADCP*, 359.
70. *LP Henry VIII*, v, no. 609; cf. *TA*, vi, 52, 54.
71. *TA*, vi, 57.
72. SRO, *ADC*, vol. 43, ff. 190–193; *ADCS*, i, f. 94
73. *ER*, xvi, 554, 565, 571, 578, 581; xvii, 742.
74. SRO, *ADC*, vol. 43, f. 192; WRH, Haigh Inventory, i, f. 67.
75. *TA*, vi, 10–15.
76. *Ibid.*, vi, 12, 14; *RSS*, ii, nos. 1250, 1299.
77. *TA*, vi, 70–1, 268; *RSS*, ii, no. 1949.
78. *RMS*, iii, no. 1326.
79. *LP Henry VIII*, v, no. 1286.
80. Murray, *Revenues*, 51–3, App. 1.
81. WRH, Haigh Inventory, i, ff. 82–3.
82. *RMS*, iii, no. 1477; SRO, *ADCS*, vii, f. 40.
83. SRO, *ADCS*, ii, f. 129.
84. WRH, Haigh Inventory, i, f. 83.
85. *Ibid.*, i, f. 69.
86. *LP Henry VIII*, v, no. 609.
87. *ER*, xv, 460, 545, *et passim*; xvi, 132, 480 F, *et passim*; xvii, 269.
88. *RMS*, iii, no. 1055–7, 1248.
89. *Ibid.*, iii, nos. 765, 1064, 1326; *RSS*, ii, no. 1435.
90. *RMS*, iii, nos. 662, 668, 702.
91. *Ibid.*, iii, no. 1008; cf. A.L. Murray, 'Account of the Kings Pursemaster, 1539–40', in *SHS Miscellany*, x (1965) [Murray, *Pursemaster*].
92. Kelley, *Tenure*, 88.
93. *RSS*, i, no. 4005.
94. *Ibid.*, i, no. 4011; *RMS*, iii, nos. 539, 1311.
95. *RSS*, ii, no. 505; *RMS*, iii, no. 885; *TA*, v, 387.
96. *RSS*, ii, no. 1335; *RMS*, iii, no. 780.
97. *RSS*, ii, nos. 1227, 1719; *RMS*, iii, nos. 648, 702, 751, 913.
98. *ADCP*, 310, 317.
99. WRH, Haigh Inventory, i, f. 37; SRO, *ADC*, vol. 43, f. 193; *TA*, v, 52.

100. *TA*, vi, 117, 120, 122.
101. *Ibid.*, vi, 105; SRO, RH 2.1.9. (*ADCS*, i, ff. 117, 120).
102. *LP Henry VIII*, vi, no. 163; cf. *ADCP*, 395; also said to be in Teviotdale were the lairds of Bagonye (? Balgonie, Fife, held by Colville of Ochiltree), Coolanre and Loughlylle (? Robert Douglas of Lochleven).
103. *LP Henry VIII*, vi, nos. 143, 217; *TA*, vi, 124.
104. *RSS*, ii, no. 2002.
105. *Ibid.*, i, no. 2203.
106. Cf. Bardgett, *op.cit.*, 10 for a discussion of this interference.
107. SRO, RH 2.1.9. (*ADC*, vo. 43, ff. 190, 193); cf. P.G.B. McNeill, 'Senators of the College of Justice: 1532–69', *J.R.*, 1978, 209–215.
108. *APS*, ii, 327.
109. *TA*, v, 70–1; *ADCP*, 50–1; *ER*, xiv, 243.
110. Cf. Kelley, *Angus*, 404.
111. *RMS*, iii, nos. 635–7, 718; *APS*, ii, 311.
112. Glasgow University, Argyll Transcripts, iii, 210; *ER*, xv, 463; *LP Henry VIII*, iv, pt. ii, nos. 4718–9.
113. *RMS*, iii, nos. 396–7.
114. SRO, *ADCS*, vi, 133v, 139v, 218; there is no royal charter to Carnock confirming this.
115. *APS*, ii, 336; *RSS*, ii, no. 7.
116. *APS*, ii, 331.
117. *LP Henry VIII*, iv, pt. ii, nos. 4718–9
118. *APS.*, ii, 329; *RSS*, ii, nos. 3967, 3971–9.
119. Pitcairn, *Trials*, i, pt. i, 138; *RSS*, i, no. 3386.
120. *RMS*, iii, nos. 402–431.
121. *RSS*, ii, no. 154.
122. *ADCP*, 352.
123. *RSS*, ii, no. 642.
124. Pitcairn, *Trials*, i, pt. i, 140; only some of these are named by Pitcairn.
125. *RSS*, i, no. 3289; he is not referred to again as holding this office during Angus' government.
126. *APS*, ii, 328.
127. *Ibid.*, ii, 331.
128. *TA*, v, 149; *Scots Peerage*, i, 189; cf. Emond, *op.cit.*, 173–6.
129. *ADCP*, 286, 293–4; Pitcairn, *Trials*, i, pt. i, 140; *Scots Peerage*, iii, 281.
130. *ADCP*, 315–6.
131. Pitcairn, *Trials*, i, pt. i, 143.
132. *HMC, Twelfth Report*, App. 8, 183.
133. *Ibid.*, 318–20; *RSS*, ii, no. 378.
134. *HMC, Twelfth Report*, 387–8, 390; *RSS*, ii, no. 1396.
135. *HMC, Twelfth Report*, App. 8, 405.
136. *RSS*, i, no. 4123; ii, no. 39.
137. *Scots Peerage*, iv, 456; Wormald, *Bonds*, App. A, 174, no. 5; cf. Emond, *op.cit.*, 173–6.
138. *ADCP*, 287; *RSS*, ii, nos. 19, 26, 27.
139. *APS*, ii, 308; *RSS*, ii, no. 1696; *RMS*, iii, no. 1480; *TA*, vi, 267; Hume's 'de facto' restoration is discussed in Emond, *op.cit.*, 306.
140. *LP Henry VIII*, vi, nos. 918, 1045, 1176; vii, nos. 647, 911.
141. *LP Henry VIII*, iv, pt. iii, no. 5844; *SP Henry VIII*, iv, pt. iv, no. ccx.
142. *LP Henry VIII*, iv, pt. iii, nos. 6077–8; *SP Henry VIII*, iv, pt. iv, no. ccxiii.
143. *SP Venetian*, iv, no. 697.
144. *ADCP*, 317.
145. *Ibid.*, 347; SRO, *ADC*, vol. 43, f. 145.
146. *ADCP*, 347.

147. *Ibid.*, 319; Pitcairn, *Trials*, i, pt. i, 140, 147.
148. *RSS*, ii, no. 39; Pitcairn, *Trials*, i, pt. i, 147; *ADCP*, 346–7.
149. *RSS*, ii, no. 713; Pitcairn, *Trials*, i, pt. i, 139.
150. *ADCP*, 319; Pitcairn, *Trials*, i, pt. i, 142.
151. *ADCP*, 318; Pitcairn, *Trials*, i, pt. i, 139.
152. Pitcairn, *Trials*, i, pt. i, 142; *Scots Peerage*, i, 190; *ADCP*, 328; *RSS*, ii, nos. 718, 722.
153. Pitcairn, *Trials*, i, pt. i, 169; *RSS*, i, no. 4016; *Scots Peerage*, viii, 434–5.
154. *SP Henry VIII*, iv, pt. iv, no. ccxix.
155. *LP Henry VIII*, v, nos. 1254, 1286, 1460.
156. *ADCP*, 328, 356.
157. *LP Henry VIII*, v, no. 1377.
158. *RSS*, ii, no. 6 (Arran); *Ibid.*, ii, no. 402 (appointment of the fourth earl of Argyll as justice general; the third earl was still alive in September 1529; cf. Glasgow University, Argyll Transcripts, iii, 231–3; *HMC*, 4th Report, 485); *RMS*; iii, no. 932 (fourth earl acting in his own right by January 1530).
159. Rae, *op.cit.*, App. 4; *RSS*, ii, no. 6 (ward of the second earl of Arran gifted to Hamilton of Finnart in 1529); *ADCP*, 356.
160. *ADCP*, 324.
161. *Ibid.*, 385, 387; *TA*, vi, 107.
162. *ADCP*, 388.
163. *Ibid.*, 385; *TA*, vi, 106, 116.
164. *LP Henry VIII*, v, no. 1460.
165. SRO, *ADCS*, ii, ff. 167, 208.
166. *ADCP*, 402–3.
167. *Ibid.*, 391–2, 394–5.
168. *LP Henry VIII*, v, no. 1246.
169. *Ibid.*, v, no. 1460.
170. *Ibid.*, v, no. 1367.
171. *Ibid.*
172. *ADCP*, 386–8; *TA*, vi, 110.
173. *LP Henry VIII*, v, no. 1558; *TA*, vi, 109–10.
174. *LP Henry VIII*, v, no. 1559.
175. *ADCP*, 390–1.
176. *SP Henry VIII*, iv, pt. iv, no. ccxxxv; Northumberland listed as 'burned, distroyed and wasted' – Oldhamstocks, Cobbirspeth (Cockburnspath), Hoprygg; Old Camers; Reidtlewes; Douglas (Dunglass); Conwodd; Honwodd; 2 Rustayns (Reston); Blak Hill (Black Law ?); Hill Ende, and 2 Atons (Ayton).
177. *Ibid.*, iv, pt. iv, no. ccxxxvi.
178. *ADCP*, 277; Pitcairn, *Trials*, i, pt. i, 158.
179. *ADCP*, 388.
180. *LP Henry VIII*, vi, nos. 260, 794.
181. *Ibid.*, vi, nos. 744, 1114; vii, no. 912; *James V Letters*, 269. By 1535 the inhabitants of Berwick-upon-Tweed and surrounding areas were grinding their corn at the mill: *ADCP*, 447. In August 1542, James ordered Cawmills to be cast down: Fraser, *Melville*, ii, no. 3.
182. *LP Henry VIII*, vi, nos. 51, 124, 143.
183. *Ibid.*, vi, nos. 143, 163, 174; and cf. above, n. 102.
184. *Ibid.*, vi, nos. 185, 217; *TA*, vi, 121, 124. The feudal host was drawn from four quarters of Scotland, each serving for one month. These came respectively from the north-east, the west, central Scotland, and the Borders: cf. *TA*, vi, 124–5; *Calendar of State Papers ... Venice* ed. R. Brown *et al* (London, 1864 -) [*SP Venetian*], iv, no. 865; Pitcairn, *Trials*, i, pt. i, 161–2; Abell, *op.cit.*, f. 120v; *Diurnal of Occurrents*, 16 (three quarters); Buchanan, *History*, ii, 248.

185. *TA*, vi, 151–2; *LP Henry VIII*, vi, nos. 113, 147; cf. Abell, *op.cit.*, f. 120v.
186. *LP Henry VIII*, vi, no. 19.
187. *Ibid.*, vi, no. 174.
188. *Ibid.*, vi, nos. 163, 185, 375, 409.
189. *Ibid.*, vi, no. 260.
190. *Ibid.*, v, no. 1460.
191. *James V Letters*, 221.
192. *Ibid.*, 203–4; *LP Henry VIII*, v, nos. 125, 1005; cf. Bapst, *op.cit.*, *passim*.
193. *SP Venetian*, iv, nos. 721, 813, 878, 894, 949.
194. *LP Henry VIII*, vii, no. 114, 214; cf. J.A. Inglis, *Sir Adam Otterburn of Redhall* (Glasgow, 1935), 49–59.
195. *SP Venetian*, iv, nos. 878, 949.
196. *James V Letters*, 207.
197. *LP Henry VIII*, vi, nos. 282, 351, 409, 675.
198. *Ibid.*, vi, no. 163.
199. *Ibid.*, vi, no. 260.
200. *Ibid.*, vi, nos. 409, 450.
201. *Ibid.*, vi, no. 753; *TA*, vi, 87, 163.
202. *LP Henry VIII*, v, nos. 453, 563; R.A. Griffiths, *The Principality of Wales in the Later Middle Ages* (Cardiff, 1972, 2 vols.), i, 164, 222.
203. *LP Henry VIII*, v, App. no. 657; vi, nos. 803, 876, 892, 1548, 1591; vii, no. 710.
204. *Ibid.*, vi, nos. 828, 902.
205. *Ibid.*, vii, nos. 656, 710, 1567; *TA*, vi, 154, 236.
206. Cf. Macdougall, *James IV*, 118–9, 122–5.
207. *Diurnal of Occurrents*, 19.
208. *LP Henry VIII*, vii, no. 1193.
209. *ADCP*, 247.
210. *RSS*, ii, nos. 1494, 1903.
211. *Ibid.*, ii, nos. 57, 1728, 3909.
212. *Ibid.*, ii, no. 4591 (Murray was the stepson of Kilspindie: cf. *Scots Peerage*, iii, 502–3).
213. SRO, *ADCS*, vi, ff. 41v, 85v, 92. (The ward of Cassillis' marriage was eventually granted to his future wife in 1538: *RSS*, ii, nos. 2614, 3834).

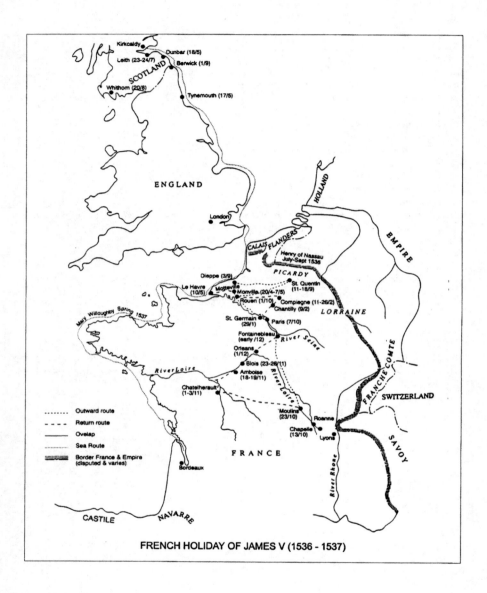

Kirkcaldy
Dunbar (18/5)
Leith (23-24/7)
Berwick (1/9)
SCOTLAND
Whithorn (20/8)
Tynemouth (17/5)

ENGLAND

London

HOLLAND

EMPIRE

CALAIS
FLANDERS
Henry of Nassau
July-Sept 1536

PICARDY

Dieppe (3/9)
Le Havre (10/5)
Motteville
Monville (20/4-7/5)
St. Quentin (11-18/9)
Rouen (1/10)
Compiegne (11-26/2)
Chantilly (9/2)
LORRAINE
St. Germain (29/1)
Paris (7/10)
Fontainebleau (early /12)
River Seine
Orleans (1/12)
Mary Willoughby Spring 1537
River Loire
Blois (23-26/11)
Amboise (18-19/11)
Chatelherault (1-3/11)
River Loire
FRANCHE-COMTE
SWITZERLAND
Moulins (23/10)
Roanne
Chapelle (13/10)
Lyons
SAVOY

FRANCE

River Rhone

Bordeaux

.... Outward route
– – – Return route
——— Overlap
·········· Sea Route
▨▨▨▨ Border France & Empire
(disputed & varies)

CASTILE
NAVARRE

FRENCH HOLIDAY OF JAMES V (1536 - 1537)

CHAPTER SEVEN

The Major Magnates and the Absentee King

I. SCOTLAND WITHOUT A KING: 1536–7

On 1 September 1536, James V set out from Kirkcaldy to sail to France to marry Mary of Bourbon, daughter of the Duke of Vêndome.[1] The marriage contract had been drawn up at Cremieu on 6 March 1536, with the Scots king represented by his uncle, the Duke of Albany; William Stewart, bishop of Aberdeen and treasurer; John, fifth lord Erskine; Sir Thomas Erskine of Brechin, royal secretary; Robert Reid, abbot of Kinloss; and the king's half-brother, the earl of Moray. It was approved by the French king on 29 March. One month later, Francis I entrusted Moray with delivery of the order of St. Michael to the Scots king[2] and both Moray and Lord Erskine appear to have stayed on in France to await James' arrival.[3]

The royal fleet consisted of six ships, the largest being the *Mary Willoughby*, and James had a force of some five hundred men. He was accompanied by the second earl of Arran; the fourth earl of Argyll; the fourth earl of Rothes; Lord Fleming, the chamberlain; David Beaton, abbot of Arbroath and keeper of the privy seal; Robert Reid, abbot of Kinloss; John Roule, prior of Pittenweem; James Douglas of Drumlanrig; and James Gordon of Lochinvar.[4] The royal fleet sailed down the east coast, passing Berwick-upon-Tweed on 3 September, and reached Dieppe on 9 or 10 September.[5] the king then 'departid the nixt dai . . . and whether he is gonne, I trust your Lordshipe knowis the better than I'. It was left to Adam Abell to supply the answer:

In a different vestement he came to the duke of Vêndome father of the lady that he should have married. He was known there by his picture.[6]

From the Duke of Vêndome's court at St. Quentin, Picardy, James returned to Rouen, where the Scots had made their headquarters,[7] and thence to Paris in early October. Rothes and Lord Erskine sailed home to Scotland.[8] By 14 October French sources were predicting that James would now be marrying the princess Madeleine, and that Mary of Bourbon would be offered by Francis I to the marquis of Lorraine, son of the Duke of Guise.[9] From Paris, James headed south, meeting with Francis I at Chapelle. The two kings then went on a tour of the Loire valley, passing through Moulins, Amboise and Châtelherault before

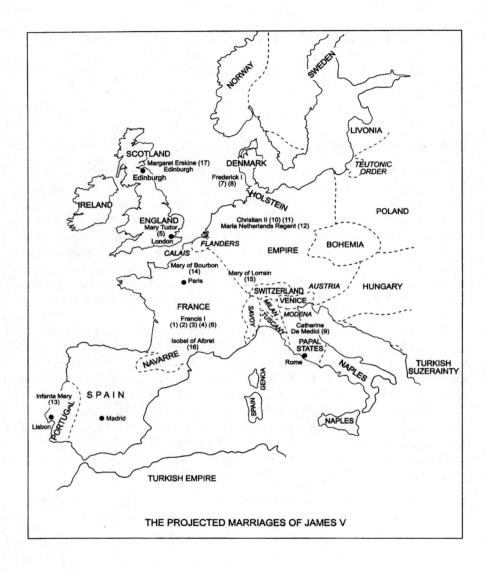

THE PROJECTED MARRIAGES OF JAMES V

returning north to Blois.[10] There, on 26 November 1536, they drew up the contract for the marriage of James to Francis' daughter, Madeleine.[11] Returning north via Orleans and Fontainebleau,[12] James entered Paris before the middle of December.[13] On 1 January 1537 he married Madeleine at Nôtre Dame.[14] After over twenty years of diplomatic negotiations during which no fewer than eighteen names had been mooted as possible brides for the Scots king, James had fulfilled the terms of the 1517 Treaty of Rouen by marrying a daughter of the king of France.[15]

From Paris the king and his bride moved to Chantilly in early February, then to Compiègne, where the king received papal approval in the form of a hat and sword, and spent 1100 crowns on a diamond for his wife's 'spousing' ring and 1600 crowns on wine from Bordeaux.[16] At Rouen, in March, Madeleine fell ill[17]; and it was there on 3 April that James issued his Act of Revocation, being just seven days short of his twenty-fifth birthday.[18] The royal party left Le Havre on 10 May, and arrived at Leith nine days later, after stopping to buy fish off Bamburgh.[19] Madeleine died at Holyrood Palace on 7 July.[20]

James V was away from Scotland for the better part of nine months. He was the first Scots king voluntarily to remain away from his realm since David II – over two hundred years earlier. His sojourn in France displayed a remarkable degree of confidence and trust in his subjects. That he remained abroad even after he had secured his marriage suggests more than simply a concentration on diplomatic relations with France rather than on domestic affairs. It indicates that Scotland was a country which could be left safely in the hands of others. The continuous presence of the king was not required to maintain law and order. It also indicates that James was not ever-vigilant and on his guard against possible sedition and challenges to his royal authority. This was a relaxed king in 1536–37, showing no anxiety about his domestic situation. Crown-magnate relations can only have been stable for James to have enjoyed a nine-month absence.

Three days before his departure for France, on 28 August 1536, James appointed as vice-regents, Gavin Dunbar, archbishop of Glasgow and Chancellor; James Beaton, archbishop of St. Andrews; George Gordon, fourth earl of Huntly; William Graham, second earl of Montrose; Hugh Montgomery, first earl of Eglinton; and Robert, fifth lord Maxwell and warden of the West March. Acting with a minimum quorum of three and always including the Chancellor, these men had powers to convene the lieges for defence of the realm, to exercise justice and punish offenders, and to receive and respond to foreign embassies. The Chancellor, with the consent of at least two others, had authority to accept resignations of land to the king and issue confirmations of charters. At Paris, on 6 January 1537 and in anticipation of his forthcoming revocation, the king confirmed this authority but excepted the power to issue remissions and infeft heirs in their father's lands.[21]

Three of these men, the two archbishops and the elderly Eglinton, had been appointed to the king's 'secret consale' by his royal ordinance of 12 November

1528.[22] Both the Chancellor and Eglinton had been regular witnesses of charters issued under the great seal in the intervening period.[23] Montrose, Huntly and Maxwell had each witnessed only one charter prior to their appointment, at Frendraught on 14 November 1535, the recipient being John Crichton of Ruthven. Montrose and Huntly were witnesses to all four charters bearing witness lists and issued during the king's absence. Maxwell missed one, on 18 November 1536.[24] None of these three was to act as witnesses after their spell as vice-regents. Gavin Dunbar continued his 100% record for the rest of the reign, and Eglinton retired in 1538. James Beaton did not appear as a witness at any point in the reign, even whilst serving as vice-regent. The total number of charters issued by the vice-regents was forty, the majority in the register being 'testified as in other charters'. Most were confirmations, although Maxwell received two grants of lands in the Stewartry of Annandale, and John Maxwell, burgess of Dumfries, also received three marks' worth of land in Dumfries. All the charters were issued from Edinburgh, save for the three to the Maxwells, issued at Glasgow.[25]

By comparison, seventy-four charters were issued in 1536, prior to the king's departure, and one hundred-and-one in 1537, after his return.[26] Thus central administration was merely ticking over during the king's absence. The court of session record stops on 25 August 1536 and resumes on 7 November 1537.[27] The privy seal register shows that two seals were in existence, one operated by David Beaton in France, and the other remaining in Edinburgh. The Edinburgh one was used mainly to issue precepts for the chancery office. Beaton issued two respites or remissions, one from Paris and the other from Montevilliers. On 7 January 1537 he gifted the marriage of Lord Innermeath to his cousin Elizabeth, one of James' mistresses.[28]

The choice of Gavin Dunbar, archbishop of Glasgow, as vice-regent during James' absence was virtually self-evident, as he was the Chancellor. James Beaton, archbishop of St. Andrews, had been in this office during the minority until he resigned in 1526. As such he had had a near 100% record as a charter witness before 1528.[29] His selection as joint vice-regent perhaps owed much to his experience in the chancery, as well as being a formal acknowledgement of his status amongst the First Estate which, after all, provided James with the bulk of his revenue from taxation.[30] However, although Beaton had been brought on to the secret council in November 1528, relations between the senior archbishop and the king had then steadily deteriorated. Writing in March 1532 to Pope Clement VII to complain about Beaton's appropriation of the fruits of Stow church in Selkirkshire, which the king wished to have leased to William, sixth lord Borthwick, James began his letter by complaining that the activities of his archbishop required him to write too many letters of this nature.[31] However, more important in financial terms for the king was the question of taxation, and by 1533 relations between the king and his senior prelate had broken down completely. On 7 May 1533 Sir George Lawson, captain of the Berwick-upon-

Tweed garrison, recorded that Beaton was then being held in ward at St. Andrews, in the custody of the earl of Rothes. According to Lawson, this was either because Beaton had written letters contrary to James' mind or because he would not lend the king any money.[32] James himself wrote in the previous month to the Cardinal of Ravenna to complain about his archbishop's lèse-majesté 'whom it least of all befitted to conspire against the commonweal'.[33] James' reference to the commonweal reflected the fact that ostensibly the 'Great Tax' of £10,000 *per annum* granted by the Pope in 1531, and commuted to a £72,000 lump sum and £1,400 *per annum* in the following year, was to pay for the foundation of the College of Justice.[34] The term 'lèse majesté' was self-effacing when used in a letter to a senior cardinal; James did not seriously suppose that his archbishop's discontent amounted to treasonable activity, but he had to find a plausible explanation as to why he should be coercing the archbishop into paying tax.[35]

In a further lengthy letter to the pope written at the same time, James went to the opposite extreme. He began by stating that:

> it is well known that this archbishop, after the death of our father and during our youth, was able, by the means and influence given him by our authority, enriched himself, his parents and his friends, both spiritual and temporal, to our great prejudice.

James then narrated how, after authority had been restored into his own hands, the archbishop, having realised that this threatened to end his chances of enriching himself, had gathered a large number of earls, lords and subjects and attacked the king's force, besieging Edinburgh castle. The king, in order to save his own life, had been forced, against his intention and will, to place himself and his authority into the hands of Beaton's accomplices, the earl of Angus, his brother and his uncle, who were allies of England. It was notorious and manifest how the archbishop was entirely evil and had never acted without the advice and counsel of the ancient English enemy. Until now, because of the archbishop's age and James' respect for the Church, no action had been taken, but he was now accurately advised and informed that these 'damnable and displeasing' wars with his uncle were principally due to the secret letters and plottings of the arch-bishop, evidence of which would be shown to the pope by the bearer. A specific instance of this was that the archbishop had had intelligence with the captain of Berwick-upon-Tweed, and had arranged to sail secretly from St. Andrews to Berwick, in under six hours, given a favourable wind. James then reiterated his request made to the cardinal of Ravenna, that Gavin Dunbar, George Crichton, bishop of Dunkeld, and William Stewart, bishop of Aberdeen and Treasurer in 1533, or others should be given a commission to try Beaton for these crimes.[36] These three men significantly were the three named by the earl of Northumber-land in September 1532 as being the only members of the Scottish spirituality who had 'ther hartes and favours to the King'.[37]

Perhaps James did believe some of this information which he was feeding to the pope. However, Beaton was not tried by his peers, nor did he try to sail to Berwick-upon-Tweed. The king was making these accusations about his Chancellor in the early summer or 1533, at a time when the confrontation between Scotland and England had passed its peak and was soon to peter out in lengthy negotiations for peace, first at Newcastle and then at London. On the other hand, Sir George Lawson did not offer any explanation as to how he had obtained his information on Beaton's warding; and the king was successful in raising a great deal of money from the Scottish Church. The archbishopric of St. Andrews made its first payment, of £200, in 1531. Two further payments, each of £441, were entered in the *Treasurer's Accounts* in 1534, with the total sum received from taxation of the Church in that year amounting to £7600.[38] The timing of these receipts may have owed much to the warding of the archbishop in the previous year. James had plenty of money when he arrived in France in 1536, to judge by the boxes of crowns unloaded at Dieppe in September; John Tennant, Oliver Sinclair, and Robert Gibb, stable master, were each given one thousand crowns to spend on items for the king.[39] The further sum of £200 was received in July 1538 from David Beaton, acting as coadjutor of the archbishopric for his uncle. This was officially paid as a tax 'frely grantit the Kingis grace being in France', but entered the account of John Scrimegeour, master of works.[40] The commutation of the earlier 'Great Tax', ostensibly earmarked for the foundation of the College of Justice, had probably been used to fund the 'Kingis grace being in France'.

Clearly, James did not like the archbishop of St. Andrews, but he trusted him enough to appoint him as one of his vice-regents. To judge by his lack of activity as a witness to great seal charters, he took little active part in exercising the office. He may also have been a counter-weight to Gavin Dunbar, who held the rival archbishopric and, as Chancellor, had the greater authority. The First Estate was not in a position to challenge royal authority. It was faced with the choice of cooperation and taxation, or non-cooperation and dissolution of its patrimony.

2. THE SECOND ESTATE

The remaining vice-regents were drawn from the ranks of the Second Estate. If there was to be a challenge to James's authority during his absence, then the likelihood was that it would come from a disaffected magnate commanding both sufficient influence and resources to mount such a challenge. For the majority, their interests were largely localised and they came into only intermittent contact with royal authority as represented either by the king in person, or through the central judicial system.

The official reason for appointing six vice-regents was to have a quorum and to cover the possibility of any one of them dying in office.[41] Having a minimum quorum of three also meant that power was not concentrated in any one magnate's hands. Again, James had to trust his appointments, and shrewdly he did not place royal authority in any one pair of hands. Geographically the chosen magnates represented areas far apart, from Huntly in the north-east to Maxwell in the south-west. This both spread royal authority throughout the country and avoided a concentration of magnatial interests in any one area. The choice was restricted by various factors, above all the fact that not all the earls were suitable people to be entrusted with office.

A starting point for identifying the available pool of magnates at this time, is the list of those earls summoned to Edinburgh in March 1537 to await the return of the king and his new bride.[42] The first omission in the list is Matthew Stewart, fourth earl of Lennox, aged about nineteen in 1536. The distinct probability is that he had been out of the country since at least 1535, possibly since 1532.[43] On 15 February 1532, he had been gifted the ward and future relief of the lands of the earldom by letter under the privy seal. The gift was made 'ay and quhill the lauchfull entre of the richtuis are or airis tharto being of lauchfull age'. Being under-age, Lennox was not served as heir to his father at that stage, the earldom being deemed on 24 May 1532 to be in the king's hands for the period since the death of the third earl at Linlithgow, in 1526. The non-entry for this period was set at £9840, with relief at £1640 (in effect valuing the earldom as producing £1640 in annual revenue).[44] The gift to Lennox, four months earlier, was made gratis, but the May assessment suggests that the position was being reviewed, possibly in the light of the assessment being taken of the Crawford earldom at the same time. In June 1539, non-entries for the barony of Tarbolton (Ayr) were assessed at £2132 for the previous thirteen years, suggesting that this part of the earldom had become detached from the remainder, and that it was still considered to be in the Crown's possession. Sasine was then assumed to be taken by the absent Lennox.[45] In fact, in the personal rule Lennox never received a great seal charter to confirm his entry as the 'richtuis are'. On the other hand, there is no entry in the accounts for any composition being paid by him, unlike Crawford, who paid £1000 to recover his estates.

On 1 July 1532 a letter of safeguard was granted to Lennox and his retinue to endure 'fra the day of is departing furth of the realme'. On 26 July 1541, the king issued a letter suspending all actions against the earl until 'his hamecuming agane within oure realme'. The implication in this second letter was that he was then overseas.[46] Given that from 1532 until the end of the personal rule, Lennox was not once summoned to Edinburgh and never appeared at parliament, not even for the 1540–41 ratification of the king's revocation and Act of Annexation, it appears as though he was completely unavailable.[47] His estates were maintained by his family – there were two dowager countesses holding terces in 1529 – with Alexander Douglas of Mains acting as factor in 1542.[48] The king's letter of 1541 shows an interest in the safe-keeping of the estate in the absence of its lord, and Lennox' brother and sister obtained gifts of livery and clothing from James.[49] More substantially, his sister, Margaret, was granted the gift of the marriage of

Alexander, Master of Hume, in October 1542, the intention presumably being that she and he were to marry.[50] The king's 'hands off' approach to the earldom in the absence of the 'richtuis heir' stands in marked contrast to his treatment of the Crawford earldom, though the Comptroller's calculation of the value of the estates shows a keen regard for its potential worth.

Neither Sutherland nor Caithness was summoned for the king's homecoming. The third earl of Caithness had died at the battle of Summerdale, and ward of the earldom was still held by Alexander Stewart, commendator-abbot of Scone and, from 1529, bishop of Moray.[51] On 4 March 1538, the ward was granted into the joint possession of the then Treasurer, James Kirkcaldy of Grange, and Oliver Sinclair, on payment of £1200. Regress was allowed to Elizabeth Sutherland, countess of Caithness, on payment to them of 2200 marks (£1467).[52]

Ward of the Sutherland earldom was gifted to Huntly on 24 March 1536 with the decease of his kinsman, Alexander Gordon, who had held it in fee since 1527. Following the king's revocation, the ward was then regranted on 1 April 1538 to Sir John Campbell of Cawdor on payment of 1000 marks.[53] In the case of both of these earldoms, the king was not concerned with who had control of the estates, but only with making money out of them, the transfer of the ward of both earldoms in 1538 achieving this.

Alexander Graham, second earl of Menteith, was another earl omitted from the summons for the king's homecoming. He had just died; his heir, William, succeeded to the estates on 14 May 1537, with relief being set at £300.[54] The elder Menteith had had financial difficulties in 1530, with sums being claimed by the assignees of his deceased grandmother. Part of the earl's estate was apprised and assigned to the countess' representatives as security for the sum of £420.[55] This was a larger amount than the annual revenue from the whole earldom in 1537, and suggests that this earldom was impoverished. There is no entry in either the great or privy seal register to confirm the sasine to the third earl, who was of age, as his daughter was old enough to marry the son of the fourth earl of Argyll in 1542.[56] It is possible that the earls of Menteith were partially over-shadowed by the creation by James in 1528 of the lordship of Methven, which bordered the earldom, on part of Margaret Tudor's conjunct-fee. In April 1542 James gifted the lordship of Menteith, with its caput at Doune castle, to his wife in liferent. This also had been part of Margaret's conjunct-fee, and Lord Methven's brother had been appointed as captain of Doune castle in April 1528.[57] Neither the second nor the third earl appeared on the political scene in the personal rule, although William did attend the 1540–41 parliament for the ratification of the king's Act of Revocation, and for the passing of the Act of Annexation.[58]

Another obvious absentee from the king's homecoming was Patrick Hepburn, third earl of Bothwell, who was in ward in Inverness castle,[59] and had been in custody since his treason of 1531.[60]

Of those earls who were summoned to the king's homecoming in 1537, some were not yet of full age.[61] The second earl of Arran was gifted the non-entry of the earldom on 15 September 1540, and was then confirmed in its possession 'for special love and for past service in France and in Scotland'.[62] This suggests that he only reached his majority of twenty-one years in or shortly before that date.[63] Ward of the earldom had been gifted to Sir James Hamilton of Finnart on 31 March 1529. On 12 September 1532 the earldom was assessed for its value in non-entry to the Crown – over £4200 – but there was no reference to any relief being taken, although sasine was made to Arran.[64] As in the case of Lennox, there is no trace of a charter being granted to Arran in 1532, nor of a composition being paid. Arran appeared in parliament in 1535, as a lord of articles, which was perhaps a reflection of his family's status as the nearest heirs to the royal Stewarts rather than of his own abilities.[65]

William Hay, sixth earl of Erroll, remained under-age until his death in 1541.[66] Gilbert Kennedy, third earl of Cassillis, was aged around eighteen or nineteen in 1536. He had attended the 1535 parliament and was to attend the 1540–41 session.[67] Granted licence to leave Scotland in 1530 in order to go on pilgrimage to France with his tutor and the Kennedy kindred,[68] he had benefited from being educated in Paris by George Buchanan.[69] He returned to Scotland in 1534–5, and began a lawsuit against his father's killer, Hugh Campbell of Loudoun, sheriff of Ayr.[70] The summons giving rise to their dispute was not recorded in the court of session records, and the case was continued four times, the last postponement being in July 1536.[71] Probably the case reopened the feud between the two families over the lands of Turnberry in Ayrshire, which had resulted in the murder of the second earl.[72] As sheriff of Ayr, Campbell was considered not to be impartial (or 'presomit in ane part suspect to be jugis to thaim'), and deputies were appointed by the Lords of Council to hear the case.[73]

In February 1538, Cassillis was pursuing Campbell over a different matter. The third earl was under pressure from the Treasurer, and facing the poinding of his goods and lands for sums owed by his grandfather. The first earl had been sheriff at the time of the justice ayre of 1511, and had been charged with the payment of sums which he had failed to collect from transgressors. At the ayre of 1516, a ruling had been made that the second earl should have the right of relief against his deceased father's debtors. Over twenty years later, James' government was still seeking full payment from the third earl. Cassillis obtained letters of poinding against Alan Lord Cathcart, and also sought relief from Campbell of Loudoun for sums owed by his deceased mother, Dame Isobel Wallace.[74] The sum involved in her instance was trivial, but the case appears to have marked the beginning of the reversal of Campbell's fortunes. By September 1538 he was in ward, and the Cardinal of Lorraine wrote to Mary of Guise, asking her to intercede on his behalf, and have James allow him to go to France.[75] Thereafter, the sheriff of Ayr disappears without trace from the records until January 1543, when Henry VIII wrote to the then officer in command at Berwick-upon-Tweed to advise:

there is a gentleman of Scotland yet in Fraunce called the shiref of Ayre, whom therle of Bothwel and also other, do repute for a man of a good sort, and oon that the said Erle Bothwel can easely trayne to our devotion. . . .[76]

The reason for Campbell's fall from grace in 1538 was probably partly because Cassillis was coming of age. In July of the same year, the king granted Cassillis' marriage to Margaret Kennedy, who then married the young earl.[77] In November of the same year, Cassillis was granted sasine to his earldom.[78] A year later, in October 1539, Campbell's lands of Milltown and Pottertown were apprised and assigned to Cassillis.[79] In 1541 the third earl was eventually discharged of his grandfather's debts on the Treasurer's receipt of the sum of £716. He still owed a further £373, but the king's officers were ordered not to pursue him for the balance.[80] In the same year, Cassillis also obtained a nine year tack to the lands of Turnberry – over which his father had fought with Campbell of Loudoun.[81] On 6 February 1541 he received two charters of confirmation of his earldom, granted for 'good service and for gratitude'. The service referred to was in the royal Isles expedition of 1540. Cassillis attended both the December 1540 parliament and its continuation in March 1541.[82]

Campbell had received a remission on 1 July 1528 for his killing of the second earl of Cassillis, and this had been ratified in the September 1528 parliament.[83] However, there is no indication that he was forced to come to a settlement with the Kennedies, in the manner of the Tweedies of Drummelzier and Lord Fleming; Scott of Buccleuch and the Kerrs;[84] or Hamilton of Finnart and Lennox.[85] The enmity between Campbell of Loudoun and Cassillis continued into the minority of Mary Queen of Scots.[86] By removing Campbell in 1538, James gained the gratitude of a magnate who was just coming of age. Thus Campbell of Loudoun, described by the English in July 1528 as 'bedfellow' of the king,[87] and who signed the 'grete aith' in November of the same year, was ten years later ousted by the son of the man he had killed.

However, in 1536, Cassillis was not yet of age. On 30 January 1537, he and several kinsmen were accused of breaking the 'King's Proclamation in his absence' by attacking John Dunbar of Blantyre and his four servants at Ayr on 9 December 1536.[88] Dunbar was apparently a harmless individual who acted as a frequent witness for land transactions carried out by Kennedies and Campbells alike,[89] but he may have been perceived by the Kennedies as being identified with the Campbell interest rather than their own.[90] The concern of the vice-regents was probably with the breach of the king's proclamation rather than with the injuries sustained in hand and thigh by two of Dunbar's servants.

Elsewhere in Ayrshire, Cuthbert Cunningham, third earl of Glencairn, was perhaps in his late fifties or early sixties in 1536.[91] He never attended parliament in the personal rule of James V, and nor did his son, William, Master of Glencairn and Lord of Kilmaurs. William succeeded as fourth earl in 1541.[92] James apparently had little regard for the third earl, who in 1529 had been threatened with warding at Blackness castle by the Lords of Council for intrusions by his illegitimate son, James Cunningham, on the lands of Andrew Auchinleck.[93] The Master was more active. In 1524 Albany had master-minded an agreement between the Cunninghams and the Montgomeries, whereby all issues between them should be resolved by marriage and a contingent penalty of £3000 for any future breaches.[94] Yet as early as 1526 Eglinton was in breach of the agreement. Edward Cunningham of Auchenharvie had been murdered by the Montgomeries and Glencairn pressed the Lords of Council to have Eglinton put to the horn.[95] In 1527 several tenants of Eglinton had their lands apprised and granted to the Master of Glencairn, who also obtained a claim to the escheated goods of Eglinton himself.[96] On 28 May 1528, the Lords of Council decreed that Eglinton should pay Glencairn £1000 in compensation.[97] On 19 June 1528, various lands in the bailiary of Cunningham belonging to Eglinton were apprised and assigned to the Master of Glencairn. Eglinton witnessed the great seal charter issued at Edinburgh on 27 June 1528 confirming this apprisal.[98] This event is curious in that it marks a degree of continuity between the last days of the Angus government, in May, and the first days of the new régime.

Possibly the Master of Glencairn had little faith in the new régime giving him satisfaction, for in June 1528 he burned down the castle of Eglinton, leaving only the barn standing. He followed this up in July by attacking Eglinton's house of Stewarton.[99] He may simply have been taking advantage of the confusion caused by the change in government. Eglinton was one of the Lords of Council who ordered Angus' servants on July 1528 to leave Edinburgh within six hours under penalty of death, and added that this also applied to the servants of the Master of Glencairn.[100] As Angus' first cousin,[101] the Master had perhaps imagined he would be penalised by the new government. This did not happen. There was no summons of treason made against the Master, and no remission required for treasonable assistance of the Douglases. However on 5 September 1528, the gift to the Master of Glencairn of Eglinton's escheat was revoked, with the explanation that the earl was innocent of the murder of Cunningham of Auchenharvie and that it had been a gift made by the king then 'being in the handis and subjectioune of Archibald Erll of Angus'.[102] This 'acquittal' parallels those granted to both Campbell of Loudoun and Scott of Buccleuch and ratified in the September parliament. There was some truth in Lord Dacre's comment of July 1528 that James was being supported by 'murderers and mysguyded men'.[103]

In November 1528 Eglinton was granted powers to hold a commission of justice in Cunningham,[104] but no recriminations appear to have followed for the Master of Glencairn. The Lords of Council set aside the first day of December for all grievances to be heard between the Cunninghams and the Montgomeries.[105] Eglinton estimated that damages to his two houses amounted to £1800,[106] but this was offset by other obligations under the 1524 agreement when he had granted a letter of reversion for £1000 to Glencairn in exchange for some of Glencairn's lands. In 1530 Glencairn paid back £500 to Eglinton, and the lands were restored.[107] The Master of Glencairn had himself been implicated in the murder of Mathew Montgomery, chaplain, and only finally settled this matter with Eglinton in February 1537 – the king then being out of the country.[108] The Eglinton-Glencairn feud over the bailiary of Cunningham, which had been at its height during the previous reign, had at last run out of steam. Both Eglinton and Glencairn were getting older and had other concerns. In 1531 Eglinton was trying to dislodge his own son from Stewarton, after repair works had been carried out.[109]

The Master of Glencairn and Hugh Campbell of Loudoun fell into a civil dispute over the intricate succession rights to the Loudoun estate in the Cunningham bailiary following the death of Sir James Campbell of Loudoun, before 1520.[110] The earl of Moray obtained possession of Nether Loudoun in 1521; the Master of Glencairn was granted a charter to West Loudoun in January 1528, and Dame Isobel Wallace, mother of Campbell of Loudoun, held East Loudoun.[111] In 1530, Campbell took sasine to West Loudoun.[112] In December 1528 the Master unsuccessfully tried to challenge Moray's claim to Nether Loudoun;[113] in December 1531 he raised a summons of error against both Moray and Campbell;[114] and by May 1532 both the Master and Campbell were complaining of partiality, the former objecting to some of the Lords of Council dealing with the matter, and the sheriff of Ayr resenting the investigation into how he had managed to serve himself as heir to West Loudoun.[115] The outcome was that Moray lost Nether Loudoun in June 1532, to the Master;[116] the Master was then ordered to return to Eglinton the houses of Kerelaw and Stevenston, which he had held in tack from Moray;[117] and Campbell was held to possess West Loudoun, receiving a charter to the lands in July 1533.[118] Perhaps the most remarkable feature of this convoluted episode was the issue of a signet letter by the king at Peebles on 23 July 1532, discharging from all error the members who had served on the first inquest (in 1527); the king's advocate for any summons of error which he had pursued; the sheriff of Ayr; and the Chancellor, president and lords of the council of session for their involvement.[119] This amounted to a strong endorsement of the Crown's justice, and of the new College of Justice, after a complete mix-up over the Loudoun inheritance. The Master of Glencairn had gained Nether Loudoun but had lost West Loudoun. He had been after both estates. Moray had lost out completely, and Campbell now held both West and East Loudoun. The outcome was unsatisfactory for both Moray and the Master. The more critical factor was that when the earl of Eglinton held a weaponshowing for the bailiary of Cunningham on the burgh muir at Irvine on 15 October 1532, practically no-one turned up.[120] Unfortunately, the English sources reporting on Moray's manoeuvres as lieutenant on the Borders in the first half of 1533 do not indicate whether or not the west quarter was present in force.[121]

It was perhaps more than coincidental that 1538 was the year in which Eglinton retired as a charter witness, at the age of seventy-eight,[122] the sheriff of Ayr was imprisoned, and the Master of Glencairn distinguished himself in the Crown's service as one of the envoys entrusted with escorting Mary of Guise from France to Scotland.[123] Prior to then the Master, like Cassillis, had been partly marginalised by Campbell.

James Douglas, third earl of Morton, was in his mid-fifties in 1536.[124] He had no male heir, but three daughters, for two of whom he arranged marriages in 1530; the eldest, Margaret, to the second earl of Arran,[125] and the middle one, Beatrice, to the Master of Maxwell.[126] Morton was himself married to the king's half-sister.[127] On 19 October 1528 he was granted a letter under the privy seal exempting him for life from all raids, wars and weaponshowings, on account of 'diverse seiknes and infirmiteis in his persoun havand ane sare leg'.[128] This may also have accounted for his complete absence from attendance at parliament in the personal rule.

The earldom was in financial straits in 1528. The reason for this was suggested in a contract dated 25 November 1531 between the earl and John Crichton, vicar of Dalkeith, entered into because of the 'extortionis wrangis and oppressionis appearand to halykirk in diminutioun and dounputting of the frutis and teyndis thereof', and because of great travel costs and expenses sustained by both the first and second earls, and the 'exorbitant expensis' sustained by the third earl in coal-mining in Dalkeith.[129] The earl was being pursued in court in December 1528 by his sister for her dowry of 3000 marks,[130] and it took him until 1535 to pay for his second daughter's marriage.[131] His impoverishment may have prompted him, after the battle of Flodden, to abscond with the gold chest held by Peter [sic] Damian, abbot of Tongland, James IV's alchemist and failed aviator. This, at any rate, was alleged in March 1531 by Henry Wemyss, bishop of Galloway and abbot commendator of Tongland, and the Lords of Council agreed with him, ordering Morton to return the missing item.[132]

It appears as though the earl was under a form of interdict, the purpose of which was to prevent the dissipation of his estates. The effect was that any alienations of land had no legal effect unless made with consent.[133] In Morton's case the consentor was the Crown. On 19 July 1530 James signetted a licence to Morton to sell the barony of Kilbucho (Broughton) to Malcolm, lord Fleming. James followed this up on 12 October 1530 with a letter to the Countess of Morton desiring her to prevail upon her husband to ensure that the sale proceeded.[134] However, the sale did not then take place. Rather, in July 1532, Morton appeared before the Session to complain that John Perdovin, royal officer, had purchased 'sinister' royal letters interdicting the earl from all alienations of his heritage in defraud of his creditors and successors. The earl alleged he was not in debt, and the lords suspended the alleged interdict pending the production of the 'sinister' royal letters.[135] Morton went on to sell lands of the earldom in February 1534 and May 1535.[136] Then, on 22 July 1535, he eventually sold Kilbucho to Fleming at a price of 4000 marks, and under a letter of reversion to himself.[137] The king again granted a licence for the interdict to be lifted and confirmed the sale by royal charter on 26 September 1535.[138] This second licence should have been unnecessary, given the earlier one of 1530, but possibly Fleming insisted upon it because of the subsequent appearance of 'sinister' royal letters, and the fact that he was lending Morton 4000 marks. It may have been the case that this impecunious earl had originally placed himself under a voluntary interdict,[139] with the king as consentor, but had then become ensnarled in a legal entanglement with the Crown's lawyers.

These lawyers were almost using the earldom as a test case for legal principles. The main estate comprised the regality of Dalkeith; powers of regality were reserved to the earldom in the royal charter of confirmation to Fleming. Morton defended these regalian powers in a case brought in March 1533 against John Bannatyne, liferenter of Roberton mill in Lanarkshire. The Lords of Council ordered suspension of letters obtained from the sheriff of Lanark against his tenants, because Morton argued that the sheriff had no jurisdiction in this part of his earldom.[140] In June of the same year Morton himself was ordered by the Lords of Council to administer impartial justice in his regality. The defence's case rested on the authority of private letters, subscribed by the king, which the Lords of Council ruled were of no avail in the regality.[141] These evidently were more 'sinister' letters circulating in a place where there was no legal justification for them to exist.

The earl and his wife held the barony of Buittle in the Stewartry of Kirkcudbright, obtaining first a nineteen-year tack in 1516, and then, in April 1527, a charter in feu farm.[142] In May 1529 James wrote to Lord Maxwell instructing him to require his brother, John Maxwell, to pay his dues for Preston house to the king's 'lovit sister'. John must have been dilatory in paying his rent. Reprovingly, James added that 'we merwell that ze thole sic manifest wrangis'. The king's real concern was that these were Crown lands where rent was not being paid.[143] But in February 1533, Morton's charter was reduced by the Lords of Council although he had been faithfully paying over £100 annually in feu duty. The grounds of reduction were that this was a grant of Crown lands made in the king's lessage and to the diminution of his rental.[144] This was perfectly legal – a provision in the September 1528 parliament allowed the king to revoke all gifts of property made in the minority[145] – but appears unfair. Possibly the king was irked by the delay in the transfer of Kilbucho to his lord chamberlain, Lord Fleming; his letter of October to his half-sister suggests this. Buittle was granted to Lord Maxwell in June 1535 at the increased annual feu farm of £245.[146]

Following the Act of Revocation at Rouen in 1537, the earldom again came under fire. In July 1538 Morton was called to defend a summons of error for the barony of Aberdour. At first he produced a precept of sasine to himself and his wife, dating from 1521, but, this proving insufficient, eventually, in March 1539, he came up with a charter to his father granted in 1509.[147] However, this summons was only a precursor of the further threat to the earldom which materialised in 1540 in the form of an intricate series of resignations and charters ultimately purporting to convey the entire earldom to the Crown.[148] It was evident that the king had a close interest in this impoverished earldom lying to the south of his capital and possessed by the lame grandson of the king's grandfather's uncle,[149] who was married to James' half-sister, and was interested in coal-mining.

Crawford, despite his pasting at the hands of the king's advocate, was able to attend parliament in both 1532 and 1535.[150] Another temporary casualty of this investigation was John Stewart, third earl of Buchan, aged around thirty-eight in 1536.[151] He had been confirmed in his lands by royal charter issued at Stirling on 2 August 1528, and 'for singular favour' the king created the lands as the free barony of Glendowachy.[152] Buchan attended the September 1528 parliament and was one of the Lords of Council on 22 October 1528, when the stratagem for the siege of Tantallon was drawn up.[153] Probably he was in the northern quarter on the Borders for defence of the realm in March 1533, although Sir George Lawson, captain at Berwick-upon-Tweed, noted only the attendance of Huntly, Marischal and Argyll.[154]

In February 1534, Buchan became involved in an extraordinary court case with Crawford, over the lands of Carnbaddy (Cairnbeddie), in the Crawford barony of Melginch, Perthshire. In 1511 the then earl of Buchan had alienated these lands to the then earl of Crawford. Twenty-three years later, Crawford required Buchan to warrant him in possession of these lands.[155] As the earldom of Crawford had recently fallen into the king's hands by reason of non-entry, the warrandice clause made at the time of the alienation was null and void. Thus, Crawford was seeking its confirmation. By May 1534, Crawford claimed to have obtained letters enabling him to have Buchan outlawed, for his failure to grant this confirmation.[156] However the Lords of Council suspended the action until Crawford produced the letters.[157] The case continued until May 1536 without a resolution.[158] Crawford, in conjunction with the Crown, then brought another, unsuccessful, action to reduce Buchan's title to lands in the barony of Platane (Forfar). These were held by Buchan of the earldom of Crawford. The non-entries had been gifted to Buchan in July 1532, following the Crown's dispossession of Crawford.[159] However, by 13 July 1537, Buchan was at the horn for his failure to grant warrandice to Crawford for Cairnbeddie. Sir John Campbell of Lundy paid the treasurer 100 marks for the gift of Buchan's escheated goods.[160] In October 1538 Crawford was granted compensation for the lack of warrandice, in the form of rents from Buchan's lands, the annual value of which amounted to four marks, three barrels of flour and two of barley.[161]

This appears to be an absurdly trivial amount for which to outlaw a magnate. It illustrates two points: firstly, that Buchan's temporary downfall was an indirect result of the Crown's earlier financial attack on Crawford and, secondly, that the king was happy to sign a letter under the privy seal denouncing an earl as a 'rebell' on the strength of a ruling from the new College of Justice.[162] Buchan's period as an outlaw probably lasted only for a short period, given the minimal sums involved.[163] He was still disputing the decision at the end of the personal rule.[164]

Buchan's namesake was John Stewart, third earl of Atholl, a man aged around twenty-nine in 1536.[165] He attended parliament in 1528, 1532, 1535 and 1540–41.[166] He was charged to serve in the Borders in January 1533 and was reported to be there by March.[167] English reports also had him accompanying the king on the royal expedition to the Isles in 1540.[168] He died of sickness between 19 October and 9 November 1542, whilst in the king's army.[169] Ward of the estate went to Henry lord Methven on 19 November 1542.[170]

Atholl's career revolved around the keeping of law and order in the Crown lands in Perthshire. As early as February 1529, he held the king's commission for executing royal justice there.[171] In October 1529 the Lords of Council considered the problem of 'heirschips, slauchteris and uthir attemptatis' in Menteith and adjacent areas 'neirer the kingis presens.'[172] Atholl gave his bond of maintenance to Campbell of Glenorchy, one of the lairds advising on the problem, at Perth in June 1532.[173] Already in December 1530, he had been granted royal authority to hold court and exact compositions for good rule from the inhabitants of his earldom and 'divers uthir landis speciffiit', in order to compensate for the expenses incurred in carrying out his commission.[174]

The main troublemakers were the Macgregor clan. At the same time as Atholl received his 1530 authority, Argyll and Sir John Campbell of Cawdor were instructed by the Lords of Council to cause the Macgregors to 'keep gude reule';[175] Atholl became involved and on 22 October 1530 expelled the Macgregors from the house of the Isle of Loch Rannoch, delivering this to the king.[176] In reward for his service, in February 1532 Atholl was granted in feu farm the lands of Fancastle (or Thayncastle) and Scheirglasl in the Crown bailiary of Apnadull.[177] The Macgregors, like the clan Chattan, lived to fight another day and in November 1533 were stealing cattle from the earl of Menteith.[178]

Atholl's interpretation of the extent of his commission was liberal. Sir Robert Menzies of that Ilk had held the bailiary of Apnadull since 1526, and in November 1529 persuaded the Lords of Council to suspend Atholl's commission in that part.[179] The rivalry between the two families in the area had its origins in the reign of James IV who had paid a 'flying visit' to Perth in 1503 to deal with the situation.[180] Possibly it was in order to take stock of the current position that James V paid a visit to the area in 1532. Pitscottie is unique amongst the 16th century chroniclers in describing a hunting trip by James to Atholl in 1529.[181] In fact both the Keeper of the Privy Seal and the Chancellor were at Perth on 8–9 September 1532, and in the same month there was a payment of £67 made by the Treasurer for the conveyance of the 'kingis bed and uthir graith to the hunting in Athole'.[182] James found things under control, and although in March 1533 the Lords of Council again suspended Atholl's commission in Apnadull and Rannoch, in response to Menzies' complaint that he held 'sinister' letters,[183] Atholl retained possession of his lands in the bailiary until March 1539. Then the grant was reduced on the grounds that it had been made during the king's lessage.[184] The reduction came just one month after Atholl had been granted the lands of Clawalg in Nairn, the entry fees being quitclaimed for the earl's past service.[185] Presumably, this gift was a compensatory one. Possibly a further confrontation had arisen between Menzies and Atholl in Apnadull, and James, like his father, was defusing the situation.

Atholl appears to have been a magnate whose royal service was appreciated by the king, notwithstanding his excessive zeal on justice commissions. There is a distinct likelihood that Atholl accompanied the king on his first, abortive, trip to France. At Pittenweem on 23 July 1536 he was granted a letter of safeguard in near identical terms to that granted to Argyll a month later.[186]

William Keith, third Earl Marischal, was around twenty-five years old in 1536.[187] He attended parliament in 1528, 1531, 1535, and 1540–41. His earlier appearances there may have been as much to carry out his honorific duties as hereditary marshal, as to make any other contribution.[188] He served alongside Huntly under the command of Moray on the Borders in March 1533, and in 1540 was reported to be on the Isles expedition.[189] It is possible that he identified himself with Huntly's interests; at Edinburgh on 27 March 1530 both parties, with the consent of their respective curators, contracted for Huntly to marry Marischal's sister, Elizabeth Keith, with a dowry of 5000 marks.[190]

Marischal also had to pay for his own marriage. In 1521 his distant kinsman, Sir William Keith of Inverugie, died, after having married three times.[191] In his estate, he left lands in Invernessshire, and the barony of Inverugie (Banff).[192] These fell to the Crown, and in 1521 ward of the barony of Inverugie was granted to the then earl of Erroll.[193] Then, in July 1527, the ward was regranted to Marischal, and at the same time the Treasurer discharged the barony from the casualty for the sum of 5000 marks.[194] In May 1529, the ward was again gifted to Marischal, and James took the comparatively rare step of warranting his possession, 'in verbo regio'.[195] This had the effect of prompting a challenge by Agnes Stewart, countess of Bothwell, and wife of Lord Maxwell, who claimed to be an assignee of the earl of Erroll. The lords held that the ward had been decided at the king's instance and thus fell to Marischal, who was to pay 1000 marks to the Treasurer.[196]

In February 1530, it was minuted in the Books of Council that Marischal had sold lands in the barony of Keith to meet heavy debts owed to the Crown, and that this alienation was lawful.[197] In September 1531, Marischal arranged to marry one of Sir William Keith's two nieces, and a letter under the privy seal was issued by the king again guaranteeing his possession of the barony. Marischal again paid 'grete soumes', and again James 'faithfullie promittis in word of ane king' that should any of the other heirs challenge his possession, the Crown would not seek to raise a summons of error. Marischal was then granted the profits of the barony, after paying £1000.[198] In May 1538, the value of the barony was assessed by the Comptroller and assessed at £480.[199] By this time Marischal was married to Margaret Keith, one of the nieces, and on 1 June 1538, at St. Andrews, they were granted a charter to half the barony, resigned by Margaret's sister, Elizabeth, a grant made for good service.[200] In September of the same year, Marischal again received from the king the gift of the ward of all of the barony, together with the remaining Inverness-shire lands in the non-entry, with the explanation that 'now after oure perfite age we have ratifiit and apprevit' the gift first made in 1529. Marischal paid the treasury £1200.[201]

The legal nicety was that, notwithstanding the fact that it was made to Marischal and to his heirs, and despite the earlier St. Andrews charter, the letter of gift ends with the note that the lands were 'decernit be decrete of the lordis of counsale to pertene to oure soverane lord as the sammyn beris'. The implication was that the Crown still regarded the ward as belonging to it; the gift was more in the form of a 'loan' until the king decided to regrant it elsewhere.

Marischal paid at least £2200 for these lands, possibly as much as £6600.[202] The transaction suggests both a willingness on the part of the Crown to sell its casualty dearly, taking full advantage of the king's Act of Revocation, and that Marischal was willing to pay the price. He was under no obligation to purchase the estate of his distant kinsman; the heart of the earldom lay in Kincardineshire. The earldom appears to have been able to bear the cost, as well as the cost of the dowry to Marischal's sister. Indeed, Marischal purchased land in Forfar from John Erskine of Dun in 1532.[203] Twice, in 1532 and in 1541, for good service and for payment, Marischal obtained charters confirming his possessions in Kincardine, and also creating Kincardine, Cowie and Durris as free burghs.[204] The king's attitude towards Marischal simply appears to have been to use the opportunity of the royal revocation to take as much money as Marischal was able comfortably to afford, but no more. There is no indication that James went back on his promise not to raise a summons of error against Inverugie.[205]

George Leslie, fourth earl of Rothes, was possibly in his early forties in 1536.[206] He attended all six full sessions of parliament in the personal rule, and also sat on various of the committee sessions, as well as acing as a lord of the articles in 1532 and 1535.[207] He was a fairly regular charter witness, the last entry in the register for him being at Stirling on 31 August 1536.[208]

The king had an ambivalent attitude to Rothes, who replaced Lord Lindsay of the Byres as sheriff of Fife in June 1529 and held on to the office throughout, his eldest son marrying Lindsay's daughter in 1541.[209] Also in June 1529, Rothes was gifted the ward of the estate of Lord Sinclair.[210] Rothes is one of the few earls to be recorded as giving James presents – three gifts of a pair of white hose at six monthly intervals in 1532–33. The royal tailor, Arthur Thomas, made a gown and doublet to match and cover the hips of the third pair.[211] Possibly due in part to the king's frequent use of Falkland palace, various members of Rothes' family can be identified in the royal Household in the later years of the personal rule.[212] The heart of the earldom lay in Fife, and between 1539 and 1542 Rothes obtained various charters of confirmation to his estates, generally for past service. There is no record or reference to his paying for these grants.[213] This was a magnate active in public service, serving on the Borders in 1533,[214] and, later in the same year, responsible for keeping the archbishop of St. Andrews under guard in St. Andrews castle.[215]

However, Rothes had been an Angus supporter. This is suggested in Pitscottie's apocryphal tale of the king's escape from Falkland [sic] in 1528. Pitscottie wrote:

> Then George [Douglas] lape on horse to ryde to Banbreich bot within twa myle he mett the earle of Rothes and schew him that the king was nocht thair. Then they passit to Falkland againe and tuik consulltatioun quhat was best to be done. . . .[216]

On 17 August 1526 Rothes had made a bond of friendship with the earl of Angus, promising his lifetime support to Angus in promoting royal authority;[217] and he may have assisted Angus against the Lennox revolt in that year.[218] This did not count for anything at the time of the royal assumption of power two years later; the first earl of Arran had also opposed Lennox. But Rothes was on the council at Edinburgh during the last few days of the Angus régime in May 1528.[219] On 6 July 1528 he was one of the lords appointed to the first secret council to attend the king daily.[220] He was on the council on 22 October to plan the Tantallon campaign.[221] On 6 November 1528 he swore the 'grete aith' for the extermination of Angus, Sir George, and Kilspindie.[222] Three days later he was dropped from the secret council, and only returned to the session on 30 December 1528.[223] When a further 'secret council' was formed in August 1529, he was not amongst it, and it was not until May 1530 that he was again designated a councillor for advising on 'grete materis'.[224] James was not concerned with Rothes' support of Angus during the minority; others, including Arran, had reached a *modus vivendi* with the Douglas régime. But he must have been furious that one of his secret counsellors had not supported him at the Tantallon siege. On 14 April 1536 Rothes, and his family and followers, received a general remission *inter alia* for his absence from the sieges of Wark (by Albany in the minority) and Tantallon. The remission was in view of his good and faithful service. Interestingly, the editor of the *Privy Seal Register* noted that the word 'faithful' appeared to be faintly scored out, possibly by a cynical clerk.[225] Rothes had a job to do in winning back the king's favour.

William Graham, second earl of Montrose, was possibly in his early thirties in 1536.[226] He attended parliament in 1532, 1535 and 1540–41, and was a lord of the articles in 1535 and 1540, as well as an occasional committee member between full sessions.[227] He had been one of the Lords of Council on 22 October 1528, and was reported as serving under Moray on the Borders in February–March 1533; by way of comparison neither Buchan nor Atholl had achieved both of these feats.[228] By 1536, Montrose also had a good track record of service as a justiciar on justice ayres, ranging from Inverness, in August 1534, to Dumfries in November 1535.[229] A rare civil litigant,[230] he was never in opposition to the king's advocate, as were, for example, Crawford, Morton and the Master of Glencairn. These factors made him a likely prospect as a vice-regent in 1536; he had never put a foot wrong. James was to designate Montrose as one of his son's tutors in June 1540, prior to the royal expedition to the Isles.[231]

Lord Maxwell's appointment reflected his criminal judicial experience in the giving of redress on the Borders. As warden of the West March, he was also, by 1535, responsible for Liddesdale.[232] Bothwell's removal from the Borders, and Lord Hume's dubious loyalties in the minority, rendered Maxwell the most important and reliable magnate on the Borders, a key figure should the vice-regents be required to defend the realm. By September 1536 Maxwell's old rival, Johnstone of that Ilk, was incarcerated in Dumbarton castle.[233]

The royal charter of 29 August 1536, granting powers to the vice-regents, considered the eventuality of any one of them dying in service.[234] The most likely one so to do was the aged Eglinton. In the selection of his vice-regents, James picked the oldest earl (Eglinton), the Chancellor (Gavin Dunbar), the former Chancellor (James Beaton), the border magnate (Maxwell), one of the earls he had neither snubbed nor had offended him (Montrose) and Huntly, possibly a man for whom the king had a certain sympathy, as well as being one of the more influential northern magnates. Huntly was possibly slightly older than the king; and, like the king, his custody had been a matter of dispute during the minority; Angus had contemplated spiriting him off to Norham castle in September 1528.[235]

The two most publicly active earls were Archibald Campbell, fourth earl of Argyll, possibly aged around twenty-seven in 1536,[236] and James Stewart, earl of Moray, about thirty-five years old.[237] Argyll had been relieved of his hereditary duties as chamberlain of Kintyre in June 1531.[238] In January 1534 Moray was interrupted in his activities as lieutenant of the north to advise on the king's wedding plans.[239] Thus, the Crown had interfered in both men's local business. However both gave their service to the Crown. Each was a potential vice-regent; indeed Argyll was appointed as regent for the duration of the king's first, abortive, trip to France in July 1536.[240] In Moray's commission as ambassador to the court of Francis I in July 1535, he was designated lieutenant-general.[241] As the king's half-brother, he contracted marriage in March 1536 on behalf of James.[242] In his youth, Moray had been tutored on the Continent by Erasmus;[243] thus he was clearly an educated man, used to travelling overseas. Hence his position and status made him the ideal choice to represent the king in France, and this may have been a more responsible task than being a vice-regent. The probable reason for Argyll's accompanying the king on his successful trip to France was that this time, unlike in the earlier attempt, James was sailing down the east coast of England, with a large force and six ships. He needed a military commander. Although Scotland and England were at peace, nevertheless the last Scots king to make such a sea journey, James I, had been kidnapped by the English.[244] Hence it was prudent on this expedition for James to have his most warlike earl with him for his protection.[245]

Rothes was on the trip to fulfil a pilgrimage at the shrine of St. John of Amiens.

This accounted for his obtaining both a general remission in April 1536 and a letter of protection for himself and his followers, on 22 July 1536, at Largo. He returned to Scotland at the end of October 1536.[246] Why James should wish to take the young second earl of Arran with him is debatable. It showed a certain amount of prudence to have his nearest heir (Albany having died in May 1536) by his side rather than leaving him at home, but the March 1537 summons to all of the earls to attend the king's homecoming shows that those whom James had taken to France had all returned home before the king of Scots himself.[247] Indeed, there is nothing to suggest that any of the magnates were at Nôtre Dame on 1 January 1537. Only Lady Fleming received fourteen elns of velvet with which to make a gown, at a cost to the treasury of £40. She was the king's half-sister.[248] Perhaps this was so that she would look good for the occasion, but the singularity of the gift suggests that the real party for the nobility was to take place on the king's entry into Edinburgh.

The fact that James took so long to return to Scotland, and sent back his lords before him, is only partially accounted for by the illness of Madeleine at Rouen. The king felt in no hurry to return. When he left in 1536, he was allied to England, and Scotland was a peaceful country, notwithstanding such incidents as the threat to outlaw Buchan, or the censuring of Crawford by the College of Justice. There was no subversive cause for any magnate to support. The last remission for treasonable assistance to the Douglases had been granted in August 1535, to Lancelot Kerr; indeed only four remissions had been given since the conclusion of peace with England on 11 May 1534.[249] In July 1535, James had sent Lord Erskine down to London both to receive the order of the Garter on his behalf, and to advise Henry VIII that the Scots king intended to treat for marriage with France.[250] Indeed, the king's attention was focused firmly on marriage; whether to Mary of Bourbon, Christiana of Denmark,[251] Mary Tudor,[252] or Margaret Erskine,[253] he alone was to decide. The eventual fulfilment of the treaty of Rouen added a French alliance to an Anglo-Scots peace. The earl of Angus, observing Scottish affairs from Berwick on 30 September 1536, had both a jaundiced and myopic view of the royal departure to France. Gloomily he reported to the English government:

I fere the King of Scottes will tary in Fraunche as shorte while He may.[254]

Quite the reverse. That James was away for nine months, latterly with none of his magnates with him,[255] demonstrates great confidence in his government back in Scotland. Individual earls may have crossed with him in court or have either given or taken offence in isolated incidents. But Crown-magnate relations were stable. In the absence of any war, or any focus for discontent, and given that the Crown was in the hands of an adult ruler with a highly efficient legal system, magnatial interest reverted – if indeed it had shifted at all – to those traditional matters which were of principal concern to them. This meant concentrating on their own local spheres of influence, and protecting their landed areas against their tenants, their neighbours, and the Crown. Conflict would manifest itself in court before it took to armed quarrels.

There was no subversion, because there was nothing to subvert; after a long minority of faction fighting, the monarch was in full control of his realm. Although this king was intrusive in some areas, this was infinitely preferable to the sudden shifts in both policy and patronage which a minority brought with it. For the majority of the magnates, the absence of their sovereign lord did not signal an opportunity for rebellion against the Crown, for their interests were local rather than national. The exceptions to this norm were those magnates in public service. It is clear that Argyll, whose influence in the Isles was diminished in 1531, and Moray, whose absence on diplomatic business took him away from the north, were loyal servants of the Crown. Temporarily, their local interests had become secondary to their public service.

The Second Estate did not consist of seditious individuals only waiting for the king to turn his back before inviting back the English and the Angus Douglases. When James left the country, he left behind a highly efficient governmental system and a body of magnates, some of whom had been on occasion the targets of typical Stewart 'sharp practice' applied through the court of session in a legalistic manner.[256] Others would experience this after 1537. But there was nothing exceptional in James' approach to Crown-magnate relations and little that was novel. The king was not generous; some of his nobility – Crawford for one, perhaps Morton and Buchan – no doubt felt a sense of grievance at the way in which they were treated at times. But their recourse was to go to court or, like Argyll and Rothes, to look for ways of recovering royal favour. Rebellion against this adult Stewart king, whether or not he was in the country, was not a constructive option. With the exception of one 'over optimistic émigré' – Bothwell in 1531 –[257] no magnate appears even to have considered rebellion as an option during the personal rule of James V.

NOTES

1. *TA*, vi, 449; *SP Henry VIII*, v, pt. iv, no. cccv.
2. *James V Letters*, 314–5, 318.
3. *TA*, vi, 453 (Erskine at Rouen, October); *LP Henry VIII*, xi, no. 916; (Moray at Rouen, October); cf *RMS*, iii, nos. 1599, 1604: (July 1536, Moray fails to appear as a witness to these two charters, exceptional for him as he was a regular witness in every other year of the personal rule).
4. *RSS*, ii, nos. 2108, 2152, 2155, 2166, 2167, 2173; *SP Henry VIII*, v, pt. iv, nos. cccv-cccvi; Abell, *op.cit.*, f. 125v.
5. *TA*, vi, 454; *SP Henry VIII*, v, pt. iv, no. cccv-cccvi.
6. *SP Henry VIII*, v, pt. iv, no. cccvi; Abell, *op.cit.*, f. 125v. This tale of a king secretly viewing his prospective bride in disguise, is elaborated upon by Buchanan, *History*, ii, 255, and liberally embroidered by Pitscottie, *Historie*, i, 358–9. Further contemporary evidence supporting the idea of a royal disguise is given in a report by John Hudson, English diplomat at Rouen, who wrote to Cromwell on 9 October advising him of the king's

landing at Dieppe in twilight. James came ashore with fifteen other gentlemen, but no-one could distinguish them apart. The next morning the king left secretly for Rouen and few knew he had been at Dieppe at all: cf. *LP Henry VIII*, xi, no. 631.

7. *TA*, vi, 454–5; *LP Henry VIII*, xi, no. 916.

8. *TA*, vi, 453, 455.

9. *LP Henry VIII*, xi, no. 711.

10. *Ibid.*, xi, no. 848 (Moulins, 23 October), 953; *James V Letters*, 324, (Amboise, 18 November); *RSS*, ii, nos. 2911–2 (Chatêlherault, 20–22 November); *RSS*, ii, nos. 2193–4 (Blois, 23–24 November); cf. also Bapst, *op.cit.*, 292 (Chapelle, 13 October) and *passim*.

11. *James V Letters*, 325–6.

12. *RSS*, ii, no. 2199 (1 December 1536, Orleans); *TA*, vi, 456. (James' coffers taken from Fontainebleau to Paris in early December).

13. *TA*, vi, 456–7; cf. Bapst, *op.cit.*, 305.

14. Teulet, *Papiers*, i, no. XXIV; *LP Henry VIII*, xii, pt. i, no. 12.

15. These negotiations are covered comprehensively in Bapst, *op.cit.*, *passim*. Several of the possibilities are referred to in *James V Letters*, 33–5, 36, 43–4, 52, 90. 99, 156. 163. 172. 234. 281. 299. 302. Other references are in *LP Henry VIII*, iv, pt. iii, nos. 5258, 5452, 5790; v, nos. 125, 941, 1004, 1367; vii, no. 957; x, nos. 423, 6061, 699, 728. The full list is Louise (1515–1517), Charlotte (1516–1524), Madeleine (1520–1537) and Marguerite (b. 1523), all daughters of Francis I; Renée (b. 1510), 3rd cousin of Francis I; Mary of Lorraine (b. 1515), daughter of Duke of Guise, married (first), Duke of Longueville, married (second) James V; Mary of Bourbon (b. 1515), daughter of Duke of Vendôme; Isobel d'Albret, sister of king of Navarre; Catherine de Medici (b. 1519), niece by marriage of John, duke of Albany and ward of Pope Clement VII; Dorothea and Christiana, daughters of Frederick, duke of Holstein and king of Denmark; Dorothea and Christiana, daughters of Christian II of Denmark and nieces of Charles V; Maria, queen of Hungary and sister of Charles V; Marie of Portugal (b. 1521), niece of Charles V, died unmarried; her namesake, Marie of Portugal (b. 1528), later married Emperor Maximilian II; Mary Tudor (b. 1516), daughter of Henry VIII; and Margaret Erskine, daughter of John, fifth lord Erskine and mistress of James V. See map on p. 132

16. *RSS*, ii, no. 2219 (Chantilly, 9 February); *TA*, vi, 462; vii, 14, 18 (Compiègne, 11, 25, February); *LP Henry VIII*, xii, pt. i, no. 496. (One crown was roughtly equal to 22s. Scots: cf. e.g., *TA*, vi, 412, 167–8).

17. *LP Henry VIII*, xii, pt. i, no. 762; *RSS*, ii, nos. 2222, 2226.

18. *APS*, ii, 357.

19. *TA*, vi, 464; vii, 24; *RSS*, ii, no. 2260.

20. *TA*, vii, 181.

21. *RMS*, iii, nos. 1618, 1640. The text of the commission of reappointment is given in Fraser, *Eglinton*, ii, no. 129.

22. *ADCP*, 294.

23. *RMS*, iii, *passim*, Appendix I.

24. *Ibid.*, iii, nos. 1523, 1632, 1643, 1645.

25. *Ibid.*, iii, nos. 1626–1666.

26. *Ibid.*, iii, nos. 1534–1625, 1667–1741.

27. *ADCP*, 459. The record is probably missing. Several court actions are 'lost' as a result. On 2 August 1536 the Chancellor, Huntly, Montrose, Eglinton and Argyll were sitting as 'lords regent', together with Rothes, Sir James Foulis of Colinton (Clerk Register), Colville of Ochiltree (Comptroller), Sir John Campbell of Lundy, Adam Otterburn of Redhall (king's advocate), and Thomas Bellenden of Auchnoule (justice clerk); *ibid.*, 458; SRO, *ADCS*, viii, f. 158. It is possible that the regents sat on the session regularly during the king's absence.

28. *RSS*, ii, nos. 2206, 2710, 2243 *et passim*; *HMC Fifteenth Report*, App. pt. viii, 92, no. 17.

29. *RMS*, iii, *passim*, cf. Emond, *op.cit.*, App. D.

30. Cf. *MW*, i, Preface and *passim*; *TA*, vi; vii, *passim*. An attempt to compile a full list of separate taxes levied in this period, has been made by Murray, *Revenues*, App. B; cf. also O'Brien, *op.cit.*, App. O.

31. *James V Letters*, 213.

32. *LP Henry VIII*, vi, no. 269; de Beauvais, French envoy to Scotland, also mentioned that the archbishop was being held for communicating with England: *ibid.*, vi, no. 918.

33. *James V Letters*, 239; cf. *HP*, i, no. 8, for original in Latin.

34. The question of taxation and the institution of the College of Justice has been examined in depth by R.K. Hannay in *The College of Justice* (Edinburgh, 1933) and *The College of Justice* (edd. The Stair Society, 1990). The figure of £72,000 for the commutation of the 'Great Tax' was calculated by Hannay using extant accounts for Kelso abbey: cf. R.K. Hannay, 'A Study in Reformation History', in *SHR*, xxiii, 223–5.

35. Cf. *Diurnal of Occurrents*, 17, where it is stated that on 19 April 1533, James Beaton was placed in the keeping of the earl of Rothes and Bishop of Galloway, suspected of the crime of lèse majesté. Cf. also *ADCP*, 400 (2 May 1533); Beaton held by virtue of a papal decree.

36. Teulet, *Papiers*, i, no. xxiii, dated wrongly; cf. D.E. Fasson, *Gavin Dunbar* (Edinburgh, 1947), 51, and *James V Letters*, 242–4.

37. *SP Henry VIII*, iv, pt. iv, no. ccxxxi.

38. *TA*, v, 450; vi, 227–8, 231.

39. *Ibid.*, vi, 450. All three appear to have acted as unofficial 'purse masters'. Cf. Murray, *Pursemaster*. Robert Gibb has been the subject of a somewhat hagiographic biography by Sir G.D. Gibb, *The Life and Times of Robert Gib Lord of Carriber, Familiar Servitor and Master of Stables to James V* (London, 1874); cf. *ER*, xvi, 270.

40. *MW*, i, 196, 199–200.

41. *RMS*, iii, no. 1618.

42. *TA*, vi, 310–12. These were Argyll, Arran, Atholl, Buchan, Cassillis, Crawford, Eglinton, Erroll, Glencairn, Huntly, Marischal, Montrose, Moray, Morton and Rothes. That Argyll, Arran and Moray were all summoned suggests that they, like Rothes, had returned from France before the king.

43. There are two items which suggest that Lennox was still in Scotland in 1534–35. In November 1534 he was charged by Argyll to appear in court for payment of 2000 marks owed as part of a marriage contract between the two parties: SRO Montrose Papers [GD 220/6], no. 1979 (3). Also, an undated letter by Lennox, writing from Edinburgh to his brother in France, has been placed in 1535 by Fraser in Fraser, *Lennox*, ii, no. 192. Neither item proves Lennox was then still in the country.

44. *RSS*, ii, no. 1163; *ER*, xvi, 548–9.

45. *ER*, xvii, 768.

46. *RSS*, ii, no. 1307; Fraser, *Lennox*, i, no. 149.

47. He had, however, been at parliament in both April 1531 and May 1532: *APS*, ii, 332–5.

48. Fraser, *Lennox*, i, no. 142; SRO, Montrose Papers [GD 220/6], no. 1980 (3).

49. *TA*, vii, 120, 280, 438, 443.

50. *RSS*, ii, no. 4909. Margaret may have been the king's mistress: cf. n. 260.

51. *Ibid.*, ii, no. 156; Watt, *Fasti*, 217.

52. *RSS*, ii, no. 2458; *TA*, vi, 372; SRO, *ADCS*, x, f. 165.

53. *RSS*, ii, nos. 1976, 2509; *RMS*, iii, no. 520; *TA*, vi, 371.

54. *ER*, xvii, 739; cf. *Scots Peerage*, vi, 151–4.

55. *RMS*, iii, no. 960.

56. *Ibid.*, iii, nos. 2343, 2811.

57. *Spalding Miscellany*, ii, 195, no. xvi; *ER*, xvii, 713; Fraser, *Menteith*, ii, no. 98.

58. *APS*, ii, 357.

59. *ADCP*, 439, 445.

60. *Ibid.*, 379–81; *LP Henry VIII*, v, no. 595.

61. An heir reached his majority at the age of twenty-one: cf. *Regiam Maj.*, 151–2.
62. *RSS*, ii, no. 3646; *RMS*, iii, no. 2202.
63. He was alive in May 1520: *James V Letters*, 76.
64. *RSS*, ii, no. 6; *ER*, xvi, 555–6.
65. *APS*, ii, 339–40. This parliament saw an outpouring of legislation reflecting matters of concern to both the royal demesne and to the burghs. There was also a tax of £2000 for ambassadorial expenses levied on all three Estates, at the rate of 3s. for every pound of land 'of auld extent': *Ibid.*, 342; cf. Murray, *Revenues*, App. (1), h. Both the Stewart earls of Lennox and the Hamilton earls of Arran were descended from James III's sister.
66. Cf. *Scots Peerage*, iii, 568 ff.
67. Cf. *Ibid.*, ii, 468; *APS*, ii, 339–40, 355–6, 368.
68. *RSS*, ii, no. 642.
69. Cf. I.D. Macfarlane, *op.cit.*, 42, 47.
70. *Scots Peerage*, ii, 465; Pitcairn, *Trials*, i, pt. i, 136; cf. *Protocol Book of Gavin Ros* (SRS, 1908), edd. J. Anderson and F.J. Ross [*Prot. Bk. Ros.*], 137, no. 775. (John Campbell in Polquhirter, parish clerk of Cumnock, to be entered 5 October 1527 at the Tolbooth, Edinburgh, for Cassillis' murder).
71. *ADCP*, 446; SRO, *ADCS*, vii, ff. 116, 181; viii, ff. 29v, 82v. This was one of the 'lost' actions: cf. n. 27.
72. *ADCP*, 258.
73. *Ibid.*, 446.
74. SRO, *ADCS*, ix, ff. 118v, 120.
75. *LP Henry VIII*, xiii, pt. ii, no. 263; *Balcarres Papers*, 9, no. v. Why the Cardinal should have so intervened is obscure; Campbell had apparently never been to France.
76. *HP*, i, no. 278. The English king was looking for people to subvert. There is no suggestion that Campbell was an English sympathiser in the personal reign; that the Cardinal of Lorraine should have interceded on his behalf in 1538 suggests the opposite.
77. *RSS*, ii, no. 2614; cf. *RMS*, iii, no. 2270.
78. *ER*, xvii, 760–2. The annual revenue of the earldom was approximately £725.
79. *RMS*, iii, no. 2135.
80. *RSS*, ii, no. 3833.
81. *Ibid.*, ii, no. 3788; Campbell had been gifted these by charter under the great seal in March 1527: *RMS*, iii, no. 431.
82. *RMS*, iii, nos. 2268–9; *LP Henry VIII*, xiii, pt. i, no. 709; *APS*, ii, 355–6, 368.
83. *RSS*, i, no. 3967; *APS*, ii, 329.
84. Wormald, *Bonds*, App. B, no. 34. Both were killed at Melrose in 1526.
85. Fraser, *Lennox*, i, no. 146. He was killed at Linlithgow in 1526.
86. *HP*, i, no. 331. The English privy council in March 1543 were thus reluctant to send Campbell into Scotland as the 'kinges majeste remembrethe that there hathe been a dedely fede between him and therle of Casselles'.
87. *LP Henry VIII*, iv, pt. II, no. 4531, the only connotation being that he was a close adviser of the king.
88. Pitcairn, *Trials*, i, pt. i, 181.
89. *Prot. Bk. Ros*, nos. 732, 909, 1078, 1263, 1265, 1288.
90. In 1528–29 he was entrusted with the safe keeping of charters and other documents relating to a marriage contract arranged between Campbell of Loudoun and Alexander Kennedy of Bargany: *ibid.*, nos. 887, 929, 977.
91. He contracted marriage to Marion Douglas in 1492: *Scots Peerage*, i, 186 ff.
92. *TA*, vii, 394 (still described as 'Master' in September 1540); *ER*, vii, 625 (described as earl in June 1541).
93. SRO, *ADC*, Vol. 40, ff. 96v, 123, 144.
94. *ADCP*, 198; Fraser, *Eglinton*, ii, no. 109; cf. Emond, *op.cit.*
95. *ADCP*, 244–5; Pitcairn, *Trials*, i, pt. i, 132–3.

96. *RMS*, iii, nos. 511–3; Fraser, *Eglinton*, ii, 115.
97. *ADCP*, 276.
98. SRO, Glencairn Muniments [GD 39], no. 42.
99. SRO, *ADC*, Vol. 39, f. 40v.
100. SRO, RH 2.1.9. (*ADC*, vol. 38, f. 129v); *ADCP*, 278.
101. *Scots Peerage*, i, 186.
102. Fraser, *Eglinton*, ii, no. 115. Eglinton was pursued for civil damages by Auchinharvie's widow in 1536: SRO, *ADCS*, xi, f. 39.
103. *APS*, ii, 328–9; *SP Henry VIII*, iv, pt. iv, no. clxxxv.
104. Fraser, *Eglinton*, ii, no. 116.
105. *ADCP*, 295.
106. SRO, *ADC*, vol. 39, f. 40v.
107. SRO, Glencairn Muniments, nos. 36, 44; *RMS*, iii, no. 273.
108. Fraser, *Eglinton*, ii, no. 130. It is not clear when Montgomery died – probably before the 1524 agreement. He was certainly dead before February 1532. His killer was Robert Cunningham of Abot: SRO, RH 2.1.15. ('Transcripts of *Acta Dominorum Concilii*'), f. 28.
109. *Ibid.*, ii, nos. 122–3.
110. The intricacies of the succession rights arose because he married twice. There was a question mark over the degree of consanguinity between himself and his second wife, Janet Cunningham. His daughter, Marion, tried to declare her sister, Christine, illegitimate: SRO, Glencairn Muniments, nos. 30, 31, 37, 29 *et passim*.
111. *Ibid.*, nos. 31, 32; *RMS*, iii, no. 541.
112. *ER*, xvi, 528; *RSS*, ii, no. 725.
113. SRO, *ADC*, vol. 39, f. 20.
114. *Ibid.*, vol. 43, ff. 103, 150v.
115. *ADCP*, 370, 372–3.
116. SRO, *ADCS*, i, f. 23v. Quite why this should have been the outcome shows a deeper investigation than had been carried out in December 1528. Probably the political partiality of the Lords of Council was more a factor in 1528 than in June 1532, when the College of Justice was first functioning as a distinct body.
117. *Ibid.*, i, ff. 48v, 88.
118. *Ibid.*, iii, f. 53v; *RMS*, iii, no. 1301.
119. *RSS*, ii, no. 1347; SRO, Glencairn Muniments, no. 39.
120. Fraser, *Eglinton*, ii, no. 125.
121. They were summoned to be at Edinburgh on 5 January 1533: *TA*, vi, 119. There is no indication that any reprisals took place for absenteeism.
122. *Scots Peerage*, iii, 434. He died in 1545.
123. *TA*, vi, 392; *LP Henry VIII*, xv, no. 704. He had served as Treasurer in 1525–6: *TA*, v, 270.
124. *Scots Peerage*, vi, 358.
125. SRO, Morton Papers, nos. 286, 288; *HMC, Fifteenth Report*, pt. VIII, no. i; *RMS*, iii, no. 1225 (Finnart acted as Arran's representative).
126. *Ibid.*, nos. 284–5; *Registrum Honoris de Morton* (Bannatyne Club, 1853) [*Mort. Reg.*], i, nos. 1–2. The date of Morton's request to James for the marriage is wrongly given as 17 June 1528 by Fraser, *Carlaverock*, ii, no. 1. (James was not then at Falkland, the place where he granted consent to the marriage).
127. He married Katherine Stewart, illegitimate daughter of James IV by Margaret Boyd, before 1507: *Scots Peerage*, vi, 358 ff.
128. *Mort. Reg.*, i, no. 4.
129. *Ibid.*, ii, no. 244. The terms of the contract were to rent certain of the parish church lands to the earl to continue his coal-mining, and also manure the fields with his livestock in return for 40 shillings *per annum*.
130. SRO, *ADC*, vol. 39, ff. 48v, 80.
131. SRO, Morton Papers, no. 289.

132. SRO, *ADC*, vol. 40, f. 130v. Peter was John Damian, alchemist in the reign of James IV: cf. Macdougall, *James IV*, 216–7, 238, 288.
133. This was a recognised legal principle in the early sixteenth century. The interdict could be voluntarily imposed by the party himself, and this may have been the case for Morton. The consent came from any friend named by the party under the interdict: Balfour, *Practicks* , i, 186–7.
134. Charter Chest of the Earldom of Wigtown, 1214–1681., ed. F.J. Grant (SRS, 1910 (Pt. 49)) [Wigtown Charter Chest], 68, no. 536; Mort. Reg., i, no. 5.
135. SRO, *ADCS*, i, f. 96v. ('Sinister' meaning 'wrong'.)
136. *RMS*, iii, nos. 1355, 1466.
137. *Wigtown Charter Chest*, 63, nos. 498–9; 67, 534; SRO, Morton Papers, no. 296.
138. *Ibid.*, 64, no. 504; SRO, *ADCS*, vi, f. 215; *RMS*, iii, no. 1512.
139. Cf. n. 133.
140. SRO, *ADCS*, i, f. 120; cf. *Acta Sessionis* (Stair), Case no. 38.
141. SRO, *ADCS*, ii, f. 185; cf. *Acta Sessionis* (Stair), Case no. 40.
142. *RSS*, i, nos. 2835, 3733.
143. *Mort. Reg.*, i, no. 3.
144. SRO, *ADCS*, ii, f. 101; *ER*, xvi, 101, 211; cf. *Acta Sessionis* (Stair), Case no. 5.
145. *APS*, ii, 329.
146. *RMS*, iii, no. 1475.
147. SRO, *ADCS*, x, f. 131; xi, 215; *TA*, vi, 407, 431.
148. *Mort. Reg.*, ii, nos. 245–258.
149. The first earl was uncle to James III: cf. Macdougall, *James III*, *passim*.
150. *APS*, ii, 334–5, 339–40.
151. *Scots Peerage*, ii, 268.
152. *RMS*, iii, no. 625.
153. *APS*, ii, 321–2; SRO, RH 2.1.9. (*ADC*, vol. 38), 184; *ADCP*, 289.
154. *LP Henry VIII*, vi, no. 269.
155. SRO, *ADCS*, iii, ff. 209–10v.
156. The principle that an affirmation of warandice was required from the original granter after the grantee was temporarily dispossessed was established at that time: cf. Balfour, *Practicks*, II, 318 ff.
157. SRO, *ADCS*, iv, f. 151.
158. *Ibid.*, vi, f. 32; viii, ff. 21, 147.
159. *Ibid.*, vi, 106v; *RSS*, ii, no. 1343.
160. *RSS*, ii, no. 2311; *TA*, vi, 323.
161. *RMS*, iii, no. 1850.
162. This is another 'lost' case and thus the composition of the session which gave the final ruling in Crawford's favour cannot be identified (cf. n. 27).
163. On 17 July 1537, he was on the assize that tried Lady Glamis: Pitcairn, *Trials*, 190.
164. SRO, *ADCS*, xvi, ff. 33, 62v; *AD*, i, 60v.
165. *Scots Peerage*, i, 443 ff.
166. *APS*, ii, 321–2, 324–5, 339–40, 355–6, 368.
167. *TA*, vi, 124; *LP Henry VIII*, vi, no. 217. (Though the name given by Sir Thomas Clifford is 'Athe' – possibly a version of Rothes, recognised as being there in February: *ibid.*, vi, no. 163).
168. *LP Henry VIII*, vi, no. 709.
169. *ADCP*, 530; *RSS*, ii, no. 4975; cf. Lesley, *History*, 164, records him as dying at Edinburgh after Fala.
170. *RSS*, ii, no. 4981.
171. SRO, *ADC*, vol. 39, f. 104v.
172. *ADCP*, 317.
173. Wormald, *Bonds*, App. A, 199, no. 1.

174. *RSS*, ii, no. 784.
175. *ADCP*, 343–4.
176. *Ibid.*, 367–8; cf. 'The Fortirgal Chronicle' in *Taymouth Bk.*, 120–1, where he was said to have achieved their expulsion with the assistance of the Donoghue clan.
177. *RMS*, iii, no. 1139; *ER*, xv, 289.
178. Pitcairn, *Trials*, i, pt. i, 164.
179. *RSS*, i, no. 3454; SRO, *ADC*, vol. 39, f. 104v.
180. Macdougall, *James IV*, 157–8.
181. Pitscottie, *Historie*, i, 335–8. Pitscottie was apparently anxious to secure the fourth earl of Atholl as a patron: *ibid.*, Pref. xlviii ff.
182. *RSS*, ii, nos. 1402–3; *RMS*, iii, no. 1221; *TA*, vi, 103.
183. SRO, *ADCS*, ii, f. 143; *Acta Sessionis* (Stair), Case 39. Menzies resigned the lands of Rannoch in favour of his son in May 1533: *RMS*, iii, 1280.
184. *Ibid.*, xi, f. 207. Presumably the real proposition was that the grant fell by virtue of the Rouen Act of Revocation.
185. *RMS*, iii, no. 1917.
186. *RSS*, ii, nos. 2113, 2150: i.e. to protect himself and kinsmen during the king's absence and for forty days afterwards.
187. He still required curatorial consent on 8 September 1531, his curators then being George Crichton, bishop of Dunkeld, and John Leslie, rector of Philorth: *RMS*, iii, no. 1068.
188. *APS*, ii, 321–2, 332–3, 339–40, 335–6, 368. The Marshal had the task of directing the order of seating of attendants, and the task was often carried out by a deputy – as indeed it was in the 1532 parliament and also at the numerous committees held between full sessions: *Ibid.*, 334–5, (Gilbert Wauchope of Niddrie-Marshall, deputy marshal in 1532); *et passim* (Andrew Baron, Patrick Baron of Spittalfield, Thomas Porteus, Robert Barton of Over-Barnton, John Grierson of Largs, at committees). Cf. R.K. Hannay, 'Observations on the Officers of the Scottish Parliament', *JR*, 44, (1932).
189. *LP Henry VIII*, vi, no. 269; xv, no. 709.
190. *Spalding Miscellany*, iv, 138, no. x. (The Gordon Papers). Gavin Dunbar, bishop of Aberdeen, acted for both parties. Huntly's other curator was Sir William Scott of Balwearie, Marischal's was the bishop of Dunkeld. Huntly did marry Elizabeth: cf. e.g. *RMS*, iii, no. 3103.
191. *RSS*, i, no. 3198; *Scots Peerage*, vi, 34; ix, 69, 94, *et passim*.
192. *ER*, xvii, 754–6.
193. *RSS*, i, no. 3198.
194. *Ibid.*, i, no. 3851; *TA*, v, 294.
195. *RSS*, ii, nos. 124, 129.
196. SRO, *ADC*, vol. 40, ff. 24v, 25, 26v, 53.
197. *ADCP*, 321.
198. *RSS*, ii, nos. 1008–9; *TA*, v, 406.
199. *ER*, xvii, 755–6. Sixteen years of non-entry totalled £7680.
200. *RMS*, iii, no. 1798.
201. *RSS*, ii, no. 2730 and n. ; *TA*, vii, 67.
202. Taking into account the 5000 marks discharged in 1527, and the 1000 marks required by the Treasury in 1529.
203. *RMS*, iii, no. 1217.
204. *Ibid.*, iii, nos. 1113, 2299. The 1541 charter was presumably obtained in the context of the ratification of the Act of Revocation in parliament in December 1540: *APS*, ii, 357.
205. Cf. SRO, *ADCS*, xiii, f. 219. (Action by Margaret and Elizabeth Keith and Marischal to reduce a pretended charter to Duffus held by Sutherland of Duffus; case continued, but there are no further details).
206. He was served heir in 1513, married by 1520, and died in 1553. See under title in *Scots Peerage*, vii.

207. *APS*, ii, 321–2, 332–5, 339–40, 355–6, 368 *et passim*.
208. *RMS*, iii, no. 1621 *et passim*.
209. *Ibid.*, iii, nos. 798, 2227, 2290. Lindsay was sacked for negligent misconduct; his dismissal does not appear to have been politically motivated.
210. *RSS*, ii, no. 151 (9 June 1529). The government appears to have thought that Lord Sinclair was killed at the battle of Summerdale.
211. *TA*, vi, 30, 76, 84. This may have been a token rent for a blenche holding. Another earl who gave James a present was Huntly, presenting the king with a gown lined with crimson silk in July 1537: *Ibid.*, vi, 339.
212. E.g., *Ibid.*, vii, 204, 275, 315; viii, 31, 37, 47 *et passim*: payments in 1540–41 for purchase of clothing. The earl's eldest son was described as 'familiar servant' in 1541 and granted the free barony of Leslie: *RMS*, iii, no. 2241.
213. *RMS*, iii, nos. 1988, 1992, 2094, 2809–10; latterly, these grants were to himself and wife in liferent and to his heir in fee.
214. SRO, *ADCS*, ii, f. 152; *LP Henry VIII*, vi, no. 163.
215. *TA*, vi, 128; *LP Henry VIII*, vi, no. 450.
216. Pitscottie, *Historie*, i, 326. Banbreich (Ballanbreich) was part of the earldom of Rothes: e.g. *RMS*, iii, nos. 1997, 2094, 2702.
217. Wormald, *Bonds*, App. B, no. 30.
218. Most of the Fife lairds appear to have supported Lennox: cf. Emond, *op.cit.*, 510, 511, and notes. Angus considered that Lord Lindsay of the Byres was a Lennox supporter.
219. SRO, RD 2.1.9; *ADC*, vol. 38, ff. 110v, 113, 117.
220. *ADCP*, 277.
221. *Ibid.*, 289; SRO, RH 2.1.9; *ADC*, vol. 38, f. 184.
222. *ADCP*, 290.
223. *Ibid.*, 294; SRO, RH 2.1.9. (*ADC*, vol. 38, f. 187; vol. 39, f. 55, *et passim*).
224. *ADCP*, 315, 327. The 'gret materis' of 1530 related to control of the Borders.
225. *RSS*, ii, no. 2002. The remission also remitted and quitclaimed Rothes of a fine for default in paying pledges for the entry before the justiciar of various persons involved in a crime committed in May 1532 at Lindores abbey and Mugdrum island. This was in connection with a dispute between Rothes and the abbot of Lindores over the right to cut the reeds growing on Mugdrum island: *Acta Sessionis* (Stair), Case 7.
226. He was born after 1492 and married c.1515: cf. *Scots Peerage*, vi, 44ff.
227. *APS*, ii, 334–5, 339–40, 355–6, 368 *et passim*.
228. SRO, RH 2.1.9. (*ADC*, vol. 38, f. 184); *LP Henry VIII*, vi, nos. 163, 217.
229. *TA*, vi, 219, 224, 265–7; Pitcairn, *Trials*, 165–6, 167–8; cf. *RSS*, ii, nos. 1824–1880 (justice ayre Dumfries, November 1535).
230. He had a dispute with David Stratoun for the latter's wrongful despoliation in late 1534: SRO, *ADCS*, v, f. 150v.
231. *HMC, Mar 38*; Kellie, i, 14–5. The other designated tutors were Lord Erskine and the absent earl of Lennox.
232. *ADCP*, 431 (January 1535); *TA*, vi, 265 (August 1535, with Lord Fleming).
233. *TA*, vi, 307.
234. *RMS*, iii, no. 1618.
235. *ADCP*, 319 (Huntly with Margaret and James), 253; *RSS*, i, no. 3538 (his ward to Angus); *SP Henry VIII*, iv, pt. iv, 510 (to Norham).
236. Argyll's age can only be estimated. He married in 1529, and succeeded as heir to his father in that year without a non-entry: cf. *Scots Peerage*, i, 377. He may have been older.
237. *RMS*, i, no. 2585 (created earl in June 1501); *James V Letters*, 54 (aged 16 or 17 in 1517).
238. *ADCP*, 356.
239. *Ibid.*, 412; *TA*, vi, 219.
240. *ADCP*, 458, on 2 August 1536.
241. *James V Letters*, 294–5.

242. *Ibid.*, 314–5. The Duke of Albany, being ill, ratified this afterwards, as did Francis.

243. *Ibid.*, 252, at Siena. According to Erasmus he was 'a boy of great promise'.

244. M. Brown, *James I* (Edinburgh, 1994), 17.

245. The appellation given Argyll by Chapuys, imperial ambassador to London, in 1534: *LP Henry VIII*, vii, no. 1057.

246. *ADCP*, 452; *RSS*, ii, nos. 2002, 2108; *TA*, vi, 453.

247. Fleming, David Beaton, and Sir Thomas Erskine would have gone to France in their official capacities. The abbot of Kinloss was one of the commissioners for marriage to Mary of Bourbon: *James V Letters*, 314–5. Sir James Douglas of Drumlanrig, married to Angus' sister, Margaret, was perhaps looking to obtain divorce from her; she had refused to live with him at Drumlanrig in 1530, and by 1539 had arranged a separation, his divorce coming through the following year: *HMC, Fifteenth Report*, pt. 8, 15–16. He received a confirmation of the non-entry of his estate at Paris on 27 January 1537: *Ibid.*, 15. Douglas of Drumlanrig fell from grace in 1541, and fled to England. This was because of his complicity in the murder of Henry Sinclair, parson of Kirkbride: *TA*, viii, 72–3; *HP*, i, no. 68; *RSS*, ii, nos. 3963, 4121; cf. Kelley, *Angus*, 517–8. The Prior of Pittenweem would be on his way to Rome to look for papal approval in his bid to secure Coldingham priory: *James V Letters*, 334–5, cf. ch. 3. There is no clear explanation as to why Gordon of Lochinvar went to France.

248. *TA*, vii, 44; *RMS*, iii, no. 515.

249. *RSS*, ii, nos. 1580, 1581, 1610, 1666; *James V Letters*, 267.

250. *James V Letters*, 297; *LP Henry VIII*, viii, nos. 1153; ix, no. 233.

251. The reason for the visit to Scotland by Peter Suevenius, envoy of Christian II, in 1535: *LP Henry VIII*, ix, no. 1178.

252. At the urging of Charles V in 1534: *James V Letters*, 265–6; cf. Bapst, *op.cit.*, 274–8.

253. In June 1536, Pope Paul III wrote to advise James that this was not possible as her divorce from her previous husband was not valid: *James V Letters*, 320. She was the daughter of Lord Erskine, and James bestowed on her an annual grant of 500 marks from the Edinburgh customs on 26 August 1536, just before leaving for France: *RSS*, ii, no. 2138. James possibly had at least six other mistresses. They are given as (1) Elizabeth Beaton, cousin of David Beaton who married Lord Innermeath: *RSS*, ii, no. 2206; *RMS*, iii, no. 3012; *HMC Fifteenth Report*, App. pt. viii, 92, no. 17; (2) Elizabeth [*sic*]Stewart, daughter of John, third earl of Lennox – perhaps Margaret, who received the gift of the marriage of the Master of Hume in 1542: *RSS*, ii, no. 4909, alternatively Eleanor, who married the sixth earl of Erroll: *ibid.*, ii, nos. 4016, 4525; (3) Elizabeth Shaw, daughter of Alexander Shaw of Sauchie, who died before 31 August 1536: *RMS*, iii, no. 1620; (4) Elizabeth Carmichael, daughter of Sir John Carmichael; (5) Euphemia Elphinstone, daughter of the first Lord Elphinstone; and (6) Christina Barclay, perhaps daughter of Barclay of Touch: cf. *RMS*, iii, no. 1620; Dunbar, *Scots Kings*, 238–9.

254. *SP Henry VIII*, v, pt. iv, no. cccvi.

255. Cf. *HP*, i, no. 41, when in April 1537, Angus was under the impression that Moray was then in France. Possibly he had returned there to escort the royal party home.

256. Wormald, *Court*, 24, uses this phrase in connection with James V.

257. Donaldson, *op.cit.*, 55.

CHAPTER EIGHT

National Politics and the Executions of 1537

During the personal rule of James V there were three individuals convicted for the treasonable crime of conspiring to kill the king. Two convictions were secured in July 1537, some two months after the king's return from France; the third occurred in August 1540, a month after the king returned from his expedition to the Isles. All three individuals, John, Master of Forbes, Janet Douglas, Lady Glamis, and Sir James Hamilton of Finnart, were sentenced to death.[1] The executions of the Master of Forbes and Lady Glamis occurred within three days of each other.

I. THE MASTER OF FORBES

The Master of Forbes was the eldest surviving son of John, sixth lord Forbes, and was probably about twenty-five years old at the time of his trial.[2] John, Lord Forbes was reported by the English to be amongst those magnates who accompanied the king on his re-entrance into Edinburgh from Stirling in late June or early July 1528.[3] On 22 October 1528 he attended the session of the Lords of Council at which the plans for the siege of Tantallon were made;[4] on 6 November 1528 he swore the 'grete aith' against the Douglases, and four days later he was on the list of those on whose service the earl of Moray could count in exterminating the clan Chattan.[5]

However, this early impression of Forbes as a royal supporter is somewhat belied by the activities of his family. In 1526 Alexander Seton of Meldrum and William Leslie of Balquhain paid £88 to the treasury to obtain a remission for the murder of William Forbes, Gavin Murray, and Andrew Stratoun. At the same time, Lord Forbes paid £182 for a remission for his part in the death of John Leslie.[6] On 27 January 1528, William and Alexander, both younger sons of Lord Forbes, were acquitted at the Aberdeen justice ayre by Sir William Scott of Balwearie, justiciar, for the murders of Meldrum, John Leslie in Kinawty (Kinaldie), and Malcom Leslie in Garioch.[7]

What lay behind these pardons was a dispute in Aberdeen which had been running for at least the last ten years of the minority and in which the Forbes kindred were ranged against almost everybody else. The disturbances were temporarily brought to a halt through the efforts of Scott of Balwearie in

February 1528, when Lord Forbes was induced to enter into a decree-arbitral with both Leslie of Balquhain and the city of Aberdeen itself.[8] Despite this settlement, and possibly because the killer of Meldrum had not yet been found, the disturbances continued. 'For ordouring and pecifying of the north cuntre and expulsioun of the kingis rebellis sa that the kingis liegis may leif in pece and rest', on 9 November 1528 the Lords of Council ordered Lord Forbes to remain at Edinburgh, in ward, until he found sufficient caution to enter the Master in his place.[9] Evidently, Forbes did not daunt the clan Chattan (who were rebels in the north country) as he left ward in March 1529, in order to pass home for good rule of the country.[10] Whether or not the Master took his place is not recorded. On 29 July 1530, the provost and bailies of Aberdeen prepared themselves for an attack by the Forbes family, and on the following day this materialised, led by the Master.[11] In September Forbes was again ordered to enter the Master under penalty of £5000 and threat of his own ward in Blackness castle.[12] On 10 October he was fined £2000 for the breach of the 1528 decree-arbitral, and his lands were apprised for this amount.[13] In December of the same year Forbes again made a bond with the city of Aberdeen for the future good behaviour of all of his kindred, under penalty of £5000 for breach.[14]

On 10 October 1530, at Dundee, the Master found caution, in his father, to underlie the law at the next Aberdeen justice ayre for his involvement in the death of Seton of Meldrum, and curiously this appeared to satisfy the king as to his innocence; for on the same day the Master received a charter under the great seal giving him a remission for this and all his other crimes to date. The charter was granted 'for gratitude and special favour', and was conditional on his future good behaviour; treason against the king's person was excepted. The gratitude expressed may have been for the £1000 fine which Forbes paid for the charter.[15] However, notwithstanding the remission, the Master was required to remain south of the Firth of Forth, Lord Forbes giving this guarantee to the king at Stirling on 2 November 1530.[16] Over the course of the next two years Forbes had his lands apprised for the sum of £600 owed to Gilbert Menzies of Findone, provost of Aberdeen, and for £2090 owed to Andrew Fraser of Kinmundy; in each case for the profits of lands appropriated by the Forbes kindred.[17] Also he was required to compensate Alexander, lord Elphinstone for an attack made on Kildrummy castle in 1525, and for general crimes committed by the Master and his accomplices.[18] Clearly the family had few friends. In December 1531, Forbes was again obliged to guarantee the security of the city of Aberdeen and undertake to enter the Master into ward for any breach of the peace, under penalty of £2000.[19] The extant evidence suggests that the Master of Forbes was far more wicked than the 'Wicked' Master of Crawford.

On 21 June 1533, Lord Forbes came up against the earl of Huntly in the civil court over a case of intromitted profits. The lands in dispute lay in the barony of Strathbogie, part of the conjunct-fee of the dowager countess of Huntly. Huntly's advocate explained to the Lords of Council and Session that for the kindness shown to the earl and to his forbears in the past by Forbes,[20] Huntly would in no way oppose him if matters could be settled by four lords of the session.[21] The earl had previously nominated two friends as arbiters,[22] but Forbes had refused to co-operate, hence the continuation of the present summons against him. Forbes then asked as a point of information the date on which Huntly had been served to the ward of the earldom, and was informed that this had been on 11 September 1529.[23] Forbes was then required to produce evidence of his rights to the profits of the lands libelled in the summons. He produced a writing by Angus.[24] Huntly's advocate instantly protested that no other evidence be allowed. In August, the lords held that Forbes was to cease his intromissions with the profits of the lands.[25]

Whilst this case was continuing, the Master wrote to Huntly from Alford (Aberdeen) on 13 July 1533. The earl had raised a summons against Forbes for an attack made on his lands of Corrennie. The purpose of the letter was to request that the case by heard in the earl's own courts. The letter ended 'Ye Glorious vergin conserve yr lop [lord]'.[26] Huntly was not impressed by this plea, which implied that the dispute between them was a civil matter, arising out of their competing land claims. Huntly treated it as a criminal offence. On 29 July 1533, the justiciar, Argyll, required Forbes, the Master, the Master's brother William, and their supporters all to find security for their appearance at the next Aberdeen justice ayre for art and part treasonable fire-raising and destruction of the earl's cattle folds in Corrennie forest. This may have sounded faintly ridiculous, but in April of the same year, one Janet Anderson had been drowned for a similar offence. Huntly had raised the stakes. However, the Forbes were not brought to trial, instead again finding caution in May 1536 to underlie the law for the same offence.[27]

The civil case over Strathbogie continued until February 1536, when the Lords of Council ruled that Forbes should pay over to Huntly all profits of the lands for the period of his intromissions, from 1528 to 1531. The figure amounted to just £200.[28] Shortly after the verdict in his favour, Huntly paid the far greater sum of 4000 marks to obtain the gift of the escheat of John Forbes of Pitsligo and his kindred, over seventy-five of whom were outlawed in January 1536 for an attack on the Frasers.[29] Probably this attack was connected with the earlier assignation, in 1532, of the Forbes' land to Andrew Fraser of Kinmundy. Huntly was also gifted the 'unlawis in the quhilkis Johnne Maister of Forbes wes adjugit for the nonentre of the said Johne Forbes of Petslego' – giving him a monetary claim against the Master.[30]

This was the background to the charge of treason made by Huntly against the Master on 11 June 1537, at Edinburgh before the king and the Lords of Council.[31] The crime was that the Master:

had imagynit and conspirit his hienes dede and Slaughter, be ane schot of ane small gwne or culvering within the burgh of Aberdine.

[163]

The Master denied the charge and offered to defend himself in single combat with Huntly.[32] The lords considered and rejected this option and ordered the Master either to enter into ward or find caution in the vast sum of 20,000 marks for his appearance at trial on 1 July.[33]

On 14 July 1537 the Master was found guilty on three counts: plotting to kill the king, treasonable sedition in the king's army at Jedburgh, and treasonable assistance of the English in imagining the destruction of that army.[34] These two latter points referred to the defence of the Borders by Moray in 1533.[35] The trial was by an assize (jury), its members including Lord Maxwell and the Master of Glencairn, as well as four Leslies. At least five of the fifteen-strong jury members were from Aberdeenshire.[36] One of these was Leslie of Balquhain, who had received a remission in 1526 alongside Seton of Meldrum, and who had entered into a decree-arbitral with Lord Forbes in 1528, in part execution of which Huntly had acted as witness in 1530.[37] One of the jury members, James Garioch of Kinstair, had given his bond of manrent to Huntly on 10 June 1536. James Leslie of Syde, son of Leslie of Balquhain, was to do the same in 1541.[38] It is possible that Huntly had rigged the jury to obtain a guilty verdict.[39] All that he required was a majority in his favour.[40] The addition of the two latter points of treason was perhaps designed to give more credence to the overall charge.[41] One of the jurors, Melville of Raith, had served on the Borders in 1533.[42] Maxwell frequently met with the English wardens. Hume of Coldenknowes, himself a border man, was kinsman to Hume of Blackadder, the man who had written to the Lords of Council from Northumberland in 1529.[43] In 1533 the Master of Glencairn had been found innocent of a 'frivol and vayne' allegation that he had sent hawks and other 'commendations' to his cousins, the Douglases.[44] For those of the jury not from Aberdeenshire, sedition and communicating with the English were possibly more tangible crimes than conspiring to shoot the king in Aberdeen. James had visited that city once in May 1534.[45]

Huntly may have manufactured the evidence. In April 1536, he acted as cautioner for John Strathauchin, young laird of Linturk, in an action for assythement brought by the relatives of the murdered Alexander Seton of Meldrum.[46] In February 1537, Lord Forbes instructed his bailie to review his tenants' tacks. Any tenant unable to produce satisfactory evidence of his holding, ran the risk of having his tenancy terminated at Whitsun. Thomas Strathauchin of Linturk and his son appeared to be unable to produce such evidence, and were contesting the position in the bailie court in April 1537, whilst at the same time protesting that the court was partial in the matter.[47] At the time of the Master's trial, John Strathauchin was briefly warded for concealing the treasonable conspiracy; on 17 July 1537, writing from Holyrood, James declared that Strathauchin should henceforth keep himself north of the river Dee, which was hardly a drastic sentence for the son of an Aberdeenshire laird. Both the author of the *Diurnal* and Buchanan credit the Strathauchin family with making the initial accusation of treason against the Master.[48]

The Master was executed on 14 July 1537.[49] Every circumstance was against him. The king had been absent from the country for nine months; he held a conditional remission from the Crown for good behaviour; he had a track record of being a complete nuisance to his Aberdeenshire neighbours; and Huntly, the former vice-regent, was after his blood. Added to this, he was married to Elizabeth Lyon, daughter of Lady Glamis – who was to be tried for treason on 17 July 1537.[50] Throughout the Master's trial James appears to have played a passive role. If anything, the evidence suggests he rather liked the Master of Forbes; this is both hinted at in the terms of the Dundee remission, and in the *Treasurer's Accounts* which record that early in 1533 (immediately before the Master served on the Borders), the Master received a payment of £40, perhaps in return for his gift to the king of a tartan jacket.[51] Not to be outdone by this, at the time of the Master's trial, Huntly presented James with crimson satin with which to line a gown.[52] Huntly's charge against the Master on 11 June presented the king with a dilemma. Two men, both his contemporaries and acquaintances, had brought their local differences under the central spotlight. Huntly had raised the stakes again. Either James was to allow his vice-regent to engage in a duel with a complete rogue, or he could refer the matter to court. The latter was the more reasoned line to take. At the time the case was being tried, Madeleine was dying,[53] writing off twenty years of diplomacy and rendering the king's own visit to France an abortive exercise. The jury returned a guilty verdict and thus satisfied Huntly; there was no reason for the king to investigate further, even were his attention fully focused on the matter.

For a period the Forbes were penalised by the Crown. Lord Forbes and his eldest son, William, were held in ward at Edinburgh at least until April 1538.[54] However, upon his marriage in January 1539, the new Master received a royal charter to part of his father's lands, suggesting a partial rehabilitation.[55] Lord Forbes attended the 1540–41 parliament.[56] The king made a circuit of the north in September 1537, visiting Ruthven, Inverness, Aberdeen, Dunnotar, and Brechin.[57] The intention was probably to impress the presence of the Crown in an area which the king only rarely visited during his personal rule.[58]

Unsurprisingly, the relationship between the Forbes family and the earl of Huntly deteriorated after 14 July 1537. In July 1538, Lord Forbes alleged that the earl's tenants were interfering with his own lands in Corrennie forest, and obtained letters from the sheriff of Aberdeen to hold a cognition to prove his ownership. However the cognition found in Huntly's favour, and in April 1539 Forbes was ordered by the Lords of Council to cease troubling the earl's tenants, under threat of ward in Blackness castle.[59] Perhaps aware that Lord Forbes was unlikely to receive impartial judgement from the sheriff's assizes in Aberdeenshire, in December 1539 the king granted him an exemption from appearing in the sheriff court in land disputes. This allowed Forbes to bring his disputes in the first instance direct to the court of session.[60] In May 1542, Lord Elphinstone was suing Lord Forbes for £2000 in wrongful intromissions since August 1540. The court of session held that it would accept jurisdiction on account of the 'deadly feud' between the Forbes and the sheriff of Aberdeen.[61] Shortly after the king's death, Henry VIII was advised by his border officers that:

> We have also understand that therle of Huntley and the Lorde Forrbuos have foughten in the northe parties of Skotland, and many men slayne betwixt theym and therle of Huntley putt to the worse.[62]

Huntly's interests lay in the 'northe parties'. The elimination of the Master of Forbes immediately after Huntly's stint as vice-regent appears to have satisfied the latter's need for employment in central government service.[63] He next appeared in this role in May 1540, when the English reported him as being one of the magnates on the royal expedition to the Isles.[64] What Huntly really wanted was to take up his grandfather's role. When the third earl of Huntly died in 1524, the fourth earl was about twelve years old.[65] His ward was disputed amongst Margaret Tudor, Angus, and Moray.[66] The death of the Master of Forbes was really the final chapter of this dispute. The death of the third earl meant that Moray was appointed to replace him as the lieutenant of the north.[67] In the early part of the personal rule, Moray was active in this role, campaigning against the clan Chattan in 1528–29;[68] conducting a raid into Sutherland and Caithness in the summer of 1530;[69] and assisting in the daunting of the Isles in 1531.[70] This service in the north was supplemented by tours of duty on the Borders early in 1530 and again in 1533. Moray was the man to whom his half-brother turned when he needed an army commander.

It is not completely clear where Huntly's career fitted into this. He served under Moray in March 1533 on the Borders.[71] In the north, Hector Macintosh, chief of the clan Chattan, saw fit to give his bond of manrent to Moray at Darnaway on 11 November 1530. Two years later, on 26 June 1532, at Pitlurg, he gave it to Huntly. The second bond promised the service of Macintosh and his kindred to Huntly, 'the Kingis graice beand excepit allanerly'.[72] This was a switch of allegiance from one magnate to another. In September 1533 the earl of Northumberland reported to Henry VIII:

> And undowbtidly there is as great discension in the realme of Scotland as ever was; the Erlys of Murrey and Argyle beyng on the one party, and the Erle of Huntley with all hys frendys beynge on the contrary perty, for the shamefull murderinge of one gentilman callyd the Lard of Lynsay. And, as I am informed owte of Scotland, the Kynge haith bene there for agrement, but it wolde take none effect amonges theyme as yet. Wherefore He doth sene Hym self to be evyll at eace, of a soore fois.[73]

As with similar earlier, over-optimistic reports of Scottish dissension made by English officers,[74] this is an example of the writer looking for potential weak points for exploitation, and in the process distorting the picture. In this instance there was no laird of Lindsay.[75] The king was in Inveraray in September-

October 1533, to receive the *Mary Willoughby* from Hector MacLean of Duart.[76] One Alan MacLean, son of the deceased Lauchlan McGillan [MacLean] of Duart, had in March 1533 received remission for fire-raising in Mull and killing John McGillan, son of John McGillan [MacLean] of Lochbuie.[77] The earl of Argyll and MacLean of Duart had exchanged bonds in 1519, and again in 1521, in perpetuity.[78] In 1536 Huntly and Hector MacLean of Duart signed an agreement for the former to infeft MacLean in Lochaber lands, and for the two to exchange bonds.[79] Possibly relations between Argyll and MacLean had deteriorated by 1533,[80] and Argyll objected to the granting of the remission. At the same time Argyll too had been granted a remission for arson in Mull, Morvern, and Tiree, along with ninety-two other people.[81] Moray had been given a licence in 1531 to grant remissions to Isles rebels,[82] but perhaps had not authorised the remission to Alan MacLean.

Northumberland's report was accurate in that it identified a tension between Moray and Huntly. In June 1534, the two registered a decree-arbitral in the books of council and session, by the terms of which the two earls agreed to 'remain heartily in love and kindness in time to be . . . and to assist together our sovereign lord's business'. A more specific term was that Moray and James Grant of Freuchy were to dissolve the bond of manrent which existed between them, and Grant's tack to Moray's lands in Abernethy was to be reduced.[83] These links between the two men were just four years old.[84]

The clan Chattan created further disturbances in 1534, attacking the lands of Ardersier (Inverness), part of the estates of the bishopric of Moray. They were said to have killed twenty men, women and children, and caused £12,000 worth of damage, assisted in these activities by Grant of Freuchy. As the Lords of Council and Session observed, they were 'nevir profittable to the kingis grace nor realme in weir nor pece'. All sheriffs and deputies in Aberdeen, Banff, Elgin, Forres, Cromarty, Nairn and Inverness were charged to warn the lieges not to communicate with those of the name of Macintosh.[85] As in 1528, Moray was instructed to proceed against them. So also was Grant of Freuchy.[86] It appears to have been the latter's support of, rather than opposition to, the Macintoshes which resulted in the dissolution of his tie with Moray. Moray was said to have dissolved the bond of his own free will, but the arbiters may have insisted on this.[87] Grant paid £2000 to obtain a general remission in 1535, and also an exemption from appearing in any court (sheriff, lieutenant or otherwise) other than the court of session. By the time of his final payment of £1000 in 1536, he was being described by the king as 'lovit' and 'familiar servant'.[88]

Where this left Huntly and Moray is not clear. Both had bonded with Hector Macintosh; Moray, as lieutenant, was required to put down the clan Chattan in 1534. The decree-arbitral suggests that Huntly was being put under pressure to co-operate with Moray, and presumably to assist him in putting down the clan. After 1534, the clan Chattan ceased to be a problem, and by 1536 Macintosh was in ward.[89]What is curious is the cordial terms James used to describe Grant of

Freuchy, when apparently he had supported the clan Chattan. As in the cases of the Master of Forbes and Master of Crawford, the king reserved some of his most cordial greetings for the prodigal sons who paid him money.

After the execution of the Master of Forbes, James visited Ruthven in Badenoch (part of the Huntly earldom), Inverness, where Huntly was sheriff and captain of the castle,[90] and Aberdeen, where the rivalry with Forbes was being played out. The likelihood is that Huntly was accompanying him. At the same time, Moray was discharged as lieutenant of the north.[91] At first this looks like a clear shift in the Crown's support, from Moray to Huntly. But it was not followed up by Huntly's formal appointment as lieutenant, nor did there appear to be any need for this military position in the north after the Macintoshes were put down. It is also worth comparing the tasks which the two men had just carried out. Arguably, going to France as the king's representative carried just as much status (or as little)[92] as staying at home as one of six vice-regents. Apart from the gift of crimson satin, and the tour of the north in September 1537, there is little in the records to indicate that Huntly established himself as a royal favourite after the death of the Master.[93] In an official capacity, he ceased to act as a charter witness after he ceased to act as vice-regent; by contrast Moray continued to witness until the end of the reign.[94] Both men lost out as a result of the king's Act of Revocation. Moray had been granted a nineteen-year tack of Ross and Ardmannoch in 1521, and ten years later secured the agreement of the king and Lords of Council that this be converted to a heritable tenancy, in return for his military service as Border lieutenant. In 1538 his tenure was reduced.[95] Huntly paid 2000 marks for the fee of Strathdee and Cromar in 1530, and had his charter revoked in March 1539.[96] So much for favouritism.

One area where Huntly did succeed in emulating his grandfather was in having himself appointed as sheriff of Aberdeen. The office had been assigned from the Crawford earldom to the earldom of Erroll in 1510, with the reversion figure set at 600 marks.[97] In January 1532 the ward of the office was gifted to Moray, and Moray acted as sheriff-principal until the end of 1538.[98] In the shrieval cognition taken for Corrennie forest, the assize held for Huntly against Forbes.[99] This suggests both impartiality in treating the evidence and neutrality in the Forbes-Huntly feud on the part of Moray. Either that, or the assize members were more scared of Huntly than of the sheriff. Where Forbes was not directly challenging Huntly over disputed areas of land, he could be successful.[100] But Huntly wanted to control the office himself, and in January 1539 contracted to that effect with the earl of Crawford, offering to lend him 1400 marks to enable him both to redeem the office from Erroll and re-assign it to Huntly. As an interim measure, pending royal confirmation, Huntly would act as deputy sheriff.[101] That this happened is suggested by the subsequent exemption from the sheriff court given to the Forbes. Huntly's confirmation as sheriff came on 2 March 1541.[102] At this time, Moray was in France.

In May 1540 the English reported that Huntly was to go on the royal expedition to the Isles, and Moray was to be assigned to guard the Borders for the duration of the trip.[103] Moray made his will at Edinburgh on 8 June 1540, being 'reddy to departit to the partis of France to recover my haill . . . in caice that God call me to his bliss'.[104] (He was then aged forty.) He was absent from that month until March 1541.[105]

In August 1542 Huntly was reported by Sir William Eure to be lieutenant of the Borders 'because therle of Murray is seke'.[106] In the same month Huntly defeated the English in battle at Hadden Rig.[107] In October 1542, the English reported 'gret dissencions ar betwen hym and the Erle of Murray',[108] and that James had 'removid him from the lieutenancy and appointid therle of Morrey to the same'.[109]

The evidence suggests a gradual building up of a rivalry between Huntly and Moray, beginning with the latter's attempts to control the wardship of the former; Huntly then coming of age and attempting to build a rival sphere of influence in the north; Moray being sent off on diplomatic business and Huntly being appointed as vice-regent; Moray being discharged as lieutenant in the wake of the execution of the Master of Forbes; Huntly being appointed as sheriff of Aberdeen whilst Moray was recovering his health in France; the two in confrontation at Lauder in October 1542, with Moray as the older, successful lieutenant of earlier years and Huntly as the victorious commander at Hadden Rig.[110] Possibly this last confrontation was a contributory factor in the decision to scale the Scots host at Lauder. What cannot be shown is that Moray was in any way a supporter of the Forbes family in their dispute with Huntly.[111] Probably the execution of the Master of Forbes had no direct effect on Crown-magnate relations; his career marked him out as a criminal, unlikely to have committed the crimes of which he was charged, but whose death, nevertheless, was welcomed by his neighbours in the north-east. However, it may have spurred Huntly on to achieve domination in the locality by taking the office of sheriff. Moray was sabotaged on two fronts. A much more politically active man in central government than Huntly, Moray found his control of the locality in Aberdeenshire weakened, and possibly also his supervision of the local assizes. In addition, he was dogged by ill health.

James favoured neither one magnate nor the other. His intervention in the locality of the north-east was minimal, a visit in 1537 followed by an exemption in 1539 for the Forbes from Huntly's jurisdiction. But this lack of input was enough to allow Huntly to develop his career to the point where he was the first choice for the lieutenancy of the Borders when the obvious man, Moray, was unavailable.

2. JANET DOUGLAS, LADY GLAMIS

Janet Douglas was one of the four sisters of the earl of Angus and Sir George Douglas.[112] She married John Lyon, sixth lord Glamis, before 1520, and he died on 17 September 1528, leaving a minor heir. The sixth lord managed to make an appearance on the council at Edinburgh at the outset of the personal rule, in early July. However, he was not at the September parliament, and was presumably dying by then.[113] In December 1528, and again in January 1529, Janet was summoned to appear before parliament to answer the charge of art and part assistance of her brothers at Edinburgh in the last week of June 1528.[114] Unlike Hugh Kennedy of Girvanmains and John Hume of Blackadder, also summoned for the same offence, she did not receive a remission for this charge. Given that her husband appeared on the council a fortnight later, it is perfectly possible that Janet was in Edinburgh at the end of June 1528.

Patrick Charteris of Cuthilgurdy, the man responsible for burning Cranston and Cousland on 10–11 September 1528, was also summoned for the same crime.[115] On 25 February 1529 Charteris found caution to underlie the law at the next Forfar justice ayre.[116] Both Charteris and Janet (described as 'our lovittis Dame Jonat Douglas') were granted licence to travel overseas on pilgrimage on 20 September 1529, and granted respite from all actions until their return. Amongst their kin, tenants and servants were Charteris' brother, and Alexander, John and Roger Charteris.[117] The deportation of undesirables appears to have been an accepted alternative to their being granted remission.[118]

It seems that Janet did not immediately go on pilgrimage, for on 9 October 1529, a case was brought on her and her 'puir barnis' behalf against their kinsman, John Lyon of Knockany, accused of intromitting with the profits of the lands of the mains of Glamis. Verdict was given in her favour in March 1530, suggesting either that she had undertaken the pilgrimage, or was yet to leave.[119] Probably the latter was the case, and she did not go at all, as in June 1531, gift was made to one Gavin Hamilton of her escheated goods:

> now pertenyng or . . . [which] may pertene to our soverane lord', Lady
> Glamis being 'fugitive fra the law and at the horne, or convictit for inter-
> commonying with our soverane lordis rebellis, or for any uthir crymes.[120]

The sense in the wording of this gift implied that a trial of Janet was being considered by the Crown. On 13 August 1531, a conditional nineteen-year respite was granted for treasonable assistance of the Douglases to Roger, Alexander and John Charteris, they 'prevand certane crymes that Jonet Lady Glammys is to be accusit, conforme to thare promitt'.[121] On 31 January 1532 Janet found security to underlie the law at the next Forfar justice ayre. The charges against her were art and part poisoning of her late husband, and reset of Patrick Charteris, rebel. Fifteen lairds were fined on 2 February for not appearing to serve on her assize; seventeen were fined for the same default on 26 February.[122] Possibly this led to the prosecution dropping the case.[123] As the Charterises were not required to give evidence, their respite fell, and on 23 April 1532 Roger was outlawed for the crime of kidnapping two Edinburgh burgesses and holding them at Tantallon castle, which event must have occurred in 1528 or early 1529.[124]

The collapse of the trial against Janet appears temporarily to have exonerated her in the eyes of the king. By July 1532 she was married to Archibald Campbell of Skipness, uncle of the fourth earl of Argyll, the justiciar of Scotland.[125] At the same time she was allowed to resume possession of her widow's terce from the Glamis estates.[126] The newly wedded couple then raised an action against John Charteris, to reduce an assignation to him of the rents of the lands of Drumgeith (Forfar).[127] John Charteris appears to have been a servant of David Beaton, abbot of Arbroath, and Janet clearly failed to obtain a verdict in her favour; for in 1533 John was on the king's service overseas, probably as part of the abbot's embassy to France in that year.[128] The case continued until July 1536, when the Lords of Council and Session held that John was to refund to her part of the profits of the lands.[129] In April 1535, Janet also obtained a similar ruling in her favour against Roger Charteris.[130] In June 1537 she was again pursuing John Lyon of Knockany over an action for payment to her; on 13 July 1537 Lyon's son was summoned to the 'Kingis grace richt diligent' for resisting the escheat of his father's goods.[131]

On 15 June 1537, the earl of Crawford, Campbell of Skipness, Robert Douglas of Lochleven, and the laird of Lawmond became cautioners for the seventh lord Glamis to remain in ward at Edinburgh castle.[132] On 17 July Janet was convicted on two points of treason. These were art and part treasonably conspiring and imagining the death of the king by poison, and assisting and communicating with her brothers. The assize which returned a guilty verdict included the earls of Atholl, Buchan and Cassillis, lords Maxwell and Semple and her first cousin, the Master of Glencairn. She was sentenced to be burned on the castle hill, Edinburgh.[133] On 18 July Lord Glamis was convicted of concealing his mother's conspiracy to poison the king, 'to quhome [his mother] he consentit and was art and part with hir thairintill'. He was sentenced to death by hanging and drawing, but in fact this was commuted to imprisonment, probably because of his youth.[134] After the personal rule was over, Lord Glamis claimed that a confession had been won from him through the use of the rack.[135] His assize included Cassillis, Lords Maxwell, Somerville, Seton and Avandale, and the Masters of Glencairn and Eglinton.[136] On 22 August 1537, John Lyon of Knockany – the man in dispute with Janet two months earlier – was convicted for concealing her conspiracy and also for treasonably plotting to use the same poison to kill the earl of Rothes. He was sentenced to hanging and beheading.[137] On the same day the supplier of the poison, one Alexander Mackie, was convicted for supplying the poison to Lyon of Knockany, in full knowledge of the use to which it would be put. He had his ears cut off and was banished to the confines of Aberdeen-shire.[138] 'After his remanyng schort tyme within oure ward' at Edinburgh castle, Campbell of Skipness was allowed to go free. Before he could receive the good news, he 'enforcit himself to brek oure said ward and tharethrow decessit hastelie'.[139] Adam Abell narrated that he tried to escape down the castle rock and fell to his death.[140]

James I had executed several members of his own family.[141] James II had murdered the eighth earl of Douglas and executed the earl of Ormond,[142] whilst his youngest son, the earl of Mar, died in suspicious circumstances in the following reign.[143] James III himself 'happinit' to be slain at the outset of his son's reign.[144] James IV's own reign was unmarred by the execution of treasonable magnates, but the minority of James V saw the forfeiture of life and lands of the third lord Hume in 1516.[145] Janet Douglas, sister of the forfeited earl of Angus, was the highest ranking individual to be executed in the personal rule of James V. She had been found guilty of treason after a trial by jury. The death penalty was the legitimate sentence. The manner of her going was horrific; had she been beheaded as had been Anne Boleyn in May 1536, or drowned as was the commoner, Janet Anderson, in April 1533,[146] then it is possible that James V's reputation would not have suffered so greatly at the hands of historians.[147] Whether or not she was of 'uncommon beauty' and, at the age of thirty-three,[148] still in her 'blooming youth' is a matter of subjective opinion. Buchanan considered this to be the case.[149] The fact that she was female possibly aroused sympathy for her.[150]

The theme of poisoning linked the earlier charge against Janet with the later charges against her, her son, and John Lyon of Knockany. If she were a genuine poisoner, then no more need be said on the matter; she was guilty.[151] However, it is difficult to imagine when the opportunity to poison the king would have arisen. Nowhere in the records is there any suggestion that she attended the royal court; her several suits in the court of session suggest that she was a woman more concerned with managing her estates and looking after her 'puir barnis'.[152] As with the charge of shooting levied against the Master of Forbes, the charge of poisoning appears spurious. Thus, the *ratio* of the case was that she was in treasonable communication with her brothers. Unlike the case in the trial of the Master, there was no obvious individual targeting her.

However, one possible candidate for this role was the earl of Rothes. This is suggested by the charge against Lyon of Knockany. Rothes' connection with the Lyon family of Glamis was first made in the minority. After the death of the fifth earl of Erroll in 1522, ward of the earldom was initially held by the earl of Huntly.[153] The ward was then assigned to the sixth lord Glamis, who contracted to sell it to Rothes.[154] Rothes received royal approval of the transaction on 4 October 1527.[155] Shortly after the new régime took power, in September 1528, Rothes paid £1000 to purchase the Glamis ward and held both it and the Erroll ward.[156] In November 1528, Glamis' tutors claimed to have a right to the Erroll ward. Accordingly Glamis and Rothes entered into a contract on 19 December 1528, whereby Rothes agreed to renounce his claim to the Erroll ward in return for £3000.[157] As the Glamis family could not afford this in cash, £3000 worth of their estates were assigned to Rothes.[158] Alexander Lyon, cantor of Moray and uncle and tutor to the seventh lord Glamis, was then gifted the ward of Erroll, whilst Rothes took him to court to have the ward of Glamis handed over to himself.[159] Rothes had to take Glamis' tutor to court again in March 1530 to claim maintenance for his ward's upkeep.[160] The Erroll ward was passed over from Glamis' tutor to his curator, John Lyon of Knockany, in July 1536.[161] Thus by the time of the execution of Lady Glamis, Rothes was holding the Glamis ward, whilst Glamis' curator was the man who was to be executed for plotting to poison him. The Glamis family held the Erroll ward which Rothes had been anxious to obtain in the minority. Possibly because of Rothes' failure to support the king at the siege of Tantallon, he was forced to relinquish his claim to it. The signs of friction in court between Rothes and the Glamis family may have indicated a deeper discord than is to be found in the extant records. One way for Rothes fully to regain the king's favour and expurge the Tantallon episode from his memory might have been to reveal a treasonable plot against James' life. Rothes could make himself the other victim and thus get rid of Glamis' curator. As a reward the grateful king would return the ward of Erroll to Rothes, which combined with his £3000 claim on the Glamis estates, would make a useful addition to the Rothes earldom.

Rothes' involvement in unmasking the plot or supposed plot is indicated by the allegation that Lyon of Knockany wanted to kill him, and he must be held partially responsible for the trial. Possibly he came up with the idea of using the charge of poison again, although it had not worked in 1532. However it is doubtful whether Rothes arranged the whole matter, the death of Lady Glamis and the forfeiture of Lord Glamis as well as Lyon's death. He needed only one plotter, not three. Whatever his hopes of territorial gain at the expense of the Glamis family were, they were not realised. The Glamis estates were forfeited, and in 1540 were annexed to the Crown's patrimony.[162] There was no indication that Rothes' financial claim was honoured. The earldom of Erroll was treated as the Crown's property, adminstered by the Exchequer.[163] Until he left for France in 1536, Rothes had been an occasional charter witness; after his return, he ceased to act as a witness. Perhaps this was a sign of protest at the outcome for him of the whole affair.

The Glamis forfeiture, including Janet Douglas' terce in Aberdeenshire, and the estate of Knockany, brought to the exchequer the recorded sum of £5770 from 1538 until the end of the reign.[164] As with the Angus regality of Kirriemuir and the Crawford earldom, the king introduced various household servants as tenants. David Wood of Craig was infeft in Drumgeith; James Kirkcaldy of Grange, Treasurer from 1537, Henry Kempt of Thomastown, pursemaster; Walter Moncur, royal baker, and James Watson, royal surgeon, were all infeft before the end of the reign.[165] The only magnate to benefit was Lord Ruthven, who in October 1542 was granted the patronage of Forgandenny chapel with one third of the lands.[166] The Erroll ward was kept intact, and from 1538 to 1541, the Comptroller responded for the sum of £1700.[167] The sixth earl died under-age in that year, and his cousin, George Hay of Logiealmond, received charter to the earldom in December 1541.[168] The annexation of Glamis and the administration of the Erroll ward greatly increased the Crown's presence in Forfarshire. Clearly a pattern was emerging; first Kirriemuir, then Crawford, and now the gain from the Glamis forfeiture. Were the earl of Angus to return to take up his estates, he would find the area full of Household servants and other tenants who owed their presence there to the Crown. If the forfeiture of Lord Glamis was not calculated, then it was a fortunate circumstance.

In fact, there exist signs of a royal clampdown in the months following the king's return from France. Archibald Douglas of Glenbervie and William Douglas of Whittinghame were summoned to Edinburgh on 4 July 1537. James Douglas of Parkhead was outlawed for treason. One Hugh Douglas was transferred from Tantallon to Borthwick castle.[169] At the end of the month, Sir Thomas Clifford, officer at Berwick-upon-Tweed, reported to Henry VIII that there were in ward – together with Lord Forbes – Lord Glamis, William, Master of Forbes, Peter Carmichael, David Strathauchin, Robert Douglas of Lochleven, and 'diverse other'.[170] On 16 August, one Alexander Hume was beheaded on the charge of assisting the Douglases, in particular at the time of the burning of Oldhamstocks and Cockburnspath in 1532.[171] Six days later, John Mathieson was beheaded for various crimes of violence and for betraying secrets of the kingdom to the Douglases after the date of his remission.[172] This took the death tally for treasonable assistance of the Douglases and/or the English up to seven.[173] Writing to Thomas Cromwell from Newcastle on 15 September 1537, the duke of Norfolk advised that he had news from Scotland, 'wherof I knowe parte to be trewe', of the daily warding and imprisonment of friends and kin of the earl of Angus. He continued:

> And it is said that suche as have londes of any good valewe shall suffre at this nexte Parliament, and suche as have litle shall refuse the name of Douglas and be called Stewardes. So sore a dred King, and so ill beloved of his subjectes, was never in that londe.[174]

In fact there was no full session of parliament until 1540. Douglas of Glenbervie and his wife were confirmed in their lands in April 1538.[175] Douglas of Lochleven, who was married to one of the king's mistresses,[176] was appointed as bailie to lands in the archbishopric of St. Andrews in January 1538.[177] The Hugh Douglas in ward at Borthwick castle may have been Douglas of Borg, who with his wife received a feu from the abbot of Holyrood in October 1538.[178] Douglas of Whittinghame was able to win a case in court in 1541 against Patrick Hepburn, Master of Hailes.[179] Over the medium term the only Douglas who fitted Norfolk's description was Douglas of Parkhead.

But, of course, Janet Douglas was dead. Summoned to Edinburgh to celebrate a royal wedding, the magnates had instead to digest two grisly treason trials. It is possible that the fact of Janet's execution held less import for crown-magnate relations than did the forfeiture of her son. On and off the king had been after her since almost the start of the personal rule. Her death signalled that the king was now prepared, after almost nine years, to put into practice the 'utir distruction of

James V: portrait by an anonymous artist, probably contemporary. (Courtesy of the Scottish National Portrait Gallery).

James V with his first wife Madeleine, daughter of Francis I of France. From the late 16th century Seton Armorial. (Reproduced by kind permission of the owner, Sir Francis Ogilvy, Bart., and of the Trustees of the National Library of Scotland).

James V with his second wife Mary of Guise. Anonymous portrait, probably contemporary. The imperial crown above the coat-of-arms between the royal couple strikingly illustrates the king's enthusiasm for imperial imagery in the latter part of the personal rule. (Courtesy of the Scottish National Portrait Gallery).

The Royal Arms of Scotland as depicted by James V's Lyon King of Arms, Sir David Lyndsay of the Mount, in his Armorial (1542). The imagery of the imperial crown is once again in evidence. (Reproduced by kind permission of the Trustees of the National Library of Scotland).

Stirling castle: contemporary sculptured figure, representing James V, at the N.E. corner of the palace. (Crown Copyright: Royal Commission on the Ancient and Historical Monuments of Scotland).

The gold 'Bonnet Piece' of 1539. The obverse bears a striking portrait of the king, while the reverse picks up the recurring theme of the imperial crown, perhaps in anticipation of the redesigning of James V's crown early in the following year. (Courtesy of the National Museums of Scotland).

Tantallon castle, East Lothian, stronghold of James V's Chancellor Archibald, sixth earl of Angus, and scene of the abortive royal siege of 1528. (Crown Copyright: Royal Commission on the Ancient and Historical Monuments of Scotland).

Craignethan castle, Lanarkshire, home of James V's familiar and Master of Works, Sir James Hamilton of Finnart, until his arrest and execution in August 1540. (Crown Copyright: Royal Commission on the Ancient and Historical Monuments of Scotland).

Holyrood Palace and Abbey. The tower at the north-west corner of the palace (in centre of photograph) was one of James V's first major buildings, constructed between 1528 and 1532. (Crown Copyright: Royal Commission on the Ancient and Historical Monuments of Scotland).

Falkland Palace from the north. The photograph shows the east and north ranges of the palace, which were remodelled from 1537 onwards by French masons. (Crown Copyright: Royal Commission on the Ancient and Historical Monuments of Scotland).

Falkland Palace from the north-west. Together with the palace within Stirling castle, Falkland was the most important and expensive of James V's building projects in the last five years of the reign. (Crown Copyright: Royal Commission on the Ancient and Historical Monuments of Scotland).

Falkland Palace: the south range, with the chapel on the second floor, the work of the French mason Nicholas Roy. (Crown Copyright: Royal Commission on the Ancient and Historical Monuments of Scotland).

Stirling Palace: the east front. The palace, which contained accommodation for James V, Mary of Guise, and their separate households, was probably incomplete at the time of James's death in 1542. (Courtesy of Historic Scotland).

Linlithgow Palace, West Lothian: the courtyard, fountain, and east facade. (Crown Copyright: Royal Commission on the Ancient and Historical Monuments of Scotland).

Linlithgow Palace: the south facade, showing the chapel on the right and king's lodging on the left. James's daughter Mary, the future Queen of Scots, was born here in December 1542, six days before James V's death. (Courtesy of Historic Scotland).

Renaissance imagery: two stone medallions (above) from the north range of Falkland Palace, and two of the so-called 'Stirling Heads' (below), a series of some forty oak medallions which originally adorned the King's presence chamber within Stirling Palace. (Above: Crown Copyright: Royal Commission on the Ancient and Historical Monuments of Scotland; below: Courtesy of the National Museums of Scotland).

. . . Archibald [Douglas] and his part takaris', as called for in terms of the 'grete aith' of 6 November 1528.[180] No longer was a remission the automatic royal response to suspected treason. This perhaps was a chilling prospect should any individual magnate wish to commit treason. However, there is no reason to suppose that any of them did, for any treasonable scenario would involve the return of the Douglases to Scotland, perhaps with English approval. The political scene had moved on from the time in which the Angus régime had dominated Scottish government; his return might mark the start of recriminations against those who had supported the king in removing him. James clearly did not want him back; adult Stewart monarchy had proved to be incompatible with magnate domination in the past, and a Douglas rehabilitation offered poor prospects. No magnate had anything to gain by their return; Angus had alienated those who had been both old enough and interested enough to participate in public affairs in the minority.[181] Furthermore, those magnates who sat on Janet's assize may have had their own reasons for finding her guilty. Cassillis had broken the King's Proclamation during his absence.[182] Buchan had just had the escheat of his goods gifted to Sir John Campbell of Lundy over the matter of warrandice for the lands of Cairnbeddie,[183] Atholl had been warded in 1534,[184] whilst the Master of Glencairn was anxious to affirm that he had not blotted his copybook by sending hawks to his Douglas cousins in 1533.[185] Maxwell, the former vice-regent, was the man responsible for interrupting the Douglas dinner party in Edinburgh in August 1528.

The forfeiture of Lord Glamis threatened the traditional magnatial interest, the cultivation of domination of their geographical spheres of interest. Unlike the aftermath of the trial of the Master of Forbes, where the Crown by and large left Huntly and Lord Forbes to fight it out between them after 1537, in this instance James used the forfeiture to intrude into the area north of the Tay estuary. Already this had brought about friction with Buchan, notably absent from public service for the entire personal rule, except on this one occasion. As with the earlier Angus forfeiture,[186] there was no redistribution of land to the magnates. The Crown was unwilling to part with anything it had won, and offset the disaffection of a loser, in this case the young Glamis, by winning support elsewhere. On the other hand, as a minor and nephew of the exiled earl of Angus, Glamis was a soft target, as had been the earl of Crawford in 1532; to undermine their power bases was not necessarily a precedent for interfering with the landed interests of magnates in other areas. The one magnate who might have objected to part of the outcome of the whole affair was the earl of Argyll, but there is no sign that he treated the death of his uncle, Campbell of Skipness, as anything other than an accident.[187]

It is apparent that James played a more active role in the trial of Janet Douglas than in the earlier trial of the Master of Forbes. The timing of her death is significant. James had been out of the country for nine months. Whilst he was away, there were three incidents in Scotland which might have been regarded as serious enough for the king to wish to return from France. In the event none of these was sufficient to prompt him to break off his wedding negotiations with Francis I and come rushing home. However, together they led him to affirm his position when he eventually did return.

The first episode concerned Margaret Tudor. For reasons best known to herself, she decided that she no longer wished to remain with her third husband, Lord Methven.[188] She was in correspondence on this subject with her brother, Henry VIII, by the end of 1536.[189] Methven was evidently approached by the English government on the matter, for he sent a politely worded letter from Edinburgh to Thomas Cromwell on 11 December of that year.[190] Henry VIII twice sent his envoy, Sir Ralph Sadler, to James to speak on Margaret's behalf.[191] However, his attitude was best expressed by his first letter to her on the subject on 7 January 1537, when he stated that he was perplexed by her representations and asked what she wanted him to do about the matter.[192] Bombarded by letters from his sister, he then sent her £200.[193] This was not enough for Margaret, who announced in June 1537 that she was divorcing Methven.[194] She then appears to have tried to make her way towards Berwick-upon-Tweed, where her former husband, Angus, was installed. On 4 October 1537 Norfolk reported to Cromwell that Lord Maxwell had intercepted her just five or six miles north of the border and escorted her back north again. Whether Norfolk, on the East March, had met with Maxwell in person (over the matter of redress) is not clear. However, according to the English officer, Maxwell had stated that relations between the two countries would be harmonious, provided that Margaret Tudor gave no further difficulties; and for good measure, he also criticised the English government for breaking with Rome.[195] The queen mother episode effectively closed with a further letter from her to her brother, dated 13 November 1537, complaining that she was now nearly forty-nine years old and having to trail around after her son from place to place like a poor woman. Accordingly, she trusted that Henry would withhold giving redress until she was satisfied.[196] He didn't.[197] The significance of the queen mother's bid for escape was revealed in a further letter by her to her brother:

> . . . He [James] leges that I vold pas in Ingland, and marry hum that vas Erll of Angus; and thys Harry Stewrt Lord off Meffen cawsys Hym to beleffe thys of Me.[198]

James' interpretation of what he thought his mother was up to is not extant, but given that he sent Maxwell to detain her, Margaret's version may well be true. Angus was at Berwick on 30 September 1536.[199] He appears to have remained there for the duration of the king's absence overseas. He was a potential focus for discontent, and undoubtedly James wanted him to move back down south. Henry VIII had his own difficulties in England in 1536–7 in the aftermath of the Pilgrimage of Grace, and in January 1537 he set up the Council of the North to control the area more effectively. He did not want to allow the issue of the Douglases to disrupt relations with Scotland. Hence on 18 September 1537 he ordered Norfolk to have the Douglases remove themselves from the Borders.[200] This was clearly the message that James was trying to get over in the execution of Janet Douglas, that Angus was gaining nothing by sitting in Berwick. It was a severe follow-up to a letter written by James to Henry VIII from Compiègne on 24 February 1537 in which he thanked his uncle for his good wishes on his marriage, and stated that he would have forgiven Angus a long time ago, but for various weighty reasons of which Henry VIII was well aware.[201]

By this time Henry was doing little more than pay lip service to the Douglas cause. James was obviously responding to a recent communication from his uncle on the subject. One John Penven was in the Scottish entourage at Rouen and Paris in October 1536. From France he sent an excited despatch to Sir George Douglas, in which he suggested that the best stratagem for the Douglases was to ask Henry VIII to use his influence with Francis I to request James V to be reconciled with the Douglases.[202] As James wanted a French bride, possibly he would accept an approach from the French king. However, there is no indication that Henry VIII did use the good offices of Francis I on the Douglases' behalf.

In his despatch, Penven also reported on activities amongst the Scots in France. James was running up and down the streets of Paris spending money; he had sent letters home to his mistress, Margaret Erskine, wife of Douglas of Lochleven; and Sir James Hamilton of Finnart was out of favour with the king. This last was possible, but one of the final things which James had done before leaving Scotland was grant his 'lovit familiar servitour' a receipt for £683 spent on works at Linlithgow palace for the past eight months.[203] For the rest, Penven was simply giving Sir George Douglas the sort of material he would want to read. Penven asserted that it was believed that the only Scottish enemy of the Douglases in France was the earl of Argyll. This did not necessarily mean that everybody else sympathised with their cause; in any case the king's enmity towards them was a sufficient barrier to their rehabilitation. Again, according to Penven, the earl of Moray appeared to consider that the king's absence from Scotland was the sort of opportunity for which the Douglases were waiting. This was a shrewd comment from the king's half-brother, but not indicative of any sympathy for them. Perhaps Penven was nearer the mark when he commented that all (in France) were weary of the king and wished him underground. As James had just returned from Picardy and come to the conclusion that he did not want to marry Mary of Bourbon, he was probably in a very bad mood.

There were two Border incidents in James' absence. The first occurred when the followers of Lord Hume and John Edmonstone of that Ilk came to blows in the Merse, shortly after the king left the country.[204] The squabble was over the right to uplift the teind sheaves from Ednam church.[205] This right pertained to Edmonstone, but as Ednam was attached to Coldingham priory,[206] the Humes considered they had some sort of moral right to its profits. The vice-regents dealt with the matter by arresting Gilbert, William and Thomas Hume, who in

February 1537 were obliged to 'observe and keip gud reul' under penalty of 500 marks and threat of ward in Edinburgh castle.[207] The principals were discharged of any liability and an assize was instructed to rule on the issue.[208] John Hume of Blackadder, the man who had run off to Northumberland in October 1529 and negotiated his own remission, was again warded, in Dumbarton castle.[209]

Lord Hume had received a charter to the Hume estate in June 1535, in reward for his good service against the English (in 1532–33) and against rebels (as lieutenant of the Merse and East March in September 1529).[210] He had paid £1000 for this, and owed a further £1000. In 1529, he had also become joint cautioner for Hume of Blackadder, with a potential liability of £3000.[211] There were no recriminations against Lord Hume when James returned from France. Rather the king entered into a contract with him, whereby the Humes were to receive a new infeftment following the Act of Revocation, and were to be remitted all sums owed to the Crown. In return, Alexander, Master of Hume, was to marry Lady Jane, the king's illegitimate daughter by Elizabeth Beaton.[212] The Humes got their charter on 1 April 1538, which was ratified in parliament in 1541.[213] However, Lady Jane remained unmarried, and the gift of the marriage of the Master of Hume went first to the earl of Morton in 1541, and then, in 1542, to Margaret Stewart, daughter of the third earl of Lennox.[214] The 1537 contract was an attempt to bind the Humes more closely to the king;[215] Lord Hume was a key magnate in the East March, whose services were required for redress and defence. Thus the only reprisal for the Ednam incident was the execution of Alexander Hume in August 1537, technically on a quite separate charge.[216] Edmonstone of that Ilk kept Ednam, and served on the assize for Janet Douglas.[217]

There was no apparent Douglas involvement in the Ednam incident, but given its close proximity to Berwick-upon-Tweed, it was potentially a politically sensitive area. So also was Edgerston, just north of the English border in south Roxburghshire. Edgerston house (or castle in the criminal record), was the subject of a siege by the vice-regents in October-November 1536.[218] The English had no involvement in this, as was clear from a report received at New Wark (Wark) castle from a merchant from Berwick-upon-Tweed, on 11 November 1536. The captain of Wark was informed that an army of 20,000 Scots was nearly at the Border, its purpose unknown.[219] The merchant had probably over-estimated the number in the Scots army, but the records suggest that the vice-regents were acting with great force. All gentlemen from Linlithgow, Stirling, Perth, Menteith, Edinburgh and Haddington were charged to pass with the vice-regents to 'the assegeing of Edzarstoun', and preparations were made to drag artillery down from Edinburgh to the siege.[220] It was over by 8 November 1536, when Walter Kerr, warden of the Middle March, was given command of the castle.[221]

Edgerston was held by the Rutherford family. In 1493 it had been held by James Rutherford of that Ilk. He had several children, but the heiresses to the estate in 1502 were his granddaughters by his eldest son, Helen and Katherine. However, sasine to Edgerston was taken in 1514 by his second son, Thomas. Thomas' possession was disputed in 1515, and in 1517 he was outlawed for failing to deliver Edgerston to Helen Rutherford.[222] In 1516, Helen had made common cause with her uncle, Mark Kerr of Dolphinton, and he obliged himself to take her part in the recovery of her heritage from Thomas. This agreement was resurrected in 1534.[223] Helen's sister, Katherine, was mother to William Stewart of Traquair, who had been given a grant in 1511 of various tenandries of the Edgerston estate.[224] Thus there were at least three separate branches of the family with a claim to Edgerston. The siege in 1536 was a Rutherford affair, with Kerr involvement. The man being expelled from Edgerston in 1536 was Robert Rutherford, either the brother or a descendant of Thomas.[225] The man charged with expelling him and taking his escheat was Kerr of Cessford.[226] What perhaps requires some explanation is the heavy-handed reaction of the vice-regents to this Rutherford family dispute.

William Stewart of Traquair – Angus' nephew by marriage – had been granted a remission in December 1528 for treasonable assistance of the Douglases.[227] His lands of Traquair had been apprised in 1529 and granted to Sir James Stewart, captain of Doune and brother to Lords Methven and Avandale. They were restored in November 1536.[228] His mother, Katherine Rutherford, had been outlawed in November 1532 for failing to underlie the law on the charge of assistance of, and daily communication with, the Douglases. In August 1536, her son became her cautioner for her to keep good rule and not communicate with the Douglases.[229] Robert Rutherford was an outlaw in 1535, one of his supporters being granted a remission at the Jedburgh justice ayre for communicating with him and all other rebels save the Douglases. Three other Rutherfords were granted remissions at the same time for crimes of oppression. Thus, at least one branch of the Rutherford family could be termed outlaws and another branch was in communication with the Douglases. The explanation for the strong measures taken by the vice-regents against Edgerston may be that they were simply at pains to do a good job of restoring law and order in the king's absence. However, it is probable that Robert Rutherford, outlaw, had made a bid to take Edgerston in September 1536, immediately after the king had left the country. Katherine might have invited him to do this, to have her sister Helen thrown out. The obvious place to find support for capturing and keeping Edgerston was from amongst Angus' retinue in Berwick. The Douglases had been able to raise a sizeable following to supplement the English force in the raid on the East coast in 1532.[230] It is feasible that four years later they could still exert some influence in the eastern part of the Borders. Even were there no direct Douglas involvement in the siege of Edgerston, Angus' presence at Berwick was still unwelcome. If the Douglases were involved, the execution of Janet Douglas upon the king's return was a direct reprisal.[231]

James did not hate the entire family of Angus. He was prevented by rules of chivalry or magnanimity from executing Douglas of Kilspindie in 1534, but he was under no obligation to restore his widow to all her conjunct-fee lands on 2 July 1537 (at the expense of the earl of Eglinton).[232] Circumstances were against Janet Douglas. She was the only one of the four sisters of Angus not to have any Border connection, either through holding lands in her own right, or through marriage. Rather, her son's estates were north of the Firth of Tay, an area less politically sensitive in terms of Anglo-Scottish relations. In this sense she was the most vulnerable of the Douglas sisters. She was the only sister to be summoned for treason in 1528, hence her loyalty was questionable from the outset of the personal rule. For this she might have expected a remission, or a brief period of warding, as had happened to her sister, Alison, Lady Wedderburn, in 1531.[233] Instead, she was charged with poisoning her first husband, one of the first magnates to support James in July 1528. Clearly whatever crime she had committed, she was being singled out, suggesting that she was more closely associated with her brothers than were her sisters. Her execution was both expedient and well timed; it brought her son's estates to the Crown, and emphasised that there was to be no reconciliation with Angus. James was set on resurrecting his French alliance; David Beaton was sent back to France on the day of Madeleine's death, and by January 1538 a royal marriage had been arranged with Mary of Guise as the new French bride.[234] This was also a policy divergent with that pursued by Angus in the minority; Janet's death firmly underlined the point.

It is unlikely that the guilt of either the Master of Forbes or of Lady Glamis can now be proven beyond reasonable doubt.[235] The two juries were satisfied in July 1537. In the instance of the Master of Forbes, the verdict was presumably reached after the leading of witness evidence, following the accusation made by Huntly. For Lady Glamis, there is no indication of how the trial proceeded – possibly by witness evidence again, as was the intention in the attempted earlier poison trial. There may have been documentary evidence as well, in the form of letters written to her brothers. Lord Glamis claimed that a confession was extracted from him, but this appears to have related only to the charge of poisoning the king. In each instance, the charge of plotting to kill the king seems spurious. The earlier attempt to try Lady Glamis on a poisoning charge had failed. However, a charge of attempted regicide added weight to what were probably the real crimes; intriguing with the English during a hostile period in the case of the Master, and, for Lady Glamis, communicating with the Douglases. The two crimes were related only by the marriage of the Master to Lady Glamis' daughter.[236] Given the divergence in the charges levied against them and in the circumstances alleged to surround each royal assassination, the marriage was purely fortuitous.

The earl of Huntly had already attempted to convict the Forbes family for the treasonable crime of arson, and brought about the trial of the Master by accusing him of treason. In this case, the verdict against him is, at best, not proven and he may be presumed innocent of the charge. For Lady Glamis, summoned for treason in 1528, and survivor of one attempt to convict her in 1532, the verdict is not proven on the charge of poisoning, and, on the balance of probability, guilty of communicating with the Douglases.

NOTES

1. Pitcairn, *Trials*, i, pt. i, 184–5, 190–1; *APS*, ii, 362.
2. *The House of Forbes*, edd. A. 38; H. Taylor (Spalding Third Club, 1937), 57. Lord Forbes was brother of Alexander, fourth lord and one of the 'Rebels without a Cause' in 1488–9: cf. Macdougall, *James IV*, 49–71, *passim*.
3. *LP Henry VIII*, iv, pt. ii, no. 4531.
4. SRO, RH 2.1.9. (*ADC*, vol. 38, f. 184); *ADCP*, 289.
5. *ADCP*, 290; Spalding, *Miscellany*, ii, 83–4; cf. chapters 3 and 4.
6. *TA*, v, 250–1.
7. SRO, Forbes Papers, [GD 52], no. 67.
8. Taylor, *op.cit.*, 62; *RMS*, iii, no. 1194; *ADCP*, 341–2.
9. *ADCP*, 290.
10. SRO, *ADC*, vol. 39, f. 163v.
11. Taylor, *op.cit.*, 65; *ADCP*, 341–2; *RMS*, iii, no. 1194.
12. SRO, *ADC*, vol. 41, ff. 112, 117v, 118v.
13. *ADCP*, 341–2; *RMS*, iii, no. 1194.
14. Taylor, *op.cit.*, 74; cf. *ADCP*, 344, where Forbes was initially reluctant to sign the agreement.
15. Pitcairn, *Trials*, i, pt. i, 149–50; *RMS*, iii, no. 971; Taylor, *op.cit.*, 66. Seventeen lairds from the north-east were fined on 27 August 1530 for failing to appear on the assize to try Lord Forbes for the same crime.
16. SRO, *ADC*, vol. 41, f. 119.
17. *RMS*, iii, nos. 1085–6, 1191–2, 1237. In Menzies' case the intromissions had been over the previous nineteen years; in Fraser's case since 1520. The *Chronicle of Aberdeen*, 32, records that Menzies' 'howise towik fyir and breintt' in August 1529, possibly attributable to the Forbes.
18. SRO, Forbes Papers, no. 127, in July 1531, cf. SRO, *ADC*, vol. 39, ff. 65, 127v. Elphinstone reached his majority in November 1532: SRO, *ADCS*, ii, f. 30. If the Master was implicated in the 1525 attack, he would have been only fourteen years old.
19. *ADCP*, 367. It appears that for the whole of 1531, the Master had been absent from the area, and had now returned.
20. Forbes gave his bond of manrent to the third earl in 1522: Wormald, *Bonds*, App. A, 283, no. 25.
21. I.e. by decree-abitral, with the arbiters being judges of the Court of Session.
22. I.e. for a private out of court settlement.
23. Cf. *RSS*, ii, no. 326. Huntly then still being a minor, he could not take sasine.
24. Probably Angus' letter to Forbes of 30 May 1528: *A.B. Ill.*, iv, 415.
25. SRO, *ADCS*, ii, ff. 197, 199; iii, f. 4.
26. SRO, Forbes Papers no. 311; cf. Taylor, *op.cit.*, 67–8.
27. Pitcairn, *Trials*, i, pt. i, 162, 163. Fire-raising was one of the four pleas pertaining to the Crown: cf. *Regiam Maj.* 255; Balfour, *Practicks*, ii, 509.
28. SRO, *ADCS*, iii, ff. 97, 172; iv, f. 136v.; vii, f. 119.
29. *RSS*, ii, no. 1977; *TA*, vi, 266, 274; Pitcairn, *Trials*, i, pt. i, 172. The Frasers were mutilated, rather than killed. Sir James Hamilton of Finnart was the specially constituted judge for the occasion.

30. Pitcairn, *Trials*, i, pt. i, 172. The Master had given caution for the appearance of Forbes of Pitsligo to underlie the law. With Pitsligo not appearing, Huntly had a claim against the Master who could seek relief from Pitsligo. Cf. Balfour, *Practicks*, i, 192 (in civil law). The amount involved as caution is not recorded by Pitcairn, but given that Forbes provided caution of £2000 for the Master, presumably the sum was considerable, though there is no comparable example for mutilation cases given by Pitcairn.

31. Pitcairn, *Trials*, i, pt. i, 185–6; cf. NLS, Adv. MSS 6.1.20, where the same account is given. The lords were Gavin Dunbar, Chancellor; James Hay, bishop of Ross; William Chisholm, bishop of Dunblane; David Beaton, abbot of Arbroath and keeper of the Privy Seal; Robert Cairncross, abbot of Holyrood; Eglinton; Crawford; Rothes; Lord Erskine; Lord Fleming, chamberlain; the Lord of St. Johns; Lord Lindsay of the Byres; Lord Somerville; Thomas Erskine of Brechin, Royal Secretary; James Colville of East Wemyss, Comptroller; and Sir John Campbell of Lundy.

32. Which was permissible for the accused in a charge of treason: cf. *Regiam Maj.*, 249–251.

33. Pitcairn, *Trials*, i, pt. i, 186. Lord Forbes and Forbes of Pitsligo acted as his cautioners. It was the defender's option to elect for either a trial by combat or by an assize: cf. *Regiam Maj.*, 250. In this instance Huntly claimed that the treason charge had been reported to him, and he offered to bring forward the persons who had made the allegation against the Master, failing which he would accept trial by combat. Because of 'the odiousnes of sa heiche ane crime', the lords accepted this offer, and Huntly also was placed under a penalty of 20,000 marks should he fail to enter those persons.

34. *Ibid.*, i, pt. i, 184–5.

35. Cf. Chapter 6. Lord Forbes was summoned to pass to the Borders with his kindred to serve in the northern quarter on 16 February 1533: *TA*, vi, 125. The charge against the Master indicates a good response from the northern quarter.

36. Pitcairn, *Trials*, i, pt. i, 184. The jury were Maxwell, the Master of Glencairn, Sir John Melville of Raith (Fife), John Hume of Coldenknowes (Berwick), George Crawford of Federate (Aberdeen), Alexander Leslie of Pitcaple (Aberdeen), John Pantoun of Pitmedden (Aberdeen), David Duncan of Standand stanes (? Standing stones), William Leslie of Balquhain (Aberdeen), Nicholas Ross of Auchlossan (Aberdeen), James Garioch of Kinstair (Aberdeen), George Leslie of New Leslie (Fife or Aberdeen), John Cumming of Culter (probably Aberdeen), Charles Dempster, William Leslie of Coclarochy (?Corrachree, Aberdeen). In theory an assize was to consist of free tenants, but in practice they were 'of like social conditions to the accused'. The members were generally drawn from the neighbourhood of the accused: *Introduction to Scottish legal History* (Stair Society, vol. 20), 440–1.

37. *TA*, v, 251; Taylor, *op.cit.*, 62.

38. Wormald, *Bonds*, 283–4, App. A, nos. 28, 31. Garioch of Kinstair was a witness of the Master's letter of 1533 to Huntly: cf. Taylor, *op.cit.*, 68.

39. Theoretically the Master could challenge the appointment of any one of the jurors on grounds of either consanguinity or affinity with the accuser: cf. discussion in *The Jury in Scotland* (Stair Society, vol. 23), 171–176. Practically, in the circumstances, this facility may have offered little comfort.

40. *Ibid.*, 230–2. However, there was a facility for examination by the Justiciar of how each member voted should there be an acquittal by the jury.

41. The trial probably worked on an adversarial basis, rather than an inquisitorial one. Thus Huntly would bring the later points into his charge against Forbes at the beginning of the trial. However, this remains a matter for conjecture, as not enough is known about criminal court procedures in the early sixteenth century.

42. *LP Henry VIII*, vi, no. 163, in the quarter *preceding* the Forbes family; the suggestion is not being made that he should have first-hand knowledge of the Master's alleged sedition.

43. *ADCP*, 318; cf. Chapter 6.

44. *Ibid.*, 407, in August 1533. The accusation was brought by one Wallace, whom the Lords

of Council and Session described as a 'crepill and failzeit' body, recommending that the king deal with him as he chose.

45. *ADCP*, 423. It is not clear when the alleged shooting was to take place. The charge narrated that the Master conspired to shoot the king 'being for the tyme in his burghe of Aberdine, for executione and administratioun of justice . . .': Pitcairn, *Trials*, i, pt. i, 184. This suggests a justice ayre. There are references to northern ayres being held in 1531, 1532 and 1535 (*TA*, v, 447; vi, 60, 106, 240). A royal charter was issued at Aberdeen on 30 September 1531, and letters under the privy seal on 26 June and 8 July (*RMS*, iii, no. 1038; *RSS*, ii, nos. 948–9, 958). However the king was at Stirling on 30 September 1531 (*James V Letters*, 192–4). James was in Badenoch on 8 September 1537 (*Ibid.*, 337). Charters under the great seal were issued from there on 10 September, from Inverness on 14 September, and from Aberdeen on 30 September (*RMS*, iii, nos. 1713–6). It is possible that the treasonable conspiracy had yet to happen at the time of the Master's trial.

46. Pitcairn, *Trials*, i, pt. i, 175; cf. SRO, *ADCS*, viii, ff. 59v, 71v, (June 1536, protest by wives of the co-accused that their husbands' goods had been escheated). Cf. also *Ibid.*, xiv, ff. 13, 43v (December 1540, action for assythment brought by Meldrum's daughters). Lord Forbes acted as cautioner for the Master.

47. *Prot. Bk. Cristisone*, nos. 234–5, 241. Alexander Strathauchin later claimed that he was thrown off at Whitsun: SRO, *ADCS*, ix, ff. 7v, 68v.

48. Pitcairn, *Trials*, i, pt. i, 200; *Diurnal of Occurents*, 22; Buchanan, *History*, ii, 356–7. Buchanan avers that Huntly bribed the judges. John's father, Thomas, was a witness: cf. the Master's letter to Huntly in July 1533 (SRO, Forbes Papers, no. 311; Taylor, *op.cit.*, 68). David Strathauchin was warded at Edinburgh castle until April 1538, when he was allowed to go to Dundee (Pitcairn, *Trials*, i, pt. i, 207; *SP Henry VIII*, v, pt. iv, no. cccxxiii).

49. *SP Henry VIII*, v, pt. iv, no. cccxxiii. He was sentenced to be hanged and quartered (presumably also drawn); Pitcairn, *Trials*, i, pt. i, 185.

50. *RMS*, iii, no. 1483 (June 1535, gift by Lord Forbes to Elizabeth 'in her virginity'); Glasgow University, Argyll Tss., iv, no. 44 (May 1536, payment of first instalment of dowry); cf. Abell, *op.cit.*, f. 126 ('goodson' of Lady Glamis). Donaldson, *op.cit.*, 37, implies that the Master of Forbes and Elizabeth were married as early as 1523, when the Master was a spokesman against the Franco-Scots alliance. This seems unlikely, given that the Master was then aged eleven and Elizabeth possibly not yet born.

51. *TA*, vi, 80, 95.

52. *Ibid.*, vi, 339. It may have been coincidental that on 31 July James wrote to the pope requesting a benefice for Huntly's son: *James V Letters*, 335.

53. Ironically, in her last letter to her father, written on 8 June 1537, Madeleine stated she was 'much recovered': *LP Henry VIII*, xii, pt. ii, no. 537.

54. Pitcairn, *Trials*, i, pt. i, 186–7; *ADCP*, 367.

55. *RMS*, iii, no. 1891.

56. *APS*, ii, 355–6, 367.

57. To judge by the itinerary of the great seal: *RMS*, iii, nos. 1713–1718; cf. *James V Letters*, 337 (8 September 1537, James at Ruthven in Badenoch, part of Huntly's earldom).

58. Again to judge by the *RMS* and *RSS* registers, there are apparently no extant letters by the king to confirm earlier visits.

59. SRO, *ADCS*, x, f. 143v; xii, f. 136; xiii, f. 6v. In this last ruling, the lords held that John (deleted), or rather, William (added in) as Master of Forbes was to desist from pasturing his livestock on Huntly's lands.

60. *RSS*, ii, no. 3233; cf. *ADCS*, 512, when, in December 1541, there being 'distence and controverseis between Huntly and Forbes', this exemption is continued. In the sheriff's assize of 2 October 1538 at Aberdeen, the members included Leslie of Balquhain, Leslie of Kincraig, Leslie of Pitcaple, Leslie of Harthill, Alexander Strathauchin, and Alexander Fraser of Philorth – all of whom were probably opposed to the Forbes: *ibid*, xiv, f. 62v (case brought by the Crown and Lord Forbes, to annul a cognition in favour of Huntly against Forbes).

61. SRO, *AD*, i, f. 5.
62. *HP*, i, no. 267.
63. To judge from his record as a witness of charters, where he only served in this capacity for the duration of his term in office: cf. *RMS*, iii, *passim*. In 1531 he was one of the Lords of Council designated to assist the chancellor in dealing with civil judicial matters, and in 1532 he was appointed as a judge in the case between Hugh Campbell of Loudoun and the Master of Glencairn, over the ownership of Loudoun: *ADCP*, 349, 368, 373. In 1534 he was a joint witness to the ratification of the peace treaty with the English: *LP Henry VIII*, vii, no. 911.
64. *LP Henry VIII*, xv, no. 709.
65. Cf. *Scots Peerage*, iv, 533 ff. Huntly was a minor as late as February 1532: *Spalding Miscellany*, iv, 152, no. xv.
66. Cf. *ADCP*, 219, 253; *RSS*, i, no. 2538; *APS*, ii, 328.
67. *ADCP*, 195-6, 200.
68. *Spalding Miscellany*, ii, 83-4.
69. *ADCP*, 330-1. A cannon from Edinburgh castle was allowed for his use in the pursuit of rebels. Probably the raid was a response to the deaths of both the earl of Sutherland and the earl of Caithness in the preceding year: cf. Chapter 3. Moray made a bond with Mackay of Strathnaver (the family which fell into feud with the earl of Sutherland) in 1535: Wormald, *Bonds*, 345, App. A, no. 4.
70. In February 1531 Moray was granted licence to come to terms with the king's rebels in the Isles: *HMC, Sixth Report*, 670.
71. *LP Henry VIII*, vi, no. 269.
72. Wormald, *Bonds*, App. A, 383, no. 26; 345, no. 3; *Spalding Miscellany*, iv, 198, no. xxviii.
73. *SP Henry VIII*, iv, pt. iv, no. cclii.
74. As with the reports in 1531 and 1532 that Crawford might come over to the English side.
75. Or at least none traceable as being shamefully murdered. The case which fits the description most closely is the killing of a Mr. George Lindsay before February 1532, at St. Laurence church, Kinnettles, Kirriemuir, by William Sinclair of Finlay. Janet Piot, wife of William, was given respite in 1537 for 'passing away with the committaris tharof with the bludy hand' of Mr. Lindsay's mutilated brother, Patrick: *RSS*, ii, nos. 1152, 2314, 3343, 3519. As this crime occurred in the regality of Kirriemuir, under royal control, it is difficult to see why Argyll (royal justiciar), Moray (lieutenant of the March) and Huntly should be involved, let alone trace a connection between one of them and either the murderer or the victim.
76. *James V Letters*, 249; *RMS*, iii, nos. 1306-10; *TA*, vi, 178-9, 215; cf Chapter 9.
77. *RSS*, ii, no. 1527. Lauchlan would be Lauchlan MacLean; the two names appear to have been interchangeable: cf. *Ibid.*, ii, Index. The killing occurred after June 1531: cf. n. 80.
78. Wormald, *Bonds*, App. A, 178-9, nos. 5, 8.
79. *Spalding Miscellany*, iv, 200, no. xxxi (John Strathauchin of Linturk and Alexander Leslie of Pitcaple were amongst the witnesses).
80. Argyll's chief rival in the Isles was Alexander 'John Cannochsoun' or Alexander Macdonald, who in 1531 was warned by the Lords of Council not to assist the sons of John McGillan of Lochbuie: *ADCP*, 358. As Macdonald entered into government service, it seems likely that he heeded this warning – meaning that the McGillans or MacLeans of Lochbuie would become his opponents.
81. *RSS*, ii, no. 1525.
82. *HMC, Sixth Report* (1877), 670.
83. SRO, *ADCS*, v, f. 31v (spelling anglicised).
84. Wormald, *Bonds*, App. A, 345, no. 2. The bond of manrent had been given for life. Grant was to bond with Huntly in 1546: *Ibid.*, App. A, 286, no. 42.
85. *ADCP*, 425; Pitcairn, *Trials*, i, pt. i, 175-6.
86. Fraser, *Grant*, i, 1. James Grant of Freuchy was instructed on 13 May 1534 to proceed against the Macintoshes and other rebels with the lieutenant or whomever he thinks best

to command. This may have been the campaign which resulted in the hanging of William Macintosh and eighteen other ringleaders (cf. Chapter 4); Pitcairn, *Trials*, i, pt. i, 176, implies that William was still alive in 1534.

87. The arbiters between Huntly and Moray were (for Huntly) Fleming and Sir John Campbell [of Lundy], and (for Moray) Robert [Reid], abbot [of Kinloss], and Sir John Campbell of Cawdor: SRO, *ADCS*, v, 31v.

88. Fraser, *Grant*, iii, nos. 83, 86; *RSS*, ii, nos. 1750, 1753; *ADCP*, 451.

89. *TA*, vi, 303. Ward of the rightful heir, William , passed to the countess of Moray in 1538: *RSS*, ii, no. 2593. Hector died before 1541: *Ibid.*, ii, no. 3956.

90. *Spalding Miscellany*, iv, 152, no. xv.

91. *TA*, vi, 345, August 1537: payment to herald to pass to Banff, Elgin, Forres, Inverness 'and utheris placis neidfull'. Cf. a report by the English envoys to Edinburgh in May 1536 who claimed that Moray was dismissed and the lieutenancy given to Huntly: *SP Henry VIII*, v, pt. v, no. ccxcvi. This is plausible as Moray was in France at that time, and Huntly was shortly to become vice-regent.

92. James kept changing his mind about marrying Mary of Bourbon, and sending conflicting instructions to his commissioners: cf. *James V Letters*, 302, 306–7. Cf. also *SP Henry VIII*, v, pt. iv, no. ccxcvi (as per preceding note) where the lieutenancy is said to be transferred to Huntly as the commissioners were all 'lytle regardyd'.

93. Edington, *op.cit.*, 207–8, discusses the possibility that Sir David Lindsay's poem 'The Complaint and Public Confessioun of Bagsche' contained a 'coded warning' to Huntly. This is feasible, but the code is extremely cryptic.

94. *RMS*, iii, *passim*, though the Chancery was at the heart of government administration, not necessarily synonymous with the king's own activities.

95. *ER*, xv, 19n.; *RSS*, i, no. 3296; *ADCP*, 211, 323.

96. *ER*, xvii, 286; *RMS*, iii, no. 923; *TA*, v, 338–9; SRO, *ADCS*, xi, f. 206.

97. WRH, Inventory of Erroll Charters [NRA (S) 0925], nos. 240, 242, 260.

98. *RSS*, ii, no. 2656, the ward being that of the sixth earl of Erroll. The office was previously exercised by the third earl of Huntly, and then assigned to Ogilvy of that Ilk. Instances of Moray acting as sheriff occur in SRO, *ADCS*, ix, f. 32 (20 November 1537); xiii, f. 214 (2 October 1538).

99. SRO, *ADCS*, xii, f. 136; cf. n.60.

100. *Ibid.*, xii, f. 3 (30 September 1538) held for Forbes against James Strathauchin . A new cognition was requested by Huntly on 28 April 1541.

101. *ADCP*, 478; cf. *RSS*, ii, no. 2656, 30 July 1538, which is a letter of regress from Erroll to Crawford, suggesting the office had reverted to Crawford at that stage. However, this letter probably resurrected the terms of 1510 contract which would have fallen with the dispossession of Crawford in 1532. The contract of January 1539 makes it clear that Erroll was still the assignee of the office.

102. *RMS*, iii, no. 2296.

103. *LP Henry VIII*, xv, no. 709.

104. *HMC, Sixth Report*, 760–1. The will records that he had two illegitimate children.

105. *TA*, vii, 315, 439; cf. *RMS*, iii, *passim* – Moray absent as a charter witness from June 1540 to February 1541.

106. *HP*, i, no. 120; cf. *TA*, viii, 116 (corroborates Huntly's appointment). Sir William Eure was English officer at Berwick-upon-Tweed.

107. *HP*, i, nos. 127–8, 146 (1).

108. *Ibid.*, no. 224 (1).

109. *Ibid.*, App. no. II.

110. Also, in 1532 Huntly was appointed as a judge in the dispute between the Master of Glencairn and Sir Hugh Campbell of Loudoun, which resulted in Moray losing West Loudoun: *ADCP*, 373.

111. The only link being in the carrying out by Moray of the office of lieutenant of the north.

On 4 September 1529, at Dunrobin castle, William Sutherland gave his bond of manrent to Alexander Gordon, Master of Sutherland, in which he bound himself to fortify the Master's authority against all others, excepting only the king, the earl of Moray, and Lord Forbes: Fraser, *Sutherland*, iii, no. 83.

112. *Scots Peerage*, i, 189–90. The others were Elizabeth, married to Lord Hay of Yester; Alison, widow of David Hume of Wedderburn; and Margaret, who was divorced from Sir James Douglas of Drumlanrig by 1541 (*RMS*, iii, no. 2313).

113. WRH, Inventory of Glamis Charters [NRA (S) 885], Box 8, no. 184, n.113; SRO, RH 2.1.9. (*ADC*, vol. 38, f. 129). The seventh lord and heir was still a minor in 1538: *Spalding Miscellany*, ii, 214, no. vi.

114. *APS*, ii, 327, 331.

115. *SP Henry VIII*, iv, pt. iv, no. clxxxix.

116. Pitcairn, *Trials*, i, pt. i, 141. The king remitted this case to the Forfar justice ayre, suggesting that central government was no longer concerned to try the case and that the crime had thus been 'downgraded'.

117. *RSS*, ii, no. 334.

118. Possibly because those deported could not afford the composition for a remission.

119. SRO, *ADC*, vol. 40, f. 119; vol. 41, f. 51.

120. *RSS*, ii, no. 951.

121. *Ibid.*, ii, no. 985.

122. Pitcairn, *Trials*, i, pt. i, 158. Her cautioner was John Drummond of Innerpeffray, her maternal uncle. Both assizes were drawn from the localities of Forfar, Perth, Aberdeen and Fife, areas in which the Glamis lordship held estates. Lords Ruthven and Oliphant were part of the second assize. Drummond of Carnock (forfeited in 1528 and shortly to be formally restored to his estates) was on the first assize.

123. It appears to have been the prosecution's job to cite the jurors: cf. *The Jury in Scotland*, (Stair Society, vol. 23), 148–9. In this instance presumably the prosecution was the Crown.

124. Pitcairn, *Trials*, i, pt. i, 159. I.e. when Angus held the castle.

125. SRO, *ADCS*, i, f. 95; *Scots Peerage*, i, 336.

126. *HMC, Sixth Report*, 630.

127. *Acta Sessionis* (Stair), case no. 78.

128. *Ibid.*, cf. *TA*, vi, 467 (1537), when the abbot of Arbroath was given £140 to make over to John Charteris for the latter's expenses 'when he passed to France'. David Beaton was on diplomatic service in 1533 and again in 1536 and 1537: cf. M.B.H. Sanderson, *Cardinal of Scotland: David Beaton c.1494–1546* (Edinburgh, 1986), 56–7.

129. SRO, *ADCS*, vi, f. 107; viii, ff. 54v, 113v, 141v. This last ruling was given in the face of the king's instructions on 23 July 1536 that no actions were to be pursued against his servant whilst overseas on the king's business.

130. *Ibid.*, vi, f. 123.

131. Glasgow University, Argyll Tss, iv, no. 53; *TA*, vi, 327–8.

132. Pitcairn, *Trials*, i, pt. i, 198. Lawmond was possibly Lamont in Argyll, and associated with Campbell of Skipness. Douglas of Lochleven was associated with the Lyon family by holding the lands of Fossoway of the earldom of Erroll, ward of which was held by Glamis: cf. SRO, *ADC*, vol. 43, f. 159v.

133. Pitcairn, *Trials.*, i, pt. i, 190–1. There were fifteen jury members. These were Cassillis; Buchan; Atholl; Semple; Maxwell; the Master of Glencairn; Melville of Raith; Hume of Coldenknowes (these last four appearing on the assize for the Master of Forbes); Kirkpatrick of Kirkmichael (Dumfries); Crichton of Ruwennis (Ruthven, Forfar); Kerr of Mersington (Roxburgh); Towers of Inverleith (Edinburgh); Barclay of Mathers (Kincardine); Edmonstone of that Ilk (Berwick) and William Maclellan, tutor of Bondby (Bombie, Kirkcudbright). There is no apparent factor to link any of these personages either with Lady Glamis or with the king. The most that can be said is that, unlike the earlier attempt to try her, this assize was not drawn entirely from the locality.

134. *Ibid.*, i, pt. i, 199; cf. *SP Henry VIII*, v, pt. iv, no. cccxxiii, where on 26 July 1537 Sir Thomas Clifford advised Henry VIII that Lord Glamis was then in ward. He possibly was around sixteen years old in 1537.
135. *APS*, ii, 422. Glamis did not claim that his mother had been innocent in 1537. Rather, he argued that the correct procedures had not been carried out at his trial and that he had been misled by the justice clerk, Thomas Scott of Pitgormo, into making a confession. He had understood that his lands would be spared.
136. Pitcairn, *Trials*, i, pt. i, 199. Again there were fifteen persons on the jury. They were Cassillis; Towers of Inverleith; Barclay of Mathers (all on Lady Glamis' assize); Maxwell; the Master of Glencairn; Melville of Raith; Hume of Coldenknowes (all four on both the assizes of the Master of Forbes and Lady Glamis); Somerville; Seton; Ochiltree (Lord Avandale); the Master of Eglinton; Gordon of Lochinvar (Dumfries); Crichton of Bellibocht (Dumfries); Stirling of Keir (Perth); Fraser of Philorth (Aberdeen). As with the assize for Lady Glamis, there is no apparent common denominator, nor a defined geographical area being represented.
137. *Ibid.*, i, pt. i, 202–3.
138. *Ibid.*, i, pt. i, 203. This perhaps was a lenient punishment in view of the fact he had committed treason: cf. Balfour, *Practicks*, ii, 506. Possibly he was induced to provide evidence against Lyon of Knockany.
139. *RSS*, ii, no. 4778.
140. NLS, Abell, *op.cit.*, f. 126v.
141. M. Brown, *op.cit.*, 72ff.
142. C. McGladdery, *James II* (Edinburgh, 1990), 66, 96.
143. Macdougall, *James III*, 130–3.
144. Macdougall, *James IV*, 59, though, of course, James IV was hardly responsible for his death.
145. Emond, *op.cit.*, 124.
146. For arson, Pitcairn, *Trials*, i, pt. i, 162. Wilful fire-raising was punishable as treason: *APS*, ii, 316.
147. Pitcairn devotes several pages of his work to citing various extracts which lament the death of the 'unfortunate' woman: Pitcairn, *Trials*, pt. i, 191–197. Bingham, *op.cit.*, 142, also draws the comparison with Anne Boleyn. Although the crime of treason carried the penalty of forfeiture of life, land and goods, the lack of a Scottish female precedent makes it impossible to assert with any degree of confidence that it was customary for noble women to be either beheaded or burned as Pitcairn claims.
148. Assuming she married at age 16 to Lord Glamis in 1520.
149. Buchanan, *History*, ii, 257. Interestingly, he is the only sixteenth century chronicler to express any strong opinion on the death of Lady Glamis. Cf. Lesley, *History*, 154; Pitscottie, *Historie*, i, 347; *Diurnal of Occurrents*, 22, all of which simply note her death in passing, as does Abell, *op.cit.*, f. 126. Apart from expressing his own political bias in his account of the reign, it is feasible that Buchanan was an eye-witness of the event. He was tutor to James' illegitimate children in 1537, probably based at Stirling rather than Edinburgh.
150. Pitcairn, *Trials*, i, pt. i, 187ff; cf. Tytler, *op.cit.*, v, 368–373, who saw this as being of no significance.
151. Which gives rise to speculation that she may have been a witch of sorts. If that were the case, possibly David Beaton, abbot of Arbroath, was involved in her first trial, assisted by his servant, John Charteris.
152. Her two daughters were taken under the wing of the Household following her death. There is a reference in September 1537 to purses, shoes and stockings being purchased for them: *TA*, vi, 349. She appears to have had just two daughters, Margaret and Elizabeth: SRO, *ADC*, vol. 40, f. 119. With the death of her husband and the warding of her father-in-law, Lord Forbes, Elizabeth had no other place to go.

153. *Scots Peerage*, iii, 568ff; *ER*, xv, 596; *RSS*, i, nos. 3883, 4019.
154. *RMS*, iii, no. 728.
155. *RSS*, i, no. 3883.
156. *ADCP*, 284, 500 marks of which was to pay the super expenses of the Treasurer in 1517–18, Sir John Campbell of Lundy: *TA*, v, 164.
157. SRO, *ADC*, vol. 38, f. 188v; *RMS*, iii, no. 728.
158. *RMS*, iii, no. 728; *RSS*, i, no. 4031.
159. *RSS*, i, no. 4029; SRO, *ADC*, vol. 39, f. 61.
160. SRO, *ADC*, vol. 41, f. 72v.
161. WRH, NRA (S) 885, Inventory of Strathmore Writs, no. 42.
162. *RMS*, iii, no. 2233.
163. *ER*, xvii, 93, 214, 360, 432.
164. *Ibid.*, xvii, 158–61, 230, 250–6, 272, 411, 418–24, 478–81, 487.
165. *RMS*, iii, nos. 1751, 1800, 1878, 2109, 2120; *ER*, xvii, 242, 407. Andrew Wood of Largo received the island of Inchkeith for an annual reddendo of 24 rabbits at the Feast of the Circumcision: *RMS*, iii, no. 1888.
166. *RMS*, iii, no. 2747.
167. *ER*, xvii, 93–8, 214–8, 361–3, 434–6.
168. *RMS*, iii, nos. 2517, 2521.
169. *TA*, vi, 329–30, 344; *RSS*, ii, no. 2317.
170. *SP Henry VIII*, v, pt. iv, no. cccxxiii. Peter Carmichael appeared as a witness to a Forbes charter in the following reign (*RMS*, iii, no. 3988). He and Strathauchin were warded for the Master of Forbes' plot. The earl of Morton was required to find caution for Douglas of Lochleven: SRO, *ADCS*, ix, f. 117.
171. Pitcairn, *Trials*, i, pt. i, 201–2; cf. Chapter 6. In the previous year the abbot of Jedburgh (John Hume) had given security of £1000 for his passing north of the river Tay: SRO, *ADCS*, viii, f. 82v.
172. *Ibid.*, i, pt. i, 202. One William Mathieson, probably his father, was granted a remission for treasonable assistance of the Douglases in February 1529 (*RSS*, ii, no. 4089).
173. David Hope and William Inglis, both hanged at Tantallon; the Master of Forbes, Lady Glamis, Alexander Hume, John Mathieson, and John Lyon of Knockany.
174. *SP Henry VIII*, v, pt. iv, no. cccxxx. A parliamentary committee, at which Rothes was present, met on 11 March 1538: *APS*, ii, 352. No business was recorded.
175. *RMS*, iii, no. 1772. He was later described as servitor of the king: *ibid.*, iii, no. 2644.
176. Margaret Erskine: *ibid.*, nos. 1620, 2259. James did explore the possibility of having them divorced: *James V Letters*, 320; cf. *SP Henry VIII*, v, pt. iv, no. ccxc: 'He wyll marye a gentyll woman in Scotland, the lord of Arskyne's daughter'.
177. SRO, Morton Papers [GD 150], box 40, nos. 958–9, probably at the instance of David Beaton, coadjutor.
178. *RMS*, iii, no. 1846; alternatively Hugh, burgess of Edinburgh, who was granted lands by James Douglas of Drumlanrig in 1540: *Ibid.*, iii, no. 2313.
179. SRO, *ADCS*, xv, f. 163.
180. *ADCP*, 290.
181. With the death of the first earl of Arran and fourth earl of Argyll in 1529 this number was somewht diminished, the remaining key players being Moray, Eglinton, Rothes and Lord Maxwell.
182. Pitcairn, *Trials*, i, pt. i, 181. There is no record of the terms of this proclamation, which was presumably for good rule in the king's absence. One Alexander Dinglay came into the king's will in December 1538 for communicating with the Douglases at Berwick during the king's absence: *Ibid.*, i, pt. i, 209.
183. *RSS*, ii, no. 2311; cf. Chapter 7.
184. *ADCP*, 424; cf. Chapter 7.
185. *ADCP*, 407.

186. Discussed *infra*.
187. Campbell was in Argyll's affinity and cited as amongst his retinue in the latter's letter of protection for the duration of his visit to France: *RSS*, ii, no. 2152. Campbell's heir experienced difficulty in being served to his father's estates in July 1542 on account of the circumstances of the death. The king directed that he should be served with 'dew executioun': *ibid.*, ii, no. 4778.
188. In one of her numerous letters to her brother, Henry VIII, on 10 February 1537, she complained that Methven 'hath spendyd my landes and profetes apon hys owne kyn and fryndes' and put her in debt to the tune of 8000 marks: *SP Henry VIII*, v, pt. iv, no. cccxi.
189. *LP Henry VIII*, xi, no. 1018.
190. *SP Henry VIII*, v, pt. iv, no. cccviii. Reading between the lines, in effect he was telling Cromwell to mind his own business.
191. *Ibid.*, v, pt. iv, nos. cccxiii, cccxx. The first time to France, in March 1537, and the second time to Edinburgh, in June 1537.
192. *Ibid.*, v, pt. iv, no. cccix.
193. *Ibid.*, v, pt. iv, no. cccxx, via Sadler.
194. *Ibid.*, v, pt. iv, no. cccxxvii.
195. *LP Henry VIII*, xii, pt. ii, no. 828.
196. *Ibid.*, xii, pt. ii, no. 1079.
197. Cf. e.g. *ibid.*, xiii, pt. i, no. 489 (list of days of truce held in 1537–8).
198. *SP Henry VIII*, v, pt. iv, no. cccxxxvii.
199. *Ibid.*, v, pt. iv, no. cccvi.
200. *LP Henry VIII*, xii, pt. ii, no. 712.
201. *Ibid.*, xii, pt. ii, App. no. 10: i.e. all the reasons given in earlier years.
202. *Ibid.*, xi, no. 916. Penven appears once to have been a servant of Sir George Douglas. Inglis, *op.cit.*, 68, describes him as one of Henry VIII's chaplains.
203. *RSS*, ii, no. 2147, paid for by contributions from the First Estate. The earl of Moray did not believe that Finnart was out of favour either, according to Penven.
204. Pitcairn, *Trials*, i, pt. i, 180.
205. *TA*, vi, 307.
206. *ADCP*, 210.
207. Pitcairn, *Trials*, i, pt. i, 180–1.
208. *TA*, vi, 307–8.
209. *Ibid.*, vi, 307. The reference to his ward is dated 25 September 1536; possibly he had been required to enter into ward prior to the king's departure, as a precautionary measure. He shared his ward with Johnston of that Ilk.
210. *RMS*, iii, no. 1480; *RSS*, ii, no. 322.
211. *HMC, Fifteenth Report*, App. viii, 92, no. 17; *ADCP*, 318–9.
212. *TA*, vi, 4111, 416–7, 430, 444; vii, 186, for references to Lady Jane, who appears to have been the king's only illegitimate daughter. The contract is undated except for the year.
213. *RMS*, iii, no. 1764; *APS*, ii, 383–3.
214. *RSS*, ii, nos. 4265, 4909. Margaret was probably one of the royal mistresses: cf. Dunbar, *Scots Kings*, 239, where Elizabeth, daughter of Lennox, is designated as such; cf. also Chapter 7, note 260. Elizabeth does not appear to have existed.
215. The contract also envisaged that Lady Jane might marry a younger son of Lord Hume. It is possible that no marriage took place before the end of the personal rule simply because Jane was still too young.
216. Pitcairn, *Trials*, i, pt. i, 210–2. He is given no designation and probably was more closely related to the Humes of Wedderburn than to Lord Hume.
217. *RMS*, iii, no. 2987 (charter 16 January 1544); Pitcairn, *Trials*, i, pt. i, 190.
218. Pitcairn, *Trials*, i, pt. i, 179; *TA*, vi, 303, 308.
219. *LP Henry VIII*, xi, no. 1004.
220. Using oxen: *TA*, vi, 303, 308. The gunners were paid for nine weeks' service: *MW*, i, 193.

221. Pitcairn, *Trials*, i, pt. i, 179.
222. *RMS*, ii, nos. 2493, 3677; *Scots Peerage*, vii, 366ff; *ER*, xiv, 573; *ADCP*, 55, 95–6.
223. SRO, *ADCS*, iv, f. 147.
224. *RMS*, ii, nos. 3576, 3761.
225. Pitcairn, *Trials*, i, pt. i, 179; *Scots Peerage*, vii, 366ff.
226. *TA.*, vi, 310.
227. *RSS*, i, no. 4016. He was married to Christine Hay, daughter of the third Lord Hay and Elizabeth Douglas, Angus' sister: *Scots Peerage*, i, 189.
228. *RMS*, iii, nos. 803, 1762.
229. Pitcairn, *Trials*, i, pt. i, 161, 177.
230. *SP Henry VIII*, iv, pt. iv, ccxxxv; cf. Chapter 6.
231. After 1536 references to the siege of Edgerston disappear, in both Scots and English records. Angus never referred to it. Robert Rutherford was still an outlaw in 1538, when, ironically, Kerr of Cessford was convicted of breaking his bonds for good rule in allowing the Rutherfords free passage through the Middle March 'for divers years past': Pitcairn, *Trials*, i, pt. i, 208.
232. *RSS*, ii, no. 2301.
233. *ADCP*, 347.
234. *James V Letters*, 333–4, 340–1; *TA*, vi, 467; *LP Henry VIII*, xii, pt. ii, no. 566 (Beaton writes to the king from France on 22 August 1537).
235. Probably a modern concept. The doctrine of standard of proof is not referred to in legal texts covering the period.
236. Taylor, *op.cit.*, 59, narrates that Lord Forbes had a natural daughter 'by one Helen Rutherford'. The source for this piece of information is not given. If true, then it is possible to assert that his mistress was the same Helen who had a claim to Edgerston castle, but to draw from this the further inference that Lord Forbes was implicated in the siege of Edgerston castle is probably a fruitless exercise.

CHAPTER NINE

The Rise and Fall of Sir James Hamilton of Finnart

I n a recent article,[1] Charles McKean examined both the architectural work of Sir James Hamilton of Finnart and his 'summary execution' in 1540. In so doing he attempted to shed some light on the character of James V. McKean concluded that 'few could withstand the king in his anti-Douglas paranoia'. Finnart's career flourished in the 1530s and the part which he played in the personal rule is somewhat ambiguous. He combined the roles both of a magnate and a Household servant, quite apart from being hailed as 'Scotland's first architect'. Furthermore, it is possible to argue that he had easy access to the king's ear and can thus be regarded as having been a royal favourite. These factors, when combined with the repercussions of his downfall, may have affected Crown-magnate relations adversely in the personal rule.

I. EARLY YEARS: HAMILTON, DOUGLAS AND LENNOX

Finnart was probably about forty-five years old when he was executed in 1540.[2] He was the illegitimate son of the first earl of Arran, and in 1507 received a royal charter to the lands of Finnart (Renfrew), part of his father's earldom.[3] Arran was created as earl by James IV in 1503, and his son appears to have entered the royal Household. From 1507 onwards there are several entries in the *Treasurer's Accounts* which record the gift of shoes and boots for James Hamilton. By 1511 he had been knighted.[4] In 1513 he and his father's two half-brothers were legitimised. At the same time all three were made joint heirs of tailzie to the earldom of Arran, as the first earl of Arran had no legitimate heirs.[5] In the same year Arran gifted his son half the lands and barony of Crawfordjohn (Lanark).[6]

In the minority of James V, Finnart strongly identified with his father's political interest. In 1516 he took part in the battle of Kittycrosshill, on Arran's side, against the Angus Douglases.[7] In 1518 he escorted Sir George Douglas, who had been forced into exile by the Arran government, to France.[8] In 1520 Finnart accompanied his father in the raid of Jedwood forest against the Kerrs.[9] Almost certainly he played an active part in the subsequent 'Cleanse the Causeway' incident, again a clash between Hamilton and Douglas supporters.[10] The tension between the two families is illustrated nicely by a letter to the king from Sir George Douglas, written at Tantallon on 19 January 1524. Sir George apologised for not being with the king at New Year as commanded. His explanation was that:

> eftir I tuk my leif fra your grace in Edinburgh that samyn day James Hamilton lay for me till haif slane me and of cais I come nocht that way.

Sir George then accused his former escort of jumping 'my cosing' in the streets of Edinburgh in a case of mistaken identity, 'and had slain him, had nocht bene his hurs bur him away throw speid'.[11]

By September 1526 Arran and Angus had reconciled their differences sufficiently for both to be opposed to the Lennox revolt. In that month John Stewart, third earl of Lennox, was killed after an armed clash at Manuel Priory, Linlithgow. Arran and Finnart both received a remission from the Angus government.[12] Ward of the Lennox earldom was divided between Angus and Arran immediately after Lennox's death.[13] The Hamiltons then entered into a phase of cooperation with the Angus régime. In October 1526 Angus sold to Finnart £80 worth of the lordship of Bothwell (Lanark) in free regality.[14] In April 1527 Angus renounced his half of the Lennox ward to Finnart. In June Finnart made this over to Andrew Stewart, Lord Avandale.[15] Finnart then induced his father, Arran, to resign the other half of the ward to Avandale.[16] By June 1527 Avandale (married to Margaret Hamilton, half-sister to Finnart) was holding the entire ward, together with the keeping of Dumbarton castle. However Finnart kept the title of captain of Dumbarton castle for himself. The two men shared the actual responsibility for the castle's keeping until 1531.[17]

Various lands of the earldom of Arran were held of the earldom of Lennox. These included Drumry (Dunbarton), held by Finnart, and also part of the lands of the barony of Avandale. These latter were held in conjunct-fee by Elizabeth Hamilton, sister of the first earl of Arran and widow of Matthew, second earl of Lennox, killed at Flodden.[18] In June 1527, Lord Avandale obtained a licence to sell 'to quhatsumever persone or personis he ples' part of his lands and own superiorities within the barony of Avandale.[19] Over the course of the next six years, he regularly sold lands to Finnart.[20] This was a trade-off for Avandale holding the ward of the Lennox earldom; Finnart had made over the ward to Avandale for 'certain conditions'.[21] The possession of the ward of the earldom of Lennox after the death of the third earl was the means by which Finnart was able to construct his own free barony of Avandale.

Even after making over the ward of the Lennox earldom to Lord Avandale, the Hamiltons retained an interest. In January 1528, the first earl of Arran received from Alan Stewart of Craighall a bond of manrent with a ten-year term.[22] Craighall was first tutor, then curator, to the young Matthew, fourth earl of Lennox, who was probably aged eleven in 1528.[23] The bond of manrent between Arran and Craighall was almost certainly intended to run for the duration of Matthew's minority. However, Arran died at the end of March 1529. The bond was not renewed, but it is likely that Craighall and Finnart were on good terms.[24]

Finnart entered the personal rule with a lawsuit against Isobel Stewart, the widow of the deceased third earl of Lennox. This was over the non-entries to the lands of Crukisfee (Renfrew). Isobel claimed that Stewart of Craighall and Elizabeth Hamilton had stolen the charter proving the third earl's title from the family's charter chest at Blackfriars kirk, Glasgow. The case went to arbitration. Finnart consented to the title of Crukisfee going to Isobel for the duration of her life, but he himself was awarded the non-entries. These were backdated to Flodden and amounted to £600.[25] It is unclear why Finnart should have had any right to them; possibly he was representing Elizabeth Hamilton's interest. He had the cooperation of both Lord Avandale and Craighall. In any event, the earldom was required to assign lands on three separate occasions between 1529 and 1531 in order to meet the debt due to Finnart.[26] Immediately after his own father's death, in April 1529, Finnart disposed of his interest in the Lennox estate of Drumry. He exchanged this with Lawrence Crawford of Kilbirnie in return for the other half of the barony of Crawfordjohn, directly from the Crown.[27] In effect the exchange robbed the Arran earldom of its tenancy of Drumry, and Finnart obtained a new freeholding. Possibly Finnart felt he was justified in carrying out this transaction, for he had lost his Bothwell lands to the earldom of Arran. The entire lordship of Bothwell had fallen to the Crown upon the forfeiture of the earldom of Angus. With it fell Angus' 1526 grant to Finnart. The lordship was then regranted in November 1528 to the first earl of Arran.[28]

Finnart concluded the Hamilton connection with the earldom of Lennox on 29 April 1531, in an agreement drawn up with the fourth earl.[29] Hamilton represented both himself and acted as tutor for his half-brother, the second earl of Arran. Lennox acted with the consent and assent of his curator, Stewart of Craighall. By the terms of the agreement, the fourteen-year-old Lennox

> remittis, forgevis and frelie dischargeis the said James [second] erle of Arrane, James Hammiltoun of Fynnart, knicht . . . and all utheris being in company with umqhile James [first] Erle of Arrange . . . the tyme of the slauchter of the (said) Johnne [third] Erle of Levenax, oure fader.[30]

In addition, Finnart was especially discharged of all cause of forfeiture of the lands of Drumry incurred by his appearing in arms against the third earl of Lennox, superior of the lands, 'in plane feild at Canathy brig, for his slauchter'.

This suggests two separate occasions in which Finnart and Lennox were in armed opposition, the first at Canathy brig,[31] the second at Linlithgow, where the earl was killed. The first incident was a land dispute, almost certainly over the rights to the profits of Drumry, which had conveniently now been disposed of by Finnart.[32] In the second incident, Lennox had been killed. In return for being forgiven by the young fourth earl, Finnart relinquished his right to Lennox' marriage, and resigned his interest in Dumbarton castle. Finnart also agreed to visit the 'thre heid pilgrimages of Scotland', and to pay for prayers to be said for the soul of the deceased third earl. In turn, Lennox agreed not to challenge

Finnart's right of possession to those lands of the barony of Avandale as were now held by him of the earldom in conjunction with Elizabeth Hamilton. It is not clear at what point Finnart came to hold these parts or the barony, but presumably this was part of the deal with Lord Avandale.[33] Over the course of the next year, Lennox was given sasine to his earldom, together with the captaincy of Dumbarton castle and the non-entry of Crukisfee.[34] In July 1532 he obtained a licence to pass overseas.[35]

The rumour that Finnart had killed the third earl of Lennox arose almost before the body had time to grow cold.[36] The English knew about it. Whilst negotiating a renewal of the Anglo-Scots truce in November 1528, Sir Thomas Magnus put forward the proposition that the English could not treat with a young king so totally guided by 'theves and murderours', amongst them 'Sir James Hamylton, whoe did sley the Erle of Lenneux'.[37] Of the sixteenth century chroniclers, Abell, the author of the *Diurnal* and Lesley simply record the death of Lennox at Linlithgow. Buchanan used the episode to illustrate the generally heinous character of all of the Hamilton family. For once, Pitscottie was undoubtedly correct in being the only chronicler to state outright that Lennox was:

> fand lyand slaine in the deid thraw [thrown] cruellie be Schir James Hammilltoun that . . . slew him withtout marcie.[38]

The subsequent manipulation of the Lennox ward by Finnart was a cynical exercise to establish a foundation for his own free landholding; the third earl was out of the way, the fourth earl was a minor. Although the decree-arbitral between Finnart and the fourth earl of Lennox was a conventional arrangement for settling a feud between families – two contemporary examples were the agreements between Lord Fleming and the Tweedies, and Scott of Buccleuch and the Kerrs – in this instance Finnart had the upper hand. Lennox was young, and his tutor, Craighall, was probably well disposed towards Finnart as were Lennox's grandmother, Elizabeth Hamilton, and Lord Avandale. For all that Finnart was obliged to give his bond of manrent to Lennox and discharge any existing Hamilton bonds made with Lennox's kindred, it was Lennox's nose rather than Finnart's which was being rubbed in the dirt.[39]

In these circumstances Lennox's departure overseas can be seen as a retreat from circumstances beyond his control. The parallel is with Cassillis, who also departed for France, abandoning the field to his father's killer, Hugh Campbell of Loudoun. The difference between the two was that Cassillis came back to challenge the sheriff of Ayr, and eventually Campbell himself was exiled. Had Lennox been in Scotland in 1540, he would have been the prime candidate for targeting Finnart's downfall. Unfortunately, the evidence suggests that Lennox remained overseas at least until after Finnart's execution, probably throughout the remainder of the personal rule.

2. THE ARRAN WARD

The second opportunity for Finnart to manipulate an earldom for his own ends came in 1529. On 25 March 1529, the first earl of Arran appointed his son as his executor. The procedure was extraordinary; Arran resigned half of the earldom to Finnart. As an obedient son, and without any compulsion or desire to flatter his father, Finnart freely resigned this back into Arran's hands. Probably this was a symbolic alienation of the estate by testator to executor.[40] Nevertheless, it demonstrates a high degree of trust and mutual regard between father and son. On the following day, at Kinneil (Linlithgow, part of the earldom of Arran), Arran drew up his last will and testament. His assets were valued at £11,700 Scots plus 480 (unvalued) cows pasturised on Bothwell moor. £4000 of this was held as cash. A further £6000 in cash was held by the earl's illegitimate son, John, abbot-commendator of Paisley (aged 18).[41] His debts amounted to £6500. His pecuniary legacies, to illegitimate sons and daughters, amounted to £3600. The various doctors who attended him were remembered; 12d. was donated to church fabric funds. Finnart was bequeathed all other jewels and goods, which with other deductions amounted to £1600. Of more pertinence, nearly £4600 of the debt was due to Finnart, in the form of intromitted rents. If Finnart was able to take what he was owed in liquid form (after paying off the pecuniary legacies), this would have given him a large cash fund. Also, Finnart was appointed as executor and tutor to his half-brother and namesake, the second earl of Arran. The first earl then died, and on 31 March 1529 Finnart was granted the ward of the earldom, on payment of 2000 marks.[42]

The second earl was nine or ten years old when his father died.[43] He had one legitimate younger brother, Gavin.[44] Finnart was second in line to the inheritance,[45] and at the age of thirty-four, with at least ten-and-a-half years of administration of the earldom ahead of him, he was in effect the acting earl of Arran. By 1526, Finnart was married to Margaret Livingstone, and together they held the lands and barony of East Wemyss (Fife).[46] The barony had passed into the earldom of Arran through the first earl's second marriage to Janet Beaton of Creich. Upon her death in 1522 Arran had regranted East Wemyss to Finnart.[47] In 1529 Finnart and Margaret had one infant son, James. Finnart had already at least four illegitimate sons.[48] Of these, his eldest son, Andrew, latterly appears to have become Finnart's right-hand man in the administration of the Arran earldom.

The first extant instance of friction over the ward came in December 1537, when the earl of Arran was about eighteen years old, and brought a suit against Andrew, claiming that the latter was interfering with his tenants in Lanarkshire. These tenants, who included a number of Hamiltons, held their lands directly from Arran. Andrew was attempting to apprise their lands to the 'great hurt and expense of their superior'. Andrew had obtained letters charging Arran to infeft him in blanche farm in the lands. Arran's procurator, Thomas Marjoribanks, argued that, as they stood, the lands were not held in blanche farm. Thus Arran was being compelled to receive Andrew as his tenant 'without any manner of profit or pleasure', failing which Arran was to be outlawed. According to Arran, the letters were 'wrongeously' and badly obtained. However, Finnart, appearing for his son, produced the letters. The court of session ruled that they were in order. Andrew should therefore be infeft as soon as possible.[49]

The second instance of friction came in February 1540. The dispute was between John Hamilton of Fairholm and David Hamilton, chaplain of St. Leonard's hospital, Lanark. David had won the case and obtained both a sheriff-court decree to apprise John and a precept of chancery to have Andrew infeft in the apprised lands. Arran, probably now aged twenty, was refusing to infeft Andrew in terms of the precept, arguing that the lands in question were held in blanche farm direct from himself, and should not have been apprised in the first place. Andrew appealed to the court of session, and a Crown action was raised against Arran. The case was continued.[50]

Each episode was simply a land dispute, typical of the hundreds being dealt with by the court of session in the personal rule. However, the implications are of interest. Firstly, it is apparent that Andrew was trying to carve out his own landholdings within the Arran earldom, aided and abetted by his father. It is remarkable that the two should have threatened to outlaw Arran in order to achieve this. Secondly, as a young adult, the second earl of Arran began to resist Finnart's family. Thirdly, Andrew's attempt to interpose himself in the feudal chain between Arran and Arran's tenants, potentially threatened their title to possess and actually did disrupt their possession. Lastly, Andrew was able to obtain legal documentation to enable him so to do. Finnart collected various offices in the personal rule, but the only three specified in royal charters as being held by him in Lanarkshire were that of coroner, bailie of Lesmahagow, and bailie of Carstairs.[51] Neither dispute was confined within the boundaries of these bailiaries, and the office of coroner involved purely criminal duties.[52] The earls of Arran were the hereditary sheriffs of Lanark.[53] Finnart had acted as deputy for his father in 1524. One James Hamilton of Stalford acted as deputy in February 1536.[54] The second earl of Arran was summoned in his capacity as sheriff in June 1533, and was represented by his curators, James Hamilton of Kingscavil, John Hamilton of Newtown, William Hamilton of Sanquhar, and Gavin Hamilton of Haggs.[55] As wardholder of the earldom, Finnart was not *ipso facto* the acting sheriff. However, he clearly had enough influence as the administrator of the earldom to obtain letters of authorisation from both the Lanark sheriff court and the chancery office.

The likelihood is that Finnart's position brought him into dispute with other members of the Hamilton kindred. The most visible dispute was with James Hamilton of Stonehouse (Lanark). Following the killing of one Thomas Fletcher in 1533, the chief suspects were the Hamiltons of Haggs. Finnart, as coroner, had the task of apprehending them in order to enter them at the Lanark justice ayre.[56]

In August 1534 two general remissions were granted at the ayre, to Thomas Morton and to Hamilton of Stonehouse. In each case the list of excepted crimes was longer than those for which each man was pardoned. The exceptions included treasonable assistance of the Douglases, arson in the forest of the lordship of Douglas, and killing Thomas Fletcher.[57] With his large cash fund inherited from his father, Finnart was able to act as guarantor, or money lender, to the Hamiltons. Finnart had lost 500 marks in giving assythement to Fletcher's widow in February; in August Finnart was compensated with the gift of the marriage of Stonehouse's eldest son.[58] Clearly, Stonehouse was implicated in the death of Fletcher.

The next clash was in the civil court. Finnart and his son, Andrew, raised an action against Stonehouse, in November 1537, over the latter's entitlement to various lands in the Stonehouse barony, which George Hamilton of Cotcastle had alienated to Stonehouse in 1536.[59] In court, Finnart protested that the charter from Cotcastle was suspect and that it threatened Andrew's land rights. It should therefore be declared invalid.[60] Stonehouse was ordered to seek warrandice from Cotcastle.[61] By July 1538, Stonehouse was being accused of deforcing a royal officer.[62] To make matters worse for himself, he then became embroiled in a dispute with his own tenant, Katherine Hepburn, over his wrongeous intromissions with the profits of her lands.[63] Additionally, Stonehouse was suspected of killing her husband, John Hamilton of Newtown.[64] Stonehouse then entered into a dispute with David Hamilton, chaplain of St. Leonard's hospital, over the lands of Spittalshiels.[65]

Both of these latter disputes were ongoing at the end of June 1540, six weeks before Finnart's execution. In the first, Stonehouse's possession of the disputed lands was now being challenged by Katherine. On 28 June 1540 Stonehouse produced an obligation by Finnart to warrant his possession, and asked for Finnart to be called to speak to it.[66] This suggests that Finnart had succeeded in displacing Cotcastle as Stonehouse's superior. Katherine's deceased husband had been Finnart's tenant in Avandale, and also a regular witness to the numerous land deals through which Finnart had built up that lordship.[67] It was highly unlikely that Finnart would wish to appear to support Stonehouse's case. Indeed, he was probably encouraging Katherine against Stonehouse. If a criminal conviction against Stonehouse for the killing of Hamilton of Newtown could not be secured, one way to compensate Katherine was to have her dispossess Stonehouse.

In the second dispute, David Hamilton had obtained letters to have Stonehouse and his tenants thrown off Spittalshiels, under penalty of being put to the horn. As David was on the royal expedition to the Isles at the time of the hearing, on 28 June, the case was continued.[68] David was associated with Finnart's son, Andrew, in the February 1540 dispute with Arran, and was a witness to Finnart's charters.[69]

3. THE AVANDALE LORDSHIP

The Stonehouse barony bordered the Avandale lordship. Over the course of the personal rule, Finnart built the lordship into a substantial freehold. He started with the various pieces of land passed over by Lord Avandale from both within and without the Lennox earldom. In 1529, Finnart swapped the Lennox lands of Drumry for half of the barony of Crawfordjohn, held direct from the Crown.[70] In December 1530, the Arran lordship of East Wemyss was exchanged with the comptroller, James Colville, for the barony of Ochiltree (Ayr), again held direct from the Crown.[71] In August 1534 Ochiltree was exchanged with Lord Avandale for the superiority of the lands and barony of Avandale, concluding the arrangement made seven years earlier.[72] In February 1536 the Crown and Finnart entered into a contract of excambion whereby the Crown would take possession of the whole barony of Crawfordjohn and receive the estimated annual revenues of 525 marks. In lieu, Finnart would receive the annual rents of the lordship of Kilmarnock, worth 600 marks.

The Crown got slightly the better deal. Although the chamberlain appointed to administrate Crawfordjohn was only able to generate an annual turnover of around 420 marks, the shortfall was made up by Finnart being required to pay the compensatory annual sum of 240 marks for the term of the excambion.[73] The lordship of Kilmarnock was part of Margaret Tudor's conjunct-fee. The Lords of Council were satisfied that she had renounced her right to her son 'of her own fre will and propir motive without any coactioun, circumventioun, fraud or gile'. An arrangement was made for her to be compensated, though the only note of any payment to her was made in 1540. Her husband, Lord Methven, intimated her consent to the Lords of Council in January 1536.[74] Later that year, Margaret attempted to divorce Methven. After being prevented from running into England, she complained to Henry VIII that Methven had spent her lands and profits on his own kin and friends to the tune of 8000 marks.[75] The exchange of Kilmarnock and Crawfordjohn may have been one incident which she had in mind.

The 1536 charter regulating the agreement between the Crown and Finnart narrated how the king had been troubled by murderers, thieves and other lawbreakers in Annandale, Ewesdale, Eskdale, Tweeddale, Crawfordmuir and Eskdale forest, which areas had now been pacified. Crawfordjohn was adjacent to these areas, with a number of strongholds viable for the purpose of maintaining the continued security of the lieges.[76] The king may also have had in mind the arson incident in the former Angus-held barony of Douglas, to the north of Crawfordjohn. His new possession was also adjacent to Crawford Douglas, again part of the forfeited earldom of Angus. By 1536 both these baronies were held by the king through his eldest illegitimate son.[77]

As in Forfarshire, so also in Lanarkshire, the Crown was extending its patrimony in an area formerly dominated by the Douglas earls of Angus. James visited his new possession in March 1536.[78] Latterly he carried out some building works at the caput, constructing kennels and stables and maintaining its defences.[79] Probably he used the place as a hunting lodge. Possessing Crawfordjohn also gave him easier access to the gold mine located on neighbouring Crawfordmuir. Over 8lbs. of gold had been extracted by May 1537, for which the Treasurer paid £840, and which provided a clear incentive for James to move into Crawfordjohn. Finnart, who had inherited a lump of gold weighing 1lb. 8oz, sold three ounces in 1534 to the Treasury 'to the mending of the Kingis croune' at a 15%-25% mark-up in the price.[80] In 1539 James imported French miners to work the mines,[81] and three ounces were presented to Mary of Guise on her visit to Crawfordjohn in 1541[82]. There was also a lead mine at Crawfordmuir, which Ninian Crichton of Bellibocht was given licence to work in June 1536.[83]

The practical effect for Finnart was that he kept the superiority of Crawfordjohn, but until his execution commuted the profits of the barony for the Kilmarnock rents.[84] Any reference to the fact that half of Crawfordjohn was technically held from the earldom of Arran was dropped after 1531.[85] After Finnart was dead and the personal rule over, Finnart's son attempted to have his father's forfeiture rescinded. The second earl of Arran was now the governor, and Finnart's son was just fourteen in 1543, a neat reversal of roles from the situation in 1529. Arran alleged that his deceased half-brother had plundered the earldom. *Inter alia* Finnart had wrongfully intromitted with the profits of half of Crawfordjohn for ten years since the death of their father.

Arran's allegation was absolutely correct. In fact Arran could legitimately have gone on to claim that his half-brother had wrongfully disposed of both the lordship of East Wemyss and the lands of Drumry, both of which had pertained to the earldom at the time of their father's death. As it was, Arran accused Finnart of having illegally possessed himself of their father's moveables, to the detriment and impoverishment of their younger brother, Gavin. This was possibly correct as well, given Finnart's responsibilities as executor. Arran then accused Finnart of having 'feinzeit' documentation, enabling him to obtain Bothwell moor with its 480 cows. Again, this appears to have been correct. The Angus lordship of Bothwell had been granted to the earldom of Arran after Angus' forfeiture. Finnart had been granted a charter from Angus on 29 October 1526, followed by a precept of sasine to the same lands on 21 October 1529. In noting this discrepancy, the editor of the *HMC Report* assumed the precept was wrongly dated, as Angus was out of the country by May 1529. The precept may well have been forged.[86]

The wrangle over Finnart's plundering of the Arran earldom continued at least until 1549, six years after Finnart's heir had been restored to his father's estates, with Arran still not compensated. In 1546 a lawyer was paid £10 for his 'labouris in seiking of the infeftments of the lands pertayning to umquhile Schir James Hammyltoun'. In total, Arran claimed that Finnart had robbed the family and earldom of over £28,400 in moveable goods and intromitted rents. In 1549 Arran had to quitclaim the entire amount, owing to the difficulties in sorting out the tangled inheritance left in the wake of Finnart's construction of the Avandale lordship and the subsequent forfeiture.[87] The figure may have been exaggerated, but the underlying point was sound. Finnart was an expert asset-stripper. Avandale was formed partly out of the Lennox earldom, mostly from the Arran earldom. However, to judge by the number of debts left in the last testament of the first earl of Arran, he had in turn intromitted with the profits of the lands bestowed by him on Finnart.[88]

The other main segment of the lordship of Avandale came from another branch of the Hamilton family. Sir Patrick Hamilton of Kingscavil, half-brother of the first earl of Arran, died in the 'Cleanse the Causeway' episode. One son, Patrick, was burned as a heretic in February 1528.[89] His brother, Sir James Hamilton of Kingscavil, was sheriff of Linlithgow until July 1534.[90] On 27 August 1534 at Holyrood, Kingscavil was tried and convicted in his absence for heresy, in the presence of the king, the earl of Argyll (the justiciar), and several members of the First Estate. Kingscavil had lapsed again after recanting in 1532. The leniency with which he was treated – compared with his brother – may have been due in part to the fact that neither the archbishop of St. Andrews, whom James disliked, nor the archbishop's nephew, David Beaton, abbot of Arbroath, was present. Kingscavil's case was turned over to the secular law and his goods were escheated.[91] He himself appears to have been in ward in Blackness castle at this time,[92] but by September 1534 was at Berwick-upon-Tweed, from where he wrote to Thomas Cromwell asking for English intercession in his case.[93] In 1535 Henry VIII responded on Kingscavil's behalf. William Stewart, bishop of Aberdeen, wrote back with a mild response, but pointed out that Kingscavil must first be reconciled with the pope.[94] In 1536 Kingscavil was given licence by the English king to travel overseas.[95] He appears to have intended to travel to Rome to ask for pardon from the pope, and James wrote to the pope to ask him to withhold granting this until the king had time to consider the matter further.[96] By March 1537, Kingscavil had communicated with the king, possibly in person in France. James wrote to the pope from Rouen on 29 March 1537, stating that he was now assured of Kingscavil's genuine repentance, and had no further objections to his seeking a pardon in Rome. Kingscavil was paid 20 crowns by the abbot of Arbroath, at the king's command,[97] and appears to have remained overseas until 1543. In April 1541, his son, James, received £200 from the Treasurer 'to furneis his fader of the realm'. Prior to this, in February, James received two of his father's properties in Linlithgow burgh, gifted out of Kingscavil's escheat.[98] The latter's absence left vacant the office of sheriff of Linlithgow. One William Hamilton of Kingscavil, possibly a son of Sir James, was the acting sheriff in July 1535.[99] However, on 10 December 1535, Finnart was granted the lands of Kingscavil together with the sheriffship of Linlithgow.[100] This was his last major acquisition.

Throughout the personal rule, Finnart's development of his lordship was punctuated with royal charters in his favour. The name of Sir James Hamilton of Finnart is ubiquitous in the registers of both the great and privy seals. Four charters of confirmation incorporated each new possession into a free baronial holding. The first was granted at Linlithgow on 3 July 1533 by the king in his 'legitimate estate of twenty-one years'. This was for Finnart's good service and in part compensation for the same.[101] The second, at Linlithgow on 17 September 1532, stated the same reason, and with the king now at his 'perfect estate of twenty-two years'.[102] The third was granted at Stirling on 21 April 1534, with the king now twenty-four years old and the same reason being given for the grant.[103] The last charter was made at Stirling on 22 September 1539. In the narrative, the good service becomes clear. The charter of confirmation was granted for past service in the completion of the palaces of Linlithgow and Stirling and elsewhere; in part compensation of the same, and for very great sums paid to the Treasurer.[104] In each charter, Finnart was described as 'familiar servant' and principal *sewer* or servitor to the king. In each case the clause of tenure narrated that the succession was to Finnart's legitimate male heirs, whom failing, his illegitimate male heirs, whom failing, the earl of Arran, and so on through the senior lines of the Hamilton family.

Finnart was expected to pay at least £4000 for the 1539 confirmation, combined with his next royal charter, granted on 2 November 1539.[105] This latest charter legitimised both himself (again) and his three oldest sons, and provided that they could become heirs of tailzie.[106] Although Finnart already had one legitimate son, it appears as if his intention was to further ensure his family's succession to the Avandale lordship. He would also have in mind the fact that his eldest son, Andrew, was seeking to establish his own landholdings within the Arran earldom. The compelling factor prompting Finnart to seek both the confirmation and the legitimisation at this stage may have been that the second earl of Arran had just reached, or was about to reach, his majority. By ensuring his own family's rights to the lordship in a royal charter, Finnart would prevent any comeback from Arran. Finnart mortgaged his estates to meet the required composition. Lord Methven and the queen mother loaned him £2000 and took the lordship lands of Glengavel as security.[107] The lands of Finnart, which until then had played no part in Finnart's transactions, were assigned to Alexander Shaw of Sauchie for 1400 marks.[108] Lands in Strathaven were sold to one Edinburgh burgess for 500 marks; a second burgess loaned 1000 marks and took further lands in the lordship in security.[109] Finnart raised almost £4000 through mortgaging. However, on 3 November 1539, he was quitclaimed and discharged of the sum of £4000:

> because for [instead of] payment of the said soume the said James hes given his obligatioun to oure soverane lord to compleit his werkis quhilkis he hes begun.[110]

Instead of paying £4000 to the treasury, Finnart received £4000 to 'compleit the Kingis wark in Striveling'.[111]

Constructing palaces for his majesty cannot have made Finnart very wealthy. He had escaped paying compositions for earlier charters because these charters compensated him for his building services. He narrowly escaped payment again in 1539, as the king decided to continue the building works. A Frenchman – Nicholas Roy – had been appointed as master mason in April 1539, possibly in order to update some of Finnart's architectural ideas.[112] Finnart himself was given his first, and only, official appointment in connection with the building programme in September 1539 when he became

> maister of werk principale to our soverane lord of all his werkis within his realme, now biggand or to be biggand.

The office carried the respectable annual fee of £200. This may have been intended to cover the cost of the three or four deputies to serve under him.[113] The duties included travelling around the country to every royal house to assess what refurbishments were necessary. All keepers were to 'suffir and lat the said James, his servandis and werkmen, to entir in the sammyn als oft as thair pleis' to survey, mend, build, and lay sand, lime, timber and other stuff.'[114] The job description sounds somewhat mundane for a son of the first earl of Arran.[115]

The annual fee or salary may have reflected the high expenditure incurred to date by Finnart in the building programme. After his execution, his escheat was worth around £5000 to the Crown. This was made up of cash, goods, the loan from Shaw of Sauchie, and the collection of profits from, and sale of rights to, various Church fruits and tenancies.[116] Oliver Sinclair and John Tennant paid 500 marks to purchase the fruits of Abercorn church.[117] James Atkinhead had risen in the Household from being in 1526 the keeper of the cups, through the rank of master of the aviary, to become captain of Dunbar castle (with an annual salary of £200) by the time of Finnart's death.[118] He paid almost £300 for Finnart's silverware, including two saltcellars inherited from the first earl of Arran.[119] Finnart appears to have been a hoarder: his ready cash was in the form of gold; £1503 was counted out of his boxes, at Holyrood palace in the presence of John Danielston, rector of Dysart, and Henry Balnavis, senator.[120] Possibly James 'fed happily upon Finnart's treasure',[121] but it is surprising that there was so little. Less than a year previously, Finnart had borrowed nearly £4000 to pay a composition which was then waived, and he had been advanced a further £4000 by the treasury. The greater part of these sums must have been expended on the building programme, possibly also on Finnart's own castle of Craignethan.

The king's real interest was in Finnart's lands; the Avandale lordship – including Crawfordjohn – was annexed to the Crown in December 1540.[122] In 1541 the Treasurer paid out £2000 (possibly not in gold coin) to Lord Methven and the queen mother to redeem the lands of Glengavel for incorporation into the lordship.[123] This payment can be contrasted with the apparent earlier non-payment to the earl of Rothes for redemption of £3000 worth of the forfeited

Glamis estates. The Avandale lordship, or barony, was worth £370 *per annum* to the exchequer in 1542.[124]

4. FINNART'S ROYAL SERVICE

Finnart entered the personal rule as the right-hand man of his father, the first earl of Arran. After Arran's death, Finnart became a prominent magnate in his place. He frequently served on the Lords of Council. He attended several sessions when that body met to deal with public affairs, rather than with judicial matters. This meant that he was one of the Lords of Council when it met to deal with law and order in the Borders,[125] Highland and Island affairs,[126] and the defence of the realm in 1532–33.[127] In this last business, Finnart was, in April 1533, leader of a band of mounted Scots cavalry, or 'prickers'.[128] Fellow members of the council included Argyll, Atholl, Eglinton, Huntly, Montrose, Moray, Rothes, Lords Erskine, Gray, Fleming, Hume, Maxwell, Ruthven and St. John, and, initially, the earls of Bothwell and Lennox.[129] From May 1532 onwards, these names gradually disappeared from the council record after the beginning of the keeping of a separate, almost purely judicial record.[130] On two occasions in 1531, Finnart was detailed to sit on the judicial sessions of the council, along with numerous others drawn from both the First and Second Estates and the royal officers.[131] Finnart also held an occasional brief in the execution of criminal justice, in 1532 within Avandale,[132] and more generally in 1536.[133] In the latter year he presided over a mutilation case perpetrated by the Forbes of Pitsligo.[134]

Finnart acted as a lord of the articles in the 1531, 1532 and 1535 sessions of parliament, on the last occasion in conjunction with his half-brother, Arran.[135] Between 1535 and 1537 he audited accounts in both the exchequer and the treasury.[136] He was an active man; perhaps surprisingly, he was never a witness to charters issued under the great seal, and thus appears to have had no direct involvement in the chancery office. This suggests that his role in government became restricted to Household business.

Various circumstances give this impression. The first is a matter of the extant records; from 1532 onwards all magnates, not just Finnart, partially disappear from view in the absence of a separate register for the Lords of Council acting in public affairs. Secondly, after 1534, Scotland and England were at peace, hence Border matters and the defence of the realm, both of relevance for politically active magnates, became of less concern. Thirdly, after 1535, parliament met intermittently in committee form until 1540; Finnart appeared once, as a judicial commissioner, on 29 April 1536, but not at all thereafter. These committees met to consider criminal cases, hence Finnart's appearance in 1536.[137]

Finally, and particular to Finnart, was the fact that his half-brother was growing up. Although Finnart held the ward of the earldom of Arran until July 1539,[138] from October 1532 Arran was under curatorial control. Finnart was not one of the curators, and thus not in charge of Arran's own person.[139] Arran attended the 1535 parliament, and was one of the magnates who accompanied the king on his visit to France in 1536. In 1537 not only did Arran begin to challenge Finnart's administration of his earldom, but also, at the age of seventeen or eighteen, he made his first appearance as a royal charter witness, on 8 June.[140] Finnart's role as *locum* for their father was beginning to evaporate.

Increasingly, in the latter half of the personal rule, Finnart began to look less like a magnate and more like a royal Household servant, anxious to make a return to the peerage by becoming a lord of parliament. His last appearance in court, on 30 July 1540, was in the capacity of superior of the lordship of Avandale.[141] Had he survived until the December 1540 parliament, he might well have achieved his aim of becoming Lord Avandale.

In the royal Household, Finnart held the positions of master of the king's stables, and principal *sewer* or server at the king's table.[142] Both were appointments made by the Angus régime in 1527. He held the former position until 1536, and the latter at least until 1539.[143] In the *Treasurer's Accounts* for 1526–7, the ledger shows payments of £177 to purchase Finnart's new liveries.[144] Similar payments were made in 1525–26 for Sir George Douglas upon his entry into the Household as carver. Substantial gifts were made at Christmas time for other members of the Household.[145] Finnart survived the changes in personnel made in the Household by the new government in the summer of 1528, when a number of other Angus appointments were removed. Thereafter Finnart received no more Christmas presents. Rather, in his role as master of the stable he was paid a token annual livery fee of twenty marks, the same sum as allowed to Lord Maxwell, chief carver; Walter Kerr of Cessford, cup-bearer; and Shaw of Sauchie, master of the wine cellar, amongst others.[146] In his role as 'familiar servant', Finnart's appointment in 1539 as principal master of works can be seen as a form of promotion within the Household.

It is not clear if Finnart's public, magnatial role in the first years of the personal rule allowed him to carry out his ceremonial duties at the royal court. The comparison can be made with Lord Maxwell, who held the Household office of Carver, but whose principal role was as the Warden of the West March. Presumably because Finnart was master of the stables this also made him the leader of the Scots 'prickers' on the Borders in April 1533. The question arises as to whether or not he was a royal favourite at court, over and beyond being both a magnate and a Household servant. Finnart was the subject of several epithets in royal charters. In 1530 and again in 1538, he was designated 'counsellor', an appropriate term for one who was carrying out a magnatial function in at least the earlier part of the personal rule. It might be added that the young David Lord Drummond, a man who appears to have had no public career, was described as a 'counsellor' in 1542.[147] The term simply acknowledged the status of a charter recipient, and did not necessarily imply any favouritism. Nor was the appellation 'lovit', frequently bestowed on Finnart,[148] in itself indicative of especial royal affection. It is worth recalling that Janet Douglas, Lady Glamis, was also addressed as such in 1529, and that James used warm terms of endearment in communicating with both the Master of Forbes and the Master of Crawford.[149]

The most consistent phrase used in connection with Finnart was 'familiar servant', a description used for him first in September 1524 and last used in December 1539.[150] This was the usual mode of address for one in the Household; in this context the word 'familiar' was synonymous with the word 'Household'. The registers of both great and privy seals are littered with references to Household servants being so addressed when they were charter recipients. The early use of the phrase in association with Finnart suggests that the first earl of Arran put his son into the Household at a time when the Hamilton faction was in the ascendant. The subsequent frequent use of the phrase reflects the fact that Finnart held Household offices obtained under the Angus régime. It also suggests a man who was at court rather more often than, say, Lord Maxwell, who was not accorded the appellation. Latterly, of course, Finnart was carrying out the task of building royal palaces, and thus was clearly a Royal servant.

There are three indications that Finnart might have been, at times, a royal favourite, or 'minion'.[151] The first is that in February 1536 he was appointed as joint curator [sic] of the king's eldest illegitimate son, James *senior*, together with Thomas Scott of Pitgormo, justice-clerk.[152] James *senior* was the product of the king's liaison with the deceased Elizabeth Shaw. In May 1535 he became the abbot-commendator of Kelso abbey at the grand old age of five.[153] Finnart's involvement with the abbey went back to 1532, when he was appointed bailie of Lesmahagow, held from the abbey. The then incumbent was Abbot Thomas Kerr, brother of Andrew Kerr of Ferniehirst. The connection between the Kerrs of Ferniehirst and Finnart went back to 1520.[154] After taking the bailiary, Finnart was granted lands in feu farm in Lesmahagow and also the keeping of Nathane (Craignethan) castle.[155] The curatorship of James *senior* probably meant that Finnart was to administer the abbey's lands in Lesmahagow and represent the abbey in the court of session. James *senior's* education at Stirling was entrusted to George Buchanan in 1536.[156]

The second indication that Finnart may have been a minion is the fact that, on 27 December 1533, James took out a float of £100 from the royal purse and spent the day playing cards at Holyrood abbey. Shortly afterwards Finnart was repaid what was for both men the relatively trivial sum of £20 which had been borrowed from him by the king. Presumably James was gambling with Finnart and losing.[157] On another occasion in October 1531, James played cards with John Stewart, chamber groom, and borrowed 40/- from him.[158] Again at Christmas time, 1535, James had delivered to him at Stirling, £44, to play cards, and this time appears to have won, as there was no loan repaid to his unknown opponent.[159] Hence the king was a man who liked to play cards with his Household servants, especially at Christmas.

The final indication of favouritism was a rather more obscure episode. On 25

April 1536, William, Lord Howard, English envoy in Edinburgh, wrote to Henry VIII stating:

> Syr, I here . . . that the maryage ys broyn betwyxt the Kynges Grace your nephewe and Monsieur de Vaindom [Mary of Bourbon being the projected bride], and that He wyll marye a gentyllwoman in Scottland, the Lord of Arskynes douhter . . . by whom He hath had a chyld, [her] havying a hosband; and Hys Grace [James] hathe found the means to devorse them. And ther ys grett lamentation made for yt yn thys contre, as farr as men dare, Syr, ther was no man made prevy to that mater but Syr James Hambylton.[160]

A minute recorded on 30 June in the Vatican noted that Pope Paul III wrote to James advising him that there could be no divorce. By 8 July, the Duke of Norfolk and Chapuys, Imperial ambassador in London, both understood that the Erskine marriage was off and a French marriage on again.[161] It appears as though the papal communication had by then reached Scotland. On 18 July, James wrote to Henry VIII requesting a safe-conduct for his servitor and counsellor, and master of the stables, who would be passing to France for 'gret and effectuus affaris'.[162] Between 23 July and mid-August James sailed round the north coast of Scotland, leaving from Pittenweem. The fleet was forced by 'contrare wyndis' and 'extreme stormis' to land at the Isle of Whithorn.[163] The intention had been to reach France. This was made clear in a subsequent entry in the *Treasurer's Accounts*:

> Item . . . for wyne and spice to the schippes quhen the Kingis grace suld have first departit to Fraunce.[164]

Abell wrote:

> On Mary Magdalenes day [22 July] our king with the consent of the lords . . . sailed to France . . . principal with him passed Sir James Hamilton but tempest raised on the west. . . .[165]

The king then sailed down the east coast to France. John Penven wrote from the Scots entourage, at Rouen in October 1536, to Sir George Douglas, claiming that on the voyage James had told his courtiers that if he once looked again [in favour] on the earl of Angus, Finnart would droop. Whenever the two met Finnart always showed Angus the back seams of his hose. Again according to Penven, the earl of Moray met the king at Rouen in October and asked him where his minion was. James replied that Finnart was out of favour, to which Moray made an incredulous and earthy response.[166] Finnart did not appear to make it to France.[167]

In some respects the first half of 1536 saw Finnart's career at its height. There is little evidence to support the assertion that, in April, James attended the wedding of Finnart's daughter to Lord Somerville [*sic*].[168] However, Finnart had just been appointed as sheriff of Linlithgow, had exchanged land rights with the Crown, was carrying out criminal commissions and was curator of James *senior*. He was also now fully involved in the royal building programme. Since 1530 he had audited accounts for Holyrood, Stirling and Falkland. In January 1536 he entered his first account for Linlithgow, the actual master of work being Thomas Johnson, chaplain. The expenditure amounted to £1973, which sum was speedily recuperated from church taxation revenues.[169] Finnart had been appointed as captain of Linlithgow palace on 14 October 1526, and owned property there; his charter of confirmation of 17 September 1534 was issued at his town house, which suggests a royal visit.[170] Intermittently the king visited Linlithgow.[171] Lord Howard gave the impression that he had learned of the divorce scheme whilst visiting the king at Stirling.[172] This suggests that Finnart was at court at Stirling in April 1536.

If Lord Howard's information was correct, then Finnart was involved in at least part of the king's marital plans in 1536. The comparison can be made with James Atkinhead, also a Household man. Atkinhead was sent off to the French court in June 1535 with instructions for the proposed marriage with Mary of Bourbon. He was to 'pas and wesie the gentyll woman that is offerit us our partye', or in other words vet her.[173] Finnart appears to have been in charge of one of the alternative marital schemes, a royal marriage with Margaret Erskine. It is probable that when that fell through, the king at first intended sending Finnart to France on a similar mission to Atkinhead's in 1535. James V then changed his mind and decided to inspect Mary of Bourbon for himself. The first voyage was a circumspect one, attempting to use the west route. Bad weather prevented this, and hence little further mention was made of it. It was an embarrassing failure. James then went public, and sailed down the east coast, taking with him a number of his magnates, including Arran. In his marriage negotiations, James operated at two levels; on the state level he appointed his half-brother, Moray, to head a commission to treat with Francis I, but Atkinhead was entrusted with further explorations. Once in France himself, James secretly inspected Mary of Bourbon for himself before openly pursuing Francis I to marry Madeleine. After his marriage, James' first communication from France to his uncle was via his pursemaster, John Tennant.[174]

Buchanan and the anonymous author of *Factum Contre Les Hamiltons* (written in 1574) both suggest that the king's first voyage was sabotaged by Finnart, who used the excuse of bad weather to prevent the expedition from reaching France. For Buchanan, this was another instance of the Hamilton family's perfidy. The inference drawn by the latter author was that Finnart was trying to prevent a French marriage.[175] However, there is little reason to suppose that this was Finnart's intention. In the minority, the first earl of Arran had at times looked both to France and England for support in his own struggle for power.[176] By the time of his first marriage, James had been in power for eight years, and had explored marital opportunities with France, England, the Empire,

Denmark, and at home. Both the foreign and domestic political situations were stable. Even were it to be conceded that the king did receive any advice from Finnart on the subject, the latter had nothing to gain by pushing for either an English or a domestic marriage.[177] Finnart was simply employed as one of the Household staff in some aspects of the marital negotiations. His career appears to have 'peaked' in 1536, because as a dutiful royal servant he was supervising building works at Linlithgow palace. It may be accepted that he can be described as a 'minion' in this period. There is no sign of his exercising or attempting to exercise any undue influence over the king in matters of state.

To deny Finnart such an influential role is to discount both the inferences in John Penven's Rouen communication and in *Factum Contre Les Hamiltons*. The two pieces of evidence are contradictory. Neither author had an objective stance. Penven was writing to please Sir George Douglas. Presumably Sir George, and his brother Angus, would be amused to read that Finnart, the son of their former rival, was scared of them. If this were true, the inference would be that Finnart would be in favour of a French marriage and against an English or domestic marriage, the two latter options affording the Douglases the better opportunity of returning to Scotland. Such a view runs contrary to the idea of Finnart's supposed anti-French stance.

Both accounts credit Finnart with a role which he did not play in the royal marriage. He was not taken on the second trip to France because this was a royal state visit to marry a French bride. King James took various Household officers with him to help him spend Church revenues in France. However the chief person in his entourage was the second earl of Arran, who as his heir[178] was the highest-ranking of his magnates. There was no particular reason either to take Finnart as part of his Household staff or to leave him behind. If Finnart had been taken, it is doubtful that Arran would have tolerated his company in France. Finnart was a notable omission in the list of 'kin, freynndis, and servandis' taken under the king's protection in his letter of 31 August 1536 to 'our lovit cousing and counsalour', the earl of Arran.[179] If Finnart was out of favour with the king, as Penven suggested in October 1536, this was because he had failed to secure a divorce for Margaret Erskine, someone whom James did appear to want to marry. James had then travelled all the way to France and discovered that he did not want to marry Mary of Bourbon. At that time, there was nobody else available.

For the rest of his life, Finnart continued to supervise building at Linlithgow, Blackness, and Stirling (where James Nicholson was master of works). Over and above the £4000 advanced to him in October 1539, Finnart received payments totalling a further £1000.[180] After his death, work continued until 1541 at Falkland and Holyrood, under the direction of John Scrimegeour, designated principal master of works in 1534.[181] Finnart appears to have finished the major work at both Stirling castle and Linlithgow palace. At the palace there was only a further £237 spent on chimneys, plumbing works and miscellaneous items after his death. Work also commenced on the fountain.[182]

5. FINNART'S EXECUTION

On 16 August 1540, Finnart was convicted by an assize at Edinburgh on two counts of treasonable conspiracy to assassinate the king.[183] There were twenty-one lords on his assize, which was presided over by Argyll, the justiciar. These lords included the earls of Arran, Huntly, Marischal, Montrose, Cassillis, Atholl, Eglinton, Lords Maxwell, Somerville, Methven, Fleming, Fraser of Lovat, Lindsay of the Byres, and the Master of Glencairn.[184] 15s. 10d. was expended on summoning the assize and supplying the jury with wine.[185] The author of the *Diurnal* recorded that Finnart was on the same day 'heided at the skaffald at the trone of Edinburgh, the kingis grace being in Seyton'.[186]

The unofficial story of Finnart's end was given by Pitscottie and Buchanan. Both chroniclers narrated that Finnart was appointed as some sort of an official lay inquisitor into heretical practices, a Crown appointment made in response to clerical pressure. Before Finnart could exercise the office, he was accused of treason by the son of James Hamilton of Kingscavil, in a form of pre-emptive strike.[187] However, there is no evidence for this. The only hint of any religious angle is in one English letter. Writing from Berwick-upon-Tweed on 4 October 1540 to Henry VIII, Sir William Eure advised that he had learned from an envoy returning from Scotland that 'the Cardinall is not in the kinge's favour so much as he was befor the dethe of Syr James Hamylton'.[188] Finnart had held lands of both the archbishoprics of Glasgow and St. Andrews.[189] David Beaton, Cardinal of Scotland in 1540, had acted as a witness to charters in favour of Finnart between 1531 and 1536. Possibly the two men were friends.[190]

Pitscottie and Buchanan may have derived their story of a lay inquisitor from a separate episode. This was the heresy trial at St. Andrews on 28 May 1540 of Sir John Borthwick, who had served as an officer of the French guard, under Francis I. In 1537, shortly after the bestowing of the papal cap and sword and title of 'Defender of the Faith' upon the Scottish king, Borthwick wrote a letter of protest to Thomas Cromwell. He was at the Scottish court in February 1540, but escaped, probably to England, before being excommunicated. In his absence, his effigy was burnt. The lay lords on the St. Andrews assize were Huntly, Arran, Marischal, Montrose; Lords Fleming, Lindsay of the Byres, Erskine, Seton, Somerville and St. John; and James Foulis of Colinton, clerk register; Thomas Bellenden, justice clerk; Finnart and 'many other lords, barons and honest persons'.[191] Neither Pitscottie nor Buchanan mentioned Borthwick's trial. On the other hand, Knox, writing a history of the Reformation, rather than of the personal rule, did refer to the trial, but not to any subsequent proposed or actual lay inquisition, let alone one led by Finnart. Of Finnart's execution Knox had no comment other than 'justly or unjustly we dispute not'.[192]

There are some attractive elements in the unofficial story. Pitscottie wrote that Finnart was initially arrested and then released.[193] This is borne out by the judicial record.[194] Buchanan remarked that Hamilton of Kingscavil, 'after a long exile, had commenced a lawsuit against James the bastard, and had obtained liberty to return home'.[195] Kingscavil appears to have remained in exile. The extant lawsuit is between Finnart and James Hamilton of Stonehouse, and Stonehouse was fighting two cases against Finnart's tenants and supporters at the end of June 1540. Probably the treason charge against Finnart was initiated by the Hamilton kindred. The likely accuser was Stonehouse rather than Kingscavil's son. Finnart had profited from the fall of Kingscavil; shrewdly he paid Kingscavil's wife 500 marks to redeem the lands of Manerstone (Linlithgow), immediately after Kingscavil's trial.[196] But Stonehouse was a near neighbour of Finnart in Lanarkshire, and the two had a dispute.[197] It can be conjectured that a great number of other Hamiltons, holding of the earldom of Arran, would be only too willing to lend Stonehouse their support. Possibly Kingscavil's son was one of them.

Probably Stonehouse's promoter was the earl of Arran. Again, this was a man with no reason to like Finnart and every reason to hate him. Finnart had killed Lennox in circumstances arising out of a land dispute. Equally, with royal cooperation, Arran could have Finnart killed, just as Huntly had had the Master of Forbes removed. The interesting point is the timing of Finnart's fall. It is not possible to ascertain Arran's precise age, but there are several indications which suggest that he came of age (twenty-one) either in the latter part of 1539, or in 1540.[198] One month after Finnart's execution, at Glamis on 15 September 1540, Arran resigned into the king's hands, and was regranted, two new charters to confirm his possession of the earldom of Arran. At the same time he was gifted the non-entries. The charters were to Arran as 'familiar counsellor' of the king, 'for especial love, and for past service to the king both in France and in Scotland'.[199]

These were virtually the first great seal charters in which Arran appears as anything other than an heir to Finnart.[200] Arran now had at least one son,[201] and the purpose of obtaining these charters may have been to formalise the succession to the earldom in his favour, and at the same time obtain legal documentation confirming his possession in the wake of Finnart's asset stripping. Furthermore, the confirmation charters made it clear to Arran which parts of his earldom he was not getting – half of Crawfordjohn and those other lands abstracted by Finnart to construct the Avandale lordship. This was the price that Arran was required to pay in order to be rid of the plunderer. Finnart would be executed and Avandale annexed to the Crown. Arran's role as a 'familiar counsellor' was apparent from 27 August 1540; from then on he was an occasional witness to great seal charters.[202] The Scottish service referred to in the confirmation charters was Arran's participation in the June-July 1540 royal expedition to the Isles.[203] The rightful heir to the earldom was now acting as an adult earl and was being treated as such by the king. This left no magnatial role for Finnart.

The first charge of treason against Finnart was of shooting arrows from a machine on the top of the peel tower at Linlithgow palace at the king and the persons in his company, the king being personally and actually present at Linlithgow at the time of the shooting, on account of which he retired from the town.[204] Possibly this was a fictitious charge; it is reminiscent of the shooting allegation made against the Master of Forbes. However, one John Crummy or Crombie had been granted a remission on a similar charge on 4 June 1540.[205] Crombie was appointed as master of entry and principal porter (probably for Linlithgow palace) in 1536.[206] He was also the bailie of Linlithgow burgh, witnessing Finnart's property transactions there. He was present when Finnart took sasine to the captaincy of Linlithgow palace in October 1526.[207] McKean has suggested that Finnart may have invented a gun which misfired in a salute to the king. Understandably James may have had a neurosis about such accidents, given the accidental death of his great-grandfather.[208]

Another option is that both Crombie's remission and Finnart's execution were connected with events in September 1526 when Lennox had been killed in the attempt to capture the king from the Hamiltons and Douglases. The Angus Douglases had been found guilty of treason in their 'exponying of our soverane lord to battell' at Linlithgow.[209] A remission was granted in 1530 to William Stirling of Glorat and nine followers for:

> treasonably coming in arms and in battle array against the king near Linlithgow, the king being actually and personally present.[210]

Crombie's 1540 remission was for:

> treasonably holding Linlithgow palace in defiance of the king and his authority, the king being actually and personally present as displayed by his banner; for attempting to shoot the king and his company then being in Linlithgow; and for all that followed from this action.[211]

In each of these items there is an almost horrified emphasis on the fact that the king was actually there. The remission to Crombie is specific in stating that royal authority was being challenged. This was more than simply a misfire from a weapon in the giving of a royal salute. Both the treason charges and the remissions were driving home the same message, which was that a confrontation took place at Linlithgow during which the king's life was threatened.

Possibly Crombie was a Lennox supporter deliberately shooting at a group of Douglases or Hamiltons guarding the royal person whilst the battle was being fought outside Manuel priory in September 1526. Alternatively Crombie thought he was firing on a group of Lennox supporters, and had not seen the royal banner. This seems more likely, given his association with Finnart. Either way, Crombie was granted a remission. The similarity between his crime and the first charge against Finnart leads to the conclusion that this was one and the same episode. If so, Crombie was pardoned because he was acting under Finnart's orders. The likelihood is that Crombie provided the evidence for, and was the chief witness in, the trial against Finnart. The precise nature of the shooting episode – an accident, a misfire, or a deliberate act – was not important. The prosecution needed an incident which could be construed as a treasonable act and be used to incriminate Finnart, and a witness to testify to Finnart's guilt. Simply to accuse Finnart of being on the side of the Angus Douglases in September 1526 was insufficient. Amongst others Eglinton, Lords Fleming and Somerville and James Douglas of Drumlanrig had opposed Lennox; these men were all on Finnart's assize.[212] This charge was not the start of an investigation into the political circumstances surrounding the Lennox revolt, or the allegiance of any individual magnate at any particular point in the turbulent minority. For the Crown to have attempted such an exercise could conceivably have led to almost everyone being found guilty. Instead, in the December 1540 parliament a general remission was issued to all lieges, excepting the four pleas of the Crown and all instances of assisting the Douglases after their forfeiture on 5 September 1528.[213] The object of the exercise was to target Finnart. Crombie had fired a gun at the wrong moment in Linlithgow in September 1526; he was granted a remission because he was persuaded or forced to 'confess' that Finnart had instructed the firing. Hence the prosecution had a case against Finnart. The fact that Crombie's remission came over two months before Finnart's execution, over a month before any arrest or accusal of treason,[214] shows that the case against Finnart was carefully planned and was not a hasty affair. The fact that Crombie should obtain a remission indicates royal approval. Finnart's execution did not come about as a knee-jerk response to a wild accusation of treason by a king paranoid about the Douglases. The execution was calculated. Arran was its promoter; James was the sponsor.

Of the second charge, there is some circumstantial evidence. Finnart was accused of plotting with Archibald Douglas of Kilspindie and James Douglas of Parkhead at St. Leonard's chapel, near Edinburgh (Arthur's Seat) at around the time of the siege of Tantallon. The plan was to enter the king's bed-chamber at Holyrood palace and kill him.[215] There was one other conspirator in the plot to imagine 'the horrablie deid of his grace which is horrablie to tell'. This was Robert Leslie of Innerpeffray (Perth), who was already dead (of natural causes) by the time his wife and nine 'bairnis' were first summoned, in October 1540, to the December 1540 parliament. It was sharp practice on the Crown's part to seek to forfeit the family's estates. One of Leslie's sons was the parson of Kinneil church in Linlithgow.[216] Leslie had been an Edinburgh lawyer, and a witness to one of Finnart's charters, together with John Crombie, in December 1530. In October of the same year he purchased from Finnart some lands in East Wemyss.[217] Parkhead, who had been master of the larder in the Household under the Angus régime, was first summoned to the December parliament on 22 September 1540, and was convicted in his absence.[218] Parkhead had, in fact, been escheated on 5 July 1537, probably for his suspected involvement in Lady Glamis' treason, and shortly afterwards he was a 'fugitive fra the law'. In 1539 he was described as having committed 'treasonable dedis', and by then had left the country and had lost his lands.[219] He appears to have gone to England and was captured at the battle of Hadden Rig in August 1542, fighting against the Scots.[220] Sir William Eure then reported that he had learned that Parkhead had had his life spared by the king, and was being held in free ward at Falkland.[221] Of Parkhead, the Duke of Norfolk wrote in September 1542: 'No lyving man was so gret with hym [Angus] as the said Jamys'.[222]

Hence Finnart was the only accessible man who could be tried in 1540 for imagining 'the horrablie deid of his grace'. The charges against his fellow conspirators revealed the date of the meeting at St. Leonard's, 2 February 1529. Parkhead had then gone to Tantallon and reported the result of the meeting to Angus and Sir George Douglas.[223] These were more specific details than had been given in the charge against Finnart, almost as if further inquiries were uncovering more information after Finnart's death. For Finnart's involvement in a plot there is no direct evidence.[224] However, there is the report made by Sir Thomas Magnus to Cardinal Wolsey on 14 November 1528 from Berwick-upon-Tweed; Magnus wrote:

> I conceive also that in the tyme of the saide sege [of Tantallon], Archebalde Douglas, uncle to the said Erle [of Angus], and George Douglas, the said Erles broder, did mete to gader at a certaine place, as I remember called Cobornespath, with Sir James Hamelton and the Shereiff of Heire, cherisshed servauntes and in grete favour with the King of Scottes, and did common to gaider for an ordour howe the said Erle and his frendes sulde be reduced and brought into the gracious favour of thaire Soveraine.[225]

Immediately after the failure of the Tantallon siege, both Campbell of Loudoun, sheriff of Ayr, and Finnart swore the 'grete aith' to pursue the Angus Douglases 'for thar utir distruction'.[226] Angus left the country almost six months later, after negotiating an agreement that his earldom should be administered by the Crown, and that the estates should not be dissipated by alienation. For Angus, this settlement held out the possibility of his restoration to the earldom if and when he regained the king's favour. However, from James' subsequent actions, not least the burning of Janet Douglas, Lady Glamis, it is clear that Angus was not going to be forgiven in a hurry.

On 22 May 1540, James' first son, James Stewart, was born at St. Andrews.[227] The royal expedition to the Isles took place in the following month. How far ahead James arranged his parliaments can only be guessed at, but the December 1540 parliament passed the Act of Annexation. This added both the lordship of the Isles and almost the entire earldom of Angus to the Crown's patrimony.[228] It is likely that the annexation was planned at least a year beforehand, probably from the point at which Mary of Guise first advised her husband that she was pregnant. It is significant that as early as 1534 – after the conclusion of the Anglo-Scots peace – parts of the Angus earldom were granted in heredity to James' illegitimate sons.[229] The greater desire to leave a substantial inheritance for his legitimate heirs led to the passing of the Act of Annexation seven months after the birth of James Stewart.

Finnart's execution fell midway between these two events. The annexation of the Angus estates effectively tore up the terms of the agreement reached over eleven years earlier, but this did not worry the king. In effect he had repudiated this agreement in November 1533 by regranting to the fourth earl of Argyll and his heirs the superiority of the former Angus regality of Abernethy. This had originally been granted to Argyll's father in December 1528 as reward for his lieutenancy in the campaign against Angus.[230] But the Act of Annexation ensured that the Angus estates became the inalienable property of the Crown, untouched by a subsequent revocation. To take this step was more than simply to forfeit a magnate in his possession. Finnart's death underlined the conviction of the annexation; by executing Finnart, the king was telling his magnates that there were to be no half-measures in the liquidation of the greater part of Angus' earldom.

Finnart represented those elements of the Scottish government who, in the protracted struggle to remove Angus in 1528–29, had been prepared to pursue the course of compromise. For much of this year the king had been under the guidance of a secret council, and placed for his own safety in Stirling. He had not been able to dictate the terms upon which he wanted to settle the struggle, by force or by diplomacy. The method which James preferred was to pursue Angus, Sir George and Kilspindie to their 'utir distruction'. But amongst those who signed the oath, probably in order simply to placate the king after the failure of the Tantallon siege, were the compromisers. Finnart had done well out of cooperating with the Angus régime. The new government had at that time little prospect of delivering the killer punch against Angus. Both Finnart and his father were masters in the art of coming to terms with their enemies, the Angus Douglases; and it is interesting to consider the first earl of Arran's own position at this time. Arran had participated in the Tantallon siege and afterwards swore the 'grete aith'. His support had been given early on to the king, during the change in circumstances in the summer of 1528. But after the failure of Tantallon, Arran had retired to the west in order to deal with his local difficulties in the Isle of Arran. This had given the new government great difficulties in finding someone who was capable of continuing the military campaign against Angus. It is entirely conceivable that Arran was dissociating himself from what he considered to be fast becoming a lost cause. It is notable that one English source reported that, shortly before his death, before Angus was out of the country, Arran had advised that Angus should be forgiven.[231]

It is also notable that Finnart's colleague at the Cockburnspath meeting, Campbell of Loudoun, had by 1540 been in exile in France for at least the past two years. His fall in 1537–38 coincided with the coming of age of Cassillis, whose father had been killed by Loudoun. There are no details of the circumstances of

Loudoun's imprisonment and eventual exile, but there is a parallel, Finnart's fall coinciding with the second earl of Arran's coming of age. This suggests that James was a patient man. Rather than simply turning as soon as he could against those whom he felt had let him down in 1528–29, he waited. Loudoun's exit allowed Cassillis' entrance; Finnart's execution brought in Arran as a 'familiar counsellor'. In each case the fallen man could be replaced; the balance of power at a magnatial local level was not disturbed. A parallel can be drawn with the court of session's intervention in Aberdeen land disputes after the fall of the Master of Forbes; Huntly was not left to achieve complete domination in the north-east. The contrast is with the fall of Lord Glamis, where the Crown deliberately went into Forfarshire to further fortify its patrimony, in order to displace the earldom of Angus as the dominant landholder. It could be added that Janet Douglas' death came after the king's long absence in France; the first summons of treason against her had gone out over eight years earlier. James could wait for his revenge. At a lower level, Robert Barton, who struck the deal with Angus in March 1529, was found guilty of deforcement by the court of session in June 1538, was committed to a year's ward and had his goods declared escheated.[232]

It is doubtful that Finnart had really plotted on two separate occasions to kill the king. Magnus' evidence points to one meeting with the Douglases in October-November 1528. The treason charges against the deceased Leslie of Innerpeffray and exiled Douglas of Parkhead point to a second meeting in February 1529 at a different location. There is no corroborating evidence for this second meeting, but there seems to be no reason why further meetings between Finnart and the Douglases should not have taken place. These might either have been sanctioned officially, as part of the diplomatic efforts to achieve Angus' withdrawal, or have been more clandestine meetings, where Finnart would be running the risk of a treason charge if found out. Either way, Finnart would be looking to see what was in it for himself if he and his father switched the Hamilton faction from supporting the Crown to again compromising with the Angus Douglases. If the Hamiltons changed allegiance, the critical thing would be to hold the king's person, not to kill him. Possibly the second charge of treason would have been more accurate if it had been one of kidnapping the king. However, over eleven years later, with an adult king completely in control of his realm, such a charge might have sounded less convincing.

A feature common to all three convictions for attempted regicide in the personal rule was the multiplicity of the points of treason. The prosecution's pragmatic approach seems to have been that so long as a conviction could be secured on one count, this was sufficient. Thus to frame two or more distinct charges was a rational step. In Finnart's case, the king probably first looked at his failure to support the Crown wholeheartedly in 1528–29. This in turn would lead to a consideration of the Hamilton position generally during the Angus régime. Possibly things worked the other way round; Finnart had been identified with the Angus régime at least since September 1526. James would be well aware that

Lennox had been killed by Finnart at Linlithgow, and that Lennox had been attempting to capture his royal person from the Angus Douglases. The failure of the Lennox revolt allowed the Angus régime to dominate Scottish government, and led to the struggle for power two years later. Clearly Finnart's murder of Lennox had been a major factor in contributing both to his own success and to that of the Douglases. In the words of the remission granted to John Crombie, Finnart was responsible 'for all that followed from this action'. Finnart had then made an accord, which had been signed by James himself,[233] with Lennox's successor. To accuse Finnart of the murder of Lennox nine years after this accord was not a viable option, nor was Lennox's death in itself a treasonable crime against the king. Thus the made-up shooting charge, based on Crombie firing a weapon at the wrong time fourteen years earlier, whilst serving under Finnart.

Professor Donaldson has written that:

Confidence [in James] may have been finally shattered by the fate of Sir James Hamilton of Finnart, the master of works.[234]

Far from it. James was not an irrational king so paranoid about the Douglases that he lashed out indiscriminately against his magnates, heedless of the consequences. Nor was he attempting to terrify his magnates into submission.[235] He needed their support to achieve the annexation of the greater part of the Angus earldom; one element in achieving this support was to execute one of the compromisers of 1528–29. But this was not an execution of everybody who had tolerated the Angus régime, nor even of those who had supported the Douglases and the Hamiltons against Lennox in 1526. Rather it was a precise targeting of one man, visibly a mover of events in 1526 and with a successful career from then onwards; Finnart had achieved too much under Angus' government to be considered simply as an individual who tolerated the Douglases.

Of those who tried Finnart, some had been on the 'wrong', or Hamilton/Douglas, side at Linlithgow in 1526. It is possible that they were on the jury in an inquisitorial role. They might have felt some unease in the fact that the first charge appeared to be probing back into the events of the minority. But the charge itself was so fantastically worded as to allay these fears. Further peace of mind would be brought by the general remission of December 1540, which again drew a veil over the events of the minority. It is doubtful in any case whether the veteran Eglinton, a survivor of political upheavals since the reign of James' grandfather, would panic at this latest episode. Lord Fleming, married to James' illegitimate sister, and Chamberlain from the outset of the personal rule,[236] would not be overly concerned either. Both he and Eglinton had a consistently high record of service as royal charter witnesses.[237]

Also on the jury were Huntly, Atholl, Marischal, Cassillis, Maxwell and the Master of Glencairn, all returned from the recent royal expedition to the Isles.[238]

Maxwell, together with Huntly and Montrose, had served as vice-regent in 1536–37. Montrose, another jury member, had not gone to the Isles but instead had been appointed as tutor to the newly-born prince. Atholl and Maxwell had served as jurors in the 1537 treason trials, as had the Master of Glencairn. James could trust the older men – Montrose, Maxwell, Fleming, Eglinton, and the Master of Glencairn – because they had already shown their loyalty, either in royal service or in returning guilty verdicts, or both. Amongst the younger magnates – Huntly, Atholl, Marischal and Cassillis – there was less need of demonstrable loyalty, though Huntly had given this in 1536–37, when he proved himself capable of having the Master of Forbes executed; and he well understood the problem of being taken advantage of as a minor. Marischal was Huntly's brother-in-law and would probably simply follow Huntly's lead. Cassillis may well have nursed his own grievance against Finnart, who had proved to be so blasé about the need to arrest his father's killer, the sheriff of Ayr, during the Angus régime.[239] All four men had been too young to have played any political role in the minority, and their careers depended on serving their contemporary and sovereign. Treasons committed twelve and sixteen years earlier meant little to them and they did not care that the former earl of Angus was about to lose his estates for good.

Of the other jurors, one who owed his position to the king was Henry Stewart, created Lord Methven at the outset of the personal rule. Lord Somerville was possibly one who, like Hamilton of Stonehouse, had been irritated by the growth of Finnart's lands in Lanarkshire.[240] Lord Lindsay may have hoped that to serve on the assize might win him some royal favour and the sheriffship of Fife, lost to Rothes. The main absentee was the earl of Moray, then ill in France. Had he been present, as the king's half-brother he would have followed James' wishes. According to John Penven, Moray did not think much of the 'minion' anyway. The main person present, probably desperate to be foreman of the jury (if such an office existed), was Arran.

To judge from the fact that several of the jury had been on the royal expedition to the Isles, this was a trial by a large segment of the politically active nobility. It is tempting to speculate that on the trip they were briefed by the king as to his future plans. The brief would be a mixture of the king's desire for revenge, and determination to demonstrate his authority and resolution in the matter of the Act of Annexation. The chosen target was Finnart, whose own career had in a sense set him up as the target. In contriving Finnart's forfeiture and execution, James was not assailing a magnatial family with a history of landholding stretching through past generations, and with expectations of passing its lands and possessions down to its heirs. In essence this magnate *cum* Household servant was a self-made man, a soft target. What the king had allowed him to have could be taken away with minimal repercussions, as probably the greater part of the Hamilton kindred disliked Finnart. Arran almost certainly loathed him, and the annexation of the Avandale lordship was a price worth paying to gain full control of the greater part of the earldom of Arran. Nobody else suffered by Finnart's fall; some gained. Lord Somerville was granted the bailiary of the lands and barony of Carstairs on 30 December 1540.[241] Lord Methven was repaid his £2000 loan to Finnart for Glengavel, and in May 1541 became the sheriff of Linlithgow.[242] On 8 December 1540, Lord Erskine received a nineteen-year tack of the church teinds of Lanark burgh and county.[243]

The distribution of Finnart's holdings was not generous; the king was hardly a generous man. But the strong possibility is that James did not need to buy support for the execution; the fact that so many magnates sat on Finnart's assize suggests a showpiece trial to underline the king's resolve to kill this man before the December 1540 parliament. Indeed, members of the Second Estate may have been queuing up outside the Tolbooth door to drink wine and try Finnart: the murderer; the asset stripper; the minion; and ultimately, the has-been who spent other people's money on his own castle and on a palace where there had been no royal wedding, birth or coronation. James could retire peacefully to Seton confident of a guilty verdict. It would be cynical to add that Finnart's execution came shortly after he had finished work at Linlithgow palace.

NOTES

1. I am grateful to Charles McKean, BA, FRSA, FSA (Scot.), Hon. FRIBA, for sharing with me the results of his research in connection with his article 'Hamilton of Finnart', in *History Today* (January 1993).
2. His age can only be estimated. He was at least 36 years old: cf. *HMC, Eleventh Report*, App. pt. vi, 53, no. 108, when in 1529 he was to receive twenty-five years worth of rents of the lands of Finnart, indicating that he was born in or before 1504. His father was born c.1475: *Scots Peerage*, iv, 355, ff., making him aged twenty in 1495, the likely birth-date of Finnart.
3. *RMS*, ii, nos. 3147, 3803 (at the age of 12).
4. *TA*, iv, 53, 82, 99, 233, *et passim*. The repeated gift of shoes suggests that Finnart was still growing. It is unlikely he would have entered into the royal Household until about the age of 12. He would thus be knighted at the age of 16, in 1511. The 'Little James', who had his horse shoed in 1507, probably was the king's illegitimate son, the earl of Moray, then aged seven: *Ibid.*, iv, 84.
5. *RMS*, ii, no. 3804. The two half-brothers were Sir Patrick Hamilton of Kingscavil and John Hamilton of Broomhill
6. *Ibid.*, ii, no. 3803; iii, no. 1192. The gift was made via an attorney, John Drummond, suggesting that Finnart was still under the age of 21 in 1513. He would be 18 years old.
7. *RSS*, i, no. 3409 (remission in 1526); Emond, *op. cit.*, 106.
8. *TA*, v, 158; *ER*, xiv, 351; Emond, *op. cit.*, 201–2.
9. *HMC, Eleventh Report*, App. pt. vi, 32, no. 66. Kerr of Cessford was the chief protagonist amongst the Kerr family in this episode: cf. Emond, *op. cit.*, 257–261.
10. For which there is a paucity of evidence: cf. Emond, *op. cit.*, 257–61. The raciest account is given in Pitscottie, *Historie*, i, 282–3, where the year is given as 1515.
11. *ADCP*, 194–5, Sir George's 'cousin' being the laird of Dalhousie.
12. *APS*, ii, 312; cf. Emond, op. cit., 512–13.
13. *RSS*, i, no. 3506.
14. *HMC, Eleventh Report*, App. pt. vi, 217, no. 149.

15. *RSS*, i, nos. 3742, 3782.
16. *HMC, Eleventh Report*, App. pt. vi.
17. *RSS*, i, nos. 3779–80, 3824; *HMC, Eleventh Report*, App. pt. vi, 37, no. 72. The gift of the castle was made 'in double forme', Finnart holding it for nine years and Avandale for nineteen years – both appointments apparently running concurrently: *Scots Peerage*, iv, 364; vi, 511 (Avandale's marriage).
18. *HMC, Eleventh Report*, App. pt. vi, 35, no. 73; 53, no. 108; *RSS*, i, no. 3518 (gift of ward of Drumry to Finnart in 1526); *Scots Peerage*, iv, 353; v, 351 (Elizabeth's marriage).
19. *RSS*, i, no. 3810.
20. *RMS*, iii, nos. 469, 881, 1291.
21. *HMC, Eleventh Report*, App. pt. vi, 34, no. 72.
22. Wormald, *Bonds*, App. A, 307, no. 6.
23. SRO, *ADC*, vol. 38, f. 44; *HMC, Eleventh Report*, App. pt. vi, 34, no. 73. On the assumption that a tutor was appointed until the age of 14 when a curator took charge (as until recently was the case in Scots Law), this gives a birthdate for Lennox between July 1514 and April 1517. *Scots Peerage*, v, 352, gives his birthdate as 21 September 1516. The assumption that a curator was appointed at age 14 is not, however, infallible: cf. n. 152.
24. *HMC, Eleventh Report*, Ap. pt. vi, 52, no. 108 (his will dated 26 March); *RSS*, ii, no. 6 (ward of the earldom gifted 31 March).
25. SRO, *ADC*, vol. 38, ff. 144, 145v; *RSS*, ii, no. 60. Crukisfee may simply be Crookston, Renfrew.
26. *RMS*, iii, nos. 894, 1203, 1229.
27. *Ibid.*, iii, nos. 768–9.
28. *Ibid.*, iii, no. 707.
29. *HMC, Eleventh Report*, App. pt. vi, 34–5, no. 108; cf. also Fraser, *Lennox*, ii, 236, no. 146, for an earlier version dated February 1531, and *ADCP*, 355, for abbreviated version.
30. *Ibid.* The others specified as forgiven were Eglinton, Lord Fleming, Lord Somerville, Hugh Campbell of Loudoun, those of the surname Wallace, Andrew Kerr of Fernieherst, Mark Kerr of Dolphinton and James Douglas of Drumlanrig.
31. It is not possible to state with confidence where Canathy brig was. McKean, *op.cit.*, 43, locates it as Cannachy bridge, by Linlithgow, but whether such a place exists or existed is unclear. There is a Cannachy bridge in Forfar but neither the Hamiltons nor the Stewart earls of Lennox had any landed interests there. The preferred option is Camlachie burn which rises (or rose) in the vicinity of Gartcraig and runs (or ran) in a south-easterly direction for 3 miles before falling into the River Clyde. Camlachie itself is a district of greater Glasgow. This is the nearest corresponding place name for a river located between Dumbartonshire (Lennox territory) and Hamilton (Arran territory), and also not too distant from Drumry (west of Clydebank).
32. When the first earl of Arran died in March 1529, amongst his debts he left three and a half years' worth of the rents of the lands of Drumry, due to Finnart: *HMC, Eleventh Report*, App. pt. vi, 53, no. 108.
33. Avandale did not alienate this portion of the barony to Finnart until 1533: *RMS*, iii, no. 1391, possibly after the death of Elizabeth Hamilton.
34. *ER*, xvi, 548–9; *RSS*, ii, nos. 889–90, 1163.
35. *RSS*, ii, no. 1309.
36. Emond, *op.cit.*, 5122–3.
37. *SP Henry VIII*, iv, pt. iv, no. cxcvii.
38. Pitscottie, *Historie*, i, 319; Buchanan, *History*, ii, 242, 255.
39. Wormald, *Bonds*, 127–8; App. A, 325, no. 8.
40. *HMC, Eleventh Report*, App. pt. vi, 217, no. 151. The editor of *HMC* suggests that Finnart thereby renounced any right of succession by himself to the earldom: *ibid.*, 204–5.
41. *James V Letters*, 113.
42. *HMC, Eleventh Report*, App. pt. vi, 52–3, no. 108; *RSS*, ii, no. 6.

43. Again, his age can only be estimated. Finnart was still Arran's tutor on 29 April 1531, which suggests that Arran was then still under the age of 14. His 'curatory' passed to the earl of Morton on 1 October 1532, suggesting that he may have then been 14 years old, and hence 21 years old in October 1539. This gives a possible birthdate in August-September 1518. However this is not an infallible assumption to make, as apparently curators were appointed under the age of 14: cf. n. 152. Arran again had 'curators' in June 1533: SRO, *ADCS*, ii, f. 109. Finnart was still acting as administrator of the earldom on 30 July 1539: *ADCS*, xii, f. 3v, suggesting the earl was then still under the age of 21 years.

44. E.g. *RMS*, iii, no. 2201.

45. By virtue of his being heir of tailzie in 1513: *ibid.*, ii, no. 3804. Sir Patrick Hamilton of Kingscavil was killed in the 'Cleanse the Causeway' episode: cf. Emond, *op.cit.*, 257-61. The other joint heir of tailzie, John Hamilton of Broomhill, also appears to have died, given the lack of reference to him after 1513. (His son, David, is first mentioned in 1539: *Prot. Bk. Johnsoun*, 182).

46. *RSS*, i, no. 3518; cf. *RMS*, iii, no. 978 (Margaret described as 'Lady of East Wemyss').

47. *HMC, Eleventh Report*, App. pt. vi, 53, no. 108; cf. *RMS*, iii, no. 117 and M.H.B. Sanderson, *Cardinal of Scotland: David Beaton c.1494-1546* (Edinburgh, 1986), 13, 286-7. Possibly Finnart was married to Margaret in 1522.

48. Finnart's legitimate son, James, is not mentioned until after the personal rule, when he acted with curatorial consent on two occasions in 1543 and 1549: *ADCP*, 536, 593. Finnart's illegitimate sons were Andrew, James *senior*, Alexander, and James *junior*: cf. *RMS*, iii, nos. 1330, 14416, 1883, 2021, 2035. James *junior* was eighteen years old in 1538 and appears to have been granted the commendatorship of Fail Church (Ayrshire) in that year. The temporality was gifted to his father on 9 January 1538: *James V Letters*, 341; *RSS*, ii, no. 2439.

49. SRO, *ADCS*, ix, f. 65.

50. *Ibid.*, xii, f. 31.

51. The first by 1531: *RMS*, iii, no. 983; the second by 1532, *ibid.*, no. 1220; the third before 1540, *RSS*, ii, no. 3775.

52. *An Introduction to Scottish Legal History* (Stair Society, 20), 427.

53. *ADCP*, 171 (first earl exercising the office in 1523); *RMS*, iii, no. 2201 (second earl confirmed in office, 1540).

54. *RMS*, iii, no. 365; SRO, *ADCS*, vii, f. 116v.

55. SRO, *ADCS*, ii, f. 109.

56. *TA*, vi, 218-9.

57. *RSS*, ii, nos. 1580-1. The specific crime for which both were granted remission was participating in the battle of Kittycrosshill.

58. SRO, *ADCS*, iii, f. 205; *RSS*, ii, no. 1582.

59. SRO, *ADCS*, ix, f. 10v.

60. *Ibid.*, ix, ff. 105, 105v, 107v, 111.

61. *Ibid.*, ix, f. 101.

62. *Ibid.*, x, f. 126.

63. *Ibid.*, xi, ff. 146v, 188, 199v.

64. *Ibid.*, xi, f. 231.

65. *Ibid.*, xii, f. 185v.

66. *Ibid.*, xiii, ff. 40, 41v.

67. *RMS*, iii, nos. 978, 980, 1255, 1284, 1291, 1382, 1407-11, 2505-6. Finnart and Newton also appeared together on the same charter list: *ibid.*, iii, no. 1134.

68. SRO, *ADCS*, xiii, f. 59.

69. *RMS*, iii, nos. 1023, 1570 (described as notary public).

70. *Ibid.*, iii, nos. 768-9.

71. *Ibid.*, iii, nos. 978, 980.

72. *Ibid.*, iii, nos. 1407-11; thereafter Lord Avandale was designated Lord Ochiltree; cf. e.g., *ibid.*, iii, no. 1413.

73. *Ibid.*, iii, no. 1543; *ER*, xvii, 126–9, 213–4, 375–6, 570–2, accounts from 1537–8 onwards.
74. *ADCP*, 449; *ER*, xvii, 285.
75. *SP Henry VIII*, vi, pt. iv, no. cccxi, in February 1537.
76. *RMS*, iii, no. 1543.
77. *Ibid.*, iii, no. 1425, since 1534, Crawfordmuir being part of the barony of Crawford Douglas.
78. *Ibid.*, iii, no. 1562; *TA*, vi, 279.
79. *ER*, xvii,124, 128–9, 213, 375, 571.
80. *TA*, vi, 332. The Treasurer was prepared to buy gold at £6 8s. per oz.: cf. *ibid*, vii, 464; *RSS*, ii, no. 3087. However, Finnart had managed to sell it to the Treasury at £8 per oz.: *TA*, vi, 179. On Arran's death the gold lump was valued at £7 per oz.: *HMC, Eleventh Report*, App. pt. vi, 52, no. 108.
81. *Ibid.*, vii, 256; cf. *Chronicle of Kings of Scotland* (Maitland Club, 1830), 86, where Chalmers writes 'At this tyme certane mynnouris come in Scotland, and found the golden mynd of Crawfuirdmuir'.
82. *TA*, vii, 464.
83. *RSS*, ii, no. 2064 – using English miners if he so chose.
84. *RMS*, iii, nos. 1575, 2021.
85. *Ibid.*, iii, no. 983.
86. *APS*, ii, 438–40; *HMC, Eleventh Report*, App. pt. vi, 217, no. 149; cf. *ADCP*, 593–4.
87. *ADCP*, 594–5; *APS*, ii, 434–6; *TA*, viii, 487. Finnart's heir then gave his bond of manrent to Arran: *HMC Eleventh Report*, App. pt. vi, 37, no. 15.
88. *HMC Eleventh Report*, App. pt. vi, 53, no. 108.
89. Emond, *op.cit.*, 257–61; Sanderson, *op.cit.*, 76–77, 287
90. SRO, *ADC*, vol. 41, f. 101; *ADCS*, v, ff. 71v, 74v.
91. *James V Letters*, 274–5; cf. *RSS*, ii, no. 1585 (first mention of escheat on 30 September 1534).
92. *Prot. Bk. Johnsoun*, no. 82, 19 September 1534.
93. *LP Henry VIII*, vii, no. 1184 (1).
94. *Ibid.*, viii, no. 734.
95. *Ibid.*, x, no. 1256.
96. *James V Letters*, 307–8.
97. *Ibid.*, 330; *TA*, vii, 20.
98. Sanderson, *op.cit.*, 276, no. 74; *TA*, vii, 444; *RMS*, iii, 2265.
99. SRO, *ADCS*, vi, f. 166; cf. *ibid.*, xi, f. 147v (in February 1539 summoned for his interest in Linlithgow lands); *RMS*, iii, no. 2069 (12 January 1540, formerly holding lands in Linlithgow).
100. *RMS*, iii, no. 1526.
101. *Ibid.*, iii, no. 1293.
102. *Ibid.*, iii, no. 1416.
103. *Ibid.*, iii, no. 1575.
104. *Ibid.*, iii, no. 2021.
105. *RSS*, ii, no. 3199.
106. *RMS*, iii, no. 2035: presumably, that is, after Finnart's son James, then aged around eleven.
107. *Ibid.*, iii, no. 2030; *TA*, vii, 455.
108. *RSS*, ii, nos. 3782, 3885; *TA*, vii, 375, 383. The lands may have been lying in limbo up until then; Finnart only took up their non-entries in December 1539: *RSS*, ii, no. 3229.
109. *Ibid.*, ii, no. 3911; *RMS*, iii, no. 2251; *ER*, xvii, 584.
110. *RSS*, ii, no. 3199.
111. *TA*, vii, 256.
112. *RSS*, ii, no. 3002; cf. McKean, *op.cit.*, 45, where he comments that Stirling castle was being built in the style of an earlier generation.
113. *RSS*, ii, no. 3145. Cf, e.g. the annual fee of £100 paid to each of the March wardens: Rae, *op.cit.*, App. 3. However the scope for bonuses, for example in the form of escheats, as a March warden was probably much greater than that for a builder.

114. *RSS*, ii, no. 3245.
115. It might be added that Finnart's successor in the role of 'principale ourseare and maister of all werkis' at Stirling was Robert Robertson, carver, who had authority to receive the keys of 'all houssis quhare his grace hes ony geir': *ibid.*, ii, no. 4191.
116. *TA*, vii, 371, 375–6, 379–81, 383–4; viii, 19.
117. *Ibid.*, vii, 379; *RSS*, ii, no. 3830.
118. *ER*, xv, 289, 477; xvii, 278.
119. *TA*, vii, 384; viii, 19; *HMC Eleventh Report*, App. pt. vi, 52, no. 108. Probably most of the silver, or silver-gilt, came from Arran's estate. Arran had four silver spoons; Finnart had eighteen.
120. *TA*, vii, 383; cf. the escheat of one William Hume, at the same time: *Ibid.*, vii, 385, who left £125 in gold and silver coins. Finnart's father left £4500 in 'numbered money', or coinage and one piece of gold worth £100: *HMC, Eleventh Report*, App. pt. vi, 52, no. 108. Possibly this 'numbered' money was gold coin, or Finnart, in the course of the following decade, was able to exchange it for gold coin. As master of works [*sic*] he received church revenues direct (cf. e.g., *RSS*, ii, nos. 1935, 2147) which may have been in the form of gold. It is unlikely that he had been able to extract gold from Crawfordmuir, and have it minted without anyone noticing. Crawfordmuir had been Douglas territory and forfeited to the Crown, which would retain the mineral rights even on subsequent sale.
121. McKean, *op.cit.*, 47.
122. *RMS*, iii, no. 2233. Crawfordjohn is listed with the earl of Angus' estates – probably because it lay next to Crawfordmuir.
123. *TA*, vii, 455.
124. *ER*, xvii, 587–8.
125. *ADCP*, 327, 338, 340–1, 323, 370; SRO, RH 2.1.9; *ADC*, vol. 41, ff. 78–9, 101–2, 105, 112, 115, 130–1; vol. 43, f. 140; *ADCS*, i, f. 110.
126. *Ibid.*, 326, 343–4, 356–8; SRO RH 2.1.9; *ADC*, vol. 41, f. 77, 134; vol. 42, ff. 185–6.
127. *Ibid.*, 384, 387, 390, 395–6; SRO, RH 2.1.9; *ADCS*, i, ff. 117, 124; ii, ff. 27, 79.
128. *LP Henry VIII*, vi, no. 322: presumably mounted lancers for raiding purposes, or, on this occasion, intercepting English raids.
129. SRO, RH 2.1.9. *passim*; the sederunt list appears to have included those lords who happened to have a court case on that particular day.
130. Cf. P.G.B. McNeill, *op.cit.*, 209–11. Extra-ordinary lords did continue to appear on an occasional basis. Rothes and lords Erskine, Ruthven, and St. John were the most frequent attenders of the session: SRO, RH 2.1.9. *passim*.
131. *ADCP*, 349, 368.
132. *ER*, xvi, 550, with Lord Avandale. *TA*, vi, 135, refers to 'the slauchter in Avindaill' (entry dated June 1533).
133. On two occasions: *ER*, xvi, 602, 604. On the first occasion he was to capture James Philips for the mutilation of Thomas Forest and generally punish thieves with James Foulis, clerk-register. On the second occasion, the remit was shared with Sir James Colville of East Wemyss, Comptroller, Adam Otterburn of Auldhame, king's advocate, 'and others'. The first commission appears to have been in Fife; the second in Kirkcudbright.
134. Pitcairn, *Trials*, i, pt. i, 172.
135. *APS*, ii, 332–3, 334–5, 339–40.
136. *ER*, xvi, 447; xvii, 7, 42; *TA*, vi, 239, 268, 365.
137. *APS*, ii, 351–2, together with Huntly; Argyll; Marischal; Sir James Colville of East Wemyss, Comptroller; James Foulis of Colinton, clerk register; Thomas Scott of Pitgormo, justice clerk; John Perdovin, deputy-constable (for Erroll); William Mowbray, deputy sheriff, and John Anderson, adjudicator. The purpose was to detain Sir Patrick Hepburn of Waughton.
138. SRO, *ADCS*, xii, f. 3v.

139. *HMC Eleventh Report*, App. pt. vi, 218, no. 155 (Arran engaged to be married to the earl of Morton's daughter, and Finnart relinquishing his ward of Arran's person). Cf, SRO, *ADCS*, ii, f. 109v (where the curators are other Hamiltons)..

140. *RMS*, iii, no. 1671, at Edinburgh, the purpose being to confirm David, Lord Drummond as the heir to his grandfather, forfeited and then restored by the Duke of Albany in the minority. Arran did not appear as a witness again until 1540.

141. SRO, *ADCS*, xiii, f. 170v.

142. The exact duties of the *sewer* or, in Latin *'dapifer'* [*RMS*, iii, no. 1575] have been taken to be those of a cup-bearer: cf. e.g. Kelley, *Angus*, 754; Lang, *op.cit.*, i, 505. *Chambers Dictionary* defines a *sewer* as the officer who superintends service at the table. James had several cup-bearers, amongst them Walter Kerr of Cessford, Walter Douglas, James Stewart, David Baverage and John Menteith, all apparently carrying out the duties in 1536: *ER*, xvi, 480E, 480 G. Kerr of Cessford was presumably principal amongst them. Oliver Sinclair of Pitcairn also became a cupbearer. There is no record of Finnart being one: cf. McKean, *op.cit.*, 42.

143. *TA*, v, 307; *RMS*, iii, no. 2021 (*sewer*); *ER*, xv, 129; xvi, 480E (master of king's stables)

144. *TA*, v, 299, 307, 312.

145. *Ibid.*, v, 260–61, 307–14.

146. *ER*, xvi, 134, 137 (1529), 480F (1536).

147. *RMS*, iii, nos. 968, 1796, 2825.

148. E.g. *RSS*, ii, nos. 1935, 2147 (both 1536).

149. *Ibid.*, ii, no. 334; *RMS*, iii, no. 971; WRH, Haigh Inventory, f. 83.

150. *RMS*, iii, nos. 276, 2044.

151. The word used by John Penven in his despatch to Sir George Douglas from Rouen in October 1536: *LP Henry VIII*, xi, no. 916.

152. SRO, *ADCS*, vii, f. 108. Presumably what was meant was tutor. If the terms tutor and curator were loosely applied and did not necessarily denote that the age of fourteen was the age at which a curator was appointed, then this gives scope for revising Arran's age downwards: cf. n. 43.

153. *RMS*, iii, no. 1620; *James V Letters*, 279, 287.

154. *RMS*, iii, no. 1220; *Scots Peerage*, v, 52–3. The Hamiltons and the Kerrs of Ferniehirst were opposed to the Kerrs of Cessford in 1520: cf. Emond, *op.cit.*, 257–61; *HMC Eleventh Report*, App. pt. vi, 32, no. 66.

155. *ADCP*, 338; *RMS*, iii, nos. 1220, 1330, 1885.

156. *TA*, vi, 275, 289; I.D. Macfarlane, *op.cit.*, 48–9.

157. *TA*, vi, 202, 206.

158. *Ibid.*, vi, 38. At the same time Stewart was given £50 'to help him with ane pak', possibly not a pack of cards.

159. *Ibid.*, vi, 255.

160. *SP Henry VIII*, v, pt. iv, no. ccxc.

161. *James V Letters*, 320; *LP Henry VIII*, xi, nos. 8, 41.

162. *James V Letters*, 321, receiving a favourable answer; *ibid.*, 322.

163. *ADCP*, 455; *SP Henry VIII*, v, pt.iv, nos. cccv, ccclxxiv (this last a letter by Margaret Tudor to Henry VIII, wrongly dated; cf. *LP Henry VIII*, xi, no. 339. Margaret had a habit of not dating her letters).

164. *TA*, vi, 451–2; corroborated by Abell, *op.cit.*, f. 125v.

165. Abell, *op.cit.*, f. 125v; *Diurnal of Occurrents*, 21, corroborates this version. Lesley, *History*, 150, suggests that the voyage was a secret from most of the lords, and does not mention Finnart.

166. *LP Henry VIII*, xi, no. 916. Moray's reply was 'by the wounds of God, he cannot fawt to you though he dryte [shit] in your hands'.

167. *Ibid.*, xiii, pt. i, no. 1252, when Sir Thomas Clifford writes in 1538 that Finnart devised a scheme to have Berwick-upon-Tweed made over to Scotland whilst James was away in

France. This suggests that Finnart got as far as England where he may have purchased hawks and hounds for the king's use: cf. *Prot. Bk. Johnsoun*, no. 143 (royal warrant for payment to Finnart of 850 marks for purchase of same, dated 30 November 1536, Edinburgh). Cf. *TA*, vi, 312 (Finnart summoned, March 1537, to attend the king's homecoming).

168. The claim made, uniquely amongst recent historians, by McKean, *op.cit.*, 44, who states that the king attended the wedding at Craignethan castle. Lord Somerville in fact was married throughout the personal rule to Janet Maitland: *RMS*, iii, no. 374; *ER*, xix, 449. His son, James, Master of Somerville, was married to an illegitimate daughter of the first earl of Arran in 1529: *HMC Eleventh Report*, App. pt. vi, 53, no. 108. On 8 April 1536, at Cowthally (Carnwath), in return for past deference by Finnart and for love etc., Lord Somerville granted lands in liferent to Finnart's daughter, Agnes. On 9 April this charter was confirmed by the king, the confirmation issued from Stirling: *RMS*, iii, no. 1570. Agnes and the master of Somerville were married by 1550, by which time he was the fifth Lord Somerville: *ibid.*, iv, no. 486. (Hugh, Lord Somerville in the personal rule, died in 1549, *Scots Peerage*, viii, 18.) James was at Stirling on 8 April – the likely date of the marriage – and at Falkland on 9 April – the date of the royal confirmation in Agnes' favour: *James V Letters*, 315. His exact movements cannot be chartered day by day in this period but he was in Crawfordjohn in March: *TA*, vi, 279; cf. *RMS*, iii, no. 1562 (16 March); *RSS*, ii, no. 1984 (18 March). The privy seal was at Stirling on 20 March: *ibid.*, ii, no. 1985, and James appears to have been at either Stirling or Falkland throughout April: *James V Letters* (8, 9, 21, 22 April); cf. *RSS*, ii, nos. 1990–2019 and *RMS*, iii, nos. 1563–1575 (both located at Stirling, or Falkland in April, one letter under the privy seal issued from Edinburgh on 4 April). It is feasible that in returning from Crawfordjohn to Stirling in the latter part of March 1536, the king stopped off at Craignethan to attend a wedding, but no reference is made of it in the *Treasurer's Accounts* or elsewhere, perhaps surprising given he was supposedly attending the wedding of his 'favourite's' daughter. There is also no reference to a wedding present for the happy couple, if they were indeed married at that time. James was not generous but would make an exception for a wedding which he attended in person. James visited Craignethan in 1542: *ER*, xvii, 583. Any earlier royal visit for a wedding should be considered purely as an assertion which remains to be substantiated.

169. *MW*, i, 55, 114, 130–1; *RSS*, ii, no. 1935. A further £683 was spent over the summer of 1536. By 18 August Finnart and Johnston were owing the Crown £54, such was the efficiency of the tax collecting system: *ibid*; ii, no. 2147.

170. *RSS*, ii, no. 3523; *Prot. Bk. Johnsoun*, nos. 40, 81; *RMS*, iii, no. 1416.

171. E.g. *TA*, vi, 55 (December 1531), 202 (September 1534); *James V Letters*, 277 (31 October 1534). Great seal charters were issued there on 8 December 1531, 25 May and 23 September 1532, 30 June 1533, 16 June 1534 and 6 December 1535: *RMS*, iii, nos. 1098, 1176, 1225, 1292, 1391, 1525. Cf. *RSS*, ii, no. 1088 (14 December 1531).

172. *SP Henry VIII*, v, pt. iv, no. ccxc.

173. *James V Letters*, 289–90.

174. *SP Henry VIII*, v, pt. iv, no. cccxv.

175. Buchanan, *History*, ii, 255; Teulet, *Papiers*, ii, no. cvii, 334–5; Pitscottie, *Historie*, i, 355, has a similar story, but does not mention Finnart.

176. Donaldson, *op.cit.*, 38–9; Emond, *op.cit.*, *passim*.

177. Presumably the inferences to be drawn from both Buchanan and the author of *Factum Contre Les Hamiltons*, especially when read in conjunction with the circumstances leading up to James' eventual marriage.

178. Albany died on 2 June 1536: M.W. Stuart, *The Scot who was a Frenchman: being the life of John Stewart, Duke of Albany, in Scotland, France and Italy* (Hodge, 1940), 284.

179. *RSS*, ii, no. 2173.

180. *TA*, vi, 304, 448; vii, 60, 91, 195, 256, 302; viii, 37, 55; *MW*, i, 227–8.

181. *MW*, i, 264–292; *TA*, vi, 213.

182. *TA*, vii, 335, 339, 401, 444, 456, 463, 478; viii, 39, 72.

183. *APS*, ii, 362.

184. *Ibid.* Also on the assize were William Lauder of Haltoun (Forfar); William Cunningham of Glengarnock (Ayr); David Ramsay of Culluche (Colluthie, Fife); James Douglas of Drumlanrig (Dumfries); Robert Mowbroy of Bernbowgall (Barnbougle, Linlithgow); Sir John Melville of Raith (Fife) and James Lundy of Balgonie (Fife). Atholl had served on Lady Glamis' assize. Maxwell, the Master of Glencairn, and Melville of Raith had served on both Lady Glamis' and the Master of Forbes' assize.

185. *TA*, vii, 329.

186. *Diurnal of Occurrents*, 23. He was dead by 21 August: *RSS*, ii, no. 3622.

187. Pitscottie, *Historie*, i, 388–93; Buchanan, *History*, ii, 260–1.

188. *HP*, i, no. 57.

189. *RSS*, ii, nos. 3622, 3775. Cardinal David Beaton acted as joint curator for Finnart's heir in 1543, in opposition to the Governor, Arran: *ADCP*, 536.

190. Sanderson, *op.cit.*, 53. Sanderson claims Beaton was a friend to Finnart. She has no insight into the supposed appointment of Finnart as a prosecutor of heretics: *ibid.*, 149. If Finnart and Beaton were on good terms in 1536 it seems unlikely that the one should be against a French marriage, and the other in favour of it.

191. *Bannatyne Miscellany*, i, 256–60; *LP Henry VIII*, xii, pt. i, no. 496; xv, nos. 248, 714; cf, Sanderson, *op.cit.*, App. 3, no. 19.

192. Knox, *History*, i, 26, 28. Neither the *Diurnal* nor Lesley refers either to Borthwick's trial or Finnart's inquisition.

193. Pitscottie, *Historie*, i, 390–1.

194. SRO, *ADCS*, xvii, f. 22 (Finnart in Edinburgh castle in July 1540); *ibid.*, xiii, f. 170v (Finnart in court on 30 July 1540); cf. *ibid.*, xiii, f. 152 (end of July, Finnart fails to appear as sheriff of Linlithgow in a case brought by Barbara Mowbray, wife of Robert Mowbray of Barnbougle, one of the men on Finnart's assize).

195. Buchanan, *History*, ii, 260.

196. *Prot. Bk. Johnsoun*, nos. 82–3.

197. Lang, *op.cit.*, i, 506, suggested the involvement of Thomas Hamilton, brother to Stonehouse: cf. *RMS*, iii, no. 864. However it was another Thomas, familiar servant in the spice house and son of Hamilton of Torrance (Lanark or Stirling)) who received gift of part of Finnart's escheat: *Prot. Bk. Johnsoun*, nos. 178, 198; *RSS*, ii, nos. 3622, 4079.

198. Cf. notes 43, 152. Finnart took up the non-entries of the lands of Finnart on 15 December 1539, prior to selling to Shaw of Sauchie, and also the non-entries of moorlands in Bothwell barony. Both charters stated that these were in non-entry 'sen the deces of umquhill James Lord Hammylton [first earl of Arran], gudschir to the said schir James . . . ay and quhill the lauchfull entre of the richtuis are or airis thareto being of lauchfull age': *RSS*, ii, nos. 3228–9. The lawful heir would be the second earl of Arran. The implication is that he was not then of age. It may have been Finnart's entry to the moorlands of Bothwell which Arran later considered to be 'feinzeit': cf. above and *ADCP*, 594.

199. *RMS*, iii, nos. 2201–2; *RSS*, ii, no. 3648. Arran had been granted sasine to the earldom in September 1532, whilst under curators: *ER*, xvi, 556. Possibly this was on reaching his fourteenth birthday and marrying.

200. He was a witness in 1537: *RMS*, iii, no. 1672, and resigned lands on 23 September 1532 in favour of his future wife, Margaret Douglas, daughter of the earl of Morton: *ibid.*, iii, no. 1225. Possibly this was the date of his marriage; his curatory passed to Morton on 1 October 1532: *HMC Eleventh Report*, App. pt. vi, 218, no. 155.

201. Cf. *RSS*, ii, no. 4941 dated 22 October 1542, by which time Arran had three sons; cf. *HMC Eleventh Report*, App. pt. vi, 21, no. 29. Arran's younger brother, Gavin, was also still alive in 1542, meaning that Finnart's prospects of succeeding to the earldom were becoming more remote in 1540.

202. *RMS*, iii, nos. 2194, 2231, 2256, 2264, 2290, 2303, 2348.
203. *LP Henry VIII*, xv, no. 634; *SP Henry VIII*, v, pt. iv, no. ccclxxiii. (As Arran accompanied the king on his sea voyage, this explains why the absent Lennox should have been appointed as joint tutor for James' heir, a position to which Arran had a stronger claim in the succession lines.)
204. *APS*, ii, 362, 434. Probably some form of crossbow. The exact formula varied between the first and second description of the crime, the reference to arrows being omitted in the second version. Possibly 'sagittationis' referred to missiles or projectiles rather than to arrows. There are numerous references to crossbow making in *TA*, vii, *passim*.
205. *RSS*, ii, no. 3544.
206. *Ibid.*, ii, no. 1934; cf. *TA*, vii, 126, 169, 333. He had a groom under him, and was assisted by his son, Patrick.
207. *Prot. Bk. Johnsoun*, nos. 66, 73, 75, 384; *HMC Eleventh Report*, App. pt. vi, 218, no. 152.
208. McKean, *op.cit.*, 47; McGladdery, *op.cit.*, 111–2. The *Treasurer's Accounts* have occasional references to compensation being paid for victims of such accidents: e.g. *TA*, vi, 41, 333.
209. Emond, *op.cit.* 572–3; *APS*, ii, 325.
210. *RSS*, ii, no. 508, probably for being on Lennox's side; Stirling of Keir was a Lennox supporter.
211. *RSS*, ii, no. 3544.
212. *HMC Eleventh Report*, App. pt. vi, 33, no. 73; *APS*, ii, 362.
213. *APS*, ii, 363.
214. McKean, *op.cit.*, 46, asserts that Kingscavil's son first waylaid James about 15 July 1540, the king then on his way to Falkland. James was at St. Andrews on 16 July: *ADCP*, 490.
215. *APS*, ii, 362.
216. *Ibid.*, ii, 355–6, 366–7, 383, 388, 423*; *TA*, vii, 402, 432. They were first summoned in October 1540. Henry Lauder, king's advocate, sought Parliament's endorsement of the validity of making such a summons against his family.
217. Kelley, *Angus*, 752; *RMS*, iii, nos. 968, 978. He was still alive in 1535: *ibid.*, iii, no. 2702.
218. *ER*, xv, 381, 460; *APS*, ii, 355, 364, 423*; *TA*, vii, 395.
219. *RSS*, ii, nos. 2317, 3063; *TA*, vi, 330; *ER*, xvii, 168.
220. *Melr. Lib.*, ii, no. 602; *HP*, i, no. 146.
221. *HP*, i, no. 147 (1).
222. *Ibid.*, i, no. 151.
223. *APS*, ii, 423* (date of the Purification of Our Lady).
224. Finnart's son was restored in 1543 as the charges against his father had been unspecified and vague: *ibid.*, ii, 434.
225. *SP Henry VIII*, iv, pt. iv, no. cxcviii.
226. *ADCP*, 290.
227. Dunbar, *Scots Kings*, 238.
228. *APS*, ii, 404; *RMS*, iii, no. 2233.
229. *RMS*, iii, nos. 1391, 1425, 1620.
230. *Ibid.*, iii, nos. 716, 1318.
231. *LP Henry VIII*, iv, pt. iii, no. 6305, Philip Dacre to Lord Dacre, writing at Morpeth on 4 April. Placed wrongly in 1530.
232. *ADCP*, 470–1, 524; cf. Murray, *Revenues*, 261–3, *et passim*, where Barton's career is given a very full treatment.
233. *RSS*, ii, no. 3544; *HMC Eleventh Report*, App. pt.vi, 35, no. 73.
234. Donaldson, *op.cit.*, 58.
235. J. Wormald, *Mary Queen of Scots: a Study in Failure* (London, 1988), 32, found the king to be 'terrifying' in general, a judgement based, no doubt, upon such incidents as the executions of the Master of Forbes, Lady Glamis, and Hamilton of Finnart.
236. *RMS*, iii, nos. 601, 1964, *et passim*.
237. *Ibid.*, iii, *passim*, Eglinton until 1537, Fleming throughout the personal rule.

238. *LP Henry VIII*, xv, nos. 634, 709.
239. *ADCP*, 269–70.
240. Cf. *Carn Ct. Bk.*, 160, 194, 205–6, 208 (1533–37); Finnart repeatedly failed to turn up at the Barony Court to answer for his lands of Liberton, which he held of Somerville: *RMS*, iii, no. 1883. Hardly a heinous crime, but the fact that Finnart bought the lands from Maxwell suggests that he was perhaps attempting to rival Somerville as a dominant local figure.
241. *RSS*, ii, no. 3775.
242. *Ibid.*, ii, no. 4021. Possibly, had Hamilton of Kingscavil recanted and returned to Scotland, he would have regained office.
243. *Ibid.*, ii, no. 3722.

CHAPTER TEN

Daunting the Isles

To attempt the daunting of the Isles was a traditional pursuit of the Stewart monarchy. By the spring of 1430 James I had won an impressive victory over Alexander MacDonald, Lord of the Isles. Lacking sufficient resources James was unable to follow up this success by further personal campaigns.[1] In the reign of James II, the lordship was held by John MacDonald, earl of Ross, who allied with the Black Douglases. The struggle with the Douglases absorbed the king, and of necessity rather than from choice, James II pursued a conciliatory policy towards MacDonald.[2] James III organised a campaign against the earl of Ross in 1475–76, and may have led this in person. Ross was forfeited, and James III gained financially from this. However, Ross' influence in the north was partially replaced by that of his illegitimate son, Angus of Islay. Also, the forfeiture allowed the Campbell Earls of Argyll and Gordon Earls of Huntly to build up their own power bases, sanctioned by the Crown.[3] James IV's government demolished the Lordship of the Isles by forfeiture in 1493 and followed this up with two royal visits to the west in 1494. By 1495 James IV had placed royal authority in the hands principally of Huntly, Argyll and MacIan of Ardnamurchan.[4] The king then apparently abandoned further interest in the Isles. From 1506 onwards, the heir to the lordship, Donald Dubh, was held in captivity in Edinburgh castle. He remained there for the remainder of the reign and throughout the entire reign of James V.[5] He cost the Crown an annual maintenance fee of £40, levied by special mandate on the Crown lands of Cowal and Rosneath.[6]

At the beginning of the personal rule of James V, the dominant figure in the west was Colin Campbell, third earl of Argyll. He was sheriff of Argyll, and in 1517 was appointed as lieutenant in the west by the duke of Albany, for a three year term.[7] In 1521 Lauchlan MacLean of Duart and ten other chieftains gave their bond of manrent to Argyll, on behalf of themselves, their heirs and all of the inhabitants of Argyll, Lorne, Knapdale, Kintyre, Breadalbane, Balquhidder, Lennox, Menteith, and Strathearn.[8] Argyll was also the chamberlain of Kintyre, Cowal and Rosneath, and in August 1528 handed in at Stirling a three-year account for these lands, producing a mere £39 for the Comptroller.[9] Control of Kintyre gave Argyll nominal control over certain of the lands of Alexander MacDonald of Islay, *alias* Alexander John Cannochissone or Alexander of Dunivaig, who held lands in Mull and Tiree.[10] Three boll measures of barley from the farms of Tiree supplied the castle of Cairn na Burgh More in the

Treshnish isles, which, like Dunoon and Tarbert (Loch Fyne) castles, was held by Argyll for the Crown."

I. REBELLION IN THE ISLES

In May 1528, Sir James Hamilton of Finnart requested permission of the Lords of Council for himself and his father, the first earl of Arran, to be exempted from the royal raid proposed by Angus against Liddesdale. The explanation given was that 'divers hieland men of Bute, Arane, Ilis and uthiris partis' had killed twenty people at the earl's house of Glenkill on the Isle of Arran. The attack on Glenkill was followed up by another on Brodick, in which the sons of Ninian Stewart, sheriff of Bute, were implicated.¹² The first year of the personal rule was also marked by a large degree of disorder in the west of the country. The Eglinton-Glencairn feud was still ongoing in the Cunningham bailiary, and, further south there was a distinct lack of response to the summons to the Tantallon siege from the Galloway and Wigtownshire lairds.¹³ These disturbances were not necessarily connected – though the incidents on the Isle of Arran appear to have been carried out with the assistance of rebels in Galloway and Wigtown¹⁴ – nor were they perpetrated by Douglas supporters. Probably there was an element of opportunism as the change in government turned the political focus towards the east coast.

One of the opportunists was MacDonald of Islay. It is not clear when the Isles revolt began, nor its objectives. In his 1525–28 Kintyre account, Argyll entered a charge figure, over the three years, of £1666. On the discharge column £32 worth of goods in kind went to the Comptroller, £15 went to Ardchattan monastery and St. Constantine's church, and £310 went to Argyll himself for the keeping of Cairn na Burgh castle. The remainder was taken up by a large number of Islesmen holding royal letters which mandated the Crown's rents to themselves. Principal amongst these were Mariota MacIan, daughter and heiress of the deceased John Brayach MacIan of Ardnamurchan, and MacDonald of Islay.¹⁵ This was not a very encouraging return for the Crown; these mandates had been obtained without the consent of the new régime. In November 1528 the king required of his Lords of Council a decree that no new infeftments should be made in the 'Ilis and fermeland' without their and Argyll's approval. All recent infeftments should be annulled, as the king understood that these 'ar his awine propir landis or ellis in his handis' as casualty.¹⁶ At the same time Argyll again became lieutenant in the west.¹⁷

However, a large part of Argyll's time in 1528–29 was taken up in being a loyal servant of the Crown, campaigning against Angus, and also acting as justiciar, secret counsellor, and Master of the Household.¹⁸ This left the field comparatively free for MacDonald of Islay. When Argyll was able to take up his lieutenancy, he may have fuelled the Isles revolt through evicting those who were intromitting with the Crown's rents in Kintyre, as he was authorised to do by the Lords of Council. By the time the 1528–31 account was handed in, almost all of the intromitters had disappeared.[19] The precise crimes of the rebels are not entirely clear. Remissions were granted in 1531 to both MacDonald and MacLean of Duart for treasonable arson in Lennox, Rosneath, Craignish and other areas, and also for the general terrorising of the king's lieges in the Isles.[20] Argyll may have been the vengeful aggressor; there is the possibly apocryphal story that MacLean of Duart attempted to drown his Campbell wife.[21]

In August 1529 Argyll's brother, Sir John Campbell of Cawdor, tabled before the Lords of Council the Campbell strategy for a successful daunting of the Isles. Argyll requested that all men of the burghs, shires and bailiaries of the west coast (Ayr, Irvine, Glasgow, Dumbarton, Renfrew, Carrick, Kyle and Cunningham) be ready at Lochranza (Arran) on 22 August with twenty days' supplies. The first earl of Arran, who might have resented the use of the Isle of Arran as a base for a Campbell-led daunting, had conveniently died in March. However, as it was harvest time, Argyll had to be content with making use of the men of his own lieutenandry. The Treasurer authorised the expense of sending one cannon, two falcons, two gunners, two wrights and three barrels of gunpowder to Dumbarton, and the Master of Argyll was allowed the expense of furnishing his ship at Dumbarton for a two-month campaign.[22] Letters were sent to MacDonald of Islay charging him to cease from convocation against the king's lieges under penalty of treason. MacDonald's response was unsatisfactory, and on 6 September 1529 Argyll was authorised to proceed with the daunting.[23] However, Argyll died before the end of the year.[24] His son, Archibald Campbell, became the fourth earl and was appointed as Justiciar and Master of the Household on 28 October 1529. He had already held the fee of the earldom since 1526. Both these factors, as also the fact that in the September 1528 parliament the Douglases demanded that he should be a hostage for their own safety, suggest that he was of age in 1529.[25]

The campaign against MacDonald continued into 1530. In April Argyll was authorised to lead not only the men of the west coast but also those of Balquhidder, Breadalbane, Rannoch, Appin (of Dull, Perth), Atholl, Menteith, Bute and Arran, all furnished with one month's supplies, against the rebels in the Isles. At the same time letters were sent to MacDonald, charging him and his accomplices to appear before the king in Edinburgh or Stirling to answer the charges of insurrection made by Argyll. The deadline of 24 May was set.[26] This brought a response from Hector MacLean of Duart, who offered 'his trew service' to the king. Encouraged by this, the Lords of Council extended the deadline until 20 June. A safe-conduct was offered to the highland chiefs to 'cum to the kingis grace'. A guarantee of safety from attack, 'stop or impediment' by the earl of Argyll was offered in the form of several Campbells pledging to remain in Edinburgh castle whilst the highland chiefs were in town. The deadline was subsequently extended to September.[27]

James first toyed with the idea of leading his own campaign in April 1530. In response to a request for naval support from Christian II, James assured the exiled Danish king that normally the Scots would be delighted to oblige, but at this juncture James needed all of his ships for a royal Isles campaign.[28] However, in the summer of 1530 James scored a personal achievement elsewhere, in the hanging of Johnnie Armstrong of Gilknockie. Probably it was the success of his 1530 Borders expedition which inspired James to follow up the idea of an Isles campaign by the king 'in propir persoun'. By November 1530 the proposals were before the Lords of Council and the details were filled in over the winter. The expedition was scheduled to take place on 1 April 1531. The army and navy were to be drawn from both the west coast and the interior. The Second Estate were to pay their own costs. The First and Third Estates were to make a contribution.[29]

The plan was altered. The date was put back to 15 May, then to 1 June. The army was now to be drawn from all parts of the realm except the Borders. The army south of the Forth was to meet the king at Ayr. Men from north of the Forth were to meet at Dunstaffnage and from north of the Moray Firth ('the north wattir') at Inverlochy. There was a further change, the object of which appears to have been to write Argyll out of the script. James was now to command all of the army south of the Moray Firth, and the earl of Moray was to lead the remainder, mustering at Kintail. Each freeholder worth over £100 was to supply two soldiers for every £100 he was worth. Each person of property worth over 200 marks was to bring his own household. The spiritual contribution was to be £5000 levied on all church benefices worth over £100. The burghs were also to make a contribution.[30] The sum of £3457 in tax revenues was entered in the 1530–31 *Treasurer's Accounts*, drawn up in September 1531. This was £66 short of the expenditure on furnishing the ships at Leith with munitions from Edinburgh castle, gunpowder from the Netherlands and supplies of food and beer. This expenditure also included £1500 on silverware.[31]

With such elaborate preparations – boats from Crail and Anstruther being required to rendezvous with the king's ships in the Pentland Firth at a wages cost of £36 per boat per month[32] – it was possibly somewhat of an anticlimax when MacDonald of Islay submitted to the king at the eleventh hour. On 27 March 1531 James wrote to Francis I to express his sentiment that the best method of dealing with the Islesmen was to use the culverin to blow them out of their boats and strongholds. For this purpose Francis was asked to send as much gunpowder as he could spare.[33] However, MacDonald sent further communications to the king, assuring him that the Islesmen wanted nothing more than 'to be his trew and obedient liegis'.[34] Parliamentary summons were issued on five occasions between 26 April and 9 June 1531 to MacDonald, MacLean of Duart and fourteen other chieftains. Safe-conducts were offered.[35] MacDonald appeared before the king in person at Stirling in June 1531, and received the sum of £100 paid out of the Isles tax as a reward for his submission, together with the present of a purple velvet gown.[36] On 8 June remissions were issued at Edinburgh to both MacDonald and MacLean, neither man apparently being required to pay for them.[37]

James was at Stirling on 25 and 31 May and 30 June, and at Edinburgh on 2 July and for the greater part of August. In mid-September he was to be found at both places.[38] There is one entry in the *Treasurer's Accounts* referring to a payment being made in April 1531 'for the Kingis passing in the Ilis'.[39] In James' letter of 27 March to Francis I, he stated that he was planning an expedition in the summer. If such an expedition did take place, the only trace of it appears in the *Treasurer's Accounts*, which detailed the expenditure on 'the furnessing of the schippis'. No summons appear to have gone out to the lieges to meet either the king or the earl of Moray. Neither the privy seal nor the great seal made the trip over to the west in the summer of 1531. Both of the king's potential military commanders, Argyll and Moray, were on the council at Edinburgh in April and May, and at Stirling in the first week of June. It is possible that James paid a visit to the Isles in April or early May 1531, but he made no subsequent reference to this, nor did the sixteenth century chroniclers.[40] The parallel is with the 1530 Borders raid against Johnnie Armstrong, for which there is little contemporary evidence. Donaldson has written of the Isles policy in this period that 'there are signs of vacillation or of conflicting counsels in the government'.[41] In fact, it appears that the policy was similar to that adopted towards the Borders in the previous year. The appointment of Moray as lieutenant in the Borders and the arrangements made for him to lead a Borders expedition achieved the desired result – almost all the border magnates entered into ward and subsequently affirmed their bonds to give good rule. The threat of aggression had been successful. In 1531, again the threat of a military campaign achieved the capitulation of the chief Isles rebel, MacDonald of Islay.

2. THE SNUBBING OF ARGYLL

Argyll bound himself in December 1530 to give good rule in the realm in the manner of his forbears. This undertaking was given in the context of daunting the clan MacGregor. At that time, the fourth earl was receiving £3 in daily expenses as the Justiciar at Perth justice ayre.[42] Intermittently Argyll was to be found on the council whilst the arrangements for the daunting of the Isles were being made. He was also one of the parliamentary lords of the Articles in April 1531 when the Islesmen were summoned.[43] On 5 June 1531 the Lords of Council met at Stirling. The lords included, as well as the usual lawyers, nine bishops; ten abbots; the earls of Moray, Argyll, Lennox, Marischal and Rothes; and the lords Fleming, Erskine, Gray, Livingston, Methven, St. John, Avandale, Somerville and Sinclair. The official business was to ensure that Fleming, as superior of William Fleming of the Bord, infeft their tenant, William Livingston, in lands in the barony of Enzie.[44] This was hardly a matter which required the presence of so many members of the council. The king's last appearance in council had been on 2 December 1530 to accept Argyll's undertaking to give good rule.[45] James was not noted as being present on the council on 5 June 1531, but the high turnout of council members suggests that this was the occasion of MacDonald's submission to the king.

The following day Argyll appeared before a body of lords elected to the 'secret council'. Its members were James Beaton, Archbishop of St. Andrews; Gavin Dunbar, Archbishop of Glasgow and Chancellor; George Crichton, bishop of Dunkeld; Gavin Dunbar, bishop of Aberdeen and clerk register; Moray, Rothes, John, fifth lord Erskine; Patrick, third lord Gray; George Dundas, lord of St. John of Torphichen; Alexander Milne, abbot of Cambuskenneth; David Beaton, abbot of Arbroath and keeper of the privy seal; Sir William Scott of Balwearie; Sir James Hamilton of Finnart; William Stewart, dean of Glasgow, provost of Lincluden and treasurer; Thomas Erskine of Haltoun, secretary; Adam Otterburn of Auldhame, king's advocate; James Foulis of Colinton; Nicholas Crawford of Oxgangs, justice clerk; James Lawson; and Francis Bothwell. All of these men were Lords of Council on the previous day, for MacDonald's submission. There was nothing novel about this 'secret council', and its composition and designation suggests an *ad hoc* body meeting to deal with Isles business, rather than something more permanent. Argyll consented 'for the plesour of the kingis grace his prince and soverane and at his noble request' to surrender his heritable office of chamberlain of Kintyre. For the forthcoming year and further if Argyll consented, the office would be exercised by the Comptroller or his depute.[46] Argyll's last account for Kintyre was submitted in 1531 and covered the three years from the last submission in 1528. His charge, made up of three years' rents, was £1166, and he could only account for £295 as discharge – £215 intromitted by MacDonald of Islay. The balance was therefore due to the Comptroller, but as there is no record of the Comptroller responding for this, the assumption must be that the rents were never collected.[47] Neither Argyll nor his father had been very successful in their administration.

Argyll did not surrender Kintyre without making a stand. On 7 June 1531 the Lords of Council were himself, Moray, Rothes, Bothwell, and the lords Erskine, Livingston and St. John, as well as Finnart, Scott of Balwearie, both archbishops, the bishops of Dunkeld, Aberdeen, Ross and Dunblane, the prior of St. Andrews and the abbots of Arbroath, Holyrood, Melrose, Cambuskenneth and Kinloss.[48] This body considered offers which had been put forward to the 'secret council' by both Argyll and Moray. Moray was anxious to protect his position as lieutenant of the north, and promised to continue to bring in the rents from the Crown lands of Ross and Ardmannoch. In March 1530 he had requested, unsuccessfully, for these to be granted to him in heritage. Moray also promised to either bring the chiefs of the north-west Isles before the king, or:

failzeing tharof sall putt thame to utir slauchter, herschip and distructioun. . . .

Moray had the legitimate targets of MacLeod of Lewis, MacLeod of Dunvegan and John of Moidart, captain of Clanranald, all of whom had been summoned to parliament together with MacDonald of Islay.[49]

Argyll in turn offered to daunt the south Isles and Kintyre as lieutenant of the Isles. However, MacDonald had already capitulated. Rather than accepting Argyll's offer, the Lords of Council affirmed the decision of the 'secret council' to allow MacDonald to continue to uplift the profits from his lands in Kintyre. In return, MacDonald was to free any Campbell prisoners he held and was to assist the king's chamberlains in the inbringing of rents.[50] On the following day MacDonald got his remission.

Argyll did not take this insult lying down. In April 1530 the Lords of Council had authorised him to convene the Crown's tenants against MacDonald and other rebels.[51] In his 1531 account for Rosneath and Cowal, Argyll withheld £41 for Rosneath, claiming that the lands had been laid waste by MacDonald.[52] More ominously, in November 1531 the newly rehabilitated MacDonald appeared before the Lords of Council in Edinburgh to answer a bill of complaint lately laid before them by Argyll. The earl claimed that MacDonald had 'done divers and sindry greit faltis to him and his freyndes'. MacDonald now had his remission, and he pointed out to the Lords of Council that, as he understood it, Argyll, assisted by Moray, was now acting without any authority in the Isles. MacDonald offered to force the earl out of Argyllshire in order that the king could take him to task. He further offered to bring to justice any person in the Isles who might have given offence to Argyll or to any other lowlander, 'siclike as utheris lawland men dois'. This was almost the same offer which Argyll had made in April 1530, and again in June 1531. MacDonald went on to claim that he and his Isles colleagues were capable of bringing just as many fighting men to the Scots host as was Argyll.[53]

MacDonald succeeded in turning the tables on Argyll. The names of Lords of Council on the November 1531 session are not recorded, but in the latter part of 1531 the council was dominated by members of the clergy who were perhaps anxious to see a return for the money paid out by them to the Treasurer for the daunting of the Isles. They would not be too concerned as to who was carrying out the daunting. Adam Stewart, pursuivant, was already on his way to the west with a message charging Argyll to come before the king to account for his intromission with rents from the Isles.[54] On 6 December 1531, the earl of Eglinton and lord Erskine offered security in the sum of 1000 marks for Argyll's remaining in Edinburgh until given royal licence to depart.[55] This prompted the earl of Bothwell to report excitedly to the earl of Northumberland on 21 December 1531 that Argyll had been imprisoned. This, coupled with the start of the investigation being made into the non-entries of the earldom of Crawford, and the alleged disregard being shown at the time by the king towards the earl of Moray, Lord Maxwell and Hamilton of Finnart, gave Bothwell grounds for supposing that there was now little obstacle to Henry VIII being crowned in Edinburgh.[56] This was gross over-optimism on Bothwell's part, more reflective of his own state of mind than of events. Possibly Moray was offended by the accusations made against him by MacDonald. Possibly Finnart was offended by the lack of respect being shown to Argyll, who was attempting to put down a rebellion that had earlier affected the Isle of Arran. Argyll appears to have been married to Finnart's half-sister, Helen Hamilton.[57] Like Bothwell, Lord Maxwell had been warded in 1530, and Bothwell was crediting him with feeling the same resentment which he, Bothwell, obviously felt. It was true that the Crawford earldom was shortly to be dismembered legally. In a rather garbled version of Bothwell's report, written over nine months later to Henry VIII, Northumberland stated that Argyll had lost the rule of the outer Isles to Mackayn [MacIan of Ardnamurchan], and the king had given Crawford's lands to the same individual.[58]

According to Bothwell the king had a problem in 1531, but in fact no threat to his authority emerged. With the exceptions of Crawford and Bothwell, all of the 'disregarded' magnates of December 1531 served on the Borders in the spring of 1533. Argyll's 'imprisonment' was not one which could compare with that of Bothwell. Argyll appeared on the council on 1, 4, 13 and 14 December 1531, and again in January and February 1532, There are only three charters in the register bearing a witness list in this period, at Edinburgh on 6 January and 21 April 1532, and at Stirling on 28 March. Argyll appeared on each list.[59] Argyll was being kept away from the Isles, not incarcerated in Edinburgh castle. By June 1532 he was free to go to Perth to oversee the settlement of a dispute between two of his kinsmen, and apparently handled this disastrously.[60] By November 1532 he was back in the west, and being summoned to return to Edinburgh to give his counsel for the defence of the realm.[61]

MacDonald's new-found cooperation with the Crown was followed by that of Hector MacLean of Duart, who twice, in October and December 1531, was offered a safe-conduct to appear before the king and council in Edinburgh.[62] In August 1532 the earl of Northumberland reported that James had sent over five hundred archers to the assistance of the Irish rebel, O'Connell.[63] In December 1532, MacDonald of Islay took delivery from the king of twelve bows and six dozen arrows. Both he and MacLean were then summoned, in February 1533, to come to 'the King weill accumpanyit for defence of the realme'.[64] MacLean was granted licence to depart for Ireland,[65] and in July 1533 he and MacDonald conducted a raid against the Isle of Man and captured the English ship the *Mary Willoughby*.[66] James instantly claimed this prize for himself, and in September 1533 travelled over to Inveraray to collect the ship.[67] He remained there until October,[68] and then sailed south to Dumbarton aboard the *Mary Willoughby*.[69] The king then went to Glasgow,[70] leaving the ship to be refurbished at Dumbarton, the cost of the whole exercise amounting to £500, paid for out of the tax of the three teinds.[71]

It was whilst the king was in Argyll, inspecting his new toy, that the earl of Northumberland sent another of his cryptic reports to Henry VIII. In this one he claimed that there was great dissension in Scotland, 'for the shamefull murderinge of one gentilman callyd the Lard of Lynsay'. Moray and Argyll were opposed to Huntly because of this, and the king had 'bene there for agrement, but it wolde take none effect amonges theyme as yet'.[72] As no laird of Lindsay had been murdered[73] and the king was in Argyll, it appears that the bone of contention, if any, was over the dispute in Mull between the MacLeans. The MacLeans of Lochbuie and the MacLeans of Duart were engaged in a minor feud. Alan, the son of Hector MacLean of Duart, was granted a remission on 21 March 1533 for treasonable fireraising on the island of Mull and for the killing of John, son of John MacLean of Lochbuie. £3000 worth of damage was caused to Lochbuie's castle. The incident took place in the summer of 1531,[74] at which time MacDonald of Islay was supporting the MacLeans of Lochbuie in opposition to Argyll.[75] Argyll and ninety-two others obtained a remission in March 1533 for fire-raising in Mull, Tiree and Morvern.[76] Unlikely though it seems (given the supposed attempted drowning of his Campbell wife by MacLean of Duart), in 1531 Argyll may have been supporting MacLean of Duart against MacLean of Lochbuie and MacDonald of Islay. Alternatively, the situation in Mull was a free-for-all in 1531. Two years later, MacLean of Duart and MacDonald were working together in the Crown's service. Argyll was now the outsider in the Isles. To a lesser extent, Moray had also an interest in this area, and in November 1531 MacDonald had accused him of assisting Argyll without royal authority. It is possible that Huntly saw his way into obtaining local influence in the area by backing MacLean of Duart; in 1536 he and MacLean exchanged bonds and Huntly promised to infeft MacLean in lands in Lochaber.[77] MacLean's reward for the capture of the *Mary Willoughby* was to be excused all payment of rent for 1532–33 for his lands in Mull, Tiree and Morvern.[78]

Both MacLean and MacDonald were deployed in royal service in 1533. What James appears to have wanted was a means of turning the Irish situation to his advantage and to the disadvantage of the English. Scots involvement in the revolts of, first, O'Connell, then the young Lord Kildare and the Geraldine league, continued throughout the reign. This provoked speculation amongst the diplomats that Charles V was behind it all, seeking to disrupt Henry VIII's control in Ireland.[79] The official Scottish line, given by James in 1534 to the imperial envoy, Godscalkus, was that the Scottish government had no knowledge of any 'private' incidents of which the English were complaining.[80] However James was quite happy to communicate with MacDonald in Ireland and to continue supplying him, and afterwards his son, James, with bows and arrows. In 1539 the English governor in Ireland recommended the deployment of two warships in the North Channel to intercept ships from the Isles.[81]

If the intention of the king in sacking Argyll as his chamberlain in Kintyre in 1531 was to improve the Crown's revenues there, then this was a modest success. The chamberlain appointed on 5 July 1531 for the 'landis of the Ilis and withint all the boundis tharof' was one Patrick Colquhoun, who died before he could submit any returns.[82] MacDonald of Islay then paid his own rents direct to the Comptroller, £40 in 1533, and £132 in 1534. MacLean of Duart also paid the sum of

£40 to the Comptroller, for lands in the 'lordship of the isles'. In 1536, William Stirling of Glorat was acting as chamberlain and submitted the sum of £174 for 'Kintyre and the Isles' to the Comptroller in 1536.[83] These figures were not spectacular, but the Crown was receiving more than it had got out of the Campbells for the period 1525–31. A further £100 in hostage fees was reimbursed to the Comptroller by the Treasurer for the 'hieland men at Ethale and Furde', who had probably been captured in Andrew Kerr of Ferniehirst's raid against Etal in January 1533.[84] Argyll continued to enter annual returns for Cowal and Rosneath.[85] James had also got the *Mary Willoughby* and regularly sent messengers to the Isles to receive hawks from MacLean and others for his royal hunting trips.[86] MacDonald's son, James, entered the royal Household in 1531.[87]

However there was no sign of MacDonald actively assisting the Comptroller's staff in the inbringing of rents, and he revealed himself in his true colours in 1535. On 30 August he and his brother, and various Mackays described as officers of Kintyre, were outlawed for three separate acts of murder, piracy and 'stouthreif' against the merchant ships of Andrew Mure, citizen of Glasgow, who traded with Ireland. Two of Andrew's sons were killed, one whilst asleep on board his vessel in harbour at Sanda off the Mull of Kintyre on 15 July. Two servants of Andrew were also killed, and Andrew himself was wounded. Over £400 worth of merchandise was stolen. If Argyll were trying the case it must have given him great satisfaction to put his rival at the horn.[88] MacDonald died in 1536 before any recriminations could take place.[89]

To replace Argyll with MacDonald as the chamberlain of Kintyre and to turn down Argyll's offer to daunt the Isles as the king's lieutenant was something of a political gamble. Argyll must have been offended; the king's acceptance of MacDonald's offer of royal service temporarily reversed the Campbell domination of the Isles. Argyll has been given a bad press by Dr. Wormald, who has called him a 'muddler', displaying at both local and national level 'inefficiency and weakness'.[90] In his defence, he was up against an active adult Stewart monarch, unlike his father whose Isles career flourished during the faction fighting of the minority. It is also not possible to determine the fourth earl's age in 1531; he might have been as young as twenty-three,[91] and lacking the experience of political in-fighting afforded to his father in the minority. Given that Wormald is correct in her assessment of the fourth earl's character, then the stakes were not high in removing him from the chamberlaincy, and temporarily restricting his movements.

But there was more to it than that. Either through incompetence or disinclination, the third earl of Argyll had failed to produce a satisfactory return for the Crown in the 1525–28 Kintyre account. He was given authority to daunt the Isles in August 1529, but not the resources for which he asked; and he then died. James adopted the policy of pressurising the Islesmen to submit to the Crown through preparing for a military campaign. Had MacDonald not appeared before the king in June 1531, then the military campaign would have been led by the king and his half-brother, Moray. The fourth earl of Argyll's involvement would at best have been in a subordinate role. James was not prepared to allow the Campbells to lead the lieges in a daunting exercise against MacDonald; the Campbells were not being given the opportunity to control the Isles for themselves. In accepting MacDonald's and MacLean's offers of royal service, the king balanced the influence of the earls of Argyll against that of the Isles chieftains. The revolt was at an end. MacDonald and MacLean acknowledged the Crown's authority in the Isles, rather than Argyll's power.

It is difficult to conceive of an alternative course of action for Argyll, other than to accept the king's decision. Bothwell appeared to imagine that Argyll could join Crawford and himself in committing treason. But James had already made a firm impression in the Borders and, with the exception of Bothwell, the border magnates had accepted being warded without retaliation. To rebel against the king would bring in the English and the Douglases, and create a reversion to a long struggle for power similar to that of 1528–29. Also, the geographic disunity of a faction led by Argyll, Bothwell and Crawford had little prospect of success. Apart from this, James had built up a royal fleet in 1531 ready to be used against the Isles. Equally it could be used against the Campbells. Argyll may not have been able to count on the support of his kindred; Campbell of Cawdor had been appointed as sheriff of Nairn by the new régime.[92]

Like his uncle, Argyll had his public career to consider. Donaldson has stated that Argyll was out of favour for several years.[93] This was true in the sense that the king did not regard him as a favourite; James had no especial favourites among his magnates.[94] However, as a leading magnate, and the son of one who had given active service to the king in the struggle for power in 1528–29, Argyll was too important to be ignored. He was a regular and very frequent witness of great seal charters from 1530 to 1542.[95] He was the Justiciar, presiding over treason and other criminal trials,[96] and active on justice ayres.[97] He was hereditary Master of the Royal Household.[98] He served on the Borders in 1533, and ratified the Anglo-Scots peace at Holyrood in June 1534.[99] He was also vice-regent for the duration of the king's first abortive trip to France.[100] The Imperial ambassador to London, Chapuys, described Argyll in 1534 as 'the most warlike earl in Scotland'.[101] As such he was the obvious choice as a bodyguard for the king on the successful voyage to France.

On a more material level, it is interesting to note that the Angus regality of Abernethy was granted, for his good service, to the third earl of Argyll in December 1528. It was then regranted, for past and future service, to the fourth earl in November 1533. A further confirmation was made to Argyll on 9 June 1537, after the Rouen Act of Revocation. In this the preamble stated that the grant was being made for Argyll's past service in France, and in part compensation for sums expended by him in that service. Finally, Abernethy was resigned by Argyll and regranted to his son and heir in October 1542.[102] This was the sole portion of the Angus earldom not to be annexed to the Crown in 1540.[103] The implication is that the king was grateful for the third earl's service in 1528–29 and, regardless of his subsequent Isles policy, he did not intend to alienate the support of the fourth earl. Argyll remained a loyal servant of the Crown.

3. FINANCIAL RETURNS FROM THE ISLES, 1536–1542

The first royal circumnavigation of the Isles was incidental to its real purpose, to go to France. On 23 July 1536 a letter of safeguard was issued to the earl of Atholl at Pittenweem, to endure from that day until forty days after the return of the king 'agane within the realme'. Probably Atholl went with the king.[104] James was intending 'god willing this day to schip', and the Lords of Council were well aware of it.[105] Wine and spices were bought to supply the ships that were to accompany him.[106] This was not a secret expedition; if James was leaving the realm, patently he was not simply intending to visit the Isles, and it was highly unlikely that he should be seeking to visit England without a strong bodyguard. There was no secrecy in Scottish government about his intentions;[107] the subsequent lack of information about this first trip to France is accounted for both by the king's lack of desire to share his marital business with the English, and by the fact that it was a complete failure.[108] The five or six ships that did leave from the Fife coast sailed north, and the king landed at the Isle of Whithorn, Galloway, in mid-August, bad weather having sabotaged the journey. The embarrassment that this caused James meant that the whole affair was hushed up. The queen mother assured her brother, Henry VIII, that the purpose of the voyage was for her son to meet the English king, but that contrary winds had forced him to sail north.[109] Chapuys' Scottish sources informed him that the king had intended not to visit France, but rather Orkney, to put down disturbances.[110] Probably the most beneficial outcome of the affair was the compilation of Alexander Lindsay's *Rutter*, which gave precise instructions for navigating around the north coast of Scotland.[111] In 1538 – perhaps appropriately given the debacle of 1536 – 18s. 6d. was expended on the purchase of 'foure horologis and ane compas' for the royal flagship, the *Salamander*.[112]

Between this unplanned circumnavigation and the deliberate expedition of 1540, the Comptroller was able to collect Crown rents from Mull, Tiree, Morvern, and parts of Islay, and also from Trotternish. In Mull Hector MacLean of Duart acted as chamberlain, with the assistance of William Stirling of Glorat. Returns from Mull and the other areas under MacLean's jurisdiction totalled £299 for the years between 1534 and 1538, but the 1540 account was in arrears to the extent of £258.[113] In the same period, 1534–38, Argyll continued to account for Cowal and Rosneath, returning £80 each year.[114] The Crown was looking for rather more revenue from the Isles. On 11 August a letter under the privy seal, addressed 'to whom it concerns', charged the lieges 'that nane of zow tak apoun hand to mak ony impediment, lett or distrublance' to the king's chamberlains in Mull, Tiree, Ulva, Scarba, Lunga, Morvern, Belnahua, Islay, Colonsay, Trotternish, or Kintyre.[115] In fact, neither MacDonald, nor MacLean (nor even Argyll), appear to have been accounting for all of these islands, and several made no returns to the exchequer.

After the 1540 royal expedition to the Isles, the financial returns improved dramatically. The 1541 accounts are incomplete, but the 1542 accounts in several cases cover the previous two years. MacLean and one Duncan Stewart accounted between them for Mull, Morvern, Tiree, and Islay, and the Comptroller received £463 in 1540–41 and £491 in 1541–42.[116] Argyll returned £120 in 1541–42 for Cowal and Rosneath.[117] Further north, the earl of Moray acted as lessee for Trotternish (Skye) and returned £53 each year from 1530 to 1539. He was succeeded in 1540 by John MacKenzie of Kintail, who in 1542 returned a two-year account, producing £400 for the Comptroller, indicating that the annual return had almost doubled for the area.[118] In Ross, Moray's chamberlaincy came to an end in 1538, and the 1538–39 account was returned by one John Sherar.[119] New areas began to make their returns for the first time in the personal rule. Jura, Colonsay, and Ardnamurchan returned £244 for 1541–42. The south, mid ward and Rhinns of Islay returned £502 for the two-year period. £57 was obtained from Sleat (Skye) over three terms, and £8 from South Uist. A two-year account was rendered for Sunart by Duncan Stewart, but the £182 collected went to Stewart's father, Alan Stewart of Lismore, by letters under the privy seal.[120] To take into account the impact of the new and existing areas, the Comptroller established a base at Saddell castle in Kintyre in June 1541, and from there moved on to Dunivaig castle in Islay.[121] An extensive survey was carried out of the rentals of Islay, Tiree, Jura, Colonsay, Mull, Ardnamurchan, Sunart, Kintyre, Morvern, North Uist and Sleat. The conclusion was that the kindly tenancies yielded just over £500 *per annum* plus a considerable amount of beef, mutton, poultry, geese, oatmeal, cheese and beer. The task of the Comptroller and his commission was to set these lands into three-year tacks.[122]

The Comptroller's survey was the natural follow-up to the annexation of the Lordship of the Isles in the December 1540 parliament. The Act of Annexation extended to the 'lordship and lands of all the Isles, north and south office; the lands and castles of Kintyre; and the lands and lordship of Orkney and Shetland'.[123] This was a comprehensive description and the annexation, in turn, was the logical outcome of the royal expedition of the summer of 1540.

4. THE MACIAN INHERITANCE

However there was another contributory factor to the increased extent of the Crown lands and the rising revenues in 1541–42. This was the MacIan inheritance. John brayach MacIan of Ardnamurchan had been killed in 1519 in a local blood feud. He had been married to the sister of Colin, third earl of Argyll. Gift of the ward of his estates, offices and captaincy of Dunivaig castle was granted to the earls of Argyll, together with the marriage of his son, Alexander.[124] Alexander was one of the Isles chieftains encompassed in the offer of 'trew service' made by MacLean of Duart to the Crown in May 1530.[125] One of Alexander's sisters, Catherine, married MacDonald of Islay, who in his June 1531 remission was designated Alexander of Dunivaig.[126] This was the background to Northumberland's garbled report of September 1532, when he stated that Crawford had lost lands to Mackayn, and Argyll had lost the rule of the outer Isles.[127] Mackayn was either Alexander MacIan of Ardnamurchan or MacDonald of Islay, married to Catherine MacIan. Possibly the underlying cause of the whole Isles rebellion of 1528–31 was the dispute between the earls of Argyll and MacDonald of Islay over control of the MacIan inheritance.

Argyll retained an interest in the MacIan succession, even after MacDonald had replaced him as chamberlain of Kintyre. In July 1532 Argyll received a bond of manrent from one Angus MacIan,[128] and in June 1534 he arranged a contract of marriage for his first cousin, Mariota MacIan, sister to both Alexander and Catherine. The intended husband was John of Moidart, captain of Clanranald. A papal dispensation was required. Alexander witnessed the contract.[129] John of Moidart was appreciative of the terms and, 'for mony gratitudes and defendnys of him', granted Argyll various lands in Moidart.[130] The marriage took place.[131] In 1535, Argyll's uncles, Donald, abbot of Coupar Angus and Campbell of Skipness, acted as arbitrators in a dispute between Clanranald and MacLean of Duart.[132] By 1538 MacDonald of Islay, Alexander MacIan and John of Moidart were all dead,[133] and Mariota MacIan became the heiress to Islay, Ardnamurchan and Sunart, valued at £418 *per annum*.

However, the non-entries were assessed at the huge sum of £7747, representing twelve years of ward, since the death of her father, and six years thereafter, during which entry had not been taken.[134] There is no record of a composition being paid by Mariota. Possibly because she could not pay to take entry, she resigned her inheritance into the king's hands in favour of her cousin, Argyll.[135] In December 1540 a messenger was sent to the Isles to take sasine of the inheritance. Again, there is no record of a composition being paid by Argyll, and in fact he did not receive a royal charter to the MacIan inheritance.[136] By this time, the Act of Annexation had just been passed. James V now had a royal garrison with artillery stationed at Dunivaig castle, and James, son of Catherine and Alexander MacDonald of Islay, was in ward at Dunbar castle.[137] The only other member of the MacIan family with a potential claim to the MacIan inheritance appears to have been a minor;[138] and so in August 1541, by special precept and command of the king, the Treasurer paid £5000 to Argyll in respect of 'all and sindrie the landis, lordschippis and dominionis quhilkis pertenit to the airis of umquhill McKane in the Ilis and now pertenyng to Archibald, Erle of Ergile, heritablie be alienatioun, and resignit be him in our soverane lordis hands ad perpetuam remanentiam simpliciter'.[139]

Six months before this payment, on 9 February 1541, for his good service, Argyll was granted a new charter for the Angus regality of Abernethy, this coming two months after both the ratification of the Rouen revocation and the passing of the Act of Annexation.[140]

The £5000 pay-out to Argyll in 1541 exceeded the entire recorded Crown revenues from the Western Isles in the personal rule, quite apart from sums dispersed on royal expeditions. It is interesting that there was no attempt made to annex the MacIan inheritance to the Crown together with the Lordship of the Isles. Further, the king bought the inheritance; James did not attempt to reduce Argyll's title by arguing that the original gift of ward in 1519 fell on the grounds of being made in the royal minority. Nor was there a royal charter in Argyll's favour which could be revoked. All that was possible legally was for the king to demand non-entry payments from either Mariota or Argyll and allow them the lands, or alternatively purchase the inheritance. When the Comptroller was carrying out his survey of rentals in the Isles in the summer of 1541, he was dealing as much with casualty about to be purchased by the Crown as with newly annexed property. The 1540 expedition to the Isles daunted both alike.

The payment made to Argyll parallels the payment of £2000 made by the Treasurer in 1541 to Lord Methven in order for the Crown to reacquire the assigned lands of Glengavel and reinstate them in the newly annexed lordship of Avandale. In both these cases, a sharp contrast can be made with the Crown's annexation of the lordship of Liddesdale, until December 1540 part of the earldom of Bothwell. There is no record of any compensatory payment being made to the imprisoned earl of Bothwell. Argyll was being bought out of the Isles in 1541, and compensated both financially and with the grant of the Angus regality of Abernethy in Perthshire. That the Crown proceeded by this method indicates that Argyll was a major player in the Isles long after he had been sacked as chamberlain of Kintyre in 1531.

5. ORKNEY AND SHETLAND

As Crown property, the Isles were thrown into the package offered by James to Francis I as a marriage dowry. In 1532, the duchy of Orkney and Shetland and the Lordship of the Isles were given an annual value of 10,000 francs, or approximately £4500 Scots.[141] The earldom of Orkney alone was valued at £1000.[142] Yet in the same year, the Comptroller received just £413 of arrears from Orkney and Shetland, £106 in arrears from Trotternish, and £80 from Cowal and Rosneath – £600 in total.[143] In 1535, Margaret Hepburn, Lady Sinclair, returned £373 to the Comptroller for Orkney and Shetland, her whole turnover being £433.[144] Obviously there was room for improvement to match the figures being quoted to Francis I. Showing royal authority in person was one method of achieving a better financial return. Apart from this, it was good for the royal image as a dispenser of law and order. As James himself wrote to Henry VIII after the expedition, on 29 July 1540, he had taken the opportunity afforded by a peaceful spell on the Borders to visit the Isles 'for the ordouring of thame in justice and gude policy'.[145]

One incident of disorder was the attack, probably in 1539, on Eilean Donan castle.[146] In March 1541 a remission was granted to twenty-six Highlanders for their treasonable arson attack on the castle and destruction of the lands of Trotternish and Kinlochawe.[147] In 1538 John MacKenzie of Kintail, who was to replace Moray as lessee of Trotternish, was granted lands in the barony of Eilean Donan, after arguing successfully that they were not part of the Crown lands of Ross and Ardmannoch.[148] He appears to have been the favoured chieftain in the area, and Moray the man who was losing out. A further twenty Highlanders were charged in December 1539 with besieging Alexander MacLeod of Dunvegan in May 1539 in his house of Summerdaill.[149] Possibly the two incidents were connected. MacLeod himself was required to pay 1000 marks in January 1540 for a remission for his involvement in the 1516–19 rebellion of Donald of Lochalsh, and in the same month he surrendered possession of part of the bailiary of Trotternish to the Crown.[150] Further south, in Mull, Hector MacLean of Duart received a royal charter in January 1540, confirming him and his son in their lands in Mull, Knapdale, and Lochaber, these being united into the free barony of Duart. At the same time he obtained a general remission for all crimes.[151] Thus, even before the king went on his expedition, the Crown's policy was to attempt to woo some chieftains into capitulation through a policy of remission and reward.

Possibly the greatest disturbance in the Isles had been the battle of Summerdale, in Orkney, in the summer of 1529. There, William, fourth lord Sinclair, had been defeated by James Sinclair of Brecks. John Sinclair, third earl of Caithness, was killed fighting in support of his cousin, the fourth lord. Summerdale marked the end of a family feud amongst the Sinclairs for the control of Orkney and Shetland.[152] Ward of the earldom of Caithness went to Alexander Stewart, abbot-commendator of Scone, on 13 June 1529. On his death, the ward passed in March 1538 into the joint possession of James Kirkcaldy of Grange, Treasurer, and Oliver Sinclair of Pitcairn, who paid £1200 for the gift.[153] Pitcairn was the logical choice as recipient, as he was the first cousin of the third earl and probably the nearest surviving adult relative of the minor fourth earl.[154] The Scottish government in the summer of 1529 either thought that Lord Sinclair was killed or irrevocably captured at Summerdale, as the earl of Rothes was granted the ward of his estates on 9 June 1529.[155] At a later date, possibly still in 1529, Lord Sinclair handed in a bill of complaint to the Lords of Council giving his version of the feud.[156] The Scots government showed no interest.

Probably what annoyed James most about the whole episode was that it had taken place over the course of 1528–29, and thus had coincided with his own struggle for power. Margaret Tudor had informed her brother in June 1528 that Lord Sinclair was one of the first lords to join the king at Stirling after his escape from Angus' control.[157] Sinclair also attended parliament in September 1528 and in 1531. Thereafter he virtually disappears from view for the remainder of the personal rule. On 23 October 1542, he was granted a remission for treasonable assistance afforded to David Hume of Wedderburn and Lord Hume in the minority.[158] His mother, Margaret Hepburn, Lady Sinclair, was granted a remission on 16 July 1536 for her treasonable absence from the army at the Tantallon siege, for usurping royal authority and convening the lieges.[159] It is curious that she should have been forgiven for her son's default, but the message was clear. At a time when the king needed support to obtain power, Lord Sinclair had obtained royal letters and gone off to deal with his own local difficulties. The king had been deserted in his hour of need.

In the first part of his personal rule, James was not interested in the internal affairs of Orkney and Shetland. Lady Sinclair – rather than her son – was charged with making the annual returns and did so from 1529 to 1535. The annual return was £373 to the Comptroller, £20 to the bishopric of Orkney, and £40 to the royal falconers to convey birds' nests from the Northern Isles for the king's aviary.[160] In the winter of 1530–31, the earl of Moray was granted the lease of the northern Isles, for the same rental, but in fact never made any returns.[161] Possibly this was the matter to which the earl of Bothwell was referring in his December 1531 letter to Northumberland, when he stated that Moray was being disregarded. Moray had carried out a raid in Caithness and Sutherland in 1530,[162] and may have had designs on extending his lieutenancy into Orkney, with James' approval. If so, the king changed his mind on the matter, and Lady Sinclair continued making the returns.[163]

The situation changed in 1535. In June of that year, Sinclair of Brecks, the victor of Summerdale, was legitimised, knighted, and granted in feu farm the islands of Sanday and Stronsay, for 200 marks *per annum*.[164] In 1536, Sinclair made the annual return – of £273 – to the exchequer.[165] He was also absolved of blame for an act of piracy against an English merchant.[166] This was a deliberate policy on the part of the king to bring the 'usurper' into royal favour, at the expense of Lord Sinclair. However Sinclair of Brecks 'wilfully slew himself' in 1536.[167] Accordingly, on 16 July 1536, Lady Sinclair was granted a seven-year tack of the earldom, at the same rental.[168] It was in this context that the terms of her remission were framed. The usurpation of royal authority and convening the lieges referred to her son's challenge to Lord Sinclair's control in Orkney in 1528–29. In 1535–36. Sinclair of Brecks had been transformed into the upholder of royal authority. Lady Sinclair continued to make returns for the northern Isles until 1540.[169] On 19 September 1539 a general remission was granted to all supporters of Sinclair of Brecks for 'gadering of oure soverane lordis lieges in arrayt batell aganis umquhill Johne Erle of Cathnes'. This was not considered to be a treasonable offence.[170]

After the royal expedition to the Isles, Oliver Sinclair of Pitcairn became the lessor of Orkney and Shetland. He received a three-year tack in April 1541, replaced with a five-year term in August 1542. The annual rental was set at £2000. He was also given the keeping of Kirkwall castle, and justiciary powers.[171] In effect, though not confirmed *de jure* by the Crown, his predecessor and kinsman, Sinclair of Brecks, had exercised similar powers with royal sanction until his suicide.[172] In Pitcairn's first return, in 1542, the Comptroller received, in arrears, the sum of £1920, representing an annual return of £960. This was a considerable improvement on previous returns, with the promise of more to follow.[173] Given that Lord Sinclair was out of favour, Pitcairn was the logical choice as lessor, as cousin of both Lord Sinclair and Sinclair of Brecks, as well as of the third earl of Caithness.[174]

6. THE ROYAL EXPEDITION TO THE ISLES

The king's expedition to the Isles took place between 13 June and 6 July 1540.[175] James first referred to it on 29 July.[176] The expedition was originally scheduled to leave in May, departing from Leith.[177] It was delayed because of the birth of Prince James at St. Andrews on 22 May, on which day James wrote from St. Andrews to advise his uncle of the happy event.[178] Details of the preparations were not as elaborately recorded as in 1531, but the fleet consisted of the *Salamander*, the *Mary Willoughby*, the *Great Unicorn*, the *Little Unicorn*, and the *Lion*. The *Salamander*, a present from Francis I, was the flagship.[179] Five more ships were detailed for conveying the royal household and troops and a further three for victuals. The whole fleet was reckoned, from English reports, to be sixteen strong.[180] There was considerable activity in fitting out the fleet at Leith, under the direction of Lord Methven, and a great quantity of gunpowder and ordinance from Edinburgh castle was taken on board. One English commentator reported that:

> In all Scottlande was nott leffte 10 peces of ordenaunce besydes that wyche the Kynge doythe take wythe Hym.[181]

This was more than simply a 'luxury cruise'.[182]

Details of the personnel involved are supplied from English reports. Estimates as to the number of men ordered to report to Leith varied between two and four thousand. The earls of Argyll, Huntly, Marischal, Atholl, Arran, Erroll and Cassillis, together with Cardinal Beaton, the Master of Glencairn, and Lord Maxwell were to accompany the king. Huntly was to command five hundred troops from the north; Arran, five hundred from the west; and Beaton, five hundred from Fife and Forfar. The earl of Moray was detailed to remain on the Borders with a further five hundred men.[183] Huntly and Marischal were summoned by name in May 1540; other magnates were probably amongst the 'certane lordis and ladyis to be in Sanctandrois at the birth of my lord prince'.[184] Lesley, who amongst the sixteenth-century chroniclers gives the most coherent account of the expedition, stated that the king was accompanied by Arran, Huntly, Argyll, 'and mony utheris erlis, lordis, baronis'.[185] If the English reports can be accepted (and there is no particular reason for doubting them), then this was the group who – with the exception of the under-age Erroll and Cardinal

Beaton – sat on the trial of Hamilton of Finnart less than two months later. It was also a group largely composed of James' contemporaries, or near-contemporaries in age. Probably the oldest amongst them was Lord Maxwell, aged around fifty, and a veteran campaigner.[186] These were younger magnates, more energetic for fighting, and probably in the same mood for adventure as their king and leader. James made his will at Leith on 11 June, nominating his son's tutors in the event of his death. These were the reliable Montrose, the absent Lennox, nearest in line to the succession should James and Arran both be drowned on the voyage, and his former tutor, Lord Erskine.[187] The Lords of Council were instructed to invoke the act of Twizelhaugh to protect the heirs of those who died in royal service, and the expedition set off.[188]

The precise itinerary cannot be plotted. The king went to Orkney, for it was there that the queen addressed her letters from St. Andrews.[189] It is likely that the king met with Robert Maxwell, bishop of Orkney;[190] for the bishops had traditionally been the main representatives of royal Stewart authority in the northern Isles, before becoming eclipsed by the Sinclair family.[191] In April 1541, James nominated as Maxwell's successor, Robert Reid, abbot of Kinloss, a man who had given good service as a judge on the session,[192] as well as being employed on diplomatic embassies to both England and France.[193] James advised the pope that Reid was the ideal person both for religious development and 'the improvement of manners'.[194] The expedition probably went from Orkney to Lewis, following the directions of Lindsay's *Rutter*. Lesley states that the king met with Rory MacLeod of Lewis,[195] who had been admitted to the barony of Lewis in June 1538. Argyll lent him 500 marks to pay the composition.[196] MacLeod was appointed as royal commissioner of justice in Lewis in 1540 and again in 1542.[197] Lewis remained outwith the scope of the Comptroller's 1541 survey of Crown lands, and does not appear to have become part of the Crown's patrimony under the Act of Annexation.

The *Treasurer's Accounts* then refer to the king being generally in the Isles.[198] No royal charters or letters were issued on the expedition. If the fleet were following the directions given in the *Rutter*, then from Lewis it would have passed to Trotternish, Kintail, Ardamurchan, Mull, Islay, Knapdale and Kintyre, and ending at Dumbarton. Bishop Lesley gives substantially the same route.[199] On 6 June 1540 a messenger had been sent to Dumbarton, Ayr and Irvine instructing these burghs to send boats 'witht victualis to meit the Kingis grace in the Ilis the vi day of Julii nixt to cum'. The king was back in Edinburgh by 6 July, so probably had favourable winds.[200] Lesley comments that the king received, in turn, MacLeod of Harris, the laird of Glengarry, John of Moidart, and also one Maclane (possibly Angus Maclan?) and James O'Neill, 'the tua principall capitanes of the small ilis'.[201] The outcome of these meetings was that a group of unidentified Highlanders was conveyed to Dunbar and Tantallon castles and to the Bass Rock. Possibly the highest ranking of these – the only named individual – was James MacDonald of Islay, who before the expedition had been the recipient of bows and arrows from the king.[202] His capture was probably to keep him out of the way whilst the Crown proceeded with the purchase and survey of the MacIan inheritance. The other Highlanders had not been so much kidnapped as handed over as hostages for the good rule of their chieftains. Probably, with the firepower at his disposal, there had been a degree of gunboat diplomacy by James and his magnates.[203] The king also left troops and cannon at Dunivaig and Iland (Port Ellen?) castles on Islay.[204]

After he had returned to Edinburgh, James informed Henry VIII that 'justice and gude policy' might be achieved in the Isles in time.[205] The magnate who rose to prominence in the Isles was William Cunningham, Master, and by May 1541 fourth earl, of Glencairn,[206] a man well suited for the task of daunting the Isles. He had financial experience as Treasurer in the minority,[207] and was also regarded as a naval commander. In 1531 he offered to furnish five ships at his own expense and sail to the assistance of Christian II of Denmark, with his king's approval. Ill health prevented him from carrying out this offer.[208] However, in 1538 he and Lord Maxwell sailed for France to escort Mary of Guise to Scotland.[209] In the 1540 expedition the Master of Glencairn was described as the vice-admiral by the English.[210] After the king's return from the Isles, the Master remained in Kintyre and the *Little Forfar* was sent there for his use.[211] In June 1541, as earl of Glencairn, he was one of the commissioners at Saddell castle in Kintyre.[212] Both he and his son, Alexander, Master of Glencairn, took entry to holdings in Kintyre.[213] Glencairn's youngest son, William, had already been appointed as bishop of Argyll and abbot-commendator of Saddell monastery in 1539.[214] Interestingly, in the same year, another son, Andrew, was forgiven by the king and remitted his goods after being 'abjurit of heresy befor the spirituale juge'.[215] The Comptroller's commission passed from Saddell to Dunivaig castle in July 1541, and possibly met with some opposition, as gunpowder barrels were sent to Glencairn's servants in the Isles.[216] In December 1541, Sir Thomas Wharton reported from Carlisle to the English privy council that the Master of Glencairn, Cassillis and the Master of Eglinton had been sent to the north of Scotland, where there had been 'somme rebellion and men slayn laitly'. The official records indicate that Glencairn was to pass to Kintyre in November 1541.[217] In May 1542 the Master of Glencairn was appointed as governor in the bounds of Kintyre with shrieval powers, the appointment being for one year or longer, 'enduring the king's will'.[218] After Solway Moss, the English officers at Berwick-upon-Tweed advised Henry VIII that:

> the Keterickes being in the northe parties be angrye with the takinge of their lorde therle of Glencarne, and that they woll come to the Bordures and make an invasion to fetche him home.[219]

The Cunninghams appear to have achieved some popularity amongst the locals for their contribution towards the daunting.

James achieved considerable success in his daunting of the Isles, both in raising

Crown revenues, and in increasing their extent, through annexation and by purchase. He also received from the Isles' chiefs at least an acknowledgement of royal authority, though for some, such as Sinclair of Brecks, the king was simply recognising the *status quo*. To a degree, the influence of his magnates was undermined, his half-brother Moray and the hapless Lord Sinclair both giving way to lesser men. In the west, the uprising of MacDonald of Islay was ended, and both he and MacLean of Duart entered into the Crown's service. Argyll's offer of 1531 to daunt the Isles, where he and his 'frennidis hes als gret experience',[220] was turned down and MacDonald capitulated. The daunting which followed in 1540 was achieved with James leading and Argyll following.

In March 1541, for his past service in France and in Scotland, Argyll received charters of confirmation to all of the lands of his earldom united in the free baronies of Lorne and Lochawe, with Dunstaffnage and Inchconnell castles as the principal seats.[221] On 22 October 1542, the Master of Argyll was infeft in fee in the earldom.[222] However, the most significant grant was again made for the earl's past service in France and for his part in resisting the English enemy. The Master was granted the offices of lieutenant, sheriff, commissioner and chamberlain of Argyll; justice and sheriff of Lorne; and justice, sheriff, coroner and chamberlain of the lands and lordship of Knapdale and Kintyre, all of which had been resigned by the earl. These offices were the same as those which Argyll had himself received in fee from the third earl in 1526.[223]

Clearly these grants and confirmations were an acknowledgement of the importance of Argyll to the king. Although Argyll had not in fact exercised the office of chamberlain of Argyll since yielding this responsibility to the Comptroller's staff in 1531, he was still the most influential magnate in the Isles, and this was recognised by James. Argyll had lost no titles or offices in the west. However, the 1542 charters came after the king had changed the balance of power in the Isles. The Crown was now the dominant player. The success of the royal 'daunting' was such that no further rebellion in the Isles took place until 1545, three years after James' death, and with Scotland again lacking an adult ruler.[224]

NOTES

1. Brown, *op.cit.*, 93–105.
2. McGladdery, *op.cit.*, 62–3, 105.
3. Macdougall, *James III*, 121–5.
4. Macdougall, *James IV*, 100–5, 115–6.
5. *Acts of the Lords of the Isles* 1336–1493, edd. J. 38; R.W. Munro [Munro, *Isles*] (SHS, 1986), 314; cf. e.g. *TA*, v, 237.
6. *ER*, xv, 430, 434; xvi, 102, 181, 242, 334, 419, 448.
7. *RMS*, iii, no. 345; *RSS*, i, nos. 3871, 3873.
8. Wormald, *Bonds*, App. A, 179, no. 8.
9. *ER*, xv, 430–434, 454.

10. Munro, *Isles*, 294: i.e. 'Alexander, son of John Cathanach'. The Macdonalds of Islay were only distant kinsmen of the Lords of the Isles; cf. *ibid.*, 292 *et passim*.
11. *ER*, xv, 430, 433; *RMS*, iii, no. 345.
12. *ADCP*, 276; Pitcairn, *Trials*, i, pt. i, 139.
13. Pitcairn, *Trials*, i, pt. i, 140 (lairds of Wigtown and Galloway).
14. *Ibid.*, i, pt. i, 139–41.
15. *ER*, xv, 431–4; cf. Munro, *Isles*, 284, for the MacIan family tree.
16. *ADCP*, 291.
17. *Ibid*; the likelihood is that he simply continued to hold office after his initial three year term expired in 1520
18. *Ibid.*, 277, 294; *HMC Fourth Report*, 485, no. 242.
19. *ER*, xvi, 104–5.
20. *RSS*, ii, nos. 938–9.
21. Donaldson, *op.cit.*, 50.
22. *ADCP*, 313–4; *TA*, v, 373.
23. *ADCP*, 314, 316–7.
24. His son was first designated as earl on 28 October 1529, though this may have been as the feuar: *RSS*, ii, no. 402. One great seal charter, *RMS*, iii, no. 861, indicates the third earl was still alive on 4 November. The fourth earl was acting fully as such by 15 January 1530: *ibid.*, iii, no. 932.
25. *RSS*, ii, no. 402; *RMS*, iii, no. 345; *APS*, ii, 325. There was an exchange of lands in August 1529 with Helen, daughter of the first earl of Arran, suggesting a marriage contract: *RMS*, iii, nos. 826–7. However by 1542 Argyll was married to Margaret Graham (daughter of the earl of Menteith) and had a son, who was then infeft as feuar of the earldom: *ibid.*, iii, nos. 2811–6.
26. *ADCP*, 326–7; *TA*, v, 379, 381.
27. *ADCP*, 328–9, 240.
28. *James V Letters*, 177–8.
29. *ADCP*, 342, 345–6.
30. *Ibid.*, 345–6, 348–9.
31. *TA*, vi, 458, 462.
32. *Ibid.*, v, 444, 461–2.
33. *James V Letters*, 189–90.
34. *ADCP*, 353.
35. *APS*, ii, 333.
36. *ADCP*, 365; *TA*, v, 435, 461–2.
37. *RSS*, ii, nos. 938–9.
38. *James V Letters*, 191–200; *ADCP*, 358.
39. *TA*, v, 458.
40. SRO, RH 2.1.9. (*ADC*, vol. 42, ff. 169, 173, 185). Cf. Pitscottie, *Historie*, i, 351, who stated that the 'king passit to the Iillis' just after James had warded the Borderers (in 1530). Pitscottie was probably referring to the 1540 expedition; his chronology is confused. He places the trip between the deaths of Lady Glamis and the Master of Forbes (in 1537) and the king's marriage to Madeleine (in 1536–7).
41. Donaldson, *op.cit.*, 50.
42. *ADCP*, 343–4; *TA*, v, 449.
43. SRO, RH 2.1.9. (*ADC*, vol. 41, f. 154; 42, f. 144); *ADCP*, 345, 353; *APS*, ii, 331.
44. SRO, *ADC*, vol. 42, f. 185.
45. *Ibid.*, vol. 41, f. 134; *ADCP*, 343–4.
46. SRO, RH 2.1.9. (*ADC*, vol. 42, f. 185); *ADCP*, 356.
47. *ER*, xvi, 104–5.
48. SRO, RH 2.1.9. (*ADC*, vol. 42, f. 186).
49. *ADCP*, 323, 357–8.

50. *Ibid.*, 356–8.
51. *Ibid.*, 326–7.
52. *ER*, xv, 103.
53. *ADCP*, 365–6.
54. *TA*, vi, 54.
55. SRO, *ADC*, vol. 43, f. 110.
56. *LP Henry VIII*, v, no. 595.
57. *Scots Peerage*, i, 337 ff.; cf. *RMS*, iii, nos. 826–7; cf. n. 25.
58. *LP Henry VIII*, v, no. 1286.
59. SRO, RH 2.1.9. (*ADC*, vol. 43, ff. 103, 106, 118, 171, 140–1, 145, 150); *RMS*, iii, nos. 1104, 1152, 1158.
60. Glasgow University, Argyll Tss., iv, no. 12; Wormald, *Bonds*, 122–3.
61. *TA*, vi, 113.
62. *RSS*, ii, nos. 1030–1083.
63. *LP Henry VIII*, v, no. 1246.
64. *TA*, vi, 95, 124.
65. SRO, *ADCS*, ii, f. 115.
66. *LP Henry VIII*, vi, no. 610; *SP Venetian*, iv, no. 956; *TA*, vi, 136; SRO, *ADCS*, iii, f. 51v; *ER*, xvi, 566; xvii, 90.
67. *TA*, vi, 98, 178, 215; *RMS*, iii, nos. 1306–8.
68. *James V Letters*, 249; *RMS*, iii, nos. 1309–10.
69. *TA*, vi, 179.
70. *Ibid.*, vi, 233; *RMS*, iii, nos. 1311–4.
71. *TA*, vi, 227–31, 233–6.
72. *SP Henry VIII*, iv, pt. iv, no. cclii.
73. Cf. Chapter 8, n. 75.
74. *RSS*, ii, no. 1527; SRO, *ADCS*, ii, f. 115; xi, f. 181.
75. *ADCS*, 358.
76. *RSS*, ii, no. 1525.
77. Wormald, *Bonds*, App. A, 300, no. 106.
78. *ER*, xvi, 566.
79. E.g. *LP Henry VIII*, vi, nos. 821, 1586; vii, nos. 211, 1350; viii, 448, 1051; ix, nos. 514–5; x, no. 822; xiii, pt. i, nos. 1138, 1447; xiii, pt. ii, nos. 159, 1032; xv, nos. 82, 736; xvi, no. 90; xvii, no. 554 *et passim*.
80. *Ibid.*, vii, no. 1336; viii, nos. 189, 429, 1009.
81. *Ibid.*, xiv. pt. i, no. 1027; *TA*, vi, 223, 262; vii, 194.
82. *RSS*, ii, nos. 953, 1192.
83. *ER*, xvi, 291, 344, 480.
84. *TA*, vi, 154; *LP Henry VIII*, vi, no. 51.
85. *ER*, xvi, 102, 129, 288, 448, 480.
86. *TA*, vi, 40, 96, 208, 304, 428.
87. *Ibid.*, 36, 92, 203, 209, 212.
88. Pitcairn, *Trials*, i, pt. i, 170–1.
89. Munro, *Isles*, 294.
90. Wormald, *Bonds*, 108.
91. On the assumption that he was twenty-one when he succeeded his father in 1529–30, without the necessity of a wardship. Equally he may have been ten or more years older than this. He was feuar of the earldom in 1526; his son was feuar in 1542: cf. notes 24–5. If a feuar was appointed invariably at his age of majority then Argyll would be over twenty-five in 1531, with his son being born in 1521, Argyll then aged fifteen or sixteen. However Argyll appears to have first married in 1529, indicating that an heir did not have to be of age to be appointed feuar. If a feuar was appointed at age fourteen or over, then Argyll could easily be just twenty-three in 1531. He died in 1558.

92. *RMS*, iii, no. 723 (3 January 1529).
93. Donaldson, *op.cit.*, 51.
94. Finnart being the one possible exception, for his role as a Household servant building royal palaces, rather than for his earlier magnatial role.
95. *RMS*, iii, nos. 939 (20 May 1530), 2828 (26 October 1542) *et passim*.
96. Pitcairn, *Trials*, i, pt. i, 183 (the trial of the Master of Forbes) *et passim*; *APS*, ii, 362 (trial of Finnart). Pitcairn does not indicate whether or not Argyll presided over Lady Glamis' trial (she being married to his uncle, Campbell of Skipness).
97. *TA*, vi, 266; vii, 338.
98. *RSS*, ii, no. 402; *RMS*, iii, nos. 972 (21 October 1530), 2343 (27 April 1541) *et passim*. The other 'masters' who appear were presumably deputies, e.g. James Learmonth of Dairsie: *ibid.*, iii, no. 1733 (10 December 1537); Patrick Wemyss of Pittencrieff: *ibid*, iii, no. 1838 (16 September 1538).
99. *LP Henry VIII*, vii, no. 911.
100. *ADCP*, 458.
101. *LP Henry VIII*, vii, no. 1057.
102. *RMS*, iii, nos. 716, 1318, 1672, 2813.
103. *Ibid.*, no. 2233; *APS*, ii, 404; Kelley, *Tenure*, 82.
104. *RSS*, ii, no. 2113; Abell, *op.cit.*, f. 125v only records the presence of Finnart.
105. *ADCP*, 455.
106. *TA*, vi, 451–2.
107. Both Abell, *op.cit.*, f. 125v, and *Diurnal of Occurrents*, 21, record that the king left for France with the consent of his Lords of Council. Cf. *SP Henry VIII*, v, pt. iv, no. cccv, where one English officer at Berwick-upon-Tweed reported the rumour that James intended to visit Henry VIII.
108. Despite this, Thomas Cromwell guessed correctly that James was intending going to France: *LP Henry VIII*, xi, nos. 220, 286.
109. *SP Henry VIII*, v, pt. iv, no. ccclxxiv (wrongly dated). It is perfectly feasible that James and his council should not have advised his mother of his plans, given her frequent communications with her brother. The number of ships was put at five in *Diurnal of Occurrents*, 21. English reports varied on the exact number probably because the fleet was dispersed by the bad weather.
110. *LP Henry VIII*, xi, nos. 220, 358.
111. Alexander Lindsay: *A Rutter of the Scottish Seas* (*Maritime Monographs and Reports* no. 44, 1980). This is an edited version of the account published by Nicholas de Nicolay entitled 'La Navigation de Roy d'Ecosse Jaques cinquiesme du nom . . .' (1583) also entitled (misleadingly) 'The Life and Death of King James the Fifth', ed. *Miscellanea Scotica* 1818–20, iv. Though the latter title suggests a chronicle source, it is nothing of the sort, being simply de Nicolay's translation of Lindsay's *Rutter*.
112. *TA*, viii, 159.
113. *ER*, xvii, 90–92, 157, 355.
114. *Ibid.*, xvi, 389, 480; xvii, 16–17; Argyll's next account was made in 1539 for a two-year period. His return was largely in the form of goods in kind, 44 *martes* each year, each one worth two marks.
115. *RSS*, ii, no. 2117.
116. *ER*, xvii, 485–6, 526–8, 535.
117. *Ibid.*, xvii, 569–70.
118. *Ibid.*, xvi, 214, 283, 327, 433; xvii, 18, 79, 218. 492.
119. *Ibid.*, xvii, 110, 227; *ADCP*, 469.
120. *ER*, xvii, 539–41, 545, 550, 556–7. Alan Stewart of Lismore was probably Stewart of Duror who gave his bond of manrent to Argyll in 1531: Wormald, *Bonds*, App. A, 181, no. 21.
121. *ER*, xvii, 611, 625, 649.
122. *Ibid.*, xvii, 611, 614, 620–2, 624–5, 649–50.

123. *RMS*, iii, no. 2233; *APS*, ii, 361, 405.
124. *RSS*, i, no. 3048; Munro, *Isles*, 285.
125. *ADCP*, 328–9.
126. Munro, *Isles*, 285; *RSS*, ii, no. 938.
127. *LP Henry VIII*, vi, no. 1286.
128. Glasgow University, Argyll Tss., iv, no. 13. It is not clear who Angus was; he does not appear in the MacIan family tree: cf. Munro, *Isles*, 284.
129. Glasgow University, Argyll Tss., iv, no. 27.
130. *Ibid.*, iv, no. 31; *HMC Fourth Report*, 482, no. 173.
131. *RMS*, iii, no. 1396.
132. SRO, *ADCS*, vi, f. 138; cf. Pitcairn, *Trials*, i, pt. i, 169–70. Campbell of Lundy and Campbell of Ardkinglass acted for MacLean of Duart.
133. Munro, *Isles*, 285, 294. MacDonald died in 1536. John of Moidart may not have died but rather had his marriage declared void. Mariota married Robert Robertson of Struan on 18 March 1539.
134. *ER*, xvii, 750–1; it is not clear why her sister, Catherine, did not appear to share in this inheritance; she was still alive: *Ibid*, xvii, 544.
135. Glasgow University, Argyll Tss., iv, no. 73, with the consent of her second husband.
136. *TA*, vii, 416, presumably for Argyll, but this is not clear. Argyll was sheriff of Argyll and Tarbert and thus responsible for responding for the non-entry.
137. *ER*, xvii, 278–9, 296.
138. Alexander, son of Somerled, cousin of James, and niece of both Mariota and Alexander MacIan deceased: Munro, *Isles*, 284.
139. *TA*, vii, 470.
140. *RMS*, iii, no. 2277.
141. The exchange rate was 9s. Scots for 2.25 francs; cf. *TA*, vi, 412, 467–8.
142. *James V Letters*, 216, 258, 298, 341.
143. *ER*, xvi, 167. Technically only Trotternish was in the Lordship: cf. Munro, *Isles*, Pref. xxx *et passim*.
144. *ER*, xvi, 434–5.
145. *James V Letters*, 404.
146. Said to have been led by Donald Gorm of Sleat, a descendant of Alexander, Lord of the Isles, who was killed in the attack. There is no trace of him in the official records, but cf. Munro, *Isles*, 309.
147. *RSS*, ii, no. 3943.
148. *RMS*, iii, no. 1832; SRO, *ADCS*, x, 4v. MacKenzie claimed that his ancestor had received a charter from James IV. Moray's charter to Ross and Ardmannoch was reduced on the grounds of their being annexed lands and thus being set out in rental required parliamentary consent. Moray's original lease had been from Margaret Tudor, in 1524: *ADCP*, 469.
149. Pitcairn, *Trials*, i, pt. i, 225.
150. *RSS*, ii, no. 3287; *TA*, vii, 243, 281; viii, 17; Munro, *Isles*, 306.
151. *RSS*, ii, no. 3338; *RMS*, iii, no. 2065.
152. Clouston, *op.cit.*, 58–9, no. xxv; Anderson, *Orkney*, 22.
153. *RSS*, ii, nos. 156, 2458.
154. The third earl and Pitcairn had the same grandfather in William Sinclair, earl of Orkney: cf. Anderson, *Orkney*, 19 and B.E. Crawford, 'William Sinclair, earl of Orkney, and his family: A Study in the Politics of Survival' in Stringer, *Nobility*, 244. The third earl had one brother, Alexander of Stamster, whose career went unremarked in the personal rule.
155. *RSS*, ii, no. 151. Alternatively he was still under the age of twenty-one at the time of the battle of Summerdale. He died in 1570: Anderson, *Orkney*, 22.
156. Clouston, *op.cit.*, 57, no. xxv.
157. *LP Henry VIII*, iv, pt. ii, no. 4532; cf. Lang *op.cit.*, i, Pref. xv-xvi (same report quoted in full).

158. *RSS*, ii, no. 4951. This either made him very young at the time that the treasonable assistance was given, or very old at the time of his death in 1570; cf. n. 155.
159. *Ibid.*, ii, no. 2091.
160. *ER*, xv, 488, 530, 540; xvi, 29–30, 434.
161. *RSS*, ii, no. 766; *RMS*, iii, no. 988.
162. *ADCP*, 331.
163. *ER*, xvi, 120, 129, 213.
164. *RSS*, ii, no. 1697; *RMS*, iii, no. 1479. Clouston, *op.cit.*, 220, points out that this charter had dubious legal validity as the land tenure system in Orkney was udal not feudal.
165. *ER*, xvi, 480.
166. *RSS*, ii, no. 1665.
167. *Ibid.*, ii, no. 2999 (gift of escheat to his wife in 1539); *ER*, xvi, 480; Anderson, *Orkney*, 27. Cf. reference to this suicide in Abell, *op.cit.*, f. 124v.
168. *RSS*, ii, no. 2088.
169. *ER*, xvii, 12–13, 354–5.
170. *RSS*, ii, no. 3151. Technically the remission was to all adherents of Edward Sinclair of Strome, brother of Sinclair of Brecks; cf. Anderson, *Orkney*, 19.
171. *RSS*, ii, nos. 3989, 4856.
172. Cf. Anderson, *Orkney*, 22, 25. It is not clear who controlled the castle thereafter; probably his brother, Edward of Strome.
173. *ER*, xvii, 523–4. This was a two year account.
174. Anderson, *Orkney*, 19 (family tree of William, earl of Orkney).
175. *James V Letters*, 401–2 (James writing from Edinburgh on 12 June and 6 July); *RMS*, iii, nos. 2177 (charter issued at Leith on 12 June), 2178 (8 July, at Edinburgh); *RSS*, ii, no. 3579 (Leith, 13 June); *TA*, vii, 353 ('departing of the schippes the xii day of Junii').
176. *James V Letters*, 404.
177. *LP Henry VIII*, xv, nos. 6322, 634; *SP Henry VIII*, v, pt. iv, no. ccclxxiii.
178. Dunbar, *Scot. Kings*, 238; *SP Henry VIII*, v, pt. iv, no. ccclxxi.
179. *TA*, vii, 352–3, 420–1, 465; *SP Henry VIII*, v, pt. iv, no. ccclxxiii; *LP Henry VIII*, xii, pt. i, no. 1286.
180. *SP Henry VIII*, v, pt. v, no. ccclxxiii.
181. *Ibid.*, v, pt. iv, no. ccclxxii; *TA*, vii, 341–358; viii, 153–4.
182. Cf. Donaldson, *op.cit.*, 58, who appears to adopt a disapproving tone at so much expenditure on 'conspicuous luxuries'.
183. *SP Henry VIII*, v, pt. v, nos. ccclxxii-iii; *LP Henry VIII*, xv, no. 634. Moray departed for France in June 1540.
184. *TA*, vii, 309.
185. Lesley, *History*, 156 (wrongly placed in 1538).
186. His age can only be estimated: cf. *Scots Peerage*, vi, 479–80. He married first in 1509.
187. The witnesses were James Learmonth of Dairsie, Master (depute) of the king's Household; Sir James Kirkcaldy of Grange, Treasurer; Sir Thomas Erskine of Brechin, Secretary; and James Foulis of Colinton, clerk register: *HMC, Mar 38*.
188. *ADCP*, 488. The royal instructions were written on 13 June, at 'the raid on seyburd', possibly meaning simply that they were written once the king had embarked and was 'on seaboard'.
189. *TA*, vii, 328.
190. Lesley, *History*, 156, states that the royal party was 'honorablie ressavit' by the bishop.
191. Anderson, *Orkney*, 13, 16–17, 20–1.
192. *ADCP*, 349, 368, 374 (as vice-president of the College of Justice), 426. He was appointed as one of the ordinary lords of session: cf. P.G.B. McNeill, *op.cit.*, 213.
193. *James V Letters*, 271–2, 298, 303–5, 314 (as procurator for James' intended marriage to Mary of Bourbon).
194. *Ibid.*, 423.

195. *Lesley*, History, 156.
196. *ER*, xvii, 758–9; *RSS*, ii, no. 2514; *ADCP*, 469. MacLeod was unable to sign his name on his bond of relief to Argyll.
197. *ER*, xvii, 770, 773.
198. *TA*, vii, 402, 420–1, 445.
199. Lesley, *History*, 156–7.
200. *TA*, vii, 317; *James V Letters*, 402.
201. Lesley, *History*, 156–7.
202. *TA*, vii, 194, 323; *ER*, xvii, 296.
203. Cf. Donaldson, *op.cit.*, 51, who states that the Highland and Island chiefs 'submitted to kidnapping as readily now as they had done under James I and were to do again under James VI'.
204. *TA*, vii, 328, 438; *ER*, xvii, 278–9. Also at Lochbrone (?Lochbroom) castle.
205. *James V Letters*, 404.
206. *ADCP*, 504; cf. *Scots Peerage*, iv, 235ff.
207. *TA*, v, 270.
208. *James V Letters*, 186–7, 198–9.
209. *TA*, vi, 392; *RSS*, ii, no. 2656; *LP Henry VIII*, xiii, pt. i, no. 757.
210. *LP Henry VIII*, xv, no. 634. Maxwell held the office of 'great admiral': *RSS*, ii, no. 2656.
211. *TA*, vii, 394, 400.
212. *ADCP*, 504; *ER*, xvii, 625.
213. *ER*, xvii, 626, 630–1.
214. *James V Letters*, 364; *RSS*, ii, no. 3364; Watt, *Fasti*, 27, in succession to a Montgomery.
215. *RSS*, ii, no. 2952.
216. *ER*, xvii, 611, 6633; *TA*, viii, 118.
217. *HP*, i, no. 106, Wharton naming them as Cassillis, Master Montgomery and Master Kilmaurs; *TA*, viii, 40.
218. *RSS*, ii, no. 4631.
219. *HP*, i, no. 254 (12 December 1542).
220. *ADCP*, 357.
221. *RMS*, iii, nos. 2305–6.
222. *Ibid.*, iii, nos. 2811–5.
223. *Ibid.*, iii, nos. 345, 2816.
224. Cf. the assessment made by Lynch, *op.cit.*, 168.

CHAPTER ELEVEN

Wealth and Patronage

I. SOURCES OF INCOME

Bishop Lesley concluded his study of the personal rule of James V with the remark that 'he by his hiech pollicye mervellouslie riched his realme and him selfe'.[1] After his death there was found over £26,000 in the king's boxes at Edinburgh Castle, marginally exceeding the sums spilling out of his grand-father's box into the Sauchieburn mud.[2] Both Pitscottie and Buchanan wrote of the king's 'covettousnes' and 'keenness for money', the latter chronicler ex-plaining that this was due to the 'utmost parsimony' with which he had been educated in his minority.[3]

A more significant comment – because it comes from a contemporary source – was made by Lord Wharton at Carlisle in a letter to Thomas Cromwell. On 5 September 1539, Wharton wrote that the king 'inclynethe daylye more and more to covitousse'. Wharton's spy had told him that the earl of Bothwell was about to leave the country and that 'the Kyng hayth takyn Liddesdaylle to hys own possession'. Moray and Huntly were also in the king's 'dysplesure', and had lost 'divers other londes'.[4] Naturally Wharton, in common with all English border officers, was looking for potential areas of weakness in the Scottish government which might be exploited by his master. It was true that Liddesdale had been administered either directly or indirectly by the Crown since 1534, after the Hepburn family had been allowed a further opportunity to control the area. Liddesdale was inalienably annexed to the Crown in 1540. Bothwell was exiled in 1541 and was successfully subverted by Henry VIII in 1542. Moray and Huntly were both casualties of the 1537 Act of Revocation, Moray losing the chamber-laincy of Ross and Ardmannoch, and Huntly his feu of Strathdee, Braemar and Cromar. These were Crown lands, and as such their loss was not comparable with the confiscation of Bothwell's heritage. James was perhaps 'covetous' in his annexing of Liddesdale, but the circumstances of the area were particular. It would be reasonable to argue that Bothwell should have forfeited his entire earldom immediately following the discovery of his treasonable communications with the earl of Northumberland in 1531.

Professors Mitchison and Donaldson have considered the pursuit of wealth to be the prime driving force behind all James' policies in the personal rule. Donaldson has argued that 'the sense of insecurity among the king's subjects must have become more acute as his 'covetousness' became more pronounced'.[5]

Such a predatory king would certainly have created a crisis in Crown-magnate relations during the personal rule; but as with Wharton's interpretation of the factors contributing to James' supposed 'covitousse' in 1539, so Donaldson's use of the downfall of Hamilton of Finnart to illustrate the adverse effects of the king's 'covoutness' on his nobility is unsustainable. Finnart was not so much an example as an isolated case.

James went through two Comptrollers – Robert Barton of Over-Barnton and James Colville of Ochiltree, latterly Sir James of East Wemyss – before the appointment of David Wood of Craig, formerly master of the larder, in 1538.[6] He had three Treasurers – Robert Cairncross, abbot of Holyrood, Robert Barton, and William Stewart, dean of Glasgow and latterly bishop of Aberdeen – before James Kirkcaldy of Grange was appointed, again in 1538.[7] The difficulties which these men faced in attempting to balance their accounts is a subject dealt with in detail by Dr. Athol L. Murray.[8] Murray also notes the various fates of James' Comptrollers. Barton faced a charge of deforcement in 1538.

In the same year Colville was called to appear before a judicial session of parliament to answer a summons of treason. The substance of this was that Colville had been implicated in a shady deal over the ward of Kennedy of Culzean in 1528. He had attempted to assign the profits of this to the former Treasurer, Archibald Douglas of Kilspindie, after the latter had been charged with treason in July 1528. The lords hearing the case ten years later were Moray (as presiding judge), Arran, Cassillis, Rothes, and Maxwell. The earls of Erroll and Marischal also sat as, respectively, Constable and Marshal of parliament.[9] Like Robert Leslie of Innerpeffray, Colville was dead when the summons was raised again in parliament in 1540, and in 1541 his estates were annexed to the Crown.[10]

1538 appears to have been the year for the downfall of royal officers. Adam Otterburn of Auldhame, latterly Sir Adam Otterburn of Redhall, the king's advocate, was replaced by Henry Lauder. Otterburn's offence was one of treasonable communications with the Douglases after their forfeiture.[11] Possibly he was in some way involved in Colville's attempt to defraud the Crown. After being warded at Dumbarton castle, he was fined £2000 and pardoned in 1539. Mr. John Chisholm, who can be identified as being involved in Colville's scam, was fined £1000 in 1541.[12] Both Otterburn and Colville were commissioners in Newcastle during the Anglo-Scots truce negotiations of 1533, and in 1538 Colville faced charges not only of fraud but also of communicating with the Douglases, who were at Newcastle in 1533.[13]

It is unlikely that the king cared greatly about the problems of his financial officers in their attempts to balance the budget, especially as some of them had not been acting in his best interests during his struggle for power in 1528–29. They were eminently replaceable from within the ranks of the Household. So too was Adam Otterburn from amongst the numerous lawyers in attendance on the Court of Session. There is one indication, in September 1528, of the Lords of

Council finding time to address the issue of unpaid super-expenses, when the Glamis ward was sold to the earl of Rothes for £1000, with the proceeds being allocated towards unpaid Household debts.[14] Much has been made of the 'desperate' financial situation of the Crown in March 1530, when James gave his personal undertaking to repay the earl of Huntly 2000 marks loaned for the purpose of financing the royal secretary's diplomatic trip to the Continent.[15] However, at the same time the Lords of Council ordered Huntly to deliver 2000 marks to the secretary, 'quhilk soume he is awand to our soverane lord' for the feu of Strathdee, Braemar and Cromar. Probably the two sums were to be offset against each other, in which case this was a sale rather than a loan – with Huntly's charter later being revoked.[16] Even if this was a genuine loan, it is interesting to note that the Stewart royal building programme had resumed in 1529–30, with £1744 being expended on refurbishments at Holyrood palace, and paid for by the Treasurer.[17] This was an item of expenditure which could have been deferred had James had any real worries about the state of the Crown's resources.

The *Treasurer's Accounts* and *Exchequer Rolls* for the personal rule are fairly full. However, there are some anomalies; for example, the charge figure entered in the 1539–40 Treasurer's account for sheriff's dues, charter compositions, and ward and relief, is £12,409, but the actual total for accounted items is only £5448.[18] Hence there are instances of royal charters being granted 'for payment of sums' where no corresponding entries can be found in the accounts. One example is that there is no entry for the repayment of Huntly's loan. In any event, the accounts reveal that both revenue and expenditure rose in the period. In 1531–32, the total income for the Crown from both casualty and property was around £24,000, with expenditure slightly less. In 1535–36 revenue increased to £25,000, again with expenditure slightly less. In 1539–40 expenditure had overtaken revenue, both figures exceeding £51,000.[19] Household costs were £10,883 in 1526–27 and first exceeded this figure in 1537–38 (£13132, in the year of James' second marriage), rising to £19,228 in 1539–40, the last period for which an account is extant.[20] After 1540, the extent of the Crown lands increased, firstly through annexation and then through the resumption of Margaret Tudor's patrimony after her death in November 1541. The reasonable assumption to make is that expenditure would have risen correspondingly. Casual income was £12,914 in 1529–30 (the previous year's account is missing) and peaked at £37,630 in 1540–41, before falling to £25,720 in 1541–42. In each case the expenditure figure was slightly above or slightly below.[21] The conclusion must be that the king simply spent whatever was available, leaving the problem of shortfalls to his Comptroller and Treasurer.

James' father had managed to drive up his annual income from the Treasury from around £4,500 in 1496 to £28,000 in 1512. In the last years of his reign he was probably receiving a total income of around £44,500, with expenditure outstripping this possibly by more than £7,000 *per annum*. In his attempts to swell royal income he had used the tactics of recognition, non-entry, feu-farm grants, compositions for charters following the 1498 revocation, the sale of remissions, and the use of regular taxations between 1488 and 1497. The assertion that James V 'tightened the financial screw further' by being the first Stewart monarch to demand compositions following his own revocation of 1537, cannot be sustained.[22] Indeed James V's legal emasculation of the Crawford earldom through the device of non-entry was mild when compared with the bills presented by his father's advocate to the fifth earl of Angus in 1510.

In James IV's reign the second earl of Rothes was also pursued for non-entries.[23] With the exception of royal demands for compositions to avoid recognition, all of James IV's tactics were employed by his son. The Rouen Act of Revocation, passed on 3 April 1537 and ratified in the December 1540 parliament, was almost a carbon copy of that passed by James IV in 1498. Interestingly, however, the highest figure for charter compositions in general in the personal rule was achieved in the 1530–31 account, at £1800 (including £500 paid by Lord Forbes). Thereafter the figure dipped to as little as £85 in 1535–36, before averaging out at around £700 *per annum* from 1536–37 to 1540–41 and rising to £1000 in 1541–42.[24] The 1530–31 account is the first one extant for the personal rule. The indication is that the king was making money out of confirming charters in the early years after assuming power, long before he felt the need to issue an act, at his 'perfect age' of twenty-five, specifically addressing the issue of grants made in his minority detrimental to the Crown's patrimony.

The question may arise as to how far inflation was a factor in the Stewart monarchy's urge to increase royal revenues. For the personal rule of James V, this did not appear to be a consideration. One boll measure of oatmeal cost half a mark in 1528 and the same in 1542.[25] One eln of black satin cost 34s. in 1529, and 36s. in 1542.[26] A barrowman engaged in the royal building programme was paid 6s. per week in 1530, and 5s. a decade later.[27] Probably the increase in revenues was sought primarily as a result of increased royal consumption. Murray has drawn attention to the rising costs of the royal Household, with the Comptroller latterly required to find funds for the queen, illegitimate offspring, and generally gestures of careless royal extravagance. The annual Household livery bill increased by £800 between 1532 and 1534, from £1940 to £2730. Household fees were raised in 1538.[28] In addition each king had to finance his own 'royal obsession'[29] as well as royal military expeditions, and, in the case of James V, a marital trip to France. The happy circumstance for James V was that the extent of the Crown lands increased substantially through the Angus, Glamis and Finnart forfeitures, and again after the Act of Annexation and death of Margaret Tudor. In 1538 a special payment of 40s. was made to purchase extra parchment rolls upon which to enter the accounts.[30] In March 1539 the Comptroller was ordered to carry out a commission into the value of the Crown tenancies, whether held of old or through forfeiture. Specifically, the commission extended to Crawfordmuir, Douglas and other areas of the Angus earldom, Crawford-john, Ross and Ardmannoch, Strathdee, Braemar and Cromar, and also the three most profitable lordships of the Crown – Fife, Strathearn and Galloway, each of which produced over £800 for the Comptroller in 1538. Later the survey extended to the Isles, Liddesdale, Ettrick forest and other parts of Margaret Tudor's terce.[31] The rental book for Strathdee, Braemar and Cromar was six-and-a-half pages long in April 1539, and took up over twenty pages in 1542. After the Comptroller's survey of Fife made in May 1541, the annual return there increased by £300, largely achieved through the conversion of kindly tenancies and tacks into feus.[32]

Early on, James V hit upon the device of taxation; this was the means by which funds were raised for the projected royal expedition to the Isles in 1531, with the tax being levied on the First and Third Estates.[33] During the personal rule, thirteen taxes were levied, the bulk of the burden falling on these two estates. In June 1535, the Second Estate was required to contribute 3s. for every pound of land held in 'the auld extent' for an embassy to France, amounting to £2,000 in total. In November 1536, a further tax of 9s. in the pound was levied on the Second Estate for the king's expenses in France, totalling 10,000 marks. A third tax of £1,600 was levied on the Second Estate in March 1538 for the expenses of bringing Mary of Guise over to Scotland. This was assessed at 30d. in the pound.[34]

In September 1536, Thomas Suthill, English officer at Berwick-upon-Tweed, reported to his government that James was embarking for France and that:

> doubtlesse both Hyme selve, with the Lordes and the residue of his company, haith maid great shift and provision for money to have with theym, and many of theym haith laid their landes in morgage for the same.[35]

This was Suthill's opinion, but it is not borne out by the extant records. Arran, Argyll, Rothes and Lord Fleming were on the French trip, and there is no sign that they were forced to mortgage their estates to pay for their passage and expenses whilst with the king. Crawford had been required to mortgage to meet his debts, but he was not on the trip. However, in February 1536 he had just finished paying his composition for his new charter. The earl of Moray, then in France as one of the Scots commissioners, had been granted leave in July 1535 to alienate, under reversion, up to £4,000 worth of his earldom on the same day as he was given a letter of protection for the duration of his overseas service. Presumably this was in order to finance his trip, and avoid a possible recognition. There is no sign that Moray was required to go ahead with these sales, although in his will of 8 June 1540, he made arrangements for payment of his 'diverss creditouris'. In October 1542 he set lands in feu to his servants in return for 'sums paid to himself'.[36] It is possible that the June 1535 tax – totalling £6,000 from all three estates – obviated the need for Moray to resort to mortgaging.

Suthill may have based his financial opinion on news of Crawford's payments and Moray's licence. No magnate appears to have been driven to sell lands to pay for the king's trip. However some of them did incur expenditure. Argyll's charter to Abernethy in June 1537 specifically explains that it was being granted in part compensation for the outlays which he had incurred whilst on royal service in France. The extant records show that some of the Second Estate paid the November 1536 tax for the king's expenses: Huntly paid £100; Montrose paid £66; Marischal, Eglinton, and Lords Seton, Erskine and Ruthven paid £30; and Lord Lindsay of the Byres paid £30. These were the total sums recorded as being received by the king from his magnates.[37] It is unlikely that James' financial staff would have allowed the remaining magnates to escape payment given their tenacity elsewhere, for example in recuperating castlewards from the earl of Bothwell in 1541. Hence it must be assumed that some taxation rolls are missing from the extant accounts for the personal rule.

The tax revenues shown in the accounts amount to over £52,000 for the period.[38] The projected revenues amounted to well over £100,000. By far the largest element was the £72,000 levied on the Church in 1532, in commutation of the 'Great Tax' of £10,000 *per annum* imposed by the Pope in 1531 for the establishment of the College of Justice.[39] Although the £72,000 was supposed to be paid off within four years, its collection, when combined with the other tax contributions made by the First Estate, provided a regular annual income for the Crown, enabling James to finance the royal building programme. So reliable was the spiritual income that the 1540 parliament proposed allocating £10,000 *per annum* towards the costs of the Royal Household.[40] For the First Estate, there was really no alternative to paying up, given the activities of Henry VIII. Some early resistance was shown by James Beaton, archbishop of St. Andrews. His nephew, Cardinal David Beaton, appears to have been rather more obsequious, and was both keeper of the privy seal and one of James' diplomats in France.[41] Gavin Dunbar, archbishop of Glasgow, served as Chancellor throughout the reign. Whether or not they liked him, the First Estate needed their king more than he needed them. In February 1540, James advised the English envoy, Sir Ralph Sadler, that he thought it 'against reason' to put down the abbeys and religious houses that maintained God's service and would give him anything he needed.[42] James chose to keep intact the capital value of his asset for the benefit of the Crown. In this sense he may have appeared to his nobles as 'ane better preistis king nor he was thairis'. He certainly had a cynical regard for the well-being of the Church.[43] Had the First Estate been less compliant, James might well have thought it more reasonable to follow his uncle's example. However, it was to his advantage to have a ready source of income which brought with it other benefits, such as the papal hat and sword (which latterly his father had lost) and an efficient court of session through which the Crown could pursue its interests in a legal manner.

How far spiritual taxation affected the Second Estate through holding from the Church is difficult to detect. In 1540 the earl of Atholl obliged himself to pay the annual sum of £63 towards the maintenance of the College of Justice on behalf of the bishop of Dunkeld. Probably the effects of indirect tax were a small penalty to pay for enjoying the fruits of benefices. Jenny Wormald has commented that James' 'onslaught on the wealthiest institution in Scotland' was scarcely a matter for lay criticism when its effect was to force the Church to feu its lands to the laity.[44] For the king, spiritual taxation provided nearly £19,000 for his boxes, unloaded at Dieppe in September 1536.[45] The English ambassador at Paris in December 1536 commented of the French dowry that James was about to receive, that he thought the Scots king had never before seen so great a sum of money all gathered together.[46] Undoubtedly this was correct, but James arrived in France with lots of money to spend.

The biggest single source of income was the two French dowries. The Scots commissioners contracted with Francis I for the sum of 100,000 gold crowns of the sun as a dowry for Madeleine. Mary of Guise' marriage was worth 100,000 *livres* of Tours. Together the dowries amounted to £168,750 Scots,[47] far outstripping the 'windfall' of £35,000 achieved by James IV through marriage with Margaret Tudor.[48] David Beaton accounted for at least £112,000, in down payments and assigned rents and pensions, paid over from 1 January 1537 onwards.[49] 34,400 crowns were paid into the king's boxes in the presence of the Treasurer at Edinburgh on 7 September 1539.[50] In effect James could, and did, spend up to and beyond his limit in ordinary and casual Crown revenues, use Church funds to pay for royal palaces, and still have money left over at the end of the reign. How far there was an interchange between the king's boxes and other accounts is not evident, but the fact that the royal reserve had been reduced to just over £26,000 by the end of the reign suggests that this king was not so much a hoarder as a man who managed his resources by occasionally dipping into his reserve fund. The ready availability of the boxes, combined with the compliance of the Church, meant that the king was freed from the necessity of preying upon the remainder of his subjects. Indeed he could well afford – legally – to buy out Argyll's interest in the MacIan inheritance and redeem the lands of Glengavel from Lord Methven.

One further method of exploiting the wealth of the Church was for James to follow the example of his father, not only in levying spiritual taxation but also in 'grooming' his illegitimate sons for a spiritual career, albeit at even younger ages than that of Alexander Stewart upon his first ecclesiastical appointment.[51] On 30 August 1534, the pope granted a dispensation permitting James' sons to receive the tonsure at the age of six. In applying to the papacy for this, James was repeating the exercise carried out by his father.[52] James *senior* had the benefit of being educated by George Buchanan,[53] before being sent to St. Andrews University with his brothers James *secundus*, John, and Robert *senior*. James *secundus* and John both appeared on the matriculation roll.[54] By April 1535, James *senior*, then aged five, was nominally provided to Kelso abbey.[55] By 1539, at the age of seven, James *secundus* was provided to the priory of St. Andrews and admitted to the temporalities.[56] In the same year Robert *senior* became abbot of Holyrood at the age of six.[57] In 1541, John was admitted, at age nine, to Melrose abbey and Coldingham priory.[58] At a very conservative estimate, the combined annual revenues from these benefices were just over £10,000. Possibly they were worth four times as much, in which case James may have been controlling funds in the region of £100,000 in the last three years of the personal rule.[59] The accounts for the benefices were operated as a separate item from the Treasury and Comptroller's office, and there is scant reference to them.[60] Hence the value of the benefices for the Crown can only be estimated.

Mention should be made of two other sources of income for the Crown. The first was gold mining, which had been ongoing at Crawfordmuir since the end of the previous reign. Both English and French miners were brought in to extract the gold.[61] Mining was operated under a licensing system, whereby the Treasurer paid for extracted gold. In 1537, £849 was paid to the captain of Crawford castle 'for gold of the myne'.[62] Presumably the Crown owned the mineral rights, and this payment reflected a purchase by the Treasurer of Crown property. Gold from the mine was used to make the queen's crown in 1539.[63] James also established a reputation as a sheep farmer, and Sir Ralph Sadler gave him a lecture on this matter in February 1540, advising him not to meddle with such a lowly and unkingly pursuit, however profitable it might be.[64] Royal flocks were maintained at Crawfordmuir, Melrose, Selkirk, Coldingham, Bunkle and Preston, and royal wood was exported from Leith. The annual profits were around 2,000 marks.[65]

The prevalent royal obsession in France and England during this period was the building of palaces. Francis I was improving Fontainebleau and Chambord; Henry VIII was emulating him in his projects for Whitehall and Nonesuch.[66] Not unnaturally, therefore, this obsession was the single biggest item of expenditure for James V. At least £41,000 was expended on new buildings at Edinburgh, Holyrood, Falkland, Linlithgow and Stirling, as well as for work on Tantallon, Blackness, Kinghorn Tower, Crawfordjohn, Hermitage and a building at Leith. Recorded annual expenditure on architecture rose from around £1,700 in 1529–30 to over £5,000 in later years.[67] There was also useful expenditure on ships – the obsession of James IV – and on artillery, totalling around £20,000. The principal dock was Leith, though Newhaven, Dumbarton, Burntisland and Lochaber were used at times. In later years expenditure on 'munitionis' – a category also embracing work by craftsmen at Edinburgh castle – averaged around £1,500 *per annum* and was accounted for separately.[68] Thus, the extant records suggest expenditure of at least £61,000 on the sort of projects in which Stewart monarchs specialised – weapons, the royal navy, and buildings. Probably the actual figure was much greater; by the end of the reign James was receiving a vast income and, unlike his grandfather, was not hoarding it.[69] Bishop Lesley's verdict was correct.

2. COURT LIFE

A Stewart monarch was expected to provide 'court life and its perquisites'.[70] The promotion of a lavish display of ostentation in the royal court served to enhance the king's prestige in the eyes of his subjects – most importantly, in the eyes of his magnates. James had the palaces and the wealth to provide such a display of kingly splendour. Although he did not go to such extremes as had his father, who had patronised the pioneering aviator and alchemist, John Damian,[71] James did provide some culture, over and above playing cards with Finnart and other Household servants. In 1531, John Bellenden received payment for translating Hector Boece's history of Scotland. The senators of the College of Justice received their first year's salaries from the Treasurer.[72] George Buchanan educated James *senior*. Sir David Lindsay of the Mount was employed as a royal herald and found time to write his poems. Murray has drawn attention to the existence of the king's purse, which was operated by John Tennant in association with Henry Kempt of Thomastown, keeper of the royal boxes.[73] Payments made from the royal purse were for trivial amounts, the sums being lifted out of the *Treasurer's Accounts* and accounted for as a separate item. Oliver Sinclair of Pitcairn was one of the accountants.[74] The only surviving *Pursemaster's Accounts* are for part of 1540, but even in these there are, as Murray has pointed out, items 'reminiscent of those picturesque passages in the Treasurer's accounts of James IV's reign, which have been the delight of the biographer and of the historical novelist.'[75] It is apparent in this reign that the full picture of income and expenditure is not revealed in the accounts of the Comptroller, Treasurer and Master of Works.

The first real opportunity for a court celebration embracing and impressing the magnates came with the king's first marriage. The nobility were summoned to Edinburgh to attend the king's homecoming in March 1537. According to Abell, Madeleine was received with 'great blitheness'.[76] However, what should have been a carnival atmosphere turned into a funeral and two treason trials. It is easy to understand why Lesley wrote of this damp squib that 'the King tuik greit displesour, and thairfor keipit him quiet ane lang tyme eftir'.[77] A second opportunity for a party arose with the arrival of Mary of Guise at St. Andrews in June 1538.[78] Preparations were made for a tournament; the king had his 'grete justing sadillis' covered with five 'blak skynnis'. Possibly he wore his six-year-old orange velvet jousting shoes.[79] The prelates, barons and lords of Fife, Angus and Strathearn were warned to appear; close writings were sent to the bishops of Dunkeld, Dunblane, Brechin, and Caithness, and to Arran, Eglinton, and Lords Fleming, Ruthven, Erskine, Ogilvie and 'certane utheris lordis to cum to Sanctandros at the quenis landing'.[80] Sir David Lindsay probably based his poem *The justing betwixt James Watsoun and Jhone Barbour* on the celebratory events. He wrote that 'mony ane Knicht, Barroun and banrent' came to view this joust between the king's barber surgeon and the royal chamber groom which took place before the king and queen at St. Andrews.[81] There are references in the *Treasurer's Accounts* to a new outfit for the 'Queen's fule' and to the subsequent entry of the new queen into Edinburgh, which the author of the *Diurnal* also describes as a splendid occasion.[82]

Thomas Bellenden, justice clerk, is the source of information about another court occasion. The news of the Epiphany performance of Lindsay's *Interlude* at Linlithgow in January 1540 was received with some excitement by William Eure, English officer at Berwick-upon-Tweed. He learned from the Scots commissioner that, after the performance, the Scots king had called his Chancellor to task and threatened that unless the clergy mended their ways 'He wolde sende sex of the proudeste of thaym unto his oncle of England'.[83] Probably this threat prompted Henry VIII to send Sadler to visit James in order to lecture him on sheep and dismantling the Church. James' answer, that he saw no reason to take his uncle's advice and that he was both 'loved and dreaded' in his own country, was probably quite true, at least for the First Estate.[84] Eure considered Bellenden to be 'a man inclyned to the soorte [of religious policy] used in our Soverains Realme of England'. However the justice clerk was shrewd enough to carry out his duties in the heresy trial of Sir John Borthwick in May 1540.[85] According to Bellenden, the *Interlude* was performed at Linlithgow before the king and queen and the whole temporal and spiritual council.[86] It is not clear who was present, other than the Chancellor, 'divers other Bishops' and Bellenden. The king and queen had spent Christmas 1539 at Linlithgow,[87] and probably the performance of the *Interlude* was laid on in the Great Hall as entertainment following the formal opening of the king's new apartments there.

The next State occasion was the queen's coronation, at Holyrood, on 22 February 1540.[88] Close writings were sent to the earls of Huntly and Marischal and their wives and to 'the lordis and ladyis'.[89] Payment was made to three carters for the carriage of 'xix draucht of buirdis and sparris, quhilk wer put up in the abbay kirk at the Quenis graces coronatioun'. Possibly this avian spectacle inspired Pitscottie later to write of David Lindsay's 'triumphant frais' devised for the queen's entrance into St. Andrews after she had first arrived in Scotland.[90] The coronation was followed three months later by the birth of Prince James at St. Andrews, on 22 May 1540.[91] Again 'certane lordis and ladyis' were warned to be present for the birth, and all lords and barons in the west and south were summoned to the baptism, as were Huntly and Marischal.[92] Prior to the birth James had been in St. Andrews for nearly a fortnight. On 5 May a bear was brought to him there; on 19 May 43s. was paid to 'tua Dugemen that playt and dansyt apone the schore of Sanctandrois before the kingis graice'. However on 21 May he went to Edinburgh, only to come rushing back the next day in order to be present himself for the birth. On the day after the birth of his son, a servant of the Earl Marischal presented him with sea-birds' eggs.[93] Grimmer business followed immediately, with Marischal, Huntly, Arran, Montrose, Fleming, Lindsay of the Byres, Seton, Erskine, Somerville and Finnart all in St. Andrews by 28 May, for the trial of Sir John Borthwick.[94]

Shortly after the birth of Prince James came what perhaps was the biggest occasion for the magnates, in the form of the Isles expedition, an opportunity for some of the younger earls to become 'blooded' in the exercise of law and order. Nearly a year later, at Falkland in 1541, Arthur, Duke of Albany, was born.[95] However, no sooner had he been baptised, with the royal heralds in attendance and the 'grete artelerie' being fired, than he died.[96] Presumably the lords were summoned to his funeral, and to that of Prince James, who died soon after.[97] The third funeral of 1541 which the magnates had to attend was that of Margaret Tudor, in November.[98] James was rather unfortunate in that what should have been joyous state occasions so often turned into mournings.

At a less elevated level, there are few traces in the *Treasurer's Accounts* of court spectacles being laid on specifically with the magnates in mind. However, there is some suggestion in the surviving *Pursemaster's Accounts* of cordial relations between the king and his nobility, if only through the medium of the latter's servants. Round about Easter 1540, and the king's twenty-eighth birthday, there were a number of gratuities paid to these servants for providing a variety of food supplies for the royal kitchens. Lady Erskine supplied lampreys; Argyll and Huntly, venison and 'aquavite'; Lord Hay donated partridge; Menteith and Morton gave pike and rays, and Marischal sent along swans. Not to be outdone, Finnart provided prawns and Oliver Sinclair supplied wild geese.[99] Perhaps one way to win the king's favour was through his stomach. These donations were in the manner of formal presents, but may have indicated that the donor was coming to dine with the king. In February 1540, Sir Ralph Sadler recorded having Sunday dinner at Holyrood with the Cardinal, Huntly, Atholl, Cassillis, Erroll, the Chancellor, the bishop of Aberdeen and Lord Erskine.[100] Some of these men would be at Court in Edinburgh at that time specifically for the Queen's coronation – Huntly for example appears to have remained in the north-east unless down on legal or parliamentary business or when summoned by the king. Nevertheless, Sadler's communication suggests that the king's court was not bereft of magnatial attendance. It is a matter for speculation what the full set of *Pursemaster's Accounts* might have revealed. For example, it would be interesting to find at least one instance of the king giving presents to his nobility, rather than the other way about.

3. PATRONAGE

At a more material level, one of the hallmarks of a successful and popular Stewart monarch was his ability and willingness to bestow patronage. In its most elevated form this could mean the creation of an earldom or lordship for a royal supporter. The earldoms of Argyll, Erroll, Huntly, Marischal, Morton and Rothes had been created in the reign of James II, largely in the aftermath of the downfall of the earls of Douglas.[101] After the downfall of the Boyds, James III created the Stewart earldom of Buchan. In reward for his support of James III at

Blackness in 1488, the fifth earl of Crawford became Duke of Montrose, and three weeks before the battle of Sauchieburn, Lord Kilmaurs was made Earl of Glencairn.[102] In the few months after Sauchieburn, Lord Hailes elevated himself to become Earl of Bothwell. James IV created the earldoms of Cassillis, Eglinton, Arran and Montrose, these last two on the occasion of his marriage in 1503.[103] By comparison, James V's record is dismal: the creation of the Methven lordship in the first few weeks of the personal rule, and the confirmation of Lord Hume's restoration in the March 1541 parliament.[104] The Methven creation was because Henry Stewart had married Margaret Tudor, whilst Hume's restoration was simply an acknowledgement of the *de facto* situation following his reinstatement in the minority.

The forfeiture of the Angus earldom provided the king with ample lands which could be redistributed amongst royal supporters;[105] and indeed, the early signs were encouraging. In the week after the September 1528 parliament, Roger Lascelles, captain of Norham castle, provided a reasonably accurate list of those who were to benefit from the share-out, and added that the king, on the advice of his council:

> bad them [the beneficiaries] goo and chaisse thErle of Angis forth of Scotland, and they shuld have ther patentes.[106]

On 5 September 1528, 'for good service', Lord Maxwell was granted the lands of Crawfordmuir (the greater part of the Angus barony of Crawford-Douglas or Crawford-Lindsay) and Dunsyre. This was a grant in heredity and was confirmed on 1 January 1530, again for good service and with the 'consent of the Treasurer'. On this second occasion the lands were united as a free barony.[107] Also on 5 September 1528, Scott of Buccleuch was granted in heredity the lordship of Jedburgh Forest, excepting rights of jurisdiction over lands held by Kerr of Ferniehirst.[108] On the same day, Stirling of Keir and Moray shared the lands and escheat of Sir George Douglas, and Keir obtained part of the Forest of Dye, formerly held by Angus. The lands of Douglas of Kilspindie were divided between Eglinton and Robert Cairncross, the Treasurer.[109] The barony of Selkirk was also part of the earldom of Angus, and James Murray of Fallowhill, sheriff, was confirmed in his holdings there.[110] Indeed, in the first few days following the September parliament, nearly forty charters were issued, either confirming Angus' former tenants in their possessions, or introducing new tenants.[111]

The next round of distributions came after the failure of the siege of Tantallon. On 16 November 1528, the first earl of Arran was granted, in heredity, the Angus barony of Bothwell. After Arran's death, in March 1529, this presumably passed to his heir, although the second earl only obtained sasine on 12 September 1532.[112] In the intervening period, Finnart complicated matters by obtaining parts of the Hepburn barony of Bothwell. The earl of Bothwell alienated further lands to Finnart in December 1539,[113] and when the second earl of Arran finally obtained a charter to his earldom in September 1540, these lands appear to have been included in the Hamilton barony of Bothwell. However, the Hepburn lands were then lost to the earldom of Arran through the December 1540 Act of Annexation, which formally annexed the Angus barony of Bothwell to the Crown.[114] During his tenure of the Arran ward, Finnart appears to have muddled up the lands of the three separate baronies for his own benefit, prompting Arran in 1543 to accuse him of having 'feinzeit' documentation to Bothwell. Kelley notes that, throughout the personal rule, the actual possession of the Angus barony was enjoyed by Janet Kennedy, former mistress of both James IV and the fifth earl of Angus, and mother of the earl of Moray.[115]

The baronies of Bunkle and Preston were promised to Lord Hume in October 1528, in return for his service in expelling the Douglases from the Merse. However, as he did not expel Angus, all he received was the gift, in September 1529, of one term's profits of the lands. This coincided with his appointment as lieutenant of the Merse, and presumably gave him some incentive.[116] In May 1531 his brother, the abbot of Jedburgh, received a five-year tack of the lands with power to hold bailiary courts.[117] The Comptroller, James Colville, was granted, for good service, half the lands of Preston and Lintlaws, on 6 September 1528.[118]

Elsewhere in the south-east, the earl of Bothwell was granted a charter to the lordship of Tantallon on 28 January 1529, again as an incentive to head the anti-Douglas campaign. This was a grant in feu farm, with the annual fee set at 100 marks. It included the lands of Reidside, and the castle itself, which was then still in the possession of the earl of Angus.[119] However, Bothwell also failed to expel Angus, and in July 1529 the lordship was set in feu farm to the royal secretary, Thomas Erskine of Haltoun, in return for 'his past services at home and overseas and for risking his life and goods in the service of the king against his enemies'. The annual fee was set at 200 marks, excluding the lands of Reidside, which were held by Hugh Johnston, principal cook, in blanche farm.[120] In August 1531, Erskine, who had now been knighted, received a further grant in heredity to Tantallon, together with the custody of the castle. The narrative in the charter described him as a 'familiar', receiving the grant for his great service in Scotland and overseas, for exposing himself to diverse dangers in the expulsion of the Douglases, and for his expenses in repairing and maintaining the castle during the recent turbulent times.[121] Later in the personal rule, Erskine was reimbursed the sum of £533 for expenditure incurred in adding to Tantallon's fortifications.[122]

The lordship of Abernethy was granted in heredity to the third earl of Argyll on 6 December 1528, this time as a reward for his 'good service' in the anti-Douglas campaign. As with Bothwell, this lordship appears to have passed to Argyll's heir, following the third earl's death in 1529. The fourth earl received his first charter to the lordship – specified as a regality – at Falkland on 2 November 1533. This was made for his past and impending service and, in addition, 'at his perfect age of twenty-one', James revoked all other grants held by others in the regality. However he preserved one charter of lands in favour of his pursemaster, John

Tennant.[123] The superiorities of Bunkle and Preston, Douglas, Selkirk and Kirriemuir remained with the Crown; in both Douglas and Kirriemuir there were numerous confirmations allowed to previous Angus tenants, and in Kirriemuir a number of Crown servants were introduced. On 22 March 1529 the Lords of Council made a specific declaration that the superiority of Kirriemuir pertained to the Crown in perpetuity.[124] Probably this was in response to a dispute between some of the newly introduced tenants and those who were dispossessed. Hence Maxwell held Crawfordmuir and Dunsyre; Buccleuch held Jedburgh Forest; Arran held Bothwell; Erskine held Tantallon, and Argyll held Abernethy. Lascelles had predicted that Finnart and Campbell of Loudoun would each receive half the lordship of Douglas and that Moray would take Bunkle and Preston, but the requisite charters did not materialise. One William Simon was confirmed as bailie and captain of Douglas castle on 28 January 1530.[125]

This distribution was adequate enough to carry James through the struggle for power and the one further critical period of the personal rule – the hostilities prior to the conclusion of the perpetual peace with England in May 1534. After this there was a reorganisation. On 16 June 1534, at the age of four, the royal bastard James *senior* was granted the lordship of Douglas. Then, on 28 October 1534, he received a further charter to Douglas, Dunsyre, Crawfordmuir, Bothwell, Jedburgh Forest, Bunkle (and Preston), Tantallon and Kirriemuir.[126] This grant comprised almost the entire estates of the earldom of Angus. The assumption is that Selkirk was also included in the charter, although not specified.[127] Thenceforth the only superiority remaining outwith the Crown's control was the regality of Abernethy, again confirmed to the fourth earl of Argyll in June 1537, following the Act of Revocation.

On 10 June 1535, for his good service and in compensation for the resignation of Crawfordmuir and Dunsyre, Lord Maxwell and his wife were granted in feu farm the lands of Buittle (Kirkcudbright) in return for the annual fee of £245, and with an entry fee of £200. This exchange was similar to that made between the king and Finnart for the neighbouring lands of Crawfordjohn. James was building a 'block' of royal lands in an area where the Angus estates had been. Maxwell's family already held lands in Buittle, and for both himself and the king the arrangement made sense; Maxwell's son was married to Beatrice Douglas, daughter of the earl of Morton, and the earl of Morton had had his charter to Buittle reduced in February 1533, on the grounds that this had been made during the king's *lessage* and was in diminution of the Crown's rental. Morton had only been paying £100 *per annum* for the lands.[128] James did not require to pass an act of revocation in order to achieve the reduction. Indeed, one of the features of several of his royal charters (for example those made to Hamilton of Finnart) was the expression of the idea that the king had now reached his perfect age of twenty-one, or twenty-two, or however old he happened to be at the time.

The other man who was compensated for his loss was Thomas Erskine. As familiar and Secretary (since 1526[129]) he was granted, in feu farm on 4 February

1534, the lands and lordship of Brechin and Navar, for the annual fee of £240. This gift was made specifically as reward for his services at Tantallon, and £200 of the annual rent was remitted to Erskine for the space of five years. The royal Secretary had acted as chamberlain for these lands since 1527. In his 1534 charter he was allowed his own coat of arms, the explanation being that he had served the king as ambassador in complex negotiations and deserved recognition of this status.[130] In his charter Erskine was designed as Sir Thomas Erskine of Kirkbuddo, lands bought from Robert Barton of Over-Barnton, held from the Crawford earldom and apprised for £662 owed by the earl to the Crown. Erskine was then gifted the non-entries to the Downie barony, in February 1532, and after the lands were apprised – for over £3,500 – he was assigned the barony as security for the debt. In January 1534, rather than pursuing the earl for full payment, Erskine entered into a contract of excambion, and received further lands from the earl in lieu of the sums owed.[131] In 1538, the seven-year period during which Crawford had the opportunity of redeeming the lands of Kirkbuddo, expired. Erskine reached a further agreement with the earl to extend the period, adding an extra 500 marks to the debt.[132] In a sense, Erskine was acting as a white knight for the ailing Crawford earldom, whilst at the same time making a profit for himself.

Erskine also bought and sold lands in Kincardine in 1531 and 1532, purchasing the barony of Murphy-Fraser from Charles Fullerton of Murphy-Fraser, and selling Haltoun to Lord Erskine.[133] By March 1534, when he was due to travel overseas on a further diplomatic embassy, the number of Erskine's 'kynnismen, frendis and servandis' was still short of the two hundred names supplied by the earl of Arran in 1536, but comfortably exceeded the number of David Beaton's friends.[134] Erskine was building up a sphere of influence in the Forfar area, and enjoyed royal favour.

Professor Hannay credited the royal Secretary with the idea of instituting the College of Justice.[135] Erskine was apparently educated at Pavia – the model for the revised Scottish central civil court – and in 1530 and 1531 he was in Rome, entrusted with the business of negotiating a royal marriage with Catherine de Medici and also with further 'secret matters', not to be disclosed, involving the Duke of Albany.[136] In view of his property deals in Forfar, it is highly likely that Erskine had the type of brain capable of devising the system of funding the College, opening the floodgates for Church revenues to come flowing to the Crown. The value of his service to the king is suggested by the narratives made in his royal charters, rather more specific than the explanations given, for example, in charters received by Finnart. After all, as one of the masters of works, Finnart spent the spiritual revenues; Erskine probably conjured up this source of wealth for the Crown. In a negative sense, this impression of valuable royal service is confirmed by an undated letter from James to his Secretary. In this James wrote:

Secretar, I commend me rycht hartly to yow and weit ye that it is murmuryt that ye sould a spolkyn with Gorge and Archebald Dougles in Ingland [this past time?] quhylk wase again my command and your promys quhan we departyt.

James went on to say that he had heard rumours that the Secretary was offered bribes and continued:

And prayeng yow to tayk thes in [parting?] for ye beand ane gud servand and lelle and trow to me I sall be ane gud tru and constant maister to yow. . . .[137]

The reference to Archibald Douglas is probably to Kilspindie, which places the letter before August 1534. Clearly Erskine had encountered the Douglases in the course of his many embassies, and this may have prompted Kilspindie to seek the king's clemency in Scotland in August 1534. James was giving Erskine a friendly warning on the matter of treasonable communications.[138] The contrast between this approach and the treatment received by Sir Adam Otterburn, and Sir James Colville, is marked, and indicates that James was not a man who immediately condemned instances of treasonable disloyalty. Erskine read and understood the message.

On 31 August 1536, Tantallon, Bunkle and Preston were granted to James *secundus*, James *senior* being sufficiently provided with the benefice of Kelso, and other resources.[139] Gradually references to these and other parts of the Angus earldom began to appear in the Comptroller's accounts. (The likelihood is that separate accounts were maintained for areas held by James *senior*.) James Gordon of Lochinvar became bailie for Douglas in 1537, and was captain of the castle.[140] This may have been a reward for accompanying the king to France. One David Wallace had returned the total of £143 as chamberlain in 1533 and 1535. Gordon's grant was to last for five years, but by 1538 a David Weir was acting as chamberlain, and returned £264 to the Comptroller on a turnover of £361.[141] David Wood of Craig carried out a rental survey in June 1539, but the turnover remained the same for the remainder of the personal rule, with one William Macmorran of Glaspen acting as chamberlain.[142]

In Crawfordmuir, the emphasis was on mining and sheep farming. The captain was John Carmichael of Meadowflat, and returns of £106 came in from the teinds in 1540.[143] In Jedburgh Forest, the chamberlain Kerr of Ferniehirst returned just £45 to the Comptroller in 1537. He claimed that Scott of Buccleuch had been intromitting with the profits up to that year – notwithstanding being held periodically in ward. The turnover for Jedburgh Forest averaged £170 *per annum*, but despite a survey in May 1541, the return to the Comptroller did not increase.[144] In May 1540, Ferniehirst received all of his lands as a free barony, including those held in Jedburgh Forest. This was for his service as warden and also for his apprehending and applying the king's justice to Nixons, Rutherfords, Turnbulls, Croziers, Routledges, Ainslies and Olivers. On 2 November 1542 he was appointed as bailie.[145] Tantallon was granted in feu farm to Oliver Sinclair of

Pitcairn on 28 February 1540, at an annual fee of 160 marks, this time including the lands of Reidside, formerly held by the king's cook. Like Erskine, he was expected to supervise building alterations at the castle. In 1538, one David Borthwick returned £128 to the Comptroller from a turnover of £162. Sinclair of Pitcairn returned £53 in 1540, and kept £53 for his expenses as keeper of the castle.[146] It appears as though the lands of Tantallon had decreased in value between the period of Erskine's and Pitcairn's control.

With the exception of Abernethy, all the Angus estates were under the king's control by the time of the passing of the Act of Annexation in the 1540 parliament. In many respects King James' career was at its peak in December 1540. He had a male heir; Mary of Guise was again pregnant; there had been a royal expedition to the Isles, in which the king had been accompanied by many of his leading nobility; Finnart had been executed, and with his death James had killed any lingering notion of a possible rapprochement with the Douglases. For James the formal annexation to the Crown of the Angus estates, together with the Isles, Glamis, Avandale, Crawfordjohn and Liddesdale, was a bold and final solution. The preamble to the Act of Annexation stated that the king was following the good example of his predecessors in specifying those lands that had come into his possession and were henceforth to be considered inalienable without the consent of parliament.[147] The closest parallel was with the 1455 parliament in James II's reign, when the forfeited estates of the Black Douglases were added to the lands of the Crown. Indeed the example set by his great-grandfather had made its impact upon James V, at least in the manner in which his Act of Annexation was drafted.[148] The annexation also effectively negated the terms of the agreement reached between Robert Barton and Angus in March 1529. In this the king had agreed that should Angus surrender his lands and houses they would be 'committ to nane utheris bot to our said thesaurer or utheris our familiaris of houshald.' His whole lands would be taken 'in our awin handis' pending the day 'quharethrow we may tak hereeftir occation to do and grant to tham grace and favouris and to remit and relax to tham in all or part the panis of law that thai haif incurrit.'[149] For Angus this had held out the promise of a possible restoration. In 1540, however, with his earldom inalienably annexed to the Crown, his future career as a magnate was finished.

The Act of Annexation – and the ratification of the forfeitures of the Douglases, Lord Glamis, and Hamilton of Finnart – were passed in a full session of parliament. Ten out of the twenty earls were present. The absentees were Moray, away in France recovering his health; Bothwell, in ward; Lennox, also overseas; Eglinton, by now very old; Sutherland and Caithness, both minors who had never attended any parliament during the personal rule; Crawford; Buchan, who had attended only the September 1528 parliament; and Morton and the third earl of Glencairn, neither of whom had attended any parliament in the personal rule. Huntly, Arran, Argyll, and Montrose were lords of articles, with Marischal, Erroll, Rothes, Atholl, Cassillis and Menteith in attendance. Nineteen out of the thirty-two lords attended, and nine bishops and thirteen abbots and priors.[150] This was a higher turnout than for any previous parliament in the personal rule. James could be said to have received a resounding endorsement from his magnates for the Act of Annexation, which, building on the achievements of his predecessors, had brought the Crown lands to their greatest extent to date.[151]

The December 1540 parliament offered James a golden opportunity to distribute patronage and reward his magnate supporters; he had both the land and the money available so to do. That James understood the art of patronage to some degree is indicated by the February 1541 charter to Argyll of the regality of Abernethy. In June of the same year, Lord Maxwell again received a feu charter to the barony of Buittle.[152] This was small beer. Maxwell might have cut a convincing figure as the earl of Liddesdale. Although the heartland of his earldom lay in the north-east, Huntly also held Gordon, Fogo, and Huntly in Berwickshire.[153] He might have received Tantallon. Lascelles had reported in 1528 that Moray was to receive Preston and Bunkle. As the king's half-brother, Moray was long-suffering; he had been granted a charter to Orkney and Shetland in January 1531, but had not carried out any role there.[154] He had been promised a heritable tenure of Ross and Ardmannoch in 1530 as reward for serving as Borders lieutenant in 1530, and had served as such in 1533, but in 1538 his tack to these Crown lands was annulled.[155] He had represented his half-brother in France in 1535–36, but lost his lieutenancy in the north in 1537. Elsewhere, Patrick, third lord Gray, had served the king as sheriff of Forfar, and might have received part of the Glamis forfeiture, as might Rothes, who had held the Glamis ward. Lord Fleming, married to the king's half-sister, and serving as both chamberlain and sheriff of Peebles, could have been granted Douglas, or Crawfordmuir. Arran, who had promoted the downfall of Finnart, may have hoped for the return of at least half of Crawfordjohn.

It was almost as if James was applying new solutions to old problems. The financial problem was largely solved through the proposition to divert £10,000 *per annum* of spiritual revenues to financing the Household. The problem of magnate patronage was solved by ignoring it outright, and keeping nearly all the forfeited lands for the Crown. The happy circumstance for James was that he had had no crisis in his personal rule since the conclusion of the perpetual peace in 1534. From his point of view his minority had largely consisted of one crisis after another, during which the magnates had argued over the possession of his royal person. Possibly the most ridiculous situation for him, looking back through the parliamentary record, had been the rotation scheme of 1525. The rivalry amongst Angus, Arran and Lennox had led to Angus holding on to James until May 1528. There had followed the struggle for power. The first earl of Arran and third earl of Lennox were now dead and Angus out of the country. James was surrounded by a group of magnates, many of whom were around his age or slightly older. There was no dominant senior figure amongst them. By choosing to act as he did in the December 1540 parliament, James was taking advantage of the strong position of the Crown, in which the possible expectations of his magnates was a secondary consideration.

The last thing James wanted was to be seen showing favouritism to anyone who might turn into an over-mighty subject. It was inconceivable that, at the age of twenty-eight, he should become beholden to a magnate in the manner in which he had been obliged to the third earl of Lennox when he was half that age.[156] To favour one man over another carried the risk of jealousy, magnatial rivalry, and political unrest. Such rivalry already existed in the north-east between Huntly and Moray, and the king deliberately treated both alike. The simplest answer was to withhold patronage. In this sense it can be conceded that James 'did not love the nobility'. Indeed he went further and applied a policy of *divide et impera*[157] in 1536–37 with the appointment of not one, but six vice-regents. The absence of patronage brings into focus the careers of lesser men, such as Sir Thomas Erskine of Brechin; Henry Kempt of Thomastown, who in January 1542 was granted the ward of the lordship of Berriedale in the earldom of Sutherland; and Oliver Sinclair of Pitcairn, who, as cousin of the earl of Caithness, was granted the ward of that earldom in March 1538, held jointly with the Treasurer.[158]

As the second son of Sir Oliver Sinclair of Roslin and brother of Sir William of Roslin,[159] Pitcairn was of a rather higher social status than some of James' other 'familiar servants' – for example Hugh Johnston, the royal cook, John Tennant, king's pursemaster, and John Murray, barber-surgeon, who as a 'familiar' was granted a feu to the lands of Kingsmeadows (Edinburgh) in August 1537.[160] Pitcairn was granted in free barony the lands of Pitcairn (Perth) in January 1538. These had previously been held by Alexander Stewart, abbot-commendator of Scone and bishop of Moray. Before his death, Moray also held the ward of the Caithness earldom.[161] In the same year Pitcairn became a cup-bearer in the Household, alongside Henry Kempt.[162] Kempt had been appointed as keeper of the royal boxes in 1526, and in the same year had been granted in feu the lands of Thomastown.[163] In 1537, this charter was confirmed, and in 1538 Kempt received a further feu of lands in the Glamis lordship.[164] Sinclair first appeared in the Household in 1536, when he received his livery. He appears to have had charge of the king's purse, together with Kempt and John Tennant, and he kept the accounts. His tenure of the office coincided with the royal spending spree in Paris.[165] Owing to his family connections, and financial experience, Pitcairn became lessee for Orkney and Shetland in 1540.[166]

Pitcairn's career was typical of that of a Household servant during the personal rule – a period in office accompanied with or followed by a grant of Crown lands. An instrument of resignation dated 7 January 1540 at Linlithgow palace reveals the profusion of such men. The instrument ran in the name of David Wood of Craig, the Comptroller, and was witnessed by James Kirkcaldy of Grange, Treasurer; Pitcairn; James Learmonth of Dairsie, Master of the

Household; John Tennant, and John Ross of Craigie, principal guard of the inner chamber, who also held a charter to lands in the Glamis lordship. The actual charter of confirmation, to William Hamilton of Sanquhar, was witnessed at Linlithgow on 8 January 1540 by the Chancellor, the bishop of Galloway, the earl of Moray, the earl of Argyll, Lord Fleming, Sir Thomas Erskine, Kirkcaldy of Grange, Master James Foulis of Colinton, the clerk register, and Master Thomas Bellenden, director of the chancery and justice clerk.[167] That Pitcairn remained round the Court is suggested by his gift of wild geese to the king in April 1540, and in February 1541 he was entrusted with the responsibility of procuring a toy whistle for Prince James.[168] In 1542, Pitcairn happened to be holding charters to two pieces of Crown land – Tantallon and Orkney and Shetland. To judge by the turnover of officials in Tantallon and elsewhere – for example, in the lordship of Douglas – this was not a sign of especial royal favour. It is perhaps worth remarking that in August 1541, according to Henry VIII, James' 'most secret counsellor ' was Thomas Bellenden, entrusted with an embassy to England at that time.[169]

4. THE KING AS PREDATOR? MORTON, GRAY, AND CRAWFORD

For the majority of his magnates, then, James was not a generous king; indeed when compared with his father, he was downright mean. Some of his nobility may have had cause to use a stronger epithet. The earl of Morton was in financial difficulties throughout the personal rule, selling lands whenever he was able to obtain royal licence so to do. He had three daughters; by 1540 the two eldest were married off. He had no sons. On 10 September 1540, at Dalkeith, he sold further lands to Thomas Bellenden, the sale being confirmed by royal charter at St. Andrews on 28 September.[170] Yet little over a month later, on 17 October, at Brechin, despite his gammy leg, Morton went down on his knees and resigned his earldom into the king's hands. This occasion was witnessed by the Cardinal, John Hepburn, bishop of Brechin, Marischal, Lord Innermeath, Sir Thomas Erskine, Andrew Wood of Largo, Pitcairn, Ross of Craigie, Henry Kempt and John Tennant. The instrument of resignation recorded that the destination was to Robert Douglas of Lochleven, and that the liferent of the earldom was reserved to Morton and his wife.[171] Morton's wife was Katherine Stewart, half-sister of the king. Lochleven was a very remote kinsman.[172] On the same day, for his good service and for payment of a composition of 4000 marks, Lochleven received a charter to the fee of the earldom, to be held by himself and his heirs, and witnessed by the Chancellor, the bishop of Galloway, Arran, Argyll, Fleming, Sir Thomas Erskine, Kirkcaldy of Grange, David Wood of Craig, Foulis of Colinton and Thomas Bellenden.[173] On 11 January 1541, Lochleven took sasine, 'for his good and faithful past service'. The appropriate life reservations were made for Morton and his wife.[174]

However, at Falkland on 20 January 1541, Lochleven got down on his knees and resigned his fee of the earldom to the king. This event was witnessed by Sir Thomas Erskine and Pitcairn, and the notarial instrument recorded that Lochleven reserved the barony of Aberdour. Before he met the king, Lochleven had another notary record that he was resigning the fee out of fear and dread for his life and heritage. After his interview he made a further statement to similar effect, noting that he reserved his rights to the succession to the earldom.[175] On the same day, for his good service as a familiar servant, Lochleven received new charters to his baronies of Kinross and Kilgour.[176] On 10 March 1541 he obliged himself to resign the barony of Aberdour to the king in exchange for a charter to some of the lands of the deceased Sir James Colville of East Wemyss. Again Erskine and Pitcairn acted as witnesses.[177] King James now held the earldom of Morton in fee. This enabled him to regrant the barony of Buittle to Lord Maxwell,[178] and also confirm the lands of Moffat as a free barony to one Patrick Douglas in May 1542.[179] On 13 September 1541, Morton made the king his assignee to all the various lands held from the earldom under letters of reversion, in effect assigning his debts to James.[180] Possibly as a reward for this, Morton was then granted the gift of the marriage of the Master of Hume, which he held until October 1542.[181]

After the personal rule was over, on 18 March 1543, Morton entered into a contract with Sir George Douglas. By the terms of this, the two agreed to seek an annulment of the 1540 charter in favour of Robert Douglas of Lochleven. Sir George would then pay Morton £2000, and in return, Morton was to marry his youngest daughter, Elizabeth, to Sir George's son, James. The two would then be infeft in the earldom, and should Morton have any male heirs, he would pay his daughter and her husband 5000 marks. Morton assigned his debts to Sir George.[182] The earl then brought an action for reduction against the queen and Lochleven.

Morton put forward a heart-rending case. He claimed that the late king had charged him to pass to Inverness in the depths of winter:

> to permut and chaunge the halsoum and warme air [of Dalkeith] with cauld and tempestious air [and] the naturale fudis with the quhilkis he was nurist all his liftyme (pike?) with rude and unganand metis . . .

Old and lame and sick, he had at last arrived as far north as Brechin and had there been kept waiting for two days, before going down on his knees before the king.[183]

This poignant tale of threats, fear and ill-health was accepted by the Lords of Council and Session. Morton made out a fresh charter granting the fee of the earldom to his daughter and James Douglas, with the succession clause carefully excluding Lochleven's family.[184] Thus the earldom passed, through marriage, to an even more remote branch of the Douglas family. The tailpiece to the saga came in 1546, when Lochleven challenged the new designations in the succession clause, and attempted to reduce the court of session ruling in Morton's favour. Sir George Douglas settled the issue by paying Lochleven 5000 marks.[185]

In his treatment of Morton, James appears to have been practising something akin to recognition. In his 1543 supplication, Morton alleged that he had been interdicted from alienating his estate without any just cause, and that the king had done this deliberately in order to keep the earldom intact for himself. He further alleged that King James had contracted with Morton's younger brother, William Douglas, to effect the transfer of the earldom to himself *ad perpetuam remanentiam*, should William have succeeded as an heir of tailzie. Unfortunately for James, William predeceased his brother, and Lochleven was used as a substitute vehicle for the conveyance to the king. Morton claimed that the threat of ward had been used by the king as a more certain method of gaining the earldom.[186]

This allegation regarding the interdict was not strictly correct. Morton had obtained royal licence to sell Kilbucho to Lord Fleming in 1535, for 4000 marks. Possibly this and other licences fell by virtue of the 1537 Act of Revocation, which contained a general catch-all clause for all detrimental things done by the king in his minority. The precept to Lochleven of the earldom referred to the charter being made by reason of the king's revocation.[187] It may have been the case that Morton's 1540 sale of lands to Thomas Bellenden, just weeks before the resignation, had tipped the earldom over the balance and made possible a finding of recognition. Rather than use 'polite blackmail'[188] to obtain a composition from an impoverished earl, James took the device to its legal limits at Brechin. It is difficult to absolve Lochleven of complicity in the affair, notwithstanding the records which he had his notary take on the day of his own resignation. Clearly, he too had his designs on the Morton earldom, but ended up being used as an intermediary by King James. Lochleven does not appear to have paid his 4000 marks for his charter, and ended up with Aberdour and the promise of other lands in exchange for the barony.

It was rather an incestuous affair. Morton was married to James' half-sister. Lochleven was married to James' mistress, Margaret Erskine.[189] It is possible that James had in mind the need to secure the long-term future for at least one of his seven identifiable illegitimate sons.[190] Although James *secundus* was by 17 October 1540 the prior of St. Andrews, he still held a charter to Tantallon, Preston and Bunkle.[191] The king may have considered it appropriate to have his son by Margaret Erskine married to Morton's youngest daughter. James *secundus* would thus be the illegitimate son holding lands in the south-east. The king may then have considered controlling the earldom through a marriage between Elizabeth, Morton's daughter, and the Master of Hume. It is apparent that James' plans for the ultimate destination of the earldom had not been finalised by the end of the personal rule. In effect he and Sir George Douglas were carrying out a similar role with regard to this impoverished earldom without a male heir; both were acting as financial administrators, whilst the earl and his wife hung on to their liferent. Clearly Morton preferred Sir George's plans. If Morton's account of his epic journey north from Dalkeith is to be believed, and not simply a fabrication contrived by the Angus Douglases, then he was one magnate who had reason to consider the king a 'terrifying' individual.[192] Perhaps it was his own fault; on 18 July 1528, Lyon King of Arms had personally apprehended the earl of Angus in Dalkeith, and charged him to appear at the September 1528 parliament.[193] Presumably Morton had given Angus shelter at Dalkeith, and twelve years later James had not forgotten this.

The sixth earl of Erroll died in April 1541. He was under-age and left an infant daughter, Jane.[194] The earldom of Erroll had been administered by the Crown since the forfeiture of Lord Glamis in 1537.[195] The heir was George Hay of Logiealmond, first cousin once-removed of the sixth earl.[196] On 30 August 1541, he was granted the ward of the earldom together with Jane's marriage. On 2 September, in return 'for certane grete gratitudes done to me by the kingis grace . . . in speciall for the gift maid be his hienes to me', Logiealmond obliged himself and his heirs to pay the sum of 4000 marks 'quhen ever it sall pleis our said soverane lord'. He also agreed to marry his son to Jane and to pay 400 marks *per annum* to the sixth earl's widow.[197] On 5 December 1541, after paying his composition, he received a charter to the earldom. The narrative was effusive in its praise of Logiealmond and his predecessors:

> ever faithful barons and servants of the Crown, not only in defending the realm and invading England but also in public affairs and for upholding the liberty of the king.[198]

As the seventh earl and hereditary constable of Scotland, Logiealmond ensured that the dowager countess received the requisite provision.[199] This was a straightforward succession case, with a composition being paid as Logiealmond was an heir of tailzie to a ward held by the Crown. The lack of any machination by the king, in view of these facts, as also that the earldom was situated to the north of the Firth of Tay, where James had earlier practised a 'saturation' policy, is refreshing, coming as it does after the Morton affair and the Act of Annexation.

The succession to the Gray lordship was more involved. The third lord died in April 1541, leaving no son.[200] In 1524 the estate had been entailed in favour of his half-brother, Gilbert Gray of Buttergask, and his heirs.[201] This destination fell by virtue of one of the clauses of the Act of Revocation.[202] The nearest heirs in 1541 were Andrew Stratoun of Lauriston, married to the third lord's sister, and the seventh Lord Glamis, grandson of a second sister.[203] The Glamis estate was annexed to the Crown by April 1541, and hence the Crown was the joint heir to the Gray lordship. At Crawfordjohn on 16 July 1541, Stratoun resigned *ad perpetuam remantiam* one part of the lordship – his share of the barony of Longforgan – to the king. In exchange and for his good service, he received a charter to another part, the lands of West Kinneff, to be held by himself and heirs as a free barony. At the same time, he was granted an exemption from military service.[204] This left the king free to make grants of lands within Longforgan.

James Ross, brother of Ross of Craigie, received Lauriston; Walter Moncur, master of the queen's aviary, also received lands.[205]

This left Patrick Gray of Buttergask, son of Gilbert, without an inheritance. The situation was remedied in April 1542 when he was granted a charter to the Gray estate, including Longforgan, as heir to the second lord Gray. At the same time he became sheriff of Forfar.[206] On 3 May Buttergask obliged himself to pay the Treasurer the sum of 10,000 marks, with the last instalment due in 1544. To raise the funds, Buttergask had to sell lands. On 14 September 1542, in return for payment of a large sum, Buttergask was confirmed as the fourth lord Gray, heir of tailzie to the third lord in terms of the 1524 charter.[207] After the personal rule, in 1543, Buttergask paid off the remaining 7000 marks. He then sought to annul the various charters granted to others of parts of the estate between April 1541 and September 1542.[208] The whole episode was a neat piece of legal footwork on the part of the king and his lawyers, making use of both the Act of Revocation and the disputed succession. Gray got his charter but had to pay for it and go to the trouble of reducing other people's charters. He may have considered his sovereign to be 'probably the most unpleasant of all the Stewarts'.[209] James' 'regard for financial efficiency'[210] easily matched the 'high-powered royal fiscal activity' of his father.[211] So efficient was the fiscal system that the governor, Arran, could reap the rewards early in the following reign. Donaldson's charge of 'cupidity' laid against James in connection with Gray's composition[212] may have been considered by Lord Gray himself as applying equally to Governor Arran.

Earlier in the personal rule, the earl of Crawford had been pursued for non-entry, just as Rothes and Angus had been pursued in the reign of James IV. The 'Wicked Master', Alexander, had renounced his succession rights in 1537. However, by June 1541, he was again designated as feuar of the earldom.[213] Presumably whatever interdict and prohibitions had been passed against him had been lifted. The Master was still alive on 1 July 1541, but dead by July 1542.[214] His father, the eighth earl, was still alive on 10 October 1542 and died the following month.[215] In October 1541 he entailed the earldom in favour of David Lindsay of Edzell, his second cousin once-removed. Crawford reserved the liferent.[216] 'Our lovit' Lindsay of Edzell – who had earlier received a remission for treasonable assistance of the Douglases and who had failed to turn out at Tantallon – was served as heir on payment of 4000 marks. He began paying this sum in 1543, but was sporting the title of 'Master' by March 1542.[217] This designation overlooked the succession by the 'Wicked Master' and his heirs. It is not certain whether or not Alexander was still alive in October 1541, but he did have a son, David.[218] It appears as though the eighth earl was deliberately attempting to exclude his son and grandson from the succession, which was perhaps understandable given the earlier feud between himself and Alexander.

On 27 September 1541, three weeks before Edzell received his royal charter to the fee of the earldom, he entered into an obligation with the king at Dundee. By this he was to take possession of the earldom, but he and his heirs were to resign it into the king's hands *ad perpetuam remanentiam*, 'als sone as he or his airis beis requirit thereto', on penalty of 100,000 marks for default.[219] For Bardgett this was a sign of the 'king's own malevolence and acquisiteness'.[220] However the document recording the obligation only emerged in August 1543 after repeated requests by the Governor Arran to Sir Thomas Erskine to surrender it to him.[221] Possibly Arran hoped to enforce its terms. Certainly, it is difficult to imagine that Edzell would have been able to come up with such a huge sum to avoid losing his charter.

The editor of *The Scots Peerage* offered the explanation that the intention of all parties concerned, including Edzell himself, was that Edzell only ever expected to hold the earldom in liferent after the death of the eighth earl. This is plausible. In fact, it is what resulted in 1546, when Edzell received a further charter to the earldom in liferent, with Alexander's son, David, as the new Master. In 1546 David was required to execute a bond agreeing that should he fail to have heirs, he would ensure that the succession would revert to Edzell's heirs. Again the stipulation was made that David should resign the earldom *ad perpetuam remanentiam*.[222] The 1541 obligation by Edzell to the king was not a mechanism for James to take the earldom for himself, but rather was intended to leave open the option of succession for Alexander's heirs. The line of succession to the Crawford earldom had already been contorted in the minority, and this had afforded the opportunity for financial exploitation by the Crown in 1532. It was further complicated by the feud between the eighth earl and the 'Wicked Master'. It is in this light that Edzell's obligation at Dundee should be regarded. The sinister phrase *ad perpetuam remanentiam*, suggesting the permanent loss of lands, had not prevented Patrick Gray of Buttergask from receiving a charter to the Gray lordship. Probably the same interpretation should be applied both to the earldom of Crawford and to the earldom of Morton.

The examples of Morton, Gray and Crawford have been used by Donaldson to illustrate the notion of a king driven solely by cupidity and covetousness.[223] All three of these succession cases occurred towards the end of the personal rule, and so the conclusion can be drawn of a king sliding into greedy degeneracy. The Erroll case refutes this idea, and in fact parallels the king's approach in the more usual circumstance of a magnate dying and leaving a male heir. For the majority of his magnates, James was not a terrifying king, although those who were old enough to remember the reign of his father may have considered him to be more unpleasant than that monarch – and possibly less popular. Certainly he was less generous. James possessed formidable legal advisers, as is illustrated particularly in the instance of the Gray succession. If there was a legal loophole James would find it. In so doing he underlined the principles of the king as feudal *suzerain* and the Crown as ultimate heir. In this sense Wormald is correct to state that 'his death removed the threat of growing autocracy'. Of the many terms she uses to describe the king, 'impressive' is perhaps the most apt.[224]

NOTES

1. Lesley, *History*, 167.
2. *RSS*, iii, no. 383; cf. *TA*. viii, 220–1 for entries for some of this money; Macdougall, *James III*, 306, 308.
3. Pitscottie, *Historie*, i, 409 ('covettousnes'); Buchanan, *History*, ii, 265.
4. *SP Henry VIII*, v, pt. iv, no. ccclx.
5. Mitchison, *op.cit.*, 93; Donaldson, *op.cit.*, 44, 54, 56, 58 and generally throughout his chapter on 'The Policy of James V'.
6. *ER*, xv, 545, *et passim*; xvi, *passim*; xvii, *passim*.
7. *TA*, v; vi; vii; viii, *passim*. William Stewart is wrongly designed William Elphinstone in contents page to volume vi; cf. Watt, *Fasti*, 4.
8. Murray, *Revenues*, 267–8.
9. *APS*, ii, 353–4; SRO, *ADCS*, x, f. 177; cf. Murray, *Revenues*, 267–8, and also Kelley, *Angus*, 748–51.
10. *APS*, ii, 376, 368–9; Murray, *Revenues*, 267–8.
11. *RSS*, ii, no. 2714, Inglis, *op.cit.*, 68.
12. *ADCP*, 479; *TA*, vii, 76, 383; *SP Henry VIII*, v, pt. iv, nos. cccli, ccclx; cf. Inglis, *op.cit.*, 68–9 and *Diurnal of Occurrents*, 23.
13. *LP Henry VIII*, vi, no. 1196; *APS*, ii, 353–4.
14. *ADCP*, 284.
15. *RSS*, ii, no. 601; Murray, *Household*, 51; Donaldson, *op.cit.*, 44; Bingham, *op.cit.*, 100. Murray describes the situation as 'desperate', but also points out that the royal building programme resumed in 1529–30.
16. *ADCP*, 325; *RMS*, iii, no. 923. Alternatively, Erskine was receiving 4000 marks in all – a considerable amount for diplomatic expenses.
17. *MW*, i, 55; *TA*, v, 389 (same funds); £110 of this was for Stirling, and £35 for Falkland.
18. *TA*, vii, 233–40.
19. *Ibid.*, vi, 64, 245, 268, 274, 287; vii, 250, 340; *ER*, xv, 171–2; 480c-480d; xvii, 276–7. Cf. Murray, *Revenues*, App. 2, k.
20. *ER*, xv, 379; xvi, 162–3; xvii, 277.
21. *TA*, v, 356, 391; vii, 338; viii, 20, 117, 135.
22. Macdougall, *James IV*, 147, 166, 168; Wormald, *Court*, 10, made the assertion regarding charter compositions.
23. Macdougall, *James IV*, 161, 163.
24. *APS*, ii, 235–6, 357–8; *TA*, v, 393–400; vi, 241, 270–71, 319–22, 368–9; vii, 68–70, 236–8, 366–370; viii, 3–6.
25. *ER*, xv, 401; xvii, 515.
26. *TA*, v, 358; viii, 112.
27. *MW*, i, 2, 279.
28. *TA*, vi, 35–7, 203–5; Murray, *Household*, 54, *et passim*.
29. The phrase used by Macdougall, *James IV*, 223, for that monarch's ship-building programme.
30. *ER*, xvii, 173.
31. *Ibid.*, xvii, 157–8, 763 and 611 ff.
32. *Ibid.*, xvii, 326–31, 512–6, 662–81, 709; *RMS*, iii, nos. 2455–82.
33. *ADCP*, 346–8; *TA*, v, 450–8; vi, 64. Members of the Second Estate were to contribute from their own households.
34. Murray, *Revenues*, App. 1, g, h, i, j; App. 2, B; O'Brien, *op.cit.*, App. O. The 'auld extent' valued land at approximately one third of its current value in the sixteenth century: cf. WRH, Glamis Charters [NRA(S), 885], Box 8, no. 184, and *Thomas Thomson's Memorial on Old Extent* (Stair Society, vol. 10), 155–6 *et passim*.
35. *SP Henry VIII*, v, pt. iv, no. cccv.

36. *RSS*, ii, nos. 1738–9; *HMC Sixth Report*, 670–1; *RMS*, iii, 2797.
37. *TA*, vi, 360. In June 1538, Lord Ruthven delivered a further £200 to David Beaton by royal mandate of the king made at Falkland: *ibid.*, vii, 3, possibly indicating a further payment of taxation, although the large sum compared with his previous payment of £30 suggests that this was not all due from him alone.
38. *TA*, v, 450–8; vi, 142–3, 150, 227, 231, 359–60; *MW*, i, 196–201; 264–9, 235–9.
39. Murray, *Revenues*, App. 2, B.
40. *APS*, ii, 424. The absence of the Comptroller's accounts for 1540–41 and 1541–2 means that this cannot be shown to have been put into practice.
41. Cf. Sanderson, *op.cit.*, *passim*, for an alternative view of Cardinal Beaton's political career during the personal rule.
42. *LP Henry VIII*, xv, no. 248.
43. Pitscottie, *Historie*, i, 402; Donaldson, *op.cit*, 54, saw James' policy as being one of 'cynical disregard'.
44. SRO, *ADCS*, xii, f. 202v; Wormald, *Court*, 15.
45. *TA*, vi, 449–50.
46. *LP Henry VIII*, xi, no. 1305.
47. *James V Letters*, 325, 340. One frank or *livre* of Tours was worth roughly 9 shillings Scots. One crown was worth 2.25 franks. The Scots accountants often simply equated one crown with £1 Scots, although technically it was worth slightly more: *TA*, vi, 412, 449–50, 467. Cf. *ibid.*, vii, Pref., xvi where one crown is wrongly stated to be the equivalent of 14 shillings Scots. Donaldson, *op.cit.*, 48, identified the correct exchange rate. Cf. also Murray, *Revenues*, 322, who wrongly equated *livres* of Tours with crown of the sun.
48. Macdougall, *James IV*, 155.
49. *TA*, vii, 2–3, 48; *ER*, xvii, 273. Cf. *APS*, ii, 424, where reference is made to further Gien rents.
50. *Ibid.*, vii, 62.
51. Macdougall, *James IV*, 214, has argued that the appointment by James IV of his illegitimate son, Alexander, as archdeacon and archbishop of St. Andrews was more than simply a sign of 'nepotism, financial corruption, and spiritual degradation within the late medieval Scottish church.' Alexander was nine years old when appointed as archdeacon in 1502. James IV raised almost £7,000 from one spiritual tax in 1512: *ibid.*, 166.
52. *Ibid.*; *HMC Sixth Report*, 670.
53. Macfarlane, *op.cit.*, 48.
54. *TA*, vii, 103, 163–4, 312–4; *HP*, i, no. 382; Anderson, *op.cit.*, 5. Anderson also notes the careers of Robert *secundus*, Adam, and James *tertius*. They appear to have been younger. James had seven identifiable illegitimate sons: *ibid.*, 1–5, and App. 2. Cf. Dunbar, *Scots Kings*, 238–9 (six) and Lynch, *op.cit.*, 164 (nine).
55. *James V Letters*, 279, 287, 342; *LP Henry VIII*, viii, no. 485. He was the son of Elizabeth Shaw: *RMS*, iii, no. 1620. He was admitted to the temporalities in August 1539: *RSS*, ii, no. 3126.
56. *Ibid.*, 342–3; *RSS*, ii, nos. 3079, 3125. He was the son of Margaret Erskine: *RMS*, iii, no. 1620.
57. *Ibid.*, 357–8; *RSS*, ii, nos. 3096, 3127. Cf. Anderson, *Orkney*, App. 1, for his date of birth and generally for his career. He was the son of Euphemia Elphinstone: *RMS*, iii, no. 1620.
58. *Ibid.*, 426–7; *St. Andrews Formulaire* (Stair Society), ii, no. 411. He was the son of Elizabeth Carmichael: Dunbar, *Scots Kings*, 239.
59. Cf. *ADCP*, 310, where the annual fruits of Coupar Angus abbey are given as 2000 marks in 1530. Coupar Angus paid £220 for one term's tax in 1533. Using the same ratio of tax to annual revenue, Holyrood and Kelso were worth £2140; Melrose was worth £2300, Coldingham £1065 and St. Andrews £2670: *TA*, vi, 143–5. Murray, 'The Revenues of the bishopric of Moray in 1538' (*Innes Review*, xix, 1968), 45–8, and Anderson, *Orkney*, 5, both give higher estimates based on 1561 figures for religious houses. Murray's estimate is over £40,000 *per annum*. The Crown managed to derive almost £3700 from Moray in 1537–8, which suggests that £10,000 is a very conservative estimate.

60. *TA*, vii, 362, refers to the 1539–40 account for St. Andrews.
61. *ADCP*, 247–9, 264; *TA*, vii, 182, 193.
62. *RSS*, ii, no. 3087: licence to Patrick Douglas of Corhead to extract gold in 1539; *TA*, vi, 332.
63. *TA*, vii, 254.
64. *LP Henry VIII*, xv, no. 248.
65. *TA*, vi, 260, 324, 349; *ER*, xvii, Pref. liv, 273, 359; *APS*, ii, 424; *HP*, i, 263.
66. Cf. G. Richardson, 'Good Friends and Brothers? Francis I and Henry VIII' (*History Today*, 44/9, September 1994).
67. *MW*, i, 55, 114, 130, 195, 234, 263, 293; *TA*, v, 433; vi, 151, 232, 363; vii, 91, 159, 195, 256, 302.
68. *TA*, vi, 233–6, 381, 441; vii, 140, 231, 257, 333, 361, 445, 474, 502; viii, 94–5, 104, 118, 35, 151–55, 162.
69. Cf. Macdougall, *James III*, 306.
70. Ibid., 306, quoting W.C. Dickinson, *Scotland from the Earliest Times to 1603*, revised by A.A.M. Duncan (3rd edn., Oxford, 1977).
71. Macdougall, *James IV*, 288.
72. *TA*, v, Pref. lxviii, 434; vi, 153; cf. Wormald, *Court*, 25, who implies that the new senators were not paid until after James' death.
73. Murray, *Pursemaster*, 24; Kempt had been keeper since 1524; *RSS*, i, no. 3268.
74. Murray, *Pursemaster*, 24; *TA*, vi, 35, 201–2, *et passim*.
75. Murray, *Pursemaster*, 21.
76. *TA*, vi, 310–3; NLS, Abell, *op.cit.*, f. 126.
77. Lesley, *History*, 153.
78. Dunbar, *Scots Kings*, 48, summarises the various dates put forward for this event, which is not pinpointed in the *Treasurer's Accounts*.
79. *TA*, vi, 73, 387, 412; *MW*, i, 221–2.
80. *Ibid.*, vi, 407–8, 418. Chronologically, the dates of their summons indicate that they were to attend the queen's homecoming, although this was only specified for Lord Erskine and 'certane uthiris lordis'.
81. Lindsay, *Works*, i, 114; *ER*, xvii, 142, 166, 142. The jousting took place on Whit Monday, according to Lindsay, which was perhaps too early for the queen's arrival in 1538; cf. Edington, *op.cit.*, 72.
82. *TA*, vi, 421, 428, 432, 435; *Diurnal of Occurrents*, 22.
83. *SP Henry VIII*, v, pt. iv, no. ccclxvi.
84. *LP Henry VIII*, xv, no. 248.
85. *SP Henry VIII*, v, pt. iv, ccclxvi; Bannatyne, *Miscellany*, i, 257.
86. Ibid.
87. *TA*, vii, 267, 287. The great seal was almost continually at Linlithgow from 30 December 1539 to 21 January: *RMS*, iii, nos. 2052–2073; and the privy seal was there as well over Christmas: *RSS*, ii, nos. 3237–3264.
88. *Diurnal of Occurrents*, 23; (followed by Dunbar, *Scots Kings*, 235), but cf. *TA*, vii, 282, which suggests that it took place on 25 January.
89. *TA*, vii, 282.
90. *Ibid.*, vii, 487; Pitscottie, *Historie*, i, 379, where he describes a cloud descending, opening up to reveal a fair lady with the keys to Scotland in her hands. The contemporary records do not reveal such a pageant.
91. Dunbar, *Scots Kings*, 239.
92. *TA*, vii, 309.
93. Murray, *Pursemaster*, 19, 47, 50, 51.
94. Bannatyne, *Miscellany*, i, 257.
95. Dunbar, *Scots Kings*, 238. Again, the exact date is not given in the contemporary records.
96. *TA*, vii, 442, 445, 495.
97. Dunbar, *Scots Kings*, 238. Both princes were dead before 17 July 1541: *Balcarres Papers*, 226, no. xxiii.
98. *TA*, viii, 39.

99. Murray, *Pursemaster*, 37–43.
100. *LP Henry VIII*, xv, no. 248.
101. McGladdery, *op.cit.*, 79, 104, 108–9, *et passim*.
102. Macdougall, *James III*, 88, 252–3, 308.
103. Macdougall, *James IV*, 54, 307, *et passim*; *HBC*, 468, 484.
104. *RMS*, iii, no. 614; *APS*, ii, 382–3. Lord Hume's brother had been forfeited in the minority, but this forfeiture was later rescinded. James confirmed the rescission by royal charter in 1535: *RMS*, iii, no. 1480. Cf. Donaldson, *op.cit.*, 55, and Wormald, *Court*, 12, who, perhaps understandably, both overlooked the creation of the Methven lordship. The grant to Methven and Margaret Tudor was made in heredity.
105. Discussed at length in Kelley, *Angus*, and *Tenure*, *passim*.
106. *SP Henry VIII*, iv, pt. iv, 511, 513.
107. *RMS*, iii, nos. 645, 875.
108. *Ibid.*, iii, no. 640.
109. *Ibid.*, iii, nos. 631, 635, 636, 643, 649, 651, 665 (this last on 6 September). Eglinton's grant was really a recovery of lands lost to Kilspindie in 1527: *RSS*, i, no. 3788. George, son of the deceased David Hume of Wedderburn, and Hugh Johnston, cook, both received a part of these distributions: *RMS*, iii, nos. 641, 644.
110. *Ibid.*, iii, no. 652.
111. *Ibid.*, iii, nos. 635–689, *et passim*.
112. *Ibid.*, iii, no. 707; *ER*, xvi, 556, the non-entry being assessed at £560.
113. *RSS*, ii, nos. 174, 3228; *RMS*, iii, no. 2045.
114. *RMS*, iii, nos. 2202, 2233; cf. *RSS*, ii, no. 4941 (charter to Arran's heir in December 1542). An attempt to explain these intricacies is made by Kelley, *Angus*, 450–51.
115. Kelley, *Angus*, 447–9; cf. Macdougall, *James IV*, 162–3.
116. *ADCP*, 268–9; *RSS*, ii, no. 322, 339.
117. *RSS*, ii, no. 896; *ER*, xvi, 490A.
118. *RMS*, iii, no. 673.
119. *Ibid.*, iii, no. 738; *ADCP*, 524. In 1551, the earl of Angus sought to reduce Bothwell's charter and also its confirmation made after the king reached his perfect age: *ibid.*, 610. No such confirmation survives, and it appears as though Bothwell never set foot in Tantallon castle, which was held by Erskine from July 1529 onwards.
120. *Ibid.*, iii, nos. 644, 806.
121. *Ibid.*, iii, no. 1049.
122. *ER*, xvi, 422–3; xvii, 120–1.
123. *RMS*, iii, nos. 716, 1318. Those who had their charters revoked were mainly Carmichaels: cf. *ibid.*, iii, nos. 610, 617, 1244 (this last a grant to William Petgrunzie).
124. Cf. Kelley, *Tenure*; SRO, ADC, vol. 40, f. 7v.
125. *SP Henry VIII*, iv, pt. iv, 513; *RSS*, ii, no. 521.
126. *RMS*, iii, nos. 1391, 1425.
127. Kelley, *Angus*, 474–5 also draws this conclusion.
128. *RMS*, iii, no. 1475; *Mort. Reg.*, i, no. 3; SRO, ADCS, ii, f. 101; *ER*, xvi, 101, 211, 480B.
129. First appointed by Arran and Margaret Tudor on 6 March 1535 and then granted office for life on 5 October 1526: *Spalding Miscellany*, ii, 177–9, nos. ii, iii.
130. *RMS*, iii, no. 1345; *Spalding Miscellany*, ii, 188–9, no. ix; *ER*, xv, 434.
131. *RMS*, iii, nos. 1064, 1326, 1336; *RSS*, ii, no. 1145; cf. also Bardgett, *op.cit.*, 10.
132. SRO, ADCS, x, f. 149.
133. *RMS*, iii, nos. 1052, 1142–3.
134. *ADCP*, 418, 420–1; cf. *RSS*, ii, nos. 2166, 2173. Cf. also *ibid.*, nos. 2152, 2155, 2167 (respectively, the retainers of Argyll, Gordon of Lochinvar and Lord Fleming).
135. Hannay, *The College of Justice* (Edinburgh, 1933), 63.
136. *LP Henry VIII*, v, no. 125; *James V Letters*, 173, 182, 189.
137. *Spalding Miscellany*, ii, 193, no. xiii, dated 14 May, Edinburgh, with no year given. The

letter is reproduced in print and facsimile, with the editors unable to transliterate the bracketed words.

138. A point made more strongly by the editors who spoke of 'the confiding, kind, and truly generous spirit which this letter breathes throughout.': *ibid.*, Pref. lxxii-iii.

139. *RMS*, iii, no. 1620.

140. *ER*, xvii, 124; *RSS*, ii, nos. 2338, 2440 (this latter to his son, John; cf. *ibid.*, ii, no. 2162).

141. *ER*, xvi, 290, 390; xvii, 121, 123, 158.

142. *Ibid.*, xvii, 222, 352-4, 560, 681.

143. *Ibid.*, xvii, 273-4, 294.

144. *Ibid.*, 129, 131-2, 264, 274, 702. John, son of Andrew Kerr of Ferniehirst made the actual returns.

145. *RMS*, iii, no. 2142; *RSS*, ii, no. 4967.

146. *RSS*, ii, noo. 3410; *ER*, xvii, 132, 158, 389-90; *TA*, vii, 256.

147. *APS*, ii, 355, 357, 360-1, 401, 404; *RMS*, iii, no. 2233.

148. *Ibid.*, ii, 358; McGladdery, *op.cit.*, 93-4.

149. *ADCP*, 524.

150. *APS*, ii, 355-6.

151. Cf. *Atlas*, no. 46, map 83.

152. *RMS*, iii, nos. 2277, 2368.

153. *HMC Twelfth Report*, App. viii, 140, no. 172.

154. *RMS*, iii, no. 988.

155. *ADCP*, 323, 469.

156. Fraser, *Lennox*, ii, no. 138.

157. Cf. Donaldson, *op.cit.*, 50, 55.

158. *RSS*, ii, nos. 2458, 4437.

159. *RMS*, iii, nos. 2600, 2768.

160. *Ibid.*, iii, no. 1702.

161. *Ibid.*, iii, nos. 727, 1743.

162. *ER*, xvii, 164, 279.

163. *RMS*, iii, no. 410; *RSS*, i, no. 3268.

164. *RMS*, iii, nos. 1702, 1800.

165. *TA*, vi, 289, 418, 450, 467; vii, 18, 19; cf. Murray, *Pursemaster*, 24.

166. *ER*, xvii, 523.

167. *RMS*, iii, no. 2064; *ER*, xvii, 135, 164, 279.

168. *TA*, vii, 427; Murray, *Pursemaster*, 43.

169. *LP Henry VIII*, xvvii, no. 1125; *HP*, i, nos. 77-8.

170. *RMS*, iii, no. 2203.

171. *Mort. Reg.*, ii, no. 245.

172. The division in the family tree occurring c.1350: *Scots Peerage*, vi, 342-3, 364-9.

173. *Mort.Reg.*, ii, no. 247; *RMS*, iii, no. 2213; *RSS*, ii, no. 3673.

174. *Mort.Reg.*, ii, nos. 248-50.

175. *Op.cit.*, ii, nos. 251-3.

176. *RMS*, iii, nos. 2259-60.

177. SRO, Morton Papers [GD 150], no. 295.

178. *RMS*, iii, no. 2368. The implication must be that as Maxwell's earlier charter of 1535 fell under the Act of Revocation, so also did the 1532 reduction by the Lords of Council of Morton's charter. Buittle was included in the estates of the Morton earldom when it was granted to Lochleven on 17 October 1540: *ibid.*, iii, no. 2213.

179. *Ibid.*, iii, no. 2677.

180. SRO, Morton Papers, no. 296.

181. *RSS*, ii, nos. 4265, 4909.

182. *Mort. Reg.*, ii, no. 255; SRO, Morton Papers, no. 301.

183. *Mort. Reg.*, ii, no. 258, 289, *et passim*.

184. *RMS*, iii, no. 2901; cf. *Scots Peerage*, *passim*, for the lack of relationship between the Morton Douglases and the Angus Douglases.
185. *Mort. Reg.*, ii, nos. 260–1; SRO, Morton Papers, no. 313.
186. *Mort. Reg.*, ii, no. 258, 290–1. William was dead by 1543; cf. *Scots Peerage*, vii, 358, where Morton is said to have had just one brother called Richard, who appeared in the 1543 charter as an heir of tailzie: *RMS*, iii, no. 290.
187. *APS*, ii, 357ff; *RSS*, ii, no. 3673.
188. The phrase used by Macdougall, *James IV*, 161.
189. *RMS*, iii, nos. 1425, 2259.
190. Cf. note 54.
191. *RMS*, iii, no. 1620, i.e. before the Act of Annexation.
192. The description of James offered by Wormald, *Mary Queen of Scots: a Study in Failure* (London, 1988), 32.
193. *RMS*, iii, no. 2232.
194. *Scots Peerage*, iii, 568, by Eleanor Stewart, daughter of the third earl of Lennox and supposedly one of James' mistresses: Dunbar, *Scots Kings*, 239; cf. Anderson, *op.cit.*, App. 2, who concluded that this could not be verified.
195. *ER*, xvii, 93, 214, 360, 432, perhaps generating over £800 in income for the Comptroller.
196. *Scots Peerage*, iii, 566.
197. *RSS*, ii, no. 4184; *ADCP*, 508, the obligation signed with Logiealmond's 'hand at the pen'.
198. *TA*, viii, 8; *RMS*, iii, no. 2517: presumably for service to the king during the minority, as Logiealmond made few public appearances in the personal rule.
199. *RMS*, ii, no. 2616.
200. *Scots Peerage*, iv, 278. He was still alive on 15 April when Sir Thomas Erskine of Brechin gave a letter of regress following a sale to him by the lord: *RSS*, ii, no. 3877; *RMS*, iii, no. 2329.
201. *RMS*, iii, no. 259; *Scots Peerage*, iv, 277.
202. *APS*, ii, 357ff (clause revoking grants in tailzie from heirs-general to heirs-male).
203. *Scots Peerage*, iv, 277; *ADCP*, 531; *RMS*, iii, no. 2503.
204. *ADCP*, 532; *RMS*, iii, nos. 2407, 2435, 2650; *RSS*, iii, no. 4125.
205. *RMS*, iii, nos. 2578, 2651; *TA*, vii, 81; *ER*, xvii, 329.
206. *RMS*, iii, no. 2650; *RSS*, ii, nos. 4605–6: i.e., as grandson of the second lord, through the lord's second marriage. The third lord, Stratoun and Glamis were connected through the first marriage of the second lord.
207. *ADCP*, 516; *RMS*, iii, nos. 2679, 2749, 2782.
208. *RSS*, ii, no. 378; *ADCP*, 531–2.
209. Cf. the description of James offered by Wormald, *Court*, 12, though not based solely on this example.
210. Donaldson, *op.cit.*, 53.
211. Macdougall, *James IV*, 165.
212. Donaldson, *op.cit.*, 53.
213. *RMS*, iii, no. 3134.
214. SRO, *ADCS*, xiii, f. 48; *Scots Peerage*, iii, 26, where it is suggested that he may have been murdered. Cf. also Bardgett, *op.cit.*, 11, who suggests that the Master died in 1537.
215. *RMS*, iii, no. 2888; *Scots Peerage*, iii, 27.
216. *RMS*, iii, no. 2484; *Scots Peerage*, iii, 18, 19, 25.
217. WRH, Haigh Inventory, ii, f. 51; *TA*, viii, 221; *RSS*, ii, no. 4558.
218. *TA*, vi, 41; *RMS*, iii, no. 3231.
219. *Spalding Miscellany*, ii, 199, no. xxi.
220. Bardgett, *op.cit.*, 12.
221. *Spalding Miscellany*, ii, 197–9, nos. xix-xxi. Edzell was one of the many friends listed on Erskine's 1534 letter of safeguard: *ADCP*, 420.
222. *Scots Peerage*, iii, 28; *RMS*, iii, no. 3231.
223. Donaldson, *op.cit.*, 53.
224. Wormald, *Court*, 10, 13.

CHAPTER TWELVE

1542

The traditional picture of James V is that he met his downfall in 1542, having entered a period of decline after the execution of Hamilton of Finnart. Driven into war by his bishops, James tried twice without success to command the loyalties of his magnates. At Fala Muir they simply failed to turn up. At Solway Moss they deserted him. James died in despair. Crown-magnate relations had completely broken down.

Such an interpretation of the last year of the personal rule relies very heavily on the accounts of the later sixteenth-century chroniclers, where James' nemesis is attributed to the counsel of evil bishops and flattering courtiers. By contrast, contemporary records suggest that Henry VIII was very much the aggressor in 1542, and that James was driven into retaliation at a very late stage. There is a minimum of Scottish contemporary material to describe the king's military activity in the latter part of 1542. English sources suggest some logistical difficulties for James in October, and a very embarrassing defeat for a large number of his magnates in November. Naturally, the English border officers described what they thought was happening in some detail. They did not conclude that Scottish Crown-magnate relations had completely broken down. But they certainly picked up a lot of fact and rumour from their spies. These sources, and the scanty Scottish contemporary records, provide a picture of the diplomatic and military activity of 1542 which is sharply at odds with the stories of the later chroniclers.

I. THE DIPLOMATIC BACKGROUND

On 10 July 1542, Francis I and Charles V went to war. England and France had been at peace since the Treaty of the More in 1525. Henry VIII and Francis I had been engaged in talks in 1541 over the possible marriage of Mary Tudor to the French king's son, but these broke down and Henry decided to join with the Empire against France. However, before invading France, Henry had to be sure of his northern border.' Through marriage, James V had identified himself with the French interest. Head suggests that Anglo-Scottish relations were tied to Henry's European policy, and whilst France and England were at peace, James' connection with Francis I was of little consequence to the English king. Indeed, the Anglo-Scots perpetual peace of 1534 was largely brokered by Francis I, through his ambassador, de Beauvais. However, when France and the Empire were at peace – as they were in 1539 – Scotland as France's ally was a threat to England. As Head puts it, Henry VIII's Scottish policy was at all times guided by the 'continental focus of his diplomacy'. Hotle's emphasis is rather different, suggesting a greater emphasis on Scottish affairs by an increasingly frustrated English monarch.[2]

The Anglo-Scottish hostilities of 1532–33 had largely arisen over a mutual failure to give redress for the debatable lands and the attempts of Henry's border officers to sponsor the Angus Douglases. However, James had also indulged in some posturing by his entertainment of James Griffyd ap Powell, who arrived in Scotland too late to become a latter-day Perkin Warbeck. Also James did not care too much what his subjects in the Highlands and Islands were doing in Ireland. James' quest for a bride went beyond France and the English alternative of Mary Tudor; he considered the various imperial options on offer, and this brought him the Order of the Golden Fleece. After the conclusion of the Perpetual Peace, it became important for Henry VIII to sound out his nephew's position. The idea that both monarchs should meet to resolve their differences in a kind of summit conference was first mooted by Francis I in February 1533.[3] It was taken up again in 1534 by Henry. He appeared to have in mind that he should meet with his nephew in England, and then the two would proceed to a three-way summit at Calais, embracing Francis I, whom Henry had already met twice. Possibly mindful of the expense of the 'Field of Cloth of Gold', Henry offered to make such a meeting as inexpensive as possible for his nephew's sake.[4] According to Margaret Tudor, her son was enthusiastic about the idea, despite being 'convalest of infermyte of pox, and fevir contenow'. The queen mother also noted the dumbfounded amazement of the Scottish Chancellor, Gavin Dunbar, archbishop of Glasgow, at this prospect.[5] In the event no meeting took place, but in July 1535 Lord Erskine collected the Order of the Garter on James' behalf.

One aspect of this Anglo-Scots diplomacy was the religious card, which Henry attempted to play without success. Henry had broken with Rome by the end of 1534. In May 1535 the English government interceded on behalf of the fugitive heretic, Sir James Hamilton of Kingscavil.[6] In March 1536, Henry sent envoys to James. According to the Flemish ambassador to London, their task was to ask the Scots king to make the break with Rome. During their audience with James, lightning flashed and thunder rolled, and the king reacted by crossing himself and saying that he did not know whether he was more scared of the storm or their proposals. The envoys were then treated to a sermon on obedience to the Church.[7] At length James responded by sending Sir Adam Otterburn to London to inquire as to why he should meet his uncle. Henry's motives were never fully expressed but concerned James' marital prospects and relations with Francis I. Henry VIII suggested York as the venue; James replied that his lords would only allow him to go as far south as Newcastle, and in consequence he did not think a meeting was likely to take place in 1536.[8] James then went to France and came back in 1537 with the Collar of St. Michael, the papal cap and sword, and the title of Defender of the Faith. Theoretically, the pope could now use the Scottish king as his instrument in carrying out the deposition of the heretical English king.

Despite Henry VIII's anxieties as to the security of his northern border in the wake of the Pilgrimage of Grace and the excited communications in France between David Beaton and the French bishops,[9] James returned to Scotland with no plans for a joint Scottish-papal crusade against England. In November 1537 he congratulated Henry on the birth of Prince Edward, and Henry felt sufficiently mellow to consider sending his nephew a lion which he had just bought in Flanders.[10] In 1538, James again secured a French marriage and dowry, despite Henry VIII's attempts to persuade Francis that Mary of Guise would make a good fourth wife for himself. Mary herself was not consulted in the matter.[11] On 20 December 1538, David Beaton was created a cardinal by the pope,[12] who sent an envoy to James with instructions to equip Beaton with a biretta, and expressed his hopes that an anti-Henry VIII bull would soon be published in Scotland.[13] Cardinal Pole, who in 1537 had threatened to return to England to play a part in the Pilgrimage of Grace, sent a similar communication to his new Scots colleague.[14] However, in March 1539, the English investigated the contents of a French ship driven by storm to South Shields. Amongst other items they discovered correspondence between Rome and Scotland to the effect that 'none indults . . . wolde take any effecte in Scotlande withoute licence of their Prynce'.[15] In the same month Henry thanked his nephew for proclaiming that no 'slandrouse rymes' defaming the English king should be circulated in Scotland, and promised to send James the lion.[16]

More alarming for Henry was the fact that Francis I and Charles V met in July 1538, and by early 1539 were contemplating carving up England with James' assistance. The rumour circulated in France that Francis was sending troops to Scotland.[17] The duke of Norfolk reported from Carlisle on 29 March 1539 to Cromwell that proclamation had been made for the Scottish host to convene at Edinburgh. James had ordinance at Edinburgh castle. According to Norfolk:

> the clergie of Scotlande be in such fare that their Kinge shold do theire, as the Kinges highnes hath done in this realme, that they do their best to bring their Master to the warr . . . [and] a great parte of the temporaltie there wold their King shold followe our insample.[18]

In fact James ordered weaponshowings in March 1539, and his expenditure on weapons continued throughout 1539, as it had in earlier years.[19] Norfolk also remarked that his envoys had been informed by James that 'He wold never breke with the King his uncle during his life'.[20] This remained the position until 1542. In January 1540 James could enjoy a performance of Sir David Lindsay's satire and allegedly threaten to send his proudest bishops to his uncle. When Thomas Bellenden met Sir William Eure at Coldstream shortly after the performance, he was most anxious to obtain copies of Henry's legislation on religious policy and 'truste the to have the King his maister to studie the same'.[21] When Sir Ralph Sadler arrived in Edinburgh to lecture James on sheepfarming and religion, his first glimpse of the Scots king was attending mass with many noblemen and bishops. Sadler's escorts were Sir David Lindsay and Sir John Borthwick. That the English envoy was shown the Scots king kneeling at prayer by two outspoken critics of the Scottish religious establishment has the semblance of a contrived tableaux.[22] According to Cardinal Pole, also in communication with the Scots king, James dramatically hurled the next heretical communications from his uncle into the fire.[23] James' religious policy was summed up in the parliamentary roll for 1540–41: declarations against heresy and proposals to fund the Household from spiritual taxation.[24]

In this sense James remained orthodox in his religious policy. Knox and Pitscottie paint a picture of a king guided by the 'evill consall of his papistis bischopis', who led him to his downfall.[25] Donaldson and Wormald consider that the king's council was dominated latterly by clergy and clerical lawyers.[26] However, the sixteenth-century Protestant chroniclers were writing in the light of events in Mary Queen of Scots' reign; and Donaldson's opinion was based on the comments of English diplomats and border officers. In March 1536, William Barlow reported from Edinburgh that the whole council consisted of 'none elles but the Papystycall cleargy', and then launched into a tirade against 'ower Popysshe enemyes'.[27] Naturally, as there was a Church council being held in Edinburgh at the time that Barlow was there, he would have received a strong dose of popery.[28] After arriving in Edinburgh in 1540, Sadler reported to the English privy council that he was made welcome; the bishop of Ross had been turfed out of his town house to provide him with lodgings; the nobility were young, and James was driven to use the advice of his bishops and clergy. Sadler wished that James had such counsellors as had Henry VIII.[29]

In July 1541, Sir William Eure, writing from Berwick, reported that the great lords, spirituality, Borderers and men of the Outer Isles desired war, but James and his privy council – men such as his Comptroller and Treasurer – desired peace.[30] In September of the same year Wharton, writing from Carlisle, advised the privy council that his spy had informed him that of the Scottish 'councell', Oliver Sinclair of Pitcairn, cup bearer, his brother, Henry, a clerical accountant, John Ross of Craigie, principal chamber groom, and the Cardinal and bishops believed that James should not meet with Henry VIII in England, whilst Kirkcaldy of Grange, the Treasurer, Thomas Bellenden, justice clerk, Henry Balnaves, judge, and 'many of the barons of the realm' thought James should meet his uncle.[31] A year later, Norfolk received the report that James and all his temporal lords wanted peace, but 'their kirkemen will not agree thereunto'.[32] Marillac, French ambassador in London, reported to Francis I in 1541 that James was not expected to meet with Henry, as his prelates feared that he would then follow his uncle's example. Marillac added that the English were displeased and had dubbed the Scots prelates 'the King's tutors'.[33]

Henry VIII went on a royal progress of the north in the summer of 1541. In the process he stopped at York in August.[34] Bellenden had travelled down to Northampton in July and obtained safeconducts for Scottish merchants from the English king. The proposal was put to him that James and Henry should meet.[35] James never actually accepted the invitation, but Henry appears to have assumed that he would, as a matter of course. However, Wharton's 'espial' in Scotland advised him that James and his queen were at Falkland on 31 August 1541 with plans to head north.[36] Henry continued to wait on in York until the end of September. On 11 October James wrote a cheeky letter to him from Aberdeen and sent him some hawks. James trusted that they would be appreciated, considering that Henry had travelled so far from his usual haunts to enjoy the recreations of the north of his realm.[37] In the meantime, Cardinal Beaton was able to report to James that Francis I had assured him that France would come to Scotland's help if Henry ever had thoughts of invasion.[38] Early in 1542, Francis I revived the idea of a three-way summit. In December 1542, Francis advised the English ambassador to France that it was clear to him that Henry meant to crush Scotland and then make war on France. For the sake of peace all three kings should meet.[39]

Henry was never enthusiastic about all three kings meeting, but in February 1542 indicated to James that he was forgiven for not showing up at York the previous summer. James' excuse, of which Henry was somewhat sceptical, was that he had had troubles in the Isles in 1541. In fact the earl of Glencairn had been sent with a force to Kintyre in November 1541. Henry then asked his privy council to advise him on the possibility of kidnapping the Scots king. The privy council 'wayed that matier aftre our symple wittes' and tactfully tried to tell Henry that, as 'we fynde in it many difficulties . . . we dare not give our advises to the following of it'.[40] Hence James never met his uncle face to face despite Henry's efforts. Henry's actual agenda for such a meeting was never made plain, but broadly all he wanted to do was make sure that James caused no trouble for him in the north whilst Henry furthered his continental ambitions.

Religion was one device used by Henry in his Scottish policy. If James were to follow his uncle's example, then he would be a more reliable northern neighbour. As James did not do so, he was condemned by the later sixteenth-century chroniclers. But it is misleading to suggest that James was dominated by his clergy simply because he refused to meet Henry and eventually went on the offensive late in 1542. In effect, all that James was doing was preserving the status quo vis à vis the Scottish Church. This suited him nicely as he got money from it. His approach was summed up in a letter of 12 April 1541 to Pope Paul III, in which he declared that he had expended much money and labour in trying to stamp out heresy. In recognition of his efforts, the First Estate had voluntarily offered him a 'pecuniary token of gratitude'. All that was required was for the pope to give his assent. James marvelled greatly at the pope's delay but, as a faithful son, was determined to come to an understanding.[41]

Had the spiritual source of income ever dried up, then James would have been in a position to review religious policy. He had available both the legal and financial expertise to make possible a dissolution. Bellenden had requested copies of English documentation which could be used as a draft. Naturally, whenever an English diplomat arrived in Edinburgh, he would receive the impression of a king dominated by a priestly council. No doubt the First Estate would flock to court to ward off yet another threat to their patrimony. It is in the context of Henry VIII's unsuccessful attempts to 'drug him with diplomacy'[42] that James appears to later Protestant chroniclers to be dominated by his clergy.

James was in a strong diplomatic position after his French marriage. He could look to Francis I for assurances of support whenever Henry appeared belligerent. He could be assured that the Vatican thought him a most faithful son compared with his uncle, an erstwhile Defender of the Faith. Henry's own ambitions lay in Europe, and he wanted to accommodate Scotland rather than conquer her. Whilst Francis I was heavily engaged in diplomatic manoeuvres with Henry in 1541, James needed to do nothing, not even meet his uncle at York. James continued to do nothing until Henry decided in 1542 to join with the Empire against France, first of all dealing with Scotland. James' diplomatic position was summed up in his letter to the pope of 11 November 1542, in which he claimed that:

the King of England rages so against him only because he refuses to desert the Holy See, and will not join with him in war against the French King.[43]

Had Henry elected to side with Francis in 1542 – as was perfectly feasible[44] – then there would have been no attack by England on Scotland. The long-vaunted meeting of the three kings could have taken place – assuming that James had lived. If the Church revenues ever looked like dwindling, then James would have been in a comfortable position to begin the alternative of dissolution. This would possibly have earned him a few reproaches from his father-in-law and would have lost him the title of Defender of the Faith. As the pope's man in the British Isles, James only went into action after Henry's attack on him in 1542. If he was under pressure from a council full of clergy to initiate a religious offensive against Henry, then he simply ignored it. The 1542 war arose because Henry was unable to receive an assurance from James that he would not support Francis in the event of an English attack on France. Henry was not concerned how he got this assurance. In September 1542 he instructed his negotiators to conclude a further perpetual peace with the Scots, omitting any reference to prior Scottish obligations towards France. Alternatively James was to meet with him personally so that the same result could be achieved. As the Scots would not agree unequivocally to either proposal, it can be concluded that James had no intention of deserting his father-in-law. For this reason James never met his uncle, not because he was prevented from such a meeting by his fearful First Estate. Religion was an element in the diplomacy leading up to the war, but the fundamental reason for the war was the Scots' adherence to the Auld Alliance.

2. THE 'CONSALL OF THE PRIESTIS AND COURTOURIS'

It is difficult to identify a body of king's councillors after 1532, when the record of the Lords of Council acting in public affairs closes. The judicial record remains, and naturally shows a flourishing of both lay and clerical lawyers – these latter said by Wormald to be dominating James' council. In fact, they dominated the court of session. Political discussion took place at other times. This is clear from the sederunt lists for the Lords of Council/court of session during the personal rule. Until 1532, Argyll, Moray, and other magnates frequently appear on the session; from then on, their names appear less regularly, and are replaced by the names of the first judges. It is true that the names of magnates crop up from time to time after 1532, and 'privy council' business occasionally intrudes into the judicial record. But the scale of this, in comparison with what had been recorded prior to 1532, is minimal. Those magnates who do appear on the session after 1532 – Rothes and Lords Erskine, Ruthven and St. John are the most frequent names – were the 'extraordinary lords' drafted in to assist with judicial business. They had been assigned this task prior to the establishment of the College of Justice – with legal assistance. The presence of magnates was also recorded when they had judicial business being dealt with on the particular day. Some may have stayed on after a political session. After 1532, then, the sederunt list of the Lords of Council and Session reflects less the presence of political advisers and more the names of judges.[45]

With the absence of a satisfactory record for the Lords of Council after 1532, the nearest thing to an identifiable royal council becomes the list of witnesses to charters issued under the great seal. This changed little throughout the personal rule. Gavin Dunbar, archbishop of Glasgow and Chancellor, appeared throughout, as did Malcolm, Lord Fleming, the chamberlain. From 1540 to 1542 the other names were those of Argyll; Moray; James Foulis of Colinton, clerk-register; Thomas Bellenden, justice-clerk; the bishops of Galloway and Dunkeld; Sir Thomas Erskine of Brechin, Secretary; James Kirkcaldy of Grange, Treasurer; and David Wood of Craig, Comptroller. Arran was also a witness in 1540 and 1541.[46] David Beaton, keeper of the privy seal, was described by Head as 'head of James' council' in 1540,[47] but he did not witness any charters after 1537, no doubt because in that year he became coadjutor of the archbishopric of St. Andrews.

On certain dates in 1542, the parliamentary roll gives an indication as to who was in Edinburgh, nominally to attend to criminal judicial matters. Thus the Chancellor and the bishops of Aberdeen and Orkney appeared with Foulis, Bellenden, the lord St. John and the abbot of Cambuskenneth – president of the College of Justice – on 6 March. On 4 May, the Chancellor, Argyll, Arran,

Moray, Foulis, Bellenden and Henry Balnaves sat. On 20 July, those present were the Chancellor, the bishop of Orkney, Moray, the lord St. John, Foulis, Cambuskenneth, Bellenden, and Kirkcaldy of Grange. On 15 September Cardinal Beaton appeared with the Chancellor, the bishops of Aberdeen and Moray, Rothes, Moray, Sir Thomas Erskine, Foulis and Bellenden. On each occasion the only recorded business was a reiteration of the summons against the relatives of the deceased Robert Leslie of Innerpeffray.[48] Possibly other unrecorded business was discussed; however the king's presence was not recorded at any of these sessions.

The only other clues as to the composition of a king's council come from the reports of the English border officers – using information gleaned from their 'espialls'. Hence, the First and Second Estates appear in 1541 and 1542 as two amorphous, anonymous bodies, the former always against the English, the latter possibly in favour of war, but possibly not, according to whichever report is to be believed. One name which stands out is that of Cardinal David Beaton, who was naturally consistently hostile to the English heretics. Also, it is interesting that the lawyers and financial officers should have been considered as being in favour of peace and a royal summit meeting. War could bring a monetary headache for the Comptroller and Treasurer. It is also possible that educated lawyers such as Bellenden and Balnaves – the former deployed in diplomatic service in England – held humanist or even Lutheran views,[49] and were in favour of their king meeting with Henry VIII. Bellenden was described in one royal charter in 1540 as 'familiar and counsellor' of the king.[50]

On 14 November 1542, Berwick Pursuivant reported arriving at Edinburgh and being brought before Moray, Cardinal Beaton, the bishop of Aberdeen, Sir John Campbell [of Lundy] 'and dyvers othere of the counsaillours of Scotlande'.[51] On occasion in the latter part of 1542, what clearly was the Scots council wrote diplomatic letters from Edinburgh addressed to the English, as a body distinct from the Scots king himself. The context was comparable with letters being sent both by Henry VIII and his privy council to the English border officers. Unfortunately, apart from the Chancellor, the Scots council remained an anonymous body even in its correspondence.[52]

It is clear that Pitcairn and Ross of Craigie were Household officers. Whilst neither man appeared on any body resembling a royal council – whether in the chancery office or as parliamentary commissioners, or on the session – both were around the Court at times to witness instruments of resignation. As courtiers, possibly they were more accessible than other figures when English spies were in Edinburgh looking for information on Scottish affairs. It is doubtful that either man was a councillor in the sense that Bellenden was; certainly neither was designated as such in royal charters, although both were termed 'familiars'.[53] When Wharton's spy made his report in September 1541, he referred to the Scottish king's 'councell aboute this affare', the affair being the matter of whether or not James should meet Henry. Both Pitcairn and Craigie were said to be 'of that councell'[54] – possibly meaning little more than 'of that opinion'. A second report, made by the earl of Hertford at Alnwick on 23 November 1542, referred to 'Olyver Syntclere, oon of his [James'] pryvye counsaill'.[55] After Solway Moss, Hertford upgraded his opinion and described Pitcairn as 'the mooste secrete man leving with the said King of Scottis'.[56]

Hertford was good at adding his own gloss to the reports he received from his subordinates. Probably a more accurate description was made on 9 December 1542 by Sir Thomas Dacre, who was in charge of the Scottish prisoners after Solway Moss, and reported to Hertford. Dacre called Pitcairn 'one in grete favour with [the Scottish] king'.[57] In a list of the prisoners taken at Solway Moss, Lords Fleming and Somerville were described as being 'of the [Scots] Consaill'. This would certainly be true of Fleming. In the same list Pitcairn was described as being of the Scots king's privy council.[58] Thus the English appeared to see a distinction between those who were Lords of Council and those who were in the Household, and hence more likely to be about the king on a day-to-day basis. Of course, the English privy council corresponded with the former group rather than the latter. It is possible that some of the English border officers, Hertford for example, considered that Pitcairn stood in the same relation to James as did the members of the English privy council to Henry VIII. There is no evidence from Scottish records to support this idea.

What is likely is that James enjoyed the company of some of these 'lesser men'. They helped him spend his money on entertainments, especially in Paris. Knox, who clearly loathed Oliver Sinclair of Pitcairn,[59] at one point described him as a 'pensioner of the priests'.[60] Pitcairn's brother, Mr. Henry Sinclair, Treasurer of Brechin, was one of the auditors for both the *Accounts of the Master of Works* and the French accounts compiled by David Beaton, after receiving James' two dowries.[61] Pitcairn himself, who occasionally acted as royal pursemaster, may have had some financial dealings with the Cardinal. Henry Sinclair was promoted to the rectory of Glasgow in 1538.[62] Pitcairn had obtained his title by the grant of the lands in the free barony after the death of Alexander Stewart, bishop of Moray. He also held the fruits of Abercorn church.[63] Hence, the family were doing well out of the Church as it stood, and as a Household officer, Pitcairn was in a position to communicate his feelings on the subject both to English spies and to the Scots king.

Uniquely, but unsurprisingly, amongst the sixteenth-century chroniclers, Knox also introduced the notion of a royal list of heretical nobles. According to Knox, this scroll was first presented to James by the Cardinal and the prelates after the royal expedition to the Isles in 1540. At that time, Kirkcaldy of Grange, the Treasurer, intervened and had the king put the list away. James then told the bishops to reform their own lives.[64] Knox had the prelates conjure up this list again at some time between Fala Muir and Solway Moss. It contained the names of those whom the prelates wished to try for heresy. Knox spoke of such accusations being made against most of the nobility. This was 'the order of justice kept by the holy fathers'. Knox was never explicit as to the reason for the king needing such a list, though presumably the idea was that he could use it to terrify his magnates with the threat of conviction and escheat of their possessions. It could serve as the lay counterpoint to threats to send the bishops off to Henry VIII. Possibly James could carry the scroll around in his pocket as a form of security blanket, or hang it round his neck like a lucky charm.[65]

The first near-contemporary reference to this 'black list' comes in March 1543. The context was that the Governor Arran was having talks with Sir Ralph Sadler, and the discussion turned to the problem of Cardinal Beaton. Sadler expressed his master's anxieties that the Cardinal was not securely locked up, and suggested that he should be placed in either Tantallon or Dunbar castle. Arran said that the Cardinal was safe enough where he was. Arran went on to comment that if the Cardinal had his way, then he, Arran, would go to the fire as a heretic, and then mentioned that the late king had written down on a roll the names of three hundred and sixty noblemen and gentlemen deemed to be heretics. The list was headed by Arran, Cassillis, Glencairn, and Marischal. The conversation turned to the papacy; Arran remarked that he considered the pope to be no more than a 'very evil bishop'. The two then discussed Franco-Scots relations. Arran did not think it likely that the Scots would be looking for French help.[66]

This discussion took place at a time when Arran was engaged in a struggle for power with the Cardinal.[67] In the course of this, Beaton produced what purported to be the late king's will. This document was executed at 7 a.m. on 14 December 1542. It appointed Cardinal Beaton, Argyll, Moray and Huntly as tutors for the princess Mary and as governors of the realm after the king's death. The will is not extant, but a copy exists. However, the copyist, one Henry Balfour N.P., was not apparently authorised as a notary public.[68] Unsurprisingly, the will excluded Arran from government. Two weeks after James' death, Arran was reported by the English to have called Cardinal Beaton a 'falce churle' before the Scots council. According to Arran, the late king had died in Beaton's arms. Beaton was now lying to the Scots council about James' dying wishes regarding the rule of the country. He was also encouraging the spread of a rumour that James had wanted to forgive the Douglases. So far as English intelligence could determine, this was simply a rumour. Arran then had the Cardinal arrested.[69] Clearly, he thought that Beaton had forged the late king's will to get power for himself. Thus the later emergence of a 'black list' appears to have been a device by Arran in retaliation for Beaton's propaganda.

In 1543 Governor Arran had abuse heaped on his head from all sides. He was called 'but a simple man', a dissembler, full of 'fantazies', capable of inconstancy, a liar, and full of 'craft, frawde, and falsitie'.[70] Probably he invented the 'black list' as part of his campaign to win Sadler's support and portray himself as the man upon whom Henry VIII could rely in Scotland. Certainly, Sadler never asked to see it, and Arran never offered to produce it. After Sadler's one reference to it in his letter of 28 March 1543, the list disappeared without trace until rediscovered by Knox over twenty years later. It was an ephemeral creation by Arran in the minority of Mary Queen of Scots, not a product of the personal rule of James V.

3. RAIDS AND NEGOTIATIONS

In February 1542, James' ambassadors to London – the bishops of Aberdeen and Orkney, Lord Erskine and Thomas Bellenden – proposed that a joint Borders commission meet to give redress. Henry VIII agreed.[71] One of the causes of contention was that Englishmen were being harboured in Liddesdale and elsewhere in the Scottish Borders. Henry VIII considered these to be rebels; James considered them refugees from religious persecution.[72] The joint commission met in June 1542 with Lords Erskine and Ruthven and Bellenden as the Scottish representatives.[73] On 28 July, Henry sent Sir Robert Bowes to the Borders with instructions to garrison the English strongholds on the East and Middle Marches, pending the arrival of the earl of Rutland. According to Henry, Lord Maxwell had missed two truce days, and incidents were still occurring, notwithstanding the recent commission. Bowes was also to find out what he could about the state of the Scottish navy.[74] Henry then instructed Rutland to proceed north and ensure that no further English raids took place unless in retaliation for raids authorised by James.[75] James sent his Master of the Household, James Learmont of Dairsie, to Henry to propose that a further commission be held at York in September. Henry agreed.[76]

In August, in response to Henry's deployment of Rutland as border lieutenant, James made his own preparations. Close writings were sent to Argyll, Arran, Atholl, Cassillis, Erroll, Glencairn, Huntly, Marischal, Montrose and Rothes, and to Lords Erskine, Fleming, Hay, Hume, Lindsay, Livingston, Oliphant, Saltoun, Somerville and Semple. Letters were sent to the sheriffs to be ready at six hours' notice. The burghs of the west coast were charged to send boats to the Isles to convey men across to the mainland. Carters in Lothian were placed on twenty-four hours notice.[77] Sir William Eure, at Berwick, reported what he had learned of these movements and noted that it was now becoming extremely difficult to find any 'goode espielles for money'. However, he advised that Huntly was appointed as Scottish lieutenant 'because therle of Murray is seke'. This was probably true; Moray had spent the winter of 1540–41 in France, 'to recover my haill'.[78]

Huntly was sent down to Lauder in August, and on 20 August the Scots council briefed Learmont to advise the English that he was arriving at Kelso with a force of 'wageours' for defensive purposes only.[79] On 17 August, John Kerr, captain of Wark, raided into Teviotdale; on the following day the Scots burned Carham and Cornhill.[80] Thus it was the English turn to retaliate, although James and Henry exchanged letters professing their mutual desire to 'continew the amyte'.[81] On 24 August, Sir Robert Bowes and his fellow officers led a force of some 3000 men into the Merse. With them were Angus and Sir George Douglas, who brought their own retinue. Two forays were sent out. One burnt Syndelais (Sunlaws) and Grymsley (Grahamslaw); the other attacked Maxwellheugh. Both parties then met at Heiton – called Heiton on the Hill by both the English and Angus. The raiders then attempted to ride back to the main force, and Bowes rode out to meet them. Huntly's force, estimated at 2000 men by the English, sallied out on foot from Kelso and caught the raiding party just as it was meeting up again with the main English force. The raiders drove off all the sheep and cattle which they had rounded up; the English main party tried to round them up again and the whole force broke up in disorder. Bowes and Angus both dismounted to fight Huntly's men, but the battle was lost. Bowes and several of his colleagues were captured, together with four or five hundred men. James Douglas of Parkhead was also captured. Angus escaped.[82] Both the author of the *Diurnal* and Lesley refer to this as the battle of Hadden Rig.[83] Interestingly, Knox, Pitscottie, and Buchanan do not give the credit for this Scots victory to Huntly.[84]

On the same day as Hadden Rig, Henry VIII commissioned the Duke of Norfolk as his lieutenant in the north with a brief to muster the English counties for war against Scotland. Even before news of the defeat had reached him, Norfolk was being commanded to assemble troops not only for defence, but also for an invasion of Scotland.[85] Back in the north, John Kerr was released by his (Kerr) captors and wrote in panic to the earl of Rutland. He believed that Huntly would now lay siege to Wark castle, and reported that the remaining English prisoners had been escorted northwards from Jedburgh by Oliver Sinclair and others of James' servants.[86] In fact, James wrote to Henry VIII from Holyrood on 25 August, claiming that 10,000 men, including the rebel Douglases, had entered Scotland with the intention of burning Kelso abbey. James had sent his lieutenant with a very small force to the Borders for defence, and Huntly had succeeded in defeating this vast army. James requested a safe-conduct for his ambassadors and asked that Henry now order his officers to stop all raids. He would do the same.[87] James sent further letters from Edinburgh to his uncle on 1 and 10 September to the same effect, and agreed that the commissioners should still meet at York on 16 September.[88] At the same time Huntly and Rutland exchanged letters in which each lieutenant assured the other that raids would cease and redress be given.[89] The Scots council wrote to Rutland on the subject of the prisoners, saying:

> My lord, we can nocht understand that ye mysknaw the cause of thare takyne, considering it is sa manifest.[90]

Down south, Norfolk continued with the plans for invasion. Lists were made for provisions to be sent to Newcastle and Berwick. A royal proclamation was made for all to attend him 'for the defence and surety of the Bordures'. Norfolk was instructed to meet the Scots commissioner at York on 18 September.[91] His further instructions from the English privy council were to postpone the date of entry into Scotland from 29 September to 6 October, to allow him the time both to meet the Scots at York and to get his army ready. The Duke of Suffolk was to have 6000 men to act as a reserve whilst Norfolk was in Scotland.[92] Angus reported from Berwick that James was at Edinburgh with 'the most part of hys gryt men with hyme, boyth spiritual and temporall . . . The Kynge of Scottes sayis he wald glaidlye have paice'. Angus considered that this was largely because James had not yet received news from France.[93]

On 18 September, Robert Reid, bishop of Orkney, Lord Erskine and Learmonth met at York with Norfolk and his colleagues. Both sides agreed that redress could wait until later. The Scots were empowered to conclude a perpetual peace. The English said that France could not be encompassed in any new Anglo-Scots agreement, unlike the case in 1534. Thus neither country should declare war on the other at the instance of a third party. The Scots stated that their old ties with France could not be broken. The English response was that both kings should meet and the Scots should provide hostages – Arran, Argyll and Huntly – as pledges; they also demanded the restoration of the prisoners taken at Hadden Rig, or 'cruell warre' might ensue. The talks were then broken off.[94] Norfolk continued with his war preparations and made his will.[95] In the meantime truce days were held on the East and Middle Marches.[96] Sir Thomas Wharton, at Carlisle, was informed by a trusty spy that the Scots were ready to invade on the West March.[97] At Alnwick, Rutland's spies informed him that James and his temporal lords wanted peace, but his kirkmen would not agree.[98]

Talks resumed on 27 September at York. The Scots claimed that they were willing for James to meet with Henry at either Newcastle or York. The English did not believe this, as James had failed to meet Henry in 1541 at York. James would have to go to London. The English insisted that a perpetual peace had to be concluded before the two kings met, as otherwise James would claim that any treaty he concluded in a personal meeting with his uncle was made under duress. They pointed out that at the 1525 treaty of the More between France and England, no cognizance had been taken by the French of their ties with Scotland. The Scots replied that if a treaty were concluded, their council would see no reason for James to meet with Henry. The English demanded the return of Bowes and his colleagues. The Scots replied that the prisoners could not be released until both sides had disarmed. Neither side could disarm until both kings had met. The talks broke off.[99]

Henry VIII then sent his final demands to Norfolk. The prisoners had to be released, as otherwise they would be used as hostages. James had to arrive in London before Christmas, without 'iffes or andes of his wief . . . considering the comen errour of women in rekonnyng ther tyme'. The Scots ambassadors were to remain as pledges. If the Scots agreed, the army would be dissolved. If not, then Norfolk was to proceed with his invasion. If the 'extreme wether and rayn' and lack of supplies did not render possible 'thole entreprise as it was fyrst mynded', then Norfolk was to 'doo summe notable exployte'.[100]

Musters were taken in the English counties.[101] The date for invasion was put back to 15 October.[102] The archbishop of York dug out records showing that the see had once held primacy over all of Scotland.[103] It is apparent that Henry envisaged a great enterprise. He had sent instructions that the English navy should sail to Orkney and Shetland to destroy all the corn and cattle there that might be used by the Scots to supply their army; but Norfolk advised that this was too risky an enterprise with little to gain.[104] In another communication, Norfolk spoke of his intention to have the army rendezvous with the English navy at Edinburgh to pick up fresh supplies. However, he doubted whether the army would get that far with its present supplies.[105] He was even finding it difficult to ensure that adequate supplies were reaching Newcastle. By 7 October, a shipment of beer and victuals from London had arrived, and Norfolk was in as ready a state as he could be.[106] Angus reported from Berwick on 2 October that James feared the coming of 'our maisters armye'. His spies told him that James was still looking for peace on any terms. Moray was being pressurised by the First Estate to intercede on their behalf with the king to prevent peace. Angus doubted the truth of all this, and concluded that the Scots 'speke miche of pece and provides them alwayes for warre like wyse men'.[107]

On 4 October the talks resumed. The Scots now had a signed commission from James authorising them to conclude a meeting at York, or some other place, on 15 January 1543. Henry VIII would have to write to James to get the prisoners back. The Scots council would rather venture battle than agree to anything further, and several of them were opposed to any meeting between James and his uncle. Norfolk advised Henry that he would now assemble the army, but allow the Scots one further chance to settle. To his mind, the two sides were only at odds on minor details.[108] James' own ambassadors wrote to him from York on 6 October. They advised that difficulties remained over the delivery of the prisoners and the place of meeting between the two kings. Norfolk was delaying his attack, and they requested that Huntly should also refrain from any warlike moves. If James did not revert to them with diligence, then war would follow.[109] The privy council wrote to Norfolk saying that Henry did not really want to go to war with his nephew, but needed 'som notable exployte' to purge the dishonour created at Hadden Rig, when the English army ran away from a smaller Scottish force. The prisoners had not been ransomed, contrary to the usual practice in peace time. This gave Norfolk a pretext to invade. Any peace terms offered after his invasion were to be no less honourable than those already put forward at York.[110] On 13 October, Learmonth departed from Greenwich after a further unsuccessful attempt to persuade Henry that James should meet him at York.[111]

Norfolk's army left Berwick on 22 October. He had perhaps between 10,000 and 20,000 men.[112] James later advised the pope that the army was 40,000 strong.

French and Venetian reports estimated 100,000 men, even 120,000.[113] The bridge at Berwick collapsed when Norfolk's army tried to cross the Tweed and five men were drowned.[114] From Berwick the army proceeded to burn its way through Paxton, Hutton, Fishwick, Ladykirk, Upsettlington, Graden and Eccles before arriving at Kelso on 25 October. Around Kelso were burned Stichill, Nenthorn, Smailholm, Floors, Muirdean, Charterhouse, Broxlawe and Statherwick (Stodrig?). On 26 October, the army set fire to Kelso itself, and to the abbey, after one soldier was killed by friendly fire whilst sightseeing from the tower. On 27 October, Ednam was burnt, the army crossed the Tweed and burned Roxburgh tower and Roxburgh Mains, and moved to Redden. On 28 October it set fire to Redden, Sprouston and Hadden, and returned to Berwick.[115] Throughout, the army was desperately short of bread and beer, and nineteen men died 'only with the drinkyng of pudle water'.[116]

Norfolk himself was attacked by a severe bout of the 'lax'.[117] On his return to Berwick, he immediately discharged himself from duty and scaled the army.[118] He then wrote to Henry VIII apologising for 'the great lacke of the not accomplisshement of this journey', blaming the lack of food and transport.[119] At the same time he informed the privy council that had the army set out two months earlier with sufficient supplies, 'we might have don what we wolde without great resistence'.[120] By 5 November, Henry had printed three dozen copies of a justification for the war, caused by James missing the meeting at York in 1541, and by the Scots not giving redress and good rule, and also laying claim to the debatable lands. The declaration also rehearsed the grounds upon which Henry was entitled to lay claim to the suzerainty of Scotland. A consultation document was drawn up for the route and method by which Henry could achieve the conquest of Scotland. The recommended time for such an invasion was June 1543.[121]

4. FALA MUIR AND LAUDER – OCTOBER 1542

The Scottish records are scant for this period; the *Treasurer's Accounts* break off in August and resume in fragmentary form on 12 November. On 19 October the terms of the act of Twizelhaugh were adopted for the protection of 'the airis of thaim that suld happin to be slane, hurt to deid, or takis siknes and deit . . . gangand, remanand, or cumand fra the army'.[122] The act was invoked in early 1543 for the heir to the earl of Atholl who died of sickness, apparently at Edinburgh, after Norfolk's raid was over. His son was taken under the king's protection at Linlithgow on 9 November. Ward of the estate went to Lord Methven on 19 November.[123] On 21 October, at Edinburgh, the earl of Rothes received royal charters infefting his son, Norman, in fee to the earldom. On the following day, Argyll and Arran received similar charters; presumably this was to define clearly the succession lines to their earldoms. Rothes had three wives in the personal rule, and heirs by at least two of them.[124] On 19 October, James gave instructions from Edinburgh to Sir Thomas Erskine of Brechin and David Lindsay of Edzell to ensure good order amongst the lieges and tenants of Dun, Brechin, Edzell, Montrose and the earldom of Crawford 'anent thair furthcoming to our army and oist'. They were also to ensure that the 'unable personis' bore the costs of furnishing 'mair able personis' that could not furnish themselves in passing to the army. Earlier instructions – probably those issued in August – were superseded.[125] On 24 October, again at Edinburgh, James granted exemptions from attendance in the army to two such 'unable personis'. On account of their frailty, Robert Hunter of Hunterston and William Montgomery of that Ilk were to send their sons to war in their place.[126]

Before Norfolk's invasion, the English border officers could rely on their spies and on Scottish ambassadors to find out what was going on in Scotland in the way of diplomatic and military activity. After Norfolk's invasion, when Henry demanded Scottish news,[127] they were forced to make their assessments relying only on spies. James' own version of events came on 9 November, when he told the pope that with God's help he had turned back an army of 40,000 and a great fleet of warships.[128] Prior to that date, the scant Scottish records leave present-day historians with only the accounts of English spies – supplemented, of course, by the histories written by chroniclers writing over twenty years later.

Sir Thomas Wharton reported on 26 October from Carlisle to the Duke of Suffolk. He simply narrated the findings of four different spies, one of them being Lord Maxwell's servant. He did not attempt to compile his intelligence, but it is possible to find a chronological sequence. All four spies agreed that the Scots intended to fight. On 22 October the king had sent out to 'the northe parties' for more troops, and had put up gallows in four counties. One of the 'wylde northelandes men' already in the field had informed one spy that the presence of more troops would mean simply that all the supplies would be consumed and 'leve their countrey waste'. Lord Maxwell's servant said that his master had made proclamation at Edinburgh on 23 October for all men to be ready to fight with twenty days' supplies. Maxwell had said openly that he had thought that there would be peace, 'but nowe bothe realmes wold be oon shortly'. Another spy said that proclamation had been made on 24 October for all men to come forward. They would be paid £4 Scots per month and all they could win from their 'old enemyes of Ingland'. This same spy also advised that the men of Fife, Angus and other 'gret power' had been commanded to be at Roslin Moor on 25 October.

The king was at the castle hill in Edinburgh on 24 October, surrounded by bishops. Cartloads of victuals, spears and axes had been sent to Haddington. Oxen stood ready to draw the ordinance. One spy reported that 'they will fyght as the common opynon is'. The priests were ready for a fight. The queen had asked the nobility that 'they do not suffer the Kyng to fight (presumably in actual person) quhilk is easly graunted'. The king had promised the nobility that the queen's friends 'shall revenge this quarrell'. The intention was to cut

Norfolk's army off from the Border. The sheriff of Aberdeen (presumably a deputy as Huntly was sheriff-principal) informed one spy somewhat cryptically that 'thay [the Scots?] had cutte [dammed?] the ryver of Twide that fotemen might passe over in a gret breade when thay com to yt'.

On the night of 24/25 October all the 'northlandes men' lay in Lauderdale. Huntly and Lord Fleming had moved north from Jedburgh to join them. One spy said that the northerners should then have been at Smailholm Crags. Huntly was to have the vanguard of the army and had quarrelled with Moray 'for the having ofyt'. There were 'gret dissencions' between the two over this matter. Huntly was to have with him Lennox (who was not even in Scotland[129]), Buchan, Lord Maxwell and Cathcart, and the men of the north, the Borders, the West March, and Lothian. Maxwell was also in Lauderdale on the same night, but arrived in Dumfries on 25 October. He then received letters from James to bring the men of the West March over to the east. They and the men of Liddesdale were to meet Maxwell at Selkirk on 28 October. One spy's opinion was that James would fight on 28 or 29 October if Maxwell reached him.[130]

Wharton gave the sole account of Scottish movements for the period in which Norfolk's army was still in Scotland. All other reports filtered through to the English after both armies had gone home. If Wharton's spies are to be believed, then it appears as though James was trying to raise two armies. The first, under Huntly, was to go to Smailholm Crags (Smailholm Tower), probably to prevent Norfolk from progressing further west along the Tweed. Maxwell would meet up with Huntly and the two could then turn Norfolk either east or north, where he would be met by a second army. Probably the Scots thought that Norfolk would be turning north towards Edinburgh in any case, rather than staying to burn around Kelso. That had been the original English intention. If Norfolk did attempt to go north, then he would be caught between two armies, the first, under Huntly and Maxwell, coming in from the west, and the second coming down from Lauder, or possibly moving all the way round the coast from Haddington to come in from the east. The first army had already mustered, and was at Lauder on 2 October, ready to move to Smailholm Tower. The second army was to meet outside Edinburgh on 25 October.

A charter under the great seal was issued at Fala on 26 October. The witnesses included Moray, Argyll and Lord Fleming – this last man returning north from the first army at Lauder.[131] It appears as though Fala Muir, and not Roslin Moor, was the place of muster for the second army. One escheat was made on 26 November of the goods of John Smith in Smithston (Ayrshire?) for his 'being absent and remanyng fra oure soverane lordis oist and army, devisit and ordanit to pas to the Est and South Bordouris of the realme for expulsioun of our ald inymeiis furth of the samin, incontrar of his hienes lettres and proclamationis maid thairupoun'.[132] It is not clear from which army Smith had remained absent. Several remissions and respites were issued after the personal rule was over. Most of these referred to the pardoned man being absent from Fala in October. Some referred to an absence from the army at Lauder. Some mentioned both. One referred to the army at Smailholm Crags. Most of the recipients hailed from the west coast, from Linlithgow, and from the north-east. The two most significant absentees were Norman Leslie, Master of Rothes, and the Earl Marischal, who were both granted a nineteen-year respite in 1544. This was for their failure to obey the late king's proclamations to attend the army convened 'for resisting of the Duke of Norfolk and army of Ingland brocht be him within this realme for invasioun of the sammyn'.

At the same time both men were also pardoned for breaking the acts of parliament of 1525, 1527 and 1535, forbidding the expounding of controversial religious opinions and holding of heretical books.[133] In neither case is it clear when this latter offence was committed. It is possible that the two culprits did not join the army in October 1542 because they were then already contaminated by religion.[134] However, the Scottish host was convened for defence, and not for an invasion of the heretical land of England, and there is no necessary causal connection between the two crimes for which both men were granted a respite. It may be added that Marischal had sat on the May 1540 heresy trial of Sir John Borthwick.

In all, 164 individuals received pardons for their absence from the Scottish host in October 1542. The majority of these were issued between 1543 and 1545, but one came in 1553, and the last – to one James Leslie – in 1563. In the pardons, the offence was being absent from the army convened either at Fala or at Lauder for the purpose of resisting Norfolk's army in Scotland. No pardon made any reference to absenteeism from an army convened for invading England.[135]

If there were indeed two armies, then it appears as though the second one was led by Moray. He was at Lauder on 31 October, 'havand charge of my soverane with his counsale to gif attendance upon his besynes'. Norfolk had written to the Scots council from Berwick on 29 October on the subject of ransoming Bowes and the other prisoners captured at Hadden Rig.[136] Presumably his letter was sent to Edinburgh. John Kerr wrote to Norfolk from Wark on 1 November 1542 to say that he had learned that James was at Lauder on 31 October, with his lords and commoners. According to Kerr's spies, James 'was very desyrous to be in Englond, but the lordes wold not agree thereunto, and upon this their returned, and are dispertcyd'.[137] Thus the Scots knew that Norfolk was back at Berwick before they scaled their own army.

A further report was made on 19 November by Sir Cuthbert Ratcliffe's servant, apparently returning from Glasgow where his master was being held prisoner, having been captured at Hadden Rig. His servant reported that Argyll had had with him in the Scottish host 12,000 Irishmen and 2000 carriage horses. Probably the numbers were exaggerated. The Scots were more afraid of these men than they were of the English army, as they destroyed corn, consumed food without paying for it and threatened to kill anyone who objected. According to the servant:

There is suche penury and skarsite aswell within the lande where the Scottish army cam throughe as also upon the Borders where he passid throughe, that there is skarsely any thing to be goten for money.

His master had been informed by the Scottish Chancellor – the archbishop of Glasgow – that he would be glad of peace, 'and doubtid not but the King and the lordes wolde agre to any reasounable thing to opteyn it'. The problem lay with the Cardinal and 'som certayn bisshops'.[138]

It appears as though these wild 'Irish', or Highlanders, were part of the second army. On 22 October MacKenzie of Kintail had been in Edinburgh receiving a grant of his lands in feu farm. Probably he was in charge of a contingent of 'wylde northelande men' in Huntly's army.[139] This force was supposed by the English to have been the vanguard; Hertford reported to the privy council from Alnwick on 5 November that one spy had told him that the Scots had intended a 'notable exploite' on the Borders after 1 November. However, on that date their army had scaled. Hertford was 'credibly enformed by diverse espialles' that this was because of 'scarcite and lac of vitaill, for theire was suche famyn emonge theym that oon was like to kill an other'. Huntly had incurred royal displeasure as he had failed to attack Norfolk in the rear when the English army crossed the Tweed on 27 October, and Moray had been appointed as lieutenant in his place. Proclamation had been made in Edinburgh on 2 November for everyone to go home except the Fife men, who were to guard the coast. Back in Alnwick, supplies were short because of the late, wet harvest, and because Norfolk's army had recently passed through.[140]

One of Sir Robert Bowes' servants returned from Scotland on 16 November, and made his report to Hertford. He said that the Scots had told him that 12,000 horsemen had been ready to attack Norfolk's foot soldiers as they crossed the Tweed. Huntly had refused the enterprise, 'wherefore the Scottes doo not spare to call the said erle a cowarde captayne'. Again the number was probably exaggerated. Hertford appended a note, from a further report he had received from another spy who had been in Huntly's army at the time. His intelligence was that Huntly had only 4000 horsemen and 3000 foot soldiers. It leads to speculation as to what the 'sheriff' of Aberdeen had meant by cutting the Tweed to allow footmen to pass over.

Bowes' servant continued with the news that a Danish ship had arrived at Edinburgh – dodging the English naval blockade – with the promise of support from Denmark in the spring. The Scots were attempting to fortify Inchkeith to resist the English navy. They had also sent a ship from the west coast to France to seek help. Some fishermen had been hanged for selling oysters to the English ships. The Scots thought that Hertford would attack Jedburgh. They were prepared themselves for a retaliatory raid. In the servant's own words:

the Scotes say that theyre lordes be faynte hartyd bycause they wold not comme with more sped agaynste the armye of Englande, and it is further said the Kinge of Scottes is displeased with the said Scottes lordes for the same, for when they were commaundid by the King of Scottes to take a muster of all the Scottes oste, they certyfyed but for every 20,000 men 12,000, because they were afraid to go any further toward the army of Englande.

Even if only three out of five men showed up, it still appears as though James managed to gather a force comparable to that of Norfolk. The spy continued that there were supposed to be over 100,000 men in the Scots host, mostly wild Irish, who were unpopular as they destroyed the corn and did not pay for it. Perhaps it was just as well that the turnout was not as high as Bowes' servant reported it should have been. The same man gave further information to the effect that only Argyll and Glencairn had the ability to command a retaliatory raid. The Scots army which had dissolved had almost 180 hand guns, eighteen larger pieces, seven field guns, and two great guns. The 'common bragg' was that had Norfolk remained one more day in Scotland, then his army 'sholde have been foughten withall by the Scottes'.[141]

It is clear that Bowes' servant had been going around Edinburgh picking up every bit of information and gossip he could find. Hence he came back with a mixture of fact and rumour. There was a naval war going on; David Galbraith, Scottish skipper at Leith, had captured an English ship in August.[142] Throughout the summer, the Scots navy had been refitted at Burntisland – the *Lion* got a new anchor. By September, the English intelligence was that James had four ships at anchor, afraid to put to sea because of the greater strength of the English navy.[143] The English fleet left Newcastle early in October 1542, and on the 25th, a landing party attacked Eyemouth and killed four or five Scots men and women. Despite rumours of a French fleet supposedly in the Firth of Forth – 'laden withe wyne' – the English fleet carried on sailing north; it was supposed to rendezvous with Norfolk's army at Edinburgh. Finding no English army and no French fleet in the Forth, the English anchored off South Queensferry and settled down to burning Aberdour. There were some French merchants from Boulogne at Leith, and they lent their artillery to the Scots for defence.[144] According to James' letter to the pope on 9 November, the fleet then sailed away again – though probably James was out of touch on the west coast. (One English report implied their fleet was still in the Forth on 12 November.) The English intention was to anchor off Lindisfarne, and engage in piracy, but they may have run short of food. Before the end of the year their navy was back in the Humber.[145] This allowed the Scots fleet to set sail on 25 or 26 November. English estimates suggested that there were five merchant ships and three warships in the convoy, and by the end of the year – but after James' death – they captured three English grainships off Scarborough. Possibly James' navy did slightly better against the English in the 1542 war, than had his father's ships in 1513.[146]

It is not clear what James intended to do with the guns of which Bowes spoke.

On 2 November, Eure reported from Berwick; his spy had been in Edinburgh on 1 November, and returned south through Haddington. On his way to Berwick he found the men of Lothian going home and the Scots ordinance 'goinge bakewarde'.[147] Presumably this was the ordinance for which the oxen had been waiting on 24 October. How much of it there had been originally, how far south it had got, and how much of it was returning are all conjectures. If there were two great guns, this might suggest that a siege was intended by the Scots. Possibly this was *Mons Meg* off on her travels again. More probably, just like his father, James had new weapons to try out;[148] latterly he had been spending in the region of £1500 *per annum* on weaponry. The hand guns and field pieces could be deployed by the army in battle, and these would be sent home when no longer required. The larger weapons were probably intended for defence. James Scrimegeour, master of works, was reported as being in charge of 300 men at Coldingham in August,[149] presumably fortifying the place, as was prudent, given the exploits of the English navy at Eyemouth.

The most damaging aspect of the report by Bowes' servant was that he said the Scots thought their lords 'faynte hartyd', and that the rumour was that the king agreed with them. Hertford simply picked up this report and added his own gloss to it. Writing to the privy council on 23 November, he stated that when James was back in Edinburgh, he was 'not a litle myscontente with his lordis and servauntis', and had accused them of being 'overmuoche faynte hartid'. They had left undone two things: the one was to attack Norfolk's army in the rear, and the other was to have invaded Northumberland and stayed there for two or three days, laying waste the country. To pacify him, the lords promised they would carry out 'suche exploytis againste the kinges magesties subjectis as the said King of Scottish shuld have cause to bee contente'.[150]

The problem is not with the fact that the magnates had promised to carry out a further campaign – this demonstrates great loyalty and support for the king. The difficulty lies with the idea that the king had apparently wanted a quicker aggressive response to Norfolk's invasion and was now calling all his lords, in effect, cowards. Bowes' spy had reported various strands of thought, one of which – the idea that the Scots would have fought had Norfolk stayed in Scotland for longer – could be interpreted as meaning that the Scots were all ready to have a battle, in which case Norfolk had had a lucky escape. However, Hertford chose to amplify the other aspect of the report – this idea of a reluctant fearful nobility. No longer was it simply Huntly who had let the Scots down; now all the magnates had let the king down. No longer were the common people calling the lords faint-hearted; now the king was doing the same.

Hertford was also amplifying, or exaggerating, John Kerr's report of 1 November, in which he said that the king was 'desyrous' to be in England, but that the lords would not agree. The notion that both James and his nobility were still inclined towards peace – as reported by Ratcliffe's servant – was dropped by Hertford. Probably he also considered that enough had been said by himself and others about the shortage of supplies experienced by both sides. He seized upon one somewhat woolly report out of Edinburgh and, in particular, liked the phrase 'faynte hartid'. Hence the birth of the bad image of Crown-magnate relations in the closing months of the personal rule of James V. Really the most important part of Hertford's report was the intelligence which he was receiving about the Scots' continuing campaign; they were about to go on to the offensive.

The earlier reports out of Scotland regarding the Scots movements in relation to Norfolk's campaign, dwelt heavily on the lack of supplies. On 3 November, at Newcastle, Norfolk reported to the privy council that he had learned that James was at Lauder with 10,000 or 12,000 men, intending to invade that night or on the next morning. A further report then reached him saying that the army had scaled, confirmed to him by John Kerr's letter. 'Many other espialles' informed Norfolk that at Lauder there was 'great scarcitie of victaille', caused by the English army's 'great wast'. James had thus given licence to his men to share out what sheep they could find. 'For lack of victailles they were constrayned to sparcle their armye, and every one go home to his house'. Perhaps Atholl fell sick through drinking 'pudle' water. Norfolk then added that in his opinion James would gladly have met with Henry, but 'his lordes woll in no wise suffre Hym so to do'. Principal amongst the objectors were Argyll, Moray and Cardinal Beaton.[151]

Thus it appears as though Huntly's army passed through Lauder first on its way south to Smailholm Tower, and it ate up all the food. A second army, probably under Moray, and with Argyll leading the Highlanders, mustered at Fala Muir and then passed to Lauder in its turn. James, asked not to fight in person by the queen, received Norfolk's letter in Edinburgh. This told him that Norfolk was already back in Berwick. James then joined the second army at Lauder on or before 31 October. He would arrive fresh on the scene, full of the news that Norfolk had departed and all ready to order the army to proceed south, possibly to rendezvous with two great guns, before crossing the Tweed. If the English had their spies, it must be imagined that Moray had his. These would inform the king that Norfolk had scaled his army, but also that Hertford, appointed as warden by 29 October, was busy strengthening the English border garrisons with its remnants.[152] They would also advise James that Norfolk had burnt all the corn to the south, along the route that any avenging Scots army might take.

Norfolk had got away over the Tweed, thanking God for fair weather that had allowed him to cross, after the army's 'so merveilouse ill passaiges' along the north bank.[153] It is interesting to speculate as to what the weather was like during this period, given that Berwick bridge had collapsed on 22 October, five English soldiers had drowned crossing the Tweed, and a further nineteen died drinking 'pudle water'. Probably it had been raining at some point, hence the late wet harvests and puddles, and also the report of Chapuys from London on 2 November that rain had stopped all play on the Borders. On 13 November, Hertford reported that his officers were ready to carry out further raids into

Teviotdale – to raid as close as they could get to Jedburgh. However they could not attack Coldstream as the 'Twede hath always been up'. By the time the Teviotdale raid was carried out, on 15 November, there was a foot of snow, fallen overnight.[154] This was not ideal weather for campaigns and river crossings.

Hence Moray's army was at Lauder whilst Norfolk was burning further south. Probably Huntly was still waiting at Smailholm Tower for Maxwell to join him from Selkirk, before attempting any attack. He was probably heavily outnumbered, otherwise he would have attempted to pull off another Hadden Rig. Perhaps he was hoping that Norfolk would come forward in force from Kelso towards him. In any event it was understandable, if the reports of the English spies are to be believed, that he should have got the blame for allowing Norfolk to escape. He was the man nearest the English army, and he had failed to effect another Hadden Rig. Back at Lauder, Moray, who as the capable border commander of 1533 had missed out on doing a Hadden Rig himself through being 'seke', would be quite willing to crow at Huntly's lack of action.

Realistically, there was little else that James could do, after Norfolk had gone home, other than to scale his army at Lauder, and return to Edinburgh to devise a new strategy. It is notable that the English border officers first put this down to lack of provisions, and only later came up with reports of faintheartedness. They had not covered themselves in glory either, and they expected James to retaliate at some point. It was more important to find out what the Scots king intended to do next than quiz their own spies for the precise reasons why James had not engaged Norfolk's army.

Of the chroniclers, the author of the *Diurnal* gives a short and succinct account. The English army caused 'a littill skaith' on Scottish soil and then dispersed homewards. James 'in lykwyiss' then scaled his army and returned to Holyrood.[155] For Lesley, James was 'verray sorye' that the two armies had not met in Scotland, as it was not honourable. Thus he wanted to invade. The lords deliberated for a long time, and pronounced that this was not a good idea, as he had no male heirs and should not risk himself in person. Besides his uncle might retaliate with greater force, and jeopardise the safety of the realm. It was sufficiently honourable to defend the country against attack. James heeded the 'wisdome of his nobilyte' and returned to Edinburgh with both army and honour intact – after Norfolk had scaled his army.[156]

According to Pitscottie, at Fala James had an army of 60,000 which moved to Lauder. Norfolk came over the Border and challenged him either to meet Henry or give battle. James was 'wondrouslie commovit' and assembled his lords at Lauder Kirk. The lords debated the issue, and Glencairn was their spokesman. James, he said, could not pass forward with honour because of the bond between Scotland and England, sealed with the great seal and signed by the lords themselves. If Norfolk invaded they would defend, but they could not support an invasion of England. James then learned that Norfolk was away again. He wanted to attack. The lords 'laide thair heidis togither' and muttered dark things about him being a better priest's king than theirs, and that maybe they should hang all his secret servants who gave him such wicked counsel contrary to the welfare of the realm. They then said that they would not attack. James returned to Edinburgh with all his secret servants. The lords waited until they were sure that Norfolk had returned south, then they went home.[157]

Buchanan's version has James camped at Fala, fourteen miles from the Borders. George Gordon [Huntly] had 10,000 soldiers to check the English rovers but 'did nothing remarkable'. James, according to Buchanan, flew into a violent passion because his nobles would not give battle, though frequently told he had done enough for his honour in preventing a great army from pillaging the country, hemming them in until they reached Kelso where they rushed into the water without order and ran home as fast as possible, George Gordon not lifting a finger to stop them.[158] Knox also introduced the notion of the lords wanting to hang the king's flatterers and priestly pensioners, in remembrance of Lauder Brig. However, they could not agree who should be hanged. James stood in no little fear. The army, according to Knox, had 18,000 men in it, assembled at Fala. Huntly, Seton and Hume led 10,000 men in the vanguard. Norfolk's army went home, the rumour being that it was short of food. James asked the lords to go on the offensive; they said they would fight for their life in defence, but not in attack, being so far away from their homes, with weary horses and short of supplies. James praised their prudent foresight and wise counsel, but secretly desired revenge.[159]

None of these accounts is too outrageous, in that they all make clear the correct fact that the magnates turned out to support the king in the defence of the realm. The problem, if there was one, only arose when it came to going into England on the offensive.[160] Hence the various attempts to explain why the Scots host went home from Lauder rather than proceeding south. The answer is that they had not moved quickly enough: by the time they were ready to advance, Norfolk was away; the weather was bad; food was in extremely short supply both at Lauder and further south; possibly the army was too big to be deployed as an effective attacking force; Atholl was dying; and Moray and Huntly in all likelihood were not communicating with each other. There was no magnate rebellion against the wicked priestly king; probably there was good advice to the effect that they should all rethink their strategy now that the immediate threat posed by Norfolk was over.

NOTES

1. Cf. J.J. Scarisbrick, *Henry VIII* (London, 1968), 434–5; D.M. Head, 'Henry VIII's Scottish Policy: a Reassessment' (*SHR*, lxi, i, no. 171, April 1982), 17.
2. Head, *op.cit.*, 11–12, 14, 24; Charles P. Hotle, 'Tradition, reform and diplomacy: Anglo-Scottish relations, 1528–42' (Ph.D. thesis, Cambridge University, 1992), *passim*.
3. *LP Henry VIII*, vi, no. 184.
4. *SP Henry VIII*, v, pt, iv, no. cclxvi.
5. *Ibid.*, v, pt. iv, no. cclxxiii.

6. *LP Henry VIII*, viii, no. 734.

7. *Ibid.*, x, no. 427.

8. *Ibid.*, x, nos. 601, 699, 740, 810, 863, 908, 928.

9. *Ibid.*, xii, pt. i, nos. 463, 665, 762, 923.

10. *James V Letters*, 338; *SP Henry VIII*, v, pt. iv, no. cccxli. According to J.N. Charteris, 'The Evolution of the English Party in Scotland 1513–44' (Ph.D. thesis, McGill University, 1973), 105, the suggestion by Thomas Scott of Pitgormo that Henry send James the lion demonstrated that legal diplomat's own pro-English sentiments.

11. *LP Henry VIII*, xii, pt. ii, nos. 1004, 1201, 1292; xiii, pt. i, nos. 56, 132, 203, 273, 611; xiii, pt. ii, no. 177. This – partly French – correspondence makes it clear that Mary's own wishes in the matter were ignored and that she preferred France to Scotland, even, possibly, Henry VIII to James.

12. Sanderson, *op.cit.*, 67.

13. *James V Letters*, 361.

14. *SP Venetian*, v, no. 194; Scarisbrick, *op.cit.*, 342, 346–7.

15. *SP Henry VIII*, v, pt. iv, no. ccclvii.

16. *LP Henry VIII*, xiv, pt. i, nos. 170, 176; *HP*, i, no. 51.

17. *LP Henry VIII*, xiii, pt. i, no. 1415; xiv, pt. i, nos. 115, 298, 418; *SP Henry VIII*, v, pt. iv, no. ccclix.

18. *SP Henry VIII*, v, pt. iv, no. ccclviii.

19. *TA*, vii, 153–4, 209–231.

20. *SP Henry VIII*, v, pt. iv, no. ccclviii.

21. *Ibid.*, v, pt. iv, no. ccclxvi.

22. *LP Henry VIII*, xv, no. 248.

23. *James V Letters*, 417.

24. *APS*, ii, 370–1, 424.

25. Knox, *History*, i, 32–3; Pitscottie, *Historie*, i, 404, 406, 408 (quotation from Pitscottie).

26. Donaldson, *op.cit.*, 55; Wormald, *Court*, 12.

27. *SP Henry VIII*, v, pt. iv, no. 36.

28. *Diurnal of Occurrents*, 20.

29. Sadler, *State Papers*, 46ff.

30. *LP Henry VIII*, xvi, no. 990.

31. *HP*, i, no. 85. Pitcairn had several brothers: *RMS*, iii, no. 2768 (William, Alexander, Arthur and James). Possibly the one referred to here is Mr. Henry, Treasurer of Brechin, rector of Glasgow and accountant; cf. *TA*, vii, 2, 36, 63, 364; *ADCP*, 526.

32. *HP*, i, no. 174.

33. *LP Henry VIII*, xvi, nos. 1183, 1253.

34. *Ibid.*, xvi, nos. 864, 990, 1084.

35. *Ibid.*, xvi, nos. 1034 (2), 1105, 1115–6, 1125.

36. *Ibid.*, xvi, no. 1115; *HP*, i, no. 85.

37. *LP Henry VIII*, xvi, nos. 1208, 1251.

38. *Ibid.*, xvi, no. 1178.

39. *Ibid.*, xvii, nos. 51, 84, 97; xvii, no. 1204.

40. *SP Henry VIII*, v, pt. iv, nos. ccclxxxviii, cccxc; *TA*, viii, 40.

41. *James V Letters*, 424.

42. Scarisbrick, *op.cit.*, 434.

43. *LP Henry VIII*, xvii, no. 1060 (anglicised); also in *James V Letters*, 444.

44. Cf. Head, *op.cit.*, 14.

45. SRO, RH 2.1.9. *passim*; Wormald, *Court*, 12; cf. generally, *ADCP*, Introduction; Hannay, 'The College of Justice' (Stair Society), 128–9 and P.G.B. MacNeill, *op.cit.* In *ADCP*, 'public affairs' from June 1528 to May 1532 (four years) occupy 197 pages. The remaining ten years occupy 247 pages, and there is a perceptable change in the quality of the 'public' material after 1532 – increasingly incidental to legal matters.

46. Cf. Appendix II.
47. Head, *op.cit.*, 15.
48. *APS*, ii, 384–5.
49. Edington, *op.cit.*, 95–98, goes into this subject in detail.
50. *RMS*, iii, no. 2203.
51. *SP Henry VIII*, v, pt. iv, no. cccciv.
52. E.g., *HP*, i, no. 147 (2).
53. *RMS*, iii, nos. 1900, 2101.
54. *HP*, i, no. 85.
55. *Ibid.*, i, App. no. xiii.
56. *Ibid.*, i, App. no. xix.
57. *Ibid.*, i, no. 252 (1).
58. *LP Henry VIII*, xvii, no. 1143. In the same report, Ross of Craigie was 'gentleman usher of the Privy Chamber, one of the Council'. This designation appears to categorise him alongside Pitcairn rather than Fleming.
59. Knox's attitude is discussed by G.A. Sinclair, 'The Scots at Solway Moss' (*SHR*, ii, 1905).
60. Knox, *History*, i, 34.
61. *MW*, i, 196–7, 235; *TA*, vii, 46, 63.
62. *James V Letters*, 377; *MW*, i, 235; *ADCP*, 526.
63. *RMS*, iii, nos. 727, 1743; *TA*, vii, 379.
64. Cf. the more elaborate version of this episode given by Melville, *op.cit.* Possibly the story is in some way connected with Buchanan's and Pitscottie's tale of Hamilton of Finnart being appointed as an Inquisitor before his execution in 1540.
65. Knox, *History*, i, 33–4. Neither Knox nor Melville went this far, but the idea that the king kept the scroll on his person at all times crops up in later histories.
66. *LP Henry VIII*, xviii, pt. i, no. 324.
67. Discussed at length by Sanderson, *op.cit.*, Chapter 10.
68. *HMC Eleventh Report*, App. pt. vi, 219–20, no. 158. Lang, 'The Cardinal and the King's Will' (*SHR*, iii, 1905–6) examines the whole issue of whether or not such a will existed.
69. *HP*, i, nos. 263, 265, 267, 271–2, 289.
70. *Ibid.*, i, nos. 259, 326, 397, 433; *LP Henry VIII*, xviii, pt. i, nos. 391, 482. His detractors included Lord Fleming (dissembler), Mary of Guise ('fantazies') and Sir George Douglas (inconstancy).
71. *LP Henry VIII*, xvii, nos. 87–8.
72. *Ibid.*, xvi, nos. 499, 511, 612–13, 840.
73. *Ibid.*, xvii, nos. 398, 415, 469; *TA*, viii, 85–6.
74. *SP Henry VIII*, v, pt. iv, no. cccxci.
75. *Ibid.*, v, pt. iv, no. cccxcv; *HP*, i, nos. 117–8.
76. *SP Henry VIII*, v, pt. iv, nos. cccxciii, cccxciv; *HP*, i, no. 115.
77. *TA*, viii, 113–116.
78. *HP*, i, no. 120; *HMC Sixth Report*, 760–1.
79. *TA*, viii, 116; *LP Henry VIII*, xvii, no. 644.
80. *HP*, i, no. 120.
81. *Ibid.*, i, nos. 121, 125.
82. *Ibid.*, i, nos. 127–8, 146 (i); *Melr. Lib.*, ii, no. 602.
83. *Diurnal of Occurrents*, 25; Lesley, *History*, 25.
84. Knox, *History*, i, 31; Pitscottie, *Historie*, i, 397–8 (credits Lord St. John); Buchanan, *History*, ii, 262 (credits Lord Hume). This attitude is probably explained by the later Catholicism of the Gordon earls of Huntly.
85. *LP Henry VIII*, xvii, nos. 661, 714 (19).
86. *HP*, i, nos. 128, 135 (i).
87. *SP Henry VIII*, v, pt. iv, no. cccxcii.
88. *Ibid.*, v, pt. iv, nos. cccxciii, cccxciv.

89. *HP*, i, nos. 147 (3), 147 (4).
90. *Ibid.*, i, no. 147 (2).
91. *Ibid.*, i, nos. 143–4, 150–5, 158.
92. *LP Henry VIII*, xvii, nos. 764, 786, 794, 800.
93. *HP*, i, no. 147 (5).
94. *Ibid.*, i, no. 167.
95. *LP Henry VIII*, xvii, nos. 808, 813–4, 820.
96. *HP*, i, nos. 169, 174.
97. *Ibid.*, i, no. 174 (1).
98. *Ibid.*, i, no. 174.
99. *Ibid.*, i, no. 181.
100. *Ibid.*, i, no. 189.
101. *LP Henry VIII*, xvii, no. 882.
102. *HP*, i, no. 193.
103. *LP Henry VIII*, xvii, no. 898.
104. *HP*, i, nos. 189, 193.
105. *Ibid.*, i, no. 211.
106. *LP Henry VIII*, xvii, nos. 813–4, 901, 920–1.
107. *HP*, i, no. 197.
108. *Ibid*; LP *Henry VIII*, xvii, no. 919.
109. *LP Henry VIII*, xvii, no. 913.
110. *HP*, i, no. 204.
111. *Ibid.*, i, no. 209.
112. The size of the army can only be estimated roughly from English papers which indicate how many men were mustered from some of the shires, how many men Norfolk conveyed from Norfolk and Suffolk to the north, and how many carts he estimated he needed for water: *LP Henry VIII*, xvii, nos. 661, 703, 750, 753, 778, 800, 882, 900, 907, 922, 927, 954, 969.
113. *James V Letters*, 444; *LP Henry VIII*, xvii, nos. 806, 978.
114. *HP*, i, no. 221.
115. *LP Henry VIII*, xvii, no. 998; *HP*, i, App. nos. xx, xxiv.
116. *HP*, i, no. 226.
117. *Ibid.*, i, no. 227.
118. *Ibid.*, i, nos. 226, 228, 239. (The letter from Henry VIII on 2 November rebuked Norfolk for his hasty decision to scale the army without consulting his master).
119. *Ibid.*, i, no. 229 (29 October 1542).
120. *Ibid.*, i, no. 227.
121. *LP Henry VIII*, xvii, nos. 1033–5.
122. *ADCP*, 530.
123. *Ibid.*; *RSS*, ii, nos. 4975, 4981; Lesley, *History*, 164.
124. *RMS*, iii, nos. 2809–16; *RSS*, ii, nos. 4941–3; *Scots Peerage*, vii, 281ff. Rothes' eventual successor was Andrew, son of his second wife. Norman, son of his first wife, was designed as his heir in 1542.
125. *Spalding Miscellany*, iv, 44, no. xxvi.
126. Fraser, *Eglinton*, ii, no. 134.
127. *HP*, i, pt. i, no. 231.
128. *James V Letters*, 444.
129. Cf. Wormald, *Bonds*, App. A, 325, no. 4, which suggests Lennox granted a bond of maintenance at Tullibardine on 11 November 1542. The bond itself excepted allegiance to the Queen (i.e. Mary), clearly indicating that it was drawn up and executed after James' personal rule was over: *Taymouth Bk*, 153–4. Cf. also, *HP*, i, nos. 295 (10 February 1543), 327 (10 March 1543), 336 (20 March 1543), which indicate that Lennox was in France, about to return to Scotland. Cf. also, Fraser, *Lennox*, i, 365–7.

130. *HP*, i, no. 224 (i).
131. *RMS*, iii, no. 2828.
132. *RSS*, ii, no. 4989.
133. *Ibid.*, iii, nos. 395, 820; *APS*, ii, 295, 341. (In 1543 the Master of Rothes received an earlier respite for his absence from the army).
134. Cf. Sanderson, *op.cit.*, App. 3, nos. 99, 114.
135. *RSS*, iii, nos. 344, 395, 397, 444, 598, 746, 757, 767, 810, 813–4, 818, 820, 829, 832, 834, 1023, 1028, 1201, 2256; iv, no. 1923; v, no. 1305.
136. *HP*, i, no. 230.
137. *SP Henry VIII*, v, pt. iv, 213.
138. *HP*, i, App. no. viii.
139. *RMS*, iii, no. 2817. MacKenzie had replaced Moray as lessor of the Crown lands of Trotternish in 1540.
140. *HP*, i, App. no. ii.
141. *Ibid.*, i, App. no. vii, and also *LP Henry VIII*, xvii, no. 1100 (2).
142. *ADCP*, 534.
143. *TA*, viii, 94–5; *HP*, i, nos. 119, 147 (1), 150.
144. *HP*, i, nos. 192, 211–2, 218, 224 (2); App. nos. iii, iv; *ADCP*, 522.
145. *HP*, i, nos. 211, 265; App. nos. iv, vi.
146. *Ibid.*, i, nos. 246 (i), 251, 265; App. nos. xv,xx – possibly *Lion, Salamander*, and *Unicorn*. Cf. Macdougall, *James IV*, 243.
147. *SP Henry VIII*, v, pt. iv, 215.
148. Macdougall, *James IV*, 136, 271.
149. *HP*, i, no. 120.
150. *Ibid.*, i, App. no. xiii.
151. *SP Henry VIII*, v, pt. iv, no. cccxcvii.
152. *LP Henry VIII*, xvii, nos. 982, 996–7, 1002, 1016.
153. *HP*, i, no. 226.
154. *Ibid.*, i, no. 236; *LP Henry VIII*, xvii, nos. 1017, 1084.
155. *Diurnal of Occurrents*, 24.
156. Lesley, *History*, 163–4.
157. Pitscottie, *Historie*, i, 400–402.
158. Buchanan, *History*, ii, 262–3.
159. Knox, *History*, i, 31–3; cf. Macdougall, *James III*, 285, who discusses the parallels being made by Knox between James III and James V.
160. Cf. Lynch, *op.cit.*, 165, who thinks that the problem was that the nobility would not muster to defend the realm.

CHAPTER THIRTEEN

The Final Weeks of the Reign

The second phase of the Anglo-Scottish war of 1542 opened immediately after the Duke of Norfolk's withdrawal to Newcastle early in November. James V redeployed his forces, and strengthened his border garrisons. Lords Hume and Hay moved to Selkirk.[1] On 12 November, letters were sent to the provost to 'mak reddy fische, flesche, breid, aill and siclike', and to find all supplies of grain stored away by the local inhabitants in their barns. Similar letters of instruction were sent to Selkirk and Lauder.[2] A tax had been levied on the burghs in September, to provide 'wageours' and weapons for the border garrisons, for one term (three months, if the 1533 precedent was followed).[3]

On 4 November, Hertford wrote to Norfolk saying that he could not possibly hope to attack Jedburgh, as the Scots lieutenant (presumably by this time Moray) was there. He considered it a far more dangerous enterprise than burning Kelso; had Norfolk done his job properly, then there would have been less need to strengthen the English garrisons.[4] According to Gilbert Swinney, captain of Cornhill castle, writing on 16 November, the Jedburgh garrison was 1600 strong, and commanded by Moray, James Scrimegeour, master of works, James Doig (of Dunrobin) and an 'Irish captain'.[5] On 15 November, Hertford reported that an attempt had been made to prevent 300 Scots from reaching Coldingham, and the English had burnt Reston. Despite the river Whiteadder being fordable, the Scots had not pursued the raiders.[6]

The *Treasurer's Accounts* are fragmentary in this period, but enough survives to indicate James' new strategy. Before 12 November, letters were sent to Lanark, Edinburgh, Haddington, Linlithgow, Stirling and to nine other burghs to be at Lauder on 20 November.[7] On 19 November, the sheriff of Wigtown was ordered to convene the lieges there, and join Lord Maxwell. On the same day all barons, landed men and others and the men of West Lothian and Lauderdale, were charged to be at Peebles on 21 November. On 20 November, Huntly, Argyll, Marischal, Rothes, and Lords Ruthven, Seton, Menteith and Livingston, and Sir John Campbell of Cawdor were also charged to come to the king at Peebles 'witht diligence'. Letters were sent from the king to the Lords of Council at Haddington. The provosts of Selkirk and Hawick were directed to find provision for 600 men of the Merse and Teviotdale.[8] Two gifts of escheats were made at Edinburgh on 29 and 30 November. In each case the culprits – a handful of men from the north-east – were guilty of failing to answer the royal proclamations and letters summoning them to attend 'our soverane lordis last oist and arme, devisit to have bene at Lauder the xx day of November instant and passand fra thyne to wart the West Bordouris for defens of the samyn and resisting of the inymeis of Ingland'. One letter added that the army had passed from Lauder to Peebles and then to the West March. There appear to have been no remissions or respites obtained for those absent from this campaign.[9]

James himself was at Falkland on 12 November, where he received a further communication from Norfolk on the subject of ransoming the Hadden Rig prisoners.[10] On 17 November he was at Linlithgow, visiting his pregnant wife.[11] His own letters to the pope on 20 and 21 November – on the subject of nominations to the vacancies at the archdeaconry of Dunblane and deanery of Brechin – suggest that he was in Edinburgh on both those dates.[12] However, English intelligence, which has to be used to complete the story of the Solway Moss campaign, indicates that the Scots king was in the field by 20 November.

James returned to Lauder, and was there on the night of 20/21 November. Clearly he had no psychological hang-ups about the place. Also he was not intending to stay, and undoubtedly had brought both more food and a smaller force. The first English information on the Scots' movements came on 16 November. At that stage all that was known was that the men of Teviotdale, the Merse and West Lothian were on the move and intending to raid in the east in two separate forces.[13] On 20 November, one of Sir George Douglas' spies was turned back by the English watch at Bylleborne. He passed his message on to a woman who got lost but eventually found Sir George, who wrote from Berwick to his brother. Proclamation had been made at Edinburgh on 17 November, and at Haddington the following day. All gentlemen with their households were to meet the king at Lauder on 20 November. 1000 horsemen were deployed in Teviotdale, a further 500 in the Merse. Sir George would try to find out more.[14]

Eure wrote from Berwick to Hertford on 21 November. The Scots were to raid in the east. Either the garrisons would stop them or the Tweed. However, Sir George then produced fresh intelligence. James was not at Selkirk or Melrose. Instead, he claimed that all the king's lords and gentlemen and their households had moved from Edinburgh to join him. Oliver Sinclair, one of the privy council, was at Hume with Lord Hume and the men of the Merse, while the Teviotdale men had moved to join the king.[15] At Alnwick, Hertford did not yet have the latest information but had warned all of the English border officers to be ready, as he had discovered that James had proclaimed that all men should join him at Lauder with enough provision for a forty day campaign.[16] On 22 November, John Kerr reported from Wark that a Scotsman had come to the garrison at 10 o'clock at night, bearing the news that James was at Peebles on the night of 21/22 November, and heading for Hawick. He intended to attack the West March and had 9,000 men.[17]

On 23 November, Hertford summed up the position for the English council, and in the same letter created the legend of the fainthearted lords. James, he said, had upbraided his nobility. Upon this 'expostulacion' with them, they had been commanded to assemble all their household servants and trusted friends, and on 21 November everybody was at either Melrose or Selkirk. Moray, the Cardinal and many other lords were there. Oliver Sinclair, one of the privy council, had gone to Hume castle with the Merse men. The Teviotdale men had come to the king. Obviously Hertford's report was based on Sir George's information, relayed by Eure, who had also told Hertford that 2,000 Scots had gone to Primside Mill on 21 November and were intending to attack Ford or Etal. One of Hertford's own spies had told him on 22 November that the Scots intended to invade in two places, one force across the rivers Esk and Leven (Lyne), the other across the Coquet water or at Glendale. His latest news from Wark was that the Scots intended to attack only in the west. However, Hertford advised that this news should be taken with a pinch of salt, as the Scots might be deliberately putting out false information. As he said himself, 'the Scottish bee Scottis'.[18]

Fortunately for the English, Hertford alerted Sir Thomas Wharton in Carlisle as to the possibility of an attack in the west. Wharton got Hertford's first letter, on 22 November, warning that the Scots were mustering. At 7 p.m. on 23 November, he received a second letter, dated 22 November, giving the information that the Scots might be attacking the Esk and Lyne. Wharton had spent the previous night raiding into the debatable lands, unsuccessfully trying to draw Lord Maxwell out of Lochmaben, and Maxwell's son out of Langholm. By 8 p.m. on 23 November he had lit the beacons. At midnight he wrote to Hertford that 'newes almost commyth howrelie' of the Scots' intention to attack. The Scots king, according to Wharton, was at Castlemilk, his army at Long Hollyn (Langholm). In a postscript, Wharton added that the Scots were assembled at Langholm and Morton Kirk, and would be invading England in the morning.[19]

On 25 November, Hertford wrote that his spies had told him that James left Edinburgh on 21 November with the gentlemen and households of Fife, Angus, and many other areas. He was at Peebles on 23 November. Moray and Lords Erskine, Fleming, and Seton with their households and the men of Lothian, the Borders, Galloway and many other parts were to enter England at Whale Causey. Hertford, by now satisfied that the Scots were going to attack the West March, then learned that Moray and the Cardinal were in the east, heading for Haddington.[20] On 28 November, Angus wrote to Hertford saying that the Cardinal and Moray were at Haddington and had intended to enter the English East March, find a church and proclaim a papal interdict of England.[21] At the same time, a report came in from Berwick Pursuivant, recently at Edinburgh to discuss the subject of the Hadden Rig prisoners with the Scots council. On his return south, after his colleague Somerset Herald was assassinated near Dunbar – according to rumour, at Cardinal Beaton's instigation – Berwick met up with one James Hamilton of Innerwick, and a William Hume. These remarkably well informed characters told him that James had not consulted the Second Estate in devising his strategy against the West March, and that consequently, there was 'contention' between them and the First Estate.[22]

Hertford wrote again on 1 December. His spies now told him that the raid had been made on the advice of the Cardinal, Lord Maxwell, Mark Kerr [of Dolphinton] and Oliver Sinclair of Pitcairn, much against the 'willes and myndes' of the rest of the council, the lords and Scotland. Another spy reported that Moray, Cardinal Beaton, and three Scots bishops had intended to move from Lauder to Coldstream, cross the Tweed and pronounce the papal interdict. Moray was then to have gone to Jedburgh to garrison the Borders.[23]

As had been the case after Lauder in October, so also after Solway Moss, the picture of Scottish activity was only gradually pieced together by the English using their spies, and with each new report the picture grew more and more distorted. It seems scarcely credible that James should have managed to mount a campaign with a large number of his magnates against the wishes of the majority of them. In particular, Hertford seems to have been mesmerised by the name of Oliver Sinclair, although he was never quite sure where he was – nor where anybody else was for that matter. To judge by English reports, the Scots army largely comprised the retinues of the Scots magnates together with contingents from the Lothians and Borders, rather than being a full feudal host. One man who received a new charter to his lands at Falkland on 12 November was Hector MacLean of Duart, who in 1536 had exchanged bonds with the earl of Huntly,[24] and was presumably part of Huntly's retinue. If it was the case that James was not using the feudal host, then he needed his magnates' cooperation to pull off his scheme, and English reports as to the number of the Scots nobles in the field suggest that he got it. A smaller non-feudal host would be more mobile and able to do what James wanted quickly.

It appears as though James' intention was to start at Lauder, to give the English the impression that he was attacking towards the east. He then rapidly moved over to Peebles, meeting the main body of the army. Possibly he found time to return to Edinburgh to attend to business on 21 November. The whole force then went to Langholm *via* Hawick, arriving there on 23 November. It was not a bad strategy, given that until 7 p.m. on 23 November, English attention was still focused on the East March. Until Wharton received Hertford's warning letter on 23 November, he had been happily conducting raids into the debatable lands.[25] Hertford himself only fully understood what the Scots were doing on the day after Solway Moss. It is possible that had James been successful in his plan to raid the West March, then he would have instructed Moray to raid in the east. A papal interdict of England would be a useful propaganda exercise in countering Henry's claims of suzerainty, and would possibly attract international attention. If this was the plan, then it was a near reversal of the situation in 1513, when James IV was excommunicated by the Cardinal of York.[26] It would also be sweet revenge for the burning of Kelso abbey, and would put James in a stronger bargaining position should he decide to come to terms with his uncle. It is interesting that even after Norfolk's raid, the English intelligence was that James was still keeping alive the possibility that he might yet make peace, even meet Henry.

There are no extant Scottish contemporary accounts of the battle of Solway Moss. There are three English reports, each written by men who were there – Wharton, Sir William Musgrove,[27] and John Musgrove. Wharton gave the most detailed account, 'fighting the battle as he saw it, with a reiver's eye, and a reiver's tactics'.[28] Unfortunately, the place names he cited are somewhat obscure. The Scots began burning one-and-a-half hours after dawn on 24 November. They started at the foot (mouth) of the Esk estuary, and burnt a two-mile strip along the south bank to a place called 'Akeshawhill' (Hornick Hill?). They were burning Graham property. Three hundred English 'prickers', or light cavalry, approached to 'pricke' at them. This drew the Scots onwards, and eastwards in a 'grete and long chace'. Wharton had drawn up his main force along the south bank of the Lyne, apparently spread out to give the impression of being larger than it actually was. The Scots and English armies thus were sideways on to each other, with the Scots in an area called 'Artureth Howes'. The Scots continued burning 'homewert', presumably north towards a place where they could cross the Esk. Twelve hundred English horsemen then crossed the Lyne, and advanced to Howpsikehill (Hopesike Woods). The Scots 'marched easily' towards them, within arrow range. Both sides dismounted. The Scots set up their field ordinance. The English knew that they had to attack the Scots' right flank, as on the left there was a 'grete mosse'. Thus the Scots were trapped between the English and the Esk estuary. Wharton suggested that this caused problems for the horsemen of both armies:

> domysedaye beyng then emongstest all prekers of both the sides and not one hedestrang horse of naythre side.

The furthermost part of the Scots force from the English began 'easely to recule', and then those in front, and lastly the ordinance.

The English then marched on foot to Artureth Howes. The Scots came near to Artureth mill dam, where there was a ford called Sandyford (Sandbed?). They now had the Esk to cross, a 'grete standyng water' in front of them, and a 'grete mosse' on their left. Clearly the English had penned them in before they could reorganise themselves to ford the Esk. The English:

> had them in a shake more then in warlike haste at that dam, the standyng water mosse and the ever of Heske.

The English prickers then charged towards them again. Rather than be driven into the Esk, the Scots surrendered. Pitscottie, the only chronicler to attempt to describe the battle in any detail, said that this whole business of the Scots becoming boxed in took all day; the Scots 'knew not the passage quhilk they might have saiflie riden'. They crossed the Esk whilst the tide was up, and the water four fathoms deep, and so came to a place called 'the Solloun mose', where the English finally attacked them.[29] All the English accounts indicate that the confrontation took place on English territory, south of the Esk. 'Dyverse men'

[318]

were drowned in the Esk; ten bodies were fished out three days later. Sir William Musgrove said that Lord Maxwell, with many other nobles and courtiers, 'lighted at the waters side and fought valiantly'.

In the numbers game, the Scots had the advantage even allowing for English exaggeration. Wharton said he had 300 prickers, six standards, 200 archers, his colleagues and his own men who were 1200 or 'nere thereaboutes'. Sir William Musgrove spoke of having all the gentlemen of the West March 'with thinhabitauntes of the same', to the number of 3000 at the most. John Musgrove, leader of the English horsemen, said that the number of Henry's subjects assembled was not above 2000. By contrast the Scots had, 'as they sey theym selvis', 17,000 men, and the English were not about to disagree with this; Sir William thought they had 18,000. Wharton said that the two Scots armies camped the night before at Langholm and Morton Kirk 'extemed in bothe there nombres' above 13,000 men, perhaps over 20,000. According to John Musgrove, James held one of these two armies in reserve, intending to send it in on 25 November to the west of Carlisle. Possibly this was the army of which Hertford had spoken, ready to enter at Whale Causey. It is clear that the force defeated at Solway was only a preliminary raid, perhaps intended to trigger off a sequence of raids along the Border, at Whale Causey, Coldstream, and Primside. In the course of this attack, England would be interdicted.

The Scots defeated at Solway appear only to have intended a minor incursion into England. They were burning between the Esk and the Lyne with field ordinance; this was not a full scale invasion with Carlisle as its objective. Possibly, had the raid been successful, and Wharton defeated, it would have been followed by a more intrusive incursion. A comparison may be made with James IV's raids of 1497 against the Middle and East Marches, gradually increasing in their intensity as the year wore on.[30] The difference, of course, was that this was the West March, and very late in the campaigning season; even had the Scots won at Solway, their short-term prospects of following up their success with a more substantive raid would have been limited. Hence the strategy was probably as English reports suggested – interdict England and then take stock.

That this was no more than a Border raid is also suggested by those who were in the Scots army. It does not appear to have been a feudal host ready for a prolonged campaign; rather – to judge from the prisoners taken – it was in the nature of a 'notable exploit' or an adventure for the Scottish nobility after a long period during which there had been little opportunity for fighting anywhere other than in the Isles. Those captured included Cassillis, Glencairn (the man whom James had latterly entrusted with daunting the Isles), Lords Maxwell, Fleming, Gray, Oliphant and Somerville, and Robert, Master of Erskine. Also amongst the prisoners were Pitcairn and Ross of Craigie. Somerville advised Wharton that the Scots had had over thirty standards in the field, including those of the earls of Erroll and Menteith. Wharton saw none of them being carried back over the Sark. One English report added that the earl of Caithness was missing.[31] Wharton thought that he had taken over 1200 prisoners; Sir William Musgrove estimated over 1000 captured, killed or drowned. Wharton said only twenty men were killed.[32] It had gone horribly wrong for the Scots – less of a disaster than Flodden, but rather more humiliating than Hadden Rig had been for the English.

A list was drawn up for the purpose of ransoming the Scots prisoners; it makes interesting reading, revealing *inter alia* that Maxwell was the richest magnate, with annual landed revenues of 4000 marks and goods worth 3000 marks, though his brother, Henry, was apparently not worth anything. Fleming was richer than either Cassillis or Glencairn. Pitcairn's landed income *per annum* was 500 marks, and he had 1500 marks worth of goods, making him richer overall than the fourth lord Gray. Ross of Craigie was richer than Pitcairn.[33] All these prisoners presented a problem for the sixteenth-century chroniclers, who could not understand how Wharton with a smaller force had managed to trap the Scottish raiders – and perhaps wondered why the Scots lords had not died, as they had at Flodden.

The author of the *Diurnal* again was succinct; the Scots had been 'discomfeist' at Solway, 'quhilk was ane unhappie raid, [and were] begylit be thair awne gyding', at which the king 'tuke greit displeisour quha past to Falkland and thair lay seik'.[34] All the other chroniclers introduced the Oliver Sinclair *motif*; Sinclair was the lieutenant, produced his commission and then sat on two spears, raised upon men's' shoulders. Lesley says that the lords thought themselves 'lichlytit our farr', such a mean man being promoted above them, and willingly became prisoners. Pitscottie thought this was another example of the king being advised by 'consaill of the priestis and courterouris', and launched into a general tirade on the matter. However, he added that the battle was lost by confusion rather than by sedition or wilful surrender. James was then struck by remorse. For Buchanan, Maxwell in particular was deeply offended, and all command ceased. Knox admitted that there was a rumour that Maxwell had devised the raid, 'but the certainty therof we have not'. Pitcairn's commission, according to Knox, was all a plot arranged beforehand by the priestly council. Maxwell said that he would rather stay at Solway than go home and be hanged.[35]

On the subject of Pitcairn's (literal) elevation, Sir George Douglas also had a contribution to make from Berwick. On 16 December, before he had the latest news that James was dead, he wrote that the king 'maykes greyt o mone for Oliver Singular mor than he doys for all the greyt men that is takyng'. Pitcairn was the 'prinsyple captayne to all the said army at that tyme', and had lost the king's banner there, for which – so Sir George was informed – the king also 'maykes greyt mone'.[36] This was a singular interpretation of the Scots defeat. Sir George had good intelligence on Scottish events; he was amongst the first to alert Hertford about the proposed attack on the West March, and also to find out that James was dead. It is possible to pinpoint him as the source for the spurious notion that Pitcairn was one of James' privy councillors.

It is very likely that Sir George was conducting a smear campaign against the Scots king. After all, he and Angus had been in control of the Scots king until James assumed personal control in 1528. The Angus earldom had been annexed to the Crown in 1540; in 1542 Pitcairn was the captain of Tantallon castle, in which Sir George and Angus had successfully withstood James' 1528 siege. It is likely that the Douglases wanted to paint a picture of James as a man being badly advised by lowly men and consequently making a mess of his military campaigns. This was the sort of thing about which Dr. Magnus had warned the king fourteen years earlier, strongly hinting that James would be much better off being reconciled with his former Chancellor. 1542 was the best opportunity for an English-sponsored Douglas return since the hostilities of 1532–33.

Sir George's version of events was not corroborated by the English commanders at Solway. Sir William Musgrove's report indicates that they thought Maxwell was in charge. James was not a fool. Throughout his personal rule, in what military campaigns there had been, he had employed the service of his magnates – in particular Moray and Huntly, but also Glencairn and, early on, the third earl of Argyll. The only appointment made to date against which there might be placed a question mark was that of Bothwell as lieutenant in early 1529. But even that had been a reasonable choice; Bothwell only proved treacherous in 1531, after James had stamped his authority on the Borders. Maxwell had been one of James' vice-regents in 1536, and was the warden of the West March. To suggest that James passed over all his magnates – many of whom had been with him on the 1540 Isles campaign – in order to appoint Pitcairn as his commander is hardly credible.

What may have happened, to give some foundation to the fiction, is that James gave his standard over to his favourite Pitcairn to hand on to Maxwell, the man most likely to have been the commander. James was not at Solway; obeying his wife's instructions he kept his 'proper person' out of the field. He may not have met up with Maxwell the night before, when he arrived in a hurry down from Hawick. As this was supposed to be a surprise raid, with the Scots not looking for organised opposition, Pitcairn may have held on to the standard until the Scots drew up to face the English. With so many 'chiefs' in the Scots army, when the time came for Maxwell to call upon Pitcairn to hand over the standard, some of the other magnates – Glencairn, for example – may have been querying Maxwell's strategy, even started squabbling about it. Then confusion would arise, and Pitcairn would be left holding the standard not knowing to whom to give it. After Solway, Wharton reported that Maxwell was 'very desirous' to speak to Pitcairn.[37] Maybe he wanted to ask him what on earth he thought he was playing at.

A second fiction is that the Scots lords all willingly surrendered rather than return to their king to face the music. In its most ludicrous form, this becomes a tale of fledgling Protestants running away from the shadow of the predatory Catholic king.[38] There is the report of one Hieronomo Zuccato, Venetian ambassador to London, writing on 16 December 1542. On this date the Scots prisoners had not even arrived in London, but were at Newark-on-Trent. Zuccato was told in the strictest confidence – he had to swear not to reveal his source – that Maxwell was a Lutheran who disagreed with Cardinal Beaton, for many years the ruler in Scotland. Maxwell had caused the defeat by running round to the rear of the army, killing a few Scots, and then returning to the front to surrender.[39] Had Zuccato let the cat out of the bag, the English propaganda machine would have had a field day. However, there seems to be no particular reason to believe his informant rather than Sir William Musgrove, who said that Maxwell and the other Scots lords 'fought valiantly'. Their stance was similar to that of Sir Robert Bowes and the other prisoners taken at Hadden Rig. This was a defeat of a raiding party led by several Scottish magnates, all acting in the service of their king and probably enjoying the campaign until Wharton's prickers arrived.

The 1542 war was not in itself about religion, though the religious stances taken by both kings played a part in their diplomatic and military strategy. The religious attitudes of the nobility – at least for James – did not matter. Of those taken, Cassillis had been educated by George Buchanan; so had James *senior*. Cassillis' uncle was the abbot of Crossraguel.[40] In 1539 one of Glencairn's sons became the bishop of Argyll; another was pardoned for being a heretic.[41] Lord Gray apparently struck a Protestant attitude in Forfar during the minority of Mary Queen of Scots.[42] Lord Fleming founded a collegiate church at Biggar in 1545 under the auspices of the archbishopric of Glasgow, and approved of by the papal legate. In it prayers were to be said for the souls of himself, the late king and Cardinal Beaton.[43] James did not care greatly what his nobility thought about religion. The Cardinal might have been allowed to burn the effigy of Sir John Borthwick, but there was no attack on Sir David Lindsay or Thomas Bellenden. It is unlikely that James would have sacrificed Maxwell – one of his chief supporters – for holding heretical opinions, whatever parliamentary legislation there was about heretics not being able to hold office. Religious postures and beliefs would only become of political relevance after James' death, when Scotland was under threat from the 'heretical' English.

It is true that Eure's spies told him on 13 December 1542 that the rumour was circulating round Edinburgh that the prisoners were 'judgede in Scotlande that they shall rather become Englishe men thene other waies'. It is surprising that they could not tell him that James was now out of circulation, dying at Falkland. It is also the case that the Douglases met Lords Maxwell and Fleming at Newcastle on or shortly after 7 November. Sir George apparently discovered that they conceded that Henry VIII could now more or less dictate his own terms to James, even force him to give up the 'Auld alliance'. Maxwell suggested that he should be allowed to go back to Scotland to move to bring this about.[44] Clearly he had no qualms about facing his own king again, and was indeed anxious to go back home. Shrewdly, the English did not succumb to this ploy, and escorted all the Scots lords to London. By January 1543, they had all signed a bond to assist Henry VIII in his Scottish strategy.[45] Thus they returned to Scotland as 'assured lords'. Of course James was now dead and buried, and no doubt Henry thought that the control of Scotland was his for the taking. It was one way for Maxwell and company to get away from the English king.

The final myth about Solway is that afterwards James crawled back home to die at Falkland – 'less of an illness than a lack of will to live'.[46] Certainly, it was very late in the campaigning season, and no doubt James and his magnates had suffered a psychological blow by the failure of their strategy and capture of a fair number of the Second Estate. However the poor king managed to struggle on for a few more days, only taking to his bed, according to Sir George Douglas, on 6 December.[47] Wharton reported that James V had watched the raid from Burnswark Hill.[48] English reports then had him making his way through Lochmaben and Dumfries back to Edinburgh, and then on to Linlithgow. One report had him go straight from the west to visit a mistress at Tantallon. Knox had him lament the loss of Pitcairn – 'O fled Oliver, is Oliver tane? O fled Oliver' – and then predict that 'on Yule day ye will be masterless'. According to Knox he then paid a visit to the earl of Crawford's daughter, who was a whore.[49]

James was back in Edinburgh by 28 November, earlier if he had to sanction the sailing of the Scots fleet. By 4 December, English reports had filtered through to the effect that he had met his council.[50] One outstanding item of business was the assassination of Somerset Herald near Dunbar on 25 November 1542. The council – once again, save for the Chancellor, an anonymous body – wrote from Edinburgh to Eure on 28 November. They denied all liability and asserted that 'na falt may be impute to His Majestie, nor nane of his liegiis yerthrow'. James himself wrote from Edinburgh to Henry VIII on 30 November. The culprits were English fugitives; he requested safeconducts for Learmonth of Dairsie, Sir John Campbell of Cawdor, and Rothesay and Ross heralds to discuss the matter. His uncle replied on 10 December, demanding that James deliver the guilty parties. He closed his letter to his nephew with the words: 'We beseche God to sende you health'.[51]

English reports also came through that James had released Scott of Buccleuch, John Hume of Blackadder and Johnston of that Ilk. Blackadder had promised the king that he would 'do many marveylous thinges within your graces [Henry's] realme orr yt be long'. This was something of a political gamble; neither Buccleuch nor Blackadder had a particularly good track record of service to the Crown in the personal rule. Eure thought it likely that Blackadder would again make common cause with Angus.[52] Possibly rather more Borderers had been captured at Solway than English prisoner lists suggest. The gamble appears to have paid off in Buccleuch's case; on 4 December the Scotts of Teviotdale raided into Northumberland. The English claimed that they were repulsed without difficulty, but an entry in the *Treasurer's Accounts* suggests that they captured some booty.[53] After James' death, Buccleuch turned his attention to the royal flocks at Melrose abbey.[54]

On 28 November, at Edinburgh, James instructed Johnston (who had been in ward at Dumbarton) to take order as, in the absence of Lord Maxwell and 'infirmite' of his son, the 'west bordouris of our realme is destitut of ane wardane and gydar'. James' further instructions from Edinburgh followed on 30 November. Johnston's kin and the sheriffs of the West March were to assist Johnston for the duration of the Master's 'infirmite' in giving good rule and in the 'resistence and invasioun maid to the inymyis of Ingland'.[55] Presumably Maxwell's son was either ill, injured or simply lacking in experience. There was no suggestion that he was being dismissed for the 'desertion' of his father. Furthermore, the instructions indicate that further Scots raids were still a possibility.

Between 8 and 12 December, there are entries in the *Treasurer's Accounts* which indicate that preparations were being made to continue the campaign. On 8 December, the sheriffs of Berwick, Lauder, and Selkirk were instructed to charge all men to 'rise' with the warden of the East Marches (Lord Hume and his kinsmen). Orders were made for the lairds in the Merse to 'furnis' their houses. On 12 December the sheriffs of the Middle and East Marches were instructed to charge all men:

> bayth on hors and on fute to be reddy at the heicht of this nixt mone be skry, bale, or uthir sing [i.e. by proclamation] to pas forwart for resisting of the Inglismen.

Similar orders were sent to the Master of Maxwell.[56] On 13 December Eure reported that proclamations had been made at Duns and Haddington on 9 and 10 December for all manner of men in the East March to assemble at Hume castle, or 'where the fier or fraye shall ryese'.[57] As he himself was making no preparations for an offensive, it appears as though the Scots were. However, this is a matter of some doubt; if Sir George's later intelligence is correct, James was on his death bed by 6 December, in which case the Scots council was now in charge and probably ensuring that the realm's defences were secure.

The official Scottish records show that business was slowing down by 6 December. Charters were issued from Edinburgh from 26 November onwards. One, on 4 December, was issued from Linlithgow. But the register closed on 6 December.[58] The privy seal register continued until 8 December; the last entry concerned a convoluted shipping case involving merchants from Flanders. One entry was dated 23 November at Moffat, suggesting that either the king or Cardinal Beaton, or both men, had passed through there on the day before Solway Moss. On 6 December, letters were issued at both Edinburgh and Kelso Abbey; perhaps James, in between seeing mistresses, had paid a flying visit there to see what damage Norfolk had done.[59] However he appears to have been at either Edinburgh or Linlithgow for most of this period.

The court of session record closed on 9 December, the last entry mentioning that 'now the quenes grace is approcheand to ly and seiklie'.[60] A Scots prisoner, taken on 5 December, reported that proclamation was made at Jedburgh of the birth of a son on 2 December. By 12 December, the English had news that a girl had been born prematurely, 'a verye weyke childe and not like to lyve, as it is thought'. On 16 December Sir George Douglas' spies corroborated this information.[61] James found time to visit Linlithgow before 7 December, and it would have been possible for him to have returned there from Edinburgh after the birth.[62] On 6 December he is to be found at Edinburgh, writing to Patrick Hepburn, bishop of Moray, and to Sir John Campbell of Cawdor, sheriff of Nairn, instructing them to desist from taking legal proceedings against Hutcheon Rose of Kilravock, who had been violently resisting the bishop's attempts to collect his rents.[63] Business as usual.

James had been ill on a number of occasions during his personal rule: in 1533 'of a sore fois'; in 1534 of the 'pox, and fevir contenew'; in Paris in 1536; and in 1540, when he wrote to his wife to say that he had been as ill as he had ever been in his life, but was now recovered.[64] Evidently his immune system had not made the same recovery. 'Pestelence' – or epidemics – had plagued Edinburgh and Linlithgow in 1530, and flared up again in Linlithgow in 1545. Perth, in 1542, had been suffering from the 'pest' for three years.[65] James had visited the fair city in November 1541 and in June 1542.[66] Alternatively, James caught whatever his last illness was from someone else – perhaps his half-brother, the earl of Moray. The most likely culprit was the thirty-five year old earl of Atholl. The disease may have been cholera. There is no need to attempt to diagnose a more esoteric cause of death.[67] James died at Falkland on 14 December 1542.[68]

NOTES

1. *TA*, viii, 136, 138.
2. *Ibid.*, viii, 136.
3. Murray, *Revenues*, App. A, no. 21 (l), 91; App. B, 106.
4. *LP Henry VIII*, xvii, no. 1031.
5. *HP*, i, App. no. vi. Doig received a charter to lands in Methven on 5 December 1542: *RMS*, iii, no. 2851.
6. *HP*, i, App. no. v.
7. *TA*, viii, 136. The entry is partly mutilated.
8. *Ibid.*, viii, 137–8.
9. *RSS*, ii, no. 4994; *Spalding Miscellany*, ii, 196, no. 27; cf. *RSS*, ii, no. 4992, being an escheat for absenteeism from the army at Lauder. This – in common with some of the remissions listed at Chapter 12, n. 135 – could refer to the army at Lauder in either October or November.
10. *TA*, viii, 136; *LP Henry VIII*, xvii, no. 1068.
11. *TA*, viii, 137–8.
12. *James V Letters*, 445–6.
13. *HP*, i, App. no. vi.
14. *Ibid.*, i, App. no. ix.
15. *Ibid.*, i, App. no. x.
16. *Ibid.*, i, App. no. xi.

17. *Ibid.*, i, App. no. xii.
18. *Ibid.*, i, App. no. xiii. Hertford estimated James' army at 14,000 or 15,000 men, but then scored this out.
19. *Ibid.*, i, App. no. xiv.
20. *Ibid.*, i, App. no. xv.
21. *Ibid.*, i, App. no. xx.
22. *SP Henry VIII*, v, pt. iv, no. cccciv; *HP*, i, no. 257.
23. *HP*, i, no. 245.
24. *RMS*, iii, no. 2835; Wormald, *Bonds*, App. A, 300, no. 106.
25. *LP Henry VIII*, xvii, no. 1052.
26. Macdougall, *James IV*, 261–2, 300.
27. *HP*, i, nos. 240, 247, App. no. xvi. Curiously, this last, by Wharton, was endorsed 'M[emoran]d. thought not true report'.
28. George Macdonald Fraser, *op.cit.*, 251.
29. Pitscottie, *Historie*, i, 405.
30. Macdougall, *James IV*, 135–40.
31. *HP*, i, no. 251 (1), App. nos. xvi, xviii.
32. *Ibid.*, i, no. 240, App. no. xvi.
33. The prisoners included Maxwell (4000 marks *per annum* in lands and 3000 marks worth in goods); Cassillis (3000/1500), Glencairn (1500/1000), Somerville (1200/1500), Gray (1000/900), Oliphant (2000/2000), Fleming (3000/4000), Oliver Sinclair of Pitcairn (500/1500), George Hume of Ayton (800/1000), Robert, Master of Erskine (500/750 plus a 3000 mark inheritance), Walter, son of Sir Ninian Seton of Touch (Stirling, 150 in lands + 600 inheritance), Patrick, son of Patrick Hume of Waughton (300 in lands + 1800), John Maitland of Auchen Castle (Dumfries, 400/1000), William Moncrieffe of that Ilk (600/1000), John Ross of Craigie (750/1500), James Pringle (sheep master, 300/1000), John Leslie, illegitimate son of Rothes (Rothes inheritance of 2500/2000), John, son of John Carmichael, captain of Crawford Castle (150/750 + 400), James Sinclair, brother of Pitcairn (150/500), Alexander, brother of Pitcairn (150/150), Walter Kerr of Graden, John Charteris, Richard and John Maxwell: *SP Henry VIII*, v, pt. iv, no. cccix; cf. also *HP*, i, no. 252 (i), App. no. xxiii and *LP Henry VIII*, xvii, no. 1143.
34. *Diurnal of Occurrents*, 25.
35. Lesley, *History*, 164–5; Pitscottie, *Historie*, i, 403–7; Buchanan, *History*, ii, 263–4; Knox, *History*, i, 35–7.
36. *HP*, i, no. 259 (i).
37. *Ibid.*, i, App. no. xviii.
38. Even partly accepted by Charteris, *op.cit.*, *passim*.
39. *LP Henry VIII*, xvii, no. 1207; *HP*, i, no. 258.
40. *RSS*, ii, no. 642; *James V Letters*, 95; *Scots Peerage*, ii, 468ff. Cf. Sanderson, *op.cit.*, App. 3, no. 33, for biographical notes on Cassillis.
41. *RSS*, ii, no. 2952; *James V Letters*, 364. Cf. Sanderson, *op.cit.*, App. 3, nos. 43, 70.
42. Bardgett, *op.cit.*, 30–1 *et passim*; Sanderson, *op.cit.*, App. 3, no. 72.
43. *Wigtown Charter Chest*, nos. 529–30.
44. *HP*, i, nos. 249, 255, 257.
45. *Ibid.*, i, no. 276.
46. Lynch, *op.cit.*, 165.
47. *HP*, i, no. 260.
48. *Ibid.*, i, App. no. xviii.
49. *Ibid.*, i, nos. 251 (i), 255; Knox, *History*, i, 38–9.
50. *HP*, i, no. 246 (i).
51. *SP Henry VIII*, v, pt. iv, nos. cccciv–vi
52. *HP*, ii, nos. 251–2, 255, 256 (i), 257.
53. *Ibid.*, i, no. 248; *TA*, viii, 139.

54. *HP*, i, no. 263.
55. Fraser, *Annandale*, i, nos. 2–4; *TA*, viii, 138.
56. *TA*, viii, 138–9.
57. *HP*, i, no. 257.
58. *RMS*, iii, nos. 2842–2853.
59. *RSS*, nos. 4988–5013; Pref. xiv ff; cf. *ADCP*, 521.
60. *ADCP*, 529.
61. *HP*, i, nos. 251, 259 (i). Dunbar, *Scots Kings*, 238, states that Mary Stewart was born on 7 or 8 December.
62. *TA*, viii, 138 (no date is given), the next entry being dated 8 December.
63. *Family of Rose*, 207–8.
64. *LP Henry VIII*, vi, no. 1187; xi, no. 596; xvi, nos. 405–6; *SP Henry VIII*, v, pt. iv, no. cclxxiii.
65. *ADCP*, 332, 340, 522, 541.
66. *HMC, Laing Report*, i, 8–9; *RMS*, iii, nos. 3501–9, 2683; *RSS*, ii, nos. 4294–4311.
67. Bingham, *op.cit.*, 173–4, suggests that he may not have recovered from a 1537 hunting accident. She also suggests that James had the rare hereditary disease of porphyria. Cf. *ibid.*, 189–91 for a nice blend of the chroniclers' versions of the death-bed scene. On 30 December, the English learned from a Scots priest that there was much sickness and diarrhoea, and that the body 'did swell very great' after death: *HP*, i, no. 267. The rumour that he was poisoned was circulating in Scotland by 19 December: *ibid.*, i, no. 261, whilst Chapuys, in London, wrote on 23 December to say that the king fell ill through 'grief, regret and rage': *LP Henry VIII*, xvii, no. 1230.
68. *Mort. Reg.*, ii, no. 254; *TA*, viii, 143; *Diurnal of Occurrents*, 25; *Spalding Miscellany*, ii, 33 (Chronicle of Aberdeen); Dunbar, *Scot. Kings*, 237, 240–3.

CHAPTER FOURTEEN

'The Most Unpleasant of all the Stewarts'?

U ntil comparatively recently, it was a fairly straightforward task to pass brief judgement on the reigns of each of the five Jameses. James I was assassinated by his nobility; James II fought the Black Douglases; and James III was twice challenged by large groups of disaffected magnates. Thus there was a breakdown in Crown-magnate relations for all three kings. By contrast, James IV wore an iron belt in penance for his role in the death of his father, and died at Flodden along with the flower of his nobility; hence he was a popular and successful king.

Of course, all four kings are now the subject of scholarly biographies, and any judgement on Crown-magnate relations in their reigns is not complete without recourse to these works. By contrast the personal rule of the last James has largely escaped attention, perhaps because the reign is sandwiched between Flodden and Mary Queen of Scots. Briefly, James V is remembered as the king who escaped from the Angus Douglases in a dramatic ride from Falkland to Stirling. He then spent the rest of his reign taking paranoid revenge against those suspected of harbouring Douglas sympathies. The beautiful and noble Lady Glamis was burned and the royal favourite and master of works, Hamilton of Finnart, was executed. The nobility were disheartened, and at Fala Muir, refused to invade England; James begged them to change their minds; they did invade and many were captured. This was all the fault of another royal favourite put in charge of the army; to add to the disgrace, James found out that his new heir was a daughter; he turned his face to the wall and died in despair. Another breakdown in Crown-magnate relations.

In place of a scholarly biography of the personal rule of James V, there is Donaldson's chapter on the king's policy in volume 3 of *The Edinburgh History of Scotland*.[1] This contribution appears to be both the starting and finishing point for other academics when they require to know something about James. Essentially, Donaldson seems to have taken the conclusion of failure as his starting point, and then structured his analysis around that theme. He moves effortlessly from discussing a king who practised 'strong royal action', with little in the way of a 'conciliatory policy', to talking about a man who was 'vindictive', who 'created a sense of insecurity' for his subjects, alienating many of them; ultimately a king who practised 'something of a reign of terror'. Possibly James had 'a streak of sadistic cruelty in his nature'; certainly his upbringing and 'tendency to excessive nervous or mental stress' did 'little to lessen the revulsion with which he must be regarded'.

This is awesome language, almost as if Donaldson were suffering from an excess of John Knox or George Buchanan when he wrote it – or perhaps he had more than one eye on the reign to follow. Certainly he cites various contemporary English comments made about James, and identifies certain instances of what Wormald was to dub 'sharp practice' carried out by the king against some of his magnates. Underpinning his whole thesis is the notion that James was primarily interested in making money; in the process, 'regard to financial efficiency could easily pass into cupidity'. Of course, the same could easily be said of the first four Jameses; acquiring sufficient revenue was one of the main tasks of the Stewart monarchs, and in the process all were guilty of sharp practice. By tapping into the wealth of the First Estate, James V came close to finding a solution which avoided the need for excessive sharp practice against the Second and Third Estates.

It is difficult to find the evidence on which Donaldson builds such a damning and influential verdict on the personal rule of James V. He finds not only a breakdown in Crown-magnate relations, but an extremely nasty king as well. Wormald – whose interpretation of the reign in volume 4 of *The New History of Scotland* echoes Donaldson's verdict – calls James 'probably the most unpleasant of all the Stewarts'.[2] This is surely a matter of personal opinion, but events in the reigns of the first three Jameses suggest that none of them was a particularly attractive character. It can be conceded that James IV's reign was devoid of 'sensational' executions which appear so grisly to twentieth-century sensibilities. Again, Wormald's assessment of James V – 'terrifying' is another term she uses – has been relied upon by other writers. Whereas Donaldson considered the king to be more Tudor than Stewart, thankfully Wormald places him in the context of his forebears.

James' policy in the personal rule was very largely shaped by events at its outset, specifically by the struggle for power against the Angus Douglases. He was not simply a man who hated all Douglases *per se*: James Douglas of Drumlanrig – married to Angus' sister – was sacked from the royal Household in 1528 but accompanied the king to France in 1537; Lord Hay – married to Angus' sister – lost his job as sheriff of Peebles in 1530, but attended parliament thereafter, sent partridges to the king in 1540, and was active in royal service during the 1542 war; Alison Douglas – Lady Wedderburn and sister to Angus – was warded in 1532 but by 1541 was in court disputing castlewards; Douglas of Kilspindie – Angus' uncle – managed to return to Scotland without penalty in 1534; one Alexander Douglas of Mains can be found as factor of the Lennox earldom in 1542, whilst Patrick Douglas of Corhead obtained a licence to mine gold and sell it to the Crown in 1539. These last two men are worthy of mention if only to counteract the wild conclusions which can be drawn from Norfolk's 1537 comment that James was 'ill-beloved' and that all his Douglas subjects wished they were called Stewart.

There had been a very long minority – fifteen years – in the course of which the king had been bundled about between one faction and another. In 1526, the Angus Douglases emerged as the pre-eminent faction, if only because they managed to keep hold of the royal person. By the middle of 1528, James had both the motive – misgovernance – and rationale – he was sixteen years old – to assume royal authority in person. His mother provided the opportunity to make the break with the Douglases, in the shape of the 'safehouse' of Stirling castle. James then sacked Angus as his Chancellor and began ruling with the aid, principally, of the first earl of Arran and the third earl of Argyll. However, instead of a decisive victory over the old régime, there followed a struggle for power. In this James and his supporters were ultimately unsuccessful in the field. Tantallon remained in Angus' hands. The English did not really believe that James was exercising royal authority in person and lent Angus their moral support. Arran and his son, Hamilton of Finnart, appear to have withdrawn their active support from the king and were prepared again to compromise with the Angus Douglases. Eventually Angus negotiated his way out of Scotland. James had had to reach a compromise; the obligations set upon his magnates in the 'grete aith' were not fulfilled. In a very real sense there was unfinished business; had the Angus Douglases been executed for treason at the outset, then James' later actions might have been different.

As it was, the later downfall of many of James' subjects can be attributed to the unsuccessful struggle for power in 1528–29. James was not concerned with those who had supported the Angus régime; however, he bore a grudge against those whom he felt had let him down when he was trying to assert his royal authority. Hence the execution of Armstrong of Gilknockie; the warding of Buccleuch and Hume of Blackadder; the sacking and harassment of James Colville of East Wemyss, Robert Barton of Over Barnton and Adam Otterburn of Redhall; the ignoring of Lord Sinclair; the exiling of Campbell of Loudoun in 1538; even the sharp practice exercised against the earl of Morton. More dramatic was the burning of Lady Glamis in 1537, shortly after the king had returned from France to find Angus sitting in Berwick, probably the man behind the siege of Edgerston. In her trial can be seen the involvement of Rothes, a man who had been closely associated with the Angus régime and who had not supported the king at the Tantallon siege. Hence also Finnart's execution in 1540 – both as the compromiser of 1528–29 and, as the murderer of the third earl of Lennox in 1526, the one man whom James attacked for his association with the Angus régime.[3] Of course, to twentieth-century eyes James does not appear to have been a particularly likeable man, but he was rational, and his policy is completely understandable when interpreted in this light.

The same idea of unfinished business led to the granting of remissions – a money-spinner for James' predecessors – and to the attempt to 'saturate' the area north of the Firth of Tay with royal tenants. The finding of non-entry against the earl of Crawford in 1532 can be attributed to the king's 'saturation' policy in an area adjacent to the heartland of the earldom of Angus. In itself, this method of harassing Crawford was not novel; James IV had raised summons of non-entry against both the second earl of Rothes and the fifth earl of Angus, demanding vast sums from the latter. Crawford managed to make it to parliament in 1535 and was not deprived of a living. The forfeiture of the seventh Lord Glamis and administration by the Crown of the earldom of Erroll were again attempts to infiltrate the area. Elsewhere, James assumed control of Crawfordjohn and Crawfordmuir – areas either part of or adjacent to Angus territory. Even the administration of Liddesdale at the expense of the treasonable earl of Bothwell can be interpreted as the king acting in the knowledge that his father had taken Liddesdale from the Angus Douglases and given it to Bothwell's predecessor. And, of course, the problem of Liddesdale had contributed towards the formulation of English policy towards Scotland in 1528–29 and again in 1532.

The Act of Annexation – a copy of James II's act appropriating the estates of the Black Douglases – underlined the king's resolve not to allow the return of the Angus Douglases, and Finnart's execution demonstrated the king's conviction in this policy. Finnart's sudden removal and the Act of Annexation have been taken by some historians – for example, Kelley – to have marked the beginning of James' 'reign of terror'. Sanderson appears to have accepted without question Knox's story of a 'blacklist' of heretical nobles.[4] Morton was required to resign the fee of his earldom into the king's hands. Crawford's heir, David Lindsay of Edzell, had to sign a contract agreeing to surrender his earldom when the king required this of him. But in neither case was there a *de facto* or *de jure* disinheritance. Both the eighth earl of Crawford and the third earl of Morton kept the liferent and actual possession of their earldoms; indeed, Lindsay of Edzell was in charge of convening the lieges in Forfar in 1542. James appears to have been threatening disinheritance through legalistic methods, but the actuality never occurred. It is also true that both of these earldoms were financially on the downward path, and had been long before the start of the personal rule. James was exploiting weak targets. The sharp practice of his predecessors was becoming ever more finely honed. Where James IV had used the unpopular device of recognition simply to make a lot of money, his son appears – in the case of the earldom of Morton – to have been threatening to carry out recognition in practice. In both instances James' eventual plans for the destinations of each earldom were not realised. The king's early death leaves open the question as to whether he intended to proceed to the threatened ultimate horror of permanent disinheritance.

All Stewart kings were good at finding legal devices to make money. Perhaps the most straightforward way was to take a composition for ward and relief upon the entry of an heir. Hence the incentive offered by the act of Twizelhaugh, used in the reign of James IV, and throughout his son's reign. Where there was no such 'tax break', it was perfectly legitimate for the Crown to seek its due. In James V's personal rule can be seen the growing sophistication of the law, promoted by the 1532 establishment of the College of Justice. This afforded James the opportunity to exploit his Act of Revocation – a carbon copy of that passed by his father in 1498. Hence the fourth Lord Gray had to pay 7000 marks to the Crown to obtain possession of the entailed estate of the third lord. The third lord himself appears to have been a man favoured by James, who overruled a finding of default by the Lords of Council and confirmed him as sheriff of Forfar in 1536. The fourth lord paid his composition off early, with the final instalment being made after the personal rule was over. He also turned out at Solway Moss in 1542. The charter to the lordship was granted notwithstanding the fact that the king had earlier temporarily appropriated part of the lands 'ad perpetuam remanentiam'. The Earl Marischal appears to have been required to pay repeatedly for the possession of Inverugie; in effect he was purchasing this estate from the Crown, together with a guarantee of title to it. He accompanied the king on the 1540 royal Isles expedition. That James, in the majority of cases, was not acting as a predator king but rather as a typical Stewart monarch looking for revenue is also illustrated with the examples of the succession to the earldom of Erroll and the parliamentary confirmation of the restoration of the fourth lord Hume, both in 1541.

James forfeited the estates of the Angus Douglases, Hamilton of Finnart and Lord Glamis. Drummond of Carnock was forfeited but restored in 1532. Bothwell lost Liddesdale, but the remainder of his earldom was kept intact, notwithstanding that he himself was in ward from 1532 to 1541. Scott of Buccleuch and Johnston of that Ilk also kept their estates despite being held in ward. No other magnate lost any part of his inheritance, although the second earl of Arran justifiably had a claim to part of the lordship of Avandale. It is true that Huntly and Moray both lost their possession of part of the Crown's patrimony. The fourth earl of Argyll surrendered the exercise of the office of chamberlain of Kintyre in 1531, but still held the actual office in 1542. At times, the English would comment on the 'disaffection' of these leading magnates. However Huntly and Argyll both served as vice-regents in 1536, the former succeeding in his aim of removing the Master of Forbes. Moray was James' ambassador in France in 1535. Argyll and Moray were regular charter witnesses throughout the personal rule. All three men were in royal service in 1542. It is true that Argyll's influence in the Isles was reduced in the course of James' 'daunting' policy; but it is notable how he was paid £5000 in 1541 by the Crown to surrender the MacIan inheritance. In like manner, Lord Methven received £2000 from the Crown through its redemption of the lands of Glengavel. In both cases James was acting legally; had he been driven only by cupidity he would certainly have attempted some form of sharp practice to obtain the estates.

Argyll was briefly detained at Edinburgh in 1531 in connection with James'

Isles policy. He was not, as Donaldson asserts, 'out of favour for several years'. He was one of the few magnates to gain permanently any lands from the Angus forfeiture. Atholl was warded briefly in 1534 in order to induce him to settle a civil dispute. He may have accompanied the king on the first abortive expedition to France in 1536, and joined the king on the 1540 Isles expedition. He died in the king's service at Edinburgh in 1542. Possibly he infected the king with his 'pestilence'. Buchan was not a magnate who played a prominent public role. Briefly, he was outlawed in 1537 over a civil dispute with Crawford, the court of session in this instance upholding Crawford's case. Nevertheless, at the same time, Buchan served on the jury in the trial of Lady Glamis. Lord Maxwell, apparently one of the casualties of the lack of a 'conciliatory policy', was warded in 1530; but he went on to become vice-regent in 1536–37 and commander of the army at Solway Moss in 1542.

Thus there are too many contradictions in the careers of individual magnates for Donaldson to single out a few bad references and draw such a one-sided conclusion. One example of unreasonable royal 'cupidity' which he offers is that in relation to castlewards demanded from the earl of Bothwell in 1541. Quite apart from the fact that reasonableness has no place in the equation, Bothwell was a treacherous man who in 1531 signed articles offering his service to Henry VIII. Thus the stepping stones used to arrive at the verdict of James's greed and unpopularity are not as wholly secure as they appear to be.

What is true is that James was not lavish in his patronage. Thus there is little to offset the image of a king who was always taking rather than giving. In contrast James IV created several earldoms, and his sharp practice towards his magnates was balanced by rewards. However, it took fifteen years before the majority of these creations appeared, in and after 1503. James V's personal rule lasted only fourteen years. Only by 1540, with the execution of Finnart and the Act of Annexation, can the 'unfinished business' of the struggle for power be seen to have been finally sorted out. In the same year was born the first royal heir. At the age of twenty-eight in 1540, undoubtedly James would have considered that he had reached the peak of his career. The Isles had been daunted with the assistance of his younger nobility. These magnates – Cassillis, Atholl, Huntly, Erroll, Marischal, Arran, possibly Argyll – were the new generation, of an age with the king and untainted by the faction fighting of the minority. Had James lived beyond 1542, these men might well have received some material rewards.

Amongst the lords it is less easy to identify younger individuals who might have been elevated to the rank of earl. James' closest supporters – Maxwell, Erskine and Fleming – were all rather older men. It is conceivable that James did not rate their service overly highly; also they were tainted with the politics of the minority. A further point is that James had faced no domestic political crisis since 1528–29, and there had been no conflict with England since 1532. Domestic problems had produced many of the creations in the reigns of James II and James III. James V did not have to buy support. James IV was exceptional in that he created two earls on a happy occasion – his marriage. For his son, happy occasions were outnumbered by sad ones – the deaths of Madeleine, Prince James and Arthur, Duke of Albany. Yet no-one could have anticipated that James would die at the age of only thirty; had he lived he might have produced male heirs, sorted out his differences with Henry VIII, and begun to use his huge income to distribute largesse.

The lack of patronage prompted Donaldson to focus on the careers of lesser men. Towards some of these, he identifies 'instances of brutality' exercised by a cruel and sadistic king. The prime example which he cites – that of the execution of George Scott of the Bog – is risible in its audacity. Scott was a nasty piece of work. His execution can only have contributed towards James' reputation as a 'puir man's king', not towards Donaldson's verdict of a king more a Tudor than a Stewart in character.[5] Add together the later chroniclers' idea of a 'puir man's king' and Abell's tale of a 1536 royal visit in disguise to the court of the Duke of Vendôme, and it becomes apparent how Sir Walter Scott could tell stories about 'the guidman of Ballengeich'.

Donaldson's other lesser men were the royal favourites, until comparatively recently also a target in discussions of James III's reign. The first was Hamilton of Finnart, but in looking closely at his career it becomes clear that his execution was an instance both of practical politics and studied revenge on the part of the king, not an illogical frightening arbitrary strike against the master of works. The other 'favourite' is Oliver Sinclair of Pitcairn. It is perfectly clear why Pitcairn, with his family connections, was in charge of the earldom of Caithness and Orkney and Shetland; it is also understandable why, as a long serving member of the royal Household, he was captain of Tantallon castle. Other Household servants were in charge of other royal castles. What cannot be accepted is that he was in command of the army at Solway Moss. None of the English officers fighting the battle thought he was in charge, and the source of this spurious tale is Sir George Douglas, a man with an axe to grind and probably with a talent for propaganda.

Side by side with the lesser men in urging the king into war in 1542, according to the chroniclers, were the Scottish clergy. Contemporary English intelligence also identified the First Estate as warmongers; but the English could never quite decide what the attitudes of the king and his magnates were. Almost inevitably the political circumstances of 1542 cast James in the light of a 'priests' king'. He taxed his Church; unlike Henry VIII he did not attempt to dissolve it, although he considered the idea. Henry VIII was the maverick monarch in 1542; James, like Charles V and Francis I, represented the prevalent Orthodoxy. Later Protestant chroniclers would condemn him for this. Furthermore Henry was the aggressor in 1542; he threatened war. James responded at a late stage to Norfolk's invasion. He was not driven into waging war by a council full of clergy; unlike his father he appears to have resisted the temptation almost to the end of his personal rule. A further point is that after the 1532 establishment of the College of Justice there is no clearly identifiable royal council. The English were probably only guessing in 1542 when they cited the names of Scottish councillors. What most closely resembles a royal council is the list of great seal charter witnesses, a body which showed no great changes in its composition throughout the personal rule.

There is an inherent contradiction in the attempts made to interpret the 1542 campaigns. Huntly won a battle in August. The nobles refused to invade England in October, yet did invade in November. What had happened to make them change their minds? The answer is that there is no contradiction once the various tales of English spies and chroniclers are stripped away. The contemporary Scottish records indicate great activity: the mobilisation of armies, and the employment of the services of several magnates. When the English border officers were not speculating on the significance of the spurious rumours picked up by their spies in Edinburgh, they also reported great activity on the part of the Scots. One army was dissolved at Lauder in October, after Norfolk had gone home. This army was a defensive one, the Scots feudal host turning out in force, and with probably too many wild Highlanders in it to make it a viable army for raiding into Northumberland. The weather was bad and there was a shortage of food. The immediate threat of full-scale invasion by the English was over. A new strategy was drawn up with the object of making an appropriate response to English aggression. This involved a series of raids conducted by the magnates and their retinues. Possibly there was also a scheme to interdict England. The first raid was on the Solway. Happily engaged in burning English territory, Maxwell and his colleagues then became aware of the presence of what appeared to be a large English army in array along the south side of the Lyne water. Wharton, its commander, used superb tactics. He boxed Maxwell in between a bog and a river. Rather than be drowned in the Esk, Maxwell and company fought valiantly and then surrendered.

One wonders how James' personal rule would have been judged had Maxwell and company fought valiantly and all been killed. Almost certainly the theory of a breakdown in Crown-magnate relations would have been jettisoned completely, and the conclusion would have been that James was a successful and popular king, just like his father. However he would still have died on 14 December 1542. As it was, when he lay on his death-bed at Falkland, James could console himself with the certain knowledge that he had enjoyed the support of almost all of his magnates throughout his personal rule.

NOTES

1. Donaldson, *op.cit.*, Ch. 4, *passim*.
2. Wormald, *Court*, 12.
3. Ch. 9, *passim*.
4. Kelley, *Angus*, 530–1; Sanderson, *op.cit.*, 91
5. Donaldson, *op.cit.*, 62.

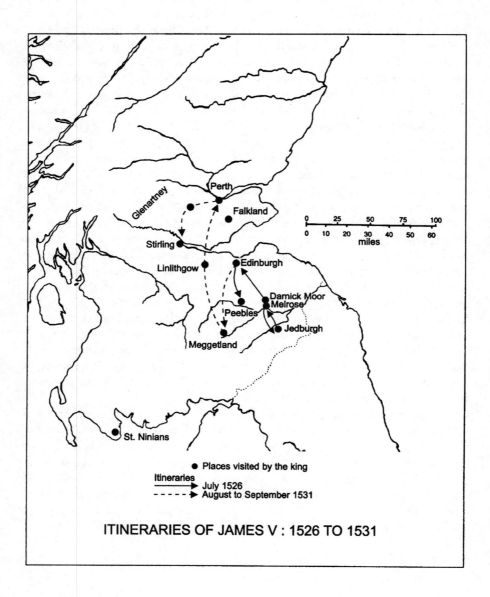

Places visited by the king

Itineraries

July 1526

August to September 1531

ITINERARIES OF JAMES V : 1526 TO 1531

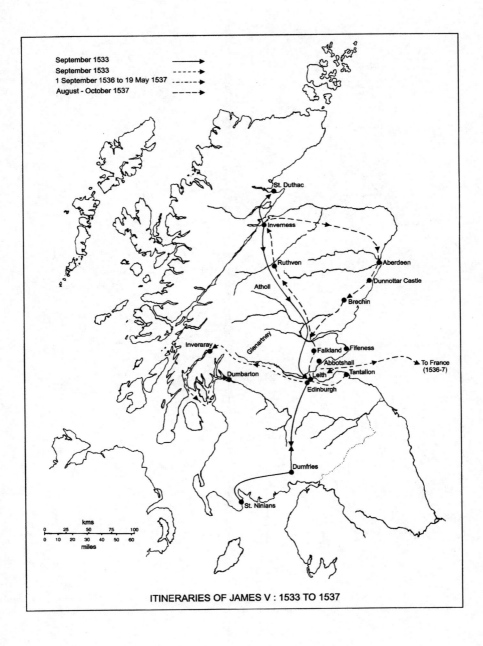

September 1533   →
September 1533   ---→
1 September 1536 to 19 May 1537   ---→
August - October 1537   ---→

St. Duthac

Inverness

Ruthven

Atholl

Aberdeen

Dunnottar Castle

Brechin

Glenartney

Inveraray

Falkland

Fifeness

Abbotshall

To France
(1536-7)

Dumbarton

Leith

Tantallon

Edinburgh

Dumfries

St. Ninians

kms
0   25   50   75   100
0   10   20   30   40   50   60
miles

ITINERARIES OF JAMES V : 1533 TO 1537

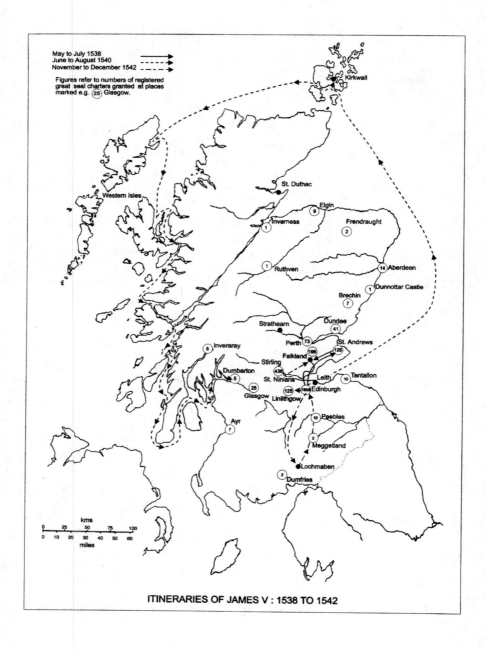

May to July 1538
June to August 1540
November to December 1542

Figures refer to numbers of registered
great seal charters granted at places
marked e.g. (25) Glasgow.

ITINERARIES OF JAMES V : 1538 TO 1542

APPENDIX I

The Sources for the Reign

A. OFFICIAL RECORDS

Many of the sources for Scottish government in this period have been collated and edited in the nineteenth and early twentieth centuries, and as a consequence exist in printed form. The major publications cover the fields of legislation, grants and revenue and are individually examined below, as is the judicial record, the bulk of which remains in manuscript form. Reference is also made to various other sources, both printed and unprinted.

(i) Acts of Parliament[1]

This is principally a list of legislation which was enacted rather than a blow-by-blow account of political debate. Much of parliament's time was taken up with the usual concerns of any Scottish administration in the fifteenth and sixteenth centuries – to provide for defence of the realm, to administer justice and to protect the Crown's patrimony. Hence there can be found provisions for the importing of firearms, for the holding of justice ayres and weapon showings, for the management of woodlands and setting of lands in feu farm, against counterfeiting of the coinage and against out of season hare hunting and salmon fishing. The presence of the Third Estate in parliament brought about trade regulations covering such matters as the holding of burgh markets, the 'stanching of masterful beggars with additioun', the standardisation of weights and measures and, in 1541, directions for upgrading harbour facilities at Leith and generally repairing 'deformities for the common passage of strangers'.

As in the reigns of Robert III, James I, and James II, so also in this reign the usual proclamation upholding the liberty of the Holy Church which opened proceedings was on occasion followed by resolutions condemning heresy.

Parliament met throughout the personal rule of James V – in contrast to the reign of his father. Full sessions were held in 1528, 1531, 1532, 1535, and in December 1540, continuing to March 1541. Between sessions a parliamentary committee sat regularly, primarily to deal with criminal judicial matters. Most of the legislative outpouring came in the 1535 and 1540/41 sessions. The 1531 parliament dealt mainly with diplomatic matters, and in 1532 the main item on the agenda was the restoration of Alexander Drummond of Carnock. The committees followed up outstanding business, most notably issuing summons to wild highlanders to appear at Edinburgh. Of prime importance for a study of the personal rule is the judicial material, beginning in the parliament of September 1528, which presided over the forfeiture of Archibald Douglas, sixth earl of Angus.

The roll also recorded attendances. One archbishop, eight bishops, twelve abbots, nine earls and nineteen lords sat in 1528; one cardinal, one archbishop, five bishops, seven abbots, ten earls and twenty-two lords attended in 1541.[2]

(ii) Great Seal Register[3]

There are over two thousand entries of charter grants for this period. The majority of these (some 43%) were royal approvals of grants or sales of lands made by third parties, with the king acting in the capacity of over-superior. A further 13% were confirmations of earlier royal charters to immediate vassals. A small number were charters of legitimisation. The remainder were largely direct grants, usually of lands resigned into the king's hands by the previous holder, who was often the grantee's parent or spouse. 5% of these redistributions came with strings attached, with the grantee's charter containing the condition that the previous owner might regain the lands within seven years should he manage to repay the monetary debt to the Crown or third party (typically non-entries) which led to his losing the lands. Grants in feu farm accounted for 14% of all charters, and it was largely in this last category that a genuine first distribution was achieved, with former royal tenants being the main beneficiaries.

Eighty-six of the recipients of charters were described either as the king's 'familiar' or 'familiar servant'. This description applied equally to Archibald Campbell, fourth earl of Argyll, and John Murray, royal barber. Household servants benefitted from feuing and, in all, the familiar servants were the beneficiaries of one hundred and fifty-eight charters, often as a reward for their 'good service'. In comparison, the magnates did not feature heavily as recipients, and for some, such as David Lindsay, eighth earl of Crawford, the register shows financial difficulties forcing him to mortgage his estates.

As well as reflecting the upturns and downswings in individual careers, the register is important for such information as it provides for witnesses to individual charters.[4] Usually the clerk simply noted that a charter had been testified *'ut in aliis cartis'*. Where cross-references can be made,[5] the witnesses cited are indeed just this. There is a paucity of full citations given in the register. For 1531 two lists are given in a total entry of one hundred and twenty-four charters (1.6%). The highest percentage is 16% in 1535 (sixteen lists). Not unexpectedly, Gavin Dunbar, Archbishop of Glasgow and Chancellor, was invariably present, whilst Malcolm Fleming, fourth lord Fleming and Great Chamberlain, achieved a 90% attendance rate over the period. Given the absence in other sources of a clearly defined body of king's counsellors, the great seal witness lists are indicative of such a body. However this hypothesis cannot be consistently sustained – charters continued to be issued in Scotland during James V's absence in France in the winter of 1536–37, although one was issued at Paris on 6 January 1537 giving powers to the vice-regents (James Beaton, archbishop of St. Andrews; the Chancellor; George Gordon, fourth earl of Huntly; William Graham, second earl of Montrose; Hugh Montgomery, first earl of Eglinton; and Robert Maxwell, fifth lord Maxwell) left in Scotland to continue business during the king's absence. Not surprisingly the vice-regents appeared as witnesses in 1536–37, but for the major part of the personal rule the most frequent witnesses were the holders of offices of state, not necessarily magnates. Nineteen persons are designated as counsellors in the register, the list including Gilbert Kennedy, second earl of Cassillis; David Drummond, fifth lord Drummond, and Sir James Hamilton of Finnart, none of whom testified a charter issued under the great seal.

Finally, the place of issue of each charter – most often, though not exclusively, Edinburgh – provides clues to a royal itinerary, though, as suggested above, this cannot be taken as being definitive.

(iii) Privy Seal Register

There are over five thousand entries in the Privy Seal Register in this period. Approximately two thousand of these serve as warrants for business to be processed by the issuing of a charter under the great seal. The rest deal largely with the disposition of feudal casualties by the king – whether by way of gift of wardship, marriage and non-entries or, in one instance in March 1542, the escheated goods of one John Pillane, 'who hanged himself'.[6]

Again, the place of issue of each letter suggests a royal itinerary, although the privy seal was under the immediate control of the keeper rather than the king, and during the king's absence in France letters were issued both from there and from Edinburgh. One entry in 1540 – subscribed by James V – referred to the theft of one of the three signet seals which were deployed respectively in the Session, on justice ayre and by the king personally. The missing signet was the 'leist' one – apparently used by James himself – and dire warnings were made as to the consequences which would befall anyone misusing it. The solution was to make a replacement and amend the two others in use.[7] This suggests the departmentalisation of government administration, with the king not necessarily supervising in person the issue of each and every document bearing the great seal or the privy seal. Unfortunately there is no surviving register of items personally signetted by James V.

(iv) Exchequer Records and Treasurer's Accounts

There is extant in published form a useful amount of financial material. The record of ordinary Crown revenues is reasonably full for this period, although there are some gaps; in particular the Comptroller's accounts for 1529–30, 1536–37, and 1538–39, and from September 1540 until the end of the reign, are missing. Supplementing the three main annual accounts (the custumars' and bailies' account for the burghs, the bailies' account for crown lands, and the Comptroller's account) are some books of rentals of Crown lands, indicating both the tenant and the rental value. There are also responde books, providing information on feudal dues to be collected by the sheriffs, as well as noting the holding of justiciary commissions. Towards the end of the reign the Comptroller commissioned surveys of new areas coming under the Crown's patrimony, particularly in the Highlands and Islands.[8] The figures indicate that both revenue and expenditure rose in the period. In the 1528–29 account of the Comptroller the charge was over £9000 Scots. Household costs amounted to over £10,000 and the total discharge was nearly £16,000. The equivalent figures in the 1539–40 account were, respectively, over £24,000, over £19,000 and some £26,800.

Increases are also indicated in the extraordinary accounts. Revenue in the 1529–30 account of the Treasurer amounted to nearly £13,000 Scots, with expenditure at over £12,000. In the 1539–40 account revenue was £28,200, and expenditure stood at nearly £31,000.[9] As with the ordinary accounts, there are gaps in the record; in particular there are no Treasurer's accounts for the period August 1527 to August 1529, during which period James V began his personal rule. The annual accounts are supplemented by other materials; David Beaton, Cardinal of Scotland, rendered one account on 12 September 1538 for the king's expenses in France, which amounted to approximately £44,000 Scots. There are also separate taxation accounts.

The Treasurer's accounts also indicate how James V spent money – on all manner of things from new artillery to clothes and other essentials for his newly born children (both legitimate and illegitimate). A separately published set of accounts records expenditure on royal palaces, and information on consumption by the royal household is also available.[10] Further, unpublished, financial material has been gathered by Dr. Athol L. Murray.[11]

(iv) Lords of Council[12]
There is for this period no extant separate record of the deliberation of a body of 'king's counsellors'. A distinct Privy council record began only in 1545. However, until 1532 there was kept a record of the regular sessions of a body of persons meeting at Edinburgh to process civil law suits. Interspersed with the voluminous judicial material is a record of other administrative matters of a more political nature. The composition of this body – described in the record as the 'lordis of counsale' – varied according to the items on the agenda. Hence the king attended on 14 July 1528, together with James Hamilton, first earl of Arran; Colin Campbell, third earl of Argyll; George Leslie, fourth earl of Rothes; Hugh Montgomery, first earl of Eglinton; Lord Maxwell and the fifth lord Erskine, all to hear Patrick Hepburn, third earl of Bothwell, pledge to answer for any misdemeanours in the lordship of Liddesdale. The following day none was present to sit through the latest episode in the ongoing wrangle amongst the representatives of the three heiresses to the Dirleton estates. (This long drawn-out case remained unresolved thirteen years later).[13]

After the institution of the College of Justice in 1532, the judicial record becomes a distinct item and there is a corresponding dearth of other material noted. The regular attenders of each session were the first senators of the College and the appearance of other persons is only intermittent. The conclusion must be that political matters continued elsewhere, and consequently it becomes difficult to identify the king's political advisers after 1532. Professor R.K. Hannay trawled the judicial record for the whole period to extract and edit what appeared to him to be of political interest. He also transcribed a list of council sederunts.[14] The extant judicial records do, however, provide some clues as to the preoccupations of the landholding classes, some of whom appear to have resorted to litigation with great regularity to resolve land disputes. In 1541 William Chirnside, son and apparent heir of Ninian Chirnside of East Nisbet, took Sir James Towers of Inverleith to court for production of William's charter to the lands of Chirnside, entrusted by Ninian to Sir James for safekeeping. Sir James alleged that his former wife '. . . has the key of the kist where the evidence lies . . .'. The lords ordained:

> . . . James to have letters charging said lady to open the kist and deliver to him the evidence wuth certification to her that [if] she should fail it shall be lawful for James to break up the said kist to effect he might have the said evidence to produce . . .

The Lords of Council had to deal with several similar instances of locked charter chests.[15]

(v) Other Records

Central criminal judicial records no longer exist. However Robert Pitcairn compiled such a record, drawing largely on the Books of Adjournal of the Court of Justiciary supplemented by other sources, both primary and second-ary.[16] This is an important work of reference for the trials of the Master of Forbes and Lady Glamis; and Pitcairn also catalogues a series of other crimes and gruesome punishments.

Foreign and diplomatic correspondence and other materials have been col-lated and edited in several works, above all the 'bible' for sixteenth century diplomatic source material, the published Letters and Papers of Henry VIII.[17] By their very nature such sources give a biased account of events, as the bulk of the surviving materials are written from an English point of view; letters exchanged amongst the wardens of the marches sometimes give the impression that all truce breakers lived north of the border. Correspondence by James V's Secretary has also been edited,[18] and provides information on Scottish relations with Europe – largely being the story of the search for a royal bride.

An account of Scotland in 1535 is given by the Danish ambassador, Peter Suevenius, who on his arrival

. . . asked if there were in Scotland trees on which birds grew and was given an account of them. There is a floating island, which goes from shore to shore with the tide. There is a place eight miles in circumference where no cocks crow, whether native or imported; taken elsewhere they crow. The gannet lays only one egg, and hatches it standing. The wild Scots live like Scythians. They know nothing of bread; when hungry they kill a stag and eat the flesh raw, just squeezing out the blood. Not far from Edinburgh is a mountain smoking like Etna which I saw. In an abbey near is a place whence oil flows out of the earth. In Irish Scotland is an island, where the sun is seen night and day.[19]

Finally, mention should be made of local sources. Various collections of unprinted family papers are held in the Scottish Record Office. Many of these have been catalogued for easier access.[20] Other collections have been edited and published in a series of Royal Commission Reports.[21] Similar work was carried out, amongst others, by Sir William Fraser. More recently Dr. Jenny Wormald has collated and published a great number of the bonds of manrent made between individuals in the sixteenth century.[22] A wealth of diverse material has been published by a number of private clubs and societies.[23]

B. CHRONICLES

Mention should be made of three published chronicles which purport to be contemporaneous with the period under study. The first of these – the Chronicle of Perth[24] – is very short, and the anonymous author is largely preoccupied with local events, such as the outbreak of a 'mallochis pest' in the city in September 1537. The siege of Tantallon on 11 October 1528 is noted as is 'Solen Moss' on 30 November 1542. Dates are given for the death of the king's mother, Margaret Tudor, at Methven; for the king's death; and for the birth of the king's daughter, Mary Stewart.

The Chronicle of Aberdeen is a similar work.[25] Noted here are the deaths of the king and of his first wife, Madeleine of France and, again, the birth of Mary. Also recorded are the departure of the king for the Isles, on 25 July 1534; his departure for France, on 15 August 1536; and the arrival at Balcomie, Fife, of his second bride, Mary of Guise. The author, Walter Cullen, also gives his own birth date as 2 November 1536.

Of considerably greater length and containing much information, is the Diurnal of Occurrents[26] The earliest manuscript for this has been estimated as being from the late sixteenth century, placing it amongst the group of works written as continuations of Boece's Scotorum Historiae. Again the authorship is anonymous, and although the events of the reign are set out with strict chronological precision, the wealth of detail as to political affairs and personages, and the style of writing, alike suggest that this is an homogeneous work written with access to contemporary records. The holding of parliaments, the trials of heretics, the movements of diplomats and the appointment of officials are given full treatment. The author makes no criticism of the king's activities, but is not averse to narrating his own perceptions. Thus after the unsuccessful siege of Tantallon castle ('bot it was still haldin and evill done'), the king is said to have 'greit suspicioun of the temporall lordis becaus thai favourit sum pairt the Douglassis', and after the 'unhappie raid' of Solway Moss (where the Scots were 'begylit be their awne gyding') the king 'took greit displeisour' before falling 'seik' and dying, at which 'thair wos greit murnying in Scotland'.

The Observantine friar, Adam Abell, abruptly breaks short his account of the 'Roit and Quheill of Tyme' in 1537 with Margaret Tudor announcing her intention to divorce her third husband, Henry Stewart, third lord Methven. Abell has just enough time to narrate in sequence the death of Queen Madeleine, the execution of the Master of Forbes, the burning of Janet Douglas, Lady Glamis, and the demise of her husband, Archibald Campbell of Skipness ('passing over the castle wall at Edinburgh he fell down suddenly'). Scottish events in Abell's account are interspersed amongst reflections on Henry VIII's divorce proceedings and reports on religious tensions in Europe. Writing at Jedburgh friary, Abell naturally also records Border incidents. Nowhere in his account is there any criticism of James V, or of his policies.[27]

Written in 1566, over twenty years after the death of the king, John Knox's account of the reign[28] is largely a diatribe against the man at the helm in the period immediately prior to the Reformation – a man who was moreover responsible for the existence of Mary Stewart. Knox (c.1514–1572) coined the deathbed phrase:

'it cam wi' a lass and it'l gang wi' a lass.'

According to Sir George Douglas, writing at Berwick on 17 December 1542, the king on his deathbed in fact 'spake bud fewe wysse wordes'.[29] However, Knox goes on to describe how James turned his face to the wall and died crying out for his favourite Oliver. Douglas had noted that the capture of Oliver Sinclair of Pitcairn at Solway did appear to distress the king more than the loss of 'all the greyt men that is takyng'.[30]

Knox also dwells at length on religious matters, cataloguing the heresy trials of the period. The king is described as:

. . . carnal and altogether given to the filthy lusts of flesh and abhorred all counsel that repugned thereto . . . most vicious and pushed on by the priests to vow that none shall be spared who is suspect of heresy . . .

Almost as though realising that his history of the Reformation is somewhat lacking in detail of the reign of James V, Knox concludes with a summary of contemporary received opinions of the king:

[345]

. . . Some rejoiced that such an enemy to God's truth was dead, called by some a good poor man's king, by others a murderer of the nobility. Some praised him for repressing theft and oppression. Others dispraised him for defouling men's wives and virgins . . .

In Knox's view there was some truth in all these statements; the virtues could not be denied, neither could the vices be cloaked.

John Lesley (c.1526–c.1596), Bishop of Ross, wrote his history in England in 1570[31], presenting it to Mary Queen of Scots, then imprisoned in Bolton Castle. His association with Mary went back to 1561, when he escorted her from France to Scotland. He was one of the 'Queen's men'.[32]

His account of the reign is considerably more substantial than that by Knox. As befits one of the co-editors of the Acts and Constitutions of Scotland in 1566, Lesley emphasises the many 'lawis and constitutionis maid for the common weill and quietnes of the cuntry' in the reign of James V, and gives a detailed account of the institution of the College of Justice. He stresses the king's ability in ordering justice, which had brought about such 'gret quietnes, tranquilitie and pollitie in Scotland as evir wer in ony Kingis tyme of befoir'. Lesley had also served as Privy councillor for Mary, and hence often points out that James' best actions were always taken on the good advice of his counsellors. His verdict on Mary's father was of a king:

. . . living all his tyme in the favour of fortune, in hiech honour, riches and glorye, and for his nobill actis and prudent pollyces worthye to be registrar in the buike of fame.

David Chalmers of Ormond (c.1526–c.1592) was another Marian who first wrote his continuation of Hector Boece's history in 1572, republished in Paris in 1579.[33] His account of the reign is brief. Again the 'gritt displeasour' of the king after the battle of Solway Moss is noted. Like Lesley, Chalmers comments that there had been a rumour that James had perhaps died of poisoning. He echoes both Knox and Lesley in reporting that the confusion at Solway was caused partly by Oliver Sinclair of Pitcairn's proclaiming himself as army commander. This prompted Lord Maxwell and other magnates to surrender willingly to the English in disgust. For Chalmers the king's death 'wes gritlie regraitted becaus of his gritt wertew and manheid. He wes callit the puir manis King, he wes also werry ritche'.

Writing in 1575, Robert Lindsay of Pitscottie (c.1532–c.1579) appears to rely principally on oral sources for his history of the reign.[34] His colourful account follows the king round the country, from the lavish party hosted by the earl of Atholl to his 'sad and remorseful' death at Falkland, via a shooting contest at St. Andrews, a daunting of the Isles, Border raids, and a trip to France. As might be expected, Pitscottie is most informative on the king's activities when in Fife, particularly on James' second wedding to Mary of Guise in St. Andrews in 1538. His Protestant convictions lead him to castigate the 'wicked Scots priests' whose 'evil and perverse' counsel prevented the king from meeting with Henry VIII. The king is praised for his building works and his purchase of artillery, but in Pitscottie's view his honest start was corrupted by both 'idollatory and adulltery'. Pitscottie also has James lamenting on his deathbed that 'it cam wi' a lass. . .' and then turning his face to the wall. This sentiment may have struck Pitscottie independently as an original idea, for Knox's history had not yet been published in 1575. Alternatively, they were using a common source. Both Knox and Pitscottie have the king sign a document thrust into his hands by Cardinal Beaton – perhaps his last will.[35] Henry VIII was advised by his officers, writing on 30th December 1542, that the Scots king died in the Cardinal's arms.[36]

George Buchanan (c.1506–1582) dedicates his history – published in the year of his death – to James VI.[37] Like Knox, he was brought up in Scotland during the minority of James V, but continued his education and career in France until circa 1535, when he was appointed as tutor to James Stewart *primus*, illegitimate son of James V, at an annual salary of £20 Scots.[38] In 1539, possibly as part of the investigations instigated by Cardinal Beaton, which led to the later trial for heresy of Sir John Borthwick, Buchanan's own religious opinions came under scrutiny and he was forced to flee to England, in his own words escaping through his bedroom window whilst his keepers were asleep. Knox (who was at this time a minor priest at Haddington), used the episode as further evidence of the king's heinous moral character.[39]

Buchanan's standpoint was strongly influenced by that of his former teacher, Hector Boece. A king had to respect the laws of the nation, should act with the consensus of his nobility, and should have no favourites. A regency was justifiable if he fell below those standards. In Buchanan's view Mary Queen of Scots acted precisely as a ruler should not. Furthermore, Buchanan disliked bishops, in particular the Marian Archbishop John Hamilton.

These attitudes are evident in his plausible account of James V's personal rule. Some sympathy is shown for the displaced Douglas régime – after all Angus was defended in the parliament of 1528 by the humanist John Bellenden, translator of Boece's history. The Hamilton family – next in line to the throne after the royal Stewarts – are portrayed as continually attempting to scupper James' marriage arrangements. The priests bribed the courtiers to persuade the king not to meet Henry VIII in person. In the year of Buchanan's own narrow escape from a possible roasting for his heretical beliefs '. . . the country had been rather quiet than contented, a leader, rather than reasons for insurrection being wanting . . .'. Once James' eldest son was born (in May 1540), the decline set in, with the king ignoring his nobility, squandering money on palaces (a praiseworthy activity in Pitscottie's opinion), and falling under the increasing influence of the clergy, who promised funds for this project. With the deaths of both of his infant sons in early 1541, the reign slid into confused diplomacy and suspicion of the nobility, culminating in Solway Moss. Here Oliver Sinclair of Pitcairn again features as the purported army commander, and Buchanan suggests that the Scots magnates deliberately surrendered rather than '. . . expose themselves to the vengeance of their own sovereign . . .'. After Solway James swithered, even considering recalling Angus '. . . on the best terms he could. . . .'. Again, this rumour had been reported to Henry VIII in the first few days after James' death.[40] There are no poignant deathbed scenes in Buchanan's account. His verdict fits his thesis: the king had fallen below the required standards and his death was largely welcomed by his nobility.

The early seventeenth-century chroniclers had little more to add to the earlier accounts.[41] In his memoirs written in 1603,[42] Sir James Melville (1549–1617) elaborates on an earlier reference by Knox to a list of heretics presented by the clergy to the king. Melville's account has James V putting the scroll in his pocket; drawing his sword on his Treasurer, Sir James Kirkcaldy of Grange; being persuaded by Grange to tax his clergy rather than burn the barons whose names were on the list; agreeing to take this course; and chasing his clergy away, brandishing a dagger and threatening to stick them. The clergy later manage to win James round by bringing him 'fair maidens and men's wives'. The story illustrates the theme, picked up by both Pitscottie and Buchanan, of the tensions in 1541 caused by the issue of whether or not James V and Henry VIII would agree to meet in person and what the repercussions of such a meeting might be. At the time, the English warden-depute, Sir Thomas Wharton, had in fact reported a division in James' council, with Grange amongst those favouring a meeting and the clergy adamantly opposing the idea.[43] First mention of a list of heretics was made by the English ambassador to Scotland, Sir Ralph Sadler, in March 1543. The list was supposedly drawn up by the late king, and had three hundred and sixty names on it, including most of the leading magnates.[44]

Writing in the middle of the seventeenth century, Patrick Anderson, Hume of Godscroft and Drummond of Hawthornden[45] rely heavily on their predecessors for their histories. Anderson notes Lesley's story of the ferry capsizing at Cambuskenneth; both Hume and Drummond mention Buchanan by name; and the Knox/Pitscottie deathbed scene is reiterated by both Drummond and Anderson. Hume – who was writing a partisan history of the Douglases – first associated the term 'witchcraft' with the treason charge against Lady Glamis.

Thus the chronicle sources give the image of a ruler who, for all his success in daunting the Isles and Borders, his financial and matrimonial successes, and his administrative successes in the legislative and judicial spheres, was ultimately unsuccessful in war, because he was unable to carry his magnates along with him. This is epitomised by the ignominious episode of Fala Muir/Lauder, where the army summoned to wage war was dissolved without seeing action. Shortly afterwards a second army was routed at Solway Moss. The image of a decline and fall fitted in well with the analysis that the Protestant chroniclers wished to present, writing in the context of the birth of the Scottish Reformation and the turbulent reign of Mary Queen of Scots. However their portrayals of the breakdown of political relations and the physical collapse of the king at the end of 1542 in part tally with contemporary English reports and accordingly cannot be dismissed as total fantasy. By and large this view of the reign has been carried into the twentieth century by subsequent historians. Caroline Bingham has written the only recent biography. Her verdict is that:

> . . . the survival of the most amiable aspect of his image was largely due to his early death, which took place before the spread of the Reformation drove him to act with the severity shown by other Catholic sovereigns in the ensuing decades.[46]

This verdict shares similarities with those of the sixteenth-century chroniclers, in that the reign is placed in the context of what was to follow rather than that which had gone before. Bingham's conclusion bears distinct echoes of those of the chroniclers: Lesley's lover of justice, Pitscottie's promising starter, and Buchanan's ill-advised king.

C. RECENT RESEARCH

Three pieces of recent research cover the period in question. Kelley's study of the Douglas earls of Angus provides a detailed breakdown of the lands forfeited by the king in the September 1528 parliament as well as useful biographies of various personages who were the subject of royal disfavour.[47]

Edington's study of Sir David Lindsay of the Mount is important for its portrayal of the royal court in this period.[48] She identifies the tensions created by the influence of humanism and Lutheranism on a number of the Crown's officials competing for favour with the more conservatively minded clergy. As indicated earlier, this had its impact on political decisions, particularly with regard to the policy to be adopted towards England. Edington also details the resurrection of the image of Stewart monarchy, with its attendant notions of chivalry, splendour and extravagance, all in abeyance since the reign of James IV. Her analysis of Lindsay's own work places it in the context of other contemporary writers, all of them analysing and elaborating on the concept of traditional mediaeval kingship. The sixteenth-century chronicle sources can also be placed in this context.

Finally, W.K. Emond's thesis[49] on the minority of James V sets the scene for the personal rule – the reassertion of the Crown's authority after a prolonged period of faction fighting amongst the leading magnates.

NOTES

1. *The Acts of the Parliaments of Scotland* [*APS*], edd. T. Thomson and C. Innes (Edinburgh, 1814–1875), vol. ii (1424–1567).
2. An evaluation of Parliament's role generally, and also of those who served as lords of articles, is given by Irene O'Brien, 'The Scottish Parliament in the Fifteenth and Sixteenth Centuries' (Ph.D., Glasgow University, 1980).

3. *Registrum Magni Sigilli Regum Scotorum* [*RMS*], vol. iii (1513–1546), edd. J.B. Paul and J.M. Thomson (Edinburgh, 1884).
4. See Appendix II.
5. E.g. cross-referencing with great seal charters noted in Argyll Transcripts (Bailie Room, Glasgow University).
6. *RSS*, ii, no. 4516.
7. *Ibid.*, ii, no. 3444; Spalding, *Miscellany* ii, 194, no. xiv; *Acts of the Lords of Council in Public Affairs* 1501–1554: Selections from *Acta Dominorum Concilii* [*ADCP*], ed. R.K. Hannay (Edinburgh, 1932), 485.
8. See also *An Historical Atlas of Scotland* c.400–c.1600 [*Atlas*], edd. P. McNeill and R. Nicholson (St. Andrews, 1975), no. 46, map 83.
9. *T.A.*, v, *passim*.
10. *Excerpta e Libris Domicilii Domini Jacobi Quinti Regis Scotorum* 1525–1533 [*Excerpta e Libris*] (Bannatyne Club, Edinburgh, 1836).
11. Athol L. Murray, 'Exchequer and Crown Revenue of Scotland, 1437–1542' (Ph.D., Edinburgh University, 1961).
12. Acts of the Lords of Council [*ADC*]; SRO, CS 5, vols. 38–43; *ADCS*, vols. 1–19 Acts and Decreets [*AD*], SRO, CS 7, vol. i.
13. SRO, CS5, vol. 38, ff. 131v-132; AD, i, f. 32v.
14. Sederunts Acta Dominorum Concilii 1518–1553 [SRO RH 2.1.9].
15. SRO, *ADCS*, xix, f. 62. Another example of a locked box being broken open was in 1530 when Sir Hugh Campbell of Loudoun robbed his sister, Marion, of her dowry of 400 marks:*ibid.*, v, 84.
16. *Criminal Trials in Scotland from* 1488 to 1624 [Pitcairn, *Trials*], ed. Robert Pitcairn (Edinburgh, 1833), i, pt. i. The justiciary record is no longer in existence; cf. also, for example, the 17th century abstract in NLS (Adv. MS, 6.1.20.).
17. Principal amongst these is *LP Henry VIII*; also, *The Hamilton Papers* [*HP*], ed. J. Bain (Edinburgh, 1890), vol. i (1532–1543) and *State Papers of Henry VIII* [*SP Henry VIII*], 11 vols. (London, 1830–1852), vols. iv-v.
18. *The Letters of James V*, 1513–1542 [*James V Letters*], edd. R.K. Hannay and D. Hay (Edinburgh, 1954).
19. *LP Henry VIII*, viii, no. 1178; also quoted in *A Source Book of Scottish History*, edd. W.C. Dickinson et al. (Nelson, 1953), ii, 6–7.
20. SRO Gifts and Deposits Collection [GD].
21. Historical Manuscripts Commission: *Reports of the Royal Commission on Historical Manuscripts* [HMC] (London, 1870–).
22. J. Wormald, *Lords and Men in Scotland: Bonds of Manrent* 1442–1603 [Wormald, *Bonds*] (Edinburgh, 1985), Appendices A-D.
23. Published in, for example, Spalding Club; Bannatyne Club; Scottish History Society Series, and as cited in Bibliography.
24. *The Chronicle of Perth* (Maitland Club, 1831).
25. 'The Chronicle of Aberdeen': *Miscellany of the Spalding Club*, vol. ii (Spalding Club, Aberdeen, 1841–1852).
26. *A Diurnal of Remarkable Occurrents that have passed within the country of Scotland, since the death of James IV till the year* 1575 (Bannatyne and Maitland Clubs, 1833). It should be noted that the continuation of the John Law Chronicle, or '*De Cronicis Scotorum Brevia*' (Edinburgh University Library, MS Dc.7.63) finishes in 1528, and the later notes added up to 1541 (including a section titled 'Of the kingdom of Neapolitana in Apulia', which also has poems about bygone kings and attempts to practise the alphabet) do not contain any reference to Scottish political events in this period. It appears as though the last pages of the volume were filled up with odds and ends – by more than one writer.
27. NLS MS. 1746; see Alasdair M. Stewart, 'The Final Folios of Adam Abell's 'Roit and

Quheill of Tyme' ', in Janet Hadley Williams (ed.), *Stewart Style: 1513–1542: Essays on the Court of James V* (East Linton, 1996), 227–253.

28. John Knox, *The History of the Reformation in Scotland*, ed. W.C. Dickinson (Edinburgh, 1949), i, 33.
29. *HP*, i, no. 260 (i).
30. *Ibid.*, i, no. 259.
31. J. Lesley, *The History of Scotland from the Death of King James I in the Year* 1436 to the Year 1561 (Bannatyne Club, 1830).
32. G. Donaldson, *All the Queen's Men* (London, 1983).
33. *Chronicle of Kings of Scotland* (Maitland Club, 1830).
34. Robert Lindsay of Pitscottie, *The Historie and Cronicles of Scotland*, ed. A.J.G. Mackay (Edinburgh, 1899), vol. i.
35. Discussed in Lang, 'The Cardinal and the King's Will', *S.H.R.*, vol. iii (Glasgow, 1905–1906).
36. *HP*, i, no. 267.
37. G. Buchanan, *The History of Scotland*, trans. J. Aikman (Glasgow and Edinburgh, 1827–9), vol. ii; for Buchanan in general, see I.D. MacFarlane, *Buchanan* (London, 1981).
38. *TA*, vi, 289, 353, 430.
39. Knox, *History*, i, 29.
40. *HP*, i, no. 265.
41. E.g., NLS, Adv. MSS 33:2:15 (Sir James Balfour, 'Annales'); 33:2:9 (George Marjoribanks, 'Annals of Scotland 1514–1594'); 33:7:25 (John Monypenny, '1612–1625, Scotis chronicle: ane abridgement or summary'); 33:7:25, folio V (Wodrow MS).
42. Sir James Melville of Halhill, *Memoirs of his Own Life 1549–1593* (Bannatyne Club, 1827).
43. *HP*, i, no. 85.
44. *LP Henry VIII*, xviii, pt. i, no. 324.
45. NLS, Adv. MSS 35:5:3(i) (Patrick Anderson, History of Scotland from death of James I to death of James VI); David Hume of Godscroft, *The History of the House and Race of Douglas and Angus* (4th edn., Edinburgh, 1748); William Drummond of Hawthornden, *History of Scotland from the Year 1423 until the Year 1542* (London edn., 1681).
46. Bingham, *op.cit.*, 192–4.
47. Michael Kelley, 'The Douglas Earls of Angus: A Study in the Social and Political Bases of Power of a Scottish Family from 1389 until 1557' (Ph.D., Edinburgh University, 1973).
48. Carol Edington, *Court and Culture in Renaissance Scotland: Sir David Lindsay of the Mount, 1486–1555* (East Linton, 1995).
49. W.K. Emond, 'The Minority of King James V, 1513–1528' (Ph.D., St. Andrews University, 1988).

APPENDIX II (*RMS*, III)

Witnesses to Charters in the *Great Seal Register*, 30 May 1528 - 6 December 1542

	1528	1529	1530	1531	1532	1533	1534	1535	1536	1537	1538	1539	1540	1541	1542
• Members of first 'daily' king's council, appointed 6 July 1528 (*ADCP*, 277)															
Total number of charters in Register	135	152	105	124	149	80	101	100	106	102	140	173	202	271	327
Cited Witness Lists															
• Gavin Dunbar (junior), archbishop of Glasgow; Chancellor; *Vice-regent, 1536-7.*	12	11	4	2	5	3	9	16	9	9	9	3	9	13	16
George Crichton, bishop of Dunkeld; *Keeper of Privy Seal, 1528.*	12	3	1	–	4	1	1	5	8	9	9	–	–	9	16
Henry Wemyss, bishop of Galloway and Chapel Royal.	–	10	3	2	5	3	9	16	9	9	9	3	9	4	–
William Stewart, dean of Glasgow, provost of Lincluden (bishop of Aberdeen, 1532→); *Treasurer, 1530–38.*	–	–	–	2	4	1	7	11	1	–	–	–	–	–	–
• Gavin Dunbar (senior), bishop of Aberdeen (d. 1532); *Clerk Register, →1532.*	12	9	4	2	1	–	–	–	–	–	–	–	–	–	–
• Alexander Myln, abbot of Cambuskenneth (*Lord President 1532→*).	10	–	–	–	–	1	5	1	1	4	8	–	–	–	–
David Beaton, abbot of Arbroath (archbishop coajd. St. Andrews, 1537→; Cardinal, 1538→; *Keeper of Privy Seal, 1529→.*	–	11	4	2	5	2	4	15	8	4	–	–	–	–	–

Members of first 'daily' king's council, appointed 6 July 1528 (ADCP, 277)	1528	1529	1530	1531	1532	1533	1534	1535	1536	1537	1538	1539	1540	1541	1542
Robert Cairncross, abbot of Holyrood; *Treasurer 1528–29.*	—	3	—	—	—	—	—	—	—	4	—	—	—	—	—
Patrick Hepburn, prior of St. Andrews (bishop of Moray, 1538→).	12	11	4	2	5	3	9	16	9	6	8	—	—	—	—
William Douglas, abbot of Holyrood (d. 1528).	1	—	—	—	—	—	—	—	—	—	—	—	—	—	—
(Sir) James Colville of Ochiltree/East Wemyss; *Comptroller and Director of Chancery 1528, 1530–38.*	12	11	4	2	5	3	9	16	9	9	5	—	—	—	—
Robert Barton of Over-Barnton; *Treasurer and Comptroller, 1529–30.*	—	6	2	—	—	—	—	—	—	—	—	—	—	—	—
David Wood of Craig; *Comptroller 1538→.*	—	—	—	—	—	—	—	—	—	—	—	—	7	13	16
James Kirkcaldy of Grange; *Treasurer, 1538→.*	—	—	—	—	—	—	—	—	—	—	4	3	9	12	15
• (Sir) Thomas Erskine of Haltoun/Brechin; *Secretary.*	12	10	3	1	2	3	3	11	3	6	9	3	9	13	15
James Foulis of Colinton; *Clerk Register, 1532→.*	—	—	—	—	3	3	9	16	9	9	9	3	9	13	16
Thomas Bellenden of Auchnoule; *Director of Chancery, 1538→; Justice-Clerk, 1540→.*	—	—	—	—	—	—	—	—	—	—	4	3	9	13	15
• James Hamilton, first earl of Arran (d. 1529).	12	5	—	—	—	—	—	—	—	—	—	—	—	—	—
James Hamilton, second earl of Arran.	–	–	—	—	—	—	—	—	—	1	—	—	2	5	—
• Colin Campbell, third earl of Argyll (d. 1529); *Master of Household; Justiciar.*	12	7	—	—	—	—	—	—	—	—	—	—	—	—	—
Archibald Campbell, fourth earl of Argyll; *Master of Household; Justiciar.*	—	—	2	2	5	3	9	14	8	5	9	3	9	13	16

Members of first 'daily' king's council, appointed 6 July 1528 (*ADCP*, 277)	1528	1529	1530	1531	1532	1533	1534	1535	1536	1537	1538	1539	1540	1541	1542
• Hugh Montgomery, first earl of Eglinton; *Vice-regent 1536–7.*	12	10	3	2	4	3	9	16	9	9	8	–	–	–	–
• James Stewart, earl of Moray (king's half-brother); *Lieutenant-General*	–	4	4	2	4	3	8	11	–	6	9	3	6	8	16
• George Leslie, fourth earl of Rothes.	–	11	2	–	–	1	–	3	6	–	–	–	–	–	–
Malcolm, third Lord Fleming; *Chamberlain.*	4	6	3	2	5	3	9	14	8	6	9	3	9	13	16
• John, fifth Lord Erskine.	–	–	–	–	1	3	4	1	–	–	–	–	–	–	–
George Gordon, fourth earl of Huntly; *Vice-regent, 1536–7.*	–	–	–	–	–	–	–	1	1	3	–	–	1	–	–
William Graham, second earl of Montrose; *Vice-regent, 1536–7.*	–	–	–	–	–	–	–	1	1	3	–	–	–	–	–
Robert, fifth Lord Maxwell; Warden West Marches; *Vice-regent, 1536–7.*	–	–	–	–	–	–	–	1	–	3	–	–	–	–	–

APPENDIX III (*APS*, II)

Magnate Sederunts Listed in Parliamentary Roll

MAGNATES	Estimated Ages in September 1528	September 1528	April 1531	May 1532	June 1535	December 1540 (Prorogued)	March 1541
(i) Earls							
Colin Campbell, third earl of Argyll (d. 1529)	40+	LA					
Archibald Campbell, fourth earl of Argyll[1]	21+	-	LA	LA	LA	LA	Yes
James Hamilton, first earl of Arran (d. 1529)	53	LA					
James Hamilton, second earl of Arran[2]	9	-	-	-	LA	LA	Yes
John Stewart, third earl of Atholl (d. 1542)	21	Yes	-	Yes	Yes	Yes	Yes
Patrick Hepburn, third earl of Bothwell (warded 1532→)[3]	16	Yes	LA	-	-	-	-
John Stewart, third earl of Buchan	30	Yes	-	-	-	-	-
John Sinclair, third earl of Caithness (d. 1529)	Adult	-					

Notes Attendances at Parliamentary Commissions

1. Fourth earl of Argyll: 28 July 1533; 29 April 1536; 25 February 1541; 2 March 1541; 9 March 1541; 4 May 1542.
2. Second earl of Arran: 18 July 1539 (summons on Colville of East Wemyss); 25 February 1541; 2 March 1541; 9 March 1541; 4 May 1542.
3. Bothwell: 22 January 1529.

LA = elected lord of articles (none elected in 1541)

—— = deceased

MAGNATES	Estimated Ages in September 1528	September 1528	April 1531	May 1532	June 1535	December 1540	March 1541
George Sinclair, fourth earl of Caithness	11	–	–	–	–	–	–
Gilbert Kennedy, third earl of Cassillis[4]	11	–	–	–	Yes	Yes	Yes
David Lindsay, eighth earl of Crawford (d. 1542)	50+	–	–	Yes	Yes	–	–
Hugh Montgomery, first earl of Eglinton	68	LA	LA	–	LA	–	–
William Hay, sixth earl of Erroll (d. 1541); hereditary constable[5]	9	–	–	–	–	Yes	Yes
Cuthbert Cunningham, third earl of Glencairn (d. 1541)	50+	–	–	–	–	–	–
George Gordon, fourth earl of Huntly[6]	18	–	Yes	LA	LA	LA	Yes
Matthew Stewart, fourth earl of Lennox (overseas 1532→)	11	–	Yes	Yes	–	–	–
William Keith, third Earl Marischal; hereditary marshal[7]	18	Yes	Yes	–	Yes	Yes	Yes
Alexander Graham, second earl of Menteith (d. 1536)	50	–	–	–	–	–	–
William Graham, third earl of Menteith	30	–	–	–	–	Yes	Yes
William Graham, second earl of Montrose[8]	30	–	–	Yes	LA	LA	Yes

LA = elected lord of articles (none elected in 1541)

— = deceased

4. Cassillis: 18 July 1539 (Colville); 2 March 1541.
5. Erroll: 18 July 1539 (Colville - as hereditary constable).
6. Huntly: 23 July 1533; 1 June 1534; 29 April 1536; 25 February 1541.
7. Marischal: 29 April 1536; 18 July 1539 (Colville); 2 March 1541 (each time as hereditary marshal).
8. Montrose: 28 July 1533.

MAGNATES	Estimated Ages in September 1528	September 1528	April 1531	May 1532	June 1535	December 1540	March 1541
James Stewart, earl of Moray[9] (overseas, 1540/41)	27	LA	LA	LA	LA	–	–
James Douglas, third earl of Morton	48	–	–	–	–	–	–
George Leslie, fourth earl of Rothes[10]		Yes	LA	LA	Yes	Yes	–
Adam Gordon, tenth earl of Sutherland (d. 1530)	Adult	–	–	–	–	–	–
John Gordon, eleventh earl of Sutherland	3						
(ii) Other Notables							
Andrew Stewart, third Lord Avandale/Ochiltree	Adult	Yes	–	–	–	–	–
John Erskine, fifth Lord Erskine[11]	Adult	Yes	LA	LA	LA	LA	Yes
Malcolm Fleming, third Lord Fleming[12]	Adult	Yes	Yes	Yes	LA	Yes	Yes
John Forbes. sixth Lord Forbes	Adult	–	–	–	–	Yes	Yes
Patrick Gray, third Lord Gray (d. 1541)	Adult	Yes	–	–	LA	–	–
John Hay, third Lord Hay of Yester	Adult	–	Yes	–	Yes	Yes	Yes
George Hume, fourth Lord Hume	Adult	Yes	–	–	–	–	Yes
John Lindsay, fifth Lord Lindsay of Byres	Adult	Yes	Yes	Yes	Yes	Yes	–

LA = elected lord of articles (none elected in 1541)

—— = deceased

9. Moray: 18 July 1539 (Colville); 4 May 1542; 15 September 1542.
10. Rothes: 1 June 1534; 11 March 1538; 15 September 1542.
11. Lord Erskine: 4 May 1534; 23 September 1534; 11 March 1538; 2 March 1541; 9 March 1541.
12. Lord Fleming: 11 August 1533; 9 March 1541.

MAGNATES	Estimated Ages in September 1528	September 1528	April 1531	May 1532	June 1535	December 1540	March 1541
Robert Maxwell, fifth Lord Maxwell[13]	38	LA	Yes	–	–	Yes	Yes
Henry Stewart, Lord Methven (creation 1528)	Adult	–	Yes	–	–	Yes	Yes
Lawrence Oliphant, third Lord Oliphant	Adult	Yes	Yes	Yes	–	–	Yes
William Ruthven, second Lord Ruthven[14]	Adult	–	Yes	–	–	LA	Yes
William Sinclair, fourth Lord Sinclair	Adult	Yes	Yes	–	–	Yes	Yes
Hugh Somerville, fourth Lord Somerville	Adult	Yes	–	–	–	Yes	Yes
Sir James Hamilton of Finnart[15]	33	–	LA	LA	LA		
Total number of Earls attending (20 earldoms, excluding Angus)		9	8	8	11	10	10
Total number of Lords attending (32 lordships)		19	13	6	7	19	22
Total number of Archbishops/Bishops attending (12 sees/dioceses)		9	9	8	10	9	7
Total number of Abbots/Priors attending (circa 30 houses)		13	10	11	11	13	8

13. Lord Maxwell: 18 July 1539 (Colville).
14. Lord Ruthven: 2 March 1541; 9 March 1541.
15. Hamilton of Finnart: 29 April 1536.

LA = elected lord of articles (none elected in 1541)
—— = deceased

[359]

Bibliography

A. PRIMARY SOURCES

(1) *Manuscripts*
National Library of Scotland [NLS]:
Adv. MS: 6:1:20   (Transcript of Books of Adjournal).
        33:2:9   (George Marjoribanks, 'Annals of Scotland, 1514–1594').
        33:2:15   (Sir James Balfour, 'Annales').
        33:7:25   (John Monypenny, '1612–1625: Scotis Chronicle, ane abridgement or summary').
        33:7:25, folio V (Wodrow MS).
        25:5:3(i)   (Patrick Anderson, 'History of Scotland from death of James I to death of James V').

Additional MS. 1746 (Adam Abell).

Scottish Record Office [SRO]:
CS 5   Acts of the Lords of Council [ADC].
CS 6   Acts of the Lords of Council and Session [ADCS].
CS 7   Acts and Decreets [*AD*].
RH 2.1.9. Sederunts Acta Dominorum Concilii 1518–1553.
RH 2.1.15. Transcript of *ADC*, 1532.
RH 2.1.28. Transcript of *ADCS*, 1532–1533.
RH 2.5.8. Statutes of Session, 1537–1541.

GD 8   Boyd Papers.
GD 28   Hay of Yester Writs.
GD 39   Glencairn Muniments.
GD 40/   Lothian Writs.
GD 52   Forbes Papers.
GD 86   Fraser Papers.
GD 150   Morton (of Dalmahoy) Papers.
GD 220/6 Montrose Papers.

West Register House [WRH]:

NRA(S) 237   Inventory of Scottish Muniments at Haigh.
NRA(S) 885   Inventory of Strathmore Writs.
NRA(S) 885   Inventory of Glamis Charters.
NRA(S) 0925   Inventory of Erroll Charters.

Edinburgh University Library:

MS Dc.7.63   (Law, De Cronicis Scotorum Brevia).

Glasgow University Library:

Argyll Transcripts.

(2) *Primary Printed Sources and Works of Reference*
Selected Cases from Acta Dominorum Concilii et Sessionis 1532–33, ed. I.H. Shearer (Stair Society, 1951).
Acts of the Lords of Council in Public Affairs, 1501–1554 [*ADCP*], ed. R.K. Hannay (Edinburgh, 1932).
Acts of the Lords of the Isles, 1336–1493, edd. J. and R.W. Munro (SHS, Edinburgh, 1986) [Munro, *Isles*].
Acts of the Parliaments of Scotland [*APS*], edd. T. Thomson and C. Innes (Edinburgh, 1814–75), vol. ii (1424–1567).
Alexander Lindsay: A Rutter of the Scottish Seas (Maritime Monographs and Reports, no. 44, 1980).
*An Historical Atlas of Scotland c.*400–c.1600, edd. P. Mcneill and R. Nicholson (St. Andrews, 1975) [*Atlas*].
Foreign Correspondence with Marie de Lorraine Queen of Scotland, from the Originals in the Balcarres Papers (SHS, 1923–25).
The Practicks of Sir James Balfour of Pittendreich, ed. P.G.B. McNeill (Stair Society, 1962).
The Chronicles of Scotland compiled by Hector Boece, translated into Scots by John Bellenden, edd. F.C. Batho and H.W. Husbands (STS, 1938–41).
The Bannatyne Miscellany (Bannatyne Club, 1827–55).
G. Buchanan, *The History of Scotland*, trans. J.Aikman (Glasgow and Edinburgh, 1827–29), vol. ii.
Calendar of State Papers and Manuscripts, relating to English affairs, existing in the Archives and Collections of Venice, edd. R. Brown *et al* (London, 1864–) [*SP Venetian*].
Records of the Convention of the Royal Burghs of Scotland [*RCRB*], ed. J.D. Marwick (Edinburgh, 1866–90).
Chronicle of the Kings of Scotland [Chalmers of Ormond] (Maitland Club, 1830).

The Chronicle of Perth (Maitland Club, 1831).

The Court Book of the Barony of Carnwath 1533–42, ed. W.C. Dickinson (SHS, 1937).

Cowan, I.B. and Easson, D.E., *Medieval Religious Houses in Scotland* (London, 1976).

Dickinson, W.C., *et al* (edd.), *A Sourcebook of Scottish History* (Nelson, 1953).

A Diurnal of Remarkable Occurrents that have passed within the country of Scotland, since the death of James IV till the year 1575 (Bannatyne and Maitland Clubs, 1833).

Drummond, William, of Hawthornden, *History of Scotland from the Year* 1423 *until the Year* 1542 (London edn., 1861).

Dunbar, A.H., *Scottish Kings: A Revised Chronology of Scottish History* 1005–1625, 2nd edn. (Edinburgh, 1906).

Excerpta e Libris Domicilii Domini Jacobi Quinti Regis Scotorum (Bannatyne Club, 1836).

The Exchequer Rolls of Scotland [ER], ed. J. Stuart *et al* (Edinburgh, 1878–1908).

Extracts from the Records of the Burgh of Edinburgh (SBRS, 1871).

The House of Forbes, edd. A. and H. Taylor (Third Spalding Club, 1937).

A Genealogical Deduction of the Family of Rose of Kilravock (Spalding Club, 1848).

Fasti Ecclesiae Scoticanae Medii Aevi ad annum 1638 ed. D.E.R. Watt (St. Andrews, 1969) [Watt, *Fasti*].

Fraser, W., *The Annandale Family Book* (Edinburgh, 1894).

Fraser, W., *The Scotts of Buccleuch* (Edinburgh, 1878).

Fraser, W., *The Book of Carlaverock* (Edinburgh, 1873).

Fraser, W., *The Douglas Book* (Edinburgh, 1885).

Fraser, W., *Memorials of the Montgomeries Earls of Eglinton* (Edinburgh 1859).

Fraser, W., *The Chiefs of Grant* (Edinburgh, 1883).

Fraser, W., *The Lennox* (Edinburgh, 1874).

Fraser, W., *The Melvilles Earls of Melville and the Leslies Earls of Leven* (Edinburgh, 1890).

Fraser. W., *The Sutherland Book* (Edinburgh, 1892).

The Hamilton Papers, ed. J. Bain (Edinburgh, 1890–92), vol. i [*HP*].

Handbook of British Chronology [HBC] edd. F.M. Powicke and E.B. Fryde (London, 1961).

Highland Papers, ed. J.R.N. Macphail (SHS, 1914–34).

Historical Manuscripts Commission: Reports of the Royal Commission on Historical Manuscripts [HMC] (London, 1870–).

Hume, David, of Godscroft, *The History of the House and Race of Douglas and Angus* (4th edn., Edinburgh, 1748).

Illustrations of the Topography and Antiquities of the Shires of Aberdeen and Banff [A.B. Ill.] (Spalding Club, 1847–69).

The Letters of James V, edd. R.K. Hannay and D. Hay (Edinburgh, 1954).

John Knox's History of the Reformation in Scotland, ed. W.C. Dickinson (Edinburgh, 1949), vol. i.

Lesley, J., *The History of Scotland from the Death of King James I in the Year 1436 to the Year 1561* (Bannatyne Club, 1830).

Letters and Papers, Foreign and Domestic, of the Reign of Henry VIII, edd. J.S. Brewer *et al*, 1862–1932 [*LP Henry VIII*].

The Works of Sir David Lindsay of the Mount 1490–1555, ed. D. Hamer (STS, 1930–36).

Genealogical Collections concerning Families in Scotland made by Walter Macfarlane (SHS, 1900).

Liber Sancte Marie de Melrose (Bannatyne Club, 1837).

Melville of Halhill, Sir James., *Memoirs of his own life, 1549–1593*, ed. T. Thomson (Bannatyne Club, 1827).

Registrum Honoris de Morton (Bannatyne Club, 1835).

Nicolay, Nicholas de, Seigneur d'Arfeuille, *La Navigation de Roy d'Ecosse Jacques cinquiesme du nom ...* (1583) [also entitled *The Life and Death of King James the Fifth* (Miscellanea Scotica, 1818)].

Pitcairn, R. (ed.), *Criminal Trials in Scotland from 1488 to 1624* (Edinburgh, 1833), vol. i, pt. i.

Pitscottie, Robert Lindsay of, *The Historie and Cronicles of Scotland* (STS, 1899–1911), vol. i.

Protocol Book of Sir John Cristisone 1518–51, ed. R.H. Lindsay (SRS, 1930).

Protocol Book of Dominus Thomas Johnsoun 1528–78 (SRS, 1920).

Protocol Book of Gavin Ros 1512–32 (SRS, 1931).

Records of the earldom of Orkney, 1299–1614, edd. J. Storer Clouston (SHS, 2nd series, 1914).

Regiam Majestatem and Quoniam Attachiamenta, ed. Lord Cooper (Stair Society, 1947).

Registrum Magni Sigilii Regum Scotorum [*RMS*], edd. J.M. Thomson *et al* (Edinburgh, 1882–1914).

Registrum Secreti Sigilii Regum Scotorum [*RSS*], edd. M. Livingstone *et al* (Edinburgh, 1908–).

St. Andrews Formulare 1514–46, edd. G. Donaldson and C. Macrae (Stair Society, 1942–4).

The Scots Peerage, ed. Sir J. Balfour Paul (Edinburgh, 1904–14).

Scottish Texts and Calendars, edd. D. and W.B. Stevenson (SHS, 1987).

Miscellany of the Spalding Club (Spalding Club, 1841–52([inc. The Chronicle of Aberdeen in vol. ii].

State Papers of Henry VIII (London 1830–52) [*SP Henry VIII*].

State Papers and Letters of Sir Ralph Sadler, ed. A. Clifford (London, 1809) [*Sadler State Papers*].

The Black Book of Taymouth (Bannatyne Club, 1855) [inc. The Chronicle of Fortingal].

Papiers d'état, pièces et documents inédits ou peu connus relatifs a l'histoire de l'Ecosse au XVIême siêcle, ed. A. Teulet (Bannatyne Club, 1852–60).

Thomson, Thomas, *Memorial on Old Extent*, ed. J.D. Mackie (Stair Society, 1946).

Accounts of the Lord High Treasurer of Scotland [TA], edd. T. Dickson and Sir J. Balfour Paul (Edinburgh, 1877–1916).

Charter Chest of the Earldom of Wigtown (SRS, 1910).

Accounts of the Masters of Works [MW], edd. H.M. Paton *et al* (Edinburgh, 1957–).

B. SECONDARY SOURCES

Anderson, P.D., *Robert Stewart, Earl of Orkney, Lord of Shetland: 1333–1593* (Edinburgh, 1982) [Anderson, *Orkney*].

Armstrong, W.A., *The Armstrong Borderland* (North Berwick, 1960).

Bapst, E., *Les Mariages de Jacques V* (Paris, 1889).

Bardgett, F.D., *Scotland Reformed: The Reformation in Angus and the Mearns* (Edinburgh, 1989).

Bingham, C., *James V: King of Scots* (London, 1971).

Brown, M., *James I* (Edinburgh, 1994).

Burton, J.H., *The History of Scotland* (2nd edn., Edinburgh, 1873).

Cosgrove, A., *Late Medieval Ireland, 1370–1541* (Dublin, 1981).

Cowan, S., *Royal House of Stuart* (London, 1908).

Cowan, I.B. and Shaw, D., (edd.), *The Renaissance and Reformation in Scotland* (Edinburgh, 1983) [*Ren. and Ref.*].

Dickinson, W.C., *Scotland from the Earliest Times to 1693* (revised by A.A.M. Duncan) (3rd edn., Oxford, 1977).

Donaldson, G., *All the Queen's Men* (London, 1983).

Donaldson, G., *Scotland James V - James VII* (*Edinburgh History of Scotland*, vol. iii, 1965).

Donaldson, G., *Scottish Kings* (London, 1967).

Easson, D.E., *Gavin Dunbar, Chancellor of Scotland, Archbishop of Glasgow* (Edinburgh, 1947).

Eaves, R.G., *Henry VIII and James V's Regency, 1524–1528: A Study in Anglo-Scottish Diplomacy* (University Press Alabama, 1987).

Edington, C., *Court and Culture in Renaissance Scotland: Sir David Lindsay of the Mount, 1486–1555* (East Linton, 1995).

Ferguson, W., *Scotland's Relations with England: a Survey to 1707* (Edinburgh, 1977).

Fraser, G.M., *The Steel Bonnets: The Story of the Anglo-Scottish Border Reivers* (London, 1971).

Gibb, G.D., *The Life and Times of Robert Gib Lord of Carriber, Familiar Servitor and Master of Stables to James V* (London, 1874).

Griffiths, R.A, *The Principality of Wales in the Later Middle Ages* (Cardiff, 1972).
Hadley Williams, J. (ed.), *Stewart Style, 1513–1542: Essays on the Court of James V* (East Linton, 1996).
Hannay, R.K., *The College of Justice* (Edinburgh, 1933).
Habsburg, Otto von, *Charles V* (translated by M. Ross, 1970).
Henderson, T.F., *The Royal Stewarts* (Edinburgh, 1914).
Hume Brown, P., *History of Scotland to the Present Time* (Cambridge, 1911).
Inglis, J.A., *Sir Adam Otterburn of Redhall* (Glasgow, 1935).
Knecht, R.J., *Francis I* (Cambridge, 1982).
Lang, A., *A History of Scotland from the Roman Occupation* (Edinburgh, 1907).
Linklater, E., *The Royal House of Scotland* (London, 1970).
Lynch, M., *Scotland: A New History* (London, 1992).
MacCurtain, M., *Tudor and Stuart Ireland* (Dublin, 1972).
Macdougall, N., *James III: A Political Study* (Edinburgh, 1982).
Macdougall, N., *James IV* (Edinburgh, 1989).
MacFarlane, I.D., *Buchanan* (London, 1981).
McGladdery, C., *James II* (Edinburgh, 1990).
MacQueen, H.L., (ed.), *The College of Justice: Essays by R.K. Hannay* (Stair Society, 1990).
Mackie, J.D., *A History of Scotland* (Penguin edn., 1969).
Palmer, M.D., *Henry VIII* (2nd edn., New York, 1983).
Paton, G.C.H. (ed.), *An Introduction to Scottish Legal History* (Stair Society, 1958).
Rae, T.I., *The Administration of the Scottish Frontier, 1513–1603* (Edinburgh, 1964).
Rait, R.S., *The Parliaments of Scotland* (Glasgow, 1924).
Reid, W.S., *Skipper from Leith: the history of Robert Barton of Over Barnton* (OUP, 1962).
Ross, S., *The Stewart Dynasty* (London, 1993).
Sanderson, M.H.B., *Scottish Rural Society in the 16th Century* (Edinburgh, 1982).
Sanderson, M.H.B., *Cardinal of Scotland: David Beaton c.1494–1546* (Edinburgh 1986).
Scott, Sir W., *Miscellaneous Works of* (II, History of Scotland, Edinburgh, 1870) [*Tales of A Grandfather*].
Scarisbrick, J.J., *Henry VIII* (London, 1968).
Shaw, A.M., *History of the Macintoshes and Clan Chattan* (London, 1880).
Stringer, K.J. (ed.), *Essays on the Nobility of Medieval Scotland* (Edinburgh, 1985) [Stringer, *Nobility*].
Stuart, M.W., *The Scot who was a Frenchman; being the life of John Stewart, Duke of Albany in Scotland, France and Italy* (Hodge, 1940).
Tytler, P.F., *A History of Scotland from the Accession of Alexander III to the Union* (Edinburgh, 1864).
Willock, I.D., *The Origins and development of the jury in Scotland* (Stair Society, 1966).

Wormald, J., *Court, Kirk and Community: Scotland* 1470–1625 (London, 1982) [Wormald, *Court*].

Wormald, J., *Lords and Men in Scotland: Bonds of Manrent*, 1442–1603 (Edinburgh, 1985) [Wormald, *Bonds*].

Wormald, J., *Mary Queen of Scots: a Study in Failure* (London, 1988).

C. ARTICLES AND BOOK CHAPTERS

Brown, A.L., 'The Scottish Establishment in the Later Fifteenth Century', *JR*, 1978.

Crawford, B.E., 'William Sinclair, Earl of Orkney and his Family: a study in the politics of survival', in Stringer, *Nobility*.

Dilworth, M., 'The Commendator System in Scotland', *IR*, xxxvii, no. 2, 1986.

Donaldson, G., 'The Legal Profession in Scottish Society in the Sixteenth and Seventeenth Centuries', *JR*, 1976.

Ellis, H. (ed.), 'Observations upon a Household Book of King James V ...', in *Archaeologia*, vol. 22, 1829.

Finnie, E., 'The House of Hamilton: Patronage, Politics and the Church in the Reformation Period', *IR*, xxxvi, no. 1, 1985.

Hannay, R.K., 'Observations on the Officers of the Scottish Parliament', *JR*, 1932.

Hannay, R.K., 'A Study in Reformation History', *SHR*, xxiii.

Head, D.M., 'Henry VIII's Scottish Policy: a Reassessment', *SHR* (1982).

Kelley, M.G., 'Land Tenure and Forfeiture: A Sixteenth Century Scottish Example', *Sixteenth Century Journal*, ix, pt. iii, 1978 [Kelley, *Tenure*].

Lang, A., 'The Cardinal and the King's Will', *SHR*, iii.

Macdougall, N., 'Crown versus Nobility: the Struggle for the Priory of Coldingham, 1472–88', in Stringer, *Nobility*.

McKean, C., 'Hamilton of Finnart', *History Today*, January 1993.

Mackenzie, W.M., 'The Debateable Land', *SHR*, xxx.

McNeill, P.G.B., 'Senators of the College of Justice: 1532–69', *JR*, 1978.

Mahoney, M., 'The Scottish Hierarchy 1513–1565', in *Ren. and Ref.*

Merriman, M., 'The Assured Scots: Scottish Collaborators with England during the Rough Wooing', *SHR*, xlvii.

Murray, A.L., 'Exchequer and Council in the Reign of James V', *JR*, v, 1960.

Murray, A.L., 'Accounts of the King's Pursemaster, 1539–40', *SHS Miscellany*, x, 1965 [Murray, *Pursemaster*].

Murray, A.L., 'The Revenues of the bishopric of Moray in 1538', *IR*, xix, no. 1, 1968.

Murray, A.L., 'Financing the Royal Household: James V and his Comptrollers, 1513–1543', in *Ren. and Ref.* [Murray, *Household*].

Nicholson, R., 'Feudal Developments in Late Medieval Scotland', *JR*, 1973.

Reid, W.S., 'Clerical Taxation: the Scottish alternative to Dissolution of the Monasteries, 1530–60', *Catholic Historical Review*, vol. 34, 1948.

Richardson, G., 'Good Friends and Brothers? Francis I and Henry VIII', *History Today*, 44 (9), September 1994.

Sinclair, G.A, 'The Scots at Solway Moss', *SHR*, ii.

Stewart, A.M., 'Adam Abell's 'Roit or Queill of Tyme' ', *Aberdeen University Review*, xliv, 1972.

Wormald, J., 'Taming the Magnates?', in Stringer, *Nobility*.

D. UNPUBLISHED THESES

Charteris, J.N., 'The Evolution of the English Party in Scotland, 1513–1544' (Ph.D., McGill University, 1973).

Emond, W.K., 'The Minority of King James V, 1513–1528' (Ph.D., St. Andrews University, 1988).

Hotle, C.P., 'Tradition, reform and diplomacy: Anglo-Scottish relations, 1528–42' (Ph.D., Cambridge University, 1992).

Kelham, C.A., 'Bases of Magnatial Power in Later Fifteenth Century Scotland' (Ph.D., Edinburgh University, 1986).

Kelley, M.G., 'The Douglas Earls of Angus: A Study in the Social and Political Bases of Power of a Scottish Family from 1389 until 1557' (Ph.D., Edinburgh University, 1973) [Kelley, *Angus*].

Murray, A.L., 'Exchequer and Crown Revenue of Scotland, 1437–1542' (Ph.D., Edinburgh University, 1961) [Murray, *Revenues*].

O'Brien, I., 'The Scottish Parliament in the Fifteenth and Sixteenth centuries' (Ph.D., Glasgow University, 1980).

Index

Abell, Adam, Franciscan friar of
Jedburgh, chronicler, 5, 7 n. 10, 10,
17, 18, 20, 24, 80, 131, 171, 206,
334, 345
Aberdeen, royal burgh of, 168, justice
ayres in (1528), 161, and Master of
Forbes, 162–3, 215
Abernethy, regality of, 4, 43, 214, 238,
241–2, 259–60, 267, 268, 272
Albany, duke of, see Stewart, John, duke
of Albany
Angus, earl of, see Douglas, Archibald,
6th earl of Angus
Annexation, Act of (December 1540),
213–4, 217, 258, 271–2, 331, 333
Apprising, 3, 4, 23, 108
Argyll, earls of, see Campbell, Colin, 3rd
earl of Argyll (d. 1529); Campbell,
Archibald, 4th earl of Argyll
Armstrong, David ('Dave the Lady'),
reiver, 72, 82
Armstrong, John (alias 'Black Jok'), thief,
hanged, 81–2
Armstrong, John (alias 'John in
Gutterholis'), reiver, drawn and
hanged, 82
Armstrong, Johnnie, of Gilknockie, x, 2,
13, 15, 92, 231, 330
hanged at Carlinrigg (1530), 79–81
posthumous reputation, 80–81
Armstrong, Simon ('Sym the Laird'),
reiver, 72, 82
Arran, earls of, see Hamilton, James, 1st
earl of Arran (d. 1529); Hamilton,
James, 2nd earl of Arran
Arran, Isle of, attacks on Hamilton earl,
53, 229
Artillery, royal, 42, 44, 48, 65, 123, 178,
231, 262, 301, 305, 306

'Assured Lords', 319–20, 322–3, 326 n. 33
Atholl, earl of, see Stewart, John, 3rd earl
of Atholl (d. 1542)
Auld Alliance, see Franco-Scottish
alliance
Avandale, Andrew Stewart, 3rd Lord, 21,
25, 198, and lordship of Avandale,
198–203

Ballad of Johnnie Armstrong, the, 80–81
Barclay, Christina, mistress of James V,
160 n. 253
Barton, Robert, of Over-Barnton,
Comptroller and Treasurer, 66–7,
108, 112, 215, 256, 330
Bastie, Antoine d'Arces, sieur de la, 58,
116
Beaton, David, abbot of Arbroath,
archbishop of St. Andrews (from
1539), Cardinal, Keeper of the privy
seal, 74, 131, 134, 180, 200, 209, 233,
245, 260, 292, 293, 295, 316
created Cardinal, 288
Beaton, Elizabeth, mistress of James V,
134, 160 n. 253, 178
Beaton, James, archbishop of
St. Andrews, 2, 9, 19, 21, 87, 200,
233
attacked by King (1532–3), 134–6, vice-
regent for James V (1536–7), 133
Bellenden, John, humanist, secretary to
6th earl of Angus, 11, 15, 17, 22, 23,
24, 26, 41, 101, 347
Bellenden, Thomas, justice clerk, 264,
274, 276, 288–9, 292, 293, 296
Belton, Elizabeth Cunningham, Lady
Belton, 101–2
Berwick, burgh of, 92, 177, 178, 299–
300, 307

[369]

Erskine, John, 5th Lord, 131, 151, 203, 218, 233, 296, 298, 333
Erskine, Margaret, mistress of James V, 151, 160 n. 253, 177, 188 n. 176, 206, 208, 276, 281 n. 56
Erskine, Sir Thomas, of Haltoun (later Brechin), royal Secretary, 12, 14, 19, 25, 33, 100, 131, 233, 273, 275, 292, 301
  career reviewed, 267, 268–270
Eure, Sir William, English officer at Berwick, 209, 213, 264, 288–9, 296, 306, 315, 324

Fala, muster point for Scottish host (1542), 302–3, 307, 308–9
Falconer, David, captain of royal footguard, killed at Tantallon, 48–9, 62, 98, 116
Falkland, royal palace, x, xi, 17, 18, 35, 148, 262
  king at (1542), 315, 325, 335
Finance, royal, 33–4
  income and expenditure reviewed, 257–262
Fleming, Malcolm 3rd Lord, 12, 19, 49, 89, 124, 131, 143–4, 203, 209, 276, 292, 333
  career reviewed, 103–4
Flodden, battle of (1513), 39, 143
Forbes, John, 6th Lord, 25, 37, 49, 165, 166
  career reviewed, 161–3
Forbes, John, Master of (ex. 1537), x, 2, 332
  career reviewed, 161–2
  trial and execution, 163–6
Francis I, King of France (1515–1547), 60, 131, 133, 231, 232, 242, 262, 286, 287, 288, 334
Franco-Scottish Alliance (The Auld Alliance), vii–viii, 60–61, 131–3, 151, 180, 261, 286–292

Glamis, Janet Douglas, Lady (ex. 1537), x, 2, 22, 116, 204–5, 330
  career reviewed, 169–170
  execution, 171–2
  and King's role in her removal, 174–5, 180–181

Glamis, John Lyon, 6th Lord (d. 1528), 169–170
Glamis, John Lyon, 7th Lord, 171–4, 331, 332
Glencairn, earl of, see Cunningham, Cuthbert, 3rd earl of Glencairn
Gordon, George, 4th earl of Huntly, x, 4, 37, 90–91, 138, 147, 203, 209, 245, 255, 317, 332, 335
  vice-regent for James V (1536–7), 133
  and Master of Forbes, 162–6
  and earl of Moray, 166–9
  royal lieutenant in 1542 campaigns, 296–309 passim
  and victory at Hadden Rig (1542), 296–7
Gordon, James, of Lochinvar, 131, 270
Gourlay, Norman, heretic, 5
Graham, Alexander, 2nd earl of Menteith (d. 1536), 40, 138
Graham, William, 3rd earl of Menteith, 138
Graham, William, 2nd earl of Montrose, 9, 40, 41, 56, 91, 203, 209
  vice-regent for James V (1536–7), 133
  career reviewed, 149–150
Gray, Patrick, 3rd Lord, 105, 109, 112, 203, 233
  death of (1541), 277
  and the Crown, 277–8, 332
'Great Tax', the (1531), 135, 260
'Great Unicorn', the, royal ship, 245
'Grete Aith', the (1528), 49, 52, 55, 62, 71, 102, 149, 213

Hadden Rig, battle of (1542), x, 169, 213, 296–7, 298, 299, 303, 316, 322
Hamilton, Andrew, illegitimate son of Sir James Hamilton of Finnart, 195–6, 197
Hamilton, Gavin, younger brother of James, 2nd earl of Arran, 195, 196, 199
Hamilton, James, 1st earl of Arran (d. 1529), viii, 9, 10, 11, 19, 21, 23, 25, 28, 32, 34, 42, 49, 52–3, Chapter 9, passim, 330
  death of, 71, 119